IDA E. MORRISON, Ed.D., Stanford University, is Professor of Education at Sacramento State College. Dr. Morrison was elementary school supervisor, Santa Barbara County; reservation principal of Carson Indian Agency Schools; and teacher of both primary and elementary school grades in San Francisco. She has taught at San Francisco State College and the University of California at Santa Barbara. She is the co-author, with Ida F. Perry, of *Kindergarten–Primary Education—Teaching Procedures,* published by The Ronald Press Company.

TEACHING READING

IN THE

ELEMENTARY SCHOOL

IDA E. MORRISON

SACRAMENTO STATE COLLEGE

THE RONALD PRESS COMPANY • NEW YORK

Library of Congress Catalog Card Number: 68–28844

PRINTED IN THE UNITED STATES OF AMERICA

Preface

This book is designed primarily for students in elementary reading methods courses, and it will also serve as a valuable guide for student teachers, in-service teachers, and reading specialists. The methods suggested throughout the book have been developed from sound objectives and currently accepted research, and have been thoroughly classroom-tested by the author during the past several years. Included in this book are materials that have not appeared elsewhere in textbook form, which the author feels deserve the close attention of teachers and students in the classrooms of today.

Our society is better educated and more affluent than ever before, yet there remains a large segment of the population whose educational gains have been minimal. Therefore, a considerable amount of attention is given in this book to the reading problems of the culturally-deprived child. Many practical ideas are suggested to help this child in his reading, especially in the important early stages when success is so vital. In addition, lists of books for all slow and retarded readers may be found in the appendices.

Also unique in this book is the chapter devoted to the various ways of organizing the first reading groups for beginners, including suggestions for helping them learn to work independently while the teacher is occupied. Finally, the linguistic approach of LeFevre and Goodman is considered basic to the reading program outlined in the book; that is, words by themselves have only limited or ambiguous meanings and in most situations must be dealt with in their relation to each other in sentences.

Several chapters have been devoted to a great variety of activities for developing reading readiness, many of which involve speaking and first-hand experience suitable for pre-school and kindergarten children. A chapter on procedures for developing readiness for word recognition has been included in addition to a chapter on techniques of teaching word recognition.

Sections are devoted to evaluating objectively the recent trends in reading, including the individualized reading program, the linguistic approach, the use of the ITA alphabet, and the use of phonics, as the total program for the early grades.

Procedures simple enough for the very slow learner are suggested throughout the book along with the ideas suitable for use with the gifted child. A variety of sample lessons has been included to illustrate actual classroom procedures for the prospective teacher. The provision of a combination of procedures to help meet the needs of each child through a balance of skills and abilities has been stressed throughout the book.

Many persons in the field of reading have helped in the preparation of this book. In particular, the author wishes to thank Dr. Mildred Dawson, past President of the International Reading Association, for her suggestions and encouragement. Mr. William Stabler of the Department of Audio-visual Education of the California State Department of Education was very helpful in his contribution of excellent pictures for illustrating the text. The Placer County School Office also kindly contributed pictures taken in the primary class of the Georgetown Elementary School. Mrs. Caryl Steere, Arizona State University, and Mrs. Caroline Gibb, New Pine Creek School, Oregon, also generously helped with the photography. The Sacramento City Schools, especially the principals of Bancroft, Sequoia, and H. W. Harkness Schools, gave permission and provided opportunities for pictures to be taken of the excellent work in their classrooms.

Dr. Warren Prentice, Director of the National Education Defense Workshop, and Mr. Robert Davis, principal of the N.D.E.A. Demonstration School, were very helpful in providing opportunities for photographs to be taken. Teachers whose fine work was photographed included Miss Clytelle Shepherd, Mrs. Peggy Gillingwater, Mrs. Barbara Pratt, Mrs. Helen Wilson, Miss Sharon Rakela, Mrs. Winifred Nyswonger, and Mrs. Mary Ellen Mello. The author also wishes to thank Miss Sally Ann Franklin and Miss Patricia Sullivan for their work on the diagrams.

IDA E. MORRISON

Sacramento, California
June, 1968

Contents

I

READING BACKGROUND

1

Teaching in the Past

Mr. and Mrs. White were concerned about the problem of their daughter's entrance into school in first grade. These parents were disturbed because of the newspaper and magazine articles which they had read about the schools and particularly about the modern reading program. They were anxious that Joan, their daughter, should have a good start in reading, especially since Mr. White's nephew had been failed in his college work due to inadequate reading ability.

CONFLICTING ISSUES

Many parents such as Mr. and Mrs. White were concerned because of the books and articles that had been published in recent years. A return to the teaching of beginning reading by means of the alphabet and intense drill on phonics to the exclusion of other procedures was urged by many of the authors of these articles. On the other hand, the number of courses in speed reading for older children and adults was rapidly increasing, indicating a need for better teaching of speed and comprehension in reading. It is not surprising that parents felt confused because they did not know what was best for their children. Few parents realized that these trends were contradictory.

Confusion in the Literature

Mr. and Mrs. White realized that the books and articles supporting a return to the older methods were written by specialists in semantics, anthropology, chemistry, and similar fields. Since most of these authorities had worked for many years only in their own professions, it seemed a little strange that they should be considered as authorities in such a specialized field as reading. Articles by other authorities described experiments in teaching very young children, even infants, to read. The development and use of a new alphabet was described by educators in England. Parents did not know what was best for their children.

Causes of Conflicts

Parents and other lay people were confused by the articles written by the critics of the schools. These people, however, had no background for understanding the gradual changes that had taken place in the teaching of reading as a result of research, nor did they consider larger social changes that had had profound effects on the schools. A review of early and more recent trends in the teaching of reading may help the student or beginning teacher understand the present situation.

READING TEACHING IN THE PAST

Some old methods that are no longer considered effective are described in this section of the chapter for whatever they may contribute to today's teaching. The modern teacher should know something about outmoded methods because parents often ask about these methods and expect them to be used, not knowing they are outmoded. Teachers who cling to these outdated techniques should also know why they are considered inadequate, and beginning teachers should know the advantages of the newer procedures. A very brief review is given of the alphabet-spelling method, the use of spelling-readers, the word method, the introduction of the graded series, the phonics approach, and the look-and-say method.

The Alphabet-Spelling Method

In the dark ages only monks and a few scholars learned to read. Serfs, soldiers, and even the nobility had no need for reading. Martin Luther, however, believed that the common man should learn to read the Bible for himself rather than to listen to it read in Latin in the churches of that day. Although a slight beginning in the teaching of reading was made at that time, several centuries followed before the common man had an opportunity to learn to read. Even today the teaching of reading is still not universal and is only recently spreading to all parts of the world.

During the colonial period the *New England Primer* was the only book used, and it was written to teach religion to children. They began to read by learning the alphabet by rote. A series of lessons were then memorized. Parts of words, sounds, and whole words were taught and recognized by spelling them aloud, as "f" "a" "l" "l," "fall" in

"In Adam's fall
We sinned all."

Although the *New England Primer* was written to teach religion, the meaning of the reading matter came last instead of first as it does today. Despite this very tedious, slow, and ineffective procedure, some adults escaped illiteracy by this spelling method of teaching reading. Even today, many adults believe the child must be able to name the letters of the alphabet in order to begin reading.

Use of Spelling-Readers

For many years in America, reading and spelling were taught from Webster's *American Spelling Book,* the famous "blue-backed speller." In this method, too, children began their work by memorizing the alphabet and learning to recognize the letters. After this step they learned to read by spelling words. First, they learned to spell and read two-letter words, then three-letter words, later four-letter words, and so on. The words were also classified by the number of syllables they contained so that children learned one-syllable words before two-syllable words, three-syllable words before four-syllable words, and so forth. As time went on, the children were required to read and spell extensive lists of long and difficult words. After tedious memorization, sentences and eventually stories were read, but children were still required to spell each word monotonously before pronouncing it.

The process was very time-consuming, since the sentence, "Baby likes to play," was read in the following manner: "B" "a" "b" "y," "Baby," "l" "i" "k" "e" "s," "likes," "t" "o," "to," "p" "l" "a" "y," "play." By the time the child had completed this ordeal of spelling and pronouncing words, he had long since lost interest and thought if he ever had any interest in or idea of the meaning of the sentence. One of the objectives of this method was to improve speech, and enunciation and pronunciation were emphasized. According to Gray [1] teachers found interest very hard to hold and behavior difficult to control except for a teacher who solved his discipline problems by eating the lunch of each pupil who misbehaved during the reading lesson.

[1] Lillian Gray, *Teaching Children to Read* (3rd ed.; New York: The Ronald Press Co., 1963).

The Word Method

In 1838 Horace Mann rebelled at the methods of the day. He condemned the alphabet method and recommended the word method in a report to the Board of Education in Massachusetts. This report has since become famous. Horace Mann had found that the child learned whole words with much greater ease and interest than reading by the old, spelling method because whole words had meaning for him. Horace Mann's method not only helped the child gain meaning from the printed word but also gave him an opportunity to see the natural grouping of letters at one glance. Reading, therefore, became more rapid, more effective, and vastly more enjoyable. When the child had gained a rather large sight vocabulary, that is, words he recognized on sight without the help of phonics, he could read sentences and eventually stories. (A sight word may first be learned by use of phonics, but later it should be recognized from memory.) Horace Mann's method provided a tremendous step forward in the teaching of reading.

Although Horace Mann brought a great advance in the teaching of reading, teachers today know that overemphasis on the word interferes with the child's ability to see the relationship among words and therefore limits comprehension and speed in reading. In the word method, the child memorized lists of isolated words before he was permitted to read sentences, which he was not taught until much later. In this method, too, the thought came as the last step in the reading process instead of coming first as it does today. No phonics procedures were taught to help the child increase his independence in recognizing words by known parts so that every word had to be learned at sight from memory.

Use of a Graded Series

The McGuffey Readers introduced in 1840 were the first series of graded readers.[2] They included a primer and a first reader for the first grade and one book each on increasingly difficult levels for each grade thereafter. These books were in use for many years and were studied by generations of children. They were still in use in some schools as late as 1920. Although the content is antiquated and the grammar is obsolete, the parents in some school districts have urged their adoption even in recent times because of the phonics approach.

Content Based on Letter Sounds. The sentences in these readers were intelligible, although rather inane because the words were selected for

2 Gertrude Hildreth, "Learning to Read with McGuffey," *The Elementary School Journal*, LXII (Apr. 1962), 363–70.

certain letter sounds. The words introduced in each lesson were printed above the sentences, and diacritical marks such as the marks for long *a* and short *a* were printed over the letters. Below these words were the letters taught in each lesson, also with the diacritical marks over them. The first lessons were especially dull. The text is illustrated by the following query, "Is the cat on the mat?" The next sentence ends the suspense by assuring the child that, "The cat is on the mat." Letter sounds were introduced systematically through the first grade, according to Hildreth, with monotonous drudgery, until drill had been given on all the consonants (*b*) and consonant blends (*bl*), the long and short vowels (*a* and *a*), the vowel digraphs (*ae*), and syllabification (*hap py*). (See chapter on phonics.) Accent marks were also taught. When the children were able to read in the second reader and had learned how to use the diacritical and accent markings, they were ready to study their lessons by themselves. As in the spelling-readers, words of one syllable were used before words of two syllables and so on. The tone of the later stories was religious, and morals were emphasized.

Shortcomings of the Series. All reading was carried on orally, and perfect enunciation and articulation were the objectives of the teaching rather than reading for meaning and understanding. The sounding of letters was formal and inflexible. No other word attack skills were given so the child was limited in his efforts to recognize words. Too many new words were introduced in each lesson, no easy reading material was provided to help the child absorb and digest his learnings, and no provision was made for individual differences. In the McGuffey and other series of the period before 1920, long drills were given on syllables without relation to meaning. As time went on, the brighter children undoubtedly learned to read for meaning by techniques of their own.

Limited Needs for Reading. Since few children went to high school and even fewer went to college at that time, the needs for rapid and efficient reading were not great. Many more people lived and worked on farms than today, and many more were employed in unskilled and skilled trades. It was not uncommon for self-made men with only an elementary school education to rise to high places in business and other fields. Today, at least a high school education is necessary for almost all workers except those in unskilled occupations, and a college degree is required for many positions. Good reading is essential today.

The Phonics Approach

Later in the nineteenth century after McGuffey's series was introduced, a number of other reading series such as the Beacon and Gordon Readers were introduced, all using a highly formal and mechanical approach to phonics. The phonics approach to reading in these programs was taught without relation to meaning. Sometimes, phonic analysis was almost the only procedure used. Lists on old charts used for this phonics program included many rhyming syllables and words, regardless of whether or not their meaning and reading level were suitable for the child. These lists included many nonsense syllables. Words such as "bad," "dad," "had," "mad," "sad," "cad," "fad," "Tad," and even such sounds as "nad," "rad," and "vad" were included. Thus, time and energy were spent on some words that the child might not meet in reading for years and on some nonsense syllables. These children learned to look at a few letters at a time and to think of the sounds of the letters and syllables. Many children taught to read by memory of letter sounds, syllables, and formal word analysis were often very handicapped in their reading speed and in their ability to comprehend and recall the meaning of selections.

The Look-and-Say Method

The alphabetical, spelling, and formal phonics techniques were questioned in time because they tended to result in slow, ineffective reading. To eliminate these inadequacies, some reading specialists and teachers adopted the word method in the late twenties and early thirties, this time under the name of the look-and-say method. This method was less formal and mechanical than that followed in Horace Mann's time.

Word Lists. A list of words was taught to the children before books were introduced. This list sometimes included as many as the first hundred words the children would meet in their beginning readers. When given primers after having learned these words, the children were able to read part of the way through the book with security and a certain degree of power. Most of this reading was oral. When the children had read as far as their preparation had taken them, they were taught another list of words and then returned to the book to read all the stories that contained this latter set of words.

A tremendous amount of repetitive drill was needed to teach these long lists of words in isolation. Many words have little meaning alone, and the child was therefore unable to use meaning as a clue to help his memory. This technique of teaching a list of so-called "sight words" was sometimes accompanied by drill on formal phonics similar to that described above, although phonics was neglected when the look-and-say method was first introduced.

Attitudes Toward This Method. To the advocates of phonics as the sole reading method, who feel that reading is actually a process of sounding each letter or syllable separately regardless of the reader's familiarity with the word, the look-and-say method seemed very superficial and of dubious value. This method has been blamed by the supporters of the alphabet and phonics methods for many reading difficulties even though it was sometimes accompanied by a supplementary program of phonics. To many parents and other adults, even today, the look-and-say method is the root of all evil, and the schools are accused of being dismal shams because many adults are sure that this method still prevails.

In some schools the parents' concern about the lack of phonics teaching was justified. Some administrators and teachers revolted against the meaningless and mechanical teaching of the previous era by turning completely away from phonics. Some children were not taught phonics during this period, which was of a very few years' duration at the most. On the other hand, the most justifiable criticism of the neglect of phonics can be leveled against teachers above the first grade who expected the first grade teachers to teach all the phonics needed. Criticism may also be leveled at those who taught phonics unsystematically without adequate review of previous learnings.

Weaknesses of This Method. The pupils taught by the look-and-say method of memorized lists of words accompanied by phonics were handicapped less by lack of ability to analyze words than by lack of ability in comprehension and speed. Although a feeling of power accompanied reading after a sight vocabulary had been developed, this reading was often a process of word pronouncing or word calling without thought or meaning. The reading of the textbook was generally oral, and the pupils tended to look at and pronounce each word singly rather than to group words into phrases for thought. Even when reading silently, this look-and-say type of reading was slow because the reader looked at only one word at a time without attention to the relationships of the words in the sentence. These pupils tended to develop considerable silent speech, as well. During silent speech the pupil produces some degree of movement in his larynx and mentally *hears* each separate word. Silent speech is discussed in Chapter Two.

The child taught by the look-and-say method acquired the habit of reading silently at the same rate at which he read orally, rather than at the much more rapid, efficient, and flexible pace of good silent reading. At this time the child was seldom given help in acquiring effective techniques in rapid silent reading.

The failure to group words for thought resulted in oral reading that was lacking in expression and fluency. The reading process was still largely mechanical, and speed and comprehension tended to be limited. Even if teachers in the upper grades tried to develop speed and meaningful reading after such a beginning, they found difficulty in replacing the inefficient habits previously acquired with more effective ones.

Early Books

During the era when children were taught lists of words before starting to read, the primer was usually the first book. These primers were more difficult than the pre-primers and primers used today. Modern books are described in a later chapter. More words in the early books were introduced in each reading selection, often from three to five on a page. Repetition was not carefully planned, and the children tended to forget words that had been learned in the early part of the reader as they moved through the book toward the end.

Elocutionary Reading

At one time much attention was given to dramatic reading, or elocution. Children practiced long hours to put the proper emotion into their oral reading and to use the most effective gestures. The teacher and children were very proud of their recitations, and readings were given for the entertainment of the parents.

The Classics

The classics were emphasized at another time. Great effort and excessive time were spent in analyzing the literary sentences for grammatical structure. Because of this activity, many children learned to dislike literature. Notes were also used extensively to clarify the meanings of archaic words, and many details were given, apparently to extend the child's interest in the era represented. The constant interruptions, however, required for the use of the notes often resulted in very negative attitudes instead of extended interests.

RESEARCH AND THE TESTING MOVEMENT

A great advance in experimentation and study of children to improve ways of teaching came during and after the nineteen twenties when the beginning of test development and standardization had taken place. The use of tests brought a great increase in the understanding of children's individual differences in physical and intellectual capacities. From this insight, an entire program of experimentation and study began to take place to help teachers understand children's growth and development and their ways of learning. Other studies were made of social and emotional differences with the result that knowledge of children, their differences, their problems, and their ways of learning became enormously enlarged. This research laid the groundwork for the modern balanced program widely accepted today. Investigations have been conducted in greater and greater numbers, but many problems are still left for solution.

Knowledge of Experimentation

As research has advanced in an effort to improve education, better methods of teaching have been introduced into the schools. An understanding of the fact that educational procedures are based on research should be made clear to students and reading teachers. Education is based on knowledge rather than on emotions. Therefore, educational beliefs are not in any way similar to religious or political beliefs. Republicans may belong to their party because their families have belonged for many years. People may also be Protestant, Roman Catholic, or Buddhist because their families, too, have been of these faiths for generations. Personal opinion, however, should not enter into such fields as education, science, or medicine. Most people do not say, "I believe in mustard plasters," or "I believe in cure-all tonics," yet these same people may say, "I don't believe in the new ideas in education." Those who fully understand educational research and the development of the study of education realize that personal opinion has very little place in making decisions about educational practices.

On the other hand, professional educators are not always objective. Some trends in education may be so new, or some studies and researches may be so inconclusive as to make it difficult to draw final conclusions regarding them. Those who experiment with new ideas or methods of working with children should try to remain objective about their procedures and to withhold conclusions until considerable evidence is collected, and teachers should carefully evaluate new trends. Some people in the field of education are inclined to let their emotions predominate and may urge that new ideas be adopted widely before their value has been proven. This failing is also true in the field of drugs. Before scientists have had adequate opportunity to try out some of the newer drugs, an occasional manufacturer may start producing these drugs in large amounts in an effort to be the first to have the medicine and therefore achieve recognition. Education should avoid similar mistakes.

Knowledge of Recent Trends

Just as some teachers tend to adopt or to spread new ideas in education before they are satisfactorily evaluated, others tend to reject all new ideas. Most differences in beliefs in the field of education are not so likely to be differences in supportable positions as they are to be differences in knowledge and understanding of the development of newer ways in education. Recent trends in the teaching of reading are discussed in a later chapter in this book.

Emphasis on Silent Reading

One of the most important and sound trends to grow out of the research and testing movements was the change toward emphasis on silent reading. As tests became commonly used, weaknesses in the reading program were discovered. Lack of comprehension and speed in silent reading was found to be prevalent. When teachers examined and evaluated the findings of these tests, they realized that skill in silent reading had been neglected. Since silent reading is much more useful than oral reading, the emphasis on oral reading was replaced by greater emphasis on silent reading skills.

At that time oral reading was almost eliminated, but its place in a well-balanced program was later re-established. Oral reading is now used more predominantly for audience situations in which the reader, only, has the book in his hands. Teachers also use motivated oral reading as a way of discovering how well the children are progressing in knowledge of the vocabulary in their readers.

Skills in silent reading are now taught even in the first grade and continue to be emphasized through the child's school life. Reading for facts alone is no longer considered adequate. Even young children can learn to recall facts, sometimes in sequence, and anticipate the endings of stories on the basis of their silent reading. Primary children can also make inferences and draw conclusions from the information they have gained from reading silently. In addition, they may also begin to pick out main ideas by choosing a name for a section of a story read silently. Many more technical skills are taught in connection with silent reading in the intermediate and upper grades.

Remedial Reading

When tests were developed sufficiently to measure a variety of abilities in reading, the production of remedial reading programs became possible. Several types of tests have been produced.

Use of Tests. A survey type of test, sometimes called an achievement test, was constructed to discover the range of reading levels to be found in a particular class. Capacity tests were developed to measure various aspects of the pupil's potential reading ability. Diagnostic tests were created to discover the skills on which the child needed help, if he did not read as well as his potential ability indicated.

Other Diagnostic Procedures. The modern teacher used other ways of diagnosing children's needs along with tests of current progress. She studied tests that were given in previous grades and compared these with more recent test results. She also observed the children during a variety of reading activities such as during discussions to test comprehension of stories and other reading selections. In addition, the teacher watched the children as they worked to discover their interests when they were encouraged to choose books for pleasure reading. She also observed them as they worked independently on various activities to check comprehension, to analyze words by means of phonics and other word analysis skills, to use the dictionary and other source materials, and to make use of other reading skills.

Present Status of Reading

As research has continued, the understanding of how children learn to read, why they seem to learn better by some methods, what methods seem to be most suitable for use, and what problems are met in helping children who have difficulties learning to read has increased to a very great extent. The causes of some problems and their remediation are still controversial because no conclusive explanation or solution for these problems has yet been discovered. The causes of some problems in reading are very difficult to find, and education must depend for some of its findings on other areas such as psychology and biology. However, the basis for a variety of effective methods of teaching reading has been established and good methods are practiced by many teachers at the present time.

INFLUENCES OF SOCIAL CHANGE

Since descriptions of many excellent procedures in teaching reading and many outstanding texts and trade books are now available, the student may wonder why the schools have been criticized so extensively in recent years. A number of social changes have resulted in serious problems for the schools. The student of reading procedures and the beginning teacher should know of these changes in order to help parents understand the problems met by the schools during the past several decades.

The Depression

In the nineteen thirties the greatest economic depression of all time began to have an influence on the lives of the people in every part of the country. As in all walks of life, positions for teachers were extremely scarce, and school districts became very selective in their choices of teachers. The schools also gained advantages through raised standards for credentials and time for research.

Selection of Teachers. Although many good teachers were unemployed and all unemployed individuals suffered during the ordeal of the depression, the schools gained some benefit from the opportunity to select the best teachers from their many applicants. The large school districts continued the selective process during the three-year probationary period before teachers were placed on tenure and also continued to select teachers carefully until the beginning of the Second World War.

Not all the teachers in the schools of that day were highly selected. Many teachers remained in the schools from the era of the First World War and the years following when teachers had been hard to secure. At that time the requirements had been dropped to high school graduation in some places. As new teachers were added during the depression, the level of achievement was gradually raised. It must be noted, however, that not all new teachers were outstanding, and not all established teachers were poor. Great variations in ability were found in both groups.

Increase in Credential Requirements. Although a few states had raised standards for credentials earlier, many more states encouraged the former two-year normal schools to raise their requirements to three and later to four years because of the over-supply of teachers during the depression. Gradually more states required a bachelor's degree for a teaching credential. All levels of education benefited from the better quality of work carried on by the more highly selected and better educated teachers of the depression.

Opportunities for Research. Because of the competition for positions during the depression, some teachers continued their college work by taking advanced degrees. These degrees usually required some course work and some research conducted under the supervision of a college professor. Other graduates who were unable to secure positions also continued their work for advanced degrees in order to use the time to advantage. College classes were small, and time permitted some college instructors as well as students to take part in advanced research. Since the testing program had provided some instruments for conducting research and the early studies had built a foundation for expanding research, education made rapid advances. As the findings of the studies were applied to the classroom, the elementary pupils benefitted from the teachers' increased understanding of how to teach.

The Progressive Education Program

Many derogatory criticisms have been made of the Progressive Education movement, which is assumed to have pervaded the schools during the thirties. Some outstanding progressive teaching was developed with small groups of children in the laboratory schools of a few of the large universities such as those at the University of Chicago, Columbia University, and the University of California, Los Angeles campus. Public school teachers in a few areas in the country and some private school teachers tried to follow the ideas and procedures developed in these laboratory schools. Some of these attempts were successful and some failed. Many of the failures were due to the supporters of this program who tried to copy the new procedures without a thorough understanding of the philosophy, psychology, and the research on which these new programs were based.

Gains Through Interest. A few good practices, especially in reading methods, were adopted by occasional teachers and by a few school districts after time had been spent in a careful study of the program. Some of the improvements brought to the field of reading by careful educators were important. Interest was stressed, and teachers tried to motivate children before they read. In other situations, children were encouraged to select books that interested them for supplementary and home reading.

Gains Through Problem Solving. Reading material was also used to stimulate thinking and to help children try to solve their own problems. They might read books to discover how to plant seeds and how to care for the plants as they began to grow. Older children might use books to discover how to make adobe bricks in a study of the history of the southwest. They might also use books to try to find out why these people used adobe for their houses instead of wood. Still older children might make use of books to find the different amounts of rainfall during a particular season in the countries of South America in order to make a large wall chart to show this information. An effort was made to balance reading skills to avoid the one-sided teaching of phonics and oral reading to the exclusion of comprehension and other important skills in silent reading.

Attacks on the Program. Before the Progressive Education movement had gained any real momentum, it was violently attacked by many teachers who feared the extra work involved, who were afraid of the more democratic control, and who had no real understanding of the program. The teachers and parents who observed the mistakes and misinterpretations made during the early superficial experiments also vigorously attacked this new program.

Evaluation of the Program. Before the Second World War ravaged the schools, some fine studies had been made in particular cities of the effects of some of the better procedures on the learning of pupils. In every case the well-planned modern program was proven to be as effective as and in many ways better than the older, formal program.

Influences of the Second World War

The attempts to apply the newer ideas concerning the utilization of children's interests, the use of activities to stimulate children to think, to explore, and to solve problems, and the effort to help children work on the level at which they could succeed at their own pace in the Progressive Education program might have been salvaged despite its many misinterpretations, had it not been for the advent of the Second World War. The war industries began to draw trained teachers from the schools in 1942 and the years following Pearl Harbor.

Lack of Trained Teachers. In most of the states that required a degree for the granting of a regular credential, provisional teachers have been required to take college courses to be able to qualify for these degrees and credentials. Some of these teachers who have qualified for regular credentials are among the best teachers in today's schools. Others learned poor ways of teaching before they were able to take education courses. When these teachers had acquired about eighty or ninety units in academic courses in such fields as history, anthropology, English, and science, they were permitted to begin their courses in teacher education. Since they were able to take only a few units each semester due to the time spent in teaching, they might have taught five or more years before they began to take courses in education. Some of the teachers were able to apply the methods they learned. Others had acquired such deeply established habits of *hunt and peck* teaching without any real methods and were so inflexible that they were unable to make use of the more modern ideas they acquired in their education courses just as *hunt and peck* typists meet difficulty if they try to learn the touch system after years of wrong habits. Still others took the necessary courses with no intention of making use of accepted methods because of the time and work needed in preparation if these methods were to be followed.

When a consultant in one situation tried to help a teacher who had no training in methods by suggesting a simple procedure to help his teaching of reading in a small way, he said in a shocked voice, "But I would have to read the story before I came to class, if I used that method."

Even older children benefit from learning about the habits of animals.
(Courtesy Georgetown Elementary School, El Dorado County Schools.)

Some of the teachers, who have failed to use the methods they have learned, wanted to teach only because of the short hours they managed to put in due to almost complete lack of preparation. Others of these teachers merely wanted to supplement their husbands' more adequate salaries with a few luxuries for the family. Teachers who fail to meet professional standards are still doing great harm to the profession, but many of these have tenure and, unfortunately, even they are needed.

According to a report of the United States Department of Health, Education and Welfare the number of teachers on provisional credentials increased by 1.7 per cent between the 1958-59 and the 1959-60 school years.[3] Even now many temporarily credentialed teachers and double sessions are still found in some schools.

Reading Methods of Poorly Trained Teachers. The teachers who failed to learn effective methods in teaching reading even today use a system called *round robin* or *barber shop*. This practice consists of calling on one pupil after another by turns to read aloud a sentence, a paragraph, or even a page of the textbook while the others usually sit by in boredom. When a child fails to recognize a particular word, either the teacher or another pupil tells him what it is, often without allowing time for the child to use clues to discover it for himself. After this process, a little phonics is usually taught. No real teaching of skills other than phonics is usually included in this practice. Many of today's youth and young adults were victims of this type of teaching.

The Deprived Generation

What has happened to these children of the war and postwar years? Have they managed to surmount the handicap of inadequately educated teachers, double sessions, and attendance at schools in several different parts of the country in one year? In an article by Lieutenant Colonel George Walton, USA, the combined rate for rejections due to failure to pass both the physical test and the Armed Forces Qualification Test (an achievement test) was about thirty per cent during the Second World War.[4] From the end of the Second World War to 1961, the rejections had increased to forty-nine per cent. For the year of 1961 alone, the rejections had grown to fifty-three per cent. For the month of May, 1961, alone, the rejection was fifty-six per cent, and for June alone it was fifty-eight per cent. These figures are based on rejections

[3] U. S. Department of Health, Education, and Welfare. *Enrollment, Teachers, and Schoolhousing*, OE 20007, Circular No. 604 (Washington, D. C.: U. S. Government Printing Office, 1959).
[4] George Walton, Lt. Col., USA, "Uncle Sam's Rejects," *The Saturday Evening Post*, CCXXXVI, No. 44 (Dec. 8, 1962), 10, 13.

of those who had registered for the draft rather than for voluntary service. For the data from the Armed Forces Qualifications Test alone, Lieutenant Colonel Walton stated that sixteen and two thirds per cent, about one in six, of the men registering for the draft from the end of the Korean conflict until the end of 1961 were rejected. These eighteen- to twenty-one year old inductees would be just the age to have been in school during the years when educational programs were suffering from tremendous handicaps. According to Austin's survey the problems were far from solved even in 1961.[5]

Influences of the Space Age

At the beginning of the space race when the Russians placed Sputnik into orbit, American people began to feel extremely insecure. People felt that something must be wrong in the modern era and naturally turned toward the schools as the source of American weakness.

Critical Reactions. American schools and the education of the children were judged to be decidedly inferior to the Russian schools and their educational products. Russia, however, had given a large proportion of money to her space activities in comparison with other phases of living. In addition, teachers in Russia received a high degree of social status and better salaries than most other members of their society. Russia was therefore able to select their teaching staff with care. Pupils and teachers were stimulated by high prestige given to devotion to work and especially to service in the government and the armed services, an important factor in Russia's favor. Another factor concerned discipline. Russian teachers were employed to teach, not to waste time on discipline. The Russian parents were held fully responsible for their children's behavior when they were in school. Any misbehavior on the part of the child resulted in a summons for both parents to go to the school immediately, although they might have to leave work in a factory or on a farm to do so. When they arrived at school, they were given full blame for the pupil's misbehavior, and the family was held in disgrace. Thus, the way was paved for the teachers to work in a highly effective situation.

Refutations. In an effort during the postwar era to counteract the accusations against the schools, some of which were irresponsible and absurd, an article was published in *Changing Times* of June, 1954, entitled, "The Truth About Our Public Schools." [6] A reprint of this article was made available for those who wished to send for it.

[5] Mary C. Austin, *et al.*, *The Torch Lighters* (Cambridge, Mass.: Harvard University Graduate School of Education, 1961).

[6] *Changing Times—The Kiplinger Magazine*, "The Truth About Our Public Schools," Washington 6, D. C., June, 1954.

A number of unbiased investigations made over a period of years were quoted. One study compared the test records of the forty best eighth grade pupils in the Cleveland schools in 1848 with records on the same test taken by the forty brightest children in the Cleveland schools in 1947. Although more of the 1947 children were younger, their average scores on the same test were considerably higher.

To compare achievement in reading, a study by Worcester and Kline was quoted.[7] These authors reported a test given to over five thousand children in Lincoln, Nebraska, in 1921 which was repeated with a comparable number of children in the same city in 1947. The average scores on the tests were compared by grade from the third through the eighth. The 1947 children made higher scores in all grades than the 1921 children who were the products of heavy emphasis on phonics. The 1921 children should have had an advantage because any child of that era who could not read on grade level by the end of the year was required to repeat the grade. On the other hand, far fewer of the 1947 children were required to repeat grades because of intervening research. It had been found that two thirds of children who repeat a particular grade achieve no better and often do not achieve as well when repeating the grade.

In 1961 Gates made a study to compare reading achievement of children tested in 1937 with those tested in 1957.[8] Data from tests of over one hundred thousand children in 1937 were compared with data from thirty-one thousand children in 1957. Vocabulary, speed, and accuracy of reading were tested. The 1957 children excelled the 1937 children by an average of one half year, although they were younger on the average than the 1937 children.

The Present Situation

These studies were made in states which had required considerable education on the part of their teachers. The results from these tests do not reflect the achievement of children who went to school in states which required only six weeks' training beyond high school graduation for their teachers, nor do they reflect the achievement of children who were taught in areas where well-educated teachers were replaced by provisional teachers who had scarcely more than a high school education.

[7] D. A. Worcester, and Anne Kline, *Reading Achievement in Lincoln, Nebraska Schools: 1921 and 1947* (Lincoln, Neb.: University of Nebraska Teachers College, 1947).

[8] Arthur I. Gates, *Reading Attainment in Elementary Schools: 1957 and 1937* (New York: Columbia University, Teachers College Bureau of Publications, 1961).

The protests of people who maintain that many children and young adults have been partially cheated of their right to a good education are justified despite the work of a considerable number of fine teachers. These children have paid a high price for their country's neglect of the schools. The people of this country are also paying a high price for their neglect because they must depend upon these young people for the social, political, mathematical, and scientific advances to be made in the years to come, as well as for the new generation of leaders. Although the teaching quality has been improving in recent years, many more improvements are still needed, and these can be accomplished with the help of an informed and forward looking public.

SUMMARY

A large amount of experimentation is now going on in the field of reading. The investigation of new ideas is involved in some of this work, whereas other so-called research is the mere regurgitation of plans formerly tried and given up as ineffective. The student and teacher should have a sound knowledge of the various ideas that have been tried in the teaching of reading in order to avoid this latter type of experimentation. Most of the important movements in the teaching of reading are described in this chapter.

The testing movement provided scientific forms of evaluation and furnished the spur to the development of more sound methods of teaching reading. Then the loss of professionally trained teachers due to the advent of the Second World War swept a large proportion of these teachers out of the schools to replace them by emergency teachers who were high school graduates or who had a few units of college courses.

The quality of teaching deteriorated profoundly, later to be blamed by self-appointed lay experts in education on the progressive movement of which these new emergency teachers had no understanding. Some of these emergency teachers became very capable with further professional education, but others either did not understand the newer ideas or did not want to put forth the work required by the new ways. Many of both types of these teachers are still in the schools today along with many of the newly graduated teachers.

2

The Reading Process

When a sportscaster asked a baseball player what he had done to improve his batting average, he replied, "I don't know, but as long as I'm doing so well I'm not going to try to find out." Most good readers would probably respond in the same way if asked how they are able to read so well. As they read, these effective readers become lost in the interest of the story or the challenge of the ideas in the reading material. The reading teacher, however, must analyze the process in order to be able to teach children to read well.

NEED FOR MEANING

Some people feel that reading is the mere process of learning sounds and blending them in order to pronounce each word. Specialists in education, on the other hand, believe that reading involves much more than the above process and that thinking is a very important part of reading.

If the ability to pronounce the sounds of the letters and to blend these to make words were true reading, everyone would be able to read a foreign language without training beyond learning the letter sounds peculiar to the language. For example, the vowel sounds in one language are as follows: *a* is sounded as *ah*, *i* as *ee*, *u* as *oo*, *e* as *ay*, and *o* as *oh*. *Aa* is merely a prolonged *ah*. The consonants are the same as those in the English language. With this help anyone should be able to read the following sentence, "Watakushi no okaasan wa yubinkyoku e ikimasu." [1] All the words in this sentence can be pronounced by fol-

[1] This sentence has meaning for the person who understands the Japanese language. It means, "My mother is going to the post office."

lowing the rules given above. What, however, does this sentence mean to one who does not know the language?

Authorities in reading feel strongly that the above process of pronouncing words is not reading, nor is the mere pronunciation of words known by the reader necessarily true reading. In fact, most authorities believe that not only the comprehension of such a sentence but its interpretation, as well, is a part of the process. A survey of the components of reading and the processes utilized may help the student understand the complexity of the reading act. Although no one component occurs separately in the reading process, four interrelated components are discussed separately below for convenience. They include perception, comprehension, integration of ideas with previous experiences, and reactions to reading material. Ways to teach reading are discussed in detail in later chapters.

PERCEPTION

Because many phases of the discussion of reading involve an understanding of the meaning of the words, maturation and maturity, these words should be defined. Maturity is used here to include the physical, mental, social, and emotional factors that result in all phases of growth. Maturity then depends upon the natural physical growth that takes place in a normal environment, and it also includes the growth provided by experience as the child is challenged to use all of his capacities. To be normal, the child must have had sufficient experience to help him develop these capacities.

Effect of Immaturity

Reading makes use of the ability to see and distinguish black letters on light paper and to perceive groups of these letters as words that stand for ideas. A certain level of maturity is necessary before the child is able to distinguish one word or letter from another. Even more maturity is required to distinguish between words containing letters that are reversed in shape from left to right, as *b* and *d* and *p* and *q*, and those that are reversed vertically as *n* and *u*. Immature children are much more able to distinguish between words and letters that are grossly different from each other, such as *b* and *w*, than they are to distinguish between words and letters that are similar to each other.

Recognition of Whole Words

A mature child who has listened to many stories knows that the marks on paper stand for words even before he knows what particular words they represent. When he begins to read, he learns to associate a group of printed letters with the sound of the word or words they represent, such as his name. These words, however, must be ones he is very familiar with when they are spoken. By the process of association, he acquires the ability to recognize such a word each time he sees the symbols that stand for it. These words are called *sight words*. This association process is very similar to the process the child follows in learning to say "cat" when he sees a small four-legged animal that says "meow."

Difficulties in Perception

Because some beginners are unable to perceive small details of shape, they may have more success at first by learning whole word configurations, even though they may identify these words by particular characteristics rather than by total shape. Another problem results because many children fail to see a pattern in the internal arrangement of the letters in a word. In addition, some children may not have had enough experience to know which details of the letters are important to the recognition of the word. Some children, too, have great difficulty in noticing the direction in which the letters face or even the order of sequence of the letters. Although many of these beginners are unable to analyze parts of words by letter sounds, they may use particular characteristics of words as clues to recognize whole words. One little girl said she recognized the word, *rabbit*, by the long ears in the middle, referring to the upper strokes of the *b's*.

Thoughts as Units

Most modern teachers teach short sentences, phrases, or words as units of thought, the process of going from the whole to the part. For example, if the child is able to recognize his own name in print, the teacher may print on the board, "Jimmy, come here." She may ask the child whose name is printed on the board to raise his hand. She may then hold up a toy, using a beckoning gesture and ask, "What do I want you to do, Jimmy?" Jimmy readily concludes that she wants him to come up to get the toy. She may then help him put the direction into words. He soon infers that the direction is "come here" and carries out the action by coming forward to take the toy. After the action she asks him to repeat or "read" the words of the direction from the board. As the teacher repeats this process using other children's names, they soon recognize the words, "come here," along with their names. In this way children start reading with meaning and thought from the very beginning.

Groups of Words Held in Mind. Unless the child is able to hold at least a small group of words in mind at one time, he will be unable to group the ideas in even a simple sentence. For example, the sentence, *The boy was at the circus,* cannot have complete meaning until the reader reaches the word, *circus.* Goins found that good readers at the end of the first grade seemed able to hold a total configuration or thought in mind while they clarified the details, that is, while they analyzed any unknown words in the sentence.[2] For example, the child may read the sentence, *The boy was beside the lion's XXXX at the circus.* He is able to grasp the thought of the boy beside the lion at the circus while he analyzes the missing word to discover that it is *cage.* He then completes the sentence by fitting the meaning of the word, *cage,* into the total thought and decides that it is appropriate.

Characteristics of Reading by Thoughts. A number of investigators have emphasized the advantages of reading in terms of whole thoughts. After reviewing many studies, Vernon states that, "To become a fluent reader, he (the child) must proceed to the stage of reading whole phrases and sentences."[3] According to Stauffer, Edmund Burke Huey pointed out in 1913 that three times as many letters could be seen at one time when combined in words than when the letters were presented separately in mixed order.[4] Vernon has stated that it is impossible for the mature reader to perceive every letter of every word since research tells us that an average adult perceives eight to ten letter spaces (letters in words and spaces between words) in a fraction of a second.

Vernon also mentions a common occurrence that emphasizes techniques used by effective readers, sometimes called "proofreaders' errors." A proofreader must look at every detail to discover errors in print. The fast reader who proofreads his own papers tends to miss many of these details because he has not been trained to observe small details in his customary reading. The professional proofreader, on the other hand, has learned to concentrate on details and usually pays comparatively little attention to the meaning of the text. A student who is able to concentrate on the details of proofreading would find that he, too, would be able to give little attention to meaning during this type of reading.

Types of Perceivers. Some investigators feel that children may fall into one of two classes of perceivers. Some read by whole thoughts, analyzing details only when necessary. Others may tend to read parts

[2] Jean Turner Goins, "Visual and Auditory Perception in Reading," *The Reading Teacher,* XIII (Oct. 1959), 9–13.

[3] M. D. Vernon, "The Perceptual Process in Reading," *The Reading Teacher,* XIII (Oct. 1959), 2–8.

[4] Russell G. Stauffer, "Old Beliefs Need Examining," *The Reading Teacher,* XIII (Oct. 1959), 1.

of words which they put together to make the whole. No proof of these types of readers yet exists, however.

Procedures of Mature Readers. In general, authorities seem to believe that an effective adult reader perceives key words and infers meaning from these and other words that he may have glimpsed vaguely. He may use a larger proportion of key words and fewer of those glimpsed vaguely, however, when reading difficult material. Obviously the process described above is vastly more streamlined than that used by a beginning reader. The long term goal of the teacher should always be directed toward the process carried on by the effective adult reader.

Introduction of Letter Sounds

Most authorities feel that the best time to point out similarities in sounds or parts of words (beginning steps in phonics) is when children have learned three or four words with the same beginning sound or with the same set of rhyming letters. For example, a group of children may have met in their pre-primer stories and learned to recognize the words, *can, car,* and *come,* by simple recall of the whole word patterns. In their next story the teacher finds that they will meet the word, *cookies.* She may introduce this word as a whole through discussion before the children read the new story.

Discovering Letter Sounds. Later at the practice period the teacher may help the children discover the similarity of the word, *cookies,* to the previously learned words. To accomplish this, she may write on the chalkboard the three words learned previously, *can, car,* and *come,* calling on children to take turns to read each word as she prints it. She may then add the word, *cookies,* which was introduced in the current lesson, and may also ask that it be read as she adds it to the list. At this point she may ask the children if someone can tell her any parts of these four words that look alike. Some child is always able to identify the *c* as the common element. She then may ask another child to read the list of words so that the members of the group can listen to see if the beginnings of these words sound as well as look alike. Most of the children who have made a successful start in reading will be able to hear the similarities in these sounds. Some children will need more practice before they are able to hear similarities in sounds.

Acquiring Auditory Acuity. The task of helping children hear the auditory sounds of beginning letters and to identify two words that begin with identical sounds among others that start with different sounds is a difficult step for them. Identifying rhyming words is also difficult. Teachers can work on this step by helping children listen to words that begin alike in the readiness stage, long before she tries to help the children associate them with visual symbols. Ideas for working on this step will be presented later.

Combining Phonics with Context Clues. If children are taught beginning reading by means of thoughts and words in context and later learn to observe distinguishing details of letters or groups of letters in words, they develop a variety of techniques and versatility in their use. Context (thought) clues should always be used to check analysis of letter sounds (phonics).

An example of this process will help distinguish between these processes of phonic analysis and the use of context clues. Children in a reading group were working on a story on the chalkboard about a birthday surprise for Billy. As the lesson progressed, the children in the story were giving Billy some hints about his present to help him guess what it was. A part of the story follows:

> Patty said, "It is little."
> Dick said, "It can walk and run."
> Ronald said, "It has two legs."
> Susan said, "I know its color.
> It is yellow."

The oral reading progressed smoothly until Fred, who was reading the last two sentences, paused because he did not recognize *yellow*, a new word. The teacher asked if he could think of another word that starts like this word. Fred suggested *yes*, a word he already knew. The teacher printed *yes* on the chalkboard near the word *yellow* and let Fred underline the beginning letters, *ye*, that were the same in both words. Then she asked, "What color begins like *yes?*" Fred thought a minute and then replied, "yellow."

The teacher reassured him and then suggested that he read the sentences again to see if they sounded right. When he read, "Susan said, 'I know its color. It is yellow.'" he added, "It does sound right because *yellow* is a color."

In order to help Fred and the children in his group identify the word, *yellow*, the teacher helped the children compare the word with another that began with the same letters, a phonic technique. She then helped Fred reread the last two sentences to be sure that the word, *yellow*, completed the thought of the sentence properly and fitted into the story, the use of a context clue. These two processes should be used together.

COMPREHENSION

The development of comprehension in reading depends first upon the child's ability to perceive the printed symbols of words and to associate

them with their sounds. The child then associates these words with
the concepts he has developed from previous experiences. These experiences may have resulted in a concept made up primarily of the physical attributes of a particular word. For example, the concept of the word,
doll, includes the size and shape of the object along with its softness
and use as a play object. Concepts, on the other hand, may be developed through experiences to arrive at an understanding of general ideas.
For example, the word, *toy,* represents a general idea of a variety of
objects that may be used for play. The child derives concepts of familiar
ideas from the material he reads, but he must also learn to understand
the relationships among the words for real comprehension. Such relationships are involved in such a sentence as, *That is my toy.* The relation of the word, *my,* has changed a general idea into a personal one.
The words, *That is,* have added the related thought of a specific toy
instead of a general idea.

INTEGRATION WITH PREVIOUS EXPERIENCES

The child must have a variety of experiences before he can gain meaning not only from reading but from all language, as well. In speaking,
the child deals with experiences that have been a part of his personal
life. In reading, however, he must deal with meaning, whether or not
it applies to incidents within his own personal experiences. Reading
will have far greater meaning for a child if he can relate it to his previous
experiences.

For example, the child who reads, "The boys were high in the tree,"
may bring rich concepts and meaning to the sentence if he has had experience playing with other boys in such a situation. He may visualize
himself with one of his playmates of similar age. He may also visualize
familiar trees. He may recall a few small fruit trees in his back yard,
but these may be too small to serve in this situation. His mind then
moves to a mental picture of the large sycamore near the street that
he and one of his friends often climb.

Enriched Experiences

He visualizes himself and his friend high in the tree sitting on sturdy
branches. He remembers the feeling of his shoes slipping on the
branches as he climbs, and the grip he takes with his hands to pull himself upward. He recalls the breathless feeling when he finally arrives
at his chosen place, followed by the feeling of lightness and temporary
freedom that comes from being high above others. He visualizes his
friend near him and recalls the pleasant feeling of comradeship and shared

secrecy because others do not know about this hiding place. He recalls the fresh feeling of the soft breeze as it rustles the leaves and the exhilaration that comes from being able to see houses, cars, and people far below like small creatures in another world. As this child reads the sentence, then, he brings images, memories, and emotions, all a part of the concept, to fill out and enrich the meaning of the sentence.

Limited Experiences

On the other hand, the child who has never climbed a tree must substitute whatever experiences with height he has had and must try to associate these with the thought of the boys in a tree. In this way each child will bring to the sentence a personal concept gained from his own personal experiences.

REACTION TO READING MATERIAL

The reaction of the reader to the material read is another component of the reading process in addition to those already discussed, that is, perception, comprehension, and integration with previous experiences. Every reader, whether an elementary school pupil, a college student, or an adult, reacts in some way to the material he reads. Most first-grade children accept the stories in their pre-primers and primers much in the unquestioning manner in which they accept bedtime stories. Some mature readers analyze and evaluate the material they read, but a large proportion of readers accept without question anything they read in newspapers, magazines, or books without regard to slant or viewpoint.

On the other hand, even children in the first grade can be guided to react toward reading in more intelligent ways, and older students must be able to react intelligently, if our democratic way of life is to be preserved. Reaction to reading materials may take one of several forms. The reader may organize the material for his own use, may evaluate material critically, or may read for enjoyment and appreciation.

The following story will serve as an example of material that may be read by children of approximately the fourth grade. It is used to illustrate ways in which children can organize and evaluate material critically.

How Some Seeds Travel

Although seeds can neither walk nor fly, they have clever ways of moving from place to place. Some of them are hitchhikers, some are gliders and spinners, and others are floaters.

Burrs are excellent examples of hitchhikers. They take rides on children's clothing. They also like to ride in the fur of animals. Since birds like to eat many types of seeds, they may carry them away as they fly from one place to another.

Spinners and gliders have other ways of traveling. The maple seed lies in a little pocket in the pod and is followed by a wing attached to it. Two seeds are usually attached to each other at the seed end of the pods. Because the ends of the pods containing the seeds are heavier, they lead the wings. The wings are shaped to cause the seed to spin as it falls to the ground. If the wind is blowing, a seed may travel for some distance. Other seeds use fuzzy parachutes that help them glide through the air. The wind may also help these seeds travel from place to place.

Most seeds are light enough to travel on water, at least until they become water soaked. If they sink to the bottom of the river or lake, they will not be able to grow because they do not have air. Some, however, are washed onto nearby banks where they are able to grow.

Organizing for Use

Some ways in which reading material may be organized for use or practical application are by selecting main ideas, classifying information and ideas, observing relationships, determining cause and effect, making inferences, predicting outcomes, arriving at generalizations, and drawing conclusions. Some of these means of organization overlap. If the teacher encourages children to organize their reading material, using some of these patterns of organization for purposes which are important to them, they will tend to understand and remember the information better than if they were carrying on practice exercises. If children read material passively in the hope that they will remember enough for a class recitation or a test, the information they recall is likely to be superficial and temporary. Some examples of the organization of the story given above are described.

Selecting Main Ideas. The story of "How Some Seeds Travel" lends itself particularly well to the selection of main ideas. A group of children in the fourth grade had been making a collection of seeds, which had originally begun in connection with a study of seeds that provide food for people and later had been extended to seeds that provide food for animals. The children had read stories in a variety of science readers and had found an occasional story in their reading texts. A few had looked up articles on seeds in junior encyclopedias. Mrs. Taylor, their teacher, had selected this story given above to provide the children with experience in organizing, since the vocabulary was rather easy and the story lent itself very well to this type of analysis. Mrs. Taylor had discussed the purpose of an introductory paragraph in previous situations. At this time she asked, "Who can tell me how to find out what is discussed in this story?"

When she called upon John, he said, "The name of the story tells us that it is about seeds and how seeds can travel."

"Good," said Mrs. Taylor, "but perhaps someone can tell us another way to find out what is discussed in the story."

She called on Laurie who said, "Sometimes the first paragraph in the story tells us about some of the things that are in the story."

"Fine," said Mrs. Taylor. "Suppose we all read the first paragraph to see if we can find out more about the topic." In a short time, most of the children had raised their hands so Mrs. Taylor said, "Good, suppose you tell us one idea that will be discussed in the story, Edward."

Edward replied, "The first paragraph said that some of the seeds are hitchhikers. That sounds funny. I don't see how seeds could hold out their thumbs for a ride."

Mrs. Taylor replied, "You have a good point, Edward. We'll read the rest of the story soon to find out how seeds can be hitchhikers. Who found another idea that will be discussed in the story? Victoria, do you have an idea?"

"The story says that some seeds are gliders and spinners," replied Victoria. "I've seen the spinners. Our maple tree has seeds that whirl round and round as they fall to the ground."

"Yes, I've seen those, too, Victoria," replied Mrs. Taylor. "We'll read some more about them pretty soon. Who found another type of seed listed?"

Mary Helen said, "The story said some are floaters. I don't know whether it means they float through the air or float on the water."

"Good," said Mrs. Taylor, "that is another type of seed. We will find out what the author meant by floaters when we read the rest of the story. Who can tell us again how most authors use the first paragraph in their stories. At least, how did this author use his first paragraph?"

Jacqueline said, "This author named the things he is going to tell us about in the rest of the story."

"Right," said Mrs. Taylor. "I'm sure you remember stories by other authors who did the same thing. Let's decide now how we can use this story to help us with our collection of seeds."

Karen said, "We decided to put our seeds in plastic bags and mount them on charts. Maybe we should have a different chart for each type of seed."

"That's an excellent idea," said Mrs. Taylor. The class then read the rest of the story to help them classify their exhibit under the titles used in the story. These titles were actually the main ideas taken from each of the paragraphs in the body of the story.

Classifying Information and Ideas. As the children picked out the main idea of each paragraph, they were actually also classifying the information in this story. Several of the children who had looked up this topic in the junior encyclopedias had drawn pictures of various types of seeds and used these to help the other children classify the seeds in their collection for placement on the charts. They found some seeds, however, that did not seem to fit on any chart. Sweet pea seeds, soy bean pods, geranium pods, and touch-me-not seeds did not fit into the classifications. One of the children suggested that they put these aside in a box until the class could discuss them.

Observing Relationships. After the children had a number of seeds placed in bags on the charts, Mrs. Taylor asked, "Do you see anything about the seeds on this chart that look alike?" as she pointed to the chart of burrs.

Ted replied, "Most of these burrs seem to have little hooks all over them. At first they looked like little slivers around all the sides of the burrs, but I looked at a burr under the magnifying glass and saw that each sliver had a hook on the end. I guess that's so they won't come out of the animal's fur too soon."

"Yes," Bob responded. "I have an awful time getting them out of my socks after I've been down at the river. No wonder they can travel so far!"

"You're right," said Mrs. Taylor. "They do have little hooks on them. When the rest of you have time, come up and look at the burrs under the magnifying glass. You can see them much more easily that way. Of course, I prefer that you come one at a time so that you will not disturb the rest of us when we are working." Mrs. Taylor guided the children to analyze the characteristics of the other types of seeds to help the children observe more relationships.

Determining Cause and Effect. On another day Mrs. Taylor decided to emphasize cause and effect in the class discussion. The work on the charts had continued, and about half the seeds had been classified, aside from the separate miscellaneous group the children had put into the box. Mrs. Taylor said, "We have already discussed some of the reasons these seeds are able to travel. Nevertheless, I think we should discuss these ideas some more. We discovered that the parachute seeds sometimes travel hundreds of miles. Does anyone know why these seeds are able to travel so far?"

Kenneth raised his hand and said, "I read about those in the encyclopedia. Those seeds are very tiny and light so that the wind can blow them easily. Sometimes they are picked up by the wind and carried into the upper currents of air. As long as the wind keeps blowing, they have to go with it. Some winds keep blowing for a long time, so the seeds don't drop to the ground until the windstorm is over. It's the same with houses and trees during cyclones, but they don't go so far."

"Excellent," said Mrs. Taylor. "Let's see if we can shorten Kenneth's story so that we can say it in two sentences. Let's start by saying, 'Two causes for seeds traveling long distances are as follows.' Who can give us one cause?"

"This type of seed is very light," responded Julie.

"Fine," said Mrs. Taylor. "Georgia, will you write that sentence on the board as the first cause. Who can give us another cause?"

"Sometimes winds blow for a long distance," said Frank, "and they take these light seeds with them."

"That's correct. Please write that sentence on the board as the second cause, Georgia." Mrs. Taylor continued to bring out cause and effect in regard to the other types of seeds on the charts. The children wrote in their notebooks about causes for seeds traveling in various ways. They had started to make notebooks so that they could keep important information for reference. They also illustrated their notes to help clarify ideas.

Making Inferences and Predicting Outcomes. To provide an opportunity for the children to make inferences, Mrs. Taylor brought up the following question one day in discussion. She said, "We have learned that coconuts sometimes float across the ocean and land in Norway. Suppose someone in Norway planted one of these coconuts. Do you think it would grow? I can help by telling you that Norway is a very cold country and that it is across the ocean from us."

James raised his hand and said, "I read about that in the encyclopedia."

Mrs. Taylor said, "Fine, James. Will you please help us with the first part of the answer, but let's see if someone else can think of the rest of the answer for himself. James, tell us what kind of a climate coconuts need to grow?"

James replied, "They grow in a hot country. I don't think they would grow in cold weather and snow."

"Good," said Mrs. Taylor. "Now, who can tell us what would happen to a coconut if someone planted it in Norway?"

Several children volunteered and Diane answered, "I don't think it would grow. James said coconuts grow in hot countries, and you just said that Norway is cold."

"Good thinking," said Mrs. Taylor. She then presented several more questions to help the children make inferences about the problem. She realized that the children had also predicted outcomes along with drawing inferences, so she worked on a different skill during the next discussion period.

Drawing Conclusions and Arriving at Generalizations. Mrs. Taylor felt the children had enough background on the problem of distribution of seeds so that she could now help them draw conclusions and arrive at generalizations. During this discussion she said, "We have learned a lot about the way seeds travel and how man has been helped because of this. I wonder if you can tell us what conditions are necessary for seeds to survive after they have traveled long distances either by water or wind. We know that many seeds don't grow because something is wrong about the place where they land. Perhaps we can make several statements that tell us what these seeds need to grow."

Phillip said, "I know one thing. Seeds have to drop into good soil so that they can grow."

"Fine," said Mrs. Taylor. "Will you please put this statement on the board and write the numeral 1 in front of it, Carolyn. Now who can think of another condition that seeds need to make them grow."

"I know something else," replied Jeanette. "The climate has to be right. If it's too cold or too hot for the seed, it won't grow. Seeds need sun, too."

"It has to have some rain," added Gary.

"Good," said Mrs. Taylor. "Did you get those conditions, Carolyn?"

"It shouldn't be buried too deep or drop in a place that's too wet all the time," said Shirley.

"That's a good one," answered Mrs. Taylor. "I wonder if we can say what it needs rather than what it shouldn't have," she added.

Randy replied, "She means the seed needs to have air."

"Good! That's a fine list," said Mrs. Taylor. "You have drawn some very good conclusions about the growing conditions of seeds."

Critical Evaluation

Critical evaluation of reading materials is an even more advanced form of reaction to reading than organization of ideas. Even in the kindergarten and first grade, the teacher may guide the children to decide whether or not a story could be true. In this way they learn to classify certain stories as fairy or fantasy stories and others as real stories, meaning that the situations and action could have occurred. Young children can also evaluate reading material from the standpoint of its adequacy in meeting their needs. Perhaps the children wish to find out how often to feed their fish. The teacher may read the directions on the package of fish food, stopping after each sentence to ask, "Does this sentence tell us what we want to know?" The teacher may deliberately read several statements that do not answer the question before she reads the needed sentence.

Evaluating Relevancy and Adequacy of Material. The story about the seeds serves to illustrate the topic, evaluating relevancy and adequacy of material, although Mrs. Taylor usually used different material to illustrate different reading skills. After the children had completed their three charts, one on hitchhikers, one on gliders and spinners, and one on floaters, June said one day, "We have quite a few seeds in our miscellaneous box. What are we going to do with these?"

Mrs. Taylor replied, "I hoped someone would bring up that problem. Why do you think we put these seeds in a box instead of making a special chart for them?"

She called on Laurie who said, "We didn't know how these seeds travel so we didn't have any titles for new charts."

"That's right," answered Mrs. Taylor. "Why didn't we read our story again to find other ways seeds travel?" she asked.

"Our story didn't tell how other seeds travel," Edward responded. "It only told three ways seeds travel."

"That's true," answered Mrs. Taylor. "What do you think about this story we read?"

Phillip said, "It didn't tell us enough. It should have told us how these other seeds travel, too."

Jacqueline raised her hand urgently and said, "This story didn't have to tell us all the ways seeds travel. The title said 'How Some Seeds Travel.' I found a story in an encyclopedia that told other ways seeds travel."

"Do you remember what it said?" asked Phillip.

"I remember some of the things it said," answered Jacqueline. "It told about seeds that pop open. It said the shells get dry and explode. That sends the seeds all over the ground."

"Do we have any of that kind in our box?" asked Victoria.

"I think I can tell if I look in the box," said Jacqueline. Mrs. Taylor nodded, so Jacqueline got the box and said, "Well I think these sweet pea pods are one kind that explode. The book said oxalis, geranium, and touch-me-not pods explode, too. I don't know if any of these seeds belong to those plants."

Julie said, "I think I can tell. We have all those flowers at home." She picked out some oxalis and geranium pods and said, "These explode, too. We could put these on a chart with the sweet pea pods."

"That's a fine idea," said Mrs. Taylor. "Who can think of a name for the chart?"

Billy, who often had original ideas, said, "Why don't we call them poppers?" The class members approved, so Mrs. Taylor asked for volunteers for a committee to print the name on a new chart and to mount these seeds on it.

She then said, "Perhaps we should wait until tomorrow to see if we have other types of seeds in our miscellaneous box. Now let's talk about our story. What did you like about it?"

"I liked the words it used to tell about the hitchhikers and gliders," said Georgia.

"Yes," replied Mrs. Taylor. "Those were interesting words to describe the seeds. Do you think the story was a good one to use to help us make our charts about how seeds travel?"

"I think so," answered Phillip. "It told us some things we needed, but it didn't tell everything we needed to know."

"I agree with you," responded Mrs. Taylor. "I wonder if the author made any mistakes in the article."

"I'm sure there were no mistakes," said Mary Helen. "I read stories in some of our science books and in two encyclopedias. They said the same things, but they told other things, too."

"Good," said Mrs. Taylor. "Did anyone else find other stories or articles in encyclopedias that agreed or disagreed with the story we read together?"

Many hands were raised and all the volunteers stated that their stories or articles agreed with the story, "How Some Seeds Travel," but most of the children said that they learned other things in addition. In this way the story was evaluated for accuracy and adequacy.

Comparing and Contrasting Reading Material. On another day Kenneth had just read to the class an article from an encyclopedia about how seeds travel. Mrs. Taylor said, "Let's compare the story we read together last week, 'How Some Seeds Travel,' with the article that Kenneth has just read to us. Do you think that they were the same or different?"

James said, "I think they both told some of the same things, but the words in the encyclopedia were harder to read. Besides, the encyclopedia story told about seeds that act like salt shakers. We don't have a chart for those. It said the top of the bluebell seed pod has little holes. When the wind blows the pod, the seeds shake out just like salt out of a shaker."

"Yes, I thought that was very interesting," replied Mrs. Taylor. "We may have to have a new chart and a new committee to work on it if we find any of those seeds in our miscellaneous box. Did Kenneth's article tell us anything else that is new?"

"Yes," June replied. "It told us about animals like squirrels that pick up nuts. Then they carry them away and bury them. It called these animals rodents," she added.

"Excellent," said Mrs. Taylor. "Now, let's review what we think about our story, 'How Some Seeds Travel.' This kind of review is often called *critical evaluation*. When we do this we should tell the good

Listening to stories outdoors can be a pleasant variation. (Courtesy California State Department of Education.)

things and the poor things about our story. We have already discussed them. Now, let's ask Georgia to write on the chalkboard some things we tell her. We will criticize the story for accuracy and completeness. Do all of you know what that means?" The children nodded their heads so Mrs. Taylor asked James to tell something good about the story.

James said, "Well, we said it was accurate as far as it went."

"Good," said Mrs. Taylor. "Georgia, please write that in a sentence on the board. Can anyone think of anything else?" she added.

Raymond said, "It left out some important things."

"That's right," answered Mrs. Taylor. "Can you say that in a more grownup way?"

"Yes," responded Raymond. "It was incomplete."

"That's a very good word," said Mrs. Taylor. "Georgia, please write that sentence on the board, too." Then she asked if anyone had any other comments to add. Since no one wanted to add anything more, Mrs. Taylor said, "I think these two ideas would be good to put in your notebooks. Suppose you look at these sentences of evaluation. Then

I'm going to erase them and write the words, *Critical Evaluation,* on the board for your title. Suppose you write a short paragraph of evaluation about our story, 'How Some Seeds Travel,' in your notebooks. When you finish the paragraph you may put an illustration on the page if you wish.

APPRECIATION

Appreciation is another component of reading, including perception, comprehension, integration with previous experiences, and reaction to reading material, discussed above. Literature must meet children's emotional and intellectual needs if they are to acquire ability to appreciate this type of writing. Children's needs have been stated in various ways; however, some of the basic needs include belonging, security, love, status, and achievement. Appreciation may be developed by stories that describe ways in which children or animals have achieved belonging. Ways in which children or animals have fulfilled other basic needs are also helpful in developing appreciation.

Many stories and books of non-fiction meet children's needs for intellectual stimulation and emotional reactions. These stories often interpret the environment, including such subjects as nature, science, accounts of the achievements of great men, and reports of industrial processes. Stories and books of this type help satisfy the intellectual needs of children.

One of the basic characteristics of literature is its tendency to make use of an indirect method of presenting thoughts. Only enough is told to challenge the imagination, arouse vivid imagery, and stimulate thought and feeling that the reader himself contributes. This stimulation of imagination is another way that literature provides intellectual challenge. Fiction of a non-literary type is direct and gives all the facts, thus leaving no challenge to the imagination. A variety of clues to stimulate thought are used in literature regarding such factors as appearance, story telling, character, feelings, and mood. The task of the teacher is to guide children to interpret these clues.

EYE MOVEMENTS

In addition to an understanding of the components of reading, the student and teacher of reading should understand the physical aspects of the process. As the individual reads, the eyes move forward, pause, make a return sweep to the previous line, and sometimes regress to clarify a point missed. These movements of the eyes are described in more detail below.

Eye Movements in the Reading Process

Reading takes place when the eye pauses. The amount of reading matter that the eye can see at one pause or fixation is called the eye-span. Usually the center of this area is seen sharply but the edges are not clearly in focus. On an adult level the average amount of material that the eye can take in at one fixation has been found to be about nine to ten letter spaces (letters and spaces between words). The eye-span for a slow reader may be six letter spaces, whereas a fast reader may average thirteen or fourteen letter spaces in one pause, according to Hildreth.[5] An example of an average eye-span is given below:

The contest was set for the end of the year. A prize was offered.

The length of the pause or fixation is about a fifth of a second for a mature reader and may last as long as two fifths of a second for a slow reader. Usually the number of pauses are approximately the same for various types of reading material but the duration of the pauses may be shorter for easier material and longer for difficult material. The eyes of a good reader move in a fairly smooth and rhythmical manner.

When the eyes reach the end of a line of printed material, they move rapidly backward to the beginning of the following line, called a return sweep. This movement usually lasts about one twenty-fifth of a second. In the case of good readers these movements are smooth and rhythmical.

Regressions

Even in the case of fast readers, the eye does not always move forward. If a key word or part of a thought is lost, the reader moves his eyes back along the line to pick up this missed word or thought. The fast reader tends to regress more often when reading difficult material than when reading easier material. The purpose of the reading also influences the regression. If the reader is searching for detailed information that he intends to use, he may regress more frequently than when reading recreational material or skimming unimportant news items.

The slow reader tends to regress frequently. Because his reading is slow, his mind many tend to wander between words or ideas. In such a case he may forget the earlier part of a sentence and may need to re-read to acquire the total thought. Children who read material that is too difficult for them must pause often to try to analyze the unfamiliar words they meet. Their eyes may move back and forth several times before they are able to put all the sounds together to make a word. If

[5] Gertrude Hildreth, *Teaching Reading* (New York: Holt, Rinehart and Winston, Inc., 1961), Chap. 4.

they are forced to analyze several of the words in a sentence, they may have to reread the sentence to get the total meaning. The necessity to read difficult material almost always increases the number of regressions on the part of the poor reader and also tends to interfere with his speed and comprehension. He moves his eyes more often, his pauses are longer, and more regressions are needed.

Effect of Training

Because some slow readers read accurately and some fast readers do not read accurately, some doubt has been cast on the importance of the size of the eye-span and the speed of the fixations. The study of such cases emphasizes the need to work simultaneously on effective comprehension and speed of reading. Increase in speed without accompanying increase in comprehension is not only useless but is even detrimental. Direct efforts to increase the eye-span have not been successful, but efforts to teach good reading habits have been quite effective.

The Eye-Voice Span

The eye-voice span in oral reading is the distance between the position at which the eyes are paused or fixated and the voice is actually reading, since the voice usually lags behind the eyes. The same lag is found for the thought in silent reading which also lags behind the eyes. According to Hildreth . . . "the mature reader does not interpret one eyeful of print at a time, but waits to perceive enough material to grasp a thought unit." [6]

The fast reader's eyes travel much farther ahead of his voice and thought than the eyes of the slow reader. The distance between the eyes and the thought or voice helps the reader grasp the thought with the greatest possible speed and accuracy because this large span is more likely to include one or more complete thought units. The reader's eyes may be almost as far as a third of a line ahead of his thought. He cannot read any faster than he can think, however. Hildreth compares this process to the tendency of an experienced motorist to drive by watching the traffic several hundred feet ahead of his car.

On the other hand, the beginning reader usually concentrates his eyes and voice on the same word. Thus, in oral reading he looks at a word and says it orally before his eyes move to the next word. He follows the same process in silent reading when he looks at a word and subvocalizes it at the same time. In this way he tends to lose the relationship between the words and, as a result, he also loses the thought.

[6] *Ibid.*

His eyes must therefore regress to discover the thought. If the beginning reader continues to read in this manner, he becomes a word-by-word reader. A good teacher works with this reader from the very beginning to increase his eye-voice and thought span. Ways of helping readers to use more mature eye and thought patterns are described in the chapter on beginning reading.

Flexibility in Reading

One of the characteristics of a good reader is his ability to adjust his pace to the type of material he is reading. To avoid the necessity of making repeated regressions, he unconsciously slows his reading to a speed that permits him successfully to comprehend a particular selection. He also adjusts his pace to his purpose in reading. The student who plans to teach may read this chapter with care because he knows he will need the information in teaching children. On the other hand, a parent might read the same material more rapidly to arrive at a general understanding of the reading process. Both the student and parent would read a detective story or light fiction with much greater speed. Most fast readers are able to reduce their reading speed almost unconsciously for difficult material and also tend to speed up their reading with little conscious thought when it is of a recreational nature. The difficulty of the material, the lack of familiarity with the vocabulary, the purpose of the reader, and the literary quality of the material may all affect the reading speed of a flexible reader.

Inflexibility of a Rapid Reader. An exception to this principle was found in the case of a student who reported that she had difficulty in comprehension because she was unable to decrease her speed when reading technical material. She stated that she had been taught in an era when speed was the prime objective, without a balanced emphasis on comprehension and other skills. The children in the primary grades had been taught to read down the center of the page without attention to the periphery. She stated that she had checked her reading speed carefully a number of times and found that she averaged a thousand words a minute. She complained, however, that her difficulty with comprehension was so great that she was often forced to read technical material at least five times in order to make sure that she understood it. This lack of flexibility is quite unusual in the case of fast readers and underscores the need for teaching a balance of skills in any good reading program.

Inflexibility of Most Slow Readers. One of the characteristics of the slow reader is his lack of ability to change his reading pace to adjust to the material that he reads. Such a reader must spend a large amount of time on assignments even in the elementary school. His comprehension may be poor because his mind tends to wander due to the slow pace of his reading. This type of student may also have poor study habits, such as lack of ability to outline or to select main thoughts, so he may reread material several times without much gain in comprehension.

Often a large proportion of students who fail to maintain the minimum grade point average in college are those who have a slow reading speed and a resultant poor vocabulary despite the fact that they may have adequate or even superior intelligence. The slow reader usually finds little satisfaction in reading for pleasure, therefore he limits his recreational reading. Since wide reading is one of the best ways to acquire an extensive vocabulary, the slow reader fails to acquire a good vocabulary. His lack of vocabulary, in turn, increases his difficulty in later reading, limiting even more his desire to read. The same principles operate in the elementary school.

Remedial reading courses are given in many colleges. While these courses are quite valuable, a semester is often too short a time to make a great improvement in reading, especially if the course is not held daily. The fact that the student must usually continue reading technical matter at his habitual slow pace at the same time often interferes with his training in this special class. Even students who spend several semesters successfully developing speed may have difficulty in maintaining this speed in later years without continuous effort. These problems again underline the need for a balance in reading skills and the establishment of good habits from the beginning of formal reading teaching.

Silent Speech

Considerable thought and research over the years have been devoted to the problem of vocalization and subvocalization or silent speech during reading. Very poor readers may move their lips and even read aloud softly as their nearest approach to silent reading. This process is called vocalization. Others make no overt movements with their lips but may have considerable movement in the vocal cords. At the same time, these readers pronounce each word mentally. This process, including some movement in the vocal cords and the mental pronunciation of words, is called subvocalization or silent speech.

Effect of Silent Speech. Reading specialists have been concerned about the process of vocalization and silent speech because of the resultant tendency to limit the speed of silent reading to the slower speed of oral reading. An oral reader is able to read a maximum of two hundred fifty words a minute. A slow silent reader may read at this same pace of two hundred fifty words or even less, whereas a fast silent reader may read five hundred or more words a minute. Although comprehension varies tremendously, the fast reader is likely to comprehend better than the slow reader. The slow reader often has other poor habits that also interfere with effective comprehension.

At times reading authorities have believed that the answer to the problem of slow reading was to eliminate silent speech. However, a study by Edfeldt who used an electrical device to record movements in the larynx found some movements in the speech muscles of even very rapid readers, although much more limited.[7] In this study brain waves of slow and fast readers were recorded during silent reading to discover possible differences between readers of differing rates. The waves of both the slow and fast readers showed fluctuations for each word, although the waves were more rapid for the fast readers.

Silent Speech of Fast Readers. The fast readers seemed to react to each word although they might use the first few letters, the last few letters, or an internal syllable or more as clues from which to fill in the rest of the word mentally. The evidence from this study shows that some silent speech is a part of the reading process. Vocalization on the level of actual pronunciation of words or overt lip movements, however, is a deterrent to rapid reading and should be prevented if possible, or at least corrected immediately if it occurs.

The selection given below has been printed to give clues only instead of words. An effective reader should be able to get the complete thought from this selection.

Wyatt Earp, southwexxxxx fronxxxx figxxx, came xx Calixxxxxx xx 1864 and drxxx a stxxx coxxx betwxxx San Bernardino xxx Prescott. Hx xxx x peace offxxxx xx x numbxx xx wesxxxx toxxx duxxxx xxx railrxxx develoxxxxx perixx. Xx died xx Los Angexxx xx Janxxxx 14, 1929.[8]

If the reader found the reading of this selection to be slower than his normal reading pace, he must remember that no individual can select the best word clues for another reader.

Word-by-Word Reading

The poor reader seems to suffer from a variety of poor reading habits. A study of reading habits that interfere with adult reading was made

[7] Ake W. Edfeldt, *Silent Speech and Silent Reading* (Chicago: The University of Chicago Press, 1960).

[8] Wyatt Earp, southwestern frontier figure, came to California in 1864 and drove a stage coach between San Bernardino and Prescott. He was a peace officer in a number of western towns during the railroad development period. He died in Los Angeles on January 14, 1929.

by Purcell, who worked with eight hundred thirty-seven college and adult students taking remedial reading courses of their own volition.[9] The difficulty listed as most serious by almost every student was that of word-by-word reading, sometimes referred to as word-calling. Purcell believes that this habit stems back to the first grade and results from many, many years of reinforcement. Too much emphasis on oral reading and practice on lists of words out of context are factors that tend to establish the habit of reading one word at a time. Overemphasis on phonics would seem to be another cause of word-by-word reading.

In word-by-word reading in the silent reading process, the individual tends to look at each word by itself and to pronounce it subvocally before he moves to the next word. In this way his speed is retarded and his thought is limited until he comes to the end of a meaningful phrase or sentence. At that time he must often look back to the beginning of the phrase or sentence to complete the entire thought.

Other Poor Reading Habits

Other difficulties reported by students in Purcell's study are listed in order of frequency by these students. They included vocalizing, backtracking (called regression in the previous chapter), clue blindness, finger following, word analysis, head swinging, and number attraction. These habits are briefly described to help those students who may have similar difficulties and to help understand the great importance of helping pupils acquire good reading habits by using good methods in teaching.

According to Purcell, backtracking often occurs when word-by-word reading results in the loss of an idea due to overconcern with the words. When defining day dreaming, Purcell included the thoughts that may enter a reader's mind during slow reading, whether they are of a practical or fantasy type. Monotonous plodding is defined as the lack of ability to pace the reading according to its difficulty or unfamiliarity. Rereading refers to the tendency to reread an entire paragraph or section due to the loss of thought, rather than backtracking over a few letters or words. The slight pause necessary to the comprehension of an unusual word constitutes word blocking. If the reader has a poor vocabulary, delays due to word blocking become frequent and seriously interfere with speed and comprehension. Word analysis as Purcell uses the term, is a more extreme process of searching for the meaning of words, even to the point of analyzing for Latin or other origins.

Clue blindness refers to the habit of ignoring the author's guides

[9] John Wallace Purcell, "Poor Reading Habits: Their Rank Order," *The Reading Teacher,* XVI (Mar. 1963), 353–58.

regarding the importance of sentences or paragraphs. Such clues include headlines, sub-titles, sentences containing main ideas, summaries, and similar guides. Finger following and head swinging are mechanical habits which tend to interfere with speed. Number attraction is low on the list of difficulties and is a tendency to stop unduly whenever a number is met. As with many other of these poor habits, this bad habit distracts the attention and results in a break in thought or the loss of thought and fluency.

Part-to-Whole Reading

Some authorities believe that words and groups of words related by thought are the best units of reading material for beginning readers, followed later by analysis of sounds to help the children become more independent in identifying words. The reasons for this belief have been described above. Others believe that letter sounds are the units most efficiently learned by beginners. Some of the linguists such as Bloomfield and Barnhart and the supporters of the all-phonics programs are proponents of this latter school.[10]

Letter Sounds as Units. Phonics is taught as a part of every well-balanced developmental reading program. It serves its purpose when taught in this way by helping children learn how to attack unfamiliar words when these are met among familiar words. When taught as a part of the program, children can learn to read for meaning, move their eyes along a line of print with reasonable smoothness, and pause only to analyze a word by its parts when this technique is needed.

Sometimes too much emphasis is placed on phonics to the neglect of other skills because ability to use phonics well gives a superficial impression of excellent reading ability in the primary grades. However, overemphasis on phonics in the primary grades can interfere with the establishment of basic habits of speed and comprehension. An all-phonics reading program will serve the purpose of developing this one type of word recognition technique only and is helpful as long as the child meets only words that he recognizes when he pronounces them orally. As soon as he begins to extend his reading vocabulary to include words that are unknown to him, even when pronounced orally, the use of phonics must be supplemented and even replaced to a certain extent by the dictionary. The child usually reaches this stage by the end of the third or during the fourth grade. By then he must learn to use diacritical marks and accents as well as definitions of words. The study of phonics at this level is usually extended to include structural analysis

[10] Leonard Bloomfield and Clarence Barnhart. *Let's Read* (Detroit: Wayne State University Press, 1961).

including the use of prefixes, suffixes, and root words. More time is also given to word origins, synonyms, antonyms, homonyms, contractions, abbreviations, and compounds.

Difficulties in Part-to-Whole Reading. Some problems arise from the part-to-whole teaching of reading. The process of blending letters to pronounce words is difficult for the younger primary children. This process also tends to focus all of the children's attention on the letters and the pronunciation of words, rather than on the meaning of a phrase or sentence. Often a great deal of emphasis on oral reading accompanies this type of phonics program. Little effort seems to be made to help children use context clues to aid them to read by thought units. In addition, the reader must try to get meaning from single words although many have little or no meaning by themselves. The example given previously made use of the sentence, "The boy was at the XXXXXX." The words *was at the* have little meaning until the reader includes the word *circus* in his thoughts.

Although some children are able to acquire meaning successfully by listening to the words that they read subvocally, other children may become handicapped in acquiring the meaning of the reading through this process. Children may also fail to acquire adequate speed for satisfactory reading on the middle and upper grade levels as a result of their tendency to analyze each word separately. The proponents of these methods of beginning reading assert that children will acquire the ability to analyze sounds at a very rapid rate. They maintain that this speed of synthesis or blending letter sounds will become so rapid and unconscious that it will not interfere with good speed and comprehension later. Neither experience nor research available at the present time seems to support this theory.

Reading Lag in Upper Grades. A study by McCollum in a school district that used one of the purely alphabetic and phonic programs of teaching reading showed the effect of the early spurt in word recognition followed by a later lag in speed and comprehension.[11] Five percent of the children tested below grade level at the end of the first grade, none at the end of the second, and four percent at the end of the third. The numbers then began to mount. The following percentages of children testing below grade level are given for the intermediate and upper grades: twelve percent by the end of the fourth grade, thirty-two percent by the end of the fifth grade, twenty-five percent by the end of the sixth grade, thirty-two percent at the end of the seventh grade, and thirty-four per-

---

[11] John A. McCollum, "An Experimental Evaluation of the Carden Method," *Challenge and Experiment in Reading* (ed.: J. Allen Figurel), Conference Proceedings VII (New York: Scholastic Magazines Press, 1962), 123–28.

cent at the end of the eighth grade. The high degree of success of the program in the primary grades seems to be due partly to the fact that some primary reading tests give heavy weight to word recognition, whereas tests for older children emphasize comprehension, speed, and study skills. Most of the school districts that have followed this particular plan of phonic training without a balance of other skills have dropped the program.

Failure To Form Thought Patterns. Some children perceive the printed symbol of the first word in a sentence well enough to pronounce the word either aloud or to themselves but then stop to begin the process with the next word. As their eyes move along the sentence, they fail to group words in order to gain the meaning from either the phrase or the sentence. For example, the child who reads the sentence, *The robin made a nest in the three,* substituting *three* for *tree,* is perceiving and recognizing words, but is not grouping them for thought. Otherwise he would discover his error and correct it to complete the thought of the sentence. This process of reading without the thought of the sentence is called word calling or word-by-word reading, described previously. Some children learn to read in this manner because their teachers have failed to teach them to group words to read for thought.

Effect of Word Calling. Many adults who report that they were taught by a method emphasizing phonics and oral reading or oral reading alone also report that they tend to read slowly and have difficulty with comprehension. Occasionally an adult who recalls having been taught primarily by phonics and oral reading reports excellent speed and good comprehension in adult reading. These individuals, however, also report reading an exceptional number of books in their childhood. One adult stated that she lived next to the library and read a book every day. Another stated that she had been given a great many books and also had attended the library frequently. She read at least five books a week. Apparently, overemphasis on letter sounds and phonics can be compensated by extensive free reading in the intermediate and upper grades. Differences in natural speed of reaction may also influence individual reading speed, but it probably can not compensate for poor habits of years' standing. Judging by the reports of most adults, few people make such a compensation.

If the child loses interest in reading because of emphasis on sounds to the neglect of meaning, he may fail to develop a desire to read widely. If he does not read widely, he fails to increase his speed and comprehension and loses an important opportunity to increase his reading vocabulary. These lacks then, in turn, tend to interfere with interest and desire to read.

Causes of Poor Reading Habits. Despite the fact that reading methods have improved considerably during the last few decades and more teachers are using better methods, far too many teachers continue to teach reading by outdated methods. First grade children who are taught new words by introducing them in isolated lists almost inevitably read orally by calling one word after another as though the sentence were made up of unrelated words, that is, by word calling or word-by-word reading. This habit is obvious when children read orally. It is harder to detect in silent reading, but it nevertheless operates to interfere with comprehension and speed.

Many primary teachers still teach children to read by introducing new words in a list, help with phonic analysis, and ask members of each group to read orally "barber shop" or "round robin" style (that is, to read orally by turns without purpose and straight down the page). These latter procedures place all the emphasis on the word as a unit to the complete neglect of methods for developing rapid reading and good comprehension. The longer the habit of concentrating on one word at a time has been established, the longer time and the more effort are needed to change the habit. Even after the children have spent only a year reading in this manner in the first grade, these habits can be changed only with difficulty. As long as many teachers continue to use the procedures just described, children will either be required to lower their educational aspirations or will be forced to take courses in remedial reading for the improvement of speed and comprehension if they are to succeed in high school and college.

Need for Balanced Skills. If children are expected to acquire and learn to use a variety of good reading skills in a flexible manner, this variety of skills must be taught correctly and in proper balance from the very beginning of the program in the first grade. No child can be expected to learn one or two basic skills out of balance in the beginning and later to change these to include other basic skills and habits. If thoroughly established, few bad habits basic to effective reading are permanently eradicated in the lifetime of an individual. Often those habits apparently eradicated gradually return after the individual ceases to work against them.

EFFECT OF ENVIRONMENT ON READING

The environment in which a child is reared may serve to raise or depress the child's ability to make use of his potential intelligence. Children whose parents use a wide vocabulary will themselves tend to have wide vocabularies, one among several important factors needed in reading. Children who live in an environment of impoverished language usage and experiences will tend to have poor vocabularies and inaccurate and inadequate language usage skills and concepts. Since vocabulary relates very closely to reading achievement, an inadequacy in one area will tend to result in an inadequacy in the other.

Interest is another factor that is affected by environment. Children who come from homes in which books and magazines are commonly found and whose parents read habitually have much more knowledge, understandings, and interest in learning to read than children whose parents take no interest in reading. In addition, children whose parents have read or told stories to them also tend to have a strong interest in books and a desire to learn to read. Conversely, children whose parents have neglected story telling have little idea of the pleasure to be gained through reading and also lack a very important language experience that they need to help them develop their own language patterns. Mayer found that children in a high socio-economic area were eight months ahead of children in a low socio-economic area on tests in both vocabulary and reading comprehension.[12]

SUMMARY

Five components of reading include perception, comprehension, integration with previous experiences, reaction to reading material, and appreciation. These components are all interacting parts of the reading process. Perception of whole words and thoughts is essential for speed and comprehension in reading. The process of comprehension depends upon the reaction of the reader to his past personal and vicarious experiences. If reading is to be of value, the reader must use a variety of techniques in organizing and evaluating the material. Appreciation is a component of all reading but is of particular value in the enjoyment of recreational reading.

Good habits of reading are reflected by efficient eye movements. The effective reader sees more at one fixation, makes shorter pauses, and has a larger eye-thought span than the slow reader. Word-by-word reading has been found to be one of the most common inefficient habits that interferes with effective reading at the college and adult levels. This habit originates in the primary grades.

The environment of the pre-school and primary child has a very basic influence on his reading progress in the primary grades. The child

[12] Martin Mayer, "The Good Slum Schools," *Harper's Magazine*, CCXXII (Apr. 1961), 267.

whose family speaks good English has a considerable advantage over the child whose family uses meager non-standard English. The child who has been given an extensive variety of experiences and who has been exposed to stories and reading as an important part of family life also has a great advantage over the child whose parents fail to provide a stimulating environment for him.

II

DEVELOPMENT OF
READING READINESS

3

Analyzing Reading Readiness

Mrs. Ashe, a kindergarten teacher, had been asked by her principal to make a list of names of the children in her class according to their reading readiness. Since the end of the kindergarten year was approaching, this list was to be prepared for the use of the first grade teacher at the beginning of the following year. Mrs. Ashe realized that she must use a reading readiness inventory because the reading readiness tests would not be given until the following fall.

The principal had discussed the advisability of giving the readiness tests at the end of the kindergarten year with Mrs. Ashe, but they had decided that the use of the tests in the fall would probably be more effective. The first grade teachers would understand the tests better if they administered them themselves. Also, some changes in readiness factors such as spurts or plateaus in maturation might take place during the summer. Any child whose mother devoted considerable time to story telling and other language activities might mature more rapidly than the average child. Other children might have opportunities for local trips or even more extended travel, which might also contribute to language growth. On the other hand some child might become disturbed by the birth of a new sibling or the illness of a member of the family, thereby resulting in a delay of his readiness. With wise handling most children should be able to recover from the disturbing effects of such an experience in a reasonable length of time, but perhaps not by the beginning of the fall term.

READINESS INVENTORY

Mrs. Ashe surveyed a number of books to find readiness traits. Since she found such a wide variety of categories, she decided to list them under the headings of language traits, intellectual traits, physical traits, emotional and social traits, and experiential background. Most of these broad topics were divided into subtopics.

Diagnosing readiness seemed to Mrs. Ashe to constitute the process of discovering how successfully each child can profit from instruction on the basis of his maturity, his mastery of a particular group of skills, and his background of experiences. Mrs. Ashe expected to find each child on different levels on the various traits. For example, a particular child might be successful in his ability to retell stories but might be unable to hear differences in sounds. In general, however, a mature child might tend to be stronger in more traits than an immature child. The score on a readiness test, thus, represents only an average of abilities, and each child needs help in terms of his own strength and weaknesses.

Readiness is not limited merely to the stage at which the child begins to read. Readiness is an ongoing process. Each reading skill that is mastered provides readiness for the strengthening and further development of these and more advanced skills. All teachers of reading, regardless of grade, are concerned with each child's readiness for the next steps.

LANGUAGE TRAITS

As Mrs. Ashe looked over her list of language traits, various children came to mind. She thought of Donald and Marjorie who told excellent stories and of Steven who retold many of his experiences from his weekly visits to his grandfather's farm. This was late in the year, and most of the children seemed to listen to stories with enjoyment, but very few could identify words in print. Marjorie's wide vocabulary came to mind along with her unusual ability to use a mature sentence structure. Mrs. Ashe decided to start with the first category in language and to begin to check off the children's names.

Relating Stories

During her experience as a teacher, Mrs. Ashe found that children who told stories well were usually quite successful in their first-grade work. Research by Morrison showed that ability to tell stories had a high relationship to success on readiness tests.[1] Mrs. Ashe had noticed

[1] Ida E. Morrison, "The Relation of Reading Readiness to Certain Language Factors," *Challenge and Experiment in Reading* (ed.: J. Allen Figurel), VII (New York: Scholastic Magazines, 1962), 119–21.

The story they are hearing on the tape recorder holds these children rapt. (Courtesy Georgetown Elementary School, El Dorado County Schools.)

that a few of her kindergarten children were able to retell stories in complete detail, especially toward the end of the kindergarten year. This year she was always able to rely on Donald and Marjorie to help during any class emergency. If a parent tended to talk unduly long at the door or if the milk balance was difficult, one of these children was always able to keep the class occupied by telling them a story. Since Donald and Marjorie had a considerable repertoire, Mrs. Ashe was not concerned that they might bore the class with repetitions.

Susan, Karen, and Mark were also able to help with stories but were more limited in the number they knew. Mrs. Ashe decided to put Donald's and Marjorie's names in the first two respective columns on her check list. She also decided to put a mark of 4 under each name opposite the category listed as *ability to tell stories,* in order to indicate that these two children had outstanding abilities in this trait. She added Susan's, Karen's, Mark's, and Steven's names in the next four columns and placed a mark of 3 under their names opposite the *ability to tell stories.*

The other children were able to tell episodes or very streamlined versions of stories, so Mrs. Ashe indicated this limited ability by a mark of 2. Some children, of course, were unable to tell any stories or even share ideas effectively. After those names she placed the symbol 1 when she added their names at the extreme right of the paper.

After jotting down these names, Mrs. Ashe wondered if she should have put them on her check list in alphabetical order. She decided, however, to continue with the plan to put the names of the most capable children first and to add the others according to her best guess of maturity. When the marks were reviewed, she might find a need to change the order of a few of the names since this list served merely as a temporary draft. A sample of the first part of the chart with the highest ten names is given in Figure 3-1, and a sample of the chart with the lowest ten names is given in Figure 3-2.

Sharing Experiences

Steven's name was the first to come to Mrs. Ashe's mind as she thought about the next trait. She immediately put a mark of 4 under his name in the row opposite the ability to tell related events. Then she looked back over the anecdotal records, brief notes of children's responses, of the first five children. She found that they were able to keep to the subject and to organize their thoughts when they told about their experiences or discussed some interesting objects they had brought to school. She then placed the symbols 4 under their names in this row. She placed the symbol 3 after the names of the eleven children next in order to indicate very good ability in these traits. She also distributed the symbols 2 and 1 to indicate the other children's ability in these traits.

Using a Variety of Sentence Structures

Mrs. Ashe had learned that some children even at five years of age still talk in single words or short phrases, especially when talking in a formal situation such as the sharing period. Other children use simple sentences or simple run-on sentences resulting from the use of the word, *and,* following each statement. Still other children are able to use sentences with compound subjects or compound predicates or a combination of these in addition to simple sentences. Very mature children use complex sentences in addition to all other forms when the situation seems appropriate.

Research by Morrison shows that a high relationship exists between children's ability to use a mature form of sentence structure and their ability to succeed on readiness tests.[2] Mrs. Ashe had kept brief anecdotal records during the sharing periods and had placed these in the children's folders in her classroom files. Rather than trust her memory, she decided to go through these folders now and to indicate on the chart the highest level of sentence structure used by each child. She took

2 *Ibid.*

Readiness Traits	Donald M.	Marjorie S.	Susan L.	Karen H.	Mark F.	Steven E.	Debbie F.	Laurie J.	Teruko W.	Richard G.
Language traits—ability to:										
Relate stories	4	4	3	3	3	3	2	2	2	2
Share experiences	4	4	4	4	4	4	3	3	3	3
Use a variety of sentence structures . .	4	4	4	4	4	3	3	3	3	3
Use a wide vocabulary	4	4	4	4	4	4	4	4	2	3
Pronounce and enunciate accurately .	4	4	4	4	4	4	3	3	1E	1E
Listen to stories with enjoyment . . .	4	4	4	4	4	4	4	4	4	4
Identify words in print	4	4								
Play with words and sounds	3	3	3	3	3	3	3	3	`3	3
Intellectual traits—ability to:										
Demonstrate mental maturity	4	4	4	4	4	4	4	4	4	4
Interpret pictures	4	4	4	4	4	4	4	4	4	4
Organize pictures	4	4	4	4	4	4	4	4	4	3
Show sustained interest in picture and story books	4	4	4	4	4	4	4	4	4	4
Show an interest in signs and labels . .	4	4	4	4	4	4	4	4	4	4
Solve simple problems	4	4	4	2	4	4	4	4	4	4
Recognize auditory likenesses and differences	4	4	4	4	4	4	4	4	4	4
Recognize visual likenesses and differences	4	4	4	4	4	4	4	4	4	4
Demonstrate a wide attention span . .	4	4	4	4	4	4	4	3	4	4
Follow directions	4	4	4	3	4	4	3	3	3	3
Demonstrate eye and hand coordination	4	4	4	4	4	4	4	4	4	4
Physical traits										
Effective vision	4	4	4	4	4	4	4	4	4	4*
Effective hearing	4	4	4	4	4	4	4	4	4	4
Emotional and Social traits										
Emotional adjustment	4	4	4	4	4	4	4	4	4	4
Social adjustment	4	4	4	4	4	4	3	4	4	4
Experiential background										

*With glasses; P, Poor pronunciation; E, Poor enunciation

Fig. 3–1. Readiness inventory.

Readiness Traits	Carolyn T.	David W.	Linda M.	Larry P.	Joe D.	Pamela Y.	Jose R.	Felicia B.	Tony R.	Carl F.
Language traits—ability to:										
Relate stories	2	2	2	1	1	1	2	2	2	1
Share experiences	2	2	2	1	1	1	2	2	2	1
Use a variety of sentence structures . .	2	2	2	1	1	1	2	2	2	1
Use a wide vocabulary	2	1	2	1	1	1	1	1	1	1
Pronounce and enunciate accurately .	1P	1E	3	1P	2	2	1E	2	1E	2
Listen to stories with enjoyment . . .	3	3	3	2	2	2	1	1	1	1
Identify words in print				(no readiness)						
Play with words and sounds				(no readiness)						
Intellectual traits—ability to:										
Demonstrate mental maturity	3	2	2	2	2	2	2	2	2	1
Interpret pictures	2	2	2	1	1	1	1	1	1	1
Organize pictures	2	2	1	1	1	1	2	2	2	1
Show sustained interest in picture and story books	2	2	1	1	1	1	2	3	2	1
Show an interest in signs and labels . .	2	2	2	1	1	1	2	2	2	1
Solve simple problems	2	2	1	1	1	1	2	2	2	1
Recognize auditory likenesses and differences	1	1	1	1	1	1	2	2	2	1
Recognize visual likenesses and differences	2	1	1	1	1	1	2	2	2	1
Demonstrate a wide attention span . .	2	2	1	1	1	1	2	2	2	1
Follow directions	2	2	1	1	1	1	1	1	1	1
Demonstrate eye and hand coordination	2	1	2	1	1	1	2	2	2	1
Physical traits										
Effective vision	4	4	4	4	4	4	4	4	4	4
Effective hearing	4	4	4	4	4	4	4	4	4	4
Emotional and Social traits										
Emotional adjustment	4	4	4	4	4	4	4	4	4	?
Social adjustment	3	3	1	4	3	3	4	4	3	1
Experiential background										

*With glasses; P, Poor pronunciation; E, Poor enunciation

Fig. 3–2. Readiness inventory.

the notes from Donald's folder and found, as she had expected, a number of notes to indicate the use of all sentence structures with considerable use of complex sentences. She therefore placed a symbol of 4 under his name to indicate that the complex sentence was his highest level of usage. She decided to give a mark of 3 to indicate the use of compound sentences and a mark of 2 to indicate the use of simple and run-on sentences. Words and phrases were indicated by the symbol 1. As she continued to look at the records, Mrs. Ashe also gave marks of 4 to Marjorie, Susan, Karen, and Mark. Steven had no notation regarding the use of complex sentences, but he had used compound as well as simple sentences so she gave him a mark of 3. Many of the other children used simple and compound sentences well, so Mrs. Ashe continued to add the symbol 3 until she came to the last twelve children. In her notations in the folders of Carl, Pamela, Joe, and Larry, she found notes to indicate that these children sometimes used phrases and often single words, but she had no notation regarding their ability to use simple sentences. Therefore she gave each of these children a mark of 1. She distributed the other marks according to her notes.

Using a Wide Vocabulary

A wide vocabulary is known to be closely related both to intelligence and to readiness for reading. If parents use a large vocabulary, their children will also tend to use such a vocabulary. Children whose parents take them on trips and plan various experiences especially for them also tend to use an enriched vocabulary. Sometimes this vocabulary happens to be especially broad when it relates to a parent's particular interest or hobby. The child's vocabulary may be average in other ways, thereby reflecting the parent's speech patterns.

As Mrs. Ashe looked over her notes, she found that at least the highest eight children could be considered to have a vocabulary decidedly better than average, so she gave them each a mark of 4. Most of the other children seemed to have more or less average vocabularies so Mrs. Ashe added marks of 3 and 2 until she came to the last nine children. David's vocabulary seemed quite limited. He used the words "that thing" to stand for quite a variety of simple objects. For this reason Mrs. Ashe put a mark of 1 under his name opposite this trait. Linda and Carolyn, on the other hand, showed no particular deficiency in vocabulary so Mrs. Ashe put a mark of 2 under their names.

Larry, Joe, Pamela, Jose, Felicia, Tony, and Carl all received marks of 1. Mrs. Ashe realized that Felicia, Tony, and Jose were bilingual. In their cases a limited vocabulary was certainly not related to low intelligence and not a true index of readiness. These children would nevertheless need extra emphasis on vocabulary to improve their readiness for reading. When looking at the other files, Mrs. Ashe had put Teruko's folder aside. Teruko's family spoke Japanese in the home. Although she was a very mature child, she suffered some handicap from her bilingualism. Mrs. Ashe put a mark of 2 under her name and decided to give special attention to Teruko's speech for a few days to see if this mark was justified.

Pronouncing and Enunciating Accurately

Lack of correct enunciation and pronunciation may be partly due to lack of maturity, but they also tend to result from other causes such as the speech in the geographical area and in the home. Children's inability to hear others' pronunciations clearly and accurately is another cause of poor pronunciation. Correct speech during the readiness period is necessary for phonics readiness. For example, children have difficulty in learning the sounds for s and th if they pronounce both of these phonemes in the same way as is done by the lisper.

Speech in the Geographical Area. In some cases children's enunciation may be due to poor enunciation in the home or by neighbors and their children. Sometimes such enunciation is the result of colloquialisms common in a particular locality. In some areas of the country G's are commonly dropped especially at the end of verbs such as comin', goin', and walkin'. An example of a more extreme enunciation irregularity such as boid for bird and hoid for heard are made by children who come from certain parts of the east coast. Another type of enunciation difficulty is the result of baby talk. Since parents have learned that school problems result from encouraging this type of enunciation, fewer such problems are met in the school.

Speech Due To Inaccurate Hearing. A third type of difficulty results from inaccurate hearing on the part of the child due either to lack of attention to details or to some actual loss of hearing particularly in the upper tone levels. Mrs. Ashe recalled that Richard used the word bome for bone and spoom for spoon. She was still helping him to enunciate these words correctly even though it was near the end of the year. This problem was a result of Richard's failure to hear the detailed differences between these two sounds. David, on the other hand, failed to enunciate S's and Sh's clearly. When David had been tested on the audiometer, the nurse had noted a deficiency in hearing on the high tone levels. Apparently David's enunciation difficulty was due to lack of ability to hear these sounds correctly. Mrs. Ashe checked with a mark of 1 the names of the children who had any of these problems, and entered an

E in the same square to indicate that the problem was a matter of enunciation.

Speech of Bilingual Children. Another type of enunciation problem that concerned Mrs. Ashe was the result of problems met by bilingual children. Because the Japanese alphabet lacks an *L* and makes use of a modified *R*, Teruko had difficulty in hearing *R's* distinctly and often substituted *L* which was closer to the Japanese *R*. Jose, who had come from Mexico, tended to say *djes* for yes and *Mizz* for Mrs. Tony had a few minor problems due to his bilingualism since the family spoke Italian at home.

Speech Due To Lack of Understanding. Mrs. Ashe met fewer difficulties resulting from misunderstanding due to lack of understanding of the meaning of words. Carolyn's mother had told Mrs. Ashe with amusement that Carolyn's favorite hymn was "The Old *Rubber* Cross," *Rubber* used instead of *Rugged*. A common mispronunciation during the Pledge of Allegiance is the pledge to one nation, *invisible*. Mrs. Ashe remembered that Larry, in particular, made this error. Mrs. Ashe put a mark of *1* under these children's names and inserted *P* to indicate that this difficulty was due to mispronunciation.

Many of the children tended to shorten some words that are naturally difficult to pronounce. Among these were *library* pronounced as *libary* and *February* pronounced as *Febuary*. These two words are difficult because many primary children have difficulty in pronouncing a clear *R*. Several other words, however, were shortened because the children did not hear the words accurately due to misunderstanding or because these words were mispronounced at home. Words falling into this category were *picture* pronounced as *pitcher, kindergarten* pronounced as *kittygarden,* and *chimney* pronounced as *chimley*. Because these errors were common, Mrs. Ashe did not check any specific names. She distributed marks of *2, 3,* and *4* under the other names, realizing that even these marks of *4* did not mean perfect pronunciation.

Listening to Stories

Mrs. Ashe realized that the ability to follow the plot of a story and to sit still long enough to enjoy listening was another phase of reading readiness. By this time of the year, kindergarten children were very enthusiastic about the story period, often requesting the retelling or rereading of favorite stories and poems. During the latter part of the year, very few children had problems in sitting still or in following the stories. Jose, Tony, and Felicia sometimes became restless when the stories were a little long. Mrs. Ashe felt that this restlessness might be partially due to the inability of these bilingual children to understand some of the vocabulary of the stories. On the other hand, Carl showed many signs of immaturity. He had particular difficulty in sitting still for a period of time. Mrs. Ashe placed him at one side of the group so that he had adequate room to change position frequently. In this way the children were less likely to be annoyed by his restlessness. Carl's inattention seemed to be due to physical immaturity as well as to lack of sufficient mental maturity to follow the plot of the story successfully. Mrs. Ashe placed a mark of 1 under these four names, realizing that the cause was different in Carl's case.

Identifying Words in Print

Marjorie and Donald were the only children who tended to point out and read words on the experience story charts or to notice the labels on such objects as the paste jar, the crayon boxes labeled by colors, the paint cans, or the numbers on the calendar. Therefore, Mrs. Ashe placed a mark of 4 for Marjorie and Donald after this category and left the others blank. After she had marked these names, Mrs. Ashe began to think about the other children. Most of the children in her class could recognize their names when they were printed in manuscript, a form of printing used with primary children, on the backs of their painting papers. They could also recognize their names when Mrs. Ashe put them on the bulletin board to indicate their turn to look for a surprise.

During the spring Mrs. Ashe had begun to use pocket charts, described below, for the planning of the work period. As each child chose the activity that interested him each day, he placed his name card in the pocket chart opposite the picture which illustrated this activity. This procedure will be more easily understood after the pocket chart has been described.

Making the Pocket Chart

Although pocket charts can be purchased from commercial school supply companies, many teachers make their own because they prefer larger charts. A pocket chart may be made from two pieces of manila tag, each approximately twenty-four by thirty-six inches in size. The top margin should be somewhat larger than the space between pockets. The margin at the bottom of the chart should be the largest in order to give the chart balance.

To make the chart, place the sheet of tag horizontally, and measure five inches from the top of the tag to make a line across the width. Score this line lightly with the point of a pair of scissors. The lines are scored in order to help fold the tag smoothly. Draw and score another line horizontally across the tag three-fourths of an inch below the first line. Fold the tag upward on the first line and downward on the second line to make a pocket three-fourths of an inch deep. Some teachers prefer to make the pockets an inch deep. This dimension is necessary if inch-ruled tag is to be used for the reading cards.

Next, measure five and a half inches from the top of the first pocket to make another horizontal line across the tag. Add a line three-fourths of an inch below this, and again score and fold the tag upward and then downward to make a second pocket. In the same way two more pockets may be made from the first sheet.

Attach the second sheet of tag to the bottom edge of the first sheet by means of some type of adhesive tape. Use good quality tape, since this joint will receive pressure because it becomes the bottom of the next pocket. Continue to make more pockets until they reach near the lower margin of the second sheet. Allow at least a six inch margin across the bottom of the completed chart. If the above directions are followed, the pocket chart will be wide enough to accommodate most needs met in the various reading steps.

The chart must be attached to some type of backing. Two or three layers of double-faced corrugated cardboard, which may be cut from large cardboard cartons, provide a sturdy but lightweight backing for the chart. The tag may be stapled to the backing along the edges, which should then be bound with some type of tape to make a neat and attractive chart. Masking tape, mystic tape, or architects' tape are suitable for this purpose. Some teachers use colored tape borders an inch in width for extra eye-appeal. A diagram of a pocket chart is found in Figure 3-3. The top of a pocket chart before folding is found in Figure 3-4.

Using the Pocket Chart

Mrs. Ashe used two of these pocket charts for planning the work period. For use in the first pocket chart, Mrs. Ashe had pasted pictures on three by five-inch cards. These pictures showed children working on the type of activities she had made available in her classroom. They included illustrations of such activities as a child painting at an easel, another working with clay, two children building with blocks, and so on. She placed each of these pictures in the left end of one of the pockets in the first chart. She then printed each child's name on a card cut from manila tag (see Figure 3-5) and placed these cards in a second pocket chart she called a card holder so that the children could find them.

During planning time when a child said that he would like to paint,

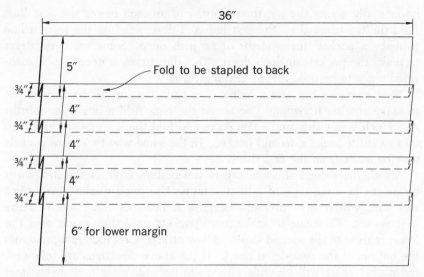

Fig. 3–3. A pocket chart made of a folded tag by stapling the edges of the fold to the back.

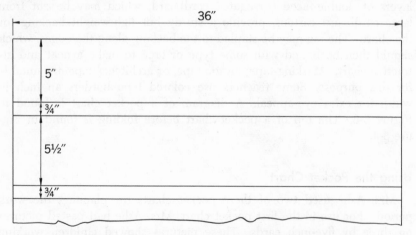

Fig. 3–4. The top of a pocket chart before folding.

he took his name card from the pocket chart used as a card holder and placed it in the other chart in the pocket headed by the picture of a child painting at an easel. He then went to the easel and began to work. Mrs. Ashe used this chart as a way of helping pictures serve as communication.

Near the end of the year, she made cards on which the name of each activity had been printed. She placed these cards beside each picture

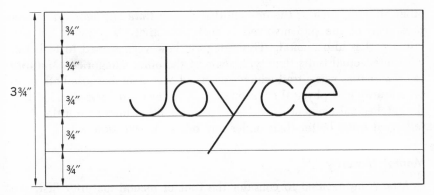

Fig. 3–5. Sample of a word card.

to help the children discover that words as well as pictures can stand for thoughts. She sometimes removed the pictures for the brighter children to see if they could find the proper pocket for their names by the printed word alone. Marjorie and Donald were able to do this. Position on the chart was of help at first. Since most of the children in her kindergarten could recognize their names in print, Mrs. Ashe decided to ignore this ability as a phase of readiness. She therefore left the symbols, 4, under Marjorie's and Donald's names after this category of ability to identify occasional words in print and left the other squares blank.

Playing with Words and Sounds

Mrs. Ashe knew that children's interest in rhyming words was another indication of readiness. Sometimes they liked to play with initial sounds. She recalled hearing Mark counting by saying, "sun, swo, sree, sour, sive, six, seven, seight, sine, and sen." When she had asked him if he could count the other way, he had nonchalantly responded by saying, "Of course." She therefore put the symbol, 4 under Mark's name. She then looked through the folders to find anecdotal notes regarding further play with words and ability to identify rhyming words in short poems. She found that Laurie had been repeating in a sing-song fashion, "Laurie, Sorry, and Torry," over and over softly as she painted at the easel. Mrs. Ashe also gave Laurie a mark of 4. The other first twelve children were able to identify rhyming words in short poems, so she gave them each a mark of 3 and left the other squares blank.

INTELLECTUAL TRAITS

Mrs. Ashe had found about fourteen traits that seemed to group themselves best under the title of intellectual traits. Actually some involved other abilities, such as the one entitled *demonstrate eye-hand co-ordination*. Part of the skill involved in such an activity is physical but certainly part is also mental. This category, however, seemed to fit better with intellectual traits than with some of the other categories. *Maturity in art activities* was a trait which concerned Mrs. Ashe because both mental maturity and physical co-ordination were involved. She decided that the intellectual element or the level of ideas fitted under the title of *intellectual traits* better than under any other classification.

Mental Maturity

Mrs. Ashe decided to consider the trait of mental maturity first. To have accurate information she needed tests. However, tests of mental maturity had been shown to be fairly unreliable when given to groups of children under eight years of age. Nevertheless, Mrs. Ashe knew that this trait was important in reading readiness.

Studies of Early Beginners. The trend toward teaching reading to very young children was of concern to her. She had found studies which seemed to offset the implications of some of the work carried on with young children. The study by Hampleman has been quoted in the chapter on *Trends in Reading*.[3] In this study children who started to school at a chronological age of six years, four months and older achieved reading scores of four months higher than the children who had started to school at six years and three months or younger. This measurement was made during the sixth grade. The IQ's of the two groups were matched. Hampleman used the criterion of chronological age rather than mental age for measuring success in reading, because he felt that this factor was easier to discuss with parents. Chronological age is an objective factor which parents are willing to accept and discuss objectively.

In order to discover the effect of entrance age on achievement, King also made a study of two groups of children whose entrance ages in first grade differed.[4] The age range of the younger group varied from five years, zero months to five years and eight months. The age range of the older group varied from six years, zero months to six years and eight months. The success of these children was also measured at the end of the sixth grade. In addition, ten of the children among those in the younger group had been retained one year, whereas only one child among those in the older group had been retained one year. The average age-grade equivalent on a general achievement test for the older group

---

[3] Richard S. Hampleman, "A Study of Comparative Reading Achievements of Early and Late School Starters," *Elementary English*, XXXVI (May 1959), 331–34.
[4] I. B. King, "Effect of Age of Entrance into Grade One upon Achievement in Elementary School," *Elementary School Journal*, LV (Feb. 1955), 331–36.

was seventh grade, seven months. An equivalent of sixth grade, two months, was found for the younger group including those retained.

Greene and Simmons also studied children whose ages differed on school entrance.[5] The younger group was under six years of age when they entered school in September and became six sometime before January first of that school year. Those children in the older group were six or older on school entrance. Fifty-nine children were selected for each group. They were matched by parental occupations and intelligence test scores. The achievement of the children in these two groups was measured during the first month of the fourth grade. The test on reading showed a difference of nine months in achievement between the scores of the older group and the younger group, and achievement in other subjects was also higher. Most other studies supported the findings of the researches quoted. The findings of the Greene and Simmons' study also showed that boys are slower to make a start in reading than girls. These findings agreed with those of other authorities.

Difference in Time Needed. Dr. Moore in a study described by Pines spent thirty-three weeks to teach the alphabet to his daughter who was less than three years old.[6] This study is described in Chapter 15, pages 8-9. Mrs. Ashe concluded from these studies that no real proof yet exists of the advantage of starting children to school at an early age. She also recalled a class that she had taught several years ago when she was teaching first grade. By the middle of the year she realized that these children were making exceptionally good progress, and even the children in the slowest group were doing very acceptable work. At first she had thought these children must be unusually intelligent. At that time intelligence tests were given to first-grade children in that school district. When she reviewed the scores for this class, she found that they were more or less average in intelligence. A few IQ's were as low as 85 and a few were near 115, but most of them were grouped around 100. These data did not support the unusual reading progress made by these children.

Mrs. Ashe then decided to check chronological age. She found that almost all of the children had been six years old when they entered first grade, and many had been six and a half or even older. The years of living had obviously been a great advantage in their ease of learning and her ease of teaching.

A number of authorities agree that children seem to learn to read more easily and progress most smoothly if they are taught beginning reading when they have time to acquire experience and interest in read-

[5] Donald Ross Greene and Sadie Vee Simmons, "Chronological Age and School Entrance," *The Elementary School Journal*, LXIII (Oct. 1962), 41–7.

[6] Maya, Pines, "How Three-Year-Olds Teach Themselves to Read—and Love It," *Harper's Magazine*, CCXXVI, No. 1356 (May 1963), 58–64.

ing. Children of less than normal intelligence and children of superior intelligence vary widely in the age when they are ready for reading. In Mrs. Ashe's class, Carl was the only child whose intelligence, judged from observation of various traits, seemed near the level of mental retardation so she put a mark of *1* under his name. About eight of the other children seemed a little below the slow normal level. Therefore, beginning with David, she put a mark of *2* under their names. She distributed marks of *3* and *4* to the other children according to her best judgment of their mental maturity.

Interpretation of Pictures

In some of the individual intelligence tests, the child's ability to interpret pictures is tested as one type of item in the total test. Mrs. Ashe had asked individual chlidren to tell her about pictures from time to time and had found a wide variety of reactions. Carl, whose mental ability was obviously low, pointed to one object in the picture and named it with a single word regardless of the variety of objects or the situation illustrated. Mrs. Ashe had used a picture of a family at the beach. Father was fishing on a point of land on a gradually sloping hillside above the beach. Mother had spread a tablecloth on the sand and had started to unpack the lunch. The boy and girl, dressed in bathing suits, were nearby piling sand to make a hill with a toy pail and shovels. When asked to tell about the picture, Carl's only reply was "man." He made no response when asked to tell more about the picture and his interest drifted immediately to other things.

Larry, Joe, Pamela, Jose, Felicia, and Tony had limited their responses to a few phrases such as, "It's a beach," "The man's fishing," "Got things to eat," and "Kids digging." These children, too, had failed to add further responses when asked to tell more about the picture. These children, including Carl, received a mark of *1* under their names in this category.

Several other children named all the people and objects in the picture, but failed to notice that the people were members of a family. They also named the pail, shovel, and pile of sand, but did not connect these to the activities of the children. Mrs. Ashe checked this category under the children's names with a mark of *2*. The next more advanced group noticed the family relationship and described the characters in terms of family. They noticed that father was fishing, that mother was preparing lunch, and that the children were making a big sand hill. Some added even more details about the picture. She gave these children a mark of *3* for their descriptions. The most mature children described the picture in greater detail than the former group. They also added imaginative touches such as, "I'll bet Daddy gets a perch," and also brought in comments from personal experience as, "My Daddy catches lots of perch at the lake we go to." These children's responses differed from those of the previous group in the imaginative touches added and in the additions from personal experiences. To these children Mrs. Ashe gave a mark of 4.

Organization of Pictures

Most of the children in the two highest groups in the above category were also able to organize pictures. Some of the less mature children were able to organize pictures if two categories were used and if the objects were simple and obvious. Many of the children were able to organize into two groups a scrambled set of simple pictures of foods and of clothing. Mrs. Ashe was careful to see that only one type of food or one type of clothing was pasted on each card respectively. For example, she had pasted a picture of a bowl of soup on a card but had cut off the rest of the meal to avoid confusion. In the same way, she pasted on another card a girl's hair ribbon without any other objects to confuse the subject. On other sets of cards she had pasted objects illustrating more subtle differences. Only a few children were able to organize all of these sets of cards. Mrs. Ashe had divided these cards into four levels of difficulty. She placed the number 4 under the names of the children who were able to successfully organize all of these types of cards. She added other numerals 3, 2, and 1 for children who were able to work on cards of less difficulty.

Interest in Books

Mrs. Ashe had kept anecdotal records regarding children's ability to show sustained interest in picture and story books. She had set up some divisions of time to show roughly how much time each child usually spent in looking at books. She made about four classifications. Level 4 indicated the ability of the child to look at a book for fifteen to twenty minutes or possibly longer. Level 3 indicated a period of ten to fifteen minutes and level 2 a period of five to ten minutes, usually for one book. Level 1 indicated that the child spent less than five minutes and often flipped through all the book on the library table in an even shorter length of time.

Mrs. Ashe had noticed that the children who were low in ability to interpret pictures were the ones who spent very little time at the library table. It was logical that a child who saw only a man in the picnic at the beach scene would also be very limited in his ability to gain meaning from pictures in books and those undoubtedly would have very little interest for him. When these children went to the library table, they were satisfied to look at only one or two pictures in a book and to glance through the other books out of idle curiosity. Some of Mrs. Ashe's friends had interpreted this tendency on the part of their own children as lack of good habits. Mrs. Ashe, however, was sure that these children were too immature to gain meaning from pictures.

Mrs. Ashe had notations concerning this lack of interest in books on the part of Linda, Larry, Joe, Pamela, and Carl, so she put the numeral 1 below their names for this trait. Although Jose, Felicia, and Tony were low on the scale in other traits, Felicia often spent ten to fifteen minutes on a book; therefore Mrs. Ashe indicated her ability as 3 on the scale. Jose and Tony usually spent more than five minutes on a book so Mrs. Ashe indicated their ability as 2 on the scale. Lack of language facility obviously did not interfere with these bilingual children's ability to interpret and enjoy pictures.

In looking over the records of the other children, she was not surprised to notice that the eleven highest children were also highest in book interest so she indicated this by the numeral 4. It seemed logical that children who perceived the total situation in pictures, who made inferences regarding possible consequences of the situation, and who identified themselves with the situation sufficiently to relate it to their own experiences would undoubtedly spend much more time in looking at picture books than children who lacked such mature ability. As she distributed 2's and 3's to indicate interest levels by the other children, she noticed that Teruko spent long periods at the library table often on one book. She therefore rated Teruko as 4 in ability despite the fact that she was lower on other traits due to her bilingual problem.

Signs and Labels

Early in the year Mrs. Ashe used picture symbols to represent children's names. She usually used bird stickers to represent boy's names and flower stickers to represent girl's names merely because these were easy to secure and because every sticker in the package showed a different bird or flower. She used the printed name in addition in each case to save the necessity of keeping a code for herself. Thus a robin sticker and Robert's name were placed on his coat hanger for easy identification by him and the teacher as well. Mothers were asked to make labels for the children's coats, rubbers, and other possessions by printing their names on a flowered or patterned piece of material. Since few mothers used the same material, these labels helped the children identify their own possessions as well as helping the teacher if errors occurred. As time went on the children learned to recognize their own names and often the names of others. When the children showed that they recognized most of the other children's names as well as their own, Mrs. Ashe felt that they were ready for the use of other printed labels.

Mrs. Ashe used the scale of 4-1 to indicate interest and ability to use printed signs regardless of whether or not the child could read them.

Auditory and Visual Differences

Perception, discussed in Chapter 2, is a basic skill needed in beginning reading. Auditory and visual perception seem to be very closely related to maturity. In a study by Durrell the ability to distinguish between pictures that are alike and those that are different seemed to have only a limited relationship to readiness for reading.[7] The ability to name and write the letters of the alphabet seemed to have a much closer relationship. Since, however, thousands of children have started to read without knowing the names of these letters and since the names of the letters do not seem to be important in facilitating the reading process, another conclusion seems to be indicated. It would seem more likely that children who are mature enough to name and write the letters of the alphabet are also mature enough to begin reading. The reversed letters, such as *b* and *d* also mentioned in Chapter 2, are the hardest to distinguish and seem to demand more maturity than the letters that have more discrete forms.

The ability to distinguish differences between sounds is another factor of perception that is needed for beginning reading. To be able to relate sounds to letters, both singly and in groups, the child must be able to hear the sounds and to distinguish between letters that have similarities in sounds. For example, *b* and *p* are made by the same position of the lips, but *b* is voiced and *p* is whispered. Other letters present the same difficulties. The tongue is placed in the same position for *d* and *t*, but *d* is voiced. Activities for helping children hear more accurately are given in Chapter 4.

Solution for Problems

Children meet many problems as they progress through the grades in school. Such problems often require the ability to read, interpret, and find solutions to abstract problems. The ability to solve problems, however, should be developed in simple action situations early in the child's life to help him acquire self-confidence and a problem-solving attitude. Children who have attended formal schools requiring only the absorption and digestion of ready-made facts tend to become dis-

[7] Donald D. Durrell, *et al.*, "Success in First Grade Reading," *Journal of Education*, CXL (Feb. 1958), 1–48.

A first-grade child is reading to the kindergarten a letter dictated and written in i.t.a. (see chapter 23). (Courtesy Georgetown School, Placer County, California.)

turbed and to react in very ineffectual ways when they are expected to think and take an active part in solving practical as well as abstract problems. This resistance is difficult to overcome and may require the large part of a school year for children who have advanced to the upper grades without being required to think actively.

Mrs. Ashe carried on a creative program requiring action based on thinking. When a child was confronted by a problem, Mrs. Ashe was careful to avoid solving the problem for him. Instead she used guiding questions to help him discover the cause of the problem and to think through to the solution for himself. When a building of blocks fell down due to poor balance, Mrs. Ashe usually guided the child to discover the cause. During the next discussion period after such an occurrence had taken place, Mrs. Ashe built two columns of blocks. She placed the blocks evenly in one column and balanced the blocks poorly in the other. She then asked the children to tell her how the "towers" were different and why one was not good. Most of the children were able to notice the irregularity in the second column compared to the evenness of the first column and knew that the second column would fall over easily. The children gradually learned to build more solid structures. If a child lacked the muscular co-ordination necessary for building a stable column of blocks, Mrs. Ashe might suggest that he build a lower building. She then guided him by questions to decide why it would be less likely to fall. Mrs. Ashe found that block building provided many situations for problem solving activities.

Work in the playhouse also provided opportunities for problem solving in social as well as other situations. Mrs. Ashe helped children with behavior difficulties by asking them to tell her a better way of solving the problem and the reasons why this latter solution would have been better. As a result of this stress on reasons for behavior, most of Mrs. Ashe's children were usually very understanding and co-operative in their social behavior.

Mrs. Ashe rated the children's levels of problem solving by their procedures in dealing with objects and materials, using her judgment in distributing marks from 1 to 4. Although advanced in other ways, Karen was given a mark of 2 because of her tendency to wait for Mrs. Ashe to guide her. She needed more confidence in dealing with problem situations. The children who were low in other traits tended to be low in this trait, too.

Attention Span

All the lists Mrs. Ashe had checked for readiness traits referred to attention span as an important factor in reading readiness. One year Mrs. Ashe had an experience that pointed up the importance of a good attention span when she had Dickie, a very immature child, in her class. Although he was large and seemed quite intelligent, he was extremely babyish in his ways. He shifted from activity to activity much more often than any other child even late in the fall. He rushed around the room with open scissors in his hand disturbing other children and in other ways demonstrating constant activity. When Mrs. Ashe lost patience with him he would come up to her, stand on the rung of her chair and put his arms around her neck. Although it was an uncomfortable position for Mrs. Ashe, she was fond of him, and he at least was inactive for a few minutes.

On investigation the attendance officer discovered that the mother had sent her three-year, nine-month old child to school so that she could seek employment. When she was required to provide a birth certificate, Mrs. Ashe's most acute attention problem ended. Her problems with Dickie made her particularly conscious of the tremendous growth made by children in extending their span of attention even in one year.

Mrs. Ashe felt that Carl, who still had difficulty in sitting still while listening to a story and who tended to move about much more often than other children, would be unlikely to have an adequate attention span for reading in first grade. The other children had grown so much in the length of time they could stay with one activity that Mrs. Ashe felt that their attention spans would be adequate for first grade reading after the lapse of two and a half months of summer vacation.

Mrs. Ashe realized that attention span was sometimes influenced by emotional insecurity as well as by immaturity. During the previous year she had taught Dan, a little boy who was disturbed apparently due to the fact that both parents worked. Dan tended to seek a great deal of attention and to change activities very often. Part of his movement around the room was made in an effort to seek attention, and part was simply due to his emotional disturbance. Mrs. Ashe noticed that he was exceptionally unstable and more extreme in his efforts to secure attention when the parents were on the swing shift at the same time. Although Mrs. Ashe was concerned about his ability to succeed in the first grade the following year, she could think of no alternate plan for him since he was very bright and large for his age. As she had feared, Dan had serious problems in the first grade and was unable to make even a beginning in reading despite his high degree of intelligence.

Because of her consciousness of the importance of a reasonable attention span, Mrs. Ashe tried to help the children grow in length of attention by providing activities of high interest. From the anecdotal notes in her files, she indicated general levels of attention by the usual symbols.

Ability to Follow Directions

Ability to follow simple directions is an important requirement for any activity in the kindergarten as well as for readiness for reading in the first grade. Mrs. Ashe worked very hard with her children early in the year in order to help them understand and follow simple directions successfully. Once this habit was established Mrs. Ashe's class work went forward with ease and smoothness.

Mrs. Ashe found that the children's ability to follow directions varied widely. Immature children might be very hesitant to try one step directions, whereas mature children with confidence were often able to carry out three and four step directions. When Mrs. Ashe used a one step direction, she might say, "Please bring me a piece of painting paper, Pamela." An example of a much more complicated direction might consist of a request to bring the stapler. Mrs. Ashe might say, "Joan, please bring me the stapler. Look in the top right-hand desk drawer in the back compartment. You will find it near my scissors." Another complicated request might be to find a book with a blue cover in the left-hand bookcase on the middle shelf. Mrs. Ashe always gave these directions in real situations.

Lack of ability to follow simple directions does not always indicate immaturity. Sometimes a shy child is afraid to try for fear he will not succeed. Children who are used to following directions from their parents issued to each one alone may find group directions difficult to follow at first. Children who are used to being waited upon and are not accustomed to carrying out requests from their parents may also be shy and fearful in attempting to carry out the teacher's directions at first. Other children may be the victims of parents who make requests without following through to be sure they are carried out. Such children may acquire the habit of ignoring requests from parents until the latter become very annoyed.

Mrs. Ashe rated her children rather informally from her notes concerning their ability to follow directions. A few children who could carry out a direction of several steps were rated highest since considerable maturity is involved in this complex activity.

Eye and Hand Co-ordination

Mrs. Ashe had noticed that children's ability to cut out pictures for scrapbooks toward the end of the kindergarten year told a great deal about their maturity. After instruction a few children were able to cut out pictures very neatly and even to paste them in an orderly manner in their books. Some children were able to paste several pictures in position so that the balance was effective, although Mrs. Ashe did not try to teach them to do so. These mature children differed from each other in a minor way in co-ordination, but the pictures were always complete; essential parts were never missing. These children were also able to organize the pictures in their scrapbooks under a variety of headings. A boy might choose various types of tractors and farm machinery for his picture collection, whereas a girl might choose various activities her mother carried on during her work in the house.

On the other end of the scale, the immature children often cut their pictures very inaccurately. Parts of heads and feet were lopped off, and parts of wheels might also be removed. The pasting was also very crude. Too many pictures might be pasted on a page, one even overlapping another. Balance was poor; a little picture might be pasted on one side of a page while the rest of the space was left blank. The ability to cut out these pictures accurately seemed to correspond to a degree to these children's abilities to interpret pictures. These children were also unable to organize their pictures under categories. Pictures of babies, policemen, and tractors would be included in the same books and even on the same pages. Mrs. Ashe found that, because of the gap in standards, the mature children resented working with immature children on the same books. She was careful to avoid such a situation. The abilities of the children in Mrs. Ashe's kindergarten seemed to vary all the way from those children who cut out and pasted very inaccurately to those who cut out and pasted pictures in a very mature way. She used this activity only near the end of the year since it demanded small muscle co-ordination. Mrs. Ashe had noted that the children who seemed very mature in other ways were usually very mature in this activity.

Block building was another activity that rather clearly showed the children's development in co-ordination. Some children merely piled one block on top of the other, often with such poor stability that the blocks soon fell down. Others made so-called buildings by jumbling a group of blocks together on the floor. Sometimes these crude structures were given names just as sometimes children give names to their art work. These children usually built structures first and named them afterward. At a later level, children might make designs with blocks; two followed by one followed by two followed by one in a rather definite pattern. These children also occasionally gave names to their groups of blocks when they were organized in designs. At the most mature level the children constructed buildings that were recognizable by an adult. Thus, in their block building, the children followed the same type of growth patterns that they followed in art. Mrs. Ashe then used her notes to record levels of co-ordination on her readiness inventory.

PHYSICAL TRAITS

Adequate vision, hearing, and general health are necessary for satisfactory work in school and are particularly important in reading readiness. The child who cannot see print clearly, who cannot hear instructions, or who lacks energy to carry on his work will find great difficulty in making a good start in school.

Hearing

If a child has a severe hearing loss, he should be recommended for tests and may be placed in a special class. Sometimes the child who does not hear well is able to carry on general activities in the classroom by alertness in watching other children and by imitating their actions or by lip reading. These procedures can take the child far, particularly on the readiness level.

When a teacher suspects that a child has some hearing loss, she may check his hearing by speaking his name when he has his back turned toward her. If he normally responds when facing her but does not respond when his back is turned, he may have some hearing loss. Inattention and loss of hearing are easily confused. The teacher should watch the child's reactions over a period of time to avoid confusing these problems.

Vision

Most young children are far-sighted. They may, therefore, have little or no difficulty when carrying on readiness activities with pictures or when reading from charts. When they begin to read in a book, their difficulties in vision may become more apparent. Many children, however, may be able to adjust to reading although their eyes are strained by the process. The young child's eyes will make accommodations, often without the child's consciousness of strain. Little children are often unable to isolate pain or discomfort. If the child squints or rubs his eyes often or if his eyes water, these symptoms indicate that he may be straining his eyes. He may even hold the book close to his face in an effort to see better. On the other hand, many children may have visual problems that are completely overlooked until they attend high school or college when the demands for reading may force them to have their eyes examined. Any of these symptoms observed during the reading period or when the child is doing close work should cause the primary teacher to refer the child for help.

Many children's visual difficulties seem to be overlooked in school because special tests are needed to discover them. Schrock and Grossman found twenty-three children with visual difficulties among thirty seventh grade pupils with reading problems.[8] These children were selected because they were reading two or more years below grade level although all had IQ's from 90 to 110. None of these defects could be identified by the *Snellen Eye Test* often used in school because of its simplicity. The *Snellen E Test* for young children is made up of capital *E's* printed in diminishing sizes. The *E's* are given in four positions with the legs facing up, down, left, and right. In this way, a young child may be given the test by asking him to show in which direction the

[8] Ralph E. Schrock and Milton Grossman, "Pilot Study: Motivation in Reading," *The Reading Teacher*, XV (Nov. 1961), 119–21.

legs are facing. With older children, the *Snellen Eye Test* uses a variety of letters. Such tests are valuable only for discovering the distance at which children can see certain rows of letters.

Schrock and Grossman administered the *Keystone Visual Skills Test* and *Lovelle Hand-Eye Co-ordination Test* for analyzing various phases of vision and the *Gray Oral Reading Test* for reading ability. Although the objective of this study was to motivate interest in reading, these authors found that twenty-three of the thirty children tested had some visual defect beyond that which could be discovered by the *Snellen Eye Test*. They also found that these children had developed a defeatist attitude as a result of failure over a period of six years. The use of thorough tests of vision in the early years of school with proper remedial help might have saved these children years of failure and unhappiness.

General Health

Lack of proper nutrition, sleep, play out of doors, or other deficiencies may handicap a pupil. The child who has been permitted to stay up beyond his normal bedtime will be sleepy and inattentive or restless on the following day. Some children never get adequate sleep because parents do not insist on good sleeping habits. The child who comes to school without breakfast or the child who is poorly nourished will have difficulty in staying alert and interested while at school.

Most schools have health services including a nurse available to make home visits. The teacher never diagnoses a child's difficulty, but merely describes the symptoms to the school nurse who will try to discover the causes of the problems and help the parents to improve the situation, if possible. Some parents must leave the home early for work or adjust to some other problem that makes proper care of the children difficult. Some parents will not put themselves out to correct a situation, whereas others are very co-operative when they understand the problem. On the other hand, the child may be suffering from a chronic difficulty such as asthma. The parent may be working with a doctor to give the child every possible help, but improvement may be very slow.

EMOTIONAL AND SOCIAL ADJUSTMENT

Children who have had a good kindergarten experience are known to succeed better on the average in first grade than children who have not attended kindergarten. The kindergarten teacher usually spends much time in helping children adjust to the school room situation in which they must work in a group of twenty-five to thirty-five peers.

After a year in a good kindergarten class, most children develop considerable initiative, independence, security, and self-confidence. They are able to obtain needed materials for themselves and to undertake most simple tasks with little help from the teacher. They have also had an opportunity to develop feelings of security which are essential if these children are to develop their maximum potential in work. Children who have not had a good kindergarten experience or who have failed to develop these social traits may have difficulty in making a successful beginning in reading. For example, a very shy first grade boy who needed time to adjust to every new situation was not ready to start reading with the first two groups. He did not advance to a higher group until after Christmas. In this way he lost the opportunity for working at his normal level until half the year was gone.

Sudden traumatic experiences, that is, experiences which seriously upset the child emotionally and which may be of several weeks or longer in duration, may seriously interfere with a child's ability to work at his normal level. A sudden traumatic experience may cause the child to regress either intellectually or emotionally as shown in his behavior. On the other hand, such an experience may block the child's further progress although he does not lose his memory or regress in any way. Instances of such cases with descriptions of their treatment are given in the following chapter.

Mrs. Ashe decided to give the children in her class a separate rating for social and emotional adjustment. Since Mrs. Ashe had no seriously emotionally disturbed children in her class at the present time, she gave all of the children the numeral 4 for emotional adjustment with the exception of Paul who had previously sought constant attention and Nancy who had been very shy. She felt that both children were well on the way toward adjustment so she gave each a mark of 2 on the chart. She omitted a mark for Carl because she was not sure whether his problem was entirely mental or partly emotional.

When Mrs. Ashe considered the children's social adjustment, she decided to put a rating of 1 on the chart under Linda's name since she felt that Linda's progress in social adjustment was not adequate to insure her success in first grade. She also gave Carl a mark of 1 since his mental immaturity limited his social adjustment. She distributed the other marks according to her notations on the children's anecdotal records.

EXPERIENTIAL BACKGROUND

Most teachers have found that a rich background of experiences is a valuable factor in reading readiness. If children's experiences have been guided and enriched by parents, these children tend to acquire a large vocabulary which in itself is valuable in readiness for reading. Parents who take children on local trips and who include them if possible when traveling are able to give these children a wide variety of knowledge as well as to increase their vocabulary. The knowledge or information acquired provides a background for understanding stories and reading material, and thereby helps children remember much that they read because it fits into a pattern of information. The children who have not had this advantage often meet ideas that are completely new to them. These ideas are therefore more difficult to understand and to remember.

The children of migratory parents who lived in lettuce crates in the San Joaquin Valley of California during the extreme shortage of housing brought practically no background which could be of help to them in understanding the stories about middle-class children in the pre-primers they read. Some of these children had lived in very crude types of homes before coming to California so that their early background was also of no help. Even the pictures presented difficulties because a two-dimensional representation of a three-dimensional object never seen by children results in a very poor concept to serve as background for reading.

As Mrs. Ashe thought about the background of the children in her class she realized that almost all of them had very adequate homes and some help from parents in building a background of experience. She stressed the values of certain experiences for children during the first two group conferences for parents. Most of the parents had since tried to make use of weekends and holidays to go to points of interest and to discuss these with their children. These children varied in their abilities, however, to gain vocabulary and to acquire a large number of concepts and understandings from these experiences. From her notes in the cumulative folders, Mrs. Ashe assigned a mark of 4 to Donald, Marjorie, Susan, Karen, Mark, and Steven. She distributed marks of 3 and 2 to most of the other children. She assigned a mark of 1 to Joe, Pamela, and Carl since their vocabulary was quite limited, their contributions during the sharing period were restricted to a very few experiences, and their background of experiences seemed to provide little help in the interpretation of many pictures. Jose, Felicia, and Tony presented a different problem because of their bilingualism. They seemed to understand experiences illustrated in pictures, but they were at a loss for enough English words to convey their ideas to other children. Mrs. Ashe put an asterisk in the place of a mark of evaluation in the squares under their names and put a note at the foot of the chart to indicate that their problem sprang from limited English due to bilingualism.

Mrs. Ashe did not usually prepare such an elaborate chart as those shown in Figures 3-1 and 3-2. She often used only the headings in the left hand column as criteria and merely made notations to indicate which children were good, average, or poor in a particular readiness trait.

SUMMARY

Readiness traits may be analyzed under several topics as follows: language, intellectual, physical, and emotional and social traits as well as experiential background. Children's levels of abilities to tell stories, to discuss their own activities, and to use mature language in this process provide opportunities for teachers to analyze their readiness for reading. Some intellectual traits also provide opportunities for diagnosis. Children's mental maturity, ability to interpret and organize pictures, their interest in books, signs, and labels, their spans of attention, their ability to recognize auditory and visual differences, and their ability to solve problems provide opportunities for teachers to recognize children's readiness for reading. Approximately normal vision and hearing and good health are essential for school learning in all areas. Children should also be stable emotionally and have ability to make social adjustments in the classroom. The extent of their experience is basic to language and intellectual development.

4

Language Activities

Suggestions for various activities given in this chapter have been arbitrarily described as language activities. Although language is needed for work with all experiences, some of these activities seem to serve more than others to stimulate thought and organization of ideas as well as to involve language.

Readiness in language is an important need in both the pre-school groups and in the primary grades. Therefore, suggestions are given for activities that are appropriate for children with the most limited background, as well as for children without such handicaps.

NEEDS OF LANGUAGE-DEPRIVED CHILDREN

Work with the culturally-deprived children in the Head Start Programs at the pre-school level has tended to focus the teacher's attention on language more intensely than before. The culturally-deprived child is often a year behind other children when he enters school and tends to drop further and further behind as he progresses through the grades.

Culturally-deprived people are strongly oriented toward action and depend to a lesser extent upon language. Directions to the children in the home may consist of gestures or single words such as "Go," or "Come." The culturally-deprived parent usually has too many children and is too busy to give lengthy directions or to explain or reason with their children. In general, they do not have the time, energy, or interest to discuss topics or exchange ideas. As a result, the culturally-deprived child does not have the opportunity to acquire anything beyond the minimum vocabulary or the simplest language structure.

Loban feels that the lack of language facility is the greatest handicap of the culturally-deprived child and that language development should be the subject of greatest stress in developing their readiness for reading and language in the grades.[1] Without skill in reading and writing the child is handicapped in all areas of learning, possibly for his entire life. In addition, his inability to succeed well will probably cause him to drop out of school at the high school level. As a result, he will be limited in his opportunities for earning a living and may be forced to remain in the poverty group because of the lack of demand in industry for uneducated labor, an increasing trend in this era of automation.

SENTENCE PATTERNS

Some authors refer to children in low socio-economic areas as "culturally-deprived." Others prefer to use the term, "language-deprived," because many have a culture of their own, although it may be different from that of the middle-class Caucasian child. Children who belong to a different racial group often have a very definite culture. One of the greatest weaknesses of these children and those brought up in a home where language is limited is the lack of mature vocabulary, concepts, and sentence structure.

Levels of Sentence Structure

The most obvious differences in language among children are found in their use of sentence patterns. In a formal situation in a classroom, such as the sharing period, some children may speak in single words or phrases. One child brought a picture of a boat every time he had his turn to share. When he showed the picture to the children, he merely said, "Boat," and no questions or comments by the teacher or members of the class could induce him to say anything more about the picture. He stayed on this level of language for over a year.

The next level found is that of the simple sentence. On this level, children may also string a series of simple sentences together with *ands*, to make run-on sentences, but these sentences are actually simple rather than compound. The next level of language may be classified as the use of simple sentences with internal compound parts, such as compound subjects, verbs, or predicates. The highest level, according to this classification, is found in complex sentences containing at least one subordinate clause along with one or more main clause. Either the main clauses

---

[1] Walter Loban, "A Sustained Program of Language Learning," *Language Problems for the Disadvantaged,* Report of the NCTE Task Force (Champaign, Ill.: National Council of Teachers of English, 1965).

or the subordinate clauses may have compound subjects, verbs, or predicates within them. According to Loban, other elements of complexity include infinitives, appositives, gerunds, and participles.

Relation of Sentence Structure to Reading

The results of a recent unpublished study of the language of second grade children sampled during the sharing period showed a very high relationship between children's levels of sentence structure and their scores on reading tests given at the end of the year. The findings from such a study suggest that children's maturity of sentence patterns is an important factor in their readiness for reading. Hunt also found complexity of sentence structure related to maturity of language.[2]

Strickland, on the other hand, did not find a relationship between the language and reading ability of second grade children.[3] Strickland, however, measured children's language by means of a linguistic analysis, which did not give recognition to complexity of sentence structure.

OBJECTIVES OF THE LANGUAGE PROGRAM

Robert F. Barnes has suggested some simple but important objectives of the program for the culturally-deprived.[4] These objectives apply equally well to the language program for middle-class children. The need for experiences and the acquisition of words to talk about them is the most basic objective for any child. Ability to listen, a knowledge of the names of various things both concrete and abstract, and ability to speak in complete sentences are also important objectives. Barnes adds to these the use of vocabulary within the child's understanding, the use of vocabulary for communication, and assimilation of information into meaningful concepts. All of these skills are needed for reading readiness.

Acquisition of Language

Crow, Murray, and Smythe stress the need for perceptual experiences of various sorts to precede language experiences in order to help the

[2] Kellogg W. Hunt, *Differences in Grammatical Structures Written at Three Grade Levels, The Structures to be Analyzed by Transformational Methods*, Cooperative Research Project, No. 1998 (Talahassee, Fla.: Florida State University, 1964).

[3] Ruth G. Strickland, *The Language of Elementary School Children: Its Relationship to the Language of Reading Textbooks and the Quality of Reading of Selected Children*, Bulletin of the School of Education, Indiana University, Vol. 38, No. 4, (Bloomington, Indiana: Bureau of Educational Studies and Testing, School of Education, Indiana University, 1962).

[4] Robert F. Barnes, "Programs for Teaching English to the Disadvantaged," *Language Programs for the Disadvantaged*, Report of the NCTE Task Force (Champaign, Ill.: National Council of Teachers of English, 1965).

child acquire the vocabulary and concepts basic to reading, thinking, and all later school work.[5] The child must also have the ability and habit of listening, if he is to profit by the language he hears.

Experiences. Experiences are of the utmost importance in building language facility. The young child needs to see, feel, hear, smell, taste, and manipulate the things around him, when such activities are possible, to acquire a knowledge of his environment. He puts things in his mouth as one way of discovering what they are like. He drops them in water, uses them for a hammer, jumps on them, and tries to swallow them if they are small enough. Adults often feel that he is destructive, but he is really trying to find what things are made of, how they react, and what he can do with them.

Development of Concepts. As the child has experience with things of various sorts, he begins to attach names to these things and to all phases of his experiences. After he learns the names of various things, he is ready to develop concepts or general ideas about them.

A concept is "A mental image of a thing formed by generalization from particulars; also, an idea of what a thing in general should be," according to Webster's Dictionary. The names of most objects are examples of concepts such as *house, automobile,* and *book* because they refer to a general class of objects rather than to a specific thing, such as *my house* or *his book.* Concepts also include ideas of relationships such as *big-little, long-short, hot-cold,* and others. Concepts also include more extended relationships such as *big, bigger,* and *biggest.*

The child needs to learn that things like milk, meat, and bread are types of food, and cats, dogs, and horses are types of animals. He must also develop concepts of qualities of things such as *pretty* or *funny.* As he learns these relationships, he gains the beginning of ability to think by means of language, the most important objective of the language program.

Ability to Listen. The culturally-deprived preschool child has more problems in learning to listen than the primary child or the one from a middle class home. All young children have short attention spans; the younger they are, the shorter the attention span. In addition, the child from the culturally-disadvantaged home has had almost no experience in extensive listening. He is told what to do by means of gestures or words and phrases. He is then expected to follow the directions into actions. In addition, a child from the culturally-disadvantaged home tends to block out sounds because of the continuous noise of various sorts

[5] Lester D. Crow, Walter I. Murray, and Hugh H. Smythe, *Educating the Culturally Disadvantaged Child* (New York: David McKay Co., Inc., 1966).

that he hears in his home. Radio or television usually blares constantly as an accompaniment to the noises made by the large number of children often found in such homes.

Assimilation and Use of Language

The child first learns the names of objects and the names for his activities as he acquires a beginning vocabulary. These words are predominantly nouns and verbs. He must continue to develop vocabulary and learn to use other parts of speech. His next goal is to learn to speak in complete sentences. He must also develop generalized ideas if he is to be able to learn to read, think, and succeed in other school work.

Ability to Speak in Complete Sentences. The ability to speak in complete sentences is acquired by children at various ages depending upon background of experiences, mental maturity, and the extent of language use in the home. The child who grows up in a verbal atmosphere may use simple but complete sentences at the age of two or three, whereas the child from a culturally-deprived home may find it difficult to use sentences even at the age of six or seven. To help the child with immature language, a great many experiences of all types should be provided.

Use of Vocabulary. The child acquires an understanding vocabulary, a term which refers to all the language he can understand, although he may be unable to use a large part of it in his speech. The understanding vocabulary has been estimated to be approximately eleven times larger than the vocabulary the child uses while speaking. As the child acquires this speaking vocabulary, he uses it for communication.

Both of these types of vocabulary are developed through a wide variety of experiences of an active as well as a listening nature. Some culturally-disadvantaged children have so few experiences, especially of a verbal nature, that their vocabulary is extremely impoverished. The school must provide many experiences, along with their verbal counterparts, to build an adequate vocabulary. Without such a vocabulary, the child's ability for thought is severely limited.

The Development of Generalizations. To function adequately with language, the child must eventually assimilate information into meaningful generalizations. The term, generalization, is used to refer to broader and more abstract ideas than the term, concept. The words, *school, woods,* and *family* are examples of such generalizations. Generalizations include words that show relationship. In addition, some words merely imply relationships. Examples of the latter are the word, *and,* which implies a relationship between two or more things, the word, *or,* which implies a relationship of one thing in contrast to another, and the word, *not,* which refers to the nonexistence of a thing.

The linguists refer to the words, *not, or,* and *and,* as "language operators" which they define as the means by which concepts and generalizations are manipulated and put into relationships with one another. Generalizations often include abstractions such as *democracy, conservation,* and *anthropology.* Many abstractions fall between the level of the "language operators" and the broad generalizations just mentioned. Some of these concepts or generalizations are simple enough for preschool and primary children to use and are needed for the thinking process.

LANGUAGE EXPERIENCES

Many activities can be provided by the school to help children increase their understanding vocabulary as well as their use of vocabulary in speech. Bereiter suggests that the programs for the culturally-disadvantaged stress the need for the school to select the activities that are of most value in developing language skills.[6] He also stresses the importance of beginning at the lowest level of the children in the program in order to build a comprehensive language program. Some language experiences which should help provide stimulation for growth and reading readiness for both the preschool and primary child are described in this chapter.

All the activities in which the child takes part are experiences that may be used for stimulating his language development. The experiences that are suggested here refer to both those that provide intake of ideas, and those that provide an opportunity for the child to express his ideas in connection with them.

Field Trips

Field trips are one of the best types of experiences for stimulating the growth of language. Some culturally-deprived children have never been beyond five or six blocks of their homes. The teacher may help the child take excursions and also help him make use of many aspects of his immediate environment to which he has previously been exposed, although he may not understand their functions. Children may have seen the neighborhood service station all their lives, but may know very little about the truck that brings the gasoline to the station and the tank into

<hr>

[6] Carl Bereiter, "Academic Instruction and Preschool Children," *Language Programs for the Disadvantaged,* Report of the NCTE Task Force (Champaign, Ill.: National Council of Teachers of English, 1965).

which it is poured. They may have seen tires all their lives, but may have no idea as to why air is put into the tires or how air functions.

A number of simple experiments can be carried on in connection with the concept of air in space and air pressure. Such a simple activity as pressing the air out of a thin plastic bag may help the children understand that air occupies space. Many experiments simple enough for young children are suggested in science books, especially those that are made up primarily of science experiments. The example of the possible knowledge that can be gained in regard to a service station may suggest the many possible aspects to be found in the immediate environment which children can explore and learn about.

Types of Trips. Extensive trips such as those to another town as taken by children in a nearby head-start program are unnecessary and wasteful for the preschool children. They should first learn as much as possible about their immediate environment. As children become a little older, they may go to the local zoo, a nearby dairy, a neighborhood bakery or creamery, a local fire station and other places of interest. Only when children have had the maximum experiences in the local environment should their trips be extended to such places as the railway depot, the airport, the central library, the main post office, and other more complicated community facilities. Trips to other towns come later still.

Plans for the Trip. Before the children take a trip, they should plan the things that they expect to see and their behavior on the trip. The use of discussion, pictures, slides, and filmstrips may give children an idea of what they expect to see and may help them acquire some of the vocabulary needed for the trip. Some kindergarten children can remember questions to ask when they are at the scene of their excursion. Many first-grade children can find questions which they want to have answered. These questions may be printed on slips of paper, one for each child who wishes to ask a question, to serve as a reminder for the children and for use as functional reading. Even though the children may be on the reading readiness level, they can usually remember the wording of their questions since they themselves dictated the questions to the teacher.

Discussion of the Trip. Often young children do not discuss their trip immediately on their return to the classroom. They seem to need a period of assimilation before they are ready to express their ideas. When the children do begin to talk about the trip, the teacher may ask them to review their questions and tell what they learned in answer to these questions. There should also be a time for a discussion of the things that interested the children aside from the answers to their questions.

The discussion of the less mature or language-deprived children will be carried on in a less structured way. The teacher, however, may ask such questions as, "What did you like best?", "What were the little bears doing when you saw them?", "Why do you think the giraffes have such long necks?" and similar questions. Younger and less experienced children cannot be expected to remember the names of all the animals, nor all the things they saw the animals do.

Values of Trips. The most obvious gain the children will have acquired from their trip is the new vocabulary. Not all of this vocabulary will be usable in their discussions. They may acquire some increased ability to stay on the topic as they discuss a subject of keen interest. Some child may, for the first time, use a more complex sentence structure than that to which he has been accustomed. For example, in answer to the question, "What were the little bears doing when you saw them?", a child may reply, "When I saw them, they were chasing each other."

Children may extend their concepts through interests gained on trips. A discussion of what the animals were fed may help some children extend their concept of food to include hay, grain, and raw meat to the foods they are accustomed to seeing people eat. Although little growth is noticed after a single field trip, children tend gradually to mature in their language facility as they acquire a wide variety of experiences.

Sharing Activities

The sharing or show and tell period is called such because children like to bring one of their toys or other treasures to show and discuss with the other children. Children may also tell about experiences without showing any objects to the class. Children from middle-class homes are able to bring a variety of treasures to show and discuss. Toys, trucks, and airplanes, often authentic models of well-known carriers, are valuable objects. Children can therefore gain some ideas of their operation. Girls enjoy bringing their dolls and discussing their knowledge of the care of babies. Boys like to bring in models of gasoline shovels, graders, and other equipment and discuss them. Much can be learned, and extensive concepts can be built around toys of various sorts.

Guidance by the Teacher. The sharing period is not necessarily limited to objects brought in by the children. Early in the year a clever teacher may initiate the activity by bringing in one thing at a time herself. She may then talk about it with the children and encourage their comments and questions. A wise teacher will pick up common objects in the environment to serve as an example to the children.

When the teacher finds a caterpillar on the shrubbery or weeds on the way to school, she may bring it to school for the children to discuss and observe as it progresses through its life cycle. Leaves from a few trees may be brought in and identified, and bugs of various sorts may be

Tom, Susan!
See Flip.
Flip.
Flip, ride

A first-grade child is matching a reading strip to a parallel story, preparatory to putting it in proper sequence in the pocket chart. (Courtesy Sacramento City Unified School District.)

observed. A grey and white streaked rock from the playground or nearby backyard may serve as an example of quartz. The children may learn that quartz often carries other minerals along with it. It is also an easily recognized rock. Older children will learn the fact that quartz is found in the form of crystals and can make crystals of their own from sugar dissolved in water into which a string is suspended.

Children should not be expected to be able to recognize many leaves, rocks, birds, or other objects found in nature. Some children at this age have difficulty in observing the differences among objects that look so much alike. Any child, however, who enjoys making a collection, should be encouraged to do so. For the culturally-deprived children, the teacher may bring toys used by her own children or borrowed from the children of friends and relatives.

As children observe the teacher who seems to enjoy bringing in things to discuss, they will very soon begin to imitate her. In this way, they discover that talking before the class is enjoyable. The shy children are slower to adopt the activity, but most normal children will request an opportunity to take part after listening to the others for a few weeks.

Schedule for the Sharing Period. Some teachers schedule children so that a few have a turn to share their experiences each day. In a class of thirty children, six children have a turn each day; in this way each child is able to have a turn once a week. In a smaller class, children may be able to have turns more frequently. Some teachers use a pocket chart described in Chapter 3, Figure 3-3. Cards with the children's names are placed in the pockets. Each child who has volunteered to share on Monday turns his card over with the blank side out after his turn. The group sharing on each following day also turn its cards over until all the children have had a turn during the week. This plan has the advantage of allowing each child to share on the day when he has something interesting to show or tell. Its weakness lies in the fact that the shy and nonverbal children usually are left until Friday. Early in the week the teacher should plan with the children in this latter group to help them have something to contribute on Friday. If any child is unwilling to do so, however, he should not be forced, since he may develop a block against the whole procedure.

Another plan for use of the pocket chart is to divide it into five vertical sections, one for each day of the week. The children may choose the day when they prefer to share. The chart then serves as a reminder for the teacher and the children. The sudden occurrence of exciting news results in a problem with either type of scheduling. New puppies, kittens, and babies tend to ignore the child's sharing schedule. Most teachers allow time for extra sharing when some unusual event has taken place.

Use of a Pupil Chairman. Some teachers have pupil chairmen to call on the children to share and to otherwise chair the proceedings. After the children are used to this procedure, the child who has just talked to the class may take this responsibility. He then calls on children who volunteer. If a question is asked, he gives the answer. If a comment is made, he learns to respond with some courteous reply.

Development of Pupil Interaction. Pupil interaction may be illustrated by the following episode. If, for example, Raymond has told the children that his cat had five kittens the night before, has given their names, and has related the fact that they cannot yet open their eyes, he may then call on other children for questions or comments. Someone may ask such a question as what the kittens are named. Another child may want to know what the kittens eat. Still another child may add the comment that his dog had three puppies last week, and they were all brown. The teacher helps the children learn to respond with some courteous reply or question as, "Can they play with you yet?" or "I think puppies are cute, too." Many of these comments will inevitably consist of the hackneyed words, "That's nice." At times the teacher may spend a few minutes with her children helping them think of comments other than "That's nice" to use as a response to someone's news.

As the children take part in the sharing of news and the questions and comments, the teacher guides them to learn what kind of news is interesting for others to hear. She also helps when one of the children in the audience takes over the conversation by telling a prolonged story about his picnic on the beach in the middle of the discussion about kittens and puppies. The teacher usually intervenes to suggest to the latter child that, although his story is interesting, we think he should wait until he has his turn to share before telling all about the picnic. Children in the first grade can begin to grasp such ideas and may realize that some children forget the topic under discussion.

Parent Co-operation. When teachers have group or individual conferences with parents, they have an excellent opportunity to explain the values of the sharing period. The teacher can then suggest that the child be allowed to bring a toy or object of interest to school on his sharing day. In this way, the mother realizes that the toys have a legitimate purpose and are not mere distractions. She should be told that many children find it easier to talk to others in the group when they have something in their hands. Parents should be told that these objects should not be new toys bought for the purpose of the sharing period. Often children's most prized possessions are their oldest ones. The caterpillar picked off the plant in the backyard or a few seed pods from the same plant have far greater potential for learning and discussion than the most expensive toy fresh from the store counter. In the case of the caterpillar and the seeds, the children have the opportunity of watching a life cycle evolve with all its learnings and opportunities for language growth. Parents are often very helpful in such situations.

Values of the Sharing Period. The opportunity to share treasures and experiences provides an excellent situation for helping children learn to talk about a specific topic. Children need to develop conversational skills, and the limiting of the number of children who share each day makes practice on this skill possible. Children develop poise and self-confidence as they find they are able to hold the attention of their peers. This situation also provides a challenge for children to speak in complete sentences and to organize their thoughts through a gradually increasing complexity of language structure. An opportunity to broaden their vocabulary is provided through the variety of objects and experiences shared by the children in the classroom. Concepts may gradually expand as the children learn that a rabbit eats vegetables and grain, whereas cats usually prefer meat. Although the words "carnivorous" and "herbivorous" may not be introduced in the early grades, the child gains the foundation for this later classification. On the other hand, children who are more nearly ready for reading pick up these words and enjoy the feeling of power that comes with their ability to use them. Suggestions for helping the shy, the overly verbal, and the problem child during the sharing period have been made by Morrison and Perry.[7]

Care of an Animal for Language Development

A trip to the zoo was discussed previously as one possible type of excursion suitable for children on the reading readiness level. Although such a trip may help children expand many of their concepts, some of the children may be overwhelmed by more ideas than they can absorb at one time. The language period, which should be informal in the preschool, is an excellent time to introduce the children to one animal at a time. If the children are able to keep the animal in the classroom, they can learn about its needs for food, water, shelter, cleanliness, and affection over an extended period of time. Since the animal needs care every day, the children acquire concepts in a much more thorough way than they do when they take one trip.

If the school is located in an area that has a junior museum, animals can be borrowed for a time and exchanged later for others. In this way, the child experiences the repetition of certain basic understandings along with contrasting ideas. For example, the children may see a squirrel running on an exercise wheel; whereas they discover that the rabbit would not use one, even if it were provided. When the children discuss the reason for the difference, they may discover that squirrels like to climb, but rabbits cannot. The children may observe the rabbit's and squirrel's legs and feet to discover why one animal is able to climb and the other is not.

[7] Ida E. Morrison and Ida F. Perry, *Kindergarten-Primary Education—Teaching Procedures* (New York: The Ronald Press Co., 1961).

Stories and Poems for Reading Readiness

Both stories and poems have value for developing reading readiness. They are both likely to contribute much toward understanding of vocabulary. They also help the child begin to appreciate literature. Poetry tends to be neglected and should have a very definite place in the program along with stories.

Stories. The lack of opportunity to hear stories read or told is one of the greatest obstacles to growth in language by the culturally-deprived child. The child who hears a bedtime story every night from the age of a year and a half until he reaches the first grade or later has a tremendous advantage. This advantage stems from his exposure to an extensive vocabulary as well as to mature sentence structures for years. He has been able to acquire a minimum vocabulary of about 2,000 to 6,000 words and may understand many thousands more.

The reading or telling of stories should be carried on daily from the time children enter school on through the grades. The new words which children meet in stories or poems should be clarified in some manner before or at the time they are first heard. If these words can be introduced at the beginning of the story without spoiling the plot or delaying the reading unnecessarily, help may be given with their meaning at that time.

Many words can be clarified by a parenthetical phrase as the teacher reads or tells a story. When the teacher reads that Peter Rabbit tore the buttons off his jacket on the blackberry vines, she may add at that point, "Those vines have long branches with lots of thorns as sharp as pins." Then she continues the story. Since children become fond of certain stories which they like to hear repeated from time to time, they will hear about blackberry vines again and again. The children who remember what blackberry vines are like may explain them to the other children.

Poems. Poetry should have a place of its own in addition to story telling and should be introduced briefly to provide a setting. The teacher may plan a short period at any time during the day for presentation and discussion of poems. As the children listen to their favorite poems, from time to time, the teacher may invite the children to participate in repeating them. Eventually, most children will be able to repeat many of these poems by themselves. They should never be required to memorize poems, nor should they be scolded for forgetting various lines. Poetry is valuable for its beauty and the pleasure it gives.

The children will enjoy learning many poems if they are taught in the following manner. To help them learn poems with ease, the teacher may repeat them during the regular period or at odd moments such as the time when children may wait at the door for the bus to arrive for them, times when they are waiting for others to finish cleaning up, or at any other times when the teacher and children must wait for a minute or two. Soon the children will join the teacher in repeating the poems, and later on they will enjoy repeating them alone.

Figurative Language. Some of the poetry that teachers will use with children will include nursery rhymes. The language of nursery rhymes are much more appropriate for 18th and 19th century England than for 20th century America. However, they form the basis for much figurative speech. Culturally-deprived children usually have difficulty with figurative speech, and therefore need acquaintance with literature of this sort, which is part of the cultural heritage. They need exposure to the early fairy and folk tales for this very reason as well as for many other values. The teacher does not try to help the children acquire the less useful vocabulary from this literature in their own speech, but it does serve to reinforce much vocabulary that is found in today's speech. Many new words are acquired by the children as they listen to stories and poems. As they repeat the poems, they gain practice in using a variety of language patterns and sentence structures.

Retelling Stories. After the children have heard the teacher read or tell stories eight or nine times over a period of time, some will be able to retell the stories. This ability of the child to retell a story he has heard in all its various details has a high relationship to reading readiness. In a study by Morrison a correlation of .79 was found between the number of items recalled in the retelling of a story and the raw scores on a reading readiness test.[8] This correlation was significant at the .01 level. A correlation of this size indicates a strong relationship between the abilities of children to recall a number of items from a story they have heard and the abilities that are measured by a reading readiness test.

Individual Differences in Retelling Stories. One of the experiences provided in the reading readiness program should be the opportunity for children to retell stories they have heard either at home or at school. Some children tell only a very few of the events in the story and may use only words and phrases rather than sentences. Others can retell stories in as good sequence and with as many details as the teacher uses. The gap can be spanned by the immature child only by hearing many stories and by having opportunities to retell stories at his own

8 Ida E. Morrison, "The Relation of Reading Readiness to Certain Language Factors," *Challenge and Experiment in Reading* (ed.: J. Allen Figurel), VII (New York: Scholastic Magazines, 1962).

level of achievement. The teacher may help the slower story-tellers by asking questions which may give them clues to remember other events in the story which they have forgotten.

Group Work in Retelling Stories. Since mature children do not enjoy listening to the immature ones, the teacher may use group work with her slowest children, while the other children are working on quiet activities. Most creative activities are quiet enough so that the teacher can work with her slow group. At this time the other children can be painting at the easel, working with clay, making collages, finger-painting, and carrying on similar activities. Suggestions for teaching children how to work in this type of situation without disturbing a reading program are given in the chapter on Independent Activities.

Values of Retelling Stories. The retelling of stories by children provides help for them in learning to recall a sequence of events in order of occurrence. This skill is needed in all later reading experiences. It is especially important in connection with social studies work in the middle grades. The study of history depends to a very great extent upon the recall of events in their proper sequence. The retelling of stories also helps children to associate related ideas. In "The Three Bears," each activity is enacted by the father bear, mother bear, and baby bear in turn. The three characters become associated in the child's mind as he retells the story. Retelling the story also provides opportunities for children to express themselves through familiar vocabulary and often provides opportunities for children to use words that they have newly learned. They make use of expanding concepts as they talk about events in the stories they have heard.

Finger Plays

Finger plays are commonly used in the kindergarten and primary grades to catch the children's attention in preparation for some group activity or for some other purpose. Good poetry that is part of today's literature serves this purpose as well or even better for middle-class children. This poetry has the value of greater beauty than is found in the usual finger plays. In addition, the children should be encouraged to create their own accompanying activities. Various children may follow their own ideas instead of copying the action suggested by the teacher.

On the other hand, finger plays with stereotyped words and actions may have a place with young, culturally-deprived children, who can acquire the ideas embodied in the language through the teacher's directed activity. Finger plays also provide language patterns, which the child with impoverished language lacks so greatly, until he can build his own language patterns. The use of memorized patterns, therefore, may have some value. An example of a finger play that teachers find helpful for getting children's attention is as follows: "Open-shut, open-shut, and give your hands a clap. Open-shut, open-shut, and put them in your lap." By the time the children have repeatedly participated in saying the rhyme with the teacher and have followed the actions, they may add some of this vocabulary to their speech.

Music

Songs have much the same contribution to make toward language and reading readiness that poetry has. They, too, need to be well introduced so that children will understand their meaning. Some authors have suggested that children with an impoverished language background should be taught English by means of some of the same techniques that are used for teaching foreign language.

Songs. The teaching of songs is valuable in foreign language instruction because it provides sentence patterns, including idiomatic expressions, which the child memorizes as he learns the song. In the same way, the child whose language is impoverished is able to learn English speaking patterns through the learning of rote songs. To be enjoyable, these songs are taught by much the same method as was suggested for the teaching of poetry in the above section. This method is the most natural and is the way children learn songs from radio and television. Children also enjoy dramatizing the actions suggested by the words of some songs, which helps to clarify their meaning and which also serves to help children develop a feeling for rhythm.

Rhythmic Activities. As children participate in activities with a rhythm band, they soon learn the names of instruments and develop very strong preferences. Since the drum is the greatest favorite of all, children learn its name and are able to ask for it in a very short time. They learn the names of the other instruments rapidly also. Interpretive rhythmic activities also help children acquire vocabulary and clarify their concepts. After the teacher has suggested that certain music sounds like trees swaying in the wind, for example, the children will demonstrate their ideas of this situation through various dancing movements to the accompaniment of the music. After several activities of this sort have been suggested by the teacher for various musical selections, the children will thereafter be able to suggest their own ideas for rhythmical activities that will interpret how music makes them feel. The children will discuss and evaluate these creative activities and in so doing will extend their language concepts. Both discussions of music played for interpretation and interpretation of this music through various art materials add to the children's concepts.

Use of Various Recorders

Tape recorders and record players may be used by the teacher to provide further opportunities for children to listen to stories, nursery rhymes, poems, and music. Sometimes the teacher makes the recording, and sometimes professional records or tapes are used.

The Listening Center. The listening center has become a common facility in many teachers' rooms. The teacher may record stories or other material on tapes. These may be used in the listening center, which may be made up of a tape recorder with six to eight or more earphones attached to it. If some adult starts the tape recorder, children as young as nursery school age may listen to these stories in small groups. Some listening centers also are provided with filmstrips and a projector. The tape or record sometimes gives a bell-like tone when the filmstrip should be turned to the next picture.

Usually the teacher or teacher's aide works with the children when both the tape recorder and filmstrip projector are used. The use of the filmstrip enriches the content of the taped material to add another type of sensory experience. Record players may be used in the same manner. Other types of audio-visual aids that are useful in the classroom include slide projectors and moving picture projectors with the sound attachment. Simple, short films are provided, which are suitable for the kindergarten-primary level. Occasionally television programs that are suitable for young children may be broadcast for the children's listening.

The Teletrainer. The teletrainer is another device for use in the classroom. Its purpose, however, is to stimulate the children's language expression rather than provide material to which they listen. The teletrainer consists of two battery-operated telephone receivers into which children may speak and to which they may listen when another child speaks. The teletrainer is provided by the Bell Telephone Company and lent to the schools for its use.

Value of Audio-Visual Aids. The use of audio-visual aids of various sorts provides experiences for the children which are often not available at first hand. The children are exposed to a review of known vocabulary through listening to these various devices and may occasionally be exposed to new vocabulary in situations that make the meaning clear to the child. Simple and more complex sentence patterns are presented over and over in various situations. When the child discusses the things he has seen and heard, he has an opportunity to make use of much of his already acquired vocabulary. He might also use an occasional new word which he has learned as a result of the various experiences he has had with this equipment. Many of the tapes and films help him add to his concepts and organize his experiences in new ways.

Dramatization

Dramatization usually refers to the portrayal of a story which has been told or read to the children. They make up the conversation as they go along, but the plot of the story is usually followed. These dramatizations are often carried on in the language period. Children volunteer for the parts and usually plan immediately to carry out the action. Such an activity demands a good recall of the sequence of the story and the ability to make up conversation as the children carry out the action.

Stage Properties. Stage properties are very crudely designated. For example, two chairs facing each other with a space between may represent the door of a house. In another situation, three chairs with their seats adjacent may represent the trolls' bridge in the story of "The Three Billygoats." Occasionally, a band around the head with two crudely-drawn horns fastened to it may be used to designate each billygoat. On another occasion, a band fastened around the head to which a visor has been attached may convert the actor into a policeman.

Adaptation for Language-Deprived Children. The language of some children is so limited that they are unable to take the part of the troll, who repeats only two sentences each time a billygoat goes across his bridge. For some children with limited language, a story like the "Gingerbread Boy" is better. Each character, such as the little old man, the dog, the cat, the rooster, and others, say only, "Stop! Stop! I'm going to eat you!" Although some children will have difficulty with this, some children who cannot manage to speak complete sentences on their own are able to repeat a stereotyped phrase, such as the one just quoted. As these language-deprived children hear others use more complex language in such dramatizations, they very slowly and gradually acquire more complex language patterns themselves.

Role Playing

Role playing or dramatic play is much less structured than dramatization. The children decide upon the characters, the need for properties, and the action by themselves in a small group. Playing in the playhouse is a good example of role playing. The teacher may ask the children who volunteer for this activity to tell what character they prefer to be and to give some idea of what they plan to do.

One child will volunteer to be the mother and will decide that she is going to make breakfast for the family. Another child may volunteer to be the little girl who says that she will set the table for breakfast. A boy may volunteer to be father and may say that he plans to shave and then read the newspaper until breakfast is ready. One child in a kindergarten chose a rather unusual activity; she said that she wanted to be grandmother and sit in the rocking chair on the porch.

Plans for Role Playing. This planning serves two purposes. It helps the children think through their future activities and communicate them to the teacher. It also helps each child plan a definite activity to avoid the disintegration in play that may occur if the children have no idea of the action that they intend to carry out.

Evaluation of Role Playing by the Children. After the play is completed, the teacher usually helps the children evaluate their play in their small group. In response to the question, "What did you like about the play in the playhouse today?", children may reply, "We put everything away.", "Mary was a good mother because she gave us breakfast.", and "Everybody worked hard." A response to a question of ways to improve the play might bring out a request for more cups and saucers because they want to have company for lunch the next day.

The language-deprived child tends to be an individualist in play, or plays parallel to others rather than with them. He therefore usually does not take part in planning an activity that requires as much cooperation as is required by role playing. He usually chooses his activity by raising his hand when the teacher asks for volunteers for such activities as painting, working with clay, or working with jigsaw puzzles. The teacher should encourage the child to talk about his work after he finishes it, if not before.

Values of Role Playing. Role playing provides an opportunity for children to make use of their known vocabulary and to use an occasional new word acquired from other experiences. It also provides opportunities for children to use names for objects which they might have called "things" before they learned the correct name. Such objects as the pancake turner, the cupboards, and the brush and dustpan are examples of names for things they may learn. They also have an opportunity to develop concepts and organize their thinking around various functions in the home, such as the utensils used for cleaning and cooking, and various types of furniture and its uses.

Puppetry

Puppets are particularly valuable for work with the shy child because he tends to speak for the puppet and forgets his self-consciousness. This child might be frustrated if he were speaking directly to a group of children. Some teachers cut a rectangle out of the front of a cardboard box, which can then be used to serve as a stage for puppets. The box can be placed on a table and the children can sit or kneel behind it as they carry on the activities with the puppets. The audience sits in front of the table so that they can see the puppets.

Types of Puppets. Small paper bags on which faces are drawn or painted may be tied around the wrists of children to serve as actors. Simple puppets can also be made by wadding newspaper over the ends of short rollers. This newspaper may then be covered with papier-mâché to make heads, and string may be glued to the top of the heads to represent hair. A tube of cloth may be tied tightly about the neck of the puppet or roller to extend over the hand to serve as clothing, and holes may be made for the little finger and thumb to serve as arms for the puppet. The child then puts his index finger into the roller and may make gestures or cause the puppet to move about the stage. Paper dolls drawn, cut out, and fastened to sticks may also be used for puppets. Children may then carry on their role playing as they speak for the puppets and move them around on the stage.

A "Television Set" for Puppets. Some teachers have used large appliance boxes to serve as television sets for role playing. The box may be large enough so that several children can stand inside of it or hold their puppet in front of the "screen." A rectangular hole is cut in the upper half of the front of the box so that the heads and shoulders of the children or their puppets may be seen. The children then carry on role playing, taking the part of television actors. In this situation, too, the child loses his identity as he or his puppet becomes an actor on the television stage. He is, therefore, less self-conscious than he would be if he faced an audience directly.

Conversation Through Activities

When children are playing with blocks or toys, working with art materials, playing informal games, or drinking milk and eating crackers during the nutrition period, opportunity arises for informal conversation among them. For example, during the work period in the kindergarten, the teacher is able to move around the room to supervise the activities. As she does so, she may engage in informal conversations with small groups of children. The children may have built a large enough boat for them to place chairs inside to sit on as they take a boat ride.

When the teacher sees them ready to leave the dock, she may ask if she may join them. At the children's usual enthusiastic welcome, the teacher may ask how she will get aboard the boat. If the children say, "Oh, just step over the side and come in," the teacher may protest that she will have to go through the water because she cannot see a gangplank or pier. When this problem arises, some children will recall boarding their father's or other people's boats and will tell about the pier or gangplank which they crossed. They will also fix a few blocks so that the teacher can go on board without getting "wet."

Clarification of Concepts Arising From Conversation. An experience such as the one described above provides a purpose for the teacher to read a story about boats during the story-telling hour or before the dramatic play the next day. In the meantime if teaching middle-class children, the teacher may have suggested that the children ask their fathers how people go on board different kinds of boats. (Parents of the culturally-deprived do not encourage children's questions.) The discussion and the short story will help children clarify their concepts about this activity and may add to their vocabulary such words as *gangplank, pier, hawser, anchor,* and similar words. Through such an activity and discussion, the children are able to clarify their concepts and build generalizations about boats.

Conversation During Creative Activities. Discussion with the teacher or other children about various types of art productions gives the child an opportunity to express his ideas. The teacher is careful to ask the child to tell her about his picture and to avoid insulting the child by asking what it is. The art production usually gives the teacher an idea of the child's maturity if she knows the developmental stages in art expression. The discussion also helps the child clarify his ideas about the things he is portraying.

If, for example, the child has painted a car with the two wheels on the near side at each end of the car, and with the two wheels on the far side of the car showing near the center, the teacher may take him to the window to look at cars parked by the sidewalk. He discusses the number of wheels he can see. If he can only see three, the teacher guides him to discuss where the other wheel must be and to tell why he is unable to see it. In such a case, the child is able to expand his concepts to some extent.

Conversation During Nutrition Period. During the nutrition period, some teachers sit with the children to encourage quiet conversations while the children have their milk or juice. Any subject that has come up during the sharing period or anything that some child has told the teacher privately because he did not have an opportunity to tell it at sharing time may serve as the beginning point for this conversation. In addition, the teacher should have in mind four or five topics of interest to the children in the group so that she can introduce a new topic if the conversation lags. This activity serves to develop language skills similar to those developed in other language activities.

Conversation for the Child With Impoverished Language. Sometimes children in nursery school and kindergarten suffer from both shyness and impoverished language. They may point or gesture to show what they want instead of talking. Some teachers have found that photographs of small group activity including this child will stimulate him to talk when nothing else seems to challenge him to make a verbal response.

Sometimes such a child can be encouraged to ask other children for things he wants such as a particular paint cup or blocks of a certain size. If the teacher is nearby, she may encourage the quiet child to tell the other what he wants and encourage the co-operating child to wait until the other expresses his request verbally. If the shy child becomes disturbed by the procedure, the matter should be dropped for the time, but should be repeated later in the hope that eventually the shy child will give his direction verbally, even though in only one word at first.

The teacher may also try working with these shy children in small groups. If she places her group near a supply of blocks, she may give them directions for making a simple structure, one block at a time. She may then take the structure apart and encourage the children to tell her how to make something. If the children respond, she will try to follow their directions as exactly as she can.

Some teachers have been successful in encouraging a shy or non-verbal child to talk by inviting him to come into the classroom a short time before school starts. She may sit down in the playhouse with the child or go to any center in which he seems interested to encourage him to talk to her. Some children will talk to the teacher when alone, although they are too shy to talk when other children are present. Other children prefer to help the teacher stir the paints or put out the materials and are able to talk with her at this time.

SUMMARY

Language ability has a close relationship to reading ability; therefore, language activities are paramount in developing reading readiness. Culturally-deprived children start to read a year behind middle-class children due to their language deprivation, especially in vocabulary and sentence structure.

Field trips, sharing activities, story telling, dramatic activities, music, and the use of audio-visual aids are helpful in improving language ability and reading readiness. Dramatic activities include dramatization, role playing, and the use of puppets. Conversation can be encouraged during many activities in the day. All these language activities further important aspects of readiness for reading.

5

Intellectual Activities

Experience stories are valuable activities for helping children develop reading readiness. Some authorities advocate formal or the planned teaching of language, especially for culturally-deprived children. Although language development is basic to reading readiness, many other activities have values in helping the child become ready for reading. A number of these activities may be classified as intellectual, although most of them include language activities as well.

INFORMAL LANGUAGE EXPERIENCES

Many of the experiences discussed in Chapter 4 were of an informal nature. The development of experience stories and the use of labels are other informal language experiences that help children become more ready for reading.

Experience Stories

Experience stories are dictated to the teacher by the children usually after they have had an interesting group experience. Field trips, the arrival of a pet in the classroom, a change in the life cycle of an insect, the sprouting of seeds planted by the children, an interesting item brought in for the sharing period, or any similar experience will serve as motivation for the writing of experience stories. Good experience stories are developed by children in a classroom in which interesting and challenging experiences take place. The daily routines of reading, unless new books arrive in the classroom, writing, and arithmetic do not usually provide a stimulating atmosphere for developing experience stories.

Example of a Topic From the Sharing Period. Often something brought in for the sharing period may serve as a good topic for the development of stories. Perhaps one of the children has brought in a tadpole which he found while on a picnic at the edge of a stream. His mother has sent it in a jar partially filled with water with holes punched in the cover to provide air. The children have washed an unused aquarium or large jar such as a large pickle jar and have placed the tadpole in the jar. They planned to give the tadpole fresh water, but decided merely to add some to the water in which the tadpole had been brought to class. This decision was made when some child told that the tadpole ate tiny bugs and plants that grew in the pond water. One of the children had volunteered to bring fish food to school on the following day for the tadpole to eat. This occasion provides an excellent topic for the dictation of one or more experience stories.

Use of Questions to Guide the Story. Some teachers ask questions to guide the writing of stories. For example, the teacher may say, "What would you like to name the story?" When a name has been decided upon, the teacher may then ask, "Who brought the tadpole to school?" followed by the question, "Where did we put the tadpole?" and finally, "What are we going to give him to eat?" This technique is advantageous for young children or those who are dictating their first few stories to the teacher.

Free Dictation. When working with more mature children, some teachers like to let the children dictate any sentence that is of interest to them. For their first sentence, they may say, "Debbie promised to bring fish food for the tadpole tomorrow." Someone may add, that they put their tadpole in their aquarium. Another child may say that they gave fresh water to the tadpole. If no one mentions who brought the tadpole to school, the teacher may suggest that this information should be included. The children may have failed to recall that the story needs a name.

Need for Reorganization. The teacher who follows the second procedure asks the children to help her reorganize the story. They may reorganize the story immediately after they have dictated the sentences if they are still interested and are not getting tired. If they are tired, the teacher may postpone the reorganization until another time during the day or even until the following day. The teacher then asks the children to recall the sentences as they were dictated by means of leading questions to help them to remember the wording of the sentences. She also asks them if they think the story could be improved. After a number of suggestions, some child may decide that the story needs a name. Another child may suggest that it should tell that George brought the tadpole to school before the other sentences.

In this way, the teacher helps the children reorganize their story for more logical sequence. As each child makes a suggestion, the teacher helps the children decide why it is a good suggestion, or helps them think of a better one. If one child, for example, suggests the sentence, "George Brought a Tadpole to School," for a title for the story, and another one suggests "George's Tadpole," the teacher may help the children select the better title. They first discuss the characteristics of a good title. The children may suggest that a good title should be short and should tell what the story is about. The children then decide that "George's Tadpole" is a good name for their story because it is shorter than the first one and also tells the subject of the story.

In the same way, the children decide which sentence should be placed first. The teacher also guides the children to tell why they feel their suggested changes are needed. For example, the children may decide that the sentence, "George brought a tadpole to school," should come first in the story because that is the first thing that happened.

Reorganization of the Sentences. If any of the sentences fail to give complete information, the teacher helps the children find the difficulty and correct it. For example, the children may have dictated the sentence, "She is going to bring fish food tomorrow." The teacher may ask the children if this sentence tells all we need to know. Someone will notice that the name of the child who promised to bring the fish food was not included. The teacher asks the children where in the sentence they will place the name. The children may suggest that Debbie's name be put at the beginning of the sentence because she promised to bring the fish food. The sentence will now read, "Debbie—she promised to bring the fish food."

The teacher may then ask the children if all the words in that sentence are necessary. She will call for suggestions until some child suggests that the word *she* be eliminated because they do not need it now that Debbie's name is in the sentence. In this way, the teacher guides the children to reorganize the story and reword the sentences when necessary.

Values of Reorganizing a Story. The teacher who accepts any statement or idea from the children without regard to sequence is able to take advantage of the children's enthusiasm and interest. If a child offers a sentence that appeals to him, the teacher does not have to refuse the suggestion because it comes in the wrong place in the sequence. By accepting each child's spontaneous contribution, the teacher is able to capture the children's enthusiasm in the wording. These stories seem to have a literary quality not usually possessed by the guided stories. As the children help the teacher reorganize the stories in sequences, they learn how to organize their ideas, and at the same time, they gradually learn the criteria for a well-written story. Teachers who have followed the plan of enlisting the children's help in reorganizing their dictated stories have found that the children eventually incorporate these procedures in their own writing.

As children become more mature, they can also learn how to condense their thought in better sentences. The children may have dictated the following sentences: "Jerry found a bowl for the tadpole"; then, "We put the tadpole in an aquarium." The teacher may ask the children if they can think of a way to put both ideas in one sentence. After a variety of suggestions, some child may suggest that they say, "When Jerry found an aquarium, we put the tadpole in it." In this way, the children may gradually learn to use more mature sentence structure.

In the language-experience program teachers help children begin to read by writing each child's individual story for him. These stories are kept in individual booklets and are read to other children. More details of this program are given in the chapter on trends.

Use of Labels for Reading Readiness

The use of labels on functional objects in the classroom is another good procedure for helping to develop reading readiness. To stimulate the children's independence and to save time needed for other work, the teacher puts materials of various sorts on low shelves or in boxes easily available to the children so that they may secure these materials when they need them. This practice also provides children with a legitimate purpose for leaving their seats at times. If children are able to do so, they can expend pent-up energy that might otherwise be used for less socially-acceptable activities.

In the preschool and kindergarten, the teacher may label these boxes with pictures of the materials contained within them. The teacher may also attach an individual sticker to each child's personal belongings along with his printed name. Gummed stickers often include a variety of flowers in one set, a variety of birds in another, and so on. Some teachers use a different flower sticker for each of the girls and a different bird sticker for each of the boys. Duplicate sets are secured so that Mary has stickers of roses on all her things, whereas George has stickers of bluebirds on all his things. Children's names and stickers may be fastened on coat hangers, lunch boxes, clothespins for attaching each

Children are scanning their readers to find answers to questions asked by a first-grade teacher. (Courtesy Sacramento City Unified School District.)

of a pair of rubbers to keep them together, and any storage places the children may have for their personal belongings.

At first the children find materials they wish through the help of the pictures on the boxes and their own things by their stickers. Later, they are able to locate the materials in the boxes and their belongings by name. After several months in the first grade, the teacher should remove the pictures and stickers in order to let the printed words stand for the materials and belongings.

FORMAL LANGUAGE INSTRUCTION

Some authors, including Bereiter, urge that formal language be taught to language-deprived preschool children, particularly from four and one half years of age.[1] They feel that the disadvantaged preschool child must acquire language more rapidly than the middle-class child because he has so much to learn. Unless the disadvantaged child is able to catch up to the middle-class child, he has very little chance to succeed

[1] Carl Bereiter, "Academic Instruction and Preschool Children," *Language Programs for the Disadvantaged*, Report of the NCTE Task Force (Champaign, Ill.: National Council of Teachers of English, 1965).

in reading in the first grade. Some of these children have poor vocabularies and are almost completely lacking in the ability to use sentence patterns. Others use street vocabulary and poor sentence construction. Although this usage is acceptable in the children's own dialect, it is not acceptable in the standard dialect of the school and other formal situations.

Correction of Errors

Loban feels that language-deprived children of eight years and under have so much to learn that they should not be urged to use formal dialect at that time.[2] He feels that the ability to use their own dialect is about all these children can handle through the primary grades. He suggests that a start be made in helping intermediate grade children use formal language patterns and that stress be placed on these skills in the junior high school. At the latter time, children should face the fact that they must acquire standard English language patterns if they are to be employed in positions demanding skill or responsibility. They should also realize that the lack of the formal English dialect is a barrier to advancement in social class and to vocational acceptance.

On the other hand, some teachers try to help young children by correcting their dialect or sentence structure. For example, a child may tell the others in the group about an experience he has had. The teacher or the child, himself, asks the other children if they have any comments or questions. After this discussion has taken place, the teacher usually makes a positive comment regarding the presentation and may then make a suggestion for expressing the idea in a better way. Some authors feel that this procedure is too inefficient in building formal dialect patterns. Others feel that corrections inhibit children's language.

Direct Language Teaching

In their discussion of language-deprived children, some authors suggest that formal English patterns should be taught even in preschool. They feel that this teaching should be direct and followed by drill. Some suggest that techniques used in foreign language teaching might serve this purpose. They suggest that the teacher say, "This is a pencil." as she holds up the object. The child should then be asked to repeat the words, "This is a pencil." The same procedure should be used with a

[2] Walter Loban, "A Sustained Program of Language Learning," *Language Problems for the Disadvantaged,* Report of the NCTE Task Force (Champaign, Ill.: National Council of Teachers of English, 1965).

few simple statements until the child is able to master these statements and use them in his own speech.

One problem with the above procedure is that children have neither the need for making such obvious statements nor does this type of statement make for realistic conversation. Because motivation for this type of language is very low, the teacher must use a great deal of drill. The children realize that they are slow in learning and tend to become bored and frustrated.

These children come to school with a rather low self-concept, that is, a low opinion of their own ability. Any school procedure that results in frustration and even temporary failure tends to increase the child's feelings of inadequacy and decreases his self-concept. Authors stress the problems that result from poor attitudes toward self and the school established in the early years. These attitudes tend to pervade the child's entire school life and tend to make for later dropouts in high school.

Functional Language Teaching. By a better procedure, one teacher with twenty-five children enthusiastically chattering in Piute, most of them able to speak only Piute, had them enthusiastically chattering in English after one year by starting in the playhouse. The teacher first gave directions which the children were asked to follow. She would place some toy forks, knives, and spoons before her near the table in the playhouse and say to the children in English, "Please put four forks on the table." Some child usually volunteered to try to carry out the directions. He might pick up three spoons and hand them to the teacher, who would then smile encouragingly, but shake her head and ask for someone else to try as she repeated the directions. When someone picked up some forks, probably by trial and error, she would praise him enthusiastically and go on to help the children discover how many should be placed on the table as she showed them the proper place to put the forks for a correct table setting.

The teacher would then go on to give directions for placing the knives and spoons on the table. When four place settings had been arranged by discovery through trial and error, she would place a small paper cup containing a little juice at each place and choose four children to be the family for that day. As time went on, she reviewed old directions and gradually added new directions for placing plates, cups and saucers, and other toy dinnerware on the table and included a cracker with the juice when the table setting became more complete. When the children were familiar with the directions, she would let them give directions to each other to place various objects on the table as they set it for a play meal.

This teacher carried on the same procedure with other activities in the playhouse such as putting on dress-up clothes, taking care of the doll, making the playhouse beds, cleaning the playhouse, caring for pets, and many others. She also gave directions for school activities, using the same discovery technique, and later asked the children to give directions to each other when they were sure of the English for the procedures she wanted carried out. In this way, the children were able to learn to tell each other to do many things in the classroom and playhouse and to acquire a useful English vocabulary while thoroughly enjoying the experience. Of course, these children were verbal in Piute before they became verbal in English. Children with impoverished language would probably learn more slowly.

Values of Teaching Through Activities. The teacher of the Piute children had an advantage over teachers who work with children who have developed a definite language pattern in their own dialect. The use of directions, however, could be used with children who are language-deprived because the teacher gives the directions first. When the children have become used to her way of giving directions, they may be asked to give the same directions to their peers. After the children have heard the teacher give the directions over and over, most of them will imitate her expressions, because children learn by imitation.

Motivation for Direct Teaching. The need for high motivation in guiding children to accept new language patterns has been stressed. Most young children who are mature enough to play together enjoy playing in the playhouse. This activity should therefore provide good motivation for them to give directions to each other. If the boys are not interested in the play directed around home activities, the teacher may use the same approach in games and activities more appropriate for boys such as driving a car made of wooden blocks, acting as a pilot on a plane also made of large wooden blocks, or acting as an engineer of a train made of large cardboard cartons fastened together. Teachers who are familiar with the interests of first-grade boys can usually extend the play to many other activities. The girls are more likely to be willing to join in the play with the boys than the reverse.

INTELLECTUAL ACTIVITIES

Some intellectual activities may help children develop ability to organize and associate ideas, to discover relationships, and to follow a sequence of ideas or events. The ability to solve problems and classify objects and ideas is also an aspect of intellectual development that may further readiness for reading.

Sequence of Events or Ideas

In an unpublished study, Winterburger tested the ability of children in the first and second grades to sort and put a number of pictures grouped by sets into proper sequence.[3] She compared this ability with reading success at the end of the first grade. The correlation between reading and sequence was found to be high, that is, .683 beyond the .01 level of significance.

This correlation means that a large proportion of the children who received a high score on the reading test were also able to put the pictures in correct order. In addition, a large proportion of the children who received low scores on the reading test also received low scores on the test of picture sequence. If the children had received exactly the same position in rank on both tests, the correlation would have been perfect. A .683 correlation indicates that many of the children did receive approximately the same rank on both tests.

The level of significance refers to the number of times a research study may be repeated with the same number of children of the same socio-economic level to secure the same results. If, for example, the investigation just described were repeated a hundred times, the same results would be secured ninety-nine times out of the hundred repetitions. The .01 refers to the one repetition when the results might be different. This level of significance is considered to be satisfactorily reliable.

The pictures used in this study were taken from a variety of workbooks. Each set consisted of from three to seven pictures planned by the authors of the workbooks to help children learn how to put these pictures in sequence. The sets were graded for difficulty before they were used. This study tends to show that children's ability to place pictures in sequence is rather closely related to the abilities required for success in reading.

Use of Pictures for Sequence.   Each readiness book produced by publishers contains some of these sets of pictures. When presented in the workbook, the pictures are out of proper sequence. The child is told to look at each of the pictures and to reorganize them by placing numbers under them from the first to the last in the series. Some teachers cut out these pictures and mount them on 3″ × 5″ or 4″ × 6″ filing cards to give the pictures durability. The child is then asked to sort the cards and place them in proper order in a logical sequence. The use of pictures on cards makes it possible for the child to move them from

[3] Oleva Winterburger, "Relationship of Ability in Picture Sequence to Beginning Reading Success." (Unpublished Master's Thesis, Sacramento State College, 1966).

one place to another until he thinks he has found their proper order. For this reason, the sorting of cards is much easier for the children than the numbering of pictures in the workbook.

Sequence in Language Activities. The teacher can find many opportunities for helping the children think in terms of a sequence of events or ideas. She finds opportunities when the children are sharing, dictating experience stories, recalling experiences during trips, or taking part in other types of experiences. When a child is telling about a trip to the shopping center, the teacher may help him think about the sequence of his activities. She will listen to his entire report first and then guide him by questions to recall the order in which he carried out these activities. When the children are dictating a story about a visit to Jimmy's home across the street to sample some of his radishes, the teacher will take the sentences in order of interest and dictation. In the reorganization, she may then help the children to put the experiences in the order of their occurrences.

Use of a Homemade "Moving Picture" Box for Sequence. Children like to make pictures to be used in a homemade "moving picture" box which may be made of cardboard or wood. A diagram of this type of box is shown in Figure 5-1. To make the box, place it on its side so that the width is greater than the height. Cut out the front, leaving a margin of several inches around the edge to serve as a frame and to conceal the rollers to which the paper will be attached. Secure two pieces of one inch or larger doweling which is long enough to extend one inch above

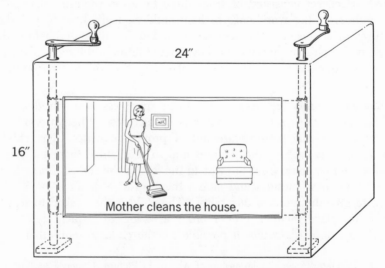

Mother cleans the house.

Fig. 5–1. Diagram of a home-made "moving picture set."

the box. Pieces of broom handle may be cut to fit the space. Make a hole large enough for each dowel rod to go through the top of the box toward the front at the extreme right and left sides. Put a small block of wood under each corner of the box directly below each hole in the top. Put each roller through the top hole and extend it down to the bottom of the box, just above the blocks. Drive a nail through each block from the under side of the box through the bottom of the box into each rod. The blocks should hold each roller in place, and the nail should allow the roller to turn freely. Attach two lengths of wood, such as two three-inch lengths of slat, by nailing each one to the top of each roller. Attach an empty spool to the other end of each piece of slat to serve as a handle.

Pictures for the "Moving Picture" Box. The children may make individual pictures of such activities as "things mother does each day," or "things we do to take care of our dog." The need for pictures should be discussed, and volunteers should be chosen to make each picture in the order in which the pictures are to be shown.

The children may then cut a long piece of heavy wrapping paper about two inches narrower than the height of the box. They then paste their drawings in sequence on this paper. Older children like to write captions and paste them at the bottoms of the pictures. Each end of the long paper is then attached to one of the rollers so that it extends across the front of the box from one roller to the other. All but the end is wound around the first roller until the children are ready to display and discuss their pictures.

Showing the "Moving Picture." The children plan the sequence of the pictures and review the sequence as they attach the pictures to the long roll of paper. One child may operate the machine by winding the paper onto the empty roller. The child moves his picture along after each child has discussed it. If the child has written a caption under his picture, he also reads it. When the pictures on the entire roll have been discussed, the paper may be rolled back onto the first roller, ready for another showing. Each time the "moving picture" is shown, the sequence is thereby reviewed. Children may also use their "moving picture" box to display their illustrations of the sequence of events in any of the stories they enjoy hearing and retelling.

Use of the Flannelboard for Sequence. Some teachers use a flannelboard when telling stories. They often cut out pictures from the books containing the stories they are using. They back these pictures with coarse flannel or felt. Sandpaper can be used, but it is rather heavy. Nylon flocking sold by some hobby houses is excellent but expensive. Two small pieces of flocking, however, one at the top and one at the bottom, are adequate for holding the pictures on the flannelboard. Some nylon flocking has an adhesive back which increases the ease of attaching it to the back of the pictures. Some teachers use pelon, a material for lining to stiffen fabrics. The pictures may be drawn directly on this material, which takes crayon or paint satisfactorily. These pictures are then cut out of the material and pressed to the board without any backing.

Use of Pictures for the Flannelboard. As the teacher tells a story, she may put each picture on the flannelboard to illustrate the steps in the story. She will have organized these pictures beforehand so that she will not have to interrupt the story to find the needed picture. The next time she repeats the story, she may spread the pictures in mixed order over another flannelboard and let children come up by turns to find a picture suitable for each episode in the story.

When the children have become used to this procedure, she may let two or three children sit by the flannelboard to place the pictures on the flannelboard in sequence by themselves. This organization of the pictures is best carried on by not more than three children at a time when the teacher is working with other children. Later on, these children may show their arrangement of pictures to the rest of the group to see if these other children agree with the arrangement. After this step, the same children or other volunteers may retell the story following the sequence of pictures on the flannelboard. Simple stories with few episodes are chosen at first. As the children increase in their ability to follow the plot, stories with more episodes may be selected.

Classification of Pictures

Some teachers prepare pictures to be classified as children sort them. These pictures are usually cut from readiness books, picture dictionaries, and magazines. The pictures may be grouped in sets of ten to twelve or more cards depending on the ability of the children. Cards $3'' \times 5''$ or $4'' \times 6''$ are practical for mounting these pictures to protect them.

The Flannelboard for Classification. If, for example, the teacher has mounted six pictures of animals that are commonly kept as pets, and six pictures of zoo animals, she may put these pictures in indiscriminate order on the flannelboard. She will ask a small group of children how they could divide these pictures into groups. After several guesses, some child will suggest that they represent pets and animals seen at the zoo. The teacher may then ask a child to place the picture of a pet at the top of the flannelboard at the left and to place a picture of the zoo animal at the top of the board at the right. Each child may then have a turn moving one of the pictures, either a pet or a zoo animal, to a position under the picture of the same type.

Evaluation of the Classification. After the pictures are arranged on the flannelboard, the children may talk about why they feel that each picture has been placed in its particular position. Some children may disagree with the position of one or two of the animals. If his reason for moving it is correct, he may change its position to the correct side of the flannelboard.

Children may work with classification cards at their seats after the cards have been introduced to the group. If the teacher uses an equal number of cards of each type, the pupils can use this criterion to sort these pictures at their seats.

Scrapbooks for Classification. Scrapbooks can be used to give children valuable experience in classifying pictures. The teacher should collect a variety of magazines. Some teachers cut off the binding of the magazines with a paper cutter. They then select pictures suitable for the children's use. This procedure is helpful because it avoids children's unhappiness when they accidentally tear a picture when trying to remove it from a magazine. It also avoids children's choices of sophisticated cartoons which they cannot understand and advertisements for alcoholic beverages.

Children who are sufficiently mature may decide to collect pictures of mothers and babies, furniture, farm machinery, automobiles, and similar topics. These scrapbooks may be made co-operatively, or each child may prefer to work on a book of his own. When children work together, the immature children should work in separate groups from the more mature. The immature children tend to mix their classifications by putting mothers and babies with farm machinery and confusing other categories to the disgust of the more mature child. The immature children also tend to cut out the pictures poorly and may cut off parts of the wheels of the car or parts of feet or heads.

Homemade Scrapbooks. Ready-made scrapbooks that can be obtained at variety stores are adequate. Books made by the teacher, however, are usually better because they can be made of a more durable paper, such as drawing paper. In addition, the pages may be limited to approximately twenty. The number of pages should be limited because children gradually raise their standards. The child may be annoyed by his earlier untidiness or poor choices which satisfied him a month or so earlier. For this reason, he should be able to finish one book in a reasonably short time. Some teachers fold twelve-by-eighteen-inch sheets of drawing paper in half, and then use a sheet of colored paper for the cover and sew them together with yarn. Yarn seems to provide the most durable material for fastening the pages together. The children may decorate the covers, and the teacher may print their names on their covers if the children are unable to do so themselves.

Topics for Classification of Pictures. Some other topics suitable for classification include the following: vegetables and fruit, animals that live on the farm and those that live in the forest, food sold in the bakery and food sold in the vegetable department of a grocery store, tools used by women and tools used by men, funny and not-funny things or situations, people wearing uniforms and people without uniforms, toys with which girls customarily play and toys with which boys play, objects that are liquid and objects that are solid, objects that are hard and objects that are soft, objects that produce heat or are warm, and objects that produce cold or are cold, objects that make sound and objects that do not make sound.

Study of Classification Ability. In an unpublished study by Baer children were tested in their ability to sort pictures in the above categories.[4] A correlation of .68 was found between the children's scores on the classification test and their mental ability. From such a correlation, it seems reasonable to assume that the activity demanded considerable thinking. A correlation of .70 was found between mental age and the scores on the classification test. A correlation of .57 was found for the relationship between the classification test and the Metropolitan Readiness Test, exclusive of the number section. All of these correlations and most of the correlations of the subtests within these tests, were significant at the .01 level. Again, it would seem that experience gained from increased mental age had some influence on the ability to succeed in this test. Apparently, the classification test also measured some of the abilities measured by the Metropolitan Readiness Test. The relationship between success in reading as measured by the Metropolitan Achievement Test and the classification test was the only relationship that was low; the correlation was .27 significant at the .05 level. The study was carried on with only fifty-one children in a somewhat deprived socio-economic area. The test will be repeated with more children and a wider range of backgrounds to discover if a better relationship between reading and the ability to classify pictures can be found. The high relationships with mental ability and reading readiness should indicate that the activity has some value for stimulating children to think and organize ideas. Such an activity seems to be of greater value than matching pictures for mere likenesses or differences.

[4] Ruth S. Baer, "Children's Ability to Classify Pictures as an Aspect of Reading Readiness." (Unpublished Master's Thesis, Sacramento State College, 1965).

Other Ways to Use Classification. Science experiments are excellent for stimulating children to classify various types of objects. Children may test a variety of objects with a magnet to discover which objects can be picked up and which cannot. They also can be guided to discover what kind of material can be picked up and what kind cannot. This conclusion is easier for children to draw if iron is the only metal used. Children on the reading readiness level are rather immature to distinguish between iron and other metals.

Another experiment for classification is an experiment with things that will float and things that will not float. The differentiation of different types of material in this experiment is difficult because anything hollow or cup-like is likely to float almost without regard to its composition. In this experiment the children merely classify the objects by name according to whether or not they will float.

A study of health has a variety of opportunities for children to classify objects. If it is related to a grocery store, the children may collect pictures of various types of food and mount them on charts according to the department in the market where they will be found. Experiments with seeds or a temporary collection of vegetables might help children to classify them according to those that have roots that are used for food, and those that have leaves or fruit that are edible. In a study of clothing, children may classify cloth according to its source, such as wool, cotton, silk, or man-made fibers.

Relationships

Pictures similar to those which are mounted for classification can also be collected for ability to see relationships among ideas. In an unpublished study by Serrano sets of pictures were collected for a test of relationships.[5] Although this test was similar to that of classification, other ideas were involved. The sets were made up of either six of one category and six of another, or six pairs of two in each category. The children were not told how many should be put in each category.

When the scores on the test of relationships were compared with tests of mental maturity, the correlation was found to be .73 significant at the .01 level. From such a correlation, it seems obvious that this type of activity demanded a good deal of thinking. When the scores on the relationships tests were compared with the Metropolitan Readiness Test, a correlation of .61 was found. When the scores on the tests of relation-

[5] Henry Serrano, "Children's Ability to Organize Pictures as a Predictor of Later Reading Competence." (Unpublished Master's Thesis, Sacramento State College, 1966).

ships was compared with success in reading at the end of the first grade, the correlation was .50, significant at the .01 level. Apparently, some of the same skills were required for the tests of relationships that are required in reading, and the relationship seems to be high enough to suggest that the use of such an activity has value.

The Categories for Relationships. Categories suitable for work with relationships may include the following topics:

1. Things usually found inside the house and those found outside.
2. Things commonly used for work at school and things used to play with.
3. Things commonly used to work with at home and things used for play.
4. Things customarily found in the same place or together, as a chicken and an egg, a coat and a coat hanger, and a turtle and a frog.
5. Parents and offspring.
6. Incomplete and complete items that belong together such as a face with only one eye and a complete eye, a bicycle with only one wheel and a complete wheel, and a boat with only one oar and a complete oar.
7. Foods and the persons or animals that commonly eat them.
8. Containers and objects that are commonly found inside them, such as a mailbox and a letter, Santa's bag and Christmas presents, a bird's nest and a bird's egg.
9. People, animals, and insects and their homes, such as a child and a house, a bird and a nest, a bear and a cave, fish and water, a bee and a hive, a spider and a web.
10. Articles of furniture and rooms in the house in which they are found.
11. Stores and kinds of things you can buy there.

Other Ways To Use Relationships. In the study of the community, community helpers and their work may be used to help children analyze this type of relationship. The uniforms they wear may add another element to this study. In a study of the farm, the foods eaten by various animals and the products derived from the animals may also help children understand another aspect of relationships. In a study of the home, the children may learn about the various types of work that can be contributed by various members of the family. Various types of equipment used by the farmer may be compared to the type of equipment used by a mechanic who repairs an automobile.

Evaluation Skills

The evaluation procedures that follow a work period in social studies or work with creative materials demand thinking and the ability to communicate satisfactorily, both of which are needed for a readiness for reading. Children's evaluation of their own and others' work should always be approached constructively in order to build up children's self-confidence and pride in their work. They should first tell what is good about other children's work. One or two constructive suggestions made after the positive evaluation may be used to help raise the child's standards.

Children should learn to state suggestions in terms of improvement, rather than in terms of criticism. If, for example, a group of children has cut out and pinned in place for mounting pictures of vegetables that are good to eat, the children's evaluation of the committee's work may consist of the offering of the following suggestions: Mary may say, "They found a lot of pictures of different kinds of vegetables." George may add, "They cut out the pictures neatly." Frances may say, "They found pictures with pretty colors."

At the teacher's request for suggestions to improve the chart, Ronald may say, "I think the pictures would look better if they were put farther apart." Perhaps the latter might be the only suggestion for the improvement of the chart. The teacher might then add, "I agree with you. They chose good pictures and the committee cut them out carefully." She might also add, "I also think Ronald's suggestion is good. Why don't you make a second chart so that you will have room for all the pictures and so that you can spread them out better? Then you may show them to us again before you paste them on the cardboard to see if we can help you with their arrangement."

If another committee has finished painting the cardboard stove for use in the playhouse, they may present their completed work to the class to report on what they have done and for evaluation. Comments regarding the stove may consist of the following statements: Debbie may say, "I like it. It's big enough so that we can really pretend we're cooking." Alex may add, "I like the burners. The pie plate's painted black almost like our stove at home." Tommy may say, "I like the way they fixed the door of the oven. It opens so we can put things into it, and they cut it straight." At the teacher's agreement and request for suggestions for improvement, Fred may say, "I like the color they painted it, but I think they should put another coat on. You can see the box through the paint. They ought to go up and down all the time with their paint brushes to make the paint look smooth."

Problem Solving

Problem solving demands that children think and gives them practice in using language to communicate their ideas. Problem solving in one classroom arose regarding a place for library books. The class had only about twenty books for free reading at the library corner and had kept them on the library table, spread so that the titles could be seen. The parent-teacher association had raised some money and had decided to spend it on library books for the primary classes.

A Problem of a Place for Books. When the books arrived, the library table was the only place available. So many books on the table took up too much space. The children suggested that the teacher ask the custodian for a bookcase. On the following day the teacher reported that no extra bookcases were available and asked the children what they thought they could do about the problem. A few children suggested putting the books in boxes, but others objected because the boxes would have to be placed on the floor and it would be difficult to find a particular book. One of the children said that his uncle had cut a board into three pieces. He had then put bricks under each end of the first board, added more bricks, then the second board, and finally made a bookcase of three shelves. The children liked the idea, but were concerned that they could not secure the boards and the bricks.

Finally a child thought of the cardboard boxes used for oranges because they are divided into two parts. He suggested that the boxes be turned on their ends so that the middle partitions would make shelves. Other members of the class approved of the idea and helped bring the boxes for their improvised bookcase. The teacher mixed liquid starch with tempera paints, which the children used to paint their bookcase dark green. The liquid starch helped prevent the paint from rubbing off onto their clothing.

A Problem in Block Building. Another problem arose when a kindergarten teacher brought her children to a circle on the rug for a cooperative block building. When the teacher asked the children what they would like to make, Marvin suggested that they build a bridge over a river. They could then put some toy boats in the water under the bridge and drive some cars over the top. The children discussed the height and length of the bridge. Then each child took a turn to bring a block to build the supports for the bridge. When they finished building the supports, they were ready to make the approaches and the roadbed for the bridge. One child started to put a long block from the supports on one side to the supports on the other. After he placed his block on the bridge, another child objected because the block slanted. The children discussed the problem and decided that their roadbed would slant unless they fixed the supports. Someone suggested that they count the blocks in each of the supports to see if they had too many on one side. Two children volunteered to count the blocks, one for each side. One child reported that there were seven blocks on his side; the other reported that he had counted six blocks. When asked what to do, one of the more mature children suggested that one block be taken away from the taller side to make them even. After this was done, the children finished the bridge.

Interpretation of Pictures

Pictures cannot take the place of first-hand experiences, and their value is limited if the child has never seen the pictured object at first hand. Nevertheless, pictures do help to bring back images and memories of experiences with objects and situations seen at first hand. A picture is a two-dimensional symbol of a three-dimensional object. Adults who look at pictures with experienced eyes can easily associate them with the image of the three-dimensional objects they represent. Young children, on the other hand, need many experiences with real objects as well as with pictures before pictures can serve to help them associate the images of the objects represented. Culturally-deprived children need to have many first-hand experiences. They also need to have access to an even greater variety of picture books and should have many opportunities to discuss pictures with their teacher.

Stages in Picture Interpretation. Children go through a number of stages in their ability to interpret pictures. Marion Monroe has described five categories that she feels can aid the teacher in determining the level of picture interpretation a child can use.[6] On the first level, the child merely names the objects in the pictures. On the second level, he describes objects in the picture and may also describe the action. On the third level, he makes inferences about the feelings and relationships shown in the picture. On the fourth level, he carries on a narrative interpretation of the picture. He may infer happenings that occurred before the action observed in the picture or may tell the possible outcome of this action. On the fifth level, he gives an evaluative interpretation of the action in the picture, that is, he may draw a conclusion or give a moral about the pictured situation.

A Study of Picture Interpretation. In an unpublished thesis Howeler evaluated Monroe's criteria with second grade children and found a correlation of .56 significant at the .01 level between ability to interpret a picture and a reading score achieved at the end of the second grade.[7]

[6] Marion Monroe, *Growing into Reading* (Chicago: Scott, Foresman & Co., 1951), p. 78.

[7] Judith E. Howeler, "Children's Ability to Interpret Pictures Compared to Their Success in Reading." (Unpublished Master's Thesis, Sacramento State College, 1966).

With a magnet tied to a string, a first-grade child is playing a fishing game that gives practice on sight words. (Courtesy Sacramento City School Summer Program.)

Such a correlation means that a large proportion of the children who were able to interpret the picture on the basis of the first four criteria were also successful in reading. The children who interpreted the picture at the lower levels achieved much lower scores on the reading test. No child in this particular grade interpreted the picture according to the fifth criteria.

Help in Learning To Interpret Pictures. Children learn to interpret pictures on a more mature level as they listen to teachers discuss various types of pictures. They also learn as they listen to children who describe pictures on a more mature level than they are able to do. The more mature children are not interested in listening to the very slow children.

The teacher should therefore put the slow children in their own readiness group when they have time to take turns describing pictures. These children should not be deprived, however, of some opportunity to listen to the more mature children.

Pictures Suitable for Interpretation. The teacher needs an extensive file of good pictures for this particular activity as well as for many others. She should choose pictures that show scenes with a few children or children with adults. The scenes should be clear-cut and obvious, such as a scene of a family having a picnic at the beach, a picture of a family packing their car getting ready to go on a trip, a picture of children getting up in the morning and dressing preparatory for going to school, and other similar scenes. Action should be involved, and the picture should be colored if possible. Children prefer clear, bright colors and realistic drawing. If possible, the picture should involve implications for activities that might occur previous to the situation portrayed and further extension of activity at a later time. In this way, the child has an opportunity to imagine activities occurring previous to the scene of the picture and others occurring afterward. Some element of suspense adds value to the picture. Monroe gives an example of a picture of a child with a dog. The ice cream is about to drop off the cone, and the dog is waiting eagerly to catch it as it falls. Such a scene offers opportunity for children to add suggestions on the level of the fifth criterion, that is, to draw conclusions, such as the statement that someone didn't fill the cone very well to prevent the ice cream from spilling.

Use of Directions for Readiness

The child who is too immature to follow directions needs help before he is required to do so in learning to read. Numbers of opportunities arise for children to follow directions in functional situations. When the teacher needs a book from the library corner, she may describe its position, such as on the top shelf, on the bottom shelf, or on the left or right side, and may add that it has a yellow cover. These directions help give children opportunity for developing concepts of such words as top and bottom, right and left, highest and lowest, smallest and largest, and so on. Some teachers put labels on children's coat hangers and on their cubicles if these are provided for storing lunch boxes and other possessions. The teacher suggests that each child put his things on the hanger or in the cubicle on which he finds his name. She will help make sure that the more immature children succeed in doing so.

Directions for Routines. Children follow directions of various sorts all day as they come into the classroom, put away their things, go to the circle, get needed materials at request, get ready to go outside to play, get ready for lunch, pass books for reading, and innumerable other activities. One advantage of heterogeneous groups is the opportunity the immature children have to watch the other children and follow them until they are sure of the directions themselves.

A homogeneous, immature group of slow learners is difficult for the teacher to handle because the group lacks enough leadership. The teacher must amplify her directions and may even need to give some physical assistance if she has only slow learning children in her group. These children are deprived of the opportunity to learn from others. In the same way, the fast moving children are deprived of opportunities for helping the less mature ones. They need this opportunity to learn to understand and to be patient with those less able than themselves. Helping other children also provides an opportunity to give status to the brighter children who may also need this reassurance. This type of help should be limited to carrying out the more routine type of activities. When children are making such articles as scrapbooks, they should work with their own maturity level. They develop pride in their projects and should therefore not be burdened with children of less ability, unless they help with the product made by the immature child for his own use.

Directions for Practice.   In a heterogeneous group, the teacher may spend some of her time in working with the slower children who need practice in following directions. She may give them help in classifying the pictures for their scrapbooks. She may also give them directions for stringing wooden beads to make patterns. At times she may give them directions for building small structures with blocks. She may then take these down and ask the children to give her directions in turn. She will follow these directions as specifically as possible even though the result was not intended by the children. In this way, they are required to give her more explicit directions in order to achieve the product desired. She may also give the children directions for making patterns with blocks. She may suggest that children put blocks in a row. The first block may be single followed by one block on top of another, followed by another single block, and so forth. Various patterns may also be suggested for the children.

Incidental Use of Directions.   Children will give each other directions. When painting, one child may ask another to pass the cup with the red paint. When playing with blocks, one child may ask another for two long blocks or three small ones. Sometimes one child may ask another to borrow his red crayon. When a child's possession has been misplaced he may ask another to help him find it. A request may be made for a mature child to button an immature child's smock when getting ready for painting or to help him fasten his paper on the easel. In this way, children give and follow their own directions.

Use of Printed Directions. Some teachers use a pocket chart for listing housekeeping duties and the children who are responsible for them. The use of such a chart constitutes a way of using printed directions rather than verbal ones. This chart also provides for children to volunteer for duties they prefer. Before children are able to read, the teacher cuts out and mounts small pictures of children carrying on various types of housekeeping activities such as wiping the tables with a damp sponge or brushing up scraps with a brush and dustpan. The pictures are inserted in a column in pockets down the left side of the chart. The children's names are printed on cards. As a child volunteers for one of the activities, he comes to the chalk rail, where the teacher has spread out the name cards, chooses his name card, and inserts it into the pocket to the right of the picture of the activity he has chosen. One or more additional children are encouraged to volunteer to help with the same activity. They also find their name cards and place them in the pocket with the picture and the first child's name.

Turns in Housekeeping. Some teachers use only one child for each clean-up activity. Other teachers, however, feel that two or more children should work in committees on one housekeeping activity. Although the use of two or more children demands more management on the part of the teacher, it provides a very important opportunity for children to learn to work together. The committee work forces them to share materials and utensils.

In the case of the committee to clean up scraps, only one brush and dustpan may be available. In this case, the teacher must guide the children to discuss a solution for this problem. They will obviously decide that one of their members will use the brush and dustpan for the smaller scraps and any spilled material such as dried clay. The other members of the committee will pick up the larger scraps by hand. The decision as to who will use the brush and dustpan must still be decided. If the children feel that its use is a status symbol, they may decide to take turns each day using it. If it is not a status symbol, the first child to get it may be the one to use it. Many similar decisions are required and much learning takes place. In the case of the use of the dustpan, the name of the first child in the pocket chart may be used to indicate the one to use these utensils. The children's names may then be rotated each day.

Housekeeping Activities. Some housekeeping activities that are suitable for children are as follows:

1. Keeping the library table in order.
2. Changing the water in the vases and throwing out dead flowers.
3. Watering the plants.
4. Erasing the boards.

5. Putting out the chalk and erasers and putting them away at night.
6. Cleaning the erasers.
7. Feeding the fish.
8. Counting the scissors to be sure they have all been returned.
9. Picking up scraps.
10. Cleaning the paint easel.
11. Cleaning the tables after nutrition or the use of paste.
12. Shapening pencils.
13. Filling paste bottles.
14. Opening the windows and closing them when needed.
15. Mixing paints, if the children are mature enough.
16. Keeping the library table in order.
17. Leading the flag salute.
18. Keeping the teacher's desk in order.
19. Taking the balls out to the play yard and returning them.
20. Checking the clay or flour dough to be sure all is returned and the plastic bags have been closed.
21. Picking up and putting away surplus material, such as pencils, drawing paper, etc.
22. Checking the puzzles to be sure they have all been returned to the proper boxes.

Rotation of Duties. If only a few children serve as housekeepers, the duties should be changed at the end of each week. If all the members in the class are able to serve on committees, the duties may not be rotated for several weeks. Since young children need help in learning how to carry out their various tasks, and since they forget their duties the first few days, some teachers have found it much better to avoid changing the duties too often. Since the children have volunteered for these duties, they are not likely to tire of them soon. If, however, one child wants to trade duties with another, all he needs to do is secure the teacher's permission and then move his card to the proper place in the chart to indicate the new committee.

SUMMARY

Most teachers make use of informal language to help children improve in their readiness for reading. A few authors suggest the use of formal or planned language activities for culturally-deprived children to try to help them catch up with middle-class children. If formal language is used, it should be closely related to the children's interests. Some intellectual activities that have a close relation to reading readiness include the ability to organize ideas in sequence, to classify pictures and ideas, to solve problems, to interpret pictures, and to follow directions.

6

Physical and Emotional Aspects

Physical aspects of readiness overlap to some extent with the language and intellectual phases of readiness. In helping children to acquire readiness skills, the physical aspects are often developed along with other procedures. For example, left-to-right eye movement is established when the teacher is working with experience stories on charts. The child must be helped to acquire maturity in the emotional and social aspects of his development as well as in the physical aspects. Without security and good emotional adjustment, even an intelligent child may be unable to learn to read.

The teaching of reading in the kindergarten is discussed in this chapter in terms of some of the facts that are known concerning children's readiness for learning. Physical, social, emotional, and intellectual aspects are all involved in the child's readiness for formal reading.

PHYSICAL ASPECTS OF READINESS

Few activities involve physical abilities or physical participation without their language and thought-provoking counterparts; however, they are grouped together for convenience in this discussion. Such aspects of readiness include eye-hand co-ordination, visual acuity, auditory acuity, and other similar abilities.

Eye-Hand Co-ordination

The value of scrapbooks and suggestions for using them were discussed in the previous chapter under the topic of classification. The experience of cutting out pictures and pasting them into scrapbooks is very valuable for helping children improve in their eye-hand co-ordination. Children who are able to cut out the pictures and paste them into books neatly and in proper position are praised for this ability. Those who are unable to do so receive praise for other things such as the selection of pictures, their colors, and so on. In this way, no child is made to feel inadequate, but the ones who are ready to improve their co-ordination may become more conscious of this need. Experience and praise for growth are the factors which help children improve in this ability.

Creative Activities for Eye-Hand Co-ordination. The use of all sorts of creative materials provide opportunities for improving eye-hand co-ordination. The children should always use these materials creatively, without directions from the teacher regarding the objects to be made. Clay, flour dough, and asbestos clay are good modeling materials. Asbestos flour is a material used by plumbers for insulating pipes and hot water heaters, among other things. The material is very light in weight, a quality which should be remembered when ordering it. The articles made of flour dough and asbestos flour are more durable than those made of clay, unless the latter is fired. The modeling activity has values for improving eye-hand co-ordination. Some teachers find the flour dough easier to handle than clay. It is easier to prevent the flour dough from becoming too sticky or crumbling too easily than ceramic clay. Asbestos flour, too, is easier to handle.

The use of finger paints, easel paints, colored chalk, and similar materials provides experiences which help children improve their eye-hand co-ordination. Collages are particularly easy for children to make and provide opportunities for the use of a great many materials. Children's collages are usually made by pasting various materials on drawing paper. Children may cut out a strip of blue construction paper for the sky. Pieces of sponge make excellent trees. Scraps of cloth may be used for children's clothing or clothing hanging on a string clothesline. Cotton makes fluffy clouds or snow. Buttons are excellent for such things as car wheels but require glue to fasten them permanently to the paper.

Potatoes cut in half may be used for block printing. Designs are made in the cut surface of the potato, which is then used to stamp these designs along the edge of a paper table cloth, on flour sack curtains, or on edging for shelf paper for use in the play house. These activities provide opportunities for improving eye-hand co-ordination. Even play with balls is useful for this purpose.

Judy Puzzles and Other Toys for Eye-Hand Co-ordination. The use of Judy puzzles is also a good activity for improving eye-hand co-ordination. Judy puzzles are a type of jig-saw puzzle made of wood and have a limited number of parts. Simple puzzles may be secured with only five, seven, or nine pieces. Others with more parts may also be secured. The child must not only place the pieces properly, but must also be able to see their relationship to other parts of the puzzle. Tinker toys also help develop eye-hand co-ordination.

Illustration of Stories for Eye-Hand Co-ordination. Children may draw or use colored crayons to illustrate many of their experiences. Some teachers make booklets similar to those used for scrapbooks for the children to keep their class experience stories. The teacher duplicates copies of the experience stories. She does not ask the children to copy these stories from the board because the values are dubious. The time and energy demanded by children at the readiness level and even by some of those in the first and second grades is unreasonable. The copying is usually poor, and the children learn to dislike the stories if this practice is continued.

The children paste the duplicated copies of these stories on one page of their booklets and draw illustrations for them on the opposite page. Even though the children cannot actually read these stories, they usually know them from memory and can select ideas for illustrating them. This reading from memory after having dictated the sentences is a stage in reading readiness.

Outlined Pictures for Eye-Hand Co-ordination. Some teachers use pictures outlined by dots which are numbered. The children then draw lines from the first dot to the second and so on. This activity is not creative, but it does give the children opportunities for reviewing numbers as long as they can read them. It also provides opportunity for eye-hand co-ordination.

Left-to-Right Eye Movement

The habit of moving the eyes from left to right along the printed line is not a great problem on the reading readiness level for teachers who use reading charts. The use of sequence pictures has been already suggested for teaching left to right progression. The teacher may also help children become conscious of left to right reading when she reads stories to them from books.

Charts for Left-to-Right Eye Movement. Teachers who use experience stories and reading charts make natural use of helping children move their eyes from left to right. The teacher or pupil leader should always stand at the left of the chart. When a teacher wishes to help the children focus their eyes on a line of print on one of these charts, she may sweep the pointer rapidly along the line and then return it to a stationary position under the line of print. For the first few times the teacher may say, "Be sure to start reading over here," as she points to the left side, "and then read along the line this way," as she moves her pointer to the right. Eventually the fact that she stands at the left and points to the right with the pointer will serve to clue the children to move their eyes in the right direction.

Avoidance of Pointing. The teacher avoids the habit of pointing to each word because this procedure tends to cause children to look at each word separately. If the child hesitates on a word, the teacher may frame it while she helps him with it, or she may ask him to frame it. This framing consists of cupping the hands around a word or sentence so that the child knows where it begins and where it ends. To help the child's eyes go along the line smoothly, and at the same time to help the child recognize each word as an entity, the teacher is careful to leave a space the size of an o between words. If a narrower space is allowed, the child may fail to see each word as an entity. Instead, he may run the words together. If too large a space is left between words, the child may move his eyes jerkily to focus on one word at a time, resulting in word by word reading.

Left-handed Children and Eye Movement. Some left-handed children tend to read from right to left and may also try to write the same way. The teacher never tries to change the dominant hand. A large amount of reading on charts while the teacher supervises the children to be sure they start at the left side of the line is usually enough to establish the proper habit, even with left-handed children. If necessary, the child may be given extra help until he establishes the correct habit.

Sequence Pictures for Left-to-Right Eye Movement. If the teacher works with sequence pictures on the flannelboard, she can help establish correct habits of eye movement. Two flannelboards are helpful. The pictures may be placed in indiscriminate order in a row across the left-hand flannelboard. A child may then volunteer to select the picture which seems to belong in first place. When he finds an appropriate picture, he may place it at the left-hand side of the second flannelboard. The child who locates the second picture may then place it at the right of the first picture, and so on until a sequence is established. If the pictures will not all fit on the first line, the children may add a second line, again starting at the left. When the children and teacher are in agreement regarding the sequence, the children may take turns telling the story of the action of each card until the story is complete. This activity gives children opportunity to review sequence and to make use of their already known verbal vocabulary as well as to practice left-to-right eye movement.

Books for Left to Right Reading. The teacher may take time occasionally to look at a large picture book with children. She may stand the book against an easel which may be a homemade device made from a cardboard carton. She may then ask for a volunteer to open the book to the first page and to tell the other children something about the picture on it. Another child may come up to discuss the second page and still another child may turn to page three and discuss that picture.

As the children take turns turning pages, the teacher helps them learn to start at the front of the book and look at pages from left to right. As she begins this procedure, she may also talk to them about the name of the book, the front page, and the name of the author as the person who wrote the book. The teacher may also remind children to start at the front of each book when they go to the library to browse. The teacher helps the children find the places in their workbook by guiding them to start at the front of the book.

Teaching Colors

In the past, the first-grade teacher's initial step was to teach the children to read the names of colors. She taught the colors so that the children would be able to color outlined pictures as independent work while she worked with other groups. This activity is no longer considered acceptable because of its stultifying effect on children's creativity and on their habits of thinking. The kindergarten teacher, however, helps language-deprived children learn the names of the colors as she helps them learn the names of various objects. Sometimes children from average families need this type of help also.

Clothing for Colors. The teacher guides children to discuss the colors of their clothing and other objects in the room. Some teachers dismiss their children to go to recess or get ready to go home by the color of their clothing. She may say, "Every girl with a blue dress or blue trimming on her dress may go out to play." She continues until all the girls have left the room. She then dismisses the boys by the colors of their shirts.

Beads for Colors. When working with stringing large colored beads, the teacher may suggest that the children tell her two colors they would like to use. She then suggests that they string beads in a design with these colors. The children may also choose two or more colors to make designs on pegboards with golf tees. When planning to play in the play house, the girls may tell the teacher what color of dress they plan to put on the doll today if the dolls have dresses of different colors.

Cards for Colors. If the teacher finds children who do not seem to know the names of the colors or who might even be colorblind, she may work with these children in a small group. Some teachers make cards by mounting colored construction paper on one side of them. The teacher may name a color and ask a volunteer to find the card of the appropriate color. Children may also serve as leaders to call on each other to find particular colors.

The teacher is watchful to discover if any of the children often confuse the colors. If these children are able to succeed well in a variety of other activities, they may be colorblind. If the teacher suspects that the child is colorblind, she may confer with the parents and probably check with the guidance counselor, who may have tests to help diagnose this problem.

Flowers for Colors.   Some flowers are very easily grown in the classroom. They may be grown in cut-down milk cartons with drainage holes punched in the bottom. Bulbs in soil in a sunny window will grow and bloom easily. Some bulbs such as hyacinths and paper white narcissus will even grow in water. The bulbs will send roots down into wet pebbles, but should not be immersed in water themselves. Sweetpea seeds will sprout in a little over two weeks. Pansy seeds will sprout in ten days, and marigolds will sprout in five days to a week. Plants such as these are interesting for children to watch, some to help develop science understandings and concepts, others to add cheerful colors to the room. Some children from culturally-deprived homes have never seen flowers and do not know their names. The pleasure of seeing flowers grow and enjoying their colors and perfume may add some cheer to the lives of these children whose homes are often drab and colorless.

Improvement of Attention Span and Listening Ability

Many children have never been taught to listen for specific sounds. Children who live in crowded homes are constantly bombarded by noises of all sorts, including children's screams as they run up and down the halls after each other, blaring television and radio, trucks with screeching brakes as they stop at boulevards, roaring motors as they start again, and jets occasionally breaking the sound barrier. These children unconsciously set up a block against noises. They often do not hear people who are talking to them. Some of them are completely unconscious of the teacher's voice unless she calls their attention to it.

Immature children usually have a short attention span, which inevitably makes listening difficult for them. These children need help before they should be required to concentrate on work for any length of time. In a review of studies on listening Duker stresses its importance and its relationship to comprehension and speed in reading.[1]

[1] Sam Duker, "Listening and Reading," *The Elementary School Journal*, LXV (Mar. 1965), 321–29.

A dynamic and enthusiastic teacher is usually able to hold these children's attention better than a quiet teacher. A good class environment helps children to listen well. The temperature of the room should be comfortable and especially not too warm. Distracting noises should be eliminated as far as possible. Articles that children play with and tend to drop should be put away.

Illustrative material used by the teacher tends to catch the children's attention and reinforces listening with a visual stimulus. Children should always have a purpose for listening. When the teacher gives directions, she gives them a purpose by asking them to listen so they will know what to do. When repeating poetry, the teacher asks the children to listen to find out what happens in the poem. For example, in Marchette Chute's poem, "Birthdays," [2] the children listen to find what favor each of the children asks for on their birthdays. A hint that the biggest surprise of all comes last adds to the interest and enjoyment. When the poem has been repeated by request from time to time, the teacher encourages the children to join her in repeating the parts they remember, another motive for listening.

Activities for Listening. A variety of activities for improving children's attention span and their ability to listen are given below:

1. Listening to flannelboard stories. Each child is given a turn to move one of the characters or a part of the scenery at appropriate places in the story.
2. Listening to find what happens next at crucial times when the teacher is telling or reading a story.
3. Following directions of various types.
4. Listening to oneself on the tape recorder. Children are fascinated by hearing their own voices on the tape recorder and will tend to listen to themselves with deep interest. They may be encouraged to listen to see if they should talk louder or more plainly.
5. Listening for rhyming words in short poems and rhymes. Some teachers suggest that children clap when they hear rhyming words. The teacher can be much more certain of their knowledge of rhyming if she asks them to identify the words that rhyme.
6. Dramatizing actions in sentences read by the teacher. The teacher may read such a sentence as, "Skip ran to Jane." One child may take the part of Skip who runs to the other child who takes the part of Jane.
7. The teacher may put a series of nine by twelve mounted pictures of baby animals on the chalk rail. She may then name one of the adult animals and ask the child to find the picture of the appropriate baby animal and tell what it is called.

[2] Marchette Chute, "Birthdays," *Story and Verse for Children* (Miriam Blanton Huber), (rev. ed.; New York: The Macmillan Co., 1955), 106.

Other activities are described below in greater detail.

The Sound Box. Children enjoy using the sound box, and it seems to have some value for helping them listen more acutely. The teacher uses an average-sized cardboard carton with a base of approximately twelve by fifteen inches. She may close all sides, but cut a large hole in the top for placing objects in the box and removing them.

When the teacher is ready to use the box with the children, she places it on its side on her table or desk with the open side toward her. She may manipulate an object inside the box, for example, a toy telephone, by dialing it. She then asks for volunteers to guess what the object is. The child who identifies the object correctly may take the teacher's place as leader to select and manipulate some other object and to call on other children to guess what it is. In this way the game continues.

Objects suitable for use in a sound box are as follows:

1. An alarm clock, hand operated. The children may listen to it as it is wound up, or may listen to the tick.
2. Sand blocks. The children listen as they are scraped together.
3. A hand bell.
4. Two dowel rods or sticks clicked together.
5. A piece of tissue paper crushed and rustled.
6. A drum, castinets, a tambourine, or other percussion instruments.
7. A pencil tapped against a piece of wood.
8. A water glass tapped with a pencil.
9. Two stones hit together.
10. An egg beater rotated rapidly.

Recordings of Sounds. A teacher made a tape recording of sounds heard around the house. She then found and cut out pictures of the objects she had used for the sounds, backed them with flannel, and put them on the flannelboard to help the children know what possible sounds they might hear. She had taped such sounds as the telephone ringing, water running, footsteps on a wooden floor, the opening and closing of a door, the grinding of an automobile starter, sounds from a piano, the noise of a jet going overhead, the ringing of the front doorbell or chimes, popcorn popping, and similar sounds.

The kindergarten children responded very enthusiastically to the tape and were soon able to identify the sounds. Some teachers are able to secure recordings of various sounds. Such a recording is *Sounds Around Us.*

Bird Songs. If children are in a suburban area, they may become interested in birds. Only one bird at a time should usually be studied, and the children should be acquainted with as much interesting information about the bird as possible. A bird seen on the school lawn or one that makes a nest in a nearby tree is a good choice. In this way, the children are assured of being able to see it often and hear its song. The teacher should never insist that all the children identify a particular bird either by sight or sound because this compulsion spoils the pleasure and the possible development of a hobby.

Sounds Near the Classroom. At times the teacher may ask the children to close their eyes while they listen to sounds around them. They may identify such objects as someone walking in the hall, an automobile or truck passing the school, the ringing of the telephone if they are near the office, a bird in a nearby tree, and similar sounds.

A Game With a Ball. One child may bounce a ball while the others close their eyes and count the number of bounces. The child bouncing the ball may call on another to tell him how many times the ball was bounced. If the second child is correct, he may have his turn to act as leader and bounce the ball.

Musical Tones and Rhythms. The teacher may play a low and a high note on the piano, the xylophone, the tone bells, or any other instrument. She then asks the children to tell her how the notes were different and to tell which was low and high. The teacher may also tap a rhythm on the desk and call on another child to repeat the tap or make an echo. Such tapping sounds might be a short-long, a long-short, two longs and a short, and so on.

A Game to Identify a Voice. Carrillo suggests a game in which the children close their eyes while the teacher chooses one of them to go behind another child and tap him on the shoulder, asking, "Who am I?" [3] If the child in his seat guesses the name of the child who tapped him on the shoulder, this child becomes the new one to take the first child's place. This author has other good suggestions for listening activities.

Animal Blindman's Buff. David and Elizabeth Russell suggest many good activities for helping the child learn to listen.[4] One of these games is called "Animal Blindman's Buff." The children are each given a name of an animal. They stand in a circle, while one child is blindfolded and stands in the middle. The child who is blindfolded calls the name of an animal. The child who represents that animal is supposed to bark, meow, or make the sound appropriate for his animal. If the blindfolded child correctly guesses who is making the animal sounds, he takes his

[3] Lawrence W. Carillo, *Informal Reading Readiness Experiences* (San Francisco: Chandler Publishing Co., 1964).

[4] David H. Russell and Elizabeth F. Russell, *Listening Aids Through the Grades* (New York: Bureau of Publications, Teachers College, Columbia University, 1959).

place in the circle; the recognized child goes to the center, and the game is continued.

Opposites. This activity is called opposites. The teacher gives a word such as *hot* and calls on a child to give a word meaning the opposite. The group may be divided into two teams, and scores may be kept for correct answers. When the children know enough words, they may take turns being the leader to give a word which calls for the opposite to the opposing team.

Auditory Acuity

Auditory acuity is very closely related to listening, but demands a greater ability to hear fine differences among sounds. Usually auditory acuity refers to the child's ability to hear letter sounds within words. The teacher first helps the children identify words that begin with the same consonants, because the consonant sounds are the most common. She also helps the child listen to and recognize words that end with the same rhyming sounds and later adds familiarity with sounds of consonant blends and digraphs as time goes on. A few suggestions for helping children hear letter sounds are given here.

Use of Children's Names. The teacher may begin with the names of the children in the class if any of their first names begin with the same letters. The children may discuss each other's names and try to think of two that begin alike. Since this discussion provides one of the first experiences with sounds, the teacher must be ready to give hints. She may tell the children that she can think of two boys' names that begin alike. If the children fail to guess which ones, she can give such clues as, "Both boys are tall, but one has dark hair and the other has red hair," or "One boy is tall, and the other is short, but their hair is the same color." In this way, the teacher helps the children think of names that begin with the same letter sounds such as Mary and Marilyn, or Tom, Terry, and Tim.

Use of Pictures. Large pictures mounted on 9″ × 12″ cardboard are very helpful in teaching children to recognize sounds. Only one object clearly illustrated without background should be placed on a card. The teacher should discuss these cards with the children to be sure that she and the children are in agreement as to the name of the object. Some pictures are ambiguous. For example, a particular picture may be correctly described as either a hen or a chicken. The teacher may place three pictures with objects beginning with the same letter sound, such as a *man*, a milk bottle representing the word *milk*, and *money*. The teacher then asks the children to tell her the names of these objects.

She may then place two or three pictures at the right of these, but separated by a large space. These pictures may show objects such as a top, a bicycle, and a marble. She then asks the children to decide which one of these three pictures belongs with the first three.

Many suggstions are given for helping children learn to recognize letter sounds of various types in Chapter 10 in connection with the development of readiness for phonics. Many additional suggestions may be found in Russell and Russell.[5]

Perception of Likenesses and Differences

The use of Judy puzzles for developing eye-hand co-ordination has been described early in this chapter. Work with these puzzles is also helpful in developing perception or visual discrimination. For another activity some teachers keep a box of nuts and bolts. Young children with a mechanical aptitude enjoy finding the right nut for the right bolt and putting them together. Some teachers use a board mounted on a wooden base for this activity. Holes are bored through the vertical piece of wood to fit a series of bolts of graded sizes. The child then fits the proper bolt to the proper hole and fastens the correct nut to the bolt.

Large colored wooden beads may be used for helping children develop perception or visual discrimination. This activity has been suggested under the section on teaching colors. Other suggestions for developing perception are given in Chapter 10 in the discussion on readiness for teaching phonics. Additional ideas may also be found in Carrillo [6] and other books on reading readiness.

The above suggestions for teaching perception and auditory acuity apply equally well to the teaching of likenesses and differences, another kind of perception. These terms are closely related and overlap in their meanings. Many exercises for teaching likenesses and difference are given in reading readiness workbooks. These exercises should be given only to the children that need them. Many children in the first grade can complete these exercises very easily and should not be required to go through the books in a routine fashion.

Vision

Children with minor defects of vision can often succeed in learning to read. The defects, however, tend to force the child to use extra energy in adjusting to the size of the print.

Farsightedness. Most preschool and primary children are farsighted. For this reason, large print on charts greatly reduces the strain of be-

[5] *Ibid.*
[6] Carillo, *op. cit.*

ginning reading. Much emphasis is placed on the use of charts in beginning reading because of the greater ease in holding children's attention on this work. The better attention achieved in teaching charts is
one result of the greater ease with which the children can see the print
on the charts.

Vision Tests. Most children are given vision tests in the kindergarten
or very early in the first grade. Some of these tests are limited to the
use of the Snellen E Charts, which are very superficial. If possible,
children should be tested by an oculist in order to make sure that their
vision is adequate.

The muscles in young children's eyes are very flexible, and they are
able to adjust to visual strains with little evidence of difficulty. In addition, young children often do not recognize the location of their discomfort. The demands for reading in the primary grades are not as
great as in upper grades, and the child is not required to use his eyes
at near vision over a very long time. For this reason, symptoms of
visual difficulty may not be evidenced until the child is in the upper
grades, high school, or even college. The lack of symptoms of eyestrain
in young children is no proof that these children's eyes have not been
strained. Oculists state that children's eyes are not completely formed
until sometime between the ages of five and seven. The teacher should
be aware of possible eye strain among her pupils.

Symptoms of Eye Strain. Some of the symptoms of eye strain are
watery-looking eyes, a tendency to rub the eyes at frequent intervals, the
habit of holding the book too close to the eyes, squinting, and frequent
headaches, especially after much use of the eyes.

Children are not usually aware of their lack of adequate vision.
Freddy was an example of this problem. When he came to first grade
Freddy was alert, co-operative, and happy. As long as he worked with
large pictures he was successful. When he started to take part in actual
reading with his group, he was completely unable to get started. In
addition, he became mischievous and increasingly unco-operative. Since
his vocabulary was good and his responses to all auditory work were
quite successful, the teacher began to suspect that his vision was not
good. When he was referred to the nurse, she tested him with the
Snellen E Chart and found that he could see nothing until he was
within about four feet of the chart instead of the normal twenty. Several conferences with the mother were necessary to convince her that
he was incapable of doing school work until he could have some help
from an oculist. The oculist found that Freddy's vision was extremely
limited. He prescribed strong lenses and a series of treatments to improve Freddy's vision. The oculist very wisely put a pair of glasses on

Freddy's mother to show her how handicapped he was. The mother confessed afterwards that she could not understand how the child could get to school and take care of himself in the room since he was almost blind. As soon as Freddy had the help of glasses, he caught up with the rest of the children and continued to make excellent progress in learning to read. Because Freddy had no way of knowing what his vision should have been, he did not know and could not tell anyone that he was almost blind.

Hearing

One of the values of the Headstart Program is the early check given the children for physical handicaps. Mild hearing loss is one of the handicaps most easily overlooked. Adults may suspect a child of being inattentive or of daydreaming. Since the child's reactions are the same in both instances, the child should be tested with an audiometer in order to discover if he has a hearing loss. If the teacher suspects that a child's lack of attention is due to inadequate hearing, she should speak to him in a normal voice when standing directly behind him. If the child fails to respond during several attempts to speak to him from the rear, the teacher may suspect his hearing effectiveness and request that he be tested for hearing loss.

Value of the Audiometer. A test on the audiometer can be used to discover whether or not the child is completely deaf or has only a partial hearing loss. Some individuals are able to hear high tones but not middle or low tones. Some, on the other hand, have a loss in the middle or lower range of tones. The audiometer gives accurate information as to the type of hearing loss. If the loss is severe, the child may be placed in a class for children with similar problems. If the loss is mild, the teacher may be able to help the child adjust to the problem.

Help in Seating the Child. Differences in hearing loss may also be found in one ear compared to the other. For this reason, the child is the best judge of where in the room he should carry on his work. When the teacher is able to work with the child alone, she should ask him to try the center front, the center rear, each side of the room, and a position near her to discover where he is best able to hear. The child should then be allowed to work in that area of the room. The idea that all children with hearing difficulty should be seated close to the teacher is erroneous since their hearing may be helped by the reflection of sound waves from one of the walls in the room.

Changes in Hearing. Some specialists say that a hearing test is only accurate for the day on which it is given. This statement is not meant to invalidate audiometer tests; rather it refers to the fact that a child's hearing may be severely limited by the accumulation of ear wax and soap in the external ear canal. In the case of the child who has this difficulty, hearing may be restored immediately after the wax is removed. This condition should always be checked by a doctor in the case of the child who has a hearing loss. In this case, too, the loss may be greater in one ear than the other.

Enunciation and Pronunciation

The problem of poor enunciation and pronunciation have been discussed in Chapter 3. A few years ago, no effort was made to help the child with speech problems until he was in the second or third grade. Part of the reason for the delay was to wait until the child had his second teeth and had overcome a temporary problem resulting from the loss of various teeth.

In the Headstart Program, the practice was changed. Since research has shown that children with severe enunciation and pronunciation problems have difficulty in learning to read, an effort has been made to give them help at the preschool level. Although young children may have greater difficulty in learning speech techniques, they learn more easily by imitation. In addition, the habits of poor speech have not become as firmly established as they have with older children. Many schools have teachers who are specially trained to help speech problems.

EMOTIONAL AND SOCIAL DEVELOPMENT

Emotional problems have been discussed in Chapter 3. Some of these problems may be severe enough to block completely the child's learning until they are alleviated. Lack of learning due to serious emotional problems may be confused with mental retardation. The need to discover the cause for lack of learning is essential if the child is to receive help. By listening to his language, the teacher can usually identify a child who is failing to learn due to emotional problems or to causes other than mental retardation. Most children seem to be able to achieve a language level somewhat equivalent to their mental development unless they are children who also have problems of language impoverishment. If a child seems unable to learn, the teacher should give as much attention as possible to his use of language. If he uses a good vocabulary for his age group and if his sentence structure is mature, the teacher can be almost certain that the difficulty is not due to low mental ability. She should then try to discover the causes.

Each day the children pinned on a calendar the appropriate number for the day of the month. (Courtesy N.D.E.A. 1967 Demonstration School and the Sacramento City Unified School District.)

Help for Children with Emotional Problems

A diplomatic conference with the parents may help the teacher discover the cause of a child's difficulty in adjustment. If the child's problem is serious, the teacher should also discuss his problem with her principal for possible referral to a psychologist, who may be able to help the family with the problem. In a case of emotional problems, pressure on the child to force him to learn should be avoided at all costs until the child himself shows evidence of security and a desire to learn.

Children with emotional problems need feelings of belonging to the group and feelings of security and love from the teacher. Often this child is the most difficult for the teacher to like, but his security depends upon her willingness to make him feel that he is loved. He needs as much attention and recognition as possible for all his attempts at good behavior and for his efforts to succeed in work. The teacher must give him status by allowing him to succeed in things which he can do and by taking every opportunity to give him praise for his successes. Some children may make progress in their adjustment with this type of help from the teacher even when the family seems unable to do much for the child.

Adjustment to New Routines

Some children need more time than others to adjust to a new school situation. No child can do his best work until he gains confidence in the teacher and acquires security by learning class routines. The first-grade teacher must help all the children as well as those who are disturbed to live comfortably in the classroom. She must also help them learn to work independently before she can begin to teach readiness in groups and later begin to teach formal reading. Suggestions for helping children learn these routines are given in the chapter on independent work.

Although some of the children may be ready to begin reading when they enter the first grade, the teacher is not able to work with them as a group until she has helped all the children to know where to find materials and how to carry on work independently. They must be able to work by themselves for a period of fifteen or twenty minutes without asking the teacher for help. When she works with a group, she must be free from interruptions except for emergencies because they distract the attention of the children in the group. After children are able to work independently, some teachers appoint a helper for the week to whom they can go for an occasional difficult word or other minor problem.

TEACHING READING IN THE KINDERGARTEN

More and more pressure is being exerted on teachers to teach reading in kindergarten. Parents, administrators, and a limited number of reading specialists are urging that a variety of procedures from readiness activities to actual instruction in formal reading be introduced in the kindergarten.

Need for Language

According to the child specialists who are working with culturally-deprived children, the lack of various aspects of language development seems to be the greatest factor that differentiates the child who is able to succeed in reading from the child who is unable to succeed. Even the child who has a good background in language, however, is not necessarily ready to learn to read. Dolores Durkin found that the children who learned to read before entering first grade were those who were very eager to read, who liked to work with pencil and paper and other quiet activities, and who had a long attention span.[7] No highly active children with a short attention span were found in this group. A degree of security and self-confidence also seems to be necessary for children to begin reading at an early age. Durkin found that only one child out of fifty had begun to undertake reading on his own initiative. Her follow-up tests show that these children were gradually losing their advantage in later grades.

Reports of Success in Early Reading Programs

More and more articles describing successful programs in either pre-reading skills or formal reading programs in kindergarten are found in educational journals. The reader must be particularly sceptical of generalizing from articles reporting success in school systems of a high socio-economic level. A larger percentage of children in such districts can succeed in some types of reading in the kindergarten than those from districts of average or lower socio-economic levels.

Means and medians are also terms of doubtful value for some children. For every child above the median there is a child below the median. Almost the same distribution occurs above and below the mean. If the program has been developed with all the children in the kindergarten, those children below the mean soon learn that they are less capable than other children. The development of a poor self-concept at the kindergarten level can interfere with the child's successful learning throughout the rest of his school life.

Statistical data without a report of the children's emotional reactions and the problems encountered by children who were not ready to enter the program can be extremely misleading and actually erroneous. The problems met by teachers in organizing formal work in the kindergarten are usually completely omitted from the statistical, success reports. Georgiady, Romano, and Baranowski have given a sensitive and understanding report of an attempt to establish one of these programs.[8] They briefly describe the problems met by the teachers who must work with children in a group while other children carry on the normal creative activities needed by the average kindergarten child and paid for in taxes by his parents.

[7] Dolores Durkin, "Children Who Learn to Read at Home," *The Elementary School Journal*, LXII (Oct. 1961), 14–19.

[8] Nicholas P. Georgiady, Louis Romano, and Arthur Baranowski, "To Read or Not to Read in Kindergarten," *The Elementary School Journal*, LXV (Mar. 1965), 306–11.

Any program that sacrifices the welfare of three quarters of a class of kindergarten children for the sake of a few who are ready to read is not meeting democratic standards and is cheating a large proportion of the children in the class. Most teachers who are required to teach a formal program to those kindergarten children who are ready force the rest of the children in the class to sit at their tables, to be quiet, and usually to carry on a lot of futile and sometimes harmful work coloring pictures out of workbooks. Coloring pictures within outlines causes children to doubt their own ability to express themselves and results in their giving up attempts to be creative. Since creativity and thinking are closely related, these children lose their drive for both types of activities.

Emotional Readiness

Georgiady, Romano, and Baranowski reported that some children in their study seemed to master the recognition symbols but did not have the emotional readiness for the activities to teach these skills. They said, "This lack was manifested in various ways—inattentiveness, boredom, nailbiting, balking, or even crying at having to participate." The teachers found a large group in the class who were emotionally unready for formal reading activities even though they were able to master the skills.

The teachers also found the demands of carrying on a rich program along with those of teaching reading to a group to be extremely difficult. These authors reported that all of the teachers believed that even the more mature children needed many of the enriching experiences provided by the kindergarten. If any real value was attained by teaching formal reading to a few of these children both they and the class would be better off if these children were taken out of the room and taught by a trained reading teacher.

Teaching Skills

Although many kindergarten teachers may know good techniques for teaching reading when they finished their work in college, they forget these techniques after a few years in the kindergarten. On the other hand, some kindergarten teachers do not know any reading techniques. Unless kindergarten teachers are carefully trained in good beginning reading procedures, they will do a great deal more harm than good.

Problems of Intellectual Maturity

The problems of reversals is one that concerns first- and even second-grade teachers. Reversals of various types are found from confusion in the perception of letters and words such as "b" with "d," "u" with "n," "p" with "q," and "was" with "saw," to mirror writing. According to authorities, almost all of these confusions are the result of children's intellectual immaturity. Children who are mature and who are actually ready to read when they are first taught have little or no trouble with these reversals. A great danger of much formal reading in kindergarten is that of the development of reversals, which may persist for some months to several years due to emotional blocks established by teachers and parents who do not know how to handle this problem.

Readiness and Reading Programs

Most readiness programs described in experimental studies are those that emphasize auditory and visual perception. The development of auditory perceptual skills has value for kindergarten children if the work is undertaken after the children are well adjusted to the kindergarten, if the periods are kept short, if the work permits the children to be active, and if the children are mature enough to be interested in what they are doing.

Reports of success with workbooks programs usually stress children's success on tests given at the end of the kindergarten year and sometimes given during the first grade. In many of the articles the actual tests are not described. If they are tests of some type of perceptual skill and if children are tested on the material they have been specifically taught, these children will obviously be ahead of children in the control groups who were not taught these skills.

In most cases, success is evaluated by tests of word recognition at the end of the first grade, since most first grade reading tests stress word recognition. Although a little attention is given to sentence and paragraph meaning in the tests, the word recognition sections are heavily weighted. The children taught any type of word recognition skills therefore have the advantage in such tests. The real question concerns whether the children will read better in the intermediate grades rather than at the end of the first grade as a result of these early programs.

Some of the investigators promise to carry on the testing through the middle grades. The worth of this type of formal teaching cannot be properly evaluated until children are old enough to be tested on a complete balance of reading skills. For this reason any attempt to rush into the use of workbooks in the kindergarten should by all means be held up until the final results of these studies are found and reported.

Values of Early Reading

The articles found more and more frequently which stress reading programs in the kindergarten all fail to tell why early reading is valuable for children. In one article this type of program was defended on the basis that children need to be able to read at an earlier age in order to be able to study science and mathematics sooner.

This defense is questionable since any good science program in the primary grades makes use of demonstration and experimentation rather than reading. After the children have had many science experiences for two or three years, they will be ready to read to add vicariously to their experiences and to further their understanding of generalizations. In any good science program, however, real experience comes first and reading comes later.

In mathematics much stress is laid on the use of pictures and diagrams and manipulation of numbers, and very little stress is laid on reading problems in the early primary grades. Again, real experiences and work with mathematical symbols should precede the use of reading material. The value of reading in the kindergarten has still not been shown.

Functional Reading in the Kindergarten

Most early readers who teach themselves or who have a little help from adults when requested learn to read functional materials such as labels on cans of food and articles in stores, signs such as those used to direct pedestrians and automobile drivers, and books of poems and nursery rhymes. In the case of the latter the children usually memorize the rhymes by listening to adults repeat them frequently. After the rhymes are memorized, the children pore over them in books and gradually begin to pick lines out of the entire poem and then words out of the lines. They locate the lines and words by finding them first in sequence and then gradually begin to recognize these same words in other contexts. Some children have help, and some learn by themselves.

The most realistic approach to reading in the kindergarten is through the use of experience stories. This approach to beginning reading has been used by many teachers over the past thirty years to help beginners acquire enough sight vocabulary to read pre-primers easily. The San Diego schools have adopted this program on a city-wide basis. Some teachers have carried the children beyond the pre-primers until they were able to read easily in primers and supplementary trade books.

This procedure has several advantages. The experience story may be dictated by members of the entire kindergarten after they have had some interesting experience. In this way all children can participate. Children who are verbally mature will probably contribute the most to these stories, but the less mature children will be exposed to the procedure. These immature children will gradually learn the function of printing through participating in records of experiences. They will also gradually become more able to take part in the dictation of the stories. The stories are memorized as wholes just as the nursery rhymes described above were learned. The most mature children who are truly ready for reading will begin to identify separate lines in the experience stories and later will identify words. In this way they are able to acquire a sight vocabulary and, in time, will be able to read pre-primers and books on the library table. Only a few children in a class will be able to function on this level. Through this experience, however, the less mature children are able to learn at their own levels.

The use of experience stories along with labels, signs, and other functional reading material provides an opportunity for the children who are ready to read to learn without working in a group. The immature children, therefore, are not required to sit still for an unreasonably long time so that the teacher can work with a few children. The children who are able to acquire a sight vocabulary are under no pressure and are not required to work on an abstract level while other children take part in more interesting and active experiences. Since no children are segregated for a particular type of work, the less mature children do not feel that they are left out of an experience because they are not as bright as the others.

SUMMARY

A variety of activities are useful in helping children grow in physical aspects of readiness for reading. Creative work such as painting and work with clay along with Judy puzzles are helpful in improving children's eye-hand co-ordination. Work with charts and pictures for sequence are valuable in helping establish habits of moving the eyes from right to left. Children may work with colored objects or other materials for perceptual discrimination. Ability to listen, attention span, and visual and auditory acuity are improved by other activities.

Some children need help in emotional and social adjustment so that they are able to learn more successfully. Teaching beginning reading in the kindergarten can be accomplished by the use of experience stories in such a way that the children who are ready to read may learn while the other children can acquire skills on their own levels without pressure on any of the children.

III

BALANCED READING PROCEDURES

7

The Pre-Primer and
Parallel Stories

BEGINNING READING

Various aspects of methods developed during the last three or four decades support and reinforce each other for an enriched and balanced program of teaching reading. Children's weaknesses in reading often seem due to the lack of a balanced approach on the part of the teacher. Some pupils may learn excellent methods of analyzing words but may be seriously handicapped by weakness in the ability to acquire thought from reading material or by lack of speed in reading. Other pupils may learn to read with speed and comprehension but have inadequate word mastery or techniques for analyzing new words. Some children are amazing in their ability to grasp meaning despite a poor sight vocabulary and a very limited ability to use clues in word recognition. Such children, however, are seriously handicapped when they must read factual or technical material in which accuracy and detail are important. Some children, too, need more help than others in developing comprehension, speed, word analysis techniques, and skill in organizing thought gained from reading. For these reasons all teachers should use variety and balance in their teaching procedures.

MODERN READING BOOKS

Children learn to recognize words most easily when they are introduced in simple sentences that are concerned with children's interests.

Words are also mastered most easily when they are repeated frequently in these simple sentences. When learned, these words are called sight words, that is, they are recognized at a glance without the necessity of using phonics, word clues, or other aids. They are called sight words after they have been learned, even though they may have been introduced by use of phonics or context clues. The plan of teaching words through their use in simple sentences incorporated in stories is followed in today's reading series.

Texts and Supplementary Readers

Short, easy, soft-backed books are written to precede the primer. These books are called pre-primers. One of these pre-primers may contain forty-five or fifty pages, but the stories are written with a very few different words. The number of words in modern pre-primers is limited to a range of between seventeen and twenty-five different words, which are frequently repeated. These words are distributed carefully throughout the booklets for repetition and review. Often three and sometimes four pre-primers in a series may be taught before the primer is introduced.

Each book in a reading series has a name, such as *At the Farm* or *In the City* to avoid using the number of the grade level conspicuously on the book. The use of names for the books tends to avoid disturbing children who may need to work in a book below the grade in which they belong by one, two, or even more years. Although the children may know they are reading an easy book, the affront is less severe when the book has a name rather than a number. Some series use a code for the numbers, which are placed on the back bindings of the books. Other similar plans are used. An average series of modern readers may consist of the following set of books:

First pre-primer	First reader, level II
Second pre-primer	Second reader, level I
Third pre-primer	Second reader, level II
Fourth pre-primer (in some series)	Third reader, level I
	Third reader, level II
Primer, level I	Fourth reader
Primer, level II	Fifth reader
First reader, level I	Sixth reader

Adopted Texts. A number of different companies publish sets of readers. One or two of these sets may be chosen by a state or a local district to be used as the adopted texts. All children are expected to read these books at some time during the year. Nevertheless, not all children in the fourth grade will read a fourth reader. Some of the children reading below grade level may read the third, second, or even first grade readers. Sometimes the more advanced children may use the reading texts for the grade or grades above. Most teachers prefer that these children read advanced books from other sets so that the teacher in the next grade may use the state text if she feels that these more advanced children need these books. Children should never be required to read a particular reader a second time. A different book on the same or an easier level should be selected for interest.

Supplementary Readers. Sets of readers by other publishers are considered as supplementary readers and may be used by reading groups before or after they use the state or district text; their use is not mandatory. Some school districts have many of these sets, that circulate from school to school or that may be withdrawn from the district library by a teacher who wishes to use these sets.

Controlled Vocabulary. Today, even the primer includes a much lower vocabulary load than the earlier books of this type, usually about a hundred words, and repetition is again carefully planned. Each booklet or book frequently repeats the words introduced in preceding books and those introduced in its own text. First readers usually introduce more words than are contained in the primers, about one hundred and fifty on the average, but continue to repeat the review vocabulary. The same procedures are followed in the second, third, and intermediate grade readers, although more words are used as the reading level increases.

To compensate for the rapid increase in the number of words utilized by the later primary books, supplementary books have been written for most reading series to follow each basic reader and to provide more stories in order to increase the repetition of words. Manuals giving carefully planned suggestions for teaching and many ideas for enrichment usually accompany these readers, and workbooks are prepared to accompany the basic readers for children's use.

The limitation of words in the texts of the pre-primers necessitates that the stories be carried primarily by the pictures, which are often clever and interesting to children. The authors have been surprisingly successful in limiting the words and yet building stories of interest and appeal to children. Many children derive a great deal of satisfaction from the power they achieve through reading the simple stories in such books. Most children are delighted when they can achieve success in reading these stories. In addition, the techniques of arousing interest and the activities followed in presenting these stories seem to be very satisfying to the children.

Quality of Pre-Primers. These pre-primers have been severely criticized, usually by those who work with advanced college students and
who have little understanding of the problems to be met in teaching
young children. Yet none of these critics has yet challenged Shake-
speare's position in the field of English literature by writing a pre-primer
with a vocabulary of twenty words on a six-year-old level of interest and
understanding. Improvement is needed and will probably be made,
perhaps not so much in literary quality as in more challenging content.
The quality of the writing in the pre-primers is probably the best that
can be produced with such a limited number of words.

Literary Values and Interest. It is true that children need to be exposed to many examples of good literature during their early school
years. The best way to provide literature at this time is through the
stories that teachers read and tell to children, which should be selected
with care. The people who feel that today's pre-primers lack quality
are usually those who extol the literary quality of the books of the late
nineteenth and early twentieth centuries. It was very common to find
selections in the books of those days that are similar to the following
excerpts of "fascinating" beginning stories:

> Baby.
> See baby.
> See, see.

The following is another story of that era, mentioned earlier:

> Is the cat on the mat?
> The cat is on the mat.

Most of today's stories are vastly more interesting than similar stories
in the early books. At the same time, the words are numerically more
limited today and therefore easier to learn.

Suggestions in Manuals and Professional Books

New methods as well as newer types of books are the outcome of
many years of work by educators and textbook writers and are based on
modern psychology. The general plan followed by most professional
authorities is called the *developmental program*. A program of this
type is planned for each series of readers in which a carefully graded
vocabulary is utilized.

Except in the beginning pre-primers, each lesson consists of a basic
plan in which the story and the new words are introduced, silent reading is carried on and checked for comprehension, selections are read
orally, rereading for some special purpose may be carried on, some type

of practice may be given, and workbooks may be used to provide a follow-up step for review. Practice is not always provided on words or sentences in context, but it is often applied to the analysis of new or difficult words. The order and number of the steps in the basic plan differ in various series, and great variety is found in the procedures used to develop each step.

These steps are discussed in detail in the chapter on teaching in the primers and more advanced books. Many suggestions for teaching these steps are described in the manuals written to serve as guides to the teacher as she plans each lesson. Some manuals offer far more ideas than the teacher can use. To select the most appropriate ideas, the teacher must understand and have skill in using good procedures. She must also know the needs of her children and be able to select the best procedures to meet their needs and to help them advance in the most effective ways.

Phonics Books

In more recent times, a series of books based entirely upon word patterns, formerly called word families, and others using an all-phonics program have been produced by most publishers of readers. These books are not the result of carefully developed research with children but have been produced and accepted by some administrators and teachers in an unconscious desire to return to an era when people felt more secure. Practically none of the writers of these books are professional reading specialists. The programs sponsored by these publishers are described and analyzed in a later chapter on reading trends.

THE FIRST PRE-PRIMER LESSONS

More simple plans than those discussed above are suggested for the children's beginning lessons in the first pre-primer. A variety of suggestions from manuals and ideas used by teachers are described to help the student and teacher decide on the plans most suitable for their use. They are listed as Procedure A, B, C, and D. Another procedure using parallel stories is also presented.

Procedure A

The suggestions for teaching the pre-primers are rather similar for most reading series. Some authorities suggest that the teacher introduce the story in the first pre-primer by means of a dramatic discussion of the pictures. The teacher then reads the one or two sentences on the pages found in the first sections of the typical pre-primers that follow the introduction of the characters in the books. Then several children are asked to repeat these sentences in an effort to achieve a modified type of oral reading before the teacher turns to the next page to repeat this process. The teacher reinforces the thought with running comments.

Some teachers read only one sentence at a time before asking a child to repeat. Others read all the sentences on the page, rarely more than three. Some authors describe the child's reading in such a case as an echo of the teacher's reading. The introductory teachnique used with the pictures in this procedure is excellent. The children's "echo" of the teacher's reading is weak because the children have no real purpose for repeating the sentence after the teacher. Therefore their attention is often poor. It is difficult for them to remember the words of the sentences after merely repeating what has been heard.

Procedure B

Some authorities suggest another technique. The teacher follows the discussion of the pictures by asking questions that lead the child to anticipate the wording of the sentences in the book. This process is actually more than guessing. By answering the teacher's skillfully worded questions the child is led to use the words of the sentences in the book in his reply.

The Anticipatory Step. For example, to help the child anticipate the line, "Jump, Pal, jump!" the teacher may ask, "What does Jimmy want Pal to do?"

The child may reply, "Jimmy wants Pal to jump."

"Fine," the teacher may respond. "What would you say to Pal if you wanted him to jump?"

The child's response may be, "Jump, Pal!"

The teacher may then say, "Good! Jimmy did say, 'Jump, Pal!' Then he told Pal to jump again. Now read it the way Jimmy said it."

The child may then respond by saying, "Jump, Pal, jump!"

"Very good!" the teacher may say, although she has virtually put the sentence into the child's mouth by this process. When the teacher has reassured the child that he has "read" the line correctly, she goes on to draw out the next line by means of further guiding questions. Enthusiasm is needed in order to maintain interest. This procedure just described is much more effective than the previous one because it holds the children's attention more adequately and stimulates them constantly to think and to concentrate on meaning.

Need for Added Procedures. As children work out the natural sequence of the conversation themselves, they tend to remember it. While this is a good procedure, it is only valuable for introducing the story. If the process is dropped at this point to go on to the next story without the use of further techniques, it may have failed to provide for establishing mastery of vocabulary for the less mature children. If this procedure, however, is followed by a variety of other techniques for vocabulary mastery, it will meet the needs of all the children including the slower ones.

Procedure C, Materials

Since Procedure C requires the use of some materials, they are described before the discussion of this procedure. Word cards are often supplied by the publishing company for their texts. A type of cardboard called tagboard or manila tag, described in Chapter 3, is used by the publishers. If word cards are not provided by the school, teachers often make their own, using the same material. If the teacher wishes to make her own cards, the following directions may be of help.

The Word Card. A card four inches wide is ruled on tag to provide adequate space for the word. The length of the card will depend upon the space demanded by the length of the word. This card is then divided into five horizontal spaces each ruled three-quarters of an inch wide except for the lowest space which is an inch in width. The first three-quarters of an inch provides a top margin. The second space is for the upper case letters, the third is for the lower case letters, and the fourth is for the down strokes that go below the line. The fifth space is used as a margin or base to be slipped into a pocket chart, mentioned below. The allowance of this lower margin is very necessary to avoid covering the down strokes in each word. These down strokes not only help the child identify the word, but they are essential to his recognition of it. A diagram of a word card is found in Chapter 3, Figure 3 5.

The Pocket Chart. The pocket chart is used to hold the word cards as the teacher discusses the story. A pocket chart is shown in Chapter 3, Figure 3-3 along with directions for making it.

Procedure C, Methods

Procedure C involves the duplication of the story on word cards described above. The teacher may first use a large picture to build interest and background for the story just as was done in the other procedures. The teacher then discusses one sentence of the story at a time, following the anticipatory step in *Procedure B*, and puts the word cards belonging to each sentence into the pocket chart as she does so. The cards are placed in correct order to build the sentences. The children find each sentence in their books after the teacher has placed these respective cards in the pocket chart. They then show the sentence to the teacher by framing it.

The children frame the sentence by placing the forefinger of each hand at the beginning and end of the sentence, which consists of only one line at this level. The framing is important to the teacher since it assures her that the children know where the sentence begins and ends. She does not have this assurance if they point to the sentence with one finger. The children may also frame each word as the teacher names it.

For additional practice, the teacher may read sentences for the children to take turns in finding on the chart. The story may also be taken from the chart, word by word, as the children take turns finding the words read by the teacher.

Review. The children may review the story on the following days by rebuilding it on the chart with the teacher's guidance. Unless the teacher is sure the children are ready to read the words at this time, she continues to read each word, asking the children to find it in an extra pocket chart where it has been placed in mixed order and to place it in correct order in the pocket chart she used originally. Two pocket charts are helpful at this point. One is used to hold the word cards from which the children select them, and the other is used to receive these cards as the children select them to build their story. The teacher also asks each child to repeat the word after he has placed it in the pocket chart, in order to be sure that he remembers it and is correct in his recall. At a later stage, the children may read the sentences without the teacher's help.

In addition to the word cards, some publishers provide sentence strips which are printed duplicates of the sentences in the pre-primer. The printing on these sentence strips is the same size as the printing on the word cards, and the sentence strips are the same dimensions as the word cards except for length. If sentence strips are not provided, many teachers make their own because of their value. The use of these sentence strips helps each child to see and read each sentence, as a whole, thereby helping to establish the habit of seeing several words at a time.

Development of Sight Vocabulary. The procedures just described in *Procedure C* have values not included in the two preceding methods. In addition to the effective techniques used in *Procedure B*, that of stimulating thought and insuring comprehension, the teacher has also provided for some practice on reading whole sentences. She has also helped the children master single words in order to provide a sight vocabulary, that is, words recognized at a glance. If the teacher gives adequate practice on the sentences and words, the children should be able to start the next story with a thorough knowledge of the review words.

The children in the advanced group may need little or no review or practice on the sentences and words. The children in the other two groups will probably profit considerably by review and practice.

Use of Books. Most of the procedures, A, B, and C just described, call for the children to have the books in their hands, at least part of the time, and to use them while they learn to recognize sentences and words as they progress through the stories in the books. This use of the books may be dull for the children who are slow in recognizing the words unless the teacher is enthusiastic and provides for some variety in the process.

Procedure D

The manuals for a few reading series introduce the new vocabulary to be met in the textbook by means of workbooks that prepare the child for the lesson to come rather than provide follow-up work to be used after the reading lesson. One of these reading series furnishes a considerable number of stories and exercises to be used before the reading lesson is taught in order thoroughly to familiarize the children with the new vocabulary. The stories and exercises are well planned and usually provide more material than is needed by the better readers. The teacher must use her judgment in selecting the proportion of this material she will use before introducing the lesson in the book.

Some publishers print the first sixteen or more pages of the material in the first pre-primer on large charts which exactly duplicate the pages in the book. These charts are bound together and may be called "the big book" or some similar name. These charts have the virtue of great attractiveness. They also make it much easier for the children to focus their attention on the large print on the charts, thus avoiding the problem of children losing their places in small books. The charts have the disadvantage of using exactly the same stories as those in the pre-primer which eliminates the purpose for the children to read the stories in the pre-primers later. They do, however, enjoy recognizing the familiar stories when they meet them in the pre-primer.

Effectiveness of Recommended Techniques

Any one or a combination of the procedures just described is usually adequately effective to teach the beginning steps in reading to children who are intelligent, mature, and ready. These mature children are able to concentrate sufficiently, to hold the books fairly still, and to keep the place reasonably well. The repetition of vocabulary provided by the book is usually sufficient to establish a sight vocabulary for these children. Also, their desire to read often carries them through some of the less challenging steps in these procedures.

Problems of Immature Children. The less mature and less stable children often need considerable help. Any observer of a reading lesson in a first-grade class has heard the teacher continuously reminding the children to keep the place. It is impossible, however, for some of these children to hold their eyes on a given line of print in a book for more than a minute or two at a time. Any distraction, a pencil dropped, an airplane overheard, someone passing by the window, or just the lapse of a little time will cause some of these children to lose the place in the book. They may find a sentence but lose it shortly just as they may catch a ball only to drop it the next moment. While the teacher is helping one child find the place another is losing it.

Need for Purpose. Unless these children are challenged by a strong purpose, they have difficulty remembering what the words say. Repeating a lesson line by line after the teacher has read it involves such slight purpose or interest that little of today's lesson is remembered tomorrow. The use of guiding questions offers more challenge than the latter procedure and may result in better retention. Even the frequent repetition of words in the best modern pre-primers is not sufficient to establish a sight vocabulary for some children.

Value of Word Cards. The use of the word cards to build sentences in a pocket chart is helpful because it gives these less mature children more opportunity for repetition of vocabulary than do the other procedures. This process is even more effective if sentence strips are introduced and used before the word cards to help the children develop the habit of reading words in groups for comprehension and speed.

Use of Workbooks for Introduction. The use of workbooks to prepare children for the vocabulary that they are to meet in their stories is an excellent procedure. The acquaintance with the new words in advance of the reading gives the children a sense of power and helps their comprehension. The introduction of the new vocabulary in workbooks on the pre-primer level results in some difficulty, however, for the immature children who have a problem in keeping the place. Most of the problems met on the pre-primer level will be minimized as the child becomes more mature and acquires increased skill in reading. If the teacher were able to help each child begin reading when he had acquired a considerable degree of maturity, fewer problems would be encountered. Unfortunately, not all teachers can spend an adequate amount of time in developing an appropriate level of readiness because of pressures from parents, from teachers of subsequent grades, and sometimes from administrators.

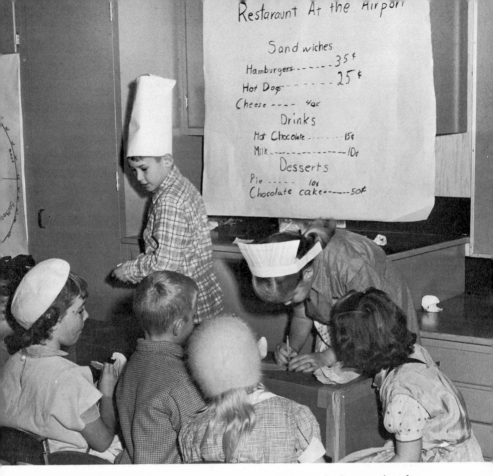

In a restaurant they have constructed in connection with their study of an airport, children are proceeding with a dramatic play. The menu also provides for exercise in the reading of text and numbers. (Courtesy California State Department of Education.)

THE PARALLEL STORY

Another plan is suggested for introducing the stories in the pre-primers. These procedures were designed to use all the best techniques in the plans described earlier and to contribute some additional suggestions.

Advantages of a Chart

The use of a chart to introduce sentences containing new words has the following important advantages:

The teacher can hold a pointer under the sentence she wishes the children to see. She therefore has an opportunity to make sure that all the children in the reading group are looking at the same place at the same time.

Children can easily find the place if their eyes wander because the print is large and the teacher is holding the pointer under the line.

Distractions caused by one child losing his place followed by another child who drops his book are eliminated because the children have nothing in their hands.

The children can go to the chart to frame a sentence (put their cupped hands around the sentence to show where it begins and ends). This activity gives them an opportunity for physical movement needed by young children. The activity also gives them a physical contact with the printed sentence to reinforce the visual contact.

Use of the Parallel Story

The parallel story is so named because it is written in the same words as those used in the pre-primer. After the first story that introduces the first words in the pre-primer, only one or two new words are introduced in each additional story, and the review words are also included. Only words that have already been learned by the children should be used in this story except for the words that need to be introduced. Although the words are parallel to those used in the pre-primer, the story may be different because the picture carries the plot of the story.

Advantages of the Parallel Story. The parallel story with a large, attractive picture has an advantage in addition to those of the chart stories in the big book, which are identical to the pre-primer stories. Although the parallel story is written with the same words but in a modified order from that of the story in the pre-primer, the picture (see page 167) changes the plot and therefore results in a different story. After the children have been introduced to and have learned the words in the parallel story, they are able to read the story in the pre-primer with ease, although it is a completely new story from their viewpoint. This ability to read a new story gives them a feeling of power not gained by reading the same story in the pre-primer that they have already read in the big book.

Use of Context Clues. Since the ability to use context clues is a valuable skill needed and used by readers from the first grade through adulthood, the story is introduced by means of guiding questions to help the children use clues to discover the wording for themselves. An example of the use of context clues is given in the following sentence: "Betty had six xxxXXxx on her birthday cake." Most children can fill in the unknown word from the total thought of the sentence. This word is obviously "candles." A picture of a cake with the candles on it will help reassure the child that his conclusion regarding the word is correct. In order to make the use of context clues possible, only one unknown word should be used in a sentence. These procedures not only help children learn to use context clues but also force close attention throughout the process. If the teacher were merely to read the line to the children, some would inevitably miss some of the words or even the whole sentence because they have no strong purpose for listening. As they try to discover the wording of the sentences for themselves, however, they are challenged to listen to the guiding questions with strong attention. In addition, the teacher should never do anything for children that they can do for themselves, another reason for these procedures. When the children do the work, they will learn and remember what they have discovered. When the teacher reads the sentence, she is the one who does most of the learning, even though she doesn't need this learning.

Influence of Teacher's Example. The story is always introduced by whole sentences, and practice is given on the individual words after all the children have learned the sentences. If the teacher needs to repeat the sentence after the children have discovered the wording, she must be sure to repeat it smoothly and with expression. This process makes use of the linguists' principles of stress, pitch, and juncture. If the teacher should repeat the sentence by accenting each word separately to help the children notice the words, they will copy her pattern of reading and will tend to become word-by-word readers. The teacher's tone and expression are strong influences in establishing fluent oral and silent reading.

Meaningful Reading. Whole sentences are taught and mastered before single words are taught to give meaning to each word in the sentence through its relationship to each other word. The lack of meaning or the ambiguity of a word standing alone was stressed in Chapter 2. Whole sentences are taught first to help the children learn to see as much of a sentence as they can at a glance. When the children practice on words later to learn to recognize them at sight, the pattern of looking at as much of the text as possible has already been established. Experience has proved that later practice on single words does not break down the habit of reading for thought with resulting fluency and expression, if children master the reading of the sentences first. In fact, some will have already learned the words before actual practice on them has begun.

Establishment of Habits. The importance of establishing the habit of reading for thought from the very first is emphasized by the large proportion of adults who have trouble from word-by-word reading. The child cannot acquire efficient reading habits if he is taught to learn single words only in his beginning steps. Reading habits that are likely to stay with the individual for the rest of his life are established in the first grade.

The time and effort needed to establish efficient habits of reading after children have been taught words in lists is far too costly for both pupils and teachers.

For example, a teacher was given a class of first-grade children during the middle of the year. A word-list, drill-sergeant type of teacher had preceded her. Some of the children were reading in a primer, others were in pre-primers, and a few slow learners had made no real start. To break the word-by-word habit, the new teacher used ordinary techniques and later rather extreme methods to be described in another section. At the end of six weeks the children were still reading like marching soldiers, each word a separate sound as of tramping feet. During the seventh week a few children began to understand and try a little to group their words, but it was not until the end of the year that most of the children were able to read orally with fluency and expression and to gain thought effectively from their silent reading. For these reasons, the plan of teaching pre-primer stories described below is strongly recommended.

Preparation for the Parallel Story

Most reading series follow the activities of a family through the pre-primers and at least part of the way through the primer. At that level other people are gradually introduced in the stories, and later the stories may depart from the particular family and involve other people entirely. When preparing to start the first group of children in the first pre-primer, teachers often pin up the paper doll family members provided by some publishers. If the publishers do not provide these paper dolls, the teacher may prepare her own from magazine pictures mounted on tag for durability. She usually pins name cards of the family members under the dolls. She discusses these dolls and their names with the children for several days before the pre-primer is introduced. She may even remove the name cards from the dolls to permit the children to match the right name to the right doll from memory. When most of the children in the first group can do this, the teacher is ready to start working with them on their pre-primer stories.

Writing the Parallel Story

The parallel story is written by using only the review words that have been introduced in the book up to the point at which the story is to be taught, along with addition of the one or two new words to be introduced. To write the first story, the teacher checks the words to be introduced in the first story in the book.

The First Story. The teacher finds the words to be taught listed in the back of the reader or in the teachers' manual. To develop the thought, she will probably need two words to be used along with the names of the story characters. The names of the characters will have been introduced before the story is presented to the children. The plot of the story will be carried by the picture. Thus, these first pre-primer stories bridge the gap between picture reading and actually reading with symbols.

For example, the picture for the first story in the pre-primer may show Mother ready to cross the street with Sam and Tippy. A car is about to turn the corner onto the street in front of them. The following story spoken in Mother's words may be found below the picture.

> Stop
> Stop, Sam.
> Stop Tippy.
> Make Tippy stop.

To change the plot and thereby virtually change the story, the teacher may make a picture of Tippy running away with one of Peggy's shoes. Peggy is shown standing on one foot because she has lost the other shoe. She is apparently calling to Sam to get her shoe for her. This first parallel story will be written in sentences of two or three words each, and the story will usually be two or three sentences long. The story to be printed on the chart may then be as follows:

> Stop
> Stop, Tippy.
> Sam, Sam!
> Make Tippy stop.

Need for Action. If the teacher has chosen or planned a picture with considerable action or one that shows some humorous situation, it will hold the children's interest despite the wording, which sounds rather inane if presented alone. Similar story plots may show a dog chasing a cat while the children call, "Run, Boots." A cat may be shown up a tree while the children are trying to get it down by calling, "Jump, Boots." In another situation the children may be shown entering a room to find the cat on the breakfast table while they call, "Stop, Boots." These stories are easily extended to two or three lines of repetition. If the picture shows an interesting or funny situation, the repetition will tend to be natural. When excited, children often repeat directions to each other or to their pets in this manner.

Although static situations are sometimes used in pre-primers, the teacher will find it more difficult to motivate the children's interest through these stories. The type of story that shows a child jumping rope followed by the story, "See Susan. Susan can jump," is certainly not very challenging.

Form of the Verbs and Nouns. If the present tense and declarative form of the verb are used in the book, however, the teacher must use this form in her parallel story. *Jump* and *jumps* are completely different words to children at this stage of reading. The same principle applies to the singular and plural forms of nouns.

Need for Review. One or two new words may be added when writing the next parallel story. At the same time the original words should be used again in order to provide review. This procedure is followed in each new chart as the teacher continues to review the old words as often as possible. As more stories are added, however, the use of all the review words in the writing of the story becomes too difficult. The teacher then tries to incorporate the review words in every other story or as often as possible so that the children do not forget these words. Once the teacher has made these charts, they may be used from year to year as long as the same text is in use in the school.

Form of Print. Manuscript is commonly used by teachers both when printing material for children to read and when teaching children to write. Most primary writing manuals give the form of manuscript used by the local school districts. Manuscript is the simplest form of writing or print known. It is therefore easy for children to read. When the teacher prepares charts for the parallel story or puts reading materials on the board, she should be careful to follow the correct form of manuscript given in the writing manuals. Each letter should not only be made correctly but should also be spaced carefully. The spacing between the letters should be uniform, and the letters should be close together enough to give the word unity. If some of the letters are spaced too far apart, the child may tend to see it as two words instead of one. The spacing between the words should also be uniform. The size of a circle, that is, round rather than oval, should be allowed between each word. If the words are spaced too closely together, the child may see two words as one. If the words are spaced too far apart, the child may be forced to look at each word separately rather than to try to group them in thought units.

Substitutes for the Parallel Story Chart

The beginning teacher will be unlikely to have time to write parallel stories and put them on charts for all of her reading groups at once. In such a case the charts should be made for the slowest group, since they will need practice of a variety of kinds before they are ready to begin reading in the book.

Use of the Flannel and Chalk Boards. For the other groups the teacher may put parallel stories on the chalkboard, or she may write each sentence or line of her parallel story on a manila tag reading strip. She may then introduce the story with a picture assembled on the flannel board and with the strips placed in the pocket chart in proper sequence for the story. All the introductory techniques may then be followed in the same way as is done with the parallel story on the chart.

Some teachers make cut-out dolls to serve as the story characters. These pictures are backed with flannel or other material and can be used repeatedly with each new parallel story. The teacher then need only supply the environmental properties for each different story. A picture of a few sprigs of grass and a tree cut out and backed with flannel will serve to suggest an outdoor scene. A cut-out picture of a chair and a table backed with flannel will serve to suggest an indoor scene. These properties may be used over and over again with different stories. Pictures of pets may also be prepared and used in the same way. The use of the flannel board and the sentence strips in the pocket chart are usually adequate for children on the more advanced levels, such as the first reader level.

Use of Sentences From the Book. The teacher who does not have time or is unable for some reason to write a parallel story may introduce the new words directly from the sentences taken from the book. She will check the words to be introduced from the list in the back of the book or in the manual and will then locate sentences in the story in the book that contain these new words. She must be careful to make sure that only one new word is introduced in each sentence so that the children can use context and phonics clues to recognize the word. She may then copy these sentences onto the chalk board and may follow all of the same techniques that are described in the introduction of the parallel story.

The above procedure has several disadvantages. Since the sentences are selected because they each contain a new word to be introduced, they lack story sequence. The use of context clues may then be somewhat more difficult and the children's interest may not be as great. On the pre-primer and primer level, the children may memorize the sentences and read them from memory when they find these sentences in their books. In some cases the uses of sentences taken directly from the book may give away the plot of the story. When the parallel story is used, however, the plot is different so there is no danger of revealing it.

Use of Words in a List. Some teachers introduce the new words by putting them on the chalkboard in a list or by printing them on separate cards. The continuous use of this practice almost invariably tends to cause the children to carry over the habit of looking at one word at a time when they read in the book, and they therefore tend to become word-by-word readers. This practice cannot be condoned even for fast readers in the primary grades since it may result in slowing down some of these readers. The fact that many teachers use this practice is not proof that it is innocuous. Many children fail to develop to their highest potential in reading power.

Another drawback to the introduction of new words in a list is due to the fact that many of them are ambiguous or without adequate meaning when presented alone. In addition, the child is unable to use context clues to help him recognize them. Even in context some words like *read* offer difficulties. The reader must judge from the other words in the sentence whether the word is *read* in the sentence "The child can read well," or *read* in the sentence "John read well yesterday." Some words such as prepositions have very little meaning alone. For example, *on* or *by* are almost meaningless without the rest of the sentence.

Use of Film Strips. In a number of effective programs the new words are presented to the children in stories on slides or film strips. To make these films, the parallel stories may be photographed and made into slides or film strips. They are then projected on a screen where they can be used in the same way as the parallel story is used on a chart. Reading strips and word cards can also be made to accompany these films so that the procedures to be described can be used to advantage in this way.

A program of this type is most easily carried on when following the split reading plan. In such a situation half of the children come to school for reading from nine to ten. The rest of the children join them at ten. The early children then go home at two o'clock, while the children who arrived at school at ten stay on until three o'clock for their reading. This plan is described in more detail in the chapter on trends in reading.

The entire room or a part of it may be darkened during the use of the film strips. Since only half of the children are in the classroom, this half of the class can be divided into two groups. In this way part of the group can work at their seats in the lightest part of the room while the others work on the film strips. Some projectors can be operated without darkening the room, a procedure which is even better than the one just described.

In some districts the pages in the book are photographed, and these are projected for the children to work with instead of using parallel stories. A program reported by Ungaro[1] made use of the above procedures with very effective results.

Outline of Beginning Steps

To help the student and teacher follow the steps involved in the early lessons in the pre-primer, the following outline is presented:

Introduction of the story through:
Interpretation of the picture.
Anticipation of action.
Guiding questions to bring out the wording of the sentences.
Practice, the identification step.
Reviewing the story (at the beginning of each reading period).
Finding or identifying the sentences in order as read by the teacher.
Finding or identifying the sentences in mixed order as read by the teacher.
Building the story in the pocket chart and identifying the sentence strips.
Playing "Guess Who" by identifying strips in children's hands.
Building the story and identifying the word cards.
Playing "Guess Who" by identifying the word cards in the children's hands.

Introduction of the Parallel Story

To help the reader follow the use of a parallel story, the procedures followed by a first-grade teacher, Mrs. Jensen, are given below. The story in the first pre-primer that Mrs. Jensen wished to introduce is illustrated by a dog named Flag, running away with a doll while the owner, a six-year-old girl named Peggy, stands calling to her brother to run after the dog, presumably to get her doll from him. The brother's name is Sam and the doll's name is Linda. The text of the story is as follows:

> Flag
> Run, Sam.
> Run, run.
> Get Linda.

Illustrating the Story. For use in the parallel story, Mrs. Jensen had changed the plot by using pictures cut from magazines. The doll, Linda, had been left on the ground and a sprinkler had been turned on. Peggy was calling to her brother, Sam, to get the doll for her. Mrs. Jensen

---

[1] Daniel Ungaro, "The Split-Vu Reading Program: A Follow-Up," *Elementary English*, XXXXII (March 1965), 254–57, 260.

had repeated the same words as those used in the original story, but had changed the order to some extent.

Because of the difficulty of finding a picture that illustrated this whole scene, Mrs. Jensen had cut out a separate boy, girl, dog, and doll from magazines. For the dog she had found a picture of an Airedale that looked much like Flag in the book. She tried to find a boy, girl, and doll somewhat like the characters in the book. She knew, however, that the pictures did not have to be identical with those in the book, since children are broad-minded about such matters. If challenged, she usually reminded the children that the two Billy's in class did not look alike.

Mrs. Jensen had pasted green paper across the bottom of the page for grass and blue paper across the top for sky. She had cut out a tree from another picture and had drawn the sprinkler and the spray of the water on the picture so that the water was splashing on the doll. Although Mrs. Jensen had no particular ability in drawing, the picture was quite effective when finished.

Printing the Parallel Story. She printed the story in manuscript below the picture. She drew lines to guide her printing and made the letters very carefully because she knew that good manuscript was necessary for children who are learning to read. Mrs. Jensen used four sentences for her story instead of three, but she felt that the first one was very easy because the children already knew the word, Sam. The text of her story is given below:

Linda

Sam, Sam!

Run, Sam.

Get Linda.

Run, run.

Introducing the Story. Mrs. Jensen had spent the first few weeks in teaching readiness and had divided the children into three groups by this time. She had also taught the children how to work independently at their seats, the procedures described in Chapter 22.

Mrs. Jensen asked the children in the fast group, called Robert's group because he was in charge of the workbooks and materials for this group, to come to the reading circle. She said, "I have something new for you today. Watch while I hang this chart on the wall." Questions and exclamations flew about as she hung up the chart, and several hands were raised when she turned around. "What do you think this is, Ronald?" she asked.

"I know," answered Ronald enthusiastically. "It's a story just like the ones in the books on the library table. I know some of the words, too."

"Fine," exclaimed Mrs. Jensen. "Don't tell what they say, yet. Let's see if some other people know what some of the words say. Suppose you tell us about something you see, Joyce."

Joyce replied, "I know the name of the story. It's 'Linda' just like the name of our paper doll on the board."

"It certainly is. Can anyone else tell us about something he sees? Ronald, I'm sure you know one of the names."

Ronald said, "I see Sam's name. It says his name twice on the first line."

"It says, 'Sam' again just under that," added Ben.

"It says Linda's name down toward the bottom of the story," said Janice.

Establishing Purposes. "My, you know all the names!" exclaimed Mrs. Jensen. "What would you like to know about the story?"

"I'd like to know if the doll gets wet," said Joyce.

"It might spoil her hair," said Janice. "My Mother doesn't like to get her hair wet after she has it fixed."

"That's right," responded Mrs. Jensen. "What else would you like to know?"

"I'd like to know if Peggy gets her doll before she gets too wet," exclaimed Sandra.

"I'd like to find out what they are all saying," added Ted.

Interpreting the Picture. "Good," said Mrs. Jensen. "I think I can help you read the story so you can find out some of these things. Now, let's talk about the picture. You already know the names of the children and the dog so that will help you. What is happening in the picture?"

"Peggy is very excited," responded Ted. "Her doll is getting all wet because it's under the sprinkler."

"Yes, I don't blame Peggy," answered Mrs. Jensen. "What do you think she is going to do?"

"I think she wants Sam to get her doll for her," said Sandra. "She is pointing at her doll."

"Why doesn't she get it?" asked Mrs. Jensen.

Milton replied, "She doesn't want to get her hair wet."

Using Guiding Questions as Clues. "I think you're right," said Mrs. Jensen. "If you had a brother named Sam and you wanted him to do something for you, what would you do?" she asked.

"I'd call him," responded Joyce.

"Right. That's what I would do, too," said Mrs. Jensen. Standing at the left, she then placed the pointer under the first line of the story and asked, "How many times did she call his name? When you know, see if you can make it sound the way Peggy would say it."

Janice said, "Sam, Sam!"

"That was very good," said Mrs. Jensen. "Janice sounded excited, didn't she?" She held her pointer under the next line as she said, "Now let's find out what the next line says. If you wanted Sam to get your doll, what would you tell him to do?" she asked.

Arlene said, "I'd tell him to hurry."

"Yes," said Mrs. Jensen. "But what do you want him to hurry to do? What would you say, Billy?"

Billy answered, "I would tell him to run."

"Very good," said Mrs. Jensen. "But whom do you want to run? Tell him what to do and then say his name so he is sure he knows who is to run."

Billy repeated, "Run," and then after hesitating said, "Sam."

"Fine!" exclaimed Mrs. Jensen. "Now try it again as though you really wanted Sam to run."

Billy tried again saying, "Run, Sam." with more expression.

"That's execellent," said Mrs. Jensen as she moved her pointer down. "Now let's try the next line. What did Peggy want Sam to do when he ran?"

"I know," said Joyce. "She wanted him to get Linda."

"Yes, that's just what she wanted him to do," said Mrs. Jensen. "Now, if you wanted Sam to get Linda what would you say?"

"I'd say, 'Go and get Linda,'" responded Victor.

"Yes," said Mrs. Jensen. "That's good, but we've already told him to run so we only need two words. Exactly what do you want to tell him to do when he runs? Can you say just two words that tell him what to do?"

"I can," said Elizabeth. "I'd say, 'Get Linda.'"

"Good," said Mrs. Jensen, "That's just what this sentence says," still holding her pointer under the words "Get Linda." "Now can you tell me what else Peggy said when Sam was a little slow to get started? What did she want him to do?"

Milton said, "She wanted him to run."

"That's just right, Milton," said Mrs. Jensen. "Now you tell him to run. How many times do you see 'run' on the chart?"

Milton said, "Two times."

"Good, then tell him to run twice," said Mrs. Jensen.

Milton responded by saying, "Run, run."

"That's just fine," said Mrs. Jensen. "We will read this story again tomorrow, and then we'll play some games."

SUMMARY

A wide variety of practices for teaching beginning reading are advocated by reading authorities and are suggested in teachers' manuals. The teacher should become familiar with these procedures and should be able to evaluate them for their values and their weaknesses. One procedure may be too brief and superficial for use in teaching slow learners but may be quite adequate for teaching fast learners. On the other hand, a procedure that provides a number of experiences for practice and review may give unnecessary repetition for the fast learner. The teacher must adapt her teaching procedures to the needs of her children.

The parallel story is a good way of introducing the new words to the children. Other procedures are also suggested. The use of context clues and thought are important in all plans for introducing the new words needed in each story to be read by the children.

8

First Steps in the
Pre-Primer

Various opinions are held regarding use of practice. Some authorities suggest that the vocabulary does not need to be mastered as the pupils work in these stories in the pre-primer. Later repetition in the books is meant to establish the vocabulary by using the same words in different contexts. For some children, however, this type of repetition is inadequate, and other activities must be used to establish a firm sight recognition vocabulary.

Games are very effective for practice since they provide high motivation for learning. Games are often more effective when children take turns as leaders when calling on others to respond. This procedure also frees the teacher to observe the needs of individual children. To be successful, the use of leaders demands the establishment of good habits on the part of the pupils when working with each other.

An easy transition may be made from reading on the charts to reading directly in the book. The children first move from the identification step to the actual reading of the charts. They are then ready for an introduction to the first pre-primer.

PRACTICE ON SIGHT VOCABULARY

Even though the vocabulary introduced in the pre-primers is repeated throughout the book, this repetition is often insufficient for average and slow readers. For this reason, a variety of techniques for practice on vocabulary is described.

The Need for Practice

Various procedures are described for the identification step. In this step the teacher uses a variety of procedures for finding sentences read by the teacher on the charts and strips and for finding words on cards to help the children become familiar with them. This step is followed by various procedures to give the children practice in the actual reading of the chart stories, strips, and word cards. These practices are described below.

Children Who Need Practice. The teacher must decide whether or not to use practice at this time on the basis of the children's ability to read the material. Practice may not be needed for all the children in the fast group. If the children are eager to read the sentences to her and if, when given the opportunity, any child can read any sentence, the teacher will decide to progress to the next parallel story. The decision at this point is quite crucial. If a few shy children fail to volunteer for any reading and if they are afraid to try when the teacher gives them the opportunity, the teacher should take the group through the next practice step, which is identification of the sentences.

The word *identification* is used to imply a half-way step; the child can find a sentence read by the teacher although he is unable to read it for himself. The identification step is especially helpful during the very first lessons in reading, particularly for slow learners or children who are afraid to try to read the sentences. They may acquire self-confidence and an association of the sentences with their oral interpretation in this step. After some repetition, they are able to remember the sentences so that they can read them for themselves.

The problem arises concerning what to do with the children in the fast group who do not need practice while the teacher works with those who do. A good compromise can be made by working with the entire group until the more competent children have their turns. The reading for these more competent children should demand the use of more thinking skills than that required for the others in the group. In that way the more competent children have been challenged and have felt that they are a part of the reading group. These faster children may then be dismissed to go to other work while the teacher works with the slower and less self-confident children in this group.

Stigma on the Word, Practice. The use of practice or drill acquired a stigma at one time because of the old type of drill, which was given on isolated words on cards that were "flashed" for the children. The problem was not with the use of cards but with the isolation of the words from context and with the process of "flashing" them. The children were drilled on the cards until they knew them from memory and could name them with considerable speed.

As has been stated, the task of learning words out of context is poor because of lack of meaning of the individual words and because the process of naming them tends to produce word-by-word readers. The demand for speed made by some teachers when using this procedure frightens some children who then become afraid of all aspects of the reading process. This demand for speed when cards are flashed is not only disturbing to some children, but the procedure also fails to give consideration to the natural differences in speed of reaction of various children. The child who is slow to react sometimes gives up trying and is often mistaken for a slow learner by the teacher.

Games have also acquired some stigma because some teachers have used them only with isolated words. Games can be adapted for use with sentences as well as with words and are excellent ways to provide practice in a highly motivated situation. Games and their advantages will be discussed in a later part of this chapter.

Perhaps some authorities are afraid of practice because they have seen it used badly. If the story in a reader is read over and over again or if the words are "flashed" day after day, children may learn to dislike the whole reading process. On the other hand, the teachers who use well-selected games have found that reading becomes one of the most enjoyable times of the day, not only for the children but for the teacher as well. Of course these teachers also give each child opportunity for success and therefore security at his own level.

Effect of Lack of Practice. Failure to provide practice for children who need it can be very harmful, especially to beginners. At this time the child is developing an attitude toward reading that may affect his interest and desire to read or the lack of it over a long period of years. If the child is forced to guess when called upon to read, he will begin to feel insecure. The longer this need to guess is permitted to continue, the more insecure the child will tend to feel. If the teacher implies blame by look, tone of voice, or such comments as, "We had that word yesterday; you should remember it," the feelings of insecurity are intensified. The teacher may tell a needed word to the child if she does so in an encouraging tone of voice. Some teachers, however, permit other children in the group to tell words on which the reader hesitates. Children have little judgment concerning the amount of time a hesitant child may need to recall a word, so they tend to hurl the needed word at him each time he takes a breath. This process tends to make the child give up trying and to fear the whole proceeding.

Dolch has said that children are expected to know about 1500 words at the end of the third grade.[1] He states, "Many do not learn 1500 but only 500. Many learn less." Perhaps this lack is the result of today's tendency to neglect most practice except on phonics.

The wise teacher gives the slower children their choice of material to read, when possible, in order to give them feelings of security. She calls on them to read a sentence they have volunteered for when she can give them time to respond—never in a hurry. She also avoids the procedure illustrated by the following example: In this situation the teacher realized near the end of the period that shy little June had not had an opportunity to read. She looked at the clock and noticed that only a minute or two remained before the class should be dismissed for recess. She therefore said, "I'll read for June today." Translated by June, this statement said, "June is so slow and she reads so poorly, I'll take her turn so she won't make us late for recess." June crawled a little lower in her chair while her feelings of adequacy sank even lower.

Suggestions for Giving Children Security. A few suggestions for helping children feel secure in their reading are given below to summarize some ideas and add others:

1. Give the hesitant child a warm smile when he is called upon.
2. Watch the shy child's eyes. They usually sparkle when he thinks he can respond.
3. Give him an opportunity to respond to something in which he feels secure.
4. Praise him sincerely for effort. The words, "That was a good try," or "You have part of it right," can almost always be said with sincerity. Children can detect insincerity with great sensitivity.
5. Praise each child warmly and generously for success. Even student teachers and regular teachers need praise, too. No one is too young or too old for sincere recognition for their achievements, but children's needs are greater.
6. If the shy child thinks he knows but fails to respond correctly, call on someone else to help him, but give him a chance to succeed very soon thereafter by asking a simple, factual question.
7. Be enthusiastic. If the teacher likes reading, the children will like it too.

First Steps in Practice

The following series of activities for helping children master each lesson is provided to give the teacher a number of steps from which to choose. The teacher may use as many steps as are necessary to give the children feelings of security during reading. She may also use different

[1] Edward W. Dolch, "Individualized Reading vs. Group Reading, I," *Elementary English*, XXXVIII (Dec. 1961), 566–75.

steps for variety so that the children do not become bored. The identification step, if needed, should precede the actual reading practice steps. The identification steps are described below in an actual reading situation.

Identifying the Sentences in Order.   Later Mrs. Jensen said, "Some of you had some questions about the story this morning. Ted wanted to know what the children said. Did you find out, Ted?"

"Yes. It was fun to read the story," replied Ted.

"I think so too," responded Mrs. Jensen. "What other questions did you ask?"

"I asked if Linda got wet," said Joyce.

"I wanted to know if her hair was spoiled," said Janice.

"I'd like to know who got her out of the water," added Ronald.

"Watch for a minute," said Mrs. Jensen, "and all your questions will be answered." She held up a picture as large as the one on the chart showing Sam holding the doll, Linda, in his hands and offering her to Peggy. "When you can read a little more," said Mrs. Jensen, "you can find your answers in the story, but this time you can find them in this picture." The children chattered excitedly about the picture and were satisfied that all their questions had been answered.

Then Mrs. Jensen said, "Now we are going to do something else with the story. You've all worked so hard I'm sure you can find the lines I'm going to read. Who can find the line that says, 'Linda'? Remember, that's the name of the story."

Robert raised his hand and went to the chart to put his hands around the word, "Linda."

Mrs. Jensen said, "Good. Now tell me what it says."

Robert said, "Linda."

"That's fine," said Mrs. Jensen. "Now I'm going to see if someone can find, 'Sam, Sam.' Jimmy, would you like to try?"

Jimmy went to the board and framed the second line.

"Very good," said Mrs. Jensen. "What does that line say?"

Jimmy said, "It says, 'Sam, Sam!' "

"Good! Now let's see if someone can find, 'Run, Sam.' "

Terry went to the board and put his hands around the third line.

"Fine," said Mrs. Jensen. "What does it say?"

Terry responded by saying, "Run, Sam."

"That's very good. Now I wonder if someone can find the sentence that says, 'Get Linda.' "

Ronald went to the board, framed the fourth line, and said, "This says, 'Get Linda.' "

"That's just fine," said Mrs. Jensen. "Can someone find, 'Run, run.'?"

As part of their study of Mexico, these children are making tortillas. Following the recipe also involves functional reading. (Courtesy California State Department of Education.)

Joyce put her hands around the last sentence and said, "Run, run."

"Excellent," said Mrs. Jensen. "I didn't even need to tell Ronald and Joyce to say the sentences after they found them."

Identifying the Sentences in Mixed Order. "Now I'm going to try something that's harder. I'm going to mix up the lines so that you will have to look very hard. I wonder if someone can find, 'Run, Sam.'"

Ben raised his hand, went to the board, and put his hands around the second line saying, "Run, Sam."

"That's exactly right. Can someone find, 'Linda.'?"

Ted went to the board and framed the title, saying, "That says, 'Linda.'"

"Very good," said the teacher. She continued this process until everyone had a turn to frame and repeat one of the sentences.

Identifying the Sentence Strips. Mrs. Jensen may not have needed to continue the practice on this story for her fast group. She might, however, work with the sentence strips and the word cards that are used in this procedure on an actual reading level as an informal test before proceeding to another story with her first reading groups. This story is told as though Mrs. Jensen continued the practice with the same group of children.

Reviewing the Story. On the following day after Mrs. Jensen had called Robert's group to the reading circle, she said, "Let's look at our chart again today. Who remembers what the story was about?"

Carl raised his hand and said, "I know. It was about Linda. Peggy left her on the lawn, and she got wet."

"That's right," said Mrs. Jensen. "Who can tell us something else about the story?"

Sandra volunteered and said, "Peggy didn't want Linda to get wet so she called to Sam to get the doll for her."

"Good. Who can tell us what she wanted Sam to do?"

"She wanted Sam to run to get the doll," said Terry.

"Why did she ask him to run?" asked Mrs. Jensen.

"I know," replied Ted. "Sam would have to run through the water or else he would get wet."

"Do you think Sam would get wet?" asked Mrs. Jensen.

Janice said, "Well, I don't think he would get too wet if he ran, but if he walked he might get pretty wet."

"If you were Sam," asked Mrs. Jensen, "would you go under the sprinkler to get the doll for Peggy?"

Ben replied, "I would, but I'd turn the sprinkler off first."

"That's a fine idea," said Mrs. Jensen. "I wonder if Sam thought of that."

Joyce said, "The story doesn't tell us."

"No, it doesn't," answered Mrs. Jensen. "Maybe we can finish the story for ourselves later."

Building the Story With Sentence Strips. "Now I have something new for you today," said Mrs. Jensen. She picked up from her desk five sentence strips printed on tag, which were exact duplicates of the sentences in the story. She had printed each by placing it below its counterpart in the story and by taking care to keep the size of the letters and the spacing exactly the same as that in the chart story. Mrs. Jensen placed these sentence strips in an extra pocket chart in mixed order. Then she went to the chart story, standing on the left to reinforce the children's reading from left to right. She moved her pointer from left to right under the word, "Linda," saying, "This word starts at the left."

Then she held the pointer steady under the word and said, "This word tells the name of our story. Do you remember what it says?"

Milton replied, "It says, 'Linda.' That's the name of the doll."

"Good," replied Mrs. Jensen. "Now I would like someone to find the word, 'Linda,' on one of these sentence strips. Look at the sentence strips, find the one that says, 'Linda,' and put it under that word on the story chart where I am holding my pointer."

Jimmy volunteered, went to the pocket chart, and picked up the sentence strip on which "Linda" had been printed. Then he moved over to the story chart and held the strip under the title of the story.

"That's very good," said Mrs. Jensen. "Now tell me what your sentence strip says."

"It says, 'Linda,'" replied Jimmy.

"Fine," said Mrs. Jensen. "Please put the sentence strip at the top of the unused pocket chart. We are going to make another story just like the one on this story chart by using these strips and putting them in the pockets. Now let's look at the next sentence." She drew the pointer smoothly under the second sentence, saying, "It says, 'Sam, Sam.'" Then she held the pointer motionless under the sentence. "Who can find 'Sam, Sam,' on one of the strips in the other pocket chart and bring it here for us?"

Ronald volunteered, went to the second pocket chart, and picked up the strip on which "Sam, Sam," had been printed. He then held it under the line, "Sam, Sam" on the story chart and looked at Mrs. Jensen for approval.

"Very good," said Mrs. Jensen. "Now tell us what it says."

Ronald replied, "It says 'Sam, Sam,'" as he put it in the pocket chart.

"Fine. Now I want someone to find the next picture." She dropped her pointer to the next sentence and said, "Who can find 'Run, Sam' among the strips? There are only three sentences left, so it is getting easier to find the sentences."

Joyce went to the extra pocket chart, picked up the sentence, "Run, Sam," and held it under the same sentence on the story chart. She said, "It says, 'Run, Sam.'" Then she put it under the second sentence in the pocket chart.

"That's very good," said Mrs. Jensen. "I don't have to ask you to tell what it says any more. Now I wonder if someone can find 'Get Linda' from the extra pocket chart."

Carl went to the chart and picked up the strip on which "Get Linda" had been printed. He held it under the sentence on the story chart and said, "It says, 'Get Linda.'"

"That's excellent," said Mrs. Jensen. "Now there is just one strip left. I wonder if anyone thinks he knows what that says."

Ben raised his hand and said, "I think it says, 'Run, run.' That's wha Peggy told him to do."

"Good, that's exactly what it says, Ben! Will you please get the sen tence strip and hold it under the line on the story chart where my pointe was."

As Ben did so, he said, "It says, 'Run, run.'" Then he placed it in the pocket chart to complete the story.

First Steps in Scanning. From the very first lesson in the first pre primer, Mrs. Jensen made use of various activities for the type of scan ning described above. The word *scanning* is not used in the conven tional sense of *scanning the newspaper* to find a specific article. A used in the discussion, scanning means to look over a variety of sentence to find a particular one. The process will then be repeated until all the lines have been found and read. As the sentences become longer, the teacher helps the children learn to look at the first word or two in each sentence until they find the correct one, rather than to read each sentence completely. She teaches the children to look at the first word or two by incorporating these words in her questions. Children soon acquire the habit of moving their eyes quickly down the page or chart until they find the desired sentences.

This scanning procedure is taught early so that the children learn to move their eyes over print with considerable speed and then to read a selected line with care and accuracy. Therefore, the child develops flexibility adapted to purposes for reading from the first lessons. The procedure is also used to avoid the thoughtless, inattentive reading that occurs so frequently when a selection is read in sequence without reference to the thought. Mrs. Jensen named the sentence to be found and then waited until each child had found it for himself before she called on a particular child to find it in the pocket chart. If any child was slow enough to force the others to wait, she gave him special help. In this way each child scanned to locate every sentence although he actually placed only one in the pocket chart. Each child also looked for a sentence with a particular thought in mind rather than automatically following the story in sequence. Young children learn this technique in a day or two, a week at the most, and become very adept at locating the answer to a question quite rapidly.

Playing "Guess Who" With Strips. "Now I think we can do some thing that is a little harder. I would like Robert, Ronald, Joyce, Milton, and Ben to come to the front of the circle, pick out one of the sentence strips from the pocket chart and stand in a line in front of the chalk board."

These children did so, each taking one of the sentence strips.

"Very good," said Mrs. Jensen. "Now I'm going to see if someone
tting down can find who is holding one of these sentences. They're
ll mixed up now because we didn't take them out of the chart in order,
) you'll have to look hard. Can anyone find 'Sam, Sam.'?"

Sandra volunteered. Mrs. Jensen said, "Fine. Now go to the children
a the front and point to the one who has the sentence strip that says,
am, Sam.'" Sandra did so and pointed to Ronald's strip. Mrs. Jensen
sked, "Is she right? Does Ronald have the card that says, 'Sam, Sam.'?
erry, what do you think?"

Terry said, "Yes, I think she's right."

"Fine," said Mrs. Jensen. "Then Sandra may have the strip. Please
ive it to her, and you may sit down, Ronald. It will be Sandra's turn
) hold the sentence strip this time. Now let's do that again with an-
ther sentence. I wonder if someone can find who has, 'Run, run.'"

Ted volunteered, went up to Milton and said, "Milton has, 'Run, run.'"

"What do you think about that?" asked Mrs. Jensen. "Is he right,
arl?"

Carl answered, "Yes, Milton does have, 'Run, run.'"

"Very good," said Mrs. Jensen. "Then Ted may have the strip and
Milton may sit down. Now let's see if someone can find who has the
trip that says, 'Linda.'" In this way she gave each child a turn to take
is place in line when he could find the strip that she named. She con-
inued until all of the children had a turn.

Building the Story With Word Cards. She then asked the children
o put the sentence strips back in the chart in order, calling for, "Linda,"
hen, "Sam, Sam," and so on until the story had been rebuilt. She then
aid to the children, "Now I have something else for you. This time it's
;oing to be even harder, but I'm sure you can do it." She picked up a
et of cards on which each word in the story had been printed. When
he was preparing these cards, she had made sure that they were exact
luplicates of the words on the strips. She made them on strips and
hen cut them apart so that they would exactly cover the space below
he words on the sentence strips. She placed the separate word cards
n the extra pocket chart in mixed order.

She then said to the children, "Now we are going to make another
.tory with the word cards just the way we did with the sentence strips.
I have left a space under each strip in the pocket chart so that we can
nake another line exactly like it. Let's start with 'Linda' again at the
op of the pocket chart." She stood at the left holding her pointer under
he word, "Linda" at the top of the pocket chart. Then she said, "Who
:an find the word 'Linda' among all of these cards? Now you will have
o look at nine cards instead of just five sentence strips as before."

Janice volunteered, went to the extra chart, and picked up the car "Linda."

"Very good," said Mrs. Jensen. "Now, put it in the space under th word to which I am pointing on the pocket chart." After Janice did s Mrs. Jensen said, "Good. Now what does it say, Janice?"

Janice said, "It says, 'Linda.'"

"Fine. Now I wonder if someone can find one of the two cards th say 'Sam.'"

Carl picked up a card that said "Sam" from the extra pocket chart an held it under the word to which Mrs. Jensen was pointing. He said, " says 'Sam,'" as he slipped it into the pocket below the sentence.

"My, that's fine," said Mrs. Jensen. "Let's see if someone can fin another card that says 'Sam.'"

Jimmy volunteered, picked up the second card that said "Sam," an slipped it into the place under the sentence that said, "Sam, Sam."

"Good. What does it say, Jimmy?" asked Mrs. Jensen.

"It says 'Sam,'" he replied.

Playing "Guess Who" With Word Cards. In this way the childre rebuilt the story with single words. After the rebuilding of the stor had been completed, Mrs. Jensen asked some of the children to com to the front of the circle and take the word cards off the pocket char Each child held a card in his hand as he stood in a row in front of th group in the same way that the children had done when they had th sentence strips before. This time they repeated the activity of findin the child who was holding a given card, naming it, and replacing th child in the row as had been done previously with sentence strips. By thi time Mrs. Jensen felt that the children were very sure of the identificatio of the words and decided that she would be able to begin the regula reading process tomorrow when the group met.

Helping in Case of Error. In one case Terry made an error by pick ing up the card for "Sam" in response to Mrs. Jensen's request to fin the word "Run," which she had framed with her fingers on the stor chart. To help Terry she said, "Bring your card up here and put it righ under my word. Mine says 'Run.'" As Terry held the word "Sam" unde the word, "Run," Mrs. Jensen asked him, "Do you think your word look like mine?"

Terry said, "It looks a little like yours. They both have big letter at the beginning."

Mrs. Jensen replied, "Let's look at the big letter in my word and th big letter in yours. Do they look just the same?"

Terry said, "No. They don't look the same. I remember now. My card says 'Sam.'"

"Fine," responded Mrs. Jensen. "Do you remember what I said my card says?" Terry had forgotten so Mrs. Jensen called on Milton to tell him that the word said "Run." "Milton is right," said Mrs. Jensen. "Now, Terry, would you like to look again to see if you can find the card that says 'Run'?"

Terry went back to the extra pocket chart and found "Run" after looking carefully at all the words. He brought it back to the story chart and said, "I think this one says 'Run.'"

"Fine!" exclaimed Mrs. Jensen. "You have it right this time. Both of our cards do say 'Run.'" In this way Mrs. Jensen helped the children correct their errors, when possible, in order to help them acquire self-confidence and to learn the correct responses.

USE OF PUPIL LEADERS

The use of pupil leaders in games serves not only as an effective type of pupil motivation but also provides some valuable social learnings. On the other hand, the student or beginning teacher should know the problems involved if she is to be able to use these procedures successfully.

Suggestions for the Use of Pupil Leaders

Children who have never worked with pupil leaders before often become very excited and eager to have a turn to be called upon and to act as a pupil leader as soon as possible. Therefore they are likely to become noisy in their demands for attention. They cry to the pupil leader, "Call on me! Call on me!" In order to still the cries, the teacher reminds the leader to call on someone who is sitting quietly. The silence then becomes intense. As this suggestion is given from time to time, the leaders themselves often adopt the technique. A leader will say, "I am going to call on someone who is sitting quietly." This statement always silences the clamor and brings the group back to order. After a few experiences the children realize that their turns depend upon their co-operation. In a week or so the problem disappears.

Control of Desire to Maintain Status. The desire of the pupil leader, who is in this position for the first time, to keep his status results in another problem. He finds the opportunity to call on children quite gratifying. Therefore, he tends to look back and forth from one child to another, holding the suspense as long as he can before he actually makes a choice. He may be in a position to dispense or withhold a favor for the first time in his life. This new power is sweet and is not easily released. The teacher is patient at first. After a pause she may remind the child that everyone is waiting for him to make a choice. If he still delays, the teacher may mention that she may have to make the choice for him if he prolongs the game too much. If he continues to delay too long, she may do so. Usually the loss of choice takes care of the problem, and the child realizes that he must make his choice within a reasonable time in fairness to the other children. He also learns that his turn will be lost if he monopolizes the time. This problem arises only at the beginning of the use of leadership procedures. In two or three days the children understand what is expected of them, and the period moves along quite smoothly.

Control of Cliques. A third problem that arises with the use of pupil leaders involves the tendency of children to call on their own particular friends. In addition, the girls call on girls, and the boys call on boys. Once a clique gets control, it holds its power as tightly as a city alderman and his henchmen.

In regard to choice of sex, the teacher may call the children's attention to the problem and ask for a solution. The children usually decide to make a rule that a boy must call on a girl, and that a girl must call on a boy. They like fairness and are willing to abide by the decision of the group. The rule should be enforced by the teacher since some of the children may forget their rule. After two or three weeks it becomes unnecessary to enforce the rule since the children develop a good understanding of fair procedures. The dropping of the rule, however, should be discussed so that the children understand and agree to this change. Since the rule was made democratically, it should be changed in the same manner.

The teacher may help the children solve the problem caused when children call only on their friends by another discussion. The children will notice or will be able to anticipate the resulting neglect of some children when others have several turns in close sequence. They usually establish a rule that no one may be chosen a second time until everyone has had one turn. Children usually agree to this plan. As they begin to develop habits of fairness, some of them will ask the children who have not yet had a turn to hold up their hands so that they can call on one of them. If they forget, the teacher reminds them. The teacher must take the responsibility of bringing such a problem to the group since they will not think of doing so themselves.

Values in Use of Pupil Leaders

One of the greatest values of the use of pupil leadership is its resulting degree of motivation. Children respond very enthusiastically in this situation, and it seems to take on the aura of a game for them. The situation also frees the teacher, as has been mentioned previously, to watch the children's reactions and to observe needs for special helps. She must still, however, keep the situation in mind and make sure that the leader and the children called upon follow the rules they have made for themselves.

Values in Physical Movement. The practice of permitting children to leave their seats to exchange cards or to carry out any other procedure is very valuable in keeping high attention on the part of the group. It is also helpful in providing them with a chance to break the strain of sitting still for a long period. Little children find the problem of either sitting or standing quietly extremely tiring; therefore any legitimate break that does not distract from their attention is valuable.

Values in Social Skills. The children acquire important social skills in taking turns as leaders and followers. They learn the importance of fairness, as has already been mentioned, so that they develop a feeling of responsibility for seeing that every child has a turn. As the children take turns acting as leaders, they acquire poise with a minimum of self-consciousness. When they take their turns as leaders, their minds are focused so strongly on the game that they forget about the fact that they are in the public eye.

The desire to succeed in giving a correct response is very strong because every child is very eager to have his turn as leader. If he fails to respond correctly, he forfeits his turn. Some teachers, however, make a rule that he must have a chance to succeed before anyone else has a second turn. Therefore he is called upon later. In this way children learn also to provide opportunities for others to succeed, another aspect of responsibility for other people.

Values in Status. Children who tend to be isolates receive recognition from others when they face the group in a position of leadership. Since the leadership role is very simple by the time the children have repeated it a number of times, the shy child is usually able to respond in this rather patterned situation. However, this position gives him an opportunity for others to get to know and respect him. He may therefore be chosen by other children for other activities and may gradually acquire a greater acceptance than he had previously.

Use of Leaders in Small Group Activities

When the children have learned thoroughly to take turns as responsible leaders and followers, this activity may be used with a few children who need extra practice. Three or four children may be permitted to go to a quiet part of the room to play one of the games, taking turns as leaders and followers. The practice that they give each other is fully as valuable as that which they receive in the larger group, yet they have more turns for responses. The teacher makes a point of setting up these small group activities with care and watches to be sure that they are successful.

The first children to take part in a small group activity while others are working in the room may be made up of children who have an unusually high sense of responsibility even though they may not need the practice activity. In this way the group activity is conducted successfully, and the teacher makes a point of giving considerable status to these children because of their willingness to work together in a cooperative and responsible manner. One small group activity at a time is a good rule for a beginning teacher. If any of the children who are permitted to take part in these small group activities become noisy or inconsiderate of the group, the teacher may stop the activity. She then asks a member of the class to repeat the rules followed in such a small group activity. She may send the noisy member to his seat to carry on other work while he is replaced by someone who feels he can accept the responsibility successfully. Although this loss of turn may seem a little harsh to the child who has not co-operated well, it is basic in setting up successful small group activities. If children are allowed to get out of hand, the activities will have to be abandoned, which penalizes co-operative children as well as the one or two who may not have been co-operative.

READING THE PARALLEL STORY

The use of a parallel story was discussed, along with the place of practice in the beginning program. The identification step was described as a way of familiarizing children with the vocabulary in a beginning story before actual reading was undertaken. The first steps in actual reading are discussed in this section of the chapter.

Up to this point Mrs. Jensen had read the sentences on the charts and on the strips for the children to find. This effort to identify the strips gave the children a strong purpose for listening and also gave them an opportunity to react physically to the reading situation. Mrs. Jensen's request to the children to repeat each sentence orally after it was identified was planned to make certain that each child had in mind the correct words of the sentence to which he pointed. The entire identification step was planned to give each child an opportunity to associate the visual and auditory stimuli with both an oral and a physical response in order to help fix the sentence and the words in his mind. Thus the child had experiences with two learning stimuli and two types of responses.

The Reading Step

By the time Mrs. Jensen moved to the reading step, the children had partially learned the words, and some knew the story from memory, although this memorization was not one of the objectives of this story. The change from the identification step to the reading was so gradual, the children often failed to realize that they were progressing to a more difficult step in the next activity.

Reviewing the Parallel Story. On the day following the last lesson described earlier in this chapter, Mrs. Jensen asked the children to review the story for her briefly. She said, "Perhaps one of you can review the story for us without help today," as she pointed to the chart on the wall.

Ted volunteered, saying, "The story is about Peggy's doll. She left it out on the lawn. Then someone turned on the sprinkler, and the doll got wet. Peggy wanted Sam to get the doll for her."

Reading Sentences Selected by Pupils. "Very good," replied Mrs. Jensen. "I think that some of you can tell me what these sentences say. Find any sentence that you would like to read and raise your hand when you are sure that you know it. Look at the whole sentence with your eyes so that you can tell me what all of it says."

Milton raised his hand and said, "I know the first line. It says, 'Linda.'"

"Fine," said Mrs. Jensen. "Please come to the chart and frame the sentence with your hands. Stand a little to the left, on my side, so that everyone can see. Then read the line for us again."

Milton went to the chart, framed the line, and said, "It says 'Linda.'"

"Excellent," said Mrs. Jensen. "Who can find another sentence that he knows? Be sure to look at all of it before you raise your hand."

Robert volunteered, went to the chart, and framed "Run, run!" Then he said, "This sentence says, 'Run, run!'"

"My! You certainly know the story well. Who can read another sentence for us? Be sure to read to the end of the sentence with your eyes."

Sandra volunteered and read the sentence that said "Sam, Sam!"

"Fine! Who else can read a sentence by looking clear to the end?"

Joyce went to the chart, framed, and read, "Run, Sam."

"Very good," said Mrs. Jensen. "There is only one sentence left. Who knows what it says?"

Jimmy said, "I know what it says." He then went to the chart, framed, and read, "Get Linda."

Choosing Sentences and Pre-reading. Mrs. Jensen continued this process until each child had had a chance to read a sentence of his choice. Each time she reminded the child to read the whole sentence silently (with his eyes) before he was ready to read it orally. Although first grade children tend to look at each word separately, they should be encouraged to pre-read the sentence, that is, to read it silently to avoid the beginning of word-by-word reading. The present vocalizing process tends to become the subvocalizing process of later reading. If the child learns to read the words in a thought sequence now, he will be much more likely to *think* the words in a thought sequence as he progresses to more mature silent reading. That is, he will learn to use a better eye-thought span.

When teaching these early stories Mrs. Jensen made a point of encouraging each child to chose the sentence he wished to read during this step in the program in order to insure the child's success. She knew that not all of the children were able to read all of the sentences at this time.

After each child had had a turn to read a sentence of his choice, Mrs. Jensen said, "I think someone can read the whole story for us." Some children are always able to read the whole story at this stage, although the process is a matter of half memory, half reading. Mrs. Jensen called on Ronald who had volunteered. She held her pointer under each sentence to help the other children keep the place as he read the story.

Practice on the Reading Step

If all the children are able to succeed in reading the sentences with ease, no further practice will be needed at this time. If, however, the children are unsure of some of the sight words in these sentences or if they fail to read the sentences with fluency, they will need further practice with the sentence strips.

Building the Story by Reading the Sentences. For the next step Mrs. Jensen had placed the sentence strips out of sequence in her second pocket chart. She now moved her first pocket chart to a position between the chart story and the second pocket chart. She said, "Let's see if you can make the story out of these sentence strips again. This time I will not read any of the sentences for you. Who would like to find the name of the story, read it for us, and put it in the top of this pocket chart?"

Janice volunteered, went to the second chart, picked out the strip that said "Linda," and placed it at the top of the first pocket chart.

"Very good," said Mrs. Jensen. "Now please tell us what it says."

"That's easy," replied Janice. "It says 'Linda.'"

"Fine," replied Mrs. Jensen. "Let's look at the chart story to see which line comes next. Then someone can find it for us."

Ted volunteered, picked up the strip that said "Sam, Sam!" and placed it under "Linda" in the first pocket chart. He said, "That strip says, 'Sam, Sam!' "

Calling on Others to Read the Sentences. Other children offered to read the rest of the sentences until the story had been rebuilt. Then Mrs. Jensen asked a child to read the completed story. Some children seemed hesitant to volunteer since they did not have the opportunity to select a particular sentence about which they felt confident. For this reason, Mrs. Jensen decided to use another practice technique. She permitted five children to select one sentence each that they were sure they could read and asked them to stand so that the sentences were in mixed order. They stood in front of the group to play a modified version of the original activity that she had called "Guess Who." This time each child had a turn to choose and call on one of the children in his seat who volunteered to read the sentence strip that he held. If the child who was called upon read the sentence correctly, he took the strip and replaced the first child in line. Then the second child in the original line had an opportunity to call on another of the seated children to read the sentence he was holding and so on until all children had a chance to take a place in the line and call on another for the reading.

Sometimes Mrs. Jensen told the children to take turns according to their order in line. In this way she was able to give full attention to the reading and to make notes concerning any particular child who seemed to need special help. At other times she called on various children in line to take their turns without regard to order. However, she always gave the children in the line their opportunity to select the child whom they wished to choose for the reading. Even in the games Mrs. Jensen encouraged the children to read the sentences with good fluency. If any child read a sentence as he would a list of words, she assured him that his reading was correct but told him that she felt sure he could make his sentence sound more like a story. The child was usually able to repeat this sentence with fluency after a second or third attempt.

She continued practice until every child could read all the strips and all the words out of context. Practice with the slower children was carried on after the faster learners had been allowed to go to other work. For this purpose Mrs. Jensen continued to use games to avoid boring the children or creating negative attitudes. If one or two of the children needed an undue amount of practice Mrs. Jensen knew that such a child belonged in a slower group.

Mrs. Jensen did not use practice on phonics at this time. The rule

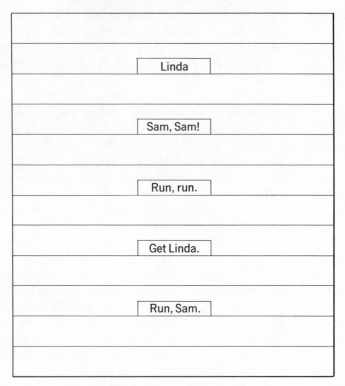

Fig. 8–1. A sample of a pocket chart with the sentence strips placed in sequence ready for the matching of words.

mentioned in Chapter 2 regarding the introduction of phonics states that beginning sounds are introduced when the children have already learned three words beginning with the same letter sound and have been introduced to the fourth in the current lesson.

Building the Story by Reading the Words.   In order to give the children practice on the actual reading of the words, Mrs. Jensen made an extra strip for each line in the parallel story. She usually placed each strip under the original and was careful to make the letters the same size and shape as those on the original strip. She was also careful to make the spacing between the letters and also between the words the same size as those on the original. If the duplicate strip is not identical with the original, the children often are unable to match them. Even a blot of ink on one may cause the children to have trouble with the matching. The teacher then cut apart the words on the duplicate strip.

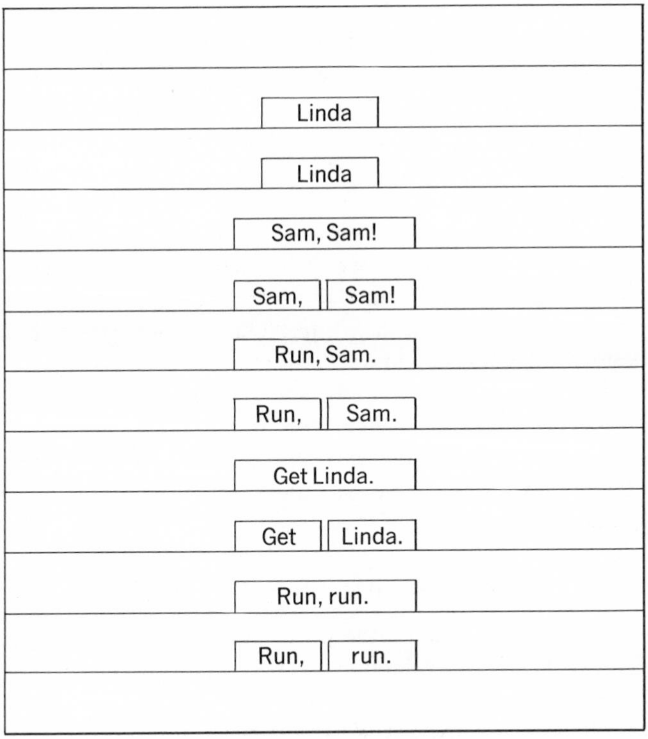

Fig. 8–2. A sample of a pocket chart after the word cards have been matched with the sentence strips in sequence.

Mrs. Jensen usually placed the strips in one pocket chart and put the words in mixed order in the second pocket chart. She then asked the children to read the story from the strips to review the sequence. She next suggested that the children might pick out any word they were able to read from the second pocket chart, read it to the class, and match it to the sentence in the pocket chart where it belonged. The child might slide the word into the pocket chart directly over its counterpart. Sometimes, however, Mrs. Jensen left a space under each sentence strip so that each could be rebuilt with the words placed directly below it. A diagram of the chart set up in this way is shown in Figure 8-1. The pocket chart as it looks after the children have placed the matching words in each sentence is shown in Figure 8-2.

Calling on Others To Read the Words. If all of the children are able to read the words with success as they match them to the story, no further practice is necessary. If they are not sure of all the words, how-

ever, they may play the "Guess Who" game. In order to carry on thi
activity Mrs. Jensen allowed each of nine children to select any of th
word cards they wished from the pocket chart. They then stood in lin
and played the game in the same way as they had played it with th
sentence strips. The first child in line chose a child in his seat to read
the card. If the chosen child was able to do so, he took the place of th
original child in the line. The second child then chose someone to read
his card and was replaced in the same way. If any child who was called
upon to read failed to read the word correctly, he remained in his sea
instead of replacing the child in line. The child in line then called o
another to read his word successfully. The teacher was careful to b
sure that the child who had failed had a second turn so that he would
be able to succeed and take his place in line. This activity can b
carried on as long as the teacher feels the practice is needed. Every
child should have at least one turn to succeed and take his place i
line, but each child may be given a number of turns if this much repeti
tion is needed.

READING IN THE FIRST PRE-PRIMERS

Some teachers permit the children to read the story in the pre-primer
immediately after the introduction of the words through the paralle
story. Other teachers introduce enough parallel stories to cover th
vocabulary of the first third of the pre-primer before putting them in the
children's hands. Still others introduce the entire eighteen to twenty-one
words used in the first pre-primer by means of about ten or twelve
charts before they give the books to the children to read.

Introducing a Section of the Book

Although some teachers permitted the children to read the first story
in the pre-primer which Mrs. Jensen had just introduced, she preferred
to introduce the first third of the book on parallel story charts before
putting it in the children's hands. In this way the children had a reasonable amount of story material to read in their pre-primer instead of the
very short, rather superficial material that they would meet in the first
story.

The ability to read a section of the book when it is first introduced
gives the children a much greater feeling of power than they achieve
when reading the first story. Since about eighteen to twenty-one words
are introduced in most pre-primers, the teacher introduces the first seven
or eight words, which may require five or six parallel stories. The children will then be able to read approximately fifteen pages in the book

Procedures for the Beginning Teacher. The beginning teacher may safely introduce approximately a third of the book with charts before giving the books to the children. A fast group of children can usually master the necessary seven or eight words in parallel stories in about two weeks. The problem of public relations with parents will usually allow this much time before the parents begin to ask why the children have not yet been given books. Although some advantages are found in the procedure of introducing the entire book at one time, the parents tend to complain if a relative's or neighbor's child is reading in a book much in advance of their own children. When the children are able to read the first third of a pre-primer, the wise teacher usually lets the children take their books home to read to their parents. This procedure completely reassures the parents and makes it possible for the teacher to introduce the next section of the book through parallel stories without the parent's concern regarding the children's progress.

Procedures Followed by an Experienced Teacher. An experienced teacher who has won the confidence of the parents in her school district may use parallel stories for the entire vocabulary of the first pre-primer before introducing this book. If a new child has entered the class, this teacher would be wise to have an informal conference with parents in order to help them understand the procedure and to know why their child does not bring a book home until he is able to read it in its entirety.

The policy of introducing each entire pre-primer on charts was followed in an eastern city. When the teacher first tried this procedure, she had planned it carefully with the parents. When the children in the fast group had completed their first set of charts at the end of about six weeks, the teacher invited the children's mothers to visit school on a particular day. At this time she presented the books to the children for the first time. They were very excited about them but rather fearful of their ability to read them.

The teacher suggested that each child take his mother to a selected part of the room and read his book aloud to her. The children were amazed and delighted to find that they were able to read the entire book, and the mothers were equally delighted. Although it was somewhat difficult for the teacher to continue her work with the other children, the appreciation of the mothers more than compensated for the slight inconvenience. The following year the mothers who were invited to share their children's first reading debut asked if they might bring the fathers. From then on it was quite common for the fathers to take a day off work in order to attend this event.

SUMMARY

After the children have mastered the vocabulary in the identification step, they will be ready to read the parallel story. If any vocabulary difficulties arise during the reading, the teacher may use other activities and games for practice on the reading level. Some teachers follow this step by the reading of a short story, two or three pages, in the pre-primer itself. Other teachers use the parallel stories to teach the vocabulary needed in about a third of the pre-primer and then put the books in the children's hands. Some experienced teachers teach the vocabulary of the entire pre-primer in parallel stories before putting the book in the children's hands.

9

Oral and Silent Reading

As more review words along with the new words are introduced in the parallel story, the identification step is dropped, and greater dependence on the use of context clues is developed. Practice on these stories is still needed by many children, but more interesting games may be used at this level because children have greater power in reading.

The use of carefully planned procedures for introducing good techniques in oral and silent reading may provide the child with efficient methods of reading and establish good reading habits that may be of value for the rest of the child's life. If the child acquires poor habits at this time, his reading may be handicapped for years, or he may be forced to spend many hours in remedial classes that could have been avoided by a careful introduction of these reading steps.

The introduction of these first steps in silent and oral reading should be successful if the child is ready for these steps. As prerequisites, he must have mastered the sight vocabulary that has been presented up to this time, and he must have acquired the skills described in Chapter 6. This is no time for the teacher to "drag the child" along in order to "cover the book."

Parental pressures are great at this time, and the teacher may also be concerned about the child's promotion at the end of the year. Some school districts insist that the child have read certain books before he is promoted. Any pressure to advance too rapidly at this time, however, may result in a lasting handicap and should be resisted. The child can much more safely progress more rapidly at a later stage.

Introducing a Longer Parallel Story

As the children progress farther along in the pre-primers, they acquire a number of sight words which are continuously reviewed in later stories after they have been introduced. Since only one new word is introduced in a sentence and since some sentences contain no new words, the identification step is no longer needed. The introduction, however, is still very important.

Purposes for the Use of the Parallel Story. At this stage the teacher uses the parallel story to introduce the new sight words in sentence context. To develop the continuity of the story, some sentences will contain only review words. The teacher guides the reading of the story line by line by means of questions. The use of guiding questions during these beginning stages is crucial in establishing reading with thought from the very beginning.

When a new word is contained in a sentence, the teacher helps the children read the known words and fill in the unknown words by means of context and picture clues. In the example of the sentence, "Betty had six xxxXXxx on her birthday cake," most children can fill in the unknown word *candles* by the use of context clues. The use of context is possible when only one new or unfamiliar word is introduced in a sentence. To summarize this step, (1) the teacher guides the reading of each sentence in sequence by means of a thought question, and (2) she helps the children fill in each unknown word through the use of context and picture clues. Occasionally an abstract word may be very difficult to introduce by means of context clues. In such a case the teacher may then directly tell the children the word.

The teacher could save time by telling the children all the new words. By using this shortcut, however, the teacher would fail to give the children opportunity to learn to use context clues, a skill that all good readers use from the first grade through adulthood.

Example of a Parallel Story. The following parallel story, which is printed on a chart, may serve as an example of a story used toward the end of the first pre-primer and in connection with the second and third pre-primers:

The Cake

Susan said,
"Get a chair, Betty.
I want the cake."

Betty said,
"Here is a chair,
I can get the cake."

Mother said, "Stop.
This cake is for dinner."

This parallel story was written to introduce the new words *chair* and *cake*. The picture should show a freshly baked cake on a high cupboard shelf. Susan, who is about three-years old, and Betty, who is about six, are shown at the left of the table. Betty has her hand on a chair. On the right side is a door through which Mother is entering.

Introduction of the Story With Discussion. A teacher may introduce this story through the following questions and their discussion: What do you see in the picture? What kind of cake is it? Why do you think Mother put it on a high shelf? What do you think Susan and Betty are going to do? Why does Betty want the chair? What do you think Mother will say when she sees Susan and Betty? What do you think Mother plans to do with the cake? In this way the general idea of the story is brought out, and the new words *chair* and *cake* are used several times in the conversation.

The children must first discover the name of the story since *cake* is a new word for them. In discussing a possible title some child is sure to suggest *The Cake* as suitable. When he does, the teacher reassures him that he has guessed the name of the new story, holds her pointer under the title, and asks him to repeat his suggestion in order to read the title to the class.

Use of the Sentences for Reading. Then the teacher asks if someone can read the name of the child who is speaking, as she holds her pointer under the words, "Susan said." Any child will be able to respond, since these words are known. The teacher reassures the child and asks if anyone knows what Susan said, as she drops her pointer to the next line. The words *Get, a,* and *Betty* are review words, but the word *chair* has been introduced only through discussion. Some child may be able to fill in the word *chair* from thought or from the picture and read the sentence successfully.

If no child is able to read the entire sentence, the teacher may ask someone to read the first two words. After a child has responded with the words *Get* and *a* the teacher may say, "Let's look at the picture. What does Susan want Betty to get?" From this question any child should be able to respond with the word *chair*. The teacher then asks the child to read the whole sentence telling her what Susan said. The child should then be able to read the whole sentence, "Get a chair, Betty." The teacher will reassure the child that his response is correct.

The teacher will drop her pointer under the next sentence and ask for a volunteer to read the sentence that tells what Susan wants. Since the first three words are review, some child will be able to read them

The listing of assignments on the board with page references for these third-grade children involves them in the functional reading of higher numbers. (Courtesy California State Department of Education.)

and will be very likely to fill in the word *cake* from context. If not, the teacher will ask what Susan wants and may even remind the child that it is on a high shelf. When the word *cake* is supplied, the teacher asks the child to reread the sentence telling what Susan says she wants. The child will then read the sentence, "I want the cake."

Dropping her pointer down to the next line, the teacher asks who spoke next. Any child in the group will be able to identify Betty as the speaker and will read this line. The teacher's next question then is, "What did Betty first say?" All of the words in this line except the last are review so a child is able to respond with the words, "Betty said, 'Here is a . . .'" If the child hesitates on the word *chair*, the teacher may suggest that he look at the picture or that he recall what Susan wanted Betty to get before she got the cake. The child will be able to conclude that the word is *chair*. The teacher may ask the child to repeat what Betty said in order to achieve expression, as follows, "Here is a chair." She may then add, "Betty said something else. I wonder if someone can read this sentence," as she moves her pointer down. Since *cake* is a colorful word, most children can remember it after the first introduction or use thought to supply it. Therefore some child is likely to be able to read, "I can get the cake." The teacher then reassures the child that he is right.

All of the words in the last two sentences are review words except the word *cake*. The teacher may now ask, "Who speaks next?," holding her pointer under the next line. Since the child knows all of the words in this sentence he may say, "Mother is talking. The sentence says, 'Mother said, "Stop."'"

After reassuring the child, the teacher may drop her pointer to the last sentence and ask if anyone knows what else Mother said. She may remind the children that the second word is new today, but it is also given in the name of the story. From this hint some child should be able to read, "This cake is for dinner." In case any child reads in a faltering manner, the teacher always asks him to reread. She may suggest that he make the reading sound the way Mother would say it.

Practice on the Parallel Story

The children in the first group will need very little practice on this story since only two words were introduced. The word *cake* has such a colorful meaning that the children may be fairly sure of it by the time the story has been introduced. The word *chair* is also somewhat colorful. In addition, it is a noun or the name of an object. Such words are usually easy for children to remember. To make sure, however, that the children are secure in this new vocabulary, the teacher may use such a game as "What's My Line?" for a brief practice on the sentences.

Practice on Sentences With the Game "What's My Line." The easiest way to introduce a new game is to start to play it, the teacher taking the leading part and giving directions as she goes along. To introduce "What's My Line" she may say, "I am thinking of one of the sentences in this story. I wonder if someone can come up, hold the pointer under a sentence, and read it to guess if I am thinking of this line." She makes sure that each child stands at the left of the chart to hold the pointer in order to reinforce the left to right process of reading. After a child has selected and read a sentence, she may say, "You read it correctly, but it is not the sentence that I am thinking about." Other children are given turns until some child guesses the teacher's particular sentence by reading it.

The teacher then tells the child who guessed the right sentence that he is to be the new leader. He must choose a line and whisper it to her so that none of the other children can hear it. This step is necessary since the child may later change his mind about his choice afte₁ he begins to play the game, or he may actually forget his choice. Occasionally a child may change his choice of sentence in order to keep the position of leader.

After the child has selected a sentence, he stands farther back to the left and calls on any child he chooses to guess his line. The chosen child comes to the left side of the chart, holds the pointer under his selected sentence, and reads it. The leader usually tells him that his sentence is or is not right without the reassurance that the sentence was read correctly. If it was not read correctly, the teacher usually offers help by reference to the story on the chart and use of context or picture clues. When some child finds the sentence that the leader has chosen, this child becomes the new leader, and the game continues until all of the children have had a chance to read a line. If more practice is needed, the game may continue until all children have had a turn to be leader.

Procedures Necessary for Practice. When playing such a game as "What's My Line," the child must actually go to the chart or board and hold the pointer under the line he is guessing. If he reads it from his seat, the teacher cannot be sure that he is actually reading. He may merely be recalling a line he remembers. In addition, when he holds the pointer under a sentence, he must actually read it. Often a child will say, "Is it this sentence?" In such a case the teacher has no assurance that the child can read it. Both steps in the process are necessary to insure learning.

The teacher always holds the pointer under an entire sentence and teaches the children to do the same. She never points to each word in the sentence, and she does not allow the children to do so. Such a procedure would cause the children to focus their attention on one word at a time, a procedure which the teacher constantly works to avoid. She also watches the children's lips to make sure that they are "reading with their eyes" and reminds them to use their eyes rather than their lips whenever he sees a child moving his lips. (Lip movement and vocalization were discussed in Chapter 2.) Even though the sentences in the second and third pre-primers are longer than those in the first pre-primer, the teacher continues to encourage the children to read the entire sentence silently before reading it orally. This practice helps the children avoid word-by-word reading.

Some teachers feel that pointing to words and lip movement are inevitable aspects of the beginning reading process. They feel that children should be permitted to point to words and to vocalize during the first grade and that the habit should be eliminated later. Many years of experience prove that children do not need to and should not be allowed to acquire either bad habit. Experience has also shown that months of strenuous effort are required by both teacher and pupil to break such bad habits. In the struggle that ensues children may lose all interest and pleasure in reading. The use of charts and games on the chalkboard seems to make reading easier for children to learn without recourse to these bad habits, but the teacher should be alert to the first signs of such habits and should eliminate them before they become established.

Practice on Words With "Tick-Tack-Toe." For practice on words, the teacher may use the "tick-tack-toe" game. The teacher draws on the board the diagram shown in Figure 9-1. Each of two squares in the

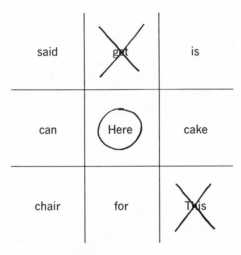

Fig. 9–1. An example of a tick-tack-toe game used for practice on sight words.

diagram are filled with one of the two new words, and other words on which the teacher feels the children need review are printed in other squares.

The teacher may divide the group into two teams according to the way the children are seated. One side may use X's for their choices, and the other side may use O's. The first child on Team A may go to the board, point to a word, and name it. If he is correct, he may place an X on the word, which may not then be chosen by the other side. Then the first child on Team B goes to the board, points to a word, and names it. If he has read it correctly, he may put an *O* on it. In this way a member of each team alternates in reading words until one group gets a series of three marks in order vertically, horizontally, or diagonally. If only part of the children have had a turn at play, the game may be played again to give every child a chance to select and read a word. The new words and the words on which the children need the most review are selected for the game.

Practice on Phonics. Since no practice is given on phonics with beginning sounds unless the children already know three sight words beginning with the particular letter involved in the new word, no phonics helps are used with the new word *chair* because it begins with the digraph *ch.* Because the children are not yet ready to learn digraphs on the pre-primer level, the teacher does not use phonics as a help with this word.

If the children already know three sight words beginning with the letter hard *c,* preferably *c* followed by long *a,* the teacher may give practice on this letter in word context in connection with the new word *cake.* At the reading level under discussion the only other words the children are likely to know beginning with small hard *c* are *came, can,* and *cat.* Therefore the teacher may decide to use these words with *cake* to help teach the beginning hard *c.*

In the lesson described the teacher put these three words on the board and asked a different child to read each one, followed by a child who read all three. She then asked, "Who can tell me what parts of these words look the same?" By this time most of the children knew the names of the commonly used letters. Any child who did not would designate the likeness by stating, "They all begin alike." Other children might say, "They all begin with *c.*" After reassuring the children, the teacher then printed the word, *cake,* at the bottom of the list, asking a child to read it. She then asked, "Now who can tell me what part looks the same in all four words?" The answer is obvious to children who know these words. The teacher asked to have all four words read to help all the children listen for the beginning sound.

To be certain that the children were able to hear the sound of the beginning *c,* this teacher used another activity. She said, "I am going to say some other words. I will then call on one of you to tell me whether or not each word begins like the words on the board. Listen carefully. My word is *catch.* Tom, does *catch* begin like *can, cat, came,* and *cake?*" Tom's reply was in the affirmative, so the teacher felt that he could probably hear the sound of *c.* She then said, "Now listen again. My next word is *baby.* Does *baby* start like *can, cat, came,* and *cake?* Sharon, what do you think?" If Sharon's reply is in the negative, the teacher is again reassured. The teacher continued this practice, using some words that begin with hard *c* and some that do not until each child had had a turn.

READING ORALLY IN THE PRE-PRIMERS

The oral reading in the first pre-primer may be carried on by permitting each child to read part or all of a page by turns, one of the very few times she uses the previously discussed "round-robin" procedure. She may use this procedure because the actual teaching has been accomplished with the charts and reading strips. The reading in the book on the first pre-primer level is planned primarily to give the children the satisfaction of reading successfully in a book. The children are very eager to read aloud to show the teacher, their friends, and their parents that they are able to read the book.

Use of Guided Scanning Procedures

The use of scanning procedures for reading in the first pre-primer would be very difficult because the short, repetitious sentences do not lend themselves to the location of answers to questions. The following text is similar to that found in most beginning pre-primers, even toward the end of the book:

> Mother said, "Come, Dan.
> Come to me.
> Come here to me.
> Come to get some cake."

If the teacher asks what Mother said to guide the scanning, the child may read any sentence and still be correct. If she asks where Mother wants Dan to come, at least three sentences may serve as the answer. If she uses the first word, *Come,* in the answering sentence, as she should at this level of reading, again three sentences can be read as the correct answer.

Even in the second pre-primer and in the beginning sections of the third pre-primer, the teacher finds stories that are difficult to adapt for use in the scanning technique because of repetition of words and ideas. With such books the best solution seems to consist of continuing to use the parallel stories and the various practice techniques with them and to reserve the book for "round-robin" reading until the children are ready to read stories with sufficient content to make scanning to answer questions a pleasure and a challenge. This stage should come toward the middle of the third pre-primer.

Scanning on the Charts. The children have already been given op-portunities to scan in the identification step in the work on charts. It will be recalled that the teacher had asked the children to locate the sentences that she read, at first in the sequence of the story and later in mixed order. She had said, "Who can find the line that says, 'Run, Sam'?" in the story found in Chapter 7 on page 172. The children were able to move their eyes down the chart until they found this line and were then able to frame it and repeat the sentence orally. This process of locating a sentence read by the teacher among three or four other sentences established the beginning of the scanning habit.

When the children came to the stories toward the end of the first pre-primer or in one of the later books, the teacher no longer used the identification technique. Instead she used questions to guide the children to find and read sentences in mixed order. This process gave the children additional skill in scanning because they were forced not only to read the sentence but also to think about its meaning.

Scanning in the Book. After the children have been introduced to the new words by means of the chart story, the teacher may introduce scanning in the oral reading process in the book. An example of a story that would be suitable for such scanning is given below:

> "We want the balls," said Betty.
> "Get the balls, Mother.
> I want the red ball."
> Susan said,
> "I want the green ball."

The picture above the story shows Mother, Betty, and Susan looking in a store window in which a large green ball is shown along with a large red ball and several other toys. After the story has been in-troduced, the teacher may ask, "What did Betty want Mother to get? The sentence starts with the word, 'Get.'" The teacher asks the children to frame the line when they have found it in their books. She walks in front of the children to be sure that each locates the correct sentence. If any child has failed to find the correct sentence, she repeats the ques-tion and says, "Look down the left side of the page," running her finger down the left margin and saying, "Show me the line that begins with the word, *Get*," for any child who fails the proper place. When all the children have framed the correct sentence she calls on one child to read it.

Her next direction may be to find the two lines that tell what Susan said. These are easy lines to find. When all the children have framed these lines, the teacher calls on the child to read, "Susan said, 'I want the green ball.'" The teacher may say, "Who can find the line that tells what Betty and Susan want? Look for the words, 'We want.'" When the children have framed the correct line, the teacher will call on some child to read, "'We want the balls,' said Betty."

The teacher may then add, "Which ball did Betty want? She said, 'I want' something. It comes before the lines that tell what Susan said she wants." Since two lines begin with the words, *I want*, the teacher may expect some children to locate the last rather than the third line. If they do so, she may say, "Your line begins correctly, but that is what Susan said. Do you see 'Susan said,' just above it? Now look up higher to find the line that tells what Betty wants. She said, 'I want' something." When all have located the third line, the teacher calls on a child to read this line that says, "I want the red ball."

Since the children have had experience in finding answers to questions on the chart stories, most of them will find little difficulty in following the same procedure in the book. However, the teacher is very patient with those who have difficulty. She may run her finger down the left margin of the page for children who have the most difficulty until they acquire the habit of looking down the left margin for themselves. For others she may give a hint such as, "Look below 'Susan said,'" or she may say, "Look for the line that starts with 'We want.' That's fine. Now look a little lower." or "Keep going. You have almost found it."

A week or so of such help should give most children considerable confidence in their abilities to locate the answers to questions using this skimming technique. If one or two children are slower than others to acquire the skill, the teacher may seat them on the end of the circle near her so that she may give her hints to them more easily. She should always check to be sure that every child has framed the correct sentence in answer to the question. If she fails to do so, the children may not develop this skill and will certainly begin to lose confidence in themselves. Every experience must end in success if the child is to feel secure.

The following suggestion may seem to contradict the above statement, but it is given for a reason. After the children have developed considerable skill in scanning and in reading the answers to questions, the teacher may allow a very secure child to frame the wrong answer without correcting him in order to give the group an opportunity to think and find answers accurately.

Perhaps the teacher may ask, "What does Betty want?" If perhaps Raymond, who is quite self-confident, should find the line following "Susan said," and frame "I want the green ball." instead of the line that starts in the same way but tells what Betty wants, the teacher may permit Raymond to read, "I want the green ball." If the children are alert and thinking, a number of hands should fly up in protest. Another child may then be allowed to read the line that he thinks is correct, that is, "I want the red ball," and may be asked to tell why he thinks his answer is correct. Very soon thereafter Raymond should have another opportunity so that he may make a correct response and be reassured.

If the teacher uses such a procedure from time to time, she should avoid calling on the same child who has made an error more than once in two or three weeks or his confidence may become undermined. An insecure child should always be helped to find the correct response before he is called upon. A thorough mastery of the vocabulary in each story is needed before the teacher guides the children to scan before reading orally.

Values of the Scanning Procedure

The need for the development of reasonable speed, the ability to see as much as possible in one eye span, and emphasis on comprehension have been stressed in this program from the very beginning. The technique of guiding children to scan over a page of material without any pressure for speed each time one sentence is read helps establish these very important habits.

Reinforcement of Oral With Silent Reading. In the "round-robin" type of reading most children read only once during the period and that is at the time when each is called on specifically to take his turn to read orally. In the scanning procedure every child must read silently before any child is permitted to read orally. Thus in a group of thirteen children, each child reads silently to frame one of the sentences thirteen times for every one opportunity to read orally. Thus each child has a great deal of experience in silent reading.

Use of Key Words. Guided scanning has other values. As the child drops his eyes from one line to the next using key words to locate the answer to a question, he is actually following one of the techniques used to help adults learn rapid reading. Scanning of this type helps develop speed of reading on the part of the young child just as the same procedure does for the adult. In this way children acquire the habit of rapid reading from the very beginning stages without pressure. The reading is not timed, and the children are not urged to use speed, but they do enjoy trying to locate a particular line and usually become quite skillful.

Reinforcement of Comprehension. Guided scanning to answer a question also forces a child to concentrate on thought, a matter badly neglected in the "round-robin" type of reading. It is impossible for a child to locate a sentence in answer to a question without careful thinking about both the question and the appropriateness of the answer he selects. By using this procedure to guide oral reading the teacher is building a cluster of important reading skills.

Reinforcement of Evaluation. In the guided scanning procedure children do not follow the sentence as it is read orally with their eyes. Instead they listen to discover whether or not the oral reader has selected the sentence that answers the question correctly. In this way no child is forced to slow down the pace of his silent reading to keep even with the oral reading of another child. In the same way no slow reader is forced to jump his eyes along a given line to keep up to the pace of the child who is reading orally. Since in the one case the fast reader is slowed down by pacing his reading to that of an oral reader and the slow reader is forced to skip words that may be essential to keep up with the oral reading, the establishment of these bad habits is eliminated by avoiding the procedure of asking children to follow each line with their eyes. At the same time the children are relieved of an onerous duty which they usually avoid in every way possible as the teacher constantly says, "Keep the place, Mary," "Johnny, keep your eyes on the book," and so forth.

SILENT READING IN THE PRE-PRIMER

The children in this program have been using silent reading from the very beginning. They read key words silently as they scanned to locate sentences on their charts in the identification step. They also read silently even more extensively as they used scanning to locate the answers to questions in the oral reading step. The teaching of guided silent reading demands a slight extension of this process already established.

Silent Reading, Sentence by Sentence

As with oral reading, a story with sufficient thought content is necessary to teach silent reading. The teacher may begin by helping the children to read one line at a time silently. In this situation she will follow the sequence of the story so that the children may understand its logical development. The parallel story shown below may serve to help describe the procedure followed in the beginning stages of silent reading.

Helping Mother

Tom and Betty said,
"We want to help you, Mother."

Mother said,
"You can help work.
Tom, get the chairs.
Susan, you can help Tom.
Betty, you get the cake."

The picture for this story shows Tom, Betty, and Susan helping
Mother get ready for dinner. Although normally the silent reading
precedes the oral reading, the teacher may reverse the steps for a few
lessons in order to be sure that the children know the vocabulary
thoroughly as they begin their first formal silent reading.

To begin this process she may say to the children, "In this story two
children are talking. Frame the first line and read it with your eyes
When you know which children are talking, raise your hand." When
most of the children have raised their hands, she may call on a child
such as George to answer her question. First she repeats the question
saying, "Which children are talking? George, can you tell us?" At this
point George will probably repeat the whole phrase, "Tom and Betty
said." To help free George from the words of the book and to help him
answer the question more naturally she may say, "That's right, George
But just tell me the names of the children." George should then reply
by saying, "Tom and Betty." The teacher may respond by saying, "That'
right, George.

"Now let's all look at the next line to find what Tom and Betty want
Frame this line. When you can tell me what it says, raise your hands."
She may call on Sharon, who responds by saying, "We want to help you
Mother." Since some children feel more secure by repeating the words
of the book and since the question was correctly answered by this re
sponse, the teacher will probably accept this sentence. She then may
say, "Look at the next line to find who talked next." She may accept
the answer of the child who responds with the word "Mother" or the
one who responds with the entire phrase, "Mother said."

The next question may be, "What did Mother say? Did she let the
children help her?" She will accept the answer, "You can help work,'
or the more informal answer, "Yes. Mother told them they could help
her work." The teacher may next say, "Look at the next line to find
what she told Tom to do." Again she may accept the line read as it is
printed in the book or the informal answer, "She told Tom to get the
chairs." She will follow the same procedure in asking what Mother
told Susan to do followed by what Mother told Betty to do.

Often the children have a strong desire to keep their eyes on the sentence in the book while answering a question in order to feel secure. The teacher's objective, however, is to establish the eventual ability to read a selection and recall the main thoughts after the book has been closed. She may help the children free themselves from the book by suggesting that they silently read the sentence in the book and then close it while keeping a finger in the place. They will then answer the question without looking at the book. The ability to answer a question with the book closed is best developed while the children are learning to read silently one sentence at a time. Without this skill they will have greater difficulty learning the next step, which is the silent reading of two sentences at a time. The teacher continues to help with one sentence at a time until the children have thoroughly mastered this skill and feel completely secure in it.

Silent Reading of Two Sentences

The following story may serve as an illustration of the teacher's approach to the problem of reading two sentences at a time in a reader.

> "Go Pony," said Susan.
> "Go fast, Pony."
> Betty said, "Stop, Susan!
> Pony is too big for you.
> Go to Tom.
> Tom wants Pony."

Three-year-old Susan is shown with Pony in front of the barn. She has the reins of his bridle in her hands and is pulling on them. Susan is shown on the left beyond Pony, and Tom is at the extreme right beyond the barn.

Mrs. Jensen used this story to help the children acquire the ability to read two sentences silently. She had introduced the story with a parallel chart and had helped the children practice on it, reading orally in order to be sure that they knew the sight vocabulary. She was now ready to help them develop the next step in silent reading. She said to the children, "Look at the first two lines of the story in your book to find what Susan said. When you have read clear to the end of the two lines and are sure you can tell me what Susan said, put your finger in the book and hold it in place while you close the book."

She helped any child who seemed to have difficulty until all had closed their books. She then called on Raymond to tell what Susan said.

Raymond answered informally by saying, "She told Pony to go."

"That's fine," responded Mrs. Jensen. "How did she want Pony to go? Do you think she wanted him to walk or run?"

"She wanted him to run," replied Raymond. "She said, 'Go fast, Pony.'"

"Fine," said Mrs. Jensen. "Now let's frame the next two lines to find what Betty said. Do you think Betty would want Susan to make Pony run while she held on to the reins?" After the children had read the next two sentences silently and closed their books, Mrs. Jensen said "What did Betty say to Susan, Charlene?"

Since Charlene was rather insecure in this new step, she tried to remember the words of the book exactly, saying, "Betty said, 'Stop, Susan, Pony is . . .'"

To help Charlene free herself from the book Mrs. Jensen asked, "What did she say about Pony? Don't worry about the words in the book. Just tell me what you remember."

Charlene replied, "Betty was afraid Pony would hurt Susan."

"That's right," answered Mrs. Jensen. "But why did she think Pony might hurt Susan?"

"Oh, I know now," said Charlene. "Pony is too big."

"That's just fine," said Mrs. Jensen. "You don't have to remember all the words. I just want you to get the ideas. Let's look at the last two lines now to see what Betty told Susan to do. Let's frame the last two lines and read clear to the end with your eyes." Mrs. Jensen gave whatever help was necessary. She then called on Karen to tell what Betty had said.

Karen responded by saying, "She told Susan to go to Tom. She told her that Tom wants Pony."

Mrs. Jensen said, "That's just right. She did tell Susan to go to Tom. Do you see now that we don't need to remember all the words in the sentences?"

Mrs. Jensen accepted the answers to her questions in the words of the book, if the children seemed to prefer to answer them this way. She knew that they would gradually learn to answer in their own words, giving the thought only, as she extended the number of sentences to be read silently. She continued to work on the silent reading of the stories using guiding questions for two sentences at a time until all of the children felt very secure in their ability to answer without looking in the book, either with informal answers or with verbatim answers. If any child was unable to give the thought of the second sentence along with the first, she let him look back in the book again, but insisted that he close it before he told her the second part of the answer. Although she praised all of the children for their responses, she stressed their success when they were able to recall the thought from two sentences without recourse to the book. She continued practicing on the two-sentence step until every child in the group could give the thought of the two sentences without referring back to the book.

Silent Reading of Three or More Sentences

When the children were completely secure in the two-sentence step, Mrs. Jensen used guiding questions to direct them to begin to read three sentences and to answer the questions with their books closed. Sometimes she found it necessary to guide them to read only two sentences instead of three because of the way the sentences in the book were grouped.

In *The Third Pre-Primer* of the Allyn and Bacon series by Sheldon, Mills and Karnes,[1] a story illustrates the problem set by the natural grouping of the sentences. The story has been paraphrased and is given below:

Is It a Fish?

"Look at it come," said Linda.
"Look at it, Bill.
It is big!"

"It looks funny to me," said Bill.
"Is it a fish?"

"See it go," said Ricky.
"It can walk.
Can fish walk?"

The picture shows Ricky, about three years old, and Bill and Linda, who are about six years old. They are fishing at the edge of a pond with a string on a stick they are using for a pole. They have pulled a turtle out of the pond.

The first three lines could be grouped naturally in answer to the question, "What did Linda say?" If the children fail to give the complete thought, the teacher might bring out the last sentence by adding the question, "What did Linda say about its size?"

The next two lines can be grouped naturally. The third line below, that is, " 'See it go,' said Ricky," does not lend itself to a combination with the two middle lines because of the change in speaker. To lead to the reading of these two lines, the fourth and fifth, the teacher might ask, "What did Bill say?," and possibly add, "What did Bill think the

[1] William Sheldon, Queenie Mills, and Merle Karnes, "Is it a Fish?" *Here and Away* (Boston: Allyn and Bacon, Inc., 1961), p. 38.

animal was?" The next three lines do group well and could be guided by the question, "What did Ricky say?" If necessary the teacher might add, "What did Ricky think it was, and what did he want to know about it?" Some stories cannot be divided into groups of three sentences. For example, the end of the story on page 42 in the book by Sheldon [2] must be grouped in two sentences at a time because the story is written in this manner.

EXTENSION OF THE SILENT READING

When the children have thoroughly mastered the technique of reading three lines silently and answering questions with the book closed, the teacher continues to expand the number of sentences included in her guiding questions. She may need to ask more than one question, however, for each set of sentences. If they are able to do so, a group of fast readers may progress almost at once to read silently and to answer questions to cover an entire page. When they can do this, the teacher usually guides the reading by asking a question that leads toward the thought at the end of the page. When the children have closed their books, they will give the answer to this question first. The teacher may then ask for other ideas in the story while the books are still closed.

If the children have failed to pick up the answers to such questions, the teacher may let them look back in the book to find the answers. She will, however, continue using questions for one page at a time until all the children are able to remember most of the ideas on a page without recourse to the book.

When the children have mastered the ability to read a page silently and answer questions with the book closed, the teacher may move gradually to the use of the same technique with two pages, then with three pages, and, finally, with the entire story of three to five pages.

The care with which the teacher works to give the children confidence in their ability and the thoroughness with which she establishes the skills with mastery on the part of every child make the difference between skillful silent reading in later grades or the lack of it. Without the ability to read silently and recall ideas from the entire context, a child will be handicapped in reading in all the content fields throughout his school life. The need for mastery in this process cannot be overemphasized.

If the children have not mastered the skills in silent reading at the beginning of the second grade, the teacher of this grade will continue work on these skills until they are completely learned. If children in the

[2] *Ibid.*, p. 42.

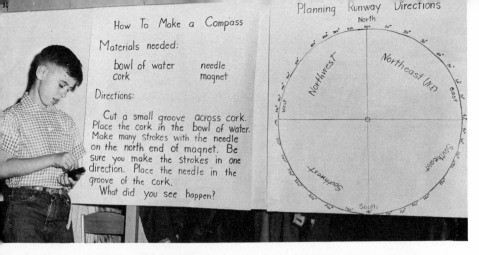

third or even higher grades have not mastered these skills, the teachers of these grades must go back to the use of beginning techniques and thoroughly establish them. A child is cheated of his birthright if he has not learned good silent reading techniques.

CHANGES IN THE READING PATTERN

Instead of introducing the story, followed by oral reading, practice on vocabulary, and silent reading, the teacher uses silent reading after the introduction. This change takes place when the children are able to read several pages silently and to recall the ideas from them. The steps then change to (1) the introduction of the story, (2) silent reading of the story followed by questions with the book closed, (3) practice on sentences, single words and phonics, and (4) oral reading with skimming. Once the children have mastered the ability to read several pages silently, this process should precede the oral reading in order to make sure that the children get the thought directly from the page rather than from hearing their peers read answers to guiding questions. The silent reading also helps the children know where to look for answers to guided questions in the skimming process used with the oral reading. In addition, the silent reading helps the child to read orally in a more intelligent manner because he has already had a chance to pick up the thought and can therefore use better expression in his reading.

Some teachers give children practice on the new sight words immediately after the introduction so that the children will have no difficulty with them when reading silently. No great objection is held to this pattern. There are several reasons, however, for some teachers' preferences for practice to follow the silent reading, although the teacher must help the children with words which they may not know as they read silently. She should keep a list of these words requested for help by the children and will make sure that these needed words are included in the practice step. In this way the children are more likely to recognize their need for practice, and the teacher has a better idea of which words are needed for practice. She may find that she needs to add a few difficult review words to the newly introduced sight words on which she has planned to give practice.

VALUES OF THE BALANCED PROGRAM

The beginning program described in Chapters 5 and 6 may seem complicated to the teacher who is accustomed to teach reading by calling on each child to read a line or a paragraph of the text followed by some practice on phonics. This program, however, has been designed to establish the basic skills necessary for reading power. The procedures have been carefully balanced to develop these skills without overemphasis on any one aspect of the program.

Overstress on Any One Skill

It has been previously stated that overstress on one type of skill may seriously handicap the child in his reading. The handicap may result from inadequate skills because they have been understressed. On the other hand, the handicap may result from overstress on one skill which may interfere with the development of another necessary skill.

The teacher who teaches by means of oral reading followed by phonics establishes the habit of reading at the rate of speech. When this habit has been established for one or two years, only the most arduous and time-consuming remedial help will break down the former habit. The longer the habit of reading at the rate of oral speech has been in effect, the greater the tendency becomes as time goes on for the child to lapse back into the old slow reading rate. In other words, the child tends to regress to old habits unless constant work is carried on to prevent this regression. In this way, the overemphasis on one skill may result in an acute handicap in another skill.

Need for Practice

The program will not seem so complex if the reader is conscious of the fact that many of the procedures described are merely ways of giving variety in practice. It has been stated that the use of practice on vocabulary has been almost eliminated from teaching because the old methods did more harm than good. It is unfortunate, however, that practice except for that on phonics has been minimized so greatly, and it is also unfortunate that teachers have been encouraged to progress through the book to new lessons before the vocabulary in the current lessons have been mastered.

Usually rapid progress through books has been geared to the learning rate of the most intelligent and mature children. When this type of teaching is used with the average and slower children, it often results in great insecurity on their part, a dislike of reading, and an inadequate ability in reading. Almost no skills, not even a rapid rate of reading, can be established by progressing from one story to the next without the development of a sound knowledge of vocabulary. The child can read rapidly only when he is thoroughly familiar with the vocabulary. Comprehension, too, depends to a tremendous extent on a thoroughly mastered vocabulary.

Need for Confidence

Dolch stresses the need for teaching remedial reading at the child's level of confidence.[3] If original teaching were carried on at the child's level of confidence, far less need for remedial teaching would be found. At the same time, more children would enjoy reading and have feelings of power in their ability to read. In addition, the need for speed reading courses for high school and college students and adults would be greatly minimized. The large proportion of college students who complain about their difficulties in comprehension and their lack of speed tend to suggest that a great need exists for better reading teaching in the elementary school and especially at the primary level.

OUTLINE OF PROCEDURES

The outline of the reading steps described in this chapter are given below. They should help to clarify the reading activities that have been presented.

    I. Teaching with the parallel story
        A. The reading step
            1. Reviewing the parallel story
            2. Reading sentences selected by the pupils
            3. Choosing sentences and prereading
        B. Practice on the reading step
            1. Building the story by reading the sentences
            2. Calling on others to read the sentences

[3] Edward W. Dolch, "Success in Remedial Reading," *Elementary English*, XXX (Mar. 1953), 133–37.

     3. Building the story by reading the words
     4. Calling on others to read the words
  C. Games for practice on the reading step
     1. Games with sentences
     2. Games with words
II. Reading in the first pre-primer
  A. Introduction of a section of the book
  B. Procedures for the beginning teacher
  C. Procedures followed by an experienced teacher
III. Introducing a longer parallel story
  A. Introduction of the story with discussion
  B. Reading the sentences
IV. Practice on the parallel story
  A. Practice on sentences
  B. Practice procedures with the sentences
  C. Practice on words
  D. Practice on phonics
V. Oral reading in the pre-primers
  A. Use of guided scanning
  B. Scanning on the charts
  C. Scanning in the book
VI. Silent reading in the pre-primers
  A. Silent reading, sentence by sentence
  B. Silent reading of two sentences
  C. Silent reading of three or more sentences
  D. Extension of the silent reading

SUMMARY

As the children progress through the parallel stories in the first pre-primer, a large proportion of the words in the stories are made up of review words. Only one new word is found in a sentence and perhaps only two or three in the entire story. At this time the identification step is no longer necessary, and the use of context clues receives more and more emphasis. Practice through games and activities is given on the sentences first and then on the single words. A phonics step may follow if the children have already learned three words beginning with a particular consonant and have been introduced to a fourth word. This letter sound may then be taught.

The basic skills needed in oral and silent reading may be taught through parallel stories. Ability to scan developed at this beginning stage helps to establish the habit of reading for thought and helps the children to think in thought units. Silent reading is taught first a sentence at a time and is gradually expanded until the children can read a short story of three to five pages. Even at this level a balance of skills is emphasized.

10

Primary Grade Procedures

In the previous chapter a description was given of teaching reading in the pre-primers. Some of the steps in the balanced program were not yet expanded to include the full program. In this chapter, a complete program is given for use with children who are reading in the primers and in more advanced books.

COMPARISON WITH SUGGESTIONS IN MANUALS

The program suggested in this chapter is similar to those used in manuals, with certain exceptions. The manuals, however, have many excellent suggestions for teaching each specific lesson and should be used by the teacher in her planning.

Addition of the Parallel Story

The parallel story has been suggested as a procedure for introducing new sight words, that is, helpful for the first steps in reading. It is of greatest value in the early steps in the pre-primers but also has values in the primers. These values have been stated but bear repeating. Words are always introduced in sentences to give them meaning and to avoid any procedure that would encourage word-by-word reading. The new words are used in a situation that is different from the one in the book. In this way, the children are unable to memorize the complete sentences that are found in the primers. They must recognize the new words in a different context. Since the parallel story makes use of a different situation and plot, the story in the book is not spoiled for the children when they read it. A chart holds the attention of the children more easily than the use of the book for the introduction.

Form of the Parallel Story. At this level, the parallel story may be printed on the chalk board. If the teacher saves copies of these stories in her plan book, she need not rewrite them. She may, however, wish to make minor changes if the children's reactions have shown that such are needed. For the slow reading children, the teacher may prefer to put the sentences on charts than to copy them on the board for several days as might be necessary with a slow group. If charts are to be saved, the name of the reader and the pages for which the chart was used should always be written on the back of the chart to save later difficulties.

Values of the Parallel Story. The use of reading charts on the pre-primer and primer level is of value in helping the teacher provide practice in scanning the chart to find answers to questions. The teacher may say, "Find the sentence that tells what Mary's dog did." When all the children have found this sentence by scanning up and down the left side of the chart and a child has read it orally, the teacher asks for the answer to another question which may be found three or four lines above or below the first one. This particular procedure seems to be one of the most effective in helping children establish the beginning of good habits in silent reading. Unless the habit has been acquired in a previous situation, no child ever moves his lips or mouths the words on the chart. This procedure also requires the child to read the sentence to himself before he reads aloud. This is essential to good oral reading.

The same habits could be established by introducing the new words taken from sentences in the book. The teacher should make minor changes in these sentences, however, to avoid children's tendency to memorize them. The teacher must also avoid using any sentence that gives away the climax of the story. The only weakness in this procedure lies in the fact that these sentences are not related to each other and therefore do not provide a story.

Addition of Extended Silent Reading

Procedures for helping children learn to read silently two sentences followed later by three sentences, then by four sentences, and then finally by a page of material were given in the previous chapter. In this chapter, suggestions are given to help children read a story of three to five pages silently at one time before discussing the story with the teacher. Suggestions in most manuals concern the combined silent and oral reading of one or two sentences at one time, or a paragraph at the most. The teacher proceeds down the page in an orderly manner combining silent reading and oral reading at each step.

Need for Pacing. The work of many teachers, both student teachers and those with a period of twenty years of experience, has proven that children are capable of reading several pages silently with good comprehension and without interruption by the time they are able to read successfully beyond the first thirty or forty pages of the primer. The individualized reading program demands even more extensive silent reading. This ability, however, presumes that children will be carefully paced on the basis of complete mastery of the sight vocabulary up to that time and will also be secure in using suitable phonics techniques on their particular level.

If children are forced to guess at many unknown words, this procedure can be disastrous. They must guess if they have not mastered the vocabulary introduced previously to their particular reading lesson. Even children with over 140 I.Q. have been found to develop serious problems as a result of placing them beyond their level of security.

Values of Uninterrupted Reading. Children enjoy reading a story without interruption because they are able to follow thought successfully. In addition, comprehension skills demanding thought can be developed when an entire story is used. Such thought skills as finding the cause and effect, finding relationships among ideas, drawing conclusions, making inferences, and following a sequence of events can be taught only in the context of a complete story. The teacher is almost forced to use factual questions for detail when she checks comprehension on one or two sentences or a short paragraph. Since children who are properly paced in the reader can be taught to read a story of three to five pages in length without pressure, these children acquire a reading power that is valuable to them in all the reading that they will do throughout their lives. Children who have learned to read an entire story can also move more rapidly and easily to reading in supplementary and library reading books than those who have been held to the silent reading of a sentence or a short paragraph. The use of step-by-step procedures to develop this skill, always at the success level, is essential if this plan is to succeed. At no time should the children feel frustrated or under pressure for any reason.

Addition of Scanning for Increased Rate

Reading specialists have developed a dislike of the word *speed* because efforts to develop speed have been misused. In addition, speed without comprehension and flexibility is valueless. However, a reasonable rate of reading is essential for flexibility. The overly slow reader is unable to be flexible in his reading because he cannot increase his speed when the situation permits or when a more rapid rate is advisable. The child wh. has developed a rapid rate of reading, on the other hand, is able to adjust his rate to the requirements of the material he is reading. The great demand for speed reading courses for adults and the many complaints of college students who have not achieved an efficient rate of reading suggest that better procedures are needed for this skill.

Regression in Rate of Reading. Many years ago William S. Gray discovered that the eye span could not be increased to a great extent with permanence after the fifth grade, even though better reading procedures were established. Those whose rate is improved after habits have been firmly established, however, are likely to find that they regress to slower reading if they do not continually force themselves to maintain the higher rate that they had once acquired. On the other hand, children who have established the basic habits of rapid reading without pressure are easily able to maintain their speed throughout their school and later life.

Lack of Time Pressure. In this section, emphasis is placed on the development of the basic habits for rapid reading by means of scanning rather than by means of artificially moving the eyes in a pattern down the page or by putting pressure by timing the children's reading, the most commonly used technique in the middle and upper grades. Again, twenty years of experience has shown that natural habits of rapid reading normal for the age level can be established by the early use of scanning.

Studies of the Value of Additional Procedures

A study by Carter evaluated the use of the balanced reading program as it is presented in this chapter.[1] Children in ten first grades who had been taught according to this reading plan in a selected variety of socio-economic levels from lowest to highest were tested in reading at the end of the first grade and again at the end of the second.

The Teachers. The tests were given after a normal teaching year, without any effort to motivate the teachers. The first-grade teachers were selected because they were using this program as a result of having taken a course in which it had been presented. Minor variations were inevitable. The children were followed through the second grade

[1] Clara Carter, "Various Techniques in the Use of Parallel Chart Stories in Beginning Reading." (Unpublished Master's Thesis, Sacramento State College, 1958).

regardless of the reading program that was followed. As a matter of chance, half of the teachers in the second grade also used this program. The other half used various procedures which they had been following for a number of years.

The Test Results. At the end of the first grade, the reading average of these children was on a par with the national norm. At the end of the second grade, the average reading ability was six months above the national norm. The first-grade tests put greater emphasis on word recognition techniques than on other reading skills. Since these children had followed a program of word recognition techniques spread over three years, they merely achieved normal growth. By the end of the second year, the test gave more recognition to the mature skills these children had learned. Because of a lack of foresight in selecting a more difficult test, one quarter of the children received maximum scores on the test. This lack of ceiling on the test may have limited the mean for the entire group.

A Second Study. Lee also carried on a study to follow the growth of children who were taught by means of this balanced program in the first grade.[2] Because the study was limited to a particular school district, these children were above average intelligence. Only one school was in a lower socio-economic area. The others were in middle-class areas. Although these children were taught by teachers using a wide variety of procedures in the second, third, and fourth grades, they achieved an average of six months above the national norm at the ends of each of the second, third, and fourth grades. Some of the procedures used in the balanced program in the first grade seem to have a lasting effect in raising the level of reading achievement. Although grade level averages are discredited by some authorities because of variations in procedures of standardization, they provide the only measure of achievement for use with a large group of children.

STEPS IN INTRODUCING A READING LESSON

Most authorities suggest four to six steps in work with a lesson in reading. These steps may be spread over a number of days. The suggested time for the development of this program is three days. The story and the sight words should be introduced and the children should be given an opportunity for silent reading; in this case, uninterrupted by discussion and oral reading. Practice is needed both at the sentence level, at the word level, and in helping children learn to apply phonics

---

[2] Gertrude W. Lee, "A Comparison of Reading Programs." (Unpublished Master's Thesis, Sacramento State College, 1966).

in analyzing new words. Oral reading is always tied to a child's purpose. Suggestions for the follow-up are given in a chapter that deals with independent activities for the children who are working at their seats while the others read with the teacher.

Suggestions are given in most manuals for introducing a story in the primer or more advanced books. The teacher wishes to arouse interest in the story, develop or clarify any necessary concepts basic to the story, and introduce any new sight vocabulary.

Development of Concepts

Children from middle- or upper-class homes may have no need for the clarifications of concepts introduced in stories that are written around the interests of such children. On the other hand, the backgrounds of children in any reading group are likely to vary considerably. If the teacher has any doubt regarding the children's understanding of any of the words in the story, she should take a little time to clarify their meaning. The word may be entirely new to the children, or a meaning of a word in addition to its common use may constitute a problem.

Fewer needs for clarification of word meanings are met in the pre-primers or primers than in the later books. The younger children, however, need more help in interpreting the pictures. Pictures are two-dimensional representations of three-dimensional objects. Even with general help on picture interpretations on the reading readiness level, some children may still need more help in interpreting the pictures accompanying the story they are going to read.

Help From Children. The teacher always makes use of explanations from the children who are more able to help those who are less able. As the more mature children discuss the picture, they are also clarifying their own thinking in this process. The teacher therefore asks such questions as, "Who are the children in this picture?" "What are they doing?" "What do you think they were doing before you saw them there?" "What do you think they are going to do?" She also asks questions about the less usual meaning of words. In a Sheldon primer, the children read a story that involves Mr. Works, who runs the school. This use of the word *runs* should be discussed with children regardless of their background. The teacher may ask such questions as, "Who do you think runs this school?" Some child will probably name the principal. Then the teacher will ask, "Who helps him run the school?" as she guides them to name the nurse, secretary, and other people. She may then ask the children what they think she means by *runs*. The discussion continues until the children seem to be clear in their understanding of this use of the word. Any other words may be clarified in the same way.

Pictures and Dramatization.   Pictures and dramatization are also help-ful ways of clarifying concepts.   Dramatization is helpful in the case of such an expression as, the horse *trotted* down the road.   Although chil-dren may have seen many horses on television, they rarely see them trotting in western pictures.   Children can trot across the room to help clarify the meaning of this type of action word.

Introduction of New Vocabulary

The introduction of new words in the parallel story or in sentences taken from the book has been discussed in the previous chapter.   A warning against the use of new words in a list on the board bears re-peating as the only form of word practice.

Cause of Word-by-Word Reading.   The children merely name these unrelated words in a list when practicing to acquire them as sight words. This habit of word calling almost inevitably carries over to the oral read-ing of the stories in the book and results in word-by-word reading.   Once this habit of word-by-word reading without conscious thought about the meaning of the selection has been established, it is very difficult to break.

Use of Phonics and Context Clues.   When new words are used in sen-tences, whether from a parallel story or from the book, the teacher may help the children use phonic analysis and context clues in recognizing these new words.   As the children acquire more phonic techniques, they will increase their ability to use these techniques in recognizing new words.   They should acquire the habit of always checking the word for its use in context before they accept it in the sentence.

If, for example, the word *ran* is a new word in the sentence, "The kitten ran to the black dog," the teacher will first ask, "What does this sentence say the kitten did?"   She may ask some child to frame the sentence that tells what the kitten did.   She may then say, "You may not know the word that tells what the kitten did.   I am going to put another word that you do know on the board to help you guess."   She may then write *an* on the board as a familiar word and ask the children to read it.   She may then say, "I am going to put a word that rhymes with *an* below it.   You have had it already in your stories."   She then writes the word *man* below *an* and calls on a child to read it.   She also adds the familiar word, *can*, to the list and asks a child to read it.

She may then say, "The word that tells what the kitten did rhymes with *an*, *man*, and *can*.   I wonder if someone can guess what it says?" as she writes the word *ran* under the other words and re-reads the words again to help the children hear them rhyme.   She then calls on some-one to guess the new word.   Some children may suggest words that do not rhyme, such as the word *jumped.* In such a case, the teacher asks the children to listen as she repeats the three known words that rhyme and continues until someone guesses the word, *ran.* She may then say, "Yes, *ran* does rhyme with the other words. Now let's try it in the sentence and see if it tells us what the kitten did." She then calls on a child to read the sentence, "The kitten ran to the black dog." She asks them to tell her if the sentence sounds right with the new word. She introduces any other new word in the same way if the children already know three words that end like it or begin like it.

If they do not, the teacher uses context clues for help. If the next sentence says, "The kitten and the black dog were friends," she will use context clues to introduce the non-phonic word *friends.* She avoids trying to work with the silent letter *i* in *friends* to use it as a rhyming word, because the children have not yet learned beginning blends such as the *fr* in *friends.*

Instead, she may say, "This sentence tells something about the kitten and the black dog. I will help you with the last word." She may then choose two children who play together frequently, and say, "Raymond, I notice that you and Frank often play together. Can anyone think of a word that means that Raymond and Frank like each other and play together?" Fred may suggest that they are pals. The teacher agrees and says, "Yes, that's a good word for boys that play together. Can anyone think of another word?"

Soon a child will suggest the word *friends.* The teacher will then say, "Yes, that's the word in our story. Let's look at the sentence again," as she holds the pointer under the line. "Let's read the sentence again, to see what it says about the kitten." She adds, "Remember the kitten and the black dog were just like Raymond and Frank." A child will then be able to read the sentence, "The kitten and the black dog were friends." The teacher continues to introduce the sentences on the board with either phonics or context clues.

Maximum New Words. The stories in the most recent readers usually present no more than about five new words in a story. Six or seven new words are the maximum that should be presented in a primer or even in a first reader, unless most of these new words can be easily analyzed by phonics. Children cannot successfully learn more than six or seven new words and apply them in their silent and oral reading, especially if they are in an average or slow reading group. If the teacher finds a story in which more words are introduced, she should cut the story in half. The greatest drawback to such a procedure is the elimination of the climax of the story. The teacher, however, may be able to use a sub-plot in the story to help guide the reading. She is wiser to limit the number of words introduced even though the climax is lost in the first part of the story.

Development of Interest

Authors of textbooks take great care in following children's interests when they write their stories. However, the children need some introduction to arouse interest in some particular plot. If, for instance, the picture shows a kitten clinging to an upper branch of a tree with children below it, the members of the reading group may discuss the picture and talk about the kitten's problem.

They may discuss why the kitten is afraid to come down. They may learn a new fact when they discover that cats cannot climb down a tree headfirst because their claws, which curve inward, cannot grip the tree. They may also discuss the fact that cats either do not like to or are afraid to come down backward. The teacher may then encourage them to think of all the things the children might do to help the kitten. Stress should be placed on the safety of the children in solving the problem. The fact that they need to get an adult will be brought out as one of the ways to help the kitten.

As the teacher is about to suggest that the children read the story, she develops a question about the climax, the climax question. She may ask the children to tell her what they want to know about the story. When a good climax question is suggested, she will help the children locate their story in the table of contents and find the correct place in the book. Teachers should always make sure that every child has found the correct place to read. She will then show them where the story ends and also suggest that the children look at the story on the board if they find a word they cannot recognize.

SILENT READING

When the children are encouraged to read an entire story, they are able to enjoy it and follow its sequence of events to the climax. They also develop a knowledge of the story that permits the development of the thought questions discussed before. To repeat, such thought questions may relate to finding cause and effect, discovering relationships among ideas, drawing conclusions, making inferences, and following the sequence of events. Children also tend to read more rapidly when they are permitted to read without interruptions. The climax question serves to challenge their curiosity to find how the story ends.

Flexibility

To balance rapid reading with reading for detail in order to develop flexibility in the silent reading, the teacher should select occasional stories for their wealth of detail. Before they read, she should tell the children that she would like them to review the story carefully because she is going to ask them a lot of questions. She may mention a few details for them to watch for in addition to the climax question. Most of these details will probably call for factual questions, but a few thought questions should be included.

Help with Forgotten Words

The teacher suggests that the children look at the story on the board that was used for introduction of new words to help them recall a forgotten word. She also reminds them that they should raise their hands if they do not remember any other words from the story. She will then go to them to tell them the forgotten word. She will discourage the children from bringing the book to her because of the resultant break in thought. She will tell them the word immediately rather than by giving help with phonics at that time.

She gives no phonics at this time because she feels that the comprehension of the story and its sequence of events is most important in the silent reading. She neither wants to interrupt their train of thought nor interfere with their speed of reading. If the word, however, is one other than the new words introduced on the chart, she will jot down this word on a piece of paper kept in her book for that purpose. She will plan to add a sentence containing this word to the others for the practice period on the following day.

Time for Silent Reading

The introduction for a story with an average number of new sight words and one or two new concepts takes from three to five minutes when the teacher becomes used to the procedure. About eight to ten minutes is an average amount of time for the silent reading and about five to seven minutes should accommodate the discussion following the reading. The teacher judges the amount of time needed for the silent reading by the time the children take to finish reading the selection.

Differences in Rate of Reading. The time needed even by children in the same reading group varies surprisingly. One or two children may finish in four or five minutes. Most will finish in six to seven minutes, and a few may take more than twelve to fifteen minutes if the teacher were able to give them this much time. These estimates of time vary with the children in the reading group and the story selected for reading. The time limits described apply to the reading of four or five pages of material that is paced at the proper level of difficulty for the children; that is, five, six, or seven new words scattered over four or five pages. In this way, the children will probably meet only one or two of these words on a page. They may occasionally need help with one or two sight words which they have forgotten, probably because of their abstract meaning or their lack of phonetic construction.

Problem of Differences in Rate. Usually, the children who finish silent reading first need wait only a short time while most of the others finish. When all but the last two or three, sometimes only one, have finished reading, the teacher stops the group. If she waited for the very slowest children, the others would become bored. They would want to read other stories in the book and would tend to forget the content of the story.

The teacher keeps these two or three slow children in this group because their sight vocabulary and comprehension are adequate. Their only weakness is their speed, which will probably improve as they work with a group of children who read somewhat faster than they do. If these slower children were put back in a slower group, they would tend to retrogress in their vocabulary and comprehension and would not gain more speed. The teacher must always work with children who are on the borderline between two groups. She must balance one factor against another to decide where the children will work best.

The children who do not have time to finish the story may take the book to their seats after the discussion and finish the story before they start other work. The teacher, however, does not insist that they finish the reading at their seats. She feels that resentment of this activity as a requirement might result in dislike for reading. In such a case, the losses would be greater than the gains. She also knows that these children will have another opportunity to read the unfinished part of the story during the oral period.

Discussion of the Story

When the teacher stops the silent reading, she combines discussion with questions to make sure of the children's comprehension. A discussion of the part of the story the children like best, the character each one would like to be, or the funniest things that happened, among other topics, brings out much of the content of the story. The teacher also plans some questions to check on the understanding of some of the details in the story and some questions to stimulate thought. She must be sure to give the readers who did not finish the story an early opportunity to take part in the discussion and to answer questions that pertain to the first part of the story.

Such questions as, "Who can tell what Jimmy did before he called father?" "How many children tried to get the kitten down from the tree?" and "What did each do?" are questions that help children recall the sequence of events in the story. "Why did Mary tell Marvin not to get the step ladder?" will help the children anticipate the consequences and develop cause-and-effect type of sequence. Such questions such as, "Who was the biggest child in the group?" and "Why was he not big enough to get the step ladder?" will help children understand relationships. Such questions as, "Do you think the children decided on the best way to get the kitten down?" helps them draw conclusions and evaluate ideas.

THE PRACTICE STEP

Often children need to practice to insure mastery of sight words that have been developed from context and also of new words that have been first analyzed by phonics techniques. The teacher may give this practice on the second day of the lesson in the story. In order to avoid the tendency to develop the habit of word-by-word reading, much of the practice is given in sentence context. The teacher wishes to give the children enough repetition of new words to assure their mastery. The children, however, have no particular desire to learn words. For this reason, games provide the ideal opportunity for repetition as well as good motivation.

Enjoyment of Practice

Some teachers question the value of games because the children enjoy playing them. The pleasure in the game, however, is very effective in helping children learn. In addition, they have no feeling of pressure, and boredom is eliminated. A follow-up of the children who had most of their drill in the form of games has been very reassuring. These children not only have good mastery of their skills, but they also enjoyed every phase of the reading program. When the teacher brought in new books, she was greeted with gasps of delight and such questions as, "When can we look at them?" "Can we look at them now?" and so on. The philosophy of John Calvin, who decreed that only those things that were laborious, unpleasant, and oppressive were good for the soul, has long since been proven wrong as far as anyone can observe here on earth. Anyone who observes adults at work usually finds that those who enjoy their work, are enthusiastic, and deeply interested are the ones who are the most successful. Those who dislike their work and who are unhappy in it rarely put enough of themselves into it to do outstanding work.

Use of Games for Practice on Sentences

The game called "What's My Line" was described in the previous chapter in connection with practice on the pre-primer level. This game is very popular with children and can be used for practice throughout the primary grades. Sentence strips may be used for this game, or the sentences may be put on the board.

Sentence Strips Used in Games

Sentences on strips of tag are needed for some games. These sentence strips may be made of pieces of tag cut the width of the cardboard, which may be secured in sheets 24″ × 36″. An adequate length for the sentence strips in the pre-primers and for most of those in the primers is 24″. When making strips for longer sentences, the tag may be cut lengthwise to make strips that are 36″ in length unless they are ruled. In this case, an extra piece may be spliced to another for greater length. The strips may be made 3¾″ in width. Lines are drawn horizontally at three-quarters of an inch intervals. In this way, five three-quarters of an inch spaces are provided on each strip.

The lower case letters are printed in the middle space. The second space is allowed for the upper case letters and the tops of the capital letters. The fourth space is allowed for the lower loops of the letters. The top space serves as a margin, and the lowest space provides room for inserting the strips into the pocket chart without covering any of the lower loops of the letters. If the folds of the pocket chart are made 1″ deep, the lower space on the strip should also be 1″ wide. A sample of a sentence strip is shown on page 64. The sentence strips may be inserted in the pocket chart in the same sequence as the words were introduced in the story in the book. The children have already been exposed to these words twice—once when they were introduced and once when the children met them in the book. Practice on sentences and words is usually needed only by the children in the middle and slow groups.

An Activity for Practice

Although it is not a real game, children enjoy the following activity. The teacher may call on children who volunteer to select one of the strips she has placed in the pocket chart, show it to the group, and read it. Each child may then take a position in front of the group at one side while others volunteer to secure cards and read them in the same manner. When about half the children are holding sentence strips in their hands at the front of the group, they may form a line in the center. Each one then takes a turn calling on a child who volunteers to read the strip. The first child in the line will choose a child who is seated to read his strip. If the child is able to do so successfully, he may replace the child in the line, and the latter will return to his seat. Each child then has his turn to read a sentence strip, and the line changes as each child is replaced.

If a child has difficulty with one of the new words the first or second time the sentence is read, the teacher may help him recognize the word by going back to the parallel chart and reviewing the context clues she used in questions to help introduce this work. If the child still does not recall the word, another may tell him but only with permission from the teacher. The teacher should never allow children to bombard a reader with words when he hesitates. No one can think while others are shouting or even whispering words at him. Some children merely become frustrated in this situation, while others get the habit of waiting for help without trying to recall the word themselves. After the children have had help in winning their cards, they may be penalized for errors. If a child is unable to read a strip after the second time around, he may forfeit his turn. Nevertheless, each child should have a turn to succeed shortly after his failure in order to rebuild his self-confidence.

Examples of Activities

Games to be adapted for practice on sentences are more difficult to find than for games for practice on words because sentence strips are awkward to use in some situations. The Train Game is good practice on sentences. This game is described below along with others.

Matching Questions and Answers. Although the matching of questions and answers is not a game, children enjoy this activity. The teacher may print questions about a story on the board or on sentence strips. She may print the answers in another column on the board or on sentence strips.

If the work is on the board, the teacher may call on a child to choose a question from the list. The child then holds the pointer under the question while he calls on another child to find the answer. The first child does not read the question out loud. Therefore, the child called upon must both read the question and find his answer silently. He may then read both the question and the answer aloud, and the original child

SPIDERS

Spiders are many colors
shapes.
They make their homes
fine thread. It is
d a web.

spiders are friends
e enemies of man.

Being studied are insects that are helpful and those that are harmful to man.
(Courtesy Sacramento City Unified School District.)

may tell him whether his answer was correct. If his answer was incorrect, the first leader will call on another child to find the correct answer. If the volunteer is able to select the right answer and can read both the question and answer correctly, he then has a turn to be the new leader to select a question and to call on still another child to find the correct answer.

This game demands a high degree of comprehension. Sometimes children are afraid to try it without help from the teacher. They particularly desire to read the question aloud before they look for the answer in order to be sure that they understand the question. The teacher may permit the children to do this when they first use this activity, but should encourage them to read the questions silently before they find the answer as soon as they feel secure in doing so.

Grab Bag. Grab bag is also an activity rather than a game. The teacher puts the sentence strips in a box through a hole cut in the top large enough for the strips to be placed in the box and for the child to put his hand in to get one. The teacher calls on a volunteer to pull a sentence strip out of the box and to read it aloud to the others. If he reads it successfully, he may keep the strip. He then calls on another child to take a turn to secure a strip and read it. The children count the strips they have won when the game is over.

Baseball. The reading group may be divided into two teams for a game like baseball for practice on sentences. "Home" and three bases may be drawn on the board. The reading group is then divided into two teams. A teacher holds up a sentence strip or points to a sentence on the board. If the first child on team A can read it, a score keeper may move an eraser to first base to keep track of the successful responses. The teacher then calls on a second child on Team A to read a sentence strip. If he can do so successfully, the scorekeeper moves the eraser to second base, and so on until a run or score is made. The game continues, and the scorekeeper chalks up homeruns as he moves the eraser around the bases. If a child misses, the scorekeeper marks an "out." When a team has made three "outs," the play goes to the other side. If the time which Team A must use for play is too long, the play may go to Team B as soon as Team A has made one run. This game is more suitable for older children who do not mind waiting until the opposing team has three outs before taking their turn. The game may also be used for practice on word cards.

The Train Game. This game is useful for giving practice on new or difficult words in context. It may be played with children in a reading circle, and sentences printed on the board or on reading strips may be used. One chair is removed, and the child who occupied it is asked to stand behind the chair of the first player. The teacher points to a sentence. If the first child is able to read the sentence, he takes the place of the child who stood behind his chair, and the latter takes his chair. The conductor, the child who read the sentence correctly, now moves behind the chair of the second child. In each case the child in his seat is given the first chance to read the sentence. If he makes an error, the child standing behind him is given an opportunity to read the sentence correctly. If he does so, he retains his place behind the circle but moves behind the child in the next chair. The game continues in the same way around the circle, the winner always taking the standing position.

The Sequence Game. This game may be used with a reading group under the teacher's supervision. The sentences each containing only one new or difficult word may be printed on the chalk board or on reading strips.

Divide the reading group into two teams. Call on a member of Team A to find the sentence which gives the first step in the story. If it is on a reading strip, he may place it in the first pocket of a pocket chart. If it is printed on the chalk board, he may place the number one before the appropriate sentence. If any of the members of Team B disagree with the choice, they may ask the first player to prove that his sentence is the first in the sequence of the story by referring to the proper place in the book and by reading it orally. If they think that another sentence should have been chosen, they may read it to convince the other team of their ideas. The teacher is the final arbiter of which team is correct.

If the first player's choice is proven correct, Team A receives a tally mark on the board to indicate one point for its side. The play then goes to the first member of Team B who selects the sentence representing the second step in the story. The play continues in the same way. When all the players have had an opportunity to select a step in the story and when all the sentences have been placed in the proper order, the points are added to discover which side has won the game.

The Practice Step for Words

After the children have had practice on the words in sentence context, they need a short practice period for recognizing words alone. In this way, the teacher is able to know that each child has mastered the words and can recognize them without the benefit of the sentence context. If at least half the period has been spent in practice on sentences, only a quarter of the period is usually needed to practice on words alone. If this proportion of time is maintained, the children will not develop the habit of reading word-by-word. Games are also practical for practice on this step. The use of tick-tack-toe for recognition of sight words has been described in Chapter 9.

The Use of a Spinner for Practice. This activity has somewhat of a game aspect and is usually enjoyed by children. A large circle about 24″ in diameter is cut from cardboard. A large pointer similar to the hands of a clock is cut out and fastened to the center of the circle. It must be fastened loosely enough so that it will spin when a child moves it and tightly enough so that it will stop from lack of momentum rather than from gravity. If it is too loose, it tends to drop to the bottom of the circle, seriously limiting practice. The movement of the hand can best be controlled by fastening it with a small bolt inserted through the center of the circle. A series of washers are put on the bolt on both sides of the cardboard. The bolt is then put through a hole in the pointer, and another one or two washers are added before the nut is placed on the bolt and tightened. The tension of the nut regulates the freedom of the pointer.

The teacher clips word cards to the outer rim of the circle. The cards should be placed so that the print is in a horizontal position regardless of its location on the spinner. A child is called upon to spin the pointer and read the word to which it points. If the teacher puts lines like spokes in a wheel between the words, confusion over the word to which the hand is pointing is avoided. The reading group may be divided into two teams. A child from each team may take turns alternating in spinning the pointer and reading the word. Each team receives a point for each word read correctly.

The Fishing Game. This game makes use of a device because the children pretend that a circle drawn in chalk on the floor is a pond and the word cards dropped inside the circle are fish. Most devices do not interest children for very long at a time, but the gadgets used in this game have a strong appeal.

The child uses a fishing pole made of a pointer or yardstick to which a magnet has been attached by means of a string. The string should be about 24" long. A reasonably strong magnet, although not necessarily a large one, should be used for this purpose. Paper clips are attached to cards to provide a metal surface so that the magnet will pick up the card. If the card does not stay in position on the magnet, two or even more paper clips will help provide more metal for the magnet to grasp. To be of use, these paper clips must be put as close together as possible. The children enjoy taking turns fishing for a card which they must be able to read in order to keep as "fish."

Some teachers make the game more elaborate by using a large fish bowl and cutting the cards in the shape of a fish. This elaboration is not necessary since the children have vivid imaginations and enjoy the game just as much without the special arrangements.

Bingo or Wordo. Two large squares may be drawn on the board or two flannel boards may be used for this game. The game may be made with places for nine words, sixteen words, or twenty-five words, depending upon the time the teacher wants to spend on the play. Review words may be added to the new words to fill in the extra spaces. For a small game, each square is divided into three spaces vertically and three horizontally. If the flannel board is used, red string may be laid across the board vertically and horizontally to provide the spaces. Words are then printed on word cards backed with flannel, and the cards are placed in the spaces on the flannel board.

The reading group is divided into two teams. The same words may be used on both charts as long as they are put in different spaces. A child from the first team reads a word for a child on the second team to find on his chart. If he finds the correct word, he reads it and puts a cross through it or takes it off the flannelboard. The child who reads the word originally is usually the one to verify his opponent's accuracy. The child on the second team then reads a word for a child on the first team to locate. The members of each team try to read words to avoid bingo for their opponents. However, when one team has crosses on a row, a column, or a diagonal group of squares, it has won the game.

Merry-Go-Round. The chairs used by children in a reading group may be placed back to back in a double row. One player who is called "It" should be without a chair. A word card is placed on each chair. The players pick up their cards off the chairs and read the words in turn. If a child misses, the child who is "It" may try to read the word. If he succeeds, he may take the chair of the player who missed, and the latter player will become "It." If both children fail, a volunteer will be called upon to read the word, but this reading of the card will not be part of the game. When all the children have read their cards, they put them on the chairs and move around one place. The child who is "It" continues to wait for his turn to get a chair by reading the word when another child misses.

Practice on Word Analysis

A variety of suggestions were given for the development of readiness for phonics in Chapters 6 and 14. Many other suggestions are given in Chapter 15 for teaching phonics in the primary grades. A few general suggestions for teaching phonics are given here although they are repeated in much greater detail in the later chapters.

When the teacher has taught three words with the beginning initial consonant, she is ready to compare these words with a fourth word with the same beginning consonant. When she meets this fourth word in a later lesson, she puts the three review words on the board and asks the children to read these words and point out the similar parts. She then adds the new word that has been introduced in the lesson, asks the children to read it, and asks them to tell how it is similar to the other words. The teacher may test the children's ability to hear this beginning consonant by naming a number of words, some of which begin with the consonant and some of which do not. She asks the children to listen to a particular word and then calls on a child to tell her whether or not it begins like the words on the board.

A Game for Beginning Consonants. A game called "Go Fish" is an excellent one to help children hear beginning consonants. The game

should be made up of sets of cards, four in a set, in which all the word
begin with the same letter. These words should be those that childre
already recognize at sight. Enough sets of four cards each may b
made to include ten or more consonants. In this way, the children ma
play with about forty cards. Four or more children may play. Th
teacher may divide a reading group into two groups and start the game
with each group after they have listened carefully to how the game i
played. The teacher may help one group, and a more mature chil
may help the other group.

The cards are shuffled and five are dealt to each player. The rest o
the cards are placed face down in the center of the table. Each chil
tries to get a book of four cards with words beginning with the sam
consonant, such as *baby, boy, big,* and *ball.* The first child may de
cide to save words beginning with *b* because he already has two. H
may then ask his neighbor at his left if he has a word that begins lik
the word *ball* in the original cards that the child possesses. If th
second child has a word beginning with *b,* he must then give it to the
first child. If he does not have such a word, he says, "Go Fish," and the
child must draw a card from the pack in the center of the table. H
must also discard one card, which is placed at one side of the origina
pack. The next child takes his turn to decide which words he wishes t
save. He may have two words in his hand that start with the sam
letter, such as *girl* and *go.* He will then say to his neighbor on the left
"Do you have any words that start like *girl?*" The third child eithe
gives him a card beginning with *g* or tells the second player to "G
Fish." The game continues in the same manner.

When a child gets a book of four cards beginning with the sam
letter, he places them in a pile beside him, and they constitute his first
book. When he gets down to one card in his hand, he may take fou
more cards from the pack in the center to bring up his number. Any
child may draw from the discard pile if he thinks he needs the card
on the top of the pile. The players continue until all the cards in the
pack in the center and in the discard pile have been drawn. The child
with the most books is the winner. This game has been simplified from
the original description to make it easier for young children to play.
This game may also be played with words that end alike or that rhyme.

A Game for Rhyming Words. An adaptation of "Concentration"
makes a good game for practice on rhyming sounds. Twenty word
cards made up of ten pairs of rhyming words such as *sing* and *ring* may
be placed in a pocket chart, facing inward. They may be made up of
five cards in a row and four rows in the pocket chart. Small number
cards from one to twenty may be placed in order behind the word cards

to help the child remember their position. Four or five players are maximum for this game, unless the teacher divides the group into two teams. Since play in teams is the most practical for a reading game, this arrangement will be described. The teacher divides the group into two teams and calls on the first child in Team *A* to take two cards, blank side up, at random off the pocket chart, read them, and decide whether or not they rhyme. If they do not rhyme, he must put them back in the places where he found them, facing in. If number cards are used, he must put the word cards in back of the numbers so that they can still be seen. If these first cards do happen to rhyme, the player puts them on a chalk rail or table, as the first book won by his team. The first player in Team *B* then has a chance to take two cards from the pocket chart, read them, and tell whether or not they rhyme. He, too, returns them to their places if they do not rhyme or places them in a book on the table if they do. The play progresses in the same manner going from one team to the other in turn.

When all the cards have been removed from the board, the number of books won by each team is counted, and the team with the most books wins the game. This game helps children develop a visual memory as well as acquire practice in identifying rhyming words. As the cards are turned over, read, and returned to the pocket chart, the children begin to remember their positions. In this way, the children can find rhyming cards more easily as the game goes on.

SUMMARY

Every reading lesson should have a well-planned introduction including the development of the meanings of unfamiliar words, introduction of new sight vocabulary in sentences, and the development of interest in the story. Over a period of time primary children should learn to read several pages silently and to be able to discuss various aspects of the story. This discussion should bring out both factual and thought provoking aspects of the story. Those children who need extra help on the new and difficult words should be given practice on each word in a complete sentence, each word alone, and phonic relationships of the new words with those previously learned.

11

Oral Reading in Primary Grades

Oral reading in the past consisted of the provision for each child to read a sentence, a paragraph, or even a page aloud. Each child was called upon to have his turn, and those who had already read often stopped participating as soon as they had had their turns. Because the reading was without purpose, children lost interest and engaged in actual reading only a fraction of the time they sat in the group with their peers.

Guidance in oral reading today should provide a strong pupil purpose. Children are guided to look for the answers to questions as one way to stimulate their interest. By scanning the sentences on a page or on several pages, children must keep meaning of the material in mind to decide whether or not it answers a particular question. In this way, oral reading tends to support good habits of comprehension. At the same time, the children gain speed as they scan the sentences on a page to answer a question. Their reading also tends to become more fluent and more expressive. Reading before an audience and the use of a chart of standards also helps improve the quality of oral reading.

Modifications of the total primary program for the fast group eliminates practice unless needed and provides for more independent reading. Books are carefully selected to fit the level of reading for each group of children. More motivated practice is provided for children in the slowest group.

Children's interests expand rapidly as they acquire increased reading power. Children read more widely in the second and third grades and acquire greater information and increased interest as they do so. Dramatic activities, exhibits, and displays on bulletin boards are some of the ways of helping children increase their interests. This wider reading also helps provide for expansion of concepts and broader vocabulary. Parents' interests in their children's reading and their help in securing books from libraries and other sources are also valuable for helping children grow in reading power.

ORAL READING

Oral reading was the only kind of reading carried on in the schools at one time, except for phonics drills. The pendulum then swung the other way, and oral reading tended to be neglected in some schools. Most primary teachers feel that oral reading is essential to give children a sense of security. It is also needed as a diagnostic procedure for teachers to discover whether the children have mastered the sight vocabulary and are able to use the particular skill she has been teaching. These values are genuine, and oral reading should be a legitimate part of the primary reading program.

The crucial problem lies in how this oral reading is carried on. Oral reading can result in very little learning, or it can contribute important skills to the child's ability to read. "Barbershop" or "round-robin" reading is described as a very poor way to conduct an oral reading lesson. Oral reading with scanning is suggested as a valuable procedure for developing good skills. Some teachers cling to a poor method of directing oral reading because they feel that children should read the story in sequence. In the balanced reading program, however, the children have already had an opportunity to read the story silently in sequence and they therefore have no need to read the story orally in the same way.

"Barbershop" Reading

Much has been said about the sins of reading down the page, one sentence after the other, in sequence to the teacher's comment of "next." Since the word *next* has been used so commonly, some unsung poet has called the procedure the "barbershop" method. Others have called it the "round-robin" procedure. It has few virtues under any name. Whether the children take turns according to their seating order or whether they are called upon in any other order, little is gained.

If the children are called on in order of seating, and unfortunately this is still commonly done, each child can estimate which of the sentences or paragraphs is his and can then "tune out" until the reader next to him reads. This serves to alert the next reader, who double checks his place, reads his part orally, and mentally retires from the circle once more. In this way, each child may spend one or two minutes on his own particular sentence and the other fifteen or twenty minutes thinking about what he has in his lunch pail, what he would like to play at the following recess, or what he wants to do after school.

If the teacher skips around, a conscientious child may stay alert until he is called upon; then he retreats to his day dreaming. The more optimistic children, however, float off into the clouds while relying on a neighbor to nudge them when their turn comes. When the teacher is trying to say "Jimmy, you should pay attention," another child points to the proper sentence, and the first child starts reading to avoid hearing more about his "sins of omission."

Lack of Comprehension

Some children develop the ability to read orally without any comprehension of, or attention to, the material they are reading. An occasional child has even reached the eighth grade without ability to get meaning from the page, although he may use good expression and read fluently. Adults refuse to believe this statement when they first hear it until reminded that they can read bedtime stories to their children with good expression and apparent sense of the drama, while making up menus for the next day's meals or recalling how many shirts have to be ironed before bedtime. Adults can also read the newspaper or chapters in assigned textbooks while solving some of tomorrow's routine problems. They may reach the bottom of a page only to wonder what the material on the page is about.

Use of Scanning

A better procedure for conducting the oral reading avoids such problems. This procedure also helps the children gradually acquire speed in reading and forces them to concentrate on the thought of the entire story. The teacher first asks a question, and tells the children to scan until they find the answer. The teacher has been following this practice on charts since the first reading lessons, so it should not be difficult for children who have this background. To help them, however, the teacher uses the first word or two of the sentences in her question. She also starts by skipping down two lines and back one. In this way, the children do not have far to scan at first.

Use of Clues for Scanning. After she asks a question such as, "Where did Mary find the black kitten?" she may say, "the line starts with 'Mary

ound.' Look down the left side of the page to find those words." She
hen illustrates this procedure by running her finger down the left hand
ide of the page in her book to show them how to find the desired line.
She may then say, "When you have found the line that tells where Mary
ound the kitten, please frame it with your fingers so that I will know
hat you are ready." The teacher walks in front of the children to help
a child having difficulty, with encouraging words. She may say, "It
comes after the line that tells what Mary said," or "Look a little lower
down." She may even point to each line for a child having difficulty
vhile she continues to ask, "Does this line start with 'Mary found'?"
until the child recognizes the sentence.

The children must silently read the sentence that answers the ques-
ion in order to make sure that it is the correct one. A sentence that
says, "Mary ran to look in the garage," might be confused with the one
hat also starts with Mary but tells where she found the kitten. When
all the children have found the correct sentence, the teacher calls on
one child to read it. If the teacher cannot use the first word or two in
her question, she may ask the question and then tell the words used at
the beginning of the sentence.

Emphasis on Thought in Scanning. The children do not follow with
their eyes the sentence that is read by one child. Although this point
was discussed in another chapter, it bears repetition since so many
teachers insist that children keep their eyes on the print while another
child reads orally. If the children do this, the faster readers must continually regress to keep pace with the slower readers. They may therefore lose their rapid rate of reading. The slower readers must skip words
in a hopscotch manner that establishes sloppy habits of reading for them.

The children who are listening to the reader should spend this time
evaluating his answer to make sure that he found the correct response
to the question. In this way, the children concentrate on the thought of
the selection and avoid developing poor reading habits.

Increase of Power in Scanning. The teacher develops increasing
power in scanning in a number of ways. At first, she limits the scanning
for finding sentences that answer questions to alternate lines, the procedure described above. When all children are able to succeed in finding these sentences, she may word her questions to require scanning up
and down the entire page with larger gaps between the sentences. When
the children are completely successful in scanning the material on one
page, she may use two pages. She always tells the children when she
extends the amount of reading matter she is covering with her question.
If children have had experience in scanning in the first grade, a faster
reader in a second grade should be able to find the answer to a question

any place in a four- or five-page story. The slower readers will probabl
be unable to scan this widely for a much longer time.

Elimination of Clues. The teacher also gradually eliminates the clue
in her questions. She asks her questions without using words with whicl
the answer begins. For a while, her questions may include some of th
words in the answer; later, she drops even this much repetition of words
When the children have begun to read short paragraphs, the teache
may direct her question to the content of each of these paragraphs. I
the second or third grade, she may ask a question that must be answere
by reading a sentence from the middle or end of a paragraph. Since thi
work is for the purpose of developing oral reading, the teacher asks th
children to read the sentence orally rather than tell the information i
their own words.

Help with Expression and Fluency

Although oral reading is no longer considered an art and is used in
frequently in later life, children should learn to read with average ex
pression and fluency. Good oral reading often shows that the chilc
understands the meaned of the selection, although some children are
exceptions to this rule. If children read in a monotone or in a haltin
manner, the teacher may suggest that they read the speaking parts a
though they were reading a play.

The teacher selects a story with considerable conversation for thi
purpose. Volunteers are chosen for the part of each character, and an
other child is chosen to read the descriptive part and is known as "Th
Book." A group of children may read a page or two as a play.

Evaluation of Oral Reading. When the children have finished, th
other children are asked to point out the good qualities of the reader
and later to suggest ways of improving. Children usually say in thi
situation, "Mary sounded like a real mother. George always knew whei
his turn came," or "I could hear all the words when Marilyn read." Fo
constructive suggestions, children may say, "Some of the children shoulc
read louder," or "Some of the children should watch more carefully fo
their turns."

Another team of volunteers may be selected to read the same page o
pages, or they may read later pages of the story. Again, their readin
is evaluated by the children. All of the children in the group shoulc
have an opportunity to take part in the dramatic reading during th
period. Children learn as effectively from reading a short part of th
story as they do from reading a long part, and the learnings are more
equally distributed when all the children take part.

If the teacher wants to help a child who has particular difficulties when reading with expression, she may ask him to repeat his line so that he sounds more like the character he represents. She may also let various other children try reading the same sentence until some child is able to read it with particularly good expression. The teacher does not prolong the experience for the child who has difficulty, since he may become embarrassed. As other stories are used in the same way to provide more practice in good reading, the child will gradually improve.

Attention to Punctuation. Young children have difficulty observing punctuation while they are carrying on a process which seems quite complicated to them. If the child does not stop at the period, the teacher may ask him to show her just how much the character said by framing it with his fingers. If he still includes more than one sentence, the teacher may tell him that the period shows how much the character said at one time and helps him find the place to stop. She may then ask him to read just that much and try to make it sound as though the character were talking. Some children have no difficulty with this problem; others need continuous help over a long period of time. Children who have been forced to read material with too many unknown words often have difficulty with expression and with fluency.

The question mark constitutes another problem. The teacher may help the children decide that Father is asking a question. One child may then ask the question while another child reads the answer. If the expression is not good, other pairs of children may try reading the same question and answer to discover if they sound more like real people talking.

Directions to children to raise their voices at the question mark and drop them at the period are often very confusing. One child in the eighth grade was still concerned about dropping her voice, although she had no difficulty dropping her pencil or eraser. This procedure probably demands too much conscious control of the voice for many children. The linguists who advocate children learning to read with attention to pitch, stress, and juncture may find difficulty using these signals even with intermediate children.

Motivation for Scanning

The use of questions to guide scanning in oral reading has been described above. Children, however, need variety in purpose or motivation to keep their interest high. Pantomime is another good means of motivating the scanning. The children's own pictures can also serve as a form of motivation.

Children who have followed the "barbershop" plan of reading in a previous grade often feel insecure when another type of reading is used. They learn to enjoy the newer procedures, however, when they are gradually guided to use them. The use of scanning in oral reading is one of the best ways of helping children comprehend the material they are reading during the oral reading process. Scanning is also a very valuable means of increasing children's reading rate and reducing word-by-word reading without putting them under pressure.

Pantomime for Scanning. When the children are able to succeed in finding answers to questions by scanning one or two pages without clues in the questions, the teacher may suggest that they take turns silently dramatizing a sentence or paragraph. The children may work individually or in small groups to dramatize sections of the reading material for other children to find. The teacher may start this procedure by calling for volunteers and by selecting the sentence or sentences for them to dramatize until they understand the procedure more clearly.

In the primer called *Our School,* one of the Sheldon Basic Reading Series books, one story tells about the children, Bill and Linda, who have walked past a store front while it was being painted red. One part of the story tells that they were later sent to the nurse to see if they had an infectious disease. The nurse turned each child's face toward her as she examined it. She then laughed at what she saw. Bill and Linda's faces were covered with red paint spots.

Three children may take the parts of Bill, Linda, and the nurse. When they have finished dramatizing the selected reading, which is chosen secretly, they call on a child in the reading circle to read the lines that they have dramatized. If the volunteer reads the wrong lines, the characters repeat the dramatization and call on another child to try to read the correct section. The child who finds and reads the correct section may then have a turn to dramatize another part of the story, either alone or with others if they are needed. In this way, each of the children has a turn to take part in a dramatization and to read a section of the story.

Use of Pictures for Scanning. Some teachers use another procedure for motivating the scanning. This procedure is valuable when the children are able to scan the entire story to find a specific section. After the children have read the story silently, the teacher helps each child choose a part of the story which he would like to illustrate. He may draw his picture during the independent work period while the children in another group are working with the teacher. The teacher helps the children select their parts for illustration to avoid repetitions of the same section and large gaps in the material which are not illustrated: She

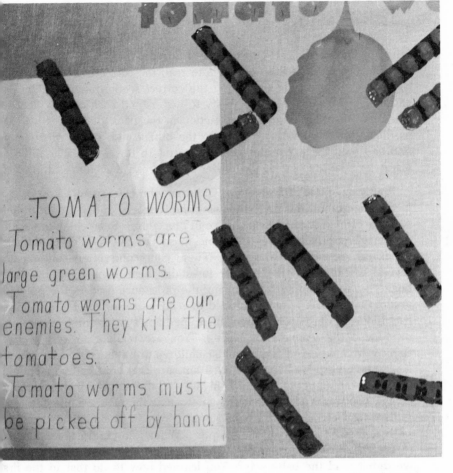

TOMATO WORMS

Tomato worms are large green worms.

Tomato worms are our enemies. They kill the tomatoes.

Tomato worms must be picked off by hand.

Children discover that tomato worms damage tomato plants. (Courtesy of Sacramento City Unified School District.)

also wishes to avoid the tendency of the children to copy the illustrations from the book.

The teacher makes sure that each child puts the number of the page he plans to illustrate on his drawing paper. Some children's pictures are difficult for the teacher to interpret, although the children are much more adept than she at recognizing the objects in their peers' drawings. The page number on the drawing helps the teacher avoid asking such an undiplomatic question as, "What is your picture about?"

Volunteers to Read the Illustrated Part of the Text. When the children are ready for their oral reading of a particular story, the teacher calls on a volunteer to show his picture to the children and to call on a child in his reading group to find the part of the story he has illustrated. The child called upon must read his section orally. If the reader has failed to find the correct section, the illustrator then calls on other children in turn until he finds one able to read the correct section. Usually the first child succeeds in locating the correct section in the reader because of children's surprising ability to understand each other's pictures. The child who reads the correct section in the book then takes his turn as illustrator to show his picture to the others and to call on them to find and read the section he has illustrated. In this way, each child has a turn to take the part of the reader and to read a section in the story.

Problems in Use of Scanning. Children who have spent a year or two in reading around the circle following the "barbershop" or "round-robin" plan are often disturbed by a change in procedure. Such children usually wait until just before they go home to say to the teacher plaintively, "Teacher, we didn't read today." These complaints often continue for several weeks unless the teacher forestalls them. One teacher usually began her oral reading by following the procedure used in the previous grade, that is, calling on each child to read by turn. After the children had time to adjust to her procedures, perhaps two or three weeks, she introduced the scanning by saying, "You are reading so very well, I think you could do something older children are able to do. Of course it may be a little hard for you, but I am sure that you read well enough to try something new. You read this way all through the first grade, and I know you want to learn something new, now that you are big children."

This teacher then began her scanning procedures similar to those described in this section of the chapter. When the children complained to her that they had not read today, she would reply, "Oh you mean we didn't read the baby way? You learned how to do that in the first grade." This statement usually ended the discussion for the moment, but the complaints usually continued for several days due to the children's insecurity resulting from a change of habit. This teacher also praised the children enthusiastically for finding the sentences in answer to her questions and for their fluent reading. If the children continued to be disturbed, she occasionally dropped back to the "barbershop" plan for a day. She stressed the fact, however, that it was too easy for the children and that she was sure they would rather read in a more grown-up way. Children really enjoy the scanning as long as the teacher moves slowly enough to make sure they feel secure. After two or three weeks, they are able to forget about their old habits and enjoy following new procedures.

Values of Scanning. Some of the values have been mentioned but bear repeating. The scanning helps the children learn to move their eyes from one key word to another. This skill is one that is taught to adult readers in speed reading courses. These adults would not need such a course if they had acquired this skill in the primary grades. When asked a question the children at first scan to find the teacher's clue to the correct sentence. Later, they must choose their own clues as the teacher broadens the questions and eliminates clues in her wording.

Through this procedure the children are required to focus on the meaning of the reading selection because they cannot find an answer to a question without comprehending the answer. This scanning procedure has served to eliminate the habit of lip movement for some children who have minor difficulty. For those with greater difficulty, more arduous methods must be used. Pointing is also eliminated by scanning because the teacher insists that the children frame an entire sentence rather than point to individual words. If the child has difficulty with pointing, the teacher may let him use a marker, a cardboard strip to place under a line of print, until he feels more secure. The scanning procedure also helps word-by-word readers if their habits are not too firmly established. The fact that the child must read the sentence silently before the teacher selects any child to read the sentence orally tends to help him read orally by phrases, although the improvement may be very slow and gradual. In cases of more extreme word-by-word readers, the teacher may need to use other methods.

Use of Markers

Some teachers hesitate to use markers because they are afraid that children may come to depend upon them permanently. Experience has shown that the reverse is true. Children are more likely to forget to use their markers while they regress to pointing than to depend upon them too much. The teacher should keep a few cardboard strips on hand. Whenever she sees a child pointing, she should hand him a marker and tell him to put it under the entire line in the text. She should watch him to make sure that he does not point to words with the end of the marker. The teacher should not give children markers when they can read without pointing.

Use of an Audience for Oral Reading

If the teacher feels that a particular group of children need extra practice on expression and fluency in oral reading, she may suggest that they read a story to another class. Some teachers are very co-operative and will help in activities of this sort to provide the children with a new and strong motivation. The children will be eager to practice so that the other class will enjoy their presentation. Some of this practicing may be carried on in small groups during the independent work period. At other times, the teacher will help them with their weaknesses.

A chart of standards described below is helpful for children to use to evaluate their own performance and that of others. The presentation may consist of a mere reading of one page by each child. As another way to present a story, the children may decide to take parts for dramatic reading of the story. It may also be presented as a television play. Suggestions are given in the chapter on the independent work period for a type of cardboard television box. At another time, the children may prefer to record their story on tape and play it for another group.

Slow children have the greatest need for good motivation. They may practice a short story until they can read it well in order to read it to the kindergarten children. The easy stories read by members of the slow group might be boring to children of their own age or those who are older. These slow children, however, seem very glamorous to those who are younger, and the story is likely to meet the interest of a younger group. The slow children will also enjoy reading the story in the various ways described above. They may need to spend more time practicing in advance of their presentations, but the time will be well spent.

Chart of Standards

A chart dictated by the children is helpful in reminding them of things they should remember to improve their oral reading. Some teachers like to put the statement on the chart in a positive form. Such a chart might include the following statements:

> We read so everyone can hear.
> We stand tall.
> We remember to keep the place.
> We read with good expression.
> We practice before we read to other children.

The teacher may suggest that the children look at the chart before they start to read to help them remember how to read well. They may also look at the chart when they are evaluating their own and others' readings.

Additional Suggestions for Oral Reading

Suggestions for procedures that may motivate children to read orally are given below:

1. Record individual dramatic reading in groups on a tape recorder to be used to entertain children in another class or to be used for listening to evaluate oral reading.
2. Read a story to find parts that can be illustrated in preparation for playing a guessing game with the illustrations when the parts will be read orally.

3. Choose different parts of a story for oral reading. Give reasons for the choices.

4. Select and read the most important event in a story. If the children disagree on the part selected, have each child read the part that seems most important to him and tell why.

5. Select and read the climax of a story. Differences of opinion provide for more oral reading and more thinking as the children justify their opinions. This suggestion is better for older children who are mature enough to understand what is meant by the climax.

6. Read and discuss several versions of a story as they are given in several books.

7. Select a sentence or paragraph which tells about some particular event and read it orally. An example of such an event might be, "What kind of a place did the kittens find to go to sleep?" or "How did Ronald and George get red paint on their clothes?"

8. Read the part in the story that proves a point.

9. Read a part of the story about which a disagreement may have arisen when the children discussed their story. Each child may read to prove his point of view. At other times, the teacher may put controversial statements on the board to stimulate children to find a part in a selection and to support their opinion by reading it orally.

10. Find selections in a story that provide answers to questions listed on the board and read these selections orally. At least some of these questions should be of the *how* and *why* type.

11. Read paragraphs or selections to children who have been absent. This activity provides a natural reason for review and is enjoyed by both the children who have returned to school after an absence and by the readers.

12. Take part in oral reading to practice parts of a play, a moving picture, or a television play.

13. Read an unfinished selection. One child may begin a paragraph telling only that it is somewhere on one of two pages which face each other. This child may stop in the middle of the paragraph and call on another child to complete it.

14. Read to the class when a parent or other person is talking to the teacher for a short time.

15. Read to visitors. A sympathetic principal can be of help to serve as an audience at times. Room mothers and other mothers who may visit may also serve as an audience at times.

16. Read a part of a story that has been read in an earlier part of the books. Call on another child to guess the name of the story from which the excerpt was taken. This reading constitutes an excellent review and is helpful when the children have finished a book or when they seem to have reached a temporary slump.

17. Read statements taken from a story written or printed on the board in mixed sequence. Read selections from the book to justify corrections in the order made by renumbering the statements on the board.
18. Read the funniest part of the story.
19. Read the part of the story that describes a doll, a pet, or some other object that appeals to a particular child.
20. Practice on Christmas poems and stories and then record them on a tape to serve as a greeting for another class.

MODIFICATION OF THE PROGRAM FOR
INDIVIDUAL DIFFERENCES

The most difficult problem for the beginning teacher is the wide range of abilities found in each grade or classroom. Programs should be adjusted and procedures varied for different levels of reading ability.

Modifications for the Fast Group

Stories for the children in all of the reading levels should have a good introduction. In addition, the children in the fast group need both oral and silent reading, but they may not need practice on some aspects of the program.

Need for Practice. If the children have no problem with new words introduced in the story, they will not need practice. The teacher should present some phonics to them occasionally, in case the children developed inefficient methods of analyzing words. This practice is given on words the children are reading in their reader because they are more likely to apply the principles learned in this case.

Independent Reading. These children are often able to read a story in one lesson without need for further procedures to develop mastery. For this reason, they may read their story silently at their seats and discuss it with the teacher when their group meets with her. The children should be able to read silently without the teacher when she is sure that none of them read with their lips or point. Most children in the fast group are free of these bad habits. These children may read silently at their seats and use some form of oral reading with the teacher for alternate stories. On other days they may read silently, followed by discussion of the story with the teacher or by use of some study procedure such as recalling the sequence of events in the story. In this way, both oral and silent reading are given attention, but not in every story. These children can also benefit from many opportunities for individualized reading of supplementary books, magazines, and other materials.

Modifications for the Middle Group

On occasion, the children in the middle group may read almost as well as those in the fast group. They may have enough reading power and strong enough skills to follow the plan of alternating silent and oral reading by stories. On the other hand, most children in middle groups need the four steps spread over three days. They need various types of motivation, so activities should be varied from time to time, but the teacher should be sure that all the skills are developed and mastered as the children go along. These children may read silently without supervision when the teacher is sure they are free of poor reading habits.

Modifications for the Slow Group

Many teachers hesitate to use a book at the proper grade level for the children in the slow group. These teachers tend to use a book that is too difficult in order to avoid hurting the feelings of the children, offending the parents, and possibly even annoying the teacher in the grade above. These children, however, need to read at their levels of confidence even more than any of the other children. They rarely make any real progress in books that are too difficult for them, and they tend to develop more and more resistance to the whole reading process when using difficult books.

Books of Mature Interest. While children can progress more easily in the regular graded developmental series of readers because of the carefully selected vocabulary, the teacher may decide to use books of easy vocabulary but written especially for older children. The format of these books may resemble readers written for more mature children such as the use of smaller print, longer sentences, and more material on a page.

These books provide an excellent solution to the problem if their vocabulary is graded. If it is not, the teacher must check the vocabulary to make sure that the children do not meet more than one or two new words on a page. *The Cowboy Sam* series, by Edna Chandler, are suitable for children in the slow group in the second or third grade. Spache lists between fifty and sixty series of books that are written for slower readers on various grade levels.[1] The publisher, a comment about the book, and the reading level are given in this very valuable book by Spache. Many trade books on an easy level of vocabulary and high interest are listed by Spache and are organized by topics.

[1] George D. Spache, *Good Reading for Poor Readers* (rev. ed.; Champaign, Ill.: Garrard Publishing Co., 1962).

Slow children who are reading at their proper level in one of the developmental series readers may need more than one day for practice, particularly when practice is given on sentences, words, and phonics skills. No problem should arise from the provision of extra practice periods as long as the activities are varied and games are heavily emphasized. The reading process has little allure for these children, but they enjoy anything that gives them an opportunity to be active and that savors of a game. Enough types of games and activities should be used to provide reasonable mastery in order to avoid difficulty for the children when they try to read the next story in their books.

OUTLINE OF THE BALANCED READING PROGRAM

Five steps in the outline are given below. The fifth step provides for the follow-up practice material which may be used after the children have read the story and includes creative and other types of activities described in the chapter on the independent work period. The outline applies to the program which is used from about the middle of the primer until the end of the third grade for children who are average readers. The outline is given below.

1. Introduction
   Arouse interest and set the climax question.
   Develop or clarify concepts.
   Introduce new vocabulary.
2. Silent reading
   Children read an entire section of a story.
   Children ask unknown words.
   Teacher keeps a list of unknown words other than those introduced for the lesson.
   Close books and discuss the story for comprehension, organization, and thought.
3. Practice on unknown words.
   Practice on unknown words in sentences.
   Practice on unknown words in isolation.
   Practice on phonics by comparing unknown with known words.
4. Oral reading with a pupil purpose.
   Scan to find the answer to a question and read the answer orally.
   Take parts in dramatic reading.
   Pantomime a sentence or a paragraph to be read.
   Draw a picture and call on others to read the part illustrated.
5. Follow-up with functional reading activities for independent work.

ACQUISITION OF READING POWER

As children advance to the second and third grades many of them acquire considerable independence and power in reading. Through experiences in school and wide reading they develop a greater variety of interests. They also acquire a greater variety of concepts and increased depth in concepts already acquired. They begin to read more widely in social studies and other content subjects and should also read more widely in recreational material. The teacher continues to help these children with a balance of skills including word analysis, word structure, synonyms, homonyms, and figurative language. These children are able to read orally to each other from a variety of books with greater fluency and expression than usually found in the first grade. Since some children are acquiring greater strength than others in various reading skills, the teacher should diagnose the weaknesses of those who cannot advance as rapidly as others and should work with these children in individual and special small groups.

Expansion of Interests

One of the most important sources for expanding reading interests is the home. It would seem that children's early desire to read arises when they see parents and older brothers and sisters finding enjoyment in reading. If the members of the family discuss ideas about which they have read, children begin to realize that information and ideas can be acquired from books. Television and radio programs help extend children's interests into various fields such as science, current affairs, and possibly music and art. If they are able to see good programs, they may also acquire interests in literature. Television plays such as "Alice in Wonderland," "Pinocchio," "The Seven Dwarfs," and "Cinderella" usually result in a heavy demand for books of these stories at the library. Teachers can help to stimulate children's interests in good programs by watching advance notices and arousing the children's interests in good programs to be shown on television.

Children also expand old interests and develop new interests when their parents take them on trips. School trips are also valuable for helping expand their interests. Third-grade children are mature enough to visit the airport, the main city library, the main postoffice, various industries, and parks and zoos. If the teacher is able to secure books about one of these topics for the children to read before as well as after their visit, they may follow one of these themes in their reading for a long time.

Teachers should also know the interests that are common to six-, seven-, and eight-year-old children. Although interests vary with different children, most children will respond to subjects of interest to their age group. Children in kindergarten and first grade enjoy hearing and later reading about pets, toys, and events in their immediate environment. They enjoy fantasy and like folk tales and fairy stories. They demand more plot and suspense than preschool children and enjoy incongruity in humor. They still like favorite stories and poems reread by the teacher, and they often read such stories a number of times themselves. They can also gain a great deal of information from pictures. Picture books are also very helpful for children who have not yet begun to read but who can acquire information from pictures.

Children in the second and third grades are also very fond of fairy stories and enjoy fables, myths, and legends. Many books are available for reading in the social studies on these levels. Usually the community is studied rather extensively in the second grade. Social studies in the third grade vary rather widely. In some cases children learn about the expanding environment and begin to learn about the physical features of land such as bays, which are used for harbors, mountains and their effect on people's lives such as the type of clothing people wear, and large agricultural areas in valleys. Children who are able to read average second and third grade material may be capable of extending their interests to reading in this type of material. The slow readers will need much help from their teacher and will acquire much of their information from the pictures in these books.

Activities for Expanding Children's Interests Through Oral Reading. Suggestions have been made earlier in the chapter for providing opportunities for children to read the funniest, most exciting, or most interesting part of a book to other children. Opportunity for children to read with good fluency and expression to other members of the class is one of the best ways of helping other children become interested in these books. Sometimes children read some of the action immediately preceding the climax of the story and then announce to the class that the book will be available on the library table. A long waiting list for this book usually follows such an announcement. Children also like to read their favorite poems and riddles to the other children.

Dramatic Activities for Arousing Interest. Seven- and eight-year-old children like to present plays to members of the class. A small group of rather mature children can plan the dramatization of a story and can prepare a few props for use in their play during an independent work period. The teacher should listen to their plans and possibly review part of their presentation before they give their play in front of the class.

They may also select stories with a large amount of dialogue for dramatic reading to the other members of the class. The teacher should help the children in the slow group prepare occasional plays to be given either before the other members of the class or for children in a lower grade. Such activity provides excellent motivation for these slower readers. The plays may be varied by providing opportunity for the children to make puppets and to present these stories behind some type of screen. Puppets of this sort may be made of paper bags or paper dolls fastened to sticks. After eight-year-olds have read a rather wide variety of books, they might each select a book to represent in a book parade. Children in one group might make their costumes and hold the parade for the other members of the class to guess which book they represent. In such a case, however, most of the children should have had an opportunity to read the same books. All the children might take part in such a book parade to be given to another class, probably to children of their own age so that they would be able to recognize the books represented by the children in the parade.

Expanding Children's Interests by Exhibits. The teacher may introduce a new book to the children. She may then place it open on the library table so that children will be likely to browse through it whenever they are at the library table. Before she introduces the book, a small group of children may wish to make paper doll stand-up figures of the important characters in the book to interest other children in the new book. They might be placed within a diorama with scenery painted around them. Mature third-grade children may enjoy making a peep show in a shoe box. The scene may represent one of the important sections of a particular book. After the scenery and stand-up figures are placed in the box, the cover is fastened on, then a hole about an inch square is covered with cellophane or some other transparent material placed on the inside through which other children may look to enjoy the peep show. The peep show may be labeled with the name of the book it represents or the originator of the show may encourage other children to guess which book the peep show illustrates. Children may make drawings or paintings to illustrate various stories. These may be illustrations to arouse the interest of other children in favorite books. A moving picture made on a strip of wrapping paper may be used to show the sequence in the plot of a particular book. A committee of children may work together to make a moving picture of this type and then may take turns telling various parts of the story as the paper is wound from one reel to the other when they present their play.

Expanding Children's Interests by Displays on Bulletin Boards. Children may make posters showing the important characters and one of the important scenes in their favorite books. These posters may be pinned on the bulletin board to stimulate interest in favorite books. Each committee may take turns to prepare posters of their own favorite books for a particular week. Children's brief book reports may be mounted on attractive backing and placed on the bulletin board for others to read to see if they think they would enjoy these stories. A few reviews may be placed on the bulletin board at one time and replaced by reviews by other children at weekly or biweekly intervals. A committee may enjoy working on a frieze or a series of pictures mounted on a strip of backing paper to show various scenes in one of their favorite books. This frieze may be pinned on the bulletin board to arouse the interest of other children to read the particular book that was illustrated.

Expansion of Concepts and Vocabulary

Stories in children's readers and in supplementary books used for recreational reading introduce many new concepts at their present reading level and also expand concepts which the children may have acquired previously. The teacher should take as much care at this level as she did with beginning readers to help the children clarify their concepts regarding the meaning of new words. The teachers of the culturally-deprived children must spend considerable time and effort in this work since reading has no meaning for children if they are frustrated by terms which are new to them.

Books for children in second and third grade often have stories about elephants, whales, monkeys, crocodiles, giraffes, swans, and other such animals and birds. Unless the children have had an opportunity to see such animals at the zoo or at a circus at some time they will need help to give them an idea of the appearance and characteristics of such animals. They need to know particularly how large an animal is, what it eats, and where it normally lives.

Fairy stories include characters such as kings, queens, princes, dwarfs, and other such people. Unless children have listened to such stories at home and have learned from their parents what these people are like, they need help with the concepts represented by these words. Stories about old-fashioned trains, carriages or stage coaches drawn by horses, buffaloes found on the plains, people who live in other times (including Indian people), and equipment used in various industries all demand help for children in visualizing the size of these things and the way they operate. Experience in viewing television may help build backgrounds of understanding for some of these things, but the children need to know much more about them than they would learn from television. Sometimes, too, the concepts developed by television are inaccurate, and the teacher finds it necessary to clarify errors in concepts. A word which is often tied to inaccurate concepts is that of the *Indian*. Many children think of Indians living today dressed in feathered head dresses and clothing made of deer or buffalo hides. Children also think of them as living in tents or hogans. Children need to learn that Indian people dress like every one else today, and that most of them live in homes like their own and that they drive automobiles just as the children's parents do. Probably the most misunderstood group of people is the Eskimo. Many people fail to realize that igloos are only used by Eskimos when camping over night or staying a few days where they are hunting. Normally, they live in wooden houses and even use outboard motors in their kayaks.

Expanding Vocabulary and Functional Reading Through the Social Studies. The social studies provide many opportunities for reading, for introducing new vocabulary and concepts, and for providing review of others. The concepts, vocabulary, and reading are used functionally and are therefore learned gradually and without conscious effort on the part of the children. Functional learning takes place as the child works on some activity or interest that has a strong purpose for him.

In a study of the airport the members of the class may decide on the things they want to know and how they can find answers to their problems. These ideas may be dictated to the teacher, who prints them in lists and places them on a bulletin board. The children may also make clocks to show the time zones which would be needed in case of a trip by plane from the west to the east coast.

Experience in reading numbers in connection with daily activities is provided for young children through the use of the calendar. If some technique for placing numbers on the calendar each day is provided, the first-grade children can have the opportunity of sorting the unused cards daily to find the new one that is needed. The less mature children can be given the opportunity to find the easier numbers, and the more mature children can find the larger numbers. Through the discussion of the number of the day, the children have practice in number sequence.

Dramatic activities in the social studies also provide opportunity for reading, including numbers. One group of children dramatized cooking and serving food for passengers in a restaurant at the airport and made use of numbers on their menus. Another group of children carried on dramatic play in their study of the bakery. Their price list also demanded the use of reading numbers. Some third-grade children made tortillas in connection with the study of Mexico. Their work with a recipe demanded the functional use of reading and numbers, although the numbers were limited in this case. A teacher often places reading and other assignments on the chalk board. She usually gives the page

numbers for each assignment, thus providing older children with an opportunity for the functional reading of numbers.

Children are able to follow directions in working with science materials. A child in the third grade knew what materials he needed and
what he had to do to make a home-made compass. He stroked a needle
in one direction against the north end of a magnet. When the needle
was magnetized it was inserted through a piece of cork and floated or
water. The northern pole then pointed to the northern magnetic pole
of the earth. The children needed to use the compass in order to place
the runway for their model airplanes in the proper position.

Other science experiences are valuable for expanding vocabulary and
concepts. Children in a first-grade class acquired many ideas through
the study of insects. They were able to recognize some of the helpful
spiders and also knew a few of the dangerous spiders. They made a
collection of insects and also made some spiders for their bulletin board
They found that the making of a web of flexible, covered wire demands
patience for a child and this work must be even more difficult for the
spider. They also learned some important facts about bees and sampled
honey from a honeycomb. They discovered that bees, too, have tedious
work to do. The children made bees from short rollers and wings of
construction paper. Painted pipe cleaners served for antenna and legs

Some first-grade children were impressed by a large tomato moth they
found. They also found some worms on tomato plants and discovered
that these worms eventually hatched into tomato moths. They learned
why tomato worms are destructive and made some models of these worms
out of halves of egg cartons to use on their bulletin board. One of the
worms was eating a large leaf. (See pages 181, 235, and 249.)

Expanding Reading Vocabulary Through Phonics. Many of the new
words met in reading by seven- and eight-year-old children are words
that are in their understanding vocabulary and many are in their speaking vocabulary. For this reason, phonics is of greatest use for children
of this age because the children know the meaning of the word when
they analyze it. Most teachers' manuals give excellent suggestions for
the development of phonics skills and include a carefully developed program of these skills from the first grade through the third. The simplest
skills are presented first, and other skills are added in increasing order
of difficulty. By the end of the third grade many of the phonics skills
have been presented, and review has been provided frequently enough
to establish these skills.

Special Help on Weaknesses. In each class a few children are found
who have failed to master certain skills and who therefore have gaps

in their ability to use phonics. Sometimes these children have been absent for several weeks when a particular skill was introduced. Sometimes, on the other hand, these children have failed to learn certain steps because of immaturity or lack of understanding. For this reason the teacher should keep a piece of paper in her book on which she jots down these difficulties as children meet them. If a child seems to have only a few gaps in his ability to use phonics skills, the teacher may give him individual help to overcome his problems. When she dismisses the reading group after their practice period she may keep with her the particular child who is having difficulties. Extra help alone for three to five minutes repeated for several days may help the child master his particular problem. If the teacher finds that some children are having difficulty with quite a number of phonics skills, she may put them in a special group to work on any problems that are common to the group until they have acquired these particular skills.

Expanding Vocabulary Through Synonyms and Homonyms. As children's vocabularies expand, they will tend to meet synonyms and homonyms from time to time. The homonyms such as *their* and *there* do not usually cause much trouble in reading but may offer considerable difficulty to the children in spelling. Whether the problem arises in spelling or reading, the best procedure is to teach one word until it is thoroughly mastered, allowing a period for its successful use before the other word of the pair is introduced. The teaching of synonyms is usually a part of the general development of expanding vocabulary.

Expanding Vocabulary Through Picture Dictionaries. Sometimes picture dictionaries for second- and third-grade children help to expand their vocabulary. The teacher must help the children use these dictionaries until they are sure of knowing how to locate words in alphabetical order. Children in the fast reading group will acquire ability to use these dictionaries independently before the other children, but the teacher always checks to be sure that they have located the word successfully and that they understand the meanings of these words.

Expanding Vocabulary Through Help in Writing. At this level, work in spelling and writing stories and other types of compositions supplements and reinforces the children's work in reading. Children tend to overuse hackneyed and rather meaningless words such as *nice* or *good*. The teacher can help the children think of other words to describe a variety of objects or situations. This activity may not only help improve their writing but may also give them a better idea of the function of a synonym. When the teacher finds a story that makes use of appropriate synonyms for a word overused by the children, she may help the children look through the story to find and discuss these words. Some child who prints well may then put these synonyms in alphabetical order on a chart for the use of the children when they are writing compositions. At various times in the reading program the teacher may use particular stories as sources of good synonyms for the children to choose and add to their growing lists.

Expanding Vocabulary Through Use of Figurative Language. Figurative language is found in reading material as children acquire ability to read more extensively. Such an expression as, "Billy flew from the horse's back when it jumped over the fence," demands help for some children. The teacher should help them understand why the author used the word *flew* in this manner.

Some of the following expressions were found in a third-grade reader used commonly in the schools: "railroad bed," "cross as two sticks," "a milk-white horse," "the waves swept the shore," "the face of the earth," "a child as light as a feather," and "held her fast." Although such expressions as these may be very familiar to the teacher, many children may have difficulty understanding them. The teacher should help the children realize that the expression "cross as two sticks" refers to two meanings of the word *cross*. Others involve similarities of one thing to another such as a horse as white as milk and a child as light as a feather.

Children are familiar with the word *milk* and know that it is white so they would easily be able to understand such a reference. In the reference to "a child as light as a feather," children meet two problems. Children who live in industrial sections of a city may never have seen a feather so this concept must be clarified, preferably by showing them a real feather. They should then discuss whether or not any child is really as light as a feather. Since they know this cannot be true, they must be helped to understand that the expression carries an exaggeration, but nevertheless implies lightness in weight.

The study of literature, including poetry, involves similar problems with which the children must have help if they are to understand the stories and poems they read. Culturally-deprived children have even greater problems than those with middle-class backgrounds. Members of culturally-deprived families rarely use figurative expressions, so the teacher must be sure to give help with all of such expressions. One first-grade teacher complained that her culturally-deprived children were completely lost when she made casual references to the common folk and fairy tales. If she made such a statement as, "My what a pretty coat you have! You look like Little Red Riding Hood," the children had no idea what she meant. She decided to plan a program to meet these children's needs since this literature is part of the cultural heritage.

Flexibility in Reading

One of the problems met by teachers of children in the middle grades is lack of flexibility. The foundation for this ability is developed in the primary grades. Some children who lack flexibility may have been taught to read easy recreational material without a balance of material requiring more detailed reading. Other children may have been taught with a great deal of emphasis on word recognition through phonics and much oral reading. They may therefore be unable to read rapidly regardless of the demands of a particular situation.

Children from the first grade on should have experiences with a variety of types of reading. At times, the teacher should tell the children before they read a particular story that she is interested only in the important happenings so they may read rapidly. At other times, she should tell the children that she will question them in considerable detail and that she therefore wishes them to read carefully and to try to remember as much as they can. The teacher will then plan questions to follow the reading which emphasize either detail or broad ideas. Perhaps more of the stories should be read for general ideas because rapid reading is difficult to establish, but reading for detail should not be neglected.

Homework and the Help of Parents

The assignment of homework has gone through a series of stages. Early in the century teachers assigned homework regularly. Then they became more conscious of children's growth and development, length of attention span, and problems encountered in the home. They therefore tended to reduce or completely eliminate homework, especially for young children. In recent times homework has again come to the fore because of the demands of some parents.

In many cases homework does not actually contribute to the child's learning. He may have no place to work, and he may have to contend with family conversation or incessant noise from television or radio. In addition, many assignments consist of practice without meaning or purpose.

Poor Approaches. If the parent helps, he may use poor reading methods which confuse the child because they are different from those used by the teacher at school. Some of these methods may establish poor reading habits which must be broken later. Often the parent is tired at the end of the day and tends to be impatient with the child. Other children may distract the reader with noisy play or talk. Sometimes a younger child leans over the older child's shoulder to tell him words that he does not know. This kind of "help" makes the older child feel inferior and resentful toward the younger one. All of the difficulties may result in poor attitudes toward reading by the child who is receiving help.

One teacher tells a story, although one representing a rather extreme situation, that underlines the harm that may come from some parent's help. The father of a first-grade boy requested that the child's book be sent home with him, although this child was reading successfully in the first group. At the end of about two weeks, the teacher met the mother in the neighborhood grocery store. She asked the teacher not to send the book home any more because the little boy's father hit him over the head every time he failed to recognize a word.

Without guidance parents do not usually teach reading well. They often read the story to the children and then demand that the children memorize it. Since this process is difficult for the children, both the parent and the child become frustrated.

Suggestions for Needed Help.   If a child has missed considerable work because he has been absent for two or three weeks, the parent may be permitted to help if she is carefully instructed in the procedures to follow. The teacher should emphasize the fact that she should help the child for a short period such as fifteen or twenty minutes only, and no other child should be allowed to interfere. She should work with the child in a quiet place and should make a strong point of working pleasantly and using praise whenever possible. She should never reprimand the child because of a forgotten letter sound or a word he has failed to recognize, no matter how many times she has previously told him the word. A parent may be allowed to work with sentence strips but should not usually be given word cards because the parent tends to over practice with them. If a neighbor child can be brought in to play with the strips in some sort of game with the reader, the practice may be more successful.

The parent should be allowed to work with only a few reading strips involving only a few new words at one time. When the child has mastered one set of reading strips, he may be permitted to take home the next set. The teacher should explain to the parent why this practice is limited. She should also be told why encouragement and praise are so necessary and why scolding and irritability are so damaging. One teacher suggested that the parents skip the practice period entirely if she was particularly tired and might therefore be irritable with the child.

SUMMARY

Oral reading should always be motivated to hold the children's interest and to give practice in comprehension. Scanning to find sentences in mixed order and to answer questions helps children keep the thought in mind and tends to help them develop more rapid habits of reading. The program must be adjusted to the needs of the reading group and to the individual within the group. Reading power is developed through an extension of interests and an expansion of concepts and vocabulary including use of figurative language and increased flexibility.

12

Intermediate and Upper Grades

Reading in the intermediate and upper grades is to some degree an extension of the various types of reading instruction carried on in the primary grades. Grouping is still very important and may be organized in a variety of ways. A developmental program including the introduction of the lesson, the silent reading, practice, and rereading for a second purpose may still serve as the backbone of the program. Much more emphasis is given to discovery of children's weaknesses or inadequacies, and special help is given in small groups.

OBJECTIVES FOR EXTENDED READING SKILLS

As the child progresses through the intermediate and upper grades, silent reading is greatly extended by means of informaticnal and recreational materials of all types. Concepts and ideas must continue to be clarified, and rate and comprehension in silent reading are gradually increased. More efficient habits of reading and studying are also developed, and thinking is given increased attention. Children gradually learn to appreciate and enjoy more mature forms of literature and also improve in their power to interpret many kinds of materials. The teacher discovers any inadequacies or poor habits and works to help the children eliminate them. Greater emphasis is placed on fluency and expression in oral reading. The children add various reference skills from time to time. Children expand their ability to use a variety of word recognition techniques including word structure and may also learn something about the origin of words.

These older children continue to have experiences with all of the balanced aspects of the reading program. Purposes should always be established for the use of any reading materials. Some children will tend to develop purposes in connection with their own interests and will seek reading material to help them meet these purposes. Silent and oral reading will continue to be a part of this program, but more emphasis will be given to silent reading.

TEACHING IN GROUPS

Intermediate grade children need work in groups as much, or even more, than primary children. In the intermediate grades the spread of total scores on a reading test usually covers five grade equivalents and sometimes as many as eight.

If the subitems on a standardized reading test are analyzed, even greater variations will be found among these items than among the total scores. Figure 20-1 shows the great range in specific skills of children who were homogeneously grouped by total scores on a reading test. The median score for the lowest homogeneously grouped class in the fifth grade was at a 3.3 grade equivalent, whereas the median for the highest of the four classes was a 6.7 grade equivalent.

When the subscores for the highest of the homogeneously grouped classes were analyzed, however, the range in the subscores in comprehension for this fifth grade class was from 3.8 to 11.2 in grade equivalents. The range in reading rate for this class was even greater; it ranged from 2.2 to 12.7 in grade equivalents. Thus, the slowest reader in the highest class in the homogeneously grouped fifth grades was approximately five years below the average child in the lowest class.

Selection of Pupils

The teacher of the intermediate grades should use a diagnostic test or an informal oral inventory described later in this chapter to help her work in groups in her own room with children according to their needs. At first, the teacher may place children in groups according to their total scores on reading tests as a basis for general work. If she uses test records, they may be taken from tests given at the end of the previous year.

Tentative Groups. As she plans her groups, the teacher considers the groupings made by the previous teacher and her comments regarding the books each child has read. She also carefully reads the previous teach-

This chart was used by second-grade children to help them in the care of their guinea pig. (Courtesy N.D.E.A. 1967 Demonstration School and Sacramento City Unified School District.)

er's notes on each child's strengths and weaknesses. After taking these factors into consideration, many teachers divide the class into three tentative groups, making the first group the largest and the third group the smallest. In this way, the sizes of her groups are adjusted to provide more time with the teacher for the slower children. The better readers can work more independently.

The first distribution of the children in the groups is always very tentative. Some children may have read extensively through the summer and may be, therefore, able to work on a higher level than during the previous year. Other children may have had no reading experiences during the summer and may have actually lost ground in some of their reading skills. As the teacher notes that some children need to work on a higher or lower level, she gradually moves them into more suitable groups. In order to avoid discouragement for the children, when in doubt, the teacher should usually place a child in a lower rather than in a higher group at first. In this way most of her changes will be toward higher groups with resultant encouragement for children.

Divergence From Basic Groups. As the teacher works with the children in each group, she begins to realize that some may have weaknesses in word recognition skills of different types, and others may have weaknesses in one or more study skills. The teacher may handle these weaknesses through the use of basic groups. She may work with a particular group for half of her scheduled time. She may then dismiss the children who do not need special help in a given skill, such as in digraphs, while she keeps the children who do need this practice with her for the last half of the period. Sometimes only one child will need special help, and at other times several children may need this type of help. The teacher usually finds these needs in the middle and low groups, but some children in the highest group may need special help with outlining, dictionary work, or other study skills.

These small groups are thus made up of children who have weaknesses in a particular skill and who can be helped together. Other needs for help in skills may be seen in weaknesses in word construction, such as in the use of prefixes and suffixes. Some children may have weaknesses in such broad skills as comprehension or adequate rate in reading. Children with weaknesses in comprehension or rate of reading should work on material that is particularly easy for them. They should meet not more than one or two new words on a page if they are to be able to improve in their ability in these two latter skills.

Use of Temporary Groups

The beginning teacher will probably find her work easier if she keeps three basic groups and adjusts to their needs according to the suggestions in the previous paragraphs. Some teachers, however, prefer to set up their groups entirely on the basis of children's needs without the use of a basic grouping plan. Such a teacher may work with five, six, or even seven temporary groups, depending upon the children's weaknesses. As the teacher finds that children in a certain group have mastered the particular skill they have been working on, she may then redistribute them, some to one group and some to another, depending on the groups she has working at that time.

A teacher who works with constantly changing groups must keep even more careful records than the teacher who works with three basic groups. Other teachers work entirely on an individualized plan described in Chapter 19. If the teacher works with a number of small groups, she must schedule them so that they work with her on alternate days.

Twenty to twenty-five minutes is a reasonable block of time to spend with each group, but each block of time should be flexible and adjusted to the work of a particular group on a particular day. The schedule for work with individualized reading is discussed in the chapter on that topic.

Help on Special Problems

A list of study type skills is given in Chapter 17. If a skill is simple and can be quickly taught, such as the use of the index, the teacher may work with a general or basic group in which most of the children seem to need this skill. When she has worked on the skill long enough to give review for the children who do not have particular difficulty with it, she may then dismiss those children to work or read at their seats. Sometimes she may call up children from other groups who need special help for further practice on such a skill as selecting main ideas and work with them along with the children in the part of her group who need practice on this skill.

One period with the children who have special needs in a particular skill such as selecting main ideas will probably be far from adequate. The teacher must repeat this type of special teaching on this particular skill for a number of days or until all of the children are able to master it. Some of this practice may be spaced over a period of days or weeks. Even then, review will be necessary from time to time, and further practice will be given when the children need to select main ideas in connection with their work in the social studies.

DEVELOPMENTAL LESSONS

The general or basic groups may work together on the developmental lessons in a reader following suggestions given in the manual. A lesson in a typical manual for a fifth-grade developmental reader lists the new words for sight recognition and for which concepts should be developed. It then lists words for independent attack and other words for developing such skills as syllabification, work on short medial vowels in one syllable words, and similar skills. Much of this instruction is given to provide review of phonics taught in previous grades.

Introduction of the Story

A lesson in the manual also provides suggestions for presenting a background for the story. If actual characters in history are involved in the story, some background facts about their lives are given to develop interest. The setting of a story may be discussed. If the story is laid in a particular geographical area, this area may be located on the map. At this time, the teacher also helps the children with words involving concepts which the children may not fully understand. The glossary is also used to help children discover the meanings and work out the pronunciation of the names of the people and other unknown words in the story.

The children may read and discuss the definition of the words so that the teacher can be sure they understand them. If the teacher has found other words in the story that may cause difficulty for her particular group of children, she helps them discuss the meanings of these words to insure understanding during the silent reading of the lesson. The teacher then helps the children develop a purpose for reading the story. A climax question may be developed through the previous discussion or through a discussion of the pictures on the first few pages of the story. The children are then ready to read the story silently.

A situation in which the teacher gave the children considerable help was described above. Some teachers believe that they should give children even in the middle grades all the help they need until they are completely secure in the use of the glossary.

The teacher also discusses the background of the story with the children in the highest group and may guide their use of the map or other helpful materials during this introduction. Often the children in this group, however, can look up the words they need to know without help. The teacher may make sure of their comprehension of these words and other ideas in the story in the discussion that follows the silent reading.

Check on Reading Habits

The teacher may supervise the silent reading of the children in each group for the first few days or even weeks of school to make sure that none of them point to the words in the book or move their lips during the silent reading. When she is sure that the children in a particular group are free from such habits, she assigns the silent reading to be carried on at the children's seats after she has introduced the story and clarified the concepts. While the children continue the silent reading at their seats, the teacher brings another group to her for the introduction of their story or for other phases of the program.

The Silent Reading

Sometimes the teacher may guide the children to read silently to discover the answer to the climax question. At other times, she may give the children specific work to be carried on in connection with the silent reading. For example, she may put a list of steps or events taken from the story on the board, arranged in an order different from that in the story. The children then reorganize the steps in the story as part of the work in silent reading. Sometimes the teacher may outline the broad topics in a story and ask the children to list all the events or ideas they find under each appropriate general topic.

At other times, she may put several questions on the board to stimulate the children to develop answers to thought questions that are not specifically answered in the text. Sometimes the teacher may assign work to help the children learn how to use the index. She may list key words found throughout the story and place them on the chalkboard in mixed order. The children must then look up each key word and list the appropriate page or pages where the idea represented by the word is located in the story.

Discussion of the Story. The teacher always takes time to discuss the assignments with the children after they have completed their work. This discussion may take place later during the day or on the following day. To be sure that the papers are available when she needs them, the teacher may collect them and pass them back to the children when she is ready for the discussion. Sometimes the teacher may suggest that the children check their own answers for accuracy. At other times, each child may pass his paper to another child to be checked. At still other times no formal checking may be used; the teacher merely skims them to find needs for help.

Corrections for Diagnostic Help. When the beginning teacher permits children to check their own or other children's papers, she may find that they tend to correct the other's errors in order to give their friends a better grade. Several procedures help avoid this practice. The teacher emphasizes the fact that the checks are meant to help each child discover his own needs. Anyone who corrects another child's paper may be cheating him out of a chance to learn what help he needs.

The teacher will also avoid using grades on papers checked by the children in her class as a basis for marks on a report card. She, herself, merely reads the papers to see which children need certain kinds of help. She should explain this procedure to the children so that they understand how to work with her and with each other. One sixth-grade teacher found cheating rampant at first. After she had worked with them for about six weeks, however, and after they had discovered that she kept her word about the avoidance of using such papers for grading purposes, the children completely gave up the practice of surreptitiously helping their friends.

The Practice Period

If the teacher has found that the children had difficulty analyzing the words in the story that was provided for word attack skills, she may spend a period with the children in this particular group helping them attack the words with which they had problems. A variety of suggestions for this type of help are given in the teachers' manuals. Some of these suggestions are for help on skills that were taught in the primary grades, but on which the children may need review. One such lesson gave review on the pronunciation of the sounds *er, ir,* and *ur* to help the children realize that these letter groups are usually pronounced exactly the same in most words.

Help on Diacritical and Accent Marks. If the teacher found that the children had difficulty in using the diacritical and accent marks in the words in the glossary, she may give some lessons on the use of these marks. She should help the children learn to use the key words at the bottoms of the pages to help them recall the sound of a particular diacritical mark. The skill in learning to pronounce unknown words by means of the glossary or dictionary is difficult for many children. Such a lesson should be repeated from time to time as the children meet new words in their stories. This skill is not completely mastered in one grade and is quickly forgotten. The teachers of the higher grades usually find it necessary to give occasional work on this skill from time to time.

Help on Organization. At other times, this practice period may be needed for help in choosing main ideas in a selection in order gradually to help children learn how to make outlines. The suggestion that children select titles for parts of stories given in an earlier chapter for use in the second grade may also be used by teachers of more advanced grades for children who have difficulty understanding how to select main ideas. Another step in helping children acquire readiness for selecting main ideas is the assignment for children to reorganize main ideas selected by the teacher. This process should be followed for a long time for children who need it to help them understand why one idea is considered to be the main thought in a paragraph, whereas other ideas are merely subordinate to the main thought.

To help children understand the concept of subordination, the teacher may put four or five points for each paragraph on the chalkboard so that the children may select the one which is predominate or which serves as the main idea. All the ideas should be discussed in detail to help the children understand why one only should be selected. This type of practice should be provided repeatedly until the teacher is sure that all of the children understand the procedure. When some of the children in a particular group understand the idea, they may be freed to work on other activities while the teacher continues to give help to those children who need it. These children, however, should have review before they are free to carry on other activities.

Help With Figurative Language. Children need help in the use of figurative language and on words that are used as figures of speech. Some of the following terms are used in *The Brave and the Free*, a sixth-grade developmental reader. In Elizabeth Coatsworth's poem "Wishes," she uses the term "an arrow of wings," to refer to the V-formation of wild geese flying in the sky. She also uses the term "Shaping a yarn" to refer to a sailor's tendency to tell stories.[1] Carl Sandburg in "A Rootabaga Story" mentions the wind that puts "its soft fingers on their foreheads." [2] In the same story, he uses the term "steam hog's nose" to refer to the engine on a railroad train.[3] In James Buckham's story "Waukewa's Eagle" he uses the words "a gentle spirit waking in the boy" to refer to Waukewa's pity for an eagle with a broken wing.[4]

Some children can infer the meanings of such expressions as these. Other children lose the thread of the story when they are unable to understand such words. Many of today's adults fail to turn to poetry for pleasure because their understanding of the poetry studied in school was limited by too many strange figures of speech. If the teacher helps with these expressions, the study of a poem may not become an exercise in reading the notes in the backs of the books. In the past, difficulties were caused by the use of too difficult material before the children were ready for it. In today's books just enough of these figurative expressions are used to give the selection verve, as long as children are given help in understanding them when needed. Selections with figurative language are usually very difficult for culturally-deprived children. Easier selections and more help should be given if these children are to enjoy literature.

Practice on Sight Words. Very few suggestions are given in the manuals for practice on sight words in the intermediate grades. Some children become lost in their reading, however, because they meet too many words which they can neither recognize at sight nor analyze. For effective word analysis children must have a backlog of sight words which they know well. These words are then used to help analyze new words with similar elements. Some children are not able to master all the word elements they need in the primary grades. For these children extra help on words recognized at sight may be necessary.

Practice in Sentence Context. As in the primary grades, these words should be introduced and practiced in sentence context. Often, the children who need help with new sight words also need help with the use

---

[1] Barbara Nolen, Paul Witty, and Ursula Bringhurst, *The Brave and the Free*, Reading for Interest Series (rev. ed.; Boston: D. C. Heath and Co., 1950), p. 81.

[2] *Ibid.*, p. 349.

[3] *Ibid.*, p. 351.

[4] *Ibid.*, p. 361.

of context clues and the reading of words in phrases or groups. Practice similar to that given in the primary grades with the game called "What's My Line" or any of those suggested in earlier chapters for practice on sentences will serve to give this help.

Experience has shown that older children enjoy these games as much as younger children, and extra practice on sight words in context gives them much needed security. Their reading must be kept on the level of confidence if they are to enjoy reading and to turn to recreational reading on their own. One or two unknown words on a page are adequate if these children are to grow in reading without frustration. Betts' suggestion for the number of words on the instructional level is usually too difficult for these rather slow-moving readers.[5]

Practice on Single Words. These children should also have practice on the sight words that they have met in the practice on sentences described above. They must be able to recognize these words in any situation or when standing alone. Most of these intermediate grade children enjoy the same games such as bingo, tick-tack-toe, and others suggested for the primary grades. These children need practice on the single words until they are mastered. Six or seven new sight words, however, are probably the maximum that these children can learn at one time. Further practice on word analysis usually follows practice on sight words.

If children have difficulty with such basic skills as comprehension or rate during the silent reading, they should be given special help. Ideas for assistance with these types of problems are given in a later section of this chapter.

Purposes for Silent Reading

Children should always have some purpose for silent reading. The best purpose is the one developed by the children themselves, because it is likely to have the most meaning for them. On the other hand, children also profit from variety in their purposes. Sometimes a selection may include references to other material to expand the children's backgrounds or concepts, which serves as a purpose for the extension of reading. Some of the suggestions given below may help the teacher provide variety in pupil purposes for silent reading.

To prove points or settle questions of disagreement.

To verify facts or opinions.

To contrast or compare facts or ideas.

[5] Emmett A. Betts, *Foundations of Reading Instruction* (New York: American Book Company, 1957).

To find the central thought, idea, or purpose of a selection.

To select parts which support a certain point of view.

To find answers to specific questions.

To solve problems connected with a unit of work in the social studies.

To make outlines using main topics.

To find books or material for use on certain topics.

To prepare reports about particular subjects to give to the group or class.

To make tests for others to answer.

To select sentences, paragraphs, or chapters on a particular problem, possibly in connection with the social studies.

To prepare a summary of main points in selections for a group or class discussion.

To prepare questions to ask a group or class.

To decide whether statements are true or false.

To find the pages on which particular facts or parts of selections are found.

To prepare notes for use in a speech or report to members of the group or class (for older children).

To find key sentences to use in discussing a topic.

To find points overlooked by members of the group or class.

To select material for original dramatizations, pantomimes, moving picture or puppet shows.

To find the most interesting or best-liked parts of stories to tell to the group or class.

To find how to construct something for class exhibits or programs.

To find and list the most important events in sequence in order to serve as reminders when telling a story to another group or class.

To find the most important or exciting part of a story.

To discover how a story ends after someone has read part of it to the group.

To find the most interesting, beautiful, or humorous part of a story.

To find unusual or beautiful word passages in a story.

To find the most beautiful description in a story.

To select and prepare a review story to read orally later to the group or class.

To decide whether a story could be true.

To plan the scenery for a puppet show or dramatization.

To decide how many scenes are necessary for a dramatization.

To find words that describe a certain character or place.

To find words or phrases that tell what some particular person in the story did.

Oral Reading

Although oral reading is given less emphasis in the intermediate grades than in the primary grades, some help on oral reading should be given through at least the intermediate grades. In the seventh and eighth grades oral reading may be carried primarily in connection with dramatic work in literature.

Everyone must read orally at times for such purposes as reading the minutes of a club meeting, or reading a paragraph aloud from the newspaper so that it may be discussed with members of the family or friends. The teacher uses oral reading in addition to check on the children's progress in word recognition and sight vocabulary. From the early primary grades the teacher works for fluency and expression in oral reading. As in the primary grades, oral reading should never consist of purposeless responses from the children as the teacher calls on the next child to read a sentence, paragraph, or page. Even in response to purposes, the use of short selections are usually better than long ones when the reading is part of group work. Oral reading may be used in audience situations or as part of the work in the developmental program.

Audience Reading. At one time, the use of the reading of a particular selection chosen by a pupil and read to the rest of the class for their enjoyment or information was called audience reading. This type of reading has considerable value in the intermediate and upper grades. Children may select either poetry or prose. The child who is reading orally is the only one who has the selection in hand, and the other children listen to this reading which should cover material which they have not read or heard before.

Work With a Partner. The children who are to take part in audience reading should have selected the material in advance and should have practiced reading it orally either with a partner in school or at home if their home situations are suitable for such work. When the partner assures the teacher that the reader can read with enough fluency and expression to hold the attention of the class, the teacher may schedule his reading before the group or class. A child should never be permitted to read material to an audience which he has not previously read to himself.

Sometimes the teacher also must help the child who is to read to an audience if this child has difficulty in reading fluently and with expression. If the teacher feels that a particular child has inadequate expression or fluency to hold the interest of the class although he has practiced as much as the teacher feels is reasonable, she may let him read a very short selection. In this way, he may receive recognition from the other children without boring them too seriously.

Standards. The emphasis on the oral reading should always be on the provision of enjoyment or information for the other children. Once the child has been screened for reading to the group, the evaluation should consist primarily of favorable comments with possibly one or two suggestions for improvement. Some teachers encourage the children to make up a list of standards which they may use in evaluating their success as they prepare for reading to the class. This list also serves to guide the children in constructively evaluating the reading of their peers. These lists serve best when they are worded in positive terms and printed on a chart. Such a list is given below:

Suggestions for Oral Reading

We stand up straight when we read.
We read loudly enough for all to hear.
We enunciate the words clearly.
We check the pronunciation of words before we read.
We group our words in phrases.
We read with expression.
We look at the class occasionally as we read.

Reading for Enjoyment. A child may select a poem that he has enjoyed and that he would like to read orally to the class. Before children read their favorite poems, the teacher should help them learn to read poetry with emphasis on thought and expression. They should learn to avoid undue emphasis on the rhyming words at the ends of the lines in order to avoid a sing-song quality. They should also learn to avoid an overemphasis on the rhythm of the poetry. Emphasis on thought and fluency will usually help prevent overemphasis on the mechanical aspects of poetry.

Children also like to read favorite stories to other members of the class. Sometimes they may read entire short stories. When they wish to present a book, they will select a particular part for the oral reading. Children enjoy reading the part of a story that immediately precedes the climax. They may then return the book to the library table with the information that the other children can discover how the story ends by securing it from the table.

Purposes for Oral Reading. Some suggestions for reading selections from books are given in a list below:

To verify or prove the correctness of statements made by individuals.
To answer specific questions.

To read facts that have been overlooked.

To locate and read specific facts in a story or selection.

To read directions for other members of the group or class to follow.

To read to show how customs, dress, transportation facilities, or other features of a country are like or different from ours.

To read to give the group information about particular topics discussed in the social studies.

To read articles of interest or current events to the members of the class.

To read sentences or paragraphs that describe a certain character.

To read a story or poem to entertain other members of a group or class.

To read a story or poem to entertain a visitor.

To read a story, poem, or take part in a dramatic reading for a class or assembly program.

To read the most humorous or exciting parts of a story to the members of a group or class.

To read beautiful word pictures to others to help in choice of words for written compositions.

To read parts for dramatizations, puppet shows, or homemade moving picture shows.

To read to take the part of a character in a story. Other children read the other parts and one child reads the action or the descriptive parts.

To read parts that have been illustrated by pictures. The child may read the part that describes his own picture or he may read to guess the part illustrated by the picture of another child.

To read descriptions to help plan the scenery for a dramatization or puppet show.

To read parts of familiar stories for other children to identify.

To read favorite poems for other children to enjoy or to illustrate after the reader has finished.

To read original poems, stories, or reports for the enjoyment or information of the group or class.

To verify how a story ends after children have made several guesses.

To find and read certain facts or parts in a story, depending upon the interests of the children.

To read a story to children who have been absent.

To read summaries of statements for discussion.

To read answers to questions made up by other children in the reading group or class.

To read parts that describe various scenes to use as backdrops for dramatic reading.

To read a description of a character so that the class can guess which one is being described.

To read descriptions of customs or dress of people in a country from two different sources and have the class decide whether or not these descriptions agree.

To read selections about the natural resources of a country from two different sources and see whether these descriptions agree.

To read a selection to the class about a story of a hero in whom the children are interested.

To read reports which have been written to answer questions about problems in the social studies.

To read data that has been selected for use in a debate or discussion for the other members of the class to evaluate.

To read the data on a map, chart, or graph for the other members of the class when this chart is presented to them.

To read a simple outline about a topic in preparation for a talk in front of the class for class evaluation.

To read a sequence of events in a story that has been organized by the pupils for presentation.

To read a description about a place in the desert and a place in the mountains so that the class may compare the various factors in the environments.

To find the cause of some particular accident or incident in a story and read it to the class.

To read material about an exhibit prepared for the class to evaluate its accuracy.

To show a collection of butterflies, rocks, leaves from trees, or insects and read the titles of the objects to the class.

To read material about health habits to be discussed by the class.

To read information to make a health poster for the class to evaluate.

To read the speech of one political candidate and compare it with the speech of another political candidate of the opposite political party.

Scanning. The term "scanning" has been used to suggest a procedure for guiding the oral reading in the primary grades. The term "skimming" has been reserved for the quick examination of an article or selection to discover if it contributes any ideas of value in relation to a particular topic. This skimming may call for only the reading of the first or last line in each paragraph or to identify the topic.

Although rate of reading depends on the type of selection to be read and the intelligence of the reader, most children and adults do not read as efficiently as they should. Success in college will result in the elimination of ineffective readers. In the past, poor reading has been one of the chief causes of failure in college.

The scanning procedure described in the chapter on oral reading in the primary grades is also very effective in the intermediate grades.

The example of a fifth-grade class which gained an average of five months in comprehension and speed in three months is given in a later section of this chapter. Some suggestions are given for scanning in the manuals, but this work is not given often enough to raise the reading rate of most children.

Some of the oral reading in the intermediate grades should consist of scanning motivated by questions. The same care in introducing this procedure should be used in the intermediate grades as was suggested for the primary grades. The children of this age also enjoy the use of pantomime and their own illustrations as motivations for skimming.

Adaptations of the Manual's Suggestions

More suggestions for help are given in the teacher's manual for any set of developmental readers than the teacher is expected to use. She selects the skills on which the children need help and teaches these thoroughly. She will also find excellent ideas for presenting the background of the story and a wide variety of suggestions for guiding the children to read and interpret stories. Far more reccommendations for word analysis are given than most children need. She selects those that will fit her children's needs. Many good ideas are also given for enrichment activities.

ACTIVITIES FOR THE INDEPENDENT WORK PERIOD

Silent reading and organizational activities are good types of experiences for children to pursue at their seats. Silent reading may be of a work or recreational type. A variety of purposes both for recreation and for work add interest and challenge to the silent reading during the independent work period. Some suggestions are given below for various purposes for silent reading.

General Independent Activities

Read for information to add to a class activity. Social studies provides for a great many purposes for reading for information.

Find answers to a problem, again related to the social studies program.

Read to find such items of interest as kinds of minerals mined in South America in order to make a chart showing these minerals.

Read to make a list of questions for a group or committee to work on in the social studies, such as the kinds of vegetation found on deserts.

Read in children's encyclopedias to add further answers to questions of interest in social studies.

Prepare notes in order to make a record of some of the things learned on a social studies trip.

Choose scenes for a dramatization from history.

Make a notebook showing the various ways that man has told time from early history to the present.

Make a notebook of different kinds of houses built around the world.

Find information for making a time line in the social studies, such as a time line of inventions from 1800 to the present.

Select sentences, paragraphs, or chapters to add information about a problem in the social studies.

Look up information in order to find cities, railroads, rivers, mountains, and so forth for either an outline map or a relief map.

Find pictures that apply to problems in the social studies. Plan and find other information in order to present the work to the class.

Prepare notes to use in a speech or report to the class about a social studies topic.

Find points overlooked by a group or committee in the social studies.

Find new and unknown words in the social studies to put on a chart entitled *A Vocabulary List.*

Organize reading books and materials according to topics needed for the social studies. List the topic, books, and pages on a chart for reference.

Read material in preparation for writing an autobiography of one of the children traveling in a wagon train across the plains.

Read to find out what kind of food the pioneers ate when traveling across the plains in covered wagons.

Read to find out what kind of clothing the pioneers wore when traveling across the plains in covered wagons. Many other interests in connection with this topic may be explored.

Find interesting customs of people who live in other parts of the world to discuss with classmates.

Select points of interest or importance in preparation for a trip, such as a trip to a museum of pioneer artifacts.

Read to find information about the lives of some of the important men in history. (Suitable for seventh- and eighth-grade students.)

Read to trace changes over a period of time in transportation systems, dress, and similar matters in order to make a booklet.

Independent Activities in Science and Other Aspects of the Curriculum

Read in relation to special topics of seasonal interest or to gain information about holidays and holiday heroes.

Conduct simple science experiments given in books. Children may read the directions and follow their plans after they have been checked by the teacher.

Read about specimens in a nature museum and make a book of reports on the habits of these specimens.

Read to compare several true stories about a particular animal such as a wolf to see if they agree or disagree in detail.

Find material for the formulation of health rules for specific situations.

Make a booklet of "Birds I Can Recognize and How I Am Sure I Know Them."

Make a notebook of clippings of jokes or clever stories.

Make notebooks of stories of heroism.

Make notebooks of stories of adventure. These may be clipped from children's old magazines and newspapers.

Take part in an imaginary travel club. Read to decide where the club is going and what they will be likely to see.

Make a booklet of ways to travel by land, another of ways to travel by water, and still another of ways to travel by air.

Make plans for an exhibit of hobbies.

Make a notebook about certain industries such as the canning or mining industries.

Make questions for others to answer about a particular story or a particular topic in one of the textbooks.

Read about a controversial issue and try to find facts to support either side of the controversy.

Gather material in relation to discussion of a controversial issue.

Read the newspapers to find significant items on current events.

Read directions to solve crossword puzzles.

Find clippings to use in making notebooks. Girls may be interested in clipping interesting items about actresses. Boys may be interested in collecting clippings from candidate's speeches, especially on the upper grade level. Other children may like to collect clippings about new inventions or similar topics.

Read to find out how to care for a new pet, which may be borrowed from the junior museum or from one of the children.

Read to find out how to play a game.

Find clippings in old newspapers and magazines at home to take to school.

Find new material to aid in the solution of problems under discussion. An example of such a problem might be the need to find out what kind of fur-bearing animals may be found in Alaska.

Make a list of books dealing with a particular subject. Such a list might be centered around the life of the gauchos in Argentina in a study of South America.

Read about insect life or lives of animals to satisfy a personal curiosity about these things.

Read to find answers to such interests as why the temperature is lower on the mountain tops than it is in the valleys.

Find material to use in making health posters.

Find good poems about birds, trees, flowers, or other interests to make a collection on filing cards for class use.

Read to make a classification of rocks, flowers, birds, insects, or trees from these specimens in order to be able to label these.

Activities in Preparation for Oral Reports and Discussions or Dramatizations

Find books, stories, or articles to report on or discuss with others.

Find the most beautiful description in a book. Discuss with others to see if they agree with the choice.

Read to plan scenery for a puppet show or dramatization.

Read to decide how many scenes may be necessary for a dramatization.

Prepare programs for special occasions or assemblies.

Read books and take notes to help give a report on the book to the other children.

Find the most interesting or most liked part of a story to tell to a class or group.

Read to select the most interesting, beautiful, or humorous part to read to the class to see if they agree to the choice.

Read a poem to select the most beautiful, humorous, or emotional part to share with the class.

Read a story to find parts to dramatize. Others guess the name of the story from which the selection was taken.

Read to select main items in an article in order to be able to report about this article to classmates.

Read to find materials which could be used for original dramatizations, pantomimes, homemade moving picture shows, and puppet shows.

Gather information for debates or discussions (especially for the seventh and eighth grades).

Independent Activities for Classroom Projects

Select interesting animal stories and make a list of those that may be placed on the library table for others who are interested.

Read directions for the making of an object for a gift.

Read to find how to construct some object for an exhibit.

Write articles for a class newspaper. Evaluate articles written by other children for a class newspaper.

The children in this school are learning to use the Dewey decimal s numbering in locating books. (Courtesy California State Department of cation.)

Read articles written for the class newspaper and evaluate them they are included in the class newspaper.

Read to find material to add to the bulletin board.

Read to write multpile-choice questions on selections for classm complete.

Check whether exhibits are geographically or historically correct. might have been set up on the bulletin board by another committe

Miscellaneous Silent Reading Activities

Collect books and materials for the class library. Some of these may be in pamphlet form. Children may bind these together cover which they may decorate.

Select a story to read for a meeting of the reading club. Childr use the name "club" for their recreational reports, and enjoy tel other stories they have read.

opriate to read for special holidays.

usual word passages or words that are help-
nés as *nice* in written compositions.

t a story could be true.

certain character to help the reader learn

vents in a story.

events that the teacher has placed on the

nould Like to Know."

t or exciting part of a story.

orally by someone else ends.

oral reading for another grade, usually a

ites when the teacher may be busy with a

s written by other children.

a story and to read this revision to the

ident to a story.

INFORMAL ORAL APPRAISAL

informal oral appraisal is one practical way of discovering the
reading level for those who enter the class at the beginning of
ar or for a child who is a new member of a class. Harris has
ed this procedure in detail.[6] It is briefly summarized here.

on of the Material

teacher begins her check with a selection near the beginning
der that belongs to a basic reading series and that seems to be
ading level which is very easy for the child. This book should
a series to which the child has not been exposed in order to
is remembering stories previously read. The teacher asks the
read at the beginning of a story and keeps a record to discover
at which he is able to read.

J. Harris, *How to Increase Reading Ability* (4th ed.; New York: David
., Inc., 1961).

Reading Levels

Reading levels have been classified as independent, instructional, and frustration. On the independent level the child should be able to read with reasonable fluency and without making more than two or three errors in a hundred words. On a check of comprehension, after the oral reading, the child should be able to retell the story with some detail or be able to answer questions to fill in gaps in the sequence. The child should feel that the material is easy for him.

On the instructional level, the child should be able to read with some fluency although he may slow down when he meets difficult words. He should not make errors on more than two to five words out of a hundred and should feel that the selection provides some challenge. He should be able to recall most of the story, although he may forget some of the details. The child who makes more than five errors in a hundred words is probably reading on the frustration level. He has difficulty recalling the ideas in the story and finds the reading arduous.

Administration of the Test

When the teacher plans to test a child, she tries to work with him by himself when the other children are out of the room if possible. If not, the teacher and the child should work as far away from the other children as they can to avoid embarrassing the child who is tested. The teacher may number the words by marking points at the ends of twenty-five, fifty, one hundred, and two hundred words before beginning the work with the child.

The teacher introduces the story as she would with a regular reading group. She points out the names of the characters whom the child has not usually met before in his reading. She also discusses the pictures with the child and helps him relax before starting to read. She then asks the child to read orally without previous silent reading so that she can discover his approach to reading and his problems. She tells the child any words he may have difficulty with if he hesitates or asks for help on the word.

After the child has read as much of the selection as the teacher feels is necessary to discover his difficulties, she asks him to retell the story. If he omits some details, she asks questions to fill in the gaps. Instead of asking the child to retell the story, the teacher may prepare ten questions to use with the child if the content permits. In this way, she can get a rough estimate of the child's comprehension. The number of questions out of ten will give a rough per cent of comprehension. If the child is able to read this selection on the independent level, the teacher repeats the process with the next higher book. If several children are to be tested, the teacher works with other selections in the early part of the book that are on approximately the same level of difficulty.

The Record

The teacher may prepare a paper in advance for keeping the record by filling in the child's name, the date, the name of the book, and the selection or pages which the child is to read. She may then make three columns, one for each word as the child misreads or mispronounces it, one for each word as it should be correctly read, and one for each word the child is unable to recognize and which the teacher therefore pronounces for him. If an error is made a second time, the teacher should check the word on which the error is made.

The teacher may also keep a record of the repetitions and omissions made by the child. She may wish to record the time required for reading the selection and the number of questions answered correctly or a description of the extent of the child's comprehension. She may then compute the number of words read per minute. She should add any remarks that might be helpful in indicating the types of problems met by the child.

If the teacher wishes, she may ask the child to read a comparable selection silently and may check his comprehension by means of questions. She will then record the time and compute the number of words read per minute. In this way, she can compare the child's speed and comprehension of oral reading with that of his silent reading. After the test, the teacher must decide on which level the child is able to read in each book checked. In this way she will know with which group the child can read most successfully.

Instructional Level for Slow Readers

Most children in the slow group in the intermediate grades have encountered many difficulties in learning to read and have often been expected to read material that is too difficult for them. One of the most important aspects of reading for these children is to help them acquire confidence in their ability. For this reason, they can work much more successfully on the independent level or even on still easier material than on higher levels. Often these children are unable to learn many new sight words at a time and may have considerable difficulty with word analysis. If the teacher works on the independent level, the children will be able to read more successfully for meaning because they will meet fewer unknown words. They will need help in analyzing only a few unknown words and, therefore, will be less likely to become discouraged. The teacher should work for maximum comprehension. These children will probably be able to read successfully both orally and silently on their proper level. The children of lower intelligence, however, may never acquire as much speed as the average and fast readers.

SUMMARY

The reading on the intermediate- and upper-grade levels calls for an expansion of the reading skills developed in the primary grades and also demands the introduction of new skills especially of the study type. The children in these grades will also learn more advanced approaches to the reading of literature. More emphasis will be placed on diagnosis of individual difficulties and help with these problems. The children should read for a wide variety of purposes both orally and silently. The teacher can help discover the reading levels of children new in her class by an individual oral appraisal.

IV

FURTHER GROWTH IN READING

13

Reading Problems

Some children are too immature to grasp some of the reading skills when they are taught, and some are unable to acquire the new sight vocabulary as rapidly as other children. The teacher may keep these children in their reading groups if they are able to acquire some of the skills. Any failure to acquire particular skills should be remedied as soon as possible. These difficulties begin to multiply as the child is taught more advanced work, and he therefore becomes increasingly discouraged and frustrated. Unless he is given help at the earliest possible time, his reading problems become accentuated by his emotional problems and he becomes more and more resistant to help.

SUGGESTIONS FOR WORK WITH READING DISABILITY

Both the daydreamer and the child who seeks attention through aggression may have reading problems. One is seeking escape from his insolvable problem, and the other is trying to compensate for his feelings of inferiority. The teacher who is able to help these children must have a deep interest in them and a great amount of patience. Interest and motivation are extremely important factors in success in helping children improve their reading. Help in reading must be begun on the level of confidence, and the progress should be very slow until the child becomes secure and develops a desire to work on his reading problems. Records are helpful to the teacher and the pupil in recognizing the progress made by the child.

Emotions Related to Reading

Often the child with reading problems has developed unhappy attitudes toward himself and his school work because poor reading causes difficulty with other subjects as well. This child learns to dislike school, his teachers, and reading, and also has a very poor attitude toward himself.

Frustration. Many cases of reading difficulty result from the use of reading material of too difficult a level. The child may have been expected to work in a group on material too difficult for him, and this condition may have existed for most of his school life. Teachers tend to use too difficult material with readers who are slow to mature because of fear of parental criticism and concern for the opinions of other teachers and administrators. Yet the child develops emotional blocks from this procedure that drastically interfere with his learning.

The Self-Concept. Studies of the self-concepts of children have shown that they develop feelings of success or failure in connection with everything they do. The more often the child fails, the more severe his self-condemnation becomes. After a series of failures in a particular subject, the child becomes thoroughly convinced that he is unable to master it. Unfortunately, a cluster of subjects is involved when the child has difficulty with reading.

The child who has a low self-concept in regard to a particular skill such as reading usually fails to learn and gradually becomes more and more handicapped. When he becomes thoroughly convinced of his inability to learn, he will avoid reading whenever possible and will become more and more afraid to make any effort. The reconstruction of a good self-concept in the field of reading is very difficult and time-consuming. The child can make almost no progress until his self-concept has been improved.

Attitudes. Some children may make good progress in improving in reading abilities but may still dislike reading and may therefore avoid reading whenever possible. Since vocabulary and improved rate are largely acquired through extensive reading, these children become increasingly handicapped. Their failure to acquire an extensive vocabulary and to increase their rate of reading in turn limits their desire to read, and the whole procedure becomes a downward spiral. The longer they remain handicapped, the more difficult is their rehabilitation. This difficulty in reading constitutes a tragedy in these children's lives, which may permanently interfere with their future education.

Confidence. In reteaching, progress slow enough to establish confidence is crucial. The children's insecurities must be overcome, and their faith in their own ability must be restored if they are to make progress in reading and if they are to acquire a permanent desire to read. This problem is probably the most difficult aspect of the improvement program for these children and one that cannot be over-emphasized.

These children should also be convinced that they are not different from many other children since this concern torments them. They should be assured that many other children have difficulty with reading for a variety of reasons and that other children also have problems with other subjects and skills such as running and throwing a ball. These children need reassurance concerning their abilities and their potential for improvement in reading.

The Teacher

A teacher who tries to help children with reading difficulties in her own class or in a special remedial situation must have a very sincere fondness for children and a strong desire to help them. Since this type of child has felt inadequate and insecure for a long period, he must be led to feel sure that the teacher respects him as a person and appreciates those abilities that he has. She should be able to show warmth and understanding and give the child a strong feeling of acceptance and approval. Some very calm, relaxed teachers succeed very well with these children. Others inspire these children by their enthusiasm and strong self-confidence. The child needs frequent praise and constant success. Any suggestions for improvement must be made in constructive terms and in a tactful manner.

Help for Insecurity. The teacher should give these children adequate opportunities to express themselves and talk about their feelings. They should also be allowed some preferences in their activities, but the teacher should be firm although understanding and sympathetic. Many of these children need security and cannot gain stability in a completely permissive environment. They should know that the teacher expects certain things of them, although she is willing to listen to their requests and give them reasonable choices. In this work the teacher needs time to get to know the child and to listen to him when he wishes to talk. Often an opportunity to express his feelings of discouragement and resentment are of help in clearing the air before he undertakes actual work. He must also feel that the teacher really cares about him and is concerned with his problems. She uses continuous praise for all his effort and is very tactful in helping him when he makes errors. She works very slowly so that he is able to feel successful at every step of the way. Even though the teacher may feel that the child can work faster, she does not try to speed up the process, since it might make him afraid of failing again. She is wiser to wait until the child asks to take on more work and to move more rapidly.

Help to Give Recognition. The teacher tries to give the child recog nition in every way possible. When he has learned a story well, the teacher may arrange for him to read it to other children, probably those who are younger and who might therefore enjoy the story more than older children. The teacher also works with the child's family and asks them to listen whenever he wishes to read anything to them. It is important that they, too, praise every effort made by the child and ignore any errors he makes.

Symptoms of Reading Problems

The child who daydreams or constantly seeks attention by annoying others may have reading difficulties. Other symptoms of difficulty are found in the actual reading itself.

Withdrawal and Aggression. The child who withdraws because of reading difficulties usually turns to daydreaming as a form of escape from frustration due to his inability to carry out the teacher's assign ments. The other type of child tends to seek attention to build up his feelings of inadequacy and insecurity. The teacher may mistake day dreaming for laziness and attention-seeking for deliberate misbehavior Neither child knows the reasons for his reactions.

A boy in a junior high school class in English continuously disturbed the children and distracted their attention. He wore rather gaudy clothes and was extremely well-groomed in a rather flashy way. He wore side burns and slicked his hair down until it looked like patent leather. He wore an air of confidence and sophistication, which caused even the teacher to fail to realize that he had a serious problem.

When she called on him to read orally one day, he blushed deeply and refused to try. The teacher then suspected that he might have a problem and tested him at a time when they were alone. She found that his reading ability was actually on the second-grade level and that his bravado had been a desperate attempt to cover up his deficiencies. He gradually lost his defensiveness when he was given help on remedial reading, but the process was slow and discouraging at times.

Problems with Independent Assignments. The child who fails to finish his work may appear lazy. Some of these children are unable to read the material and may not know how to proceed with their assign ments. This situation can exist even though the teacher has been careful to explain the work. If the child has a weakness in word analysis, he may not be able to do the work even though the directions were clear Sometimes these children guess erratically, and their poor work may be taken for carelessness. Some children fail to learn the common, small words because of immaturity or some other problem during the first or second year of school. The lack of knowledge of these words causes constant difficulty. The teacher should look for a reading problem when the child seems lazy or careless in his work on a reading assignment.

Vision. The teacher should check the child's permanent records for health problems. Some children are able to make progress in reading with minor problems in vision, whereas other children do not overcome these handicaps. If the visual difficulty causes children to be uncomfortable when they read, they may try to avoid reading when they can. Other children may have problems resulting from nearsightedness, farsightedness, astigmatism, muscular imbalance, or other difficulty. Symptoms of eye difficulties were given in Chapter 3. The Snellen test is the test most commonly used in some schools. It serves only to show at what distance the child can read the chart. More serious eye difficulties cannot usually be discovered through this test. If the child gives evidence of having problems with his eyes, he should be referred for examination and help if needed.

Hearing. Problems in hearing can also interfere with the child's success in learning to read. These problems have also been discussed in Chapter 3. The teacher should remember that children who have good hearing at one time may have difficulty with hearing later on. The teacher should consider hearing loss as a possible cause in cases of inattentiveness. The child's physical condition should also be taken into consideration.

Lack of Sleep. A child's inattentiveness may be due to lack of sleep from watching television too long at night. Inadequate sleep may cause the child to be listless and uninterested in his work. Parents have been heard to say, "I just can't get Jimmy to go to bed before the ten o'clock show. You know, his favorite program comes on at nine thirty." A better plan for parents to use would be to let Jimmy select one favorite show within the proper time limit, such as before eight o'clock if he is six or seven years old. When that show is over the television should be firmly turned off, and Jimmy should be on his way to bed. A parent who isn't able to send his child to bed at a reasonable time is likely to have severe difficulties when the child becomes an adolescent.

Nutrition. Poor nutrition can sometimes result in reading problems. If the child does not have adequate food or goes to school without breakfast, he is likely to lack energy and interest in any of the activities in school. Since reading takes considerable energy, it is very likely to be affected. Sometimes children eat enough food but are not provided with the right food elements. Children who live on starches often do not have the proper proteins, minerals, and vitamins they need. A change in diet sometimes has remarkable results in improving the child's energy and his ability to learn. The co-operation of the school nurse may be needed to check various problems of health before the child can be helped with his reading.

Examples of Corrective Reading Procedures

Some children are willing to begin their corrective work on the primary levels of a basic reading series, although these children realize that this material really belongs in the early grades. Other children are too insecure for such a beginning. Sometimes the use of their own dictated stories provides a good place for these children to start. Occasionally, a child is found who is handicapped in his ability to acquire even a beginning vocabulary or who is emotionally disturbed when confronted with any printed material. In such a case, Fernald's tracing procedures are of help.[1] The teacher who helps children improve their reading must pattern each program to meet the needs of each child.

Work With a Basic Series. Tony was extremely handicapped in reading but was otherwise a rather well-adjusted child of normal intelligence who was willing to work in the basic series. He was in the seventh grade in a junior high school and was so handicapped that he had only three words in his sight vocabulary. He was entirely without any other reading techniques. When he entered school, Tony was bilingual, rather shy, and spoke little English. He was in a large first-grade class. Either the teacher failed to realize his lack of success in beginning to read or felt that she did not have the time to work with him individually. He was passed on to the second grade where the teacher may have had little time to help him and may not have known how to work with a beginning reader. Thereafter, Tony drifted from grade to grade learning as much subject matter as he could from his ability to listen, which was exceptionally good. He also succeeded well in mathematics, so he acquired a certain status from this success. His homeroom teacher in junior high school had an extensive conference with him to try to discover what his learning problems were and had thus found out that Tony was unable to read.

Tony's tutor was a teacher who had some time during the summer. In a man-to-man discussion she told Tony that the easiest and quickest approach to his problem was to put him in a "baby" pre-primer, although the content would be nauseating for a thirteen-year-old boy. The teacher told him she did not have time to prepare material for

[1] Grace M. Fernald, *Remedial Techniques in Basic School Subjects* (McGraw-Hill Book Co., 1943).

work with dictated stories. Tony was very good-natured and was willing to go along with this reading material. The teacher used a balance of good procedures suitable for primary teaching. Tony responded exceptionally well and was reading in the middle of a second reader by the end of summer. At that time, he had to go back to school and to his after-school job, so he was unable to continue the reading work.

Dictated Stories. Gary was an unhappy second-grade child. He had an I.Q. of 145 and a great deal of personal charm. His kindergarten experience, however, had been rather traumatic.

Gary's kindergarten teacher felt that she should be working on reading readiness, but had a very unorthodox idea of the procedures to use. She secured dittoed seat work from the second-grade teacher to use with her kindergarten children. This material consisted of about twelve to fifteen small pictures, each in a square on the paper. In each of the four corners of each square, letters representing beginning sounds were printed, one of which belonged to the word represented by the picture. For example, a picture of a bear might be shown in one square. The letters c, f, j, and b might be found one in each respective corner. In such a case the children were required to circle the letter, b, that represented the appropriate beginning sound for the word, *bear*. After selecting the proper letter, they were required to color the tiny pictures.

Despite his intelligence, Gary was too immature to have any notion of why one particular letter would be more appropriate than another. He also had poor co-ordination and had great difficulty in coloring within the lines of these little pictures. Although the other children must have failed to succeed to select the letters by any other manner than guessing, Gary seemed to draw down the teacher's wrath more often than any other child. The teacher would hold up his paper and say, "This is what I told you not to do."

By the end of the kindergarten Gary had lost all his joy in life and his avid curiosity about things in the world around him. In the first grade, Gary would have nothing to do with reading activities, but managed to make his way on his personal charm and co-operation in every other activity. His teacher was very understanding but was afraid to work with Gary on reading because of his extreme reaction against it.

Gary's second-grade teacher had four children of her own and had married a man who also had two. Her problems at home were so great that she had little energy left to cope with the problems at school, such as Gary. Her reading program consisted of directing the children to read orally down the page by turns. Gary was completely lost in the reading material, but was able to figure out the line he would be called upon to read. He then held a secret conversation with a neighbor, who told him what the sentence said. When his turn came, Gary was able to read the sentence successfully and thus avoid a problem with the teacher.

Gary's mother knew, however, that he was making no headway in reading and so secured a tutor for him. Gary seemed so unhappy in any work in a book that the tutor started with Gary's own dictated stories. He dictated a story at one lesson and was able to read the story back to her at the next session. She then made sentence strips and word cards of the material in the story. She read the sentences, which he matched to the story and later read the words that he matched to the sentences. In a short time he was able to read the sentences in mixed order for himself and soon learned the words on the cards so that he could read them when they were in mixed order.

After a few weeks of this procedure, Gary was ready to start work in an easy reader. From then on Gary's tutor used a completely balanced program with him because he needed help in all reading skills. She helped him gradually learn to analyze words from beginning sounds and worked on the development of silent reading abilities as well as fluency in oral reading. After a time, Gary was able to read the sentence in the book when his turn came in class without consulting his neighbor to find out what it said.

Work With Matching. Tom was a child of average intelligence, who was working in the fifth grade, although his reading was on the second-grade level. His tutor tried dictated stories with Tom but he resented them. She then secured an interesting second reader and tried to work with him on this book. Tom, however, was extremely unhappy and strongly resisted this help. She finally discovered that he wanted to read in the fifth-grade book that his group was using in school. When the tutor secured the book, she found that Tom could recognize only about one word out of three or four running words.

Since Tom refused to co-operate on any other material, the teacher decided as a last resort to try to work with this material, a few lines at a time. She printed the sentences on strips of paper and started with matching. She would read one of the sentence strips and ask Tom to find it in the book and repeat the sentence. Tom was successful in this process. She then made duplicate sentence strips and cut them into words. She read each word and again asked Tom to match these words to the words in the sentence strips. Tom was also successful in this activity.

After several lessons of matching sentences to words, Tom's tutor asked him if he could read any of the strips by himself. He succeeded in reading two of the strips, although the process was primarily that of repeating the sentences that he had memorized. He had a feeling of success, however, and was later able to read all of the strips and finally recognize all of the words.

Tom's tutor then put the words on cards that fitted into a shoe box. Tom made alphabetical dividers at her request and placed the words which he knew at sight under the proper letter of the alphabet. In this way, he gained a feeling of accomplishment as he watched the number of known words begin to grow in the box.

As Tom was able to recognize more words at sight, his tutor began to balance the procedures using silent reading and adding phonic techniques. Tom seemed to have a strong block against phonics. Each time he met a word with the combinations of the *e* and *a* vowels, he pronounced the *e* as though it were short and ignored the *a*. When his tutor would start to remind him of the rule of these two vowels, he would immediately respond with the long vowel pronunciation, but never applied this rule without a reminder. This block was typical of Tom's reaction to all types of phonetic analysis, but he was very successful in learning many words at sight. He seemed to have some phonics system of his own for initial consonants and some letter combinations. The tutor suspected that Tom had been given too much phonics before he was mature enough to grasp it. Tom eventually was able to read successfully on the fifth level and was able to return to work in his fifth-grade reading group. Tom, however, did not enjoy reading and never turned to reading for recreation.

The Tracing Procedure. Few children need help with the tracing procedures developed by Fernald,[2] but a very limited number of children may have such great difficulty in learning to recognize words at sight or such strong emotional rejection of printed words that the teacher may find it helpful to resort to the tracing procedure.

After rapport had been established, the child is asked to select a word he would like to know, usually in connection with some interest he has been discussing. In order to help him learn the word, the teacher prints or writes it on a strip of paper in letters three or four inches high. The child is then asked to trace the word with his finger. He is required to trace the word on the paper, rather than in the air as is sometimes done in teaching spelling in order to get the feeling of the movement of his finger on the paper. After he has traced the word several times, the teacher covers it up and asks him to write it from memory. If he cannot, he goes back to the tracing of the word and again tries to write it on the paper. He is asked to pronounce each part of the word as he writes it.

[2] *Ibid.*

When the child has succeeded in learning to write one word, he is taught to write several more along the line of his interest. When he has learned these words, he is asked to dictate a story containing them. This story is typed, and the child is asked to read it. As each word in the story is learned, the child writes it on a large card, which he then places under the proper letter in the box with alphabetical headings. The child gains security and a feeling of accomplishment as his card file of words grows.

As the child progresses and writes more stories, the teacher may find that he is able to learn the words merely by looking at them carefully several times and pronouncing them as he does so. Part of the value of this tracing and writing procedure lies in the fact that the child learns to look at the inner details within a word and is therefore able to develop an accurate visual memory of the word. Some teachers print the words learned by the child on the front of each card in the alphabetical file and write them in cursive form on the back of the card. In this way the child becomes familiar with both forms.

When the child is able to add words to his sight vocabulary without tracing them, he may be able to start work in a reader. Phonics procedures are gradually added, and the program is balanced with oral and silent reading. Grace Fernald was very successful with her use of this procedure at the University of California, Los Angeles campus, in the reading clinic where these procedures are still followed.

The teacher should make a strong effort to discover the child's special interests and should secure easy materials for him to read when he is able to begin reading independently. She also uses material along his lines of interest in her day-to-day work. In addition, the teacher should help the child develop new interests and work with his family to try to help him extend his interests.

Use of Records and Charts

One of the best motivations for children who need special help with reading is the use of some type of record of their improvement. Usually the record represents steps in the child's progress. At other times, however, the best record may be one that shows a decrease in errors of a particular type. These records may be in the form of graphs or charts using pictures. A mere line graph is helpful, but children usually enjoy making pictorial charts. For example, the child may make a map of an area where he would like to travel and mark his destination. He may mark off each five or ten miles on the map each time he reads a story successfully, adds a given number of words to his sight vocabulary, or is able to apply a phonics rule without error. He may draw a small car

A map is being made in class by a sixth-grader for the study of the local water supply. (Courtesy California State Department of Education.)

and put it on the highway to show how far he has progressed toward his destination. On the other hand, he may want to travel to the moon and may draw a picture of the rocket in which he would travel. He may then mark off distances on his chart and place the rocket on the path to show how far he has progressed. The teacher may help the child picture any special aspect of his interest and use this chart for a record of his progress. The help of the family should be enlisted to celebrate steps in the child's progress and to plan special activities to give him prestige and a feeling of success.

PROBLEMS WITH READING SKILLS

One of the most common problems in reading is the tendency to read one word at a time, called word-by-word reading. Some children who have this problem also point to each word, whisper each word, or move their lips in a soundless pronunciation as they read. This habit is accompanied by poor comprehension and an unduly slow rate of reading. Some children have extreme difficulty with comprehension, although in some cases they are able to read orally with considerable success. Some of these specific problems are discussed, and a few suggestions for help are given in the following section of this chapter.

Lack of Comprehension

Some children are able to understand reading material when they read orally, but they comprehend inadequately or completely fail to comprehend when they read silently. A mother reported that her little girl in the second grade read everything aloud, although she enjoyed reading for recreation. When her mother asked her why she did not read to herself, she replied that she did not know what the print said unless she read it aloud. She refused, however, to allow her mother who was a teacher to help her acquire good habits. This difficulty can be very serious as the child progresses through the grades when he must use silent reading more and more widely.

Causes of Poor Comprehension. Children who have spent too much time on oral reading in the early primary grades without a balance of silent reading may have difficulty with comprehension to a lesser or greater extent. On the other hand, the child may give too little attention to the meaning of the material when he reads orally. Lack of interest or purpose in reading may result in daydreaming during either the oral or silent reading period with resultant lack of comprehension. Word-by-word reading may limit the child's comprehension because he does not group words into phrases, and thought is thereby lost. Overemphasis on phonics to the neglect of meaning may also result in the lack of comprehension.

Ways to Improve Comprehension. To help develop comprehension the child should be given very easy reading material related as far as possible to his interests. Scanning to find answers to questions aimed at particular phrases at first, later at sentences, and much later at paragraphs may give some help in improving the child's comprehension. He should be encouraged to give the answer to questions in his own words to avoid the thoughtless repetition of the words in the book. The procedures used for helping children take their first steps in silent reading, described in Chapter 10, may be utilized if the child's handicap is severe.

Work on the Level of Confidence. All the suggestions for help in reading are more effective if they are carried out on the level of confidence. This level is even easier than the level of independence, described earlier in the chapter. The child is working on his level of confidence when he meets only one or two new words out of 100, when he understands the material he is reading, and when he has adequate skills to analyze the unknown words he meets, if these words are subject to analysis. Some children may be so handicapped that they are unable to work on their levels of confidence. The teacher must then build the needed skills that permit them to read at this level.

Use of a Check on Meaning. As the child improves in comprehension he should be given strong motives for silent reading, and he should be asked to report simple ideas gained from the material with the book closed. An assignment to read and organize statements from the board or on paper that have been given in mixed sequence may be helpful if the child is able to comprehend adequately. The use of multiple-choice sentences to check his reading of easy material may also be of value. The child should also be provided with easy reading of recreational material of high interest. He may retell some of the stories to his teacher and others.

Use of Printed Directions. Children who seem to have little or no power to comprehend material read silently have sometimes responded to directions printed in sight words with which they are familiar. These directions, printed on strips, must not be read orally. They are used to secure immediate, active responses from the child, who shows his comprehension by carrying out the direction. Such a direction may consist of a request to "Bring a book to me."

Most, if not all, of the words the child is able to recognize at sight in his reader can be incorporated in these action strips. Praise should be given for correct responses to these directions in order to build security and confidence. When the child has complete confidence in his ability to read silently and to carry out directions, the teacher may return him to silent reading in the book.

The child may start with the primary techniques of reading only one or two sentences silently in response to a question by the teacher. The child should give the answer in his own words, if possible. He should not be criticized, however, for using the words of the book. When he is able to answer a question on two lines with the book closed, he may then be directed to read three lines to answer a question and to respond in his own words. This procedure is continued until the child is able to read several pages and answer questions with the book closed.

Difficulty with Word-by-Word Reading

Word-by-word reading is the process of reading words in sentence context as though they were presented in a list. Thus the child pronounces each word without grouping by phrases or according to the meaning of the words. Sometimes, children who read in this way understand what they are reading despite the monotony of their voices. Other children do no thinking as they read, thereby failing to understand the meaning of the text. Children with either type of problem need help, but the problem of the latter child is by far the most serious because he may be unable to get the meaning from the text either when reading orally or when reading silently. If a child stops on occasional words but reads smoothly otherwise, he may merely need help in word attack. His pauses may be the result of his efforts to analyze words. If, on the other hand, the child always reads each word separately, his reading is the result of very inefficient reading habits.

Causes of Word-by-Word Reading. The child who has a true case of word calling may read this way because he analyzes the sounds of each word from habit. He may also have difficulty in word recognition; he may be uncertain of the sounds of some letters or may attack the word in the wrong way. Some children become word-by-word readers because they were given practice on words in lists on the board or on cards in the primary grades, rather than in sentence context. Some of these children may also have had too much practice on meaningless oral reading of the "barbershop" type without help in meaning. The habit of reading one word at a time followed by its pronunciation is carried over to the reading in the text book.

Help for Word-by-Word Reading. A good model is important in overcoming word-by-word reading. Some primary teachers direct the children to find a sentence by doing the reading, one word at a time. In this way they set a poor example that the children will inevitably follow. Some teachers read this way because they want to be sure that the children are able to recognize each word. They should read with good expression at this time, however, and leave the identification of single words for a later step.

Use of Phrases. One of the best ways to help children read orally in words grouped according to thought is to ask questions which call for the reading of phrases or short sentences in answer to these questions. The child who has had experience in reading of this sort from the early primary grades is not likely to be a word-by-word reader. If the children are only moderately handicapped, the teacher may ask questions which call for them to select phrases out of particular sentences and read these in answer to her questions. Later, they should be able to find and read entire sentences in this manner.

The teacher should insist that all the children find and read silently the phrase or sentence that answers her question before she calls on any child to read it orally. She should then help the child read it fluently.

If all of the children find and locate a phrase or sentence and read it silently before the teacher calls on one child to read it orally, they will all profit from the silent reading.

Development of Fluency. Good primary teachers develop fluency from the very beginning steps in the first grade. Effective silent reading leads to fluency in oral reading. The teacher tries to develop fluency in oral reading with the hope that this skill will carry back to the silent reading.

The teacher should use phrases to begin her work in the development of fluency. She may ask a question which will be answered by a phrase on one of the phrase cards she has printed. All of the children look for the appropriate phrase to answer the question. When they have located it, the teacher asks one child to read the phrase.

If he reads the phrase haltingly, the teacher may ask other children to try to read it to give a fluent answer to the question or to read it "the way we talk." Each child usually improves slightly over the other. The teacher praises each response but continues to call on other children until they give the phrase with real fluency. She repeats this process for the reading of each phrase, continuing until each phrase is read satisfactorily.

Although the procedure may be somewhat frustrating to the children, the teacher continues to give short periods of practice until each child can read a phrase in answer to a question with satisfactory fluency. The teacher then repeats the process with short sentences and later with longer sentences, while she helps the children learn how to group the words. Although this procedure may require several months for complete success, it seems to have some carry-over to the silent reading.

Guides for Phrasing. Some teachers use diagonal lines to separate phrases from each other in reading matter to help the intermediate child group words in both silent and oral reading. Others copy reading material allowing several spaces between phrase groups as a way of calling the child's attention to the grouping. Later, the child should be able to mark off these phrases for himself. His ability to do this phrasing assures the teacher that he is able to separate the groups of words according to their meaning and must therefore be developing greater comprehension.

Use of Sentence Strips. Some teachers print meaningful phrases or short sentences on strips of tag cardboard. These cards are held up for the child to read silently. The teacher tells the child to read the whole card silently or "with his eyes." She then turns the card over, and the child reads the whole phrase or sentence from recall. At first, the teacher should make no attempt to emphasize speed. The child should be given all the time he needs to read the phrase silently. If the child has a long-established habit of reading one word at a time, he will read only the first word orally after the teacher has turned down the strip. The teacher then repeats her directions to read the whole phrase "with his eyes" and shows him the card once more. Such a child then usually reads the first and second words but stops at that point. At the third trial he usually reads three words, and the process continues until he is able to read the whole strip orally by recall on the last trial. These practice periods should be kept short. This process is frustrating for both the pupil and teacher but seems to be an effective way to help the child gradually read by word groupings. Speed should be added to this step only when the child is completely successful at his own pace.

One teacher worked during the second half of the year with first-grade children who were confirmed word callers. She worked with short sentences on strips for six weeks before the first child was able to read silently and repeat orally at one time all the words on any strip. Several months were required before most of the slower children had acquired this skill and read the strips fluently. The teacher must use much shorter phrases or sentences for slow children than for rapid learners since their memory spans are usually shorter.

Homemade Tachistoscope. A tachistoscope is a machine that flashes a word or phrase at a controlled rate of speed at anywhere from a second to a hundredth of a second. This machine is often used with older children and adults to help them learn to perceive words rapidly.

Harris suggests the use of a homemade device for flashing words. A square large enough to expose a word is cut in a large piece of stiff cardboard. A pointer made of a rectangle of cardboard wide enough to completely cover the word is attached to the left-hand corner of the square so that it may be dropped down over the word. The teacher can raise and lower the strip of cardboard or pointer to expose a word for a brief period of time.

Although these devices or commercial machines are frequently of help in developing a more rapid rate of recognition of phrases, this increased rate may not transfer to reading in a book unless the teacher helps the child make the transfer. The intermediate child should be encouraged to use a strip of cardboard such as a 3″ × 5″ index card to slide down the page above the reading material in order to keep his eyes moving down the page. Older children are usually better able to use this card effectively than younger children.

Motivation

A variety of machines for helping improve rate are provided commercially. These machines are described and discussed in detail by Harris, who agrees with most authorities regarding their value.[3] As has been stated before, children must be helped to use their more rapid recognition ability in books after they have acquired this ability by means of the machines. Authors, in general, agree that reading rate may be improved without machines as effectively as through the use of machines.

Word Perception

Some children have difficulty noticing details in words. They may be able to make a successful beginning in reading when the configuration of words tends to have gross differences. When the gross configurations of added new words are similar to the words that these children already know, a problem may arise.

Difficulty with Configuration. A child who fails to see internal details of words may be able to recognize the word *ball* when first taught. When the word *doll* is added, however, he may fail to notice the internal details and may therefore mistake one word for the other. As the child's vocabulary increases, more and more words present this type of problem.

Causes of Poor Perception. In some cases, the failure to notice internal details is due to immaturity. If children are not discouraged, and are not forced to progress too rapidly for their rate of development, the problem may disappear as the child becomes increasingly able to notice internal details. If introduced when the child is ready, phonics techniques may help this child improve in his ability to perceive words more accurately.

A few children seem to be unable to develop the skill of perceiving words accurately even in later grades. Sometimes the difficulty seems to be due to fear, if the child has been forced to progress too rapidly in his reading. These children may be introduced to new words in the same manner that was used in good, original primary teaching or those described below.

Help in Observing Details. One of the words causing difficulty should be first presented in a sentence on a cardboard sentence strip, which the child is encouraged to read. The sentence should be made up of familiar words with only one unknown word. The teacher may help the child recognize the difficult word by context clues and by observing the beginning letter and inner details of the word. The child then rereads the sentence smoothly using the new word.

Matching. If the child needs more help, matching may be used. The teacher may make word cards to duplicate the words in the sen-

[3] Albert J. Harris, *How To Increase Reading Ability* (4th ed.; New York: David McKay Co., Inc., 1961), pp. 525–29.

tence. She may place the reading strip in a pocket chart and guide the child to match the words in the sentence by placing each word card under the same word in the strip. Most children can do this work successfully since only matching is required. The child may then read the sentence. The teacher may then take the word card representing the difficult word out of the sentence and ask the child to read it without the sentence context. If he has difficulty, the procedure may be repeated until he can read the word.

Tracing. If the child has great difficulty recalling words, the teacher may ask him to trace each word with his finger and to look carefully at all the letters in sequence as he traces it. She may then cover up the word and ask him to write it from memory. If he is unable to recall all the letters or their sequence in the word, the teacher should ask him to trace the word again and try once more to reproduce it when the original word is covered. He should continue the process until he is able to write the word accurately, unless too many repetitions are needed or the child becomes too frustrated. In such a case, the process may be repeated on the following day. This child needs constant encouragement.

Rereading. After the child has been able to reproduce the difficult word, he should reread the original sentence and then continue his reading in the book where he had the difficulty. In this way, the child is able to meet the word in a variety of situations in order to give him practice in recognizing it. If the word is not repeated soon again in the reader, the teacher may compose sentences using this word for the child to read.

The tracing and writing procedure can usually be discontinued after a month or so. By that time, the child has usually acquired the ability to observe the inner details in words and can acquire new words visually. New words should always be presented in context and mastered before the child goes on to learn further new words. New words met in experience stories are an exception to this rule since they may not be met in the child's developmental reading material.

Lip Movement and Subvocalization

Lip movement consists of the moving of the lips, sometimes silently and sometimes with an audible whisper or even soft mumble. Lip movement and subvocalization constitute a problem for the reader because they tend to limit his speed to the speed of oral reading or speech. He is likely, therefore, to be unable to read more rapidly than 150 to 200 words a minute. This speed may be adequate for the child in the intermediate grades, but it is not adequate for students to succeed in work in high school and college.

Prevention. Primary children tend to use lip movement but this habit need not be acquired. Lip movement often results from overemphasis on oral reading. Some authors feel that lip movement is an essential step in beginning reading, but years of experience using good beginning techniques, such as those described in the previous chapters, have proved that children can learn to read more effectively without these movements. The scanning on charts in the identification step seems to be one of the important procedures that helps children avoid lip movement. The continuous use of scanning in the oral reading step in the readers also helps prevent the acquisition of this habit. Since the habit is not essential, it should be avoided.

Subvocalization. Lip movement in young children seems to result in subvocalization as the children become older. Subvocalization has been described in Chapter 2. It is the process of minute movements in the larynx which accompany the mental reproduction of the words as they are read. Many people can "hear" the words as they read silently. All readers have very small degrees of subvocalization, but rapid readers have much less movement than slower readers. Those who subvocalize extensively fail to make use of clues in words.

Ways to Reduce Poor Habits. If a child in the intermediate grades moves his lips as he reads, he should be reminded to read "with his eyes" and try to avoid lip and tongue movement. The provision of a great deal of easy reading material will help reduce lip movement and excessive subvocalization. Scanning to find answers to questions is usually helpful because the child does not have time to read every word on the page when looking for an answer to a question. He should be taught to look for key words at the beginning of sentences to improve his scanning. This child should also carry on his silent reading under the teacher's supervision.

Some teachers merely remind the child to close his lips when they see him moving them. In many cases, reminders seem to be adequate. Some children have overcome the habit by pressing the tongue against the roof of the mouth, although this procedure seems to be frustrating in some cases. According to Harris, the child who subvocalizes when reading silently is unable to comprehend what he reads when he is chewing gum or candy.[4] Conversely, it is possible that gum chewing might help a child reduce his lip and tongue movements.

Many of the same techniques that were suggested for the improve-

[4] Ibid., p. 208.

ment of word-by-word reading are helpful in eliminating lip movement and reducing subvocalization.

Use of Direction Strips. One of the best ways to help children eliminate subvocalization is the use of reading strips similar to those employed in the primary grades and described in this chapter. The teacher prints directions for some type of action on these strips. She uses the words the children meet in their regular reading lessons along with review words. She asks the children to read these strips "with their eyes" to try to find out what they are supposed to do. Only the children who read without moving their lips are called on to carry out the direction. In the fifth grade such a direction might say, "Draw on the board a mosquito that might carry yellow fever." Another direction might say, "Point to Cuba on the map." The latter direction presupposes that the children have already located Cuba on the map as the teacher built the background for the reading of the story. The directions should always be given for things which the children already know how to do.

Reversion to Lip Movements and Subvocalization. The child in the upper primary and intermediate grades may tend to revert to lip movements if he feels insecure in such a situation as work with a new teacher or if he is reading in a new and more difficult book. If children in a reading group are given a new book that is too difficult for them or if a section in the book becomes too difficult because of too many words on which inadequate review has been given, they may revert to lip movement, although these habits may have been eliminated previously. Sometimes these habits develop when children are under stress even though they were not acquired in earlier grades. Established habits of word-by-word reading and lack of ability to read in phrases may also tend to be accompanied by lip movement.

Word Pointing

Word pointing consists of the child's pointing to each word, usually as he reads orally. Beginners often point to words because of their insecurity in reading.

Causes of Word Pointing. Word pointing may be caused by material that is too difficult for children, particularly on the basis of too many difficult or new sight words that the child cannot analyze at his level of phonic ability. The child who reads word-by-word also tends to point to words as he reads. Lack of ability to get thought from the reading material also causes the child to point to words. This lack of ability to comprehend is usually in turn caused by material that is too difficult for the child or that he cannot analyze with phonics. Nervousness or insecurity may also cause the child to point to words. Word pointing results in limiting the child's reading speed in the same way that lip movement or subvocalization serves as a limit.

Help in Reducing Pointing. To help the child overcome the habit of pointing, simple, interesting reading material with a minimum of new or difficult words should be used. When reading this material, the child may be given a marker to place under the sentence he is reading. A marker is a piece of lightweight cardboard or tag about an inch wide and long enough to extend across the page, probably five or six inches. If an older child objects to the use of a marker, he should be encouraged to frame particular sentences with the forefinger of each hand. Some teachers are afraid that children will depend upon markers too long and therefore become handicapped in their reading. Experience has proved that this is not a danger. Strong purposes should be given for silent reading, and it should be carried on under the supervision of the teacher to prevent the child from reverting to pointing either with his finger or with the end of the marker.

No emphasis should be placed on speed, but the scanning procedure described above is very helpful in eliminating pointing. Since this work is given on the board or on charts at first, the child is unable to point.

Adequate Reading Rate

One of the major causes of lack of adequate rate of reading is the demand that the child read material that is too difficult for him. The child may have an inadequate sight vocabulary for the material, or the material may have too many new words on one page. The child may also meet too many new words that demand phonics clues for their identification or clues that he may be unable to use. The child's lack of speed may be also due to excessive subvocalization, lip movement, or word pointing. Too much oral reading may also result in an excessively slow rate of reading. The child who reads too slowly often has not developed the ability to group words by phrases and to read in such groups.

Improvement of Reading Rate

The amount of oral reading which the child engages in should be very much reduced. The teacher should work to eliminate vocalization, lip movement, and pointing in order to help establish better habits which are basic to an adequate rate of reading. Easy materials that are of strong interest and that meet his need should be given to the child. If the habit of word-by-word reading is too thoroughly established, phrase and sentence strips, described above, can be of help for this child.

Although rate of reading depends on the type of material the children read, many children are able to use a more rapid rate than they habitually use. Both scanning and timed exercises can be used to improve reading rate.

Scanning. In an attempt to discover the value of scanning a teacher worked with his class for a period of three months. He used scanning with his group of thirty-two children of 112 average I.Q. He spent fifteen minutes a day using questions to guide the reading in the regular developmental reader. At first the questions were limited to one page, but the children were required to search up and down the page for the correct responses. Later they were guided to find the answers on either of two pages. Still later, the scanning was extended until the answers to the questions might be found on any page in a six to eight page story. This scanning was carried on after the children had read the selection silently, and usually after they had worked on one or more study skills in connection with the story.

A standardized test was given before the beginning of the study. Another form of the test was given at the end of the three months. The average gain for this group of children was 5.2 months in both speed and comprehension. The range in gain was from one to nine months.

Timed Exercises. A more commonly used method of improving rate of reading makes use of timed exercises. The child reads a selection of several paragraphs beginning and stopping on signals from the instructor. He then checks the answers to an objective test on the thought of the selection. His reading score is computed by the proportion of correct answers of the total number of correct answers possible. Each child keeps his own record and tries to improve his rate of speed and percentage of comprehension as time goes on. Some children respond well to this work, and the improvement in scores serves as a motivation. This procedure is also effective with high school and college students.

SUMMARY

Regardless of cause, a child with reading problems inevitably suffers from frustration, a low self-concept, a lack of confidence, and poor attitudes toward reading. The teacher's first task is to help the child regain his confidence and improve his self-concept. Symptoms of reading problems include both emotional and physical difficulties. The teacher must diagnose the child's weaknesses and then strengthen these needed skills.

14

Readiness for Word Recognition

The preparation for teaching of word recognition skills in a balanced program includes a variety of procedures. Before children are ready for help in word analysis in the beginning of the first grade, some words are taught at sight in sentence context. During this time children are taught to use picture clues, configuration clues, and context clues. As the children advance in achievement, they are taught the use of phonic clues.

USE OF INFORMAL CLUES

The child may get clues to the meanings of words by use of pictures, word configuration (the size or shape of words), and context before he develops phonics as a technique for recognizing words. The use of picture and configuration clues in reading are helpful only in the beginning steps. Context clues are valuable throughout the individual's reading life.

Picture Clues

The development of the use of picture clues with children has a number of values. Children learn to observe an increased number of details and to grow in their ability to observe relationships among the people or objects shown in the picture. Children may develop new concepts and clarify old ones and may learn to draw inferences from the objects or action shown in a picture. This use of pictures helps children develop visual acuity as well as to learn to draw inferences to help them interpret the meanings of pictures.

A wise teacher uses pictures as a means of developing readiness for reading as well as a method of introducing words in a story that are new to the children. She also teaches them techniques for reading pictures, that is, observation of activities portrayed in pictures and other details. The ability to draw conclusions from various aspects of a picture, such as rain clothes to suggest a rainy day, and to imagine possible future outcomes of the activities illustrated in a picture are also encouraged by the teacher.

If, for example, two six-year-old children are shown playing with a sailboat at one end of a pond and a younger child is shown playing with another boat which is just out of reach at the other end of the pond, the teacher will help the children relate the situation to their own experiences in playing with boats. She will also help them discuss the older children's responsibility for the safety of the younger child. Moreover, the teacher may help the children discuss the possible danger to the younger child from lack of experience and lack of judgment of distance. The children may then anticipate the danger of the younger child's falling into the water, the probable depth of the water, and the reaction of the child's mother to such a situation.

The teacher will help the children use pictures as clues to words they meet in their story. If, for example, the children forget the word *pond* as they read silently, the teacher may suggest that they look at the picture again to see where the children are sailing their boats. In this way, the teacher helps the children make use of the picture as a clue to help them recall some of the words in the story.

The use of picture clues is very limited because many words do not lend themselves to illustration and because children become crippled if they try completely to depend on pictures to help them remember sight words. The use of these clues, however, is helpful in the early stages of reading and gives children their first taste of a similar skill, that of using context clues, with which they will later become familiar.

Configuration Clues

Configuration clues are the hints the children gain from the shapes of words. Children are often very conscious of the upstrokes of such letters as *b, f, h, k,* and *l,* and also of the downstrokes in such letters as *g, p,* and *y.* The configuration of a word can be best understood by the adult if he were to draw a line around the upper and lower edges of the letters in a word to show a type of block shape. The following three words illustrate this idea:

was saw elephant

Children learn to recognize the word *elephant* with ease because it is one of the longest words they are likely to meet in their early reading. By noting the outlines surrounding *was* and *saw*, the teacher will be able to understand why children so frequently confuse these words and also why they are difficult to remember.

Other peculiarities in shape are also used by children to help them recognize some words. Some may think of the two *oo's* in *look* as eyes which they use as clues to the word. An occasional child may notice the two upper loops and the shorter *t* in the word *rabbit* and may think of these as long ears and a short tail. Children sometimes differentiate between *cat* and *dog* because the cat has a tail going up and the dog has a tail hanging down.

Many of such clues have meaning only for the child who originates the thought. Configuration clues along with picture clues are of value primarily in the very early stages of reading before the child has met enough words to become confused by their similarities in shapes. As long as the teacher makes use of adequate practice techniques to develop sight words, these temporary clues can be of value to a child.

Context Clues

Context clues are aids to the identity of an unrecognized word through the meaning of the rest of the sentence. In the following sentence, "Jane helped mother put the food on the XxXXx," only a few words are possible to complete the thought. Such possibilities are the words *sink, stove,* and *table.* If no picture is available to help the child, the teacher may explain that Jane is helping Mother take the food to the place where the family will eat. The words *eating place* were used because some children live in homes with dining rooms, some with dinettes, and some with eating areas in the kitchen. When the word *table* has been identified by the thought, that is, by the context clue, the teacher will ask the child to reread the sentence in order to be sure that the meaning is complete.

Context clues are very important since they are of value throughout the reader's lifetime. Nouns and words toward the ends of sentences are easiest to identify by means of context clues. They are more difficult to use when the reader is looking for a clue to an abstract word or to the less obvious parts of speech, such as prepositions, conjunctions, and pronouns. Nouns, adjectives, verbs, and adverbs are easier to identify through context clues. After the children begin to recognize sounds at the beginnings of words, the combination of a context clue with a phonic clue is the best means of identifying a new word correctly. The child, however, should be helped to use context clues from the beginning so that he may add the use of phonics clues later without the difficulty of learning two skills at one time.

READINESS FOR PHONICS

Most authors agree on a number of abilities which the child must have acquired before he is ready to begin work on phonics. Ability to hear similarities and differences among sounds and to recognize the symbols for each is one important skill. Ability to hear rhyming words is another readiness skill. In addition, children who learn sight words easily seem to be more ready for phonics than those who have difficulty. Cordts includes these and other phases of reading as essential aspects of readiness for phonics.[1]

Auditory Acuity

Ability to hear similarities and differences among sounds in various positions in words should precede work with printed symbols. The child should be able to recognize and identify rhyming words when he hears them in games, poems, and jingles and should be able to name some rhyming words himself. The child must also be able to hear similarities and differences among beginning consonants in words, and he should later be able to identify words that end with the same consonant sounds.

Although all first-grade children with normal hearing are able to recognize and understand a wide variety of the words they hear in language spoken around them, the ability to detect similarities. and differences in parts of words demands considerably more maturity and experience than that needed in the mere ability to recognize spoken words. While most children have begun to recognize spoken words at two years of age and even younger, children tend to acquire the ability to hear separate sounds within words at a much later age.

Visual Perception

Ability to recognize similarities and differences among printed letters and words is easier for some children than ability to hear these sounds. If, however, they learn to perceive differences among letters before they

[1] Anna D. Cordts, *Phonics for the Reading Teacher* (New York: Holt, Rinehart and Winston, Inc., 1965).

have acquired the ability to hear these differences, the learning may become purely mechanical. Most children can acquire the ability to underline two words starting with *b* among words starting with other letters as a purely mechanical skill which has little meaning without the knowledge of the sound. If phonics is introduced before children are able to hear differences among sounds, the instruction in recognizing visual similarities and differences may be a waste of time for such a child because he cannot apply his instruction in recognizing words.

When the child is ready, one of the best ways of teaching phonics while developing visual acuity is to present sentences to him with multiple-choice endings. At least two of the words in the multiple-choice sentence should begin with the same consonant when teaching beginning consonants. The same is true of medial or ending sounds. An example of such a sentence is given as follows:

Jimmy liked to play with
a ball
a box
Bill
a cake

If this sentence depends upon the comprehension of a story as well as upon phonic ability, the child will practice on these two skills at one time. After reading the story, he will read a sentence similar to the one above and will underline the word that is correct according to the story. The similarities among the sounds of the words in the multiple-choice endings force careful visual discrimination. A series of these sentences may be given to the child after he has read a story in order to check his comprehension and encourage visual discrimination at the same time.

Reversals

Immature children often have considerable difficulty with words that are similar in shape, especially those that involve either a reversal of letter shapes, such as words starting with *b* and *d*, or a reversal of the entire word, such as *was* and *saw*. Such letters as *u* and *n* and *p* and *q* are also difficult. Except for a very small percentage of children, those making reversals are usually immature for the level of reading which they may be trying to do.

The construction of the eye and the need for children to learn to interpret the positions of objects they see are responsible for this confusion. All visual stimuli or light waves enter the eye through the pupil and strike the optic lens in the eye. This optic lens is circular in shape and is thick in the middle and tapering toward the edge. The retina is made up of sensitive nerve endings in the back of the eye which receive the image focused by the lens and which are connected with the brain by the optic nerve. As each light ray strikes the optic lens in the eye, it is bent at an angle and is thrown on the retina on the opposite side from that at which it entered.

Thus, the light rays from the right side of an object are recorded on the left side of the retina, and the rays from the left side of the object are recorded on the right side of the retina. In the same way, the light rays from the top of an object cross in the lens and reach the lower part of the retina, whereas the light rays from the bottom of the object also cross over in the lens and reach the upper section of the retina. This process takes place in both eyes at one time. Thus all objects are recorded on the retina upside down and backward.

At first the baby has no concept of space or distance and reaches as confidently for the moon as he does for the rattles strung above his head in the crib. As time goes on, he gradually develops better ideas of distance and learns to interpret his upside-down images as he gropes for things and stumbles over them. Little by little, he unconsciously translates his visual image and becomes able to locate the top, bottom, and sides of objects as they are located in space, rather than as he sees them. In this learning process he is unconscious of the fact that his visual images are interpreted rather than direct copies of objects as seen in space. Just as the type-setter becomes able to read type upside down and backwards without consciously thinking about its position, so the young child learns to interpret his visual images without consciousness of his interpretation.

The child learns to make this visual adjustment with large objects at first and may not have learned to interpret very small things, such as print, by the time he is six. The ability to interpret the position of smaller and smaller visual images seems to be rather closely related to levels of maturity. Only a few of the younger or more immature children have difficulty with reversals in print, and most of these make the adjustment before they are seven years old.

Sometimes this lack of interpretation shows itself in the way in which the child first writes his name when it is his first writing act. When the child writes as he sees, this writing is called mirror writing and is actually upside down and backward.

Help with Reversals

This tendency will gradually disappear if the teacher appears to ignore it and merely helps the child to write and read in the correct direction. Except in rare cases no permanent difficulty is encountered

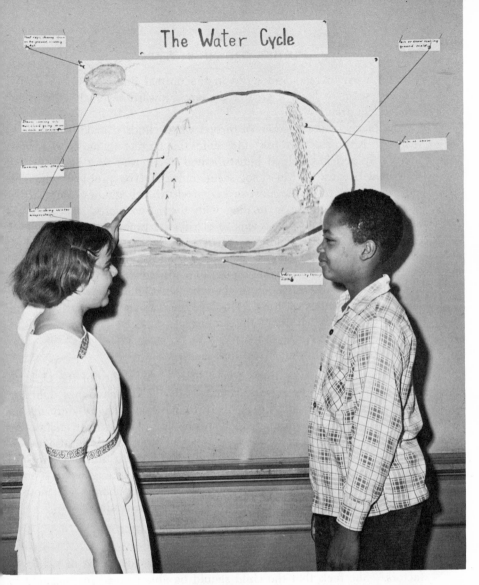

The Water Cycle

Children in a fourth grade made a diagram of the water cycle that helps them understand its progression and gives them experience in the use of graphic representations. (Courtesy California State Department of Education.)

unless the teacher or parents become emotionally disturbed and thereby disturb the child.

If the child is made to feel that his reaction is abnormal, a block to further learning of the particular words with which the child has trouble may interfere with his correct learning for a long time. To repeat, the teacher must meet the situation as a stage in normal development and work calmly to help the child continue his normal development and thereby learn to read and write in the normal direction. Left-handed children seem to have a greater tendency toward reversals than right-handed children.

The teacher may become disturbed when children make reversals in reading. After she has told the child the correct name of the word repeatedly and has helped him to sound it out, she may begin to feel disturbed because he does not seem to learn. The problem with *was* and *saw* seems to be the most severe. Help with beginning sounds does not seem to be of use in dealing with these two words. The thought of the sentence, however, seems to clarify the problem in almost every case if used patiently as long as needed. If the teacher guides the child to reread the sentence while concentrating on the thought, his error will be obvious and will probably amuse him. If she will continue to guide the child to use the criterion of thought, he usually overcomes the difficulty in a matter of time. This recovery is especially easy if the teacher is very casual about the problem.

Sight Words for Phonic Readiness

Another aspect of readiness for phonics is the ability of the child to learn words at sight successfully and easily. If the child has difficulty in learning sight words, he is likely to have even more difficulty in recognizing parts of words needed in phonics. As has been mentioned previously, the mastery of a fair number of sight words is also necessary to provide the child with opportunity for substituting letters in similar words and for making generalizations concerning word sounds. According to Hildreth, these signs of readiness for phonics are most in evidence when a pupil is ready to read in the first reader.[2]

Ability To Read for Meaning

Cordts adds a number of reading skills to the above list of readiness factors.[3] She feels that the child should be able to read for meaning in sentences, phrases, and whole words and that he should be able to answer questions from his reading. This skill rests upon his ability to read silently with comprehension. He should be sufficiently mature to read silently by the time he reads orally.

Use of Context Clues and Left-to-Right Perception

Cordts feels that the child should also be able to use context clues successfully. If he is to use context clues to check the accuracy of his

[2] Gertrude Hildreth, *Teaching Reading* (New York: Holt, Rinehart and Winston, Inc., 1961).

[3] Cordts, *op. cit.*

word analysis, he obviously must have developed some skill in their use. He should also be able to read rhythmically and have developed a desire to read. In addition, he should have developed the habit of left-to-right sequence of perception since he must learn to analyze words in a sequence from left to right. If these criteria for readiness for phonics were observed and carried into action, children might have less difficulty in learning phonics skills.

EXAMPLES OF TEACHING PROCEDURES FOR READINESS

Although some examples of teaching procedures have been given in connection with the previous topics, the teaching procedures useful in connection with a number of the aspects of phonics readiness listed above are described in detail here. Some discussion of the teaching of auditory and visual perception was given in Chapter 6, "Physical and Emotional Aspects," and further suggestions are given below.

Teaching Auditory Acuity

Some aspects of auditory acuity may be taught in the kindergarten for those children who are sufficiently mature to profit by this teaching. A variety of games for the first grade are also suggested to hold the children's interest on this rather abstract type of learnig.

Guessing Objects to Match Consonants. Children always enjoy guessing and like the following activities. The teacher may say, "I am thinking of something in this room that begins like *boy*." She is careful to pronounce the word *boy* naturally but may give a slight emphasis to the beginning sound. At first the children will name objects at random. After naming such objects as chairs, table, desk, windows, toy wagons, and so on, someone is certain to mention the word, *book*. As each child guesses, the teacher assures him that his idea was good but that he has not guessed the object about which she is thinking. When a child mentions *book*, she reacts enthusiastically and gives him a turn to be the leader.

Instead of letting the new leader choose his words unguided, the teacher should help him select the key word and the word to be guessed. Later the children will develop enough knowledge of beginning sounds to think of these words for themselves. Each time a child guesses the answer to a new puzzle, he is given a turn to be the new leader.

If the child should mention the word *blocks* when guessing a word that begins like *boy*, the teacher will accept this guess, although the word *blocks* really begins with a blend rather than a single consonant. The teacher will not make distinctions between single and blended consonants until the children have developed a good understanding of beginning sounds and are ready to work on blends. After that, she will not accept a blend as a substitute for an initial consonant.

Finding Pairs of Pictures to Match Consonants. Another game for teaching auditory acuity enjoyed by children makes use of pictures. Pictures of large, brightly colored objects mounted on nine-by-twelve tag cardboard are needed for this activity. The objects must be pasted separately, one to a card, so that the children are not confused by several objects on a page. Brightly colored pictures from magazines and objects cut from color books, mounted on tag cardboard and painted, are effective for this work. Although these pictures take time in preparation, they should last for a long time. The children enjoy the colors so much that the teacher will find it worthwhile to paint the objects with bright tempera colors if they are not already colored.

The teacher may place three pairs of these large pictures on the chalk rail or stand them up in some convenient place easy to reach by the children. The teacher will choose pictures that represent beginning consonants that usually have only one sound or phoneme. These consonants include *b, f, h, j, k, l, m, n, p, r, t, v, w* when used as a consonant and initial *y*. Among the first set may be the pictures of a ball, a boat, a fish, a fence, a kite, and a kitten. The teacher will be sure to show the pictures to the children and talk about them before she uses them in a game in order to be certain that the children identify the correct word with each picture. They might be likely to use the word *cat* for the picture of the kitten. In this case, the sounds would be the same, but the word *cat* would not serve as a comparison with *kite,* to be used later when the children are ready for the visual phase of perception. Some children may not recognize the picture of an object such as a fence, and culturally-deprived children may lack experience with many other pictured words.

The supplementation of the pictures with three-dimensional toys is valuable for work with deprived children in order to expand their concepts of these objects. The printed letter representing the beginning consonant is not combined with the picture or object. If it were added to the picture, children might match pictures by matching the shapes of the letters rather than by listening for the sounds. This point is very important in teaching auditory acuity.

After the pictures have been spread out in a convenient place, the teacher selects a child to choose one of these pictures. She guides him to show the picture to the other children and tell its name. For example, the child may choose the picture of the kitten. He then asks for someone to find the picture with a name that begins with the same sound. In this situation, too, the children will guess at random. When a child selects kite to match the word, *kitten,* he is told that he has found the right picture. He may then be the new leader to choose another picture after he replaces the pictures of the kite and kitten on the chalk rail. The guessing then continues.

After the children have played this game with the same pictures until they have become accurate in matching sounds, the teacher may introduce another pair of pictures and go on with the game for several more days. She may alternate this activity with others in order to prevent the children from becoming tired of it. As she repeats the game, however, from time to time, she may add more pairs of pictures, thus forcing the children to select pairs from a continuously enlarging group.

After the children have learned to match pairs with considerable accuracy, the teacher will add a third picture to each original pair, such as a picture of a boy added to the picture set of the ball and boat. The children are now required to find three pictures in this set. Later on another picture is added to the pair beginning with *f,* such as a picture showing a campfire. In this case, the teacher must be careful to be sure that the children use the word *fire* in connection with this word rather than *campfire,* which might be confused with the words *kite* and *kitten.* In this way the teacher continues to add pictures both to introduce new consonants and to review consonant sounds already learned. Although the children may memorize the pictures in pairs at first, the addition of a third picture beginning with the same consonant will help them learn to listen carefully for the beginning sound. The addition of still another picture beginning with the same sound will gradually reinforce this skill.

Naming Objects to Match Consonants. After the children have become familiar with the objects and pictures beginning with certain specific sounds, the teacher may call for volunteers to help her name other objects. She may start with the word *ball* and ask the children to see how many words they can name that begin with the same sound. Since this activity will probably be used in the first grade, the teacher may also help the children learn the name of the letter heard in the beginning of the word *ball* so that they may associate this letter with the names of other objects they identify.

Sorting Cards to Match Consonants. The teacher may paste pictures from readiness books on 3" × 5" cards for the children to work with at their seats. Two sets of pictures may be included in one envelope. The children may then be guided to sort the pictures according to beginning sounds. Pictures of objects beginning with *b* might be put in an envelope along with pictures of objects beginning with the sound of *f*. An even number of pictures of each letter helps the children have some idea of whether or not their sorting has been correct and also helps the teacher check the sorting quickly. As with the large pictures, these cards should first be shown to the children and discussed to make sure that they use the correct name for each picture. The teacher may work with a small group of children for a few times until she is sure that they understand how the pictures should be sorted.

If pictures of the key words to represent the initial sounds of the names of the pictures are pasted on the outside of the envelope, the children can be taught how to use these key words to help them in their sorting. For example, a picture of a ball and another of a leaf might be pasted on the front of an envelope to show that they represent two sets of pictures each beginning with one of these sounds which would be found in the envelope. The teacher may use these same key words to represent these particular initial sounds later when she teaches the children to discriminate visually between them. As in the case with the large pictures, the teacher omits placing any identifying letters on each envelope or the pictures within it so that they can be used to develop auditory acuity.

"The Train Game" to Match Consonants. An activity called "The Train Game" may be adapted for use in teaching children to hear and name beginning sounds. The teacher places on the chalk rail pictures representing a variety of pairs of beginning consonants from which the children will choose as they play the game. She may then hold up one of the large pictures representing the initial sound *b,* preferably the key word she has selected for this letter, which may be a picture of a ball.

She then selects a child to be the conductor. He will stand behind the chair of the first child in the row or semicircle. The first seated child must select a picture representing the same initial consonant sound as that held up by the teacher. He will then use this picture as his ticket, which he gives to the "conductor" standing behind him. If he has chosen correctly a picture representing a matching sound, the conductor will move on behind the chair of the second child. The teacher may then hold up a picture representing a key word of another initial consonant, and the second child will find his "ticket" from among the pictures on the chalk rail and will give it to the "conductor."

If he fails to select a picture representing the correct consonant sound, he will take the place of the conductor who will take his seat and find the correct "ticket." The conductor will then proceed along the row until another child makes an error, when he will be replaced.

"Twenty Questions" for Matching Consonants. An adaptation of the game of "Twenty Questions" may serve to help children listen for beginning consonants. The teacher may hold a picture in her hands with the back toward the children. She may then give them each a turn to guess the name of the object pictured on her card by giving them a key word as a hint. For example, she may say, "The picture I am holding begins like the word *dog*. Can anybody guess what I have?" The children may take turns responding with such questions as, "Is it a doll?," "Is it a duck?," "Is it a door?," until someone discovers that it is a dish.

Picture Dictionaries to Match Consonants. Although the picture dictionary is not a game, it has values in helping children in the first grade learn to hear beginning sounds. To make the dictionary, pictures are cut out, sorted, and pasted in booklets. Even in the first grade this activity may be too difficult for some of the children, especially early in the year.

Some teachers make booklets for this activity by folding seven sheets of 12″ × 18″ drawing or gray bogus paper (a less expensive and softer paper than drawing paper). The procedures followed in making this dictionary are described in Chapter 16, on page 370, under "Making dictionaries." Pictures from magazines or pictures drawn by the children may be used in these dictionaries in the same way that their use was described in Chapter 11. The ability to hear beginning consonant sounds becomes functional as the children sort their pictures and arrange them under the right letter.

The teacher should check the children's classifications before they paste the pictures into their books. To make the supervision easier and to pace the activity to the children's maturity, the teacher may guide her highest group to work on this activity first. The children in the second group may make their dictionaries somewhat later, and those in the third group may not be ready for this activity until near the end of the first grade or even early in the second grade. After the children in the first group have made their dictionaries, they may be able to help with the supervision of the work of the other children, always subject to the teacher's final approval.

Picture Dictionaries to Match Vowels. Work with the beginning vowels in making the dictionaries usually offers the greatest problems because of the variety of sounds of these vowels and because they are sometimes combined in digraphs and diphthongs. Therefore, the children may have difficulty in classifying them. Since this activity is meant primarily for help with beginning consonants, the teacher may give the most help with the pages on which the beginning vowels are listed. With commonly pictured objects such as airplane, eggs, and ice cream, involving a mixture of vowel types, the teacher may tell the children on what pages these pictures go without spending much time trying to help them hear the sounds. Children who have had alphabet books at home may already have some ideas regarding where the vowel pictures should be placed.

Jigsaw Puzzles to Match Consonants. An adaptation of the idea of working with jigsaw puzzles may be adapted to listening for beginning consonants. The teacher may make use of 3" × 5" or 4" × 6" cards. She may paste two pictures representing words beginning with the consonant *b*, preferably followed by short *a*, as in *bag* and *bat*. She may place the cards vertically, pasting the picture of the bag at the top of the card, and the picture of the bat on the lower half of the card. She may then cut the two pictures apart (See Figure 9-1), following a zigzag line. When the child has succeeded placing together the two parts that fit together, he will know that he has found two pictures with names beginning with the same sound. A picture of a cat and cap may be pasted on another puzzle card, and so on. These cut parts of pictures may be placed in an envelope or box with a picture of one of the cards on the outside to serve as a label for the children. When this set of cards is first introduced, the teacher may include five or six picture puzzles in one game. As the children develop skill in this activity, she may put more puzzle cards in each envelope.

Teaching Visual Perception

Although auditory discrimination can be developed without visual discrimination, effective visual discrimination cannot be taught effectively without its auditory counterpart. Unless the children learn the sounds of the letters while they learn to discriminate among their shapes, there may be no carry over to the actual function of the skill in reading.

Matching for Likenesses and Differences. From research studies, such as Goins',[4] the matching of likenesses and differences among pictures seems to have little effect on children's visual acuity in actual word discrimination. There seems to be no proof that formal exercises in matching letters, parts of words, and words carried on before the children begin to read have any appreciable effect upon their visual discrimination in the reading act, although a few authors advocate their use. These exercises may have more value as one aspect of a readiness test.

One of the shortcomings in the use of formal exercises in letter and word discriminations previous to reading is the lack of meaning they have for the child. An example of such an exercise is the presentation of several letters such as *P   S R P V*. The child is told to find the letter in the group at the right that looks like the first letter standing alone at

⁴ Jean Turner Goins, *Visual Perceptual Abilities and Early Reading Progress*, Supplementary Education Monograph No. 87 (Chicago: The University of Chicago Press, Feb. 1958).

the left. Since the letters have no meaning for the child, these exercises become merely mechanical manipulations. Geometric forms have been used in the same manner and have been found to have little value in developing visual discrimination. Since such exercises have no meaning for the child, he tends to become bored with their use. Smith states that there is no value in teaching the child to perceive likenesses and differences in words unless he knows the sounds of the letters in these words.[5]

One of the basic goals in developing reading readiness is to arouse interest in the reading process. Intelligent children tend to resent and become bored by these mechanical exercises. Children of less than normal intelligence are often satisfied to work on such exercises because they give these children feelings of success, but these exercises are of doubtful value even with such children. Other, more valuable procedures are suggested for this purpose.

According to Tinker and McCullough practice in observing likenesses and differences among geometric forms and pictures should be used only with children who have an almost total lack of ability to distinguish between these forms.[6] According to Hildreth exercises requiring the matching of word forms should be given after the children have done some reading, and they should be used in meaningful ways.[7]

A variety of matching procedures are included in formal readiness tests along with tests of ability to distinguish reversals. These tests seem to have some minor value in identifying the level of readiness for beginning reading.

Naming the Letters of the Alphabet. The results of research studies have shown that such factors as ability to name the letters of the alphabet, to recognize them in printed form, and to write them on dictation have some value in identifying the child's level of readiness. There is a great danger, however, in concluding that the teaching of such skills will result in the necessary maturity for beginning reading. In actuality, this research shows that the child who is mature enough to name, recognize, and write the letters of the alphabet is probably also mature enough to learn to read. Studies showing the value of such tests for measuring maturity should be followed by other research to discover if teaching to develop these skills actually results in reading readiness. In such cases cause may be confused with effect.

Many children have learned to read without a knowledge of the letters of the alphabet. Therefore, no one can logically conclude that this knowledge is necessary to the teaching of reading. In the modern

[5] Nila Banton Smith, *Reading Instruction for Today's Children* (Englewood Cliffs, N. J.: Prentice–Hall, Inc., 1963).

[6] Miles Tinker and Constance M. McCullough, *Teaching Elementary Reading* (2nd ed.; New York: Appleton–Century–Crofts, 1962).

[7] Hildreth, *op. cit.*

program the names of the letters are learned as the children need to use them in learning to recognize the sounds of the consonants and vowels. They also learn their names as they write the letters when they need them in functional writing. More study is needed to discover what activities really have value in developing readiness.

Use of Workbooks for Visual Discrimination. A variety of activities for developing particular aspects of reading readiness are found in workbooks. Some of today's busy teachers tend to use these workbooks with children without regard for individual needs. Some children may benefit from work in these books. Other activities should be provided for children too mature to need some of the activities in the workbook. These books are of value only if the activities are suited to the use of children. If the teacher finds that the children in the fast group are able to succeed with the activities in the nonexpendable readiness books, she should omit all these activities in the workbook. If children in the fast group actually need any of these exercises, the teacher may tear out the appropriate pages and give them to the children. The same use of the workbooks should be made for children in the other groups.

Matching with Experience Stories. A variety of experiences for developing readiness are described in Chapter 6, "Physical and Emotional Aspects." A few of those that may be valuable for developing visual discrimination are suggested here. Sentence and meaningful word matching experiences can be provided for use with experience stories on charts. Very little work with this type of activity is needed for the children who are nearly ready for reading. This type of experience, however, is valuable for children who are quite immature and who are likely to need help for a number of months before readiness is developed.

Since the children dictate the sentences in experience stories in their own words, they tend to remember them verbatim. These stories should be printed on charts and made up of only two or three sentences in the beginning. Strips made to match each sentence in a particular story may be prepared for use with this story. The same procedures are followed as those described in Chapters 7 and 8 under the heading of "The Identification Step." At first the children may match whole sentences. The teacher reads each sentence strip and asks the children to find it in the story and to match the strip to it. Later the sentences may be cut into phrases or units of thought for matching, and eventually they may be cut apart into words. These parts may also be read and matched.

Matching with Experience Stories for Slow Learners. Most slow-learning children in the first grade are usually able to match successfully unless their intelligence is low enough for them to be eligible for work in special classes. Although this matching is used with memorized sentences from the experience story and does not involve any actual reading, it seems to help these immature children gain feelings of success. They do not seem to realize that they are not participating in the complete reading activity, which is followed by the children in the other groups.

Five boys in one class took part in this type of activity varied with other reading readiness activities for a year and a half before they actually were able to recognize and read any of the sentences or words. They never seemed to become bored with these activities. Perhaps the use of a variety of their own stories and matching games helped provide satisfaction in such activities. When these boys finally succeeded in reaching the level of maturity needed for reading, they made very rapid strides. None of them had difficulty with visual discrimination after reaching this level.

Experience Stories for Visual Discrimination. The use of experience stories with average and rapid learners is also very valuable. These stories are usually printed on charts and reread occasionally for interest and pleasure. They are usually reviewed during the few days immediately following their dictation and then referred to occasionally at later times.

As the children dictate and reread the chart stories, they begin to notice the unusual characteristics of some of the words, such as those described in the section on configuration clues. As time goes on, they tend to observe more detail in the print. Often children notice words with beginning letters that are similar to the beginning letters of their own names, especially if these words in their stories happen to start with capital letters.

For example, the children may have dictated a story about their pet guinea pig named Pinky. A child named Patty is very likely to point out the fact that her name starts with the same letter as Pinky's. She may also notice that it ends the same. Other children then begin to point out letters that are similar to the beginnings of their names. Later, they will recognize a word at the beginning or end of a sentence in their experience story such as the word *school* in the sentence, "Mary brought her guinea pig to school." As time goes on, the most mature children will become able to pick out and read most of the words in the sentences in these stories.

All of this work with experience stories provides excellent opportunities for developing visual acuity in natural and meaningful situations without the use of mechanical exercises. The children who are slower to recognize words in experience stories can then profit from the matching of strips, phrases, and single words, always in the framework of the total sentence and story. The use of experience stories also provides excellent opportunities for children to learn to read from left to right without the use of artificial exercises.

Other types of visual discrimination skills are best taught in actual reading as the child develops a sight word vocabulary. At this time he is able to discriminate among words as they are used in sentences. The meaning of the words is then clear from their use in context, and misunderstanding of the use of any of the words is avoided.

Games and Activities for Visual Discrimination. Another activity may have some value in helping children develop visual discrimination of beginning consonants. When the children have acquired enough auditory discrimination to be able to dictate to the teacher words that begin with the same consonant sounds, she may print these in a list on the board in connection with the consonant, *b*. Each child who suggests a word beginning with *b* may also give a sentence containing this word.

If the children have been talking about playing with a ball or have dictated a story about it, usually in a small group, the teacher may print this word on the board. As she does so, she may ask the children if any of them can think of other words that begin with the same sound as *ball*. She may also hold up a picture of a ball as she talks. The children may name such words as *bell, baby, box, boat, bed, big, be,* and *book*.

If any of the children suggest words that do not belong in this list, the teacher may encourage them by telling them that their suggestions are good, but they do not begin like *ball*. They can be used later with words beginning with other letters. The teacher then asks the children to tell her what parts of all these words look exactly alike. Most children will be able to point out the letter *b* at the beginning of each word. The teacher may let children take turns putting a circle around or a line under each beginning letter *b* until all the beginning consonants are circled. She may then ask the children to listen while she reads the list to be sure that all the words begin with the correct sound. As the children become more mature and gain confidence in their ability to choose words beginning with a particular consonant, the teacher may accept a suggestion for a word that does not belong with the others to encourage alertness.

Most children will protest immediately as she writes the incorrect word. The teacher should praise the children enthusiastically for their ability to recognize an error and then erase the word that does not belong in the list. Although only a few children may be able to dictate correct words at first, the others will gradually learn from those that succeed until all are able to carry on this activity successfully. The teacher should develop the consonants in a planned sequence, adding one at a time and reviewing others frequently.

BASIS FOR WORD RECOGNITION SKILLS

Informal procedures for teaching the use of picture clues, configuration clues, and context clues have been suggested for helping children learn to recognize unknown words. The development of auditory acuity and visual perception has also been suggested for helping children acquire readiness. A sight word vocabulary provides the best basis for developing word recognition skills.

Need for Sight Words

For several reasons children are taught a number of sight words in their early steps in reading. The ability to recognize words at sight helps children read for thought from the very beginning. By starting in this manner, they also enjoy reading and develop feelings of confidence in this activity. Sight words are important to the beginner in checking the accuracy of his phonics applications. Sight words are also helpful to the child when he learns to compare unknown words with known words for identical parts or substitute a letter or letters of known words in unknown words.

Sight Words for Meaning. Instant recognition of words at sight is necessary if the child is to get thought from the printed page. The child must also see words in groups in order to gain thought. By beginning reading with sight words the child is able to get the meaning from his first contact with print.

Sight Words for Comparisons. Word analysis is taught by the process of making a rule from a series of examples. This process makes use of inductive reasoning and is easier for the child to use than the deductive process formerly used. For example, the child may have learned *boy, baby,* and *big* as sight words. When a new word with the same beginning consonant is met, the teacher may put the above words on the board. She will then ask the children to tell her how they are alike. When the children tell her that they all begin with the same letter, *b,* the teacher will add the new word from their lesson, such as *box,* and ask them how this word is like the others. When they tell her that *box* begins like *boy,* they have discovered the sound of a common beginning consonant and will gradually learn to apply this sound to other words that begin with *b.* In this way children start with familiar examples and draw generalizations from them.

Sight Words to Provide Context Clues. The child also needs a stock of sight words to help him use context clues to check his phonics. To be able to use context clues in this way the child must have enough sight words to get the thought. He can then apply and check his phonics generalizations. If the child tries to read the sentence, "Tommy put his new cap on his head," in which *head* is an unknown word, he will first try to read the word as *heed* because of the rule for the *ea*. According to this rule the first letter takes the long sound and the second is silent. When he realizes that the word *heed* does not make sense, he will check for thought from the known words and decide that the word is *head*, taking the short sound of *e*.

Beginning Sight Word Vocabulary

Authors are not in complete agreement in regard to the number of sight words needed by beginners before phonics is introduced. Estimates vary from fifty to two hundred or more sight words. The principle supported in this text agrees with those held by Goins, Hildreth, and Smith. These authorities agree that children should know several words beginning with the same consonant sound before they are helped to recognize these sounds in unknown words. Children should also know several sight words ending with the same consonant sound or letter groups before introducing for recognition a new word ending with these sounds. The same principle holds for medial or middle sounds and vowels in various positions.

Some of the differences of opinion among authors regarding the need for a solid background of sight words as a prerequisite for phonics instruction depend upon the type of phonic program these authors support. To those who have taught phonics or word analysis to first grade children, an obvious need is felt for an adequate background of known words upon which they can depend for the application of this substitution technique with whole words.

AIDS IN LEARNING SIGHT WORDS

Sight words are learned as the child associates the name and meaning of the word with its printed symbol. Ease of visualization, conspicuous characteristics of configuration, and pleasant emotional associations help the child recall words.

Value of Meaning

The more experience the child has had with the meaning of words, the easier it will be for him to recall. Every child has had considerable

Charts of various types were made by students for the recording of information on how oil is secured and refined. (Courtesy California State Department of Education.)

experience with food. For this reason the words *ice cream, cake,* and *cookies* are very easy for him to learn. *Mother* and *father* are also words that tie in with his experience and are therefore easy to learn.

If the meaning of a word is not clear to the child, he will tend to have more difficulty learning it. Since culturally-deprived children do not have as many experiences as other children, they have more difficulty in learning words that are easier for other children. Meaning also helps the child form a firm image of a word so that he can distinguish it more easily from other words. Children remember words that have more meaning for them and forget words that have less meaning.

Use of Words in Sentences. The child learns words when they are introduced in sentences more easily than when they are introduced alone. A list of single words is very difficult for a child to learn to read because many of these words have little meaning when printed alone. Words in a sentence take on meaning from others in context of the sentence and are therefore much easier to learn. When they are presented in sentences, the child also learns to read them in meaningful groups. If he learns words from a list on the chalkboard, he usually develops the habit of repeating them without thought and tends to carry over this habit to word-by-word reading in sentence context. Although the child should learn words in context, he should eventually be able to recognize such words when he meets them singly.

Dramatic Quality of Words.   Words that can be dramatized are also easier for a child to remember than more abstract words. If the child is given an opportunity to come when he is shown the word *come,* and to go when he is shown this word, he will tend to remember these words more easily. Children enjoy pantomime as one form of practice on sight vocabulary. A child may choose one of the words on the board to pantomime. He may then call on another child to guess which word he is dramatizing. The child may rush across the room to dramatize the word *fast* or extend his hands as far as possible to suggest the word *big.* The word *car* calls for a dramatization of driving down the street shown by pretending to steer the car. The words *jump* and *run* are obvious, and the word *funny* may be portrayed by dramatizing laughter. Children are very imaginative and can think of many ways to dramatize the meanings of words. They will remember the words much better if they create their own ideas for expressing them.

Emotional Association.   The dramatization of a word serves another purpose in helping reinforce the word, that of pleasant emotional association. Children enjoy dramatic activities, and this pleasant association helps them remember words such as *walk, jump,* and *fly.* The words *party, birthday,* and *picnic* are other examples of words that have pleasant associations for children. Any word that is tied in with the child's interests or desires tends to be fairly easy for him to remember. On the other hand, unpleasant associations with words according to Hildreth tend to block association with printed words. A child who is never allowed to go beyond his own fence to play with other children may develop a block against a recall of this word.

Visualization and Configuration Aids.   If a word has a meaning that can be visualized, it will be easier for the child to learn than one that cannot be visualized. The words *rabbit, doll,* and *car* form associations with vivid pictures in the child's mind. Some children can learn these words after one or two exposures. Outstanding configuration characteristics of a word also make it easier for the child to learn. The word *airplane* has an easy configuration to remember. The length of the word and the upper and lower strokes help the child identify it.

Reinforcement by Senses.   The child learns sight words better when they are supplemented and reinforced by hearing as well as sight. He remembers them even better if he sees the word, hears it, and also repeats it. He should say it, however, in response to a purpose so that he thinks about it as he speaks. Memory for words may be reinforced by various activities. A word such as *soft* may be reinforced by allowing the child to feel a piece of cloth when this word is introduced, and the word *rough* might be reinforced by the feel of a piece of sandpaper. A child may be encouraged to blow on his hands to reinforce the meaning of *blow* and to stand near an object of his choice to help him remember the word, *near*.

Repetition in New Situations. One of the best techniques for helping the child learn sight words is for him to meet them frequently in new sentences and stories. Repetition is of the utmost importance in helping the child develop a sight vocabulary, and the best repetition occurs in sentences and stories that appeal to his interests. Anyone who has studied a foreign language knows how essential repetition is to the recall of foreign words. He also knows how rapidly a foreign language is forgotten when it is not used. A child who is absent from school for two weeks tends to forget some of the sight vocabulary he was learning while in school.

Difficulty of Abstract Words

Words that have little meaning alone are the most difficult for the child to learn. Adverbs, prepositions, and conjunctions fall in this class. Such a word as *to* has almost no meaning when it stands alone. This word is more easily learned in connection with a noun in a phrase, such as *to the store* or *to school*. When it is learned in connection with such words, the child has an opportunity to visualize his movement toward a place with which he is familiar. The word *for* is another meaningless word unless it is associated with such a word as *you*. If the child reads the sentence, *The cake is for you*, he not only visualizes the word *cake* but he also associates it with his ownership and the pleasure received.

SUMMARY

A knowledge of some sight words serves as the basis for phonics when it is taught as an inductive skill and when the child is guided to draw the generalizations for himself. This background of sight words was not needed when phonics was taught by giving the child a generalization which he was required to apply. Ability to use picture, configuration, and context clues is taught before the child is taught to use phonics clues. Meaning is emphasized even in the readiness stages of phonics when auditory acuity has an important place. Ability to hear sounds accurately in words has been found to be necessary before formal phonics is taught. Visual perception can be improved by means of experience stories because they have meaning for the child. Some knowledge of factors that affect the learning of sight words are of value to the teacher.

Much can be done with young children to develop readiness for word recognition. Some readiness activities may be carried on in the kindergarten as long as the co-ordination of finer muscles is not demanded. Informal aids to word recognition include the use of picture, configuration, and context clues. Some of the mental aspects of readiness for phonics involves auditory and visual perception. Other aspects involve some maturity in mental qualities. A basis of sight words is needed before the child can build phonic generalizations.

15

Word Recognition Skills

The reasons for helping the child acquire a stock of sight words before he is given phonics techniques have been discussed in Chapter 14. Some of the differences between the way phonics was taught when the teaching of reading consisted of intensified phonics with oral reading and the way phonics is taught in the balanced developmental program may help the student understand the advantages of the modern program. An analysis of the various skills to be taught are given to provide suggestions for procedures in teaching phonics.

FORMAL WORD RECOGNITION PROCEDURES

The use of phonic clues as a technique of word recognition is very important. The teaching of phonics, however, should be carried on in a balanced program in order to help the child apply his learnings and to avoid loss of comprehension and lack of a good reading rate. A capable reader uses phonic clues only when he needs them to identify an unrecognized word. After most readers have analyzed a word by means of phonic clues once or even several times if necessary, the word becomes a sight word and is read as a whole or at least by major parts rather than by the phonic analysis of each sound in the word. The reader who has been taught to look for and analyze the sounds of every word he reads, regardless of need, is likely to be an extremely inefficient reader.

Comparison of Phonic Programs

One of the differences between the older, formal phonic program and the use of phonics in a modern balanced program concerns the blending of letter sounds to make whole words as opposed to the comparison of whole words for similarities within each. The emphasis on meaning is another difference between these programs. Rules or generalizations are also used in different ways. In some formal programs vowels are introduced before consonants.

Relation to the Reading Program. When phonics was taught formerly, phonic skills were presented in an intensified program concentrated in the first grade, whereas in the developmental program phonic skills are spread over the first three grades and followed by the study of word structure and dictionary use in the intermediate grades. In the intensified program all the phonic sounds and most of the rules were taught in the first grade. It was impossible to apply all of these skills to the work in reading and at the same time to give adequate review and application of the skills.

While some children were able to learn all of the skills in the first grade, many children were unable to do so. In an unpublished study, promotion procedures were investigated in a large county in a populous area during the school year 1921-1922. Although children entered school at an average age of six years and seven months and classes were small in size, one-third of the children were failed at the end of the first grade and were required to repeat the year. Moreover, one-third of the children who were enrolled in this first grade had failed the year before and were repeating the grade at this time. Therefore, during this year two-thirds of the children enrolled in the first grades at these schools had either been failed the year before or were required to repeat the current year.

Memory of Letter Patterns. In the formal phonics program, children learned to read by blending each letter in sequence in order to pronounce each word. Attention was on the letters and parts of the word followed by the recognition of the word. Reading consisted of the pronunciation of one word after another. This process tended to encourage word-by-word reading and lip movement.

In this formal program the first step in teaching beginners was to teach them the names and sounds of the letters. This step was usually followed by help in blending letter sounds to make words or nonsense syllables without attention to the meanings of these syllables or words. Practice was given through meaningless repetition of letter groups. Phonics charts and flash cards of letter groups were used to help the child memorize these letter combinations, and in some systems pressure was placed upon speed of recognition. This type of phonics along with oral reading usually made up the entire program. This procedure often killed the child's interest and enthusiasm before he started to read.

Some of today's programs have returned to the use of some of these procedures.

Development and Application of Rules. In the early phonic programs, such as that followed in the McGuffey readers, diacritical marks were placed over the letters in order to help the children identify the correct sounds. The children also learned a large number of rules and tried to remember them in order to be able to apply them to the pronunciation of new words.

In today's program the children are helped to discover the most common rules by observing their operation in a number of known words. For example, after the children have learned *made, cape,* and *same* as sight words, the teacher may put these words in a list on the chalkboard. She may then place a list with the words, *mad, cap,* and *Sam,* on the left opposite the first list. She may ask the children to look at the two lists to find out how they are different. The children will notice that each word in the list on the right ends with an *e,* but those on the left do not.

The teacher will also ask how the words in the two lists are alike. The children will notice the second list has the same words as the first list, except that the second list has an *e* added to the end of each word. After this conclusion the teacher will ask a volunteer to read the first words in each list, that is, opposite pairs, and the children will be asked to tell the difference in sound between them. Some child will be able to tell that the word in the first list has a short *a* in the middle, and the word in the second list has a long *a.* Children who do not yet know the terms, short and long *a,* may say that the second *a* "says its name," but the first *a* does not. This step will be repeated with each of the pairs of words. The teacher will then ask the children to see if they can make a rule to cover the situation. The children may decide that the *e* on the ends of the words in the list on the right has no sound. They may also add that the letter *e* on the ends of the words makes the vowels in the middle long or "makes them say their names."

Use of Consonants and Vowels. In the formal phonics program reading texts were based on a purely phonic approach. Vowel sounds were often introduced before consonants. The short sound of each vowel was taught first because these sounds are the most common. The long sounds of the vowels were taught at a later time. Words containing diphthongs and digraphs were also introduced later. The sounds of the consonants, including consonant blends and consonant digraphs, were introduced after the children had learned the long and short vowel sounds. These sounds were introduced in words but were usually pronounced separately as well as in words. The text of the stories was limited to words which were used to introduce particular vowels under study. The sentences and so-called stories in the first books therefore tended to have very little meaning.

In the balanced program consonants are introduced before vowels for several reasons. Many more words begin with consonants than with vowels. Learning to read from left to right is an important aspect of the reading program. If the children begin phonics instruction by learning the beginning consonant sounds, they will acquire the habit of reading from left to right. This process is reversed when vowels are taught first. The child looks at the vowel, usually in second or third place in the word, and then moves his eyes back to the initial consonant before he can read the word. This process forces the habit of making reversals on the child, a habit which is considered a reading handicap by most reading specialists.

Consonant sounds are the most consistent and therefore the most satisfactory for beginning instruction in phonics. Another reason for learning consonants first is concerned with the influence of the consonant on the sound of the vowel. For example, the *a* in *saw* is neither long nor short because of the influence of the final *w*. In the same way, the *a* in the words, *call* and *car,* are neither long nor short because of the influence of the double *ll* and the *r* on these vowels. For the above reasons, consonants are taught before vowels in today's program. These consonants, of course, are introduced and taught by means of whole words from sentence context.

Whole Versus Part Learning. In the formal program of phonics the child learned the sounds of the letters and then learned to blend these sounds to produce words. This process was known as part-to-whole learning or synthesis. The fact that some consonants cannot be pronounced alone resulted in a blending problem. Since the consonants such as *c* and *n* are difficult to hear when pronounced alone, the child learned to include a vowel sound with each consonant. Therefore he tried to blend the distorted sounds of *cuh a nun* in an effort to sound the word, *can.* Mature and intelligent children seem to be able to manage this awkward and unnatural procedure, but average and slow children find it very difficult.

In the modern program children learn the sound of *can* by comparing it with such known words as *cat* and *cap.* They check their analysis of the word by reading the sentence containing it to see if it suits the meaning. This process is known as substitution (of ending sounds in this case) or analysis.

Use with Meaning. In the formal program texts were written to provide experience with certain vowels and later with certain consonants rather than to provide reading with meaning on the child's level of interest. Today's texts are written to provide stories with meaning on children's levels of interest and with the use of words that are common in children's own vocabulary. As a result, the teacher must wait until the children have several sight words involving a given sound before she is able to give practice on this sound. This delay is actually beneficial because children begin to learn about sounds more successfully after they have had a background of understanding and when they are mature enough to be able to apply these sounds to new words which they will meet later. Word recognition techniques are balanced with other procedures for developing silent reading comprehension and other skills.

Steps in Teaching the Sounds

When the child has learned an adequate number of sight words, he is ready to begin to learn the sounds of letters and letter groups with understanding as they are found in words. Each letter sound is called a phoneme, and this sound in print is called a grapheme. The analysis techniques used in phonics consist of a comparison of similar word forms and substitution of one sound for another in order to change one word to a similar one. Examples of this substitution are found in the change of *bead* to *read, part* to *park,* and *map* to *mop.* In the first case the initial consonant was substituted, in the second the final consonant was substituted, and in the last case the middle or medial vowel was substituted. The child should be taught to start at the beginning of an unknown word and to analyze it all the way through from left to right, regardless of the place of substitution.

Most authors agree in general concerning the steps in teaching phonics and the order in which they should occur. Some authors have suggested the following steps in teaching the sounds:

1. The child learns a stock of sight words.
2. The child identifies recurring parts within these words which serve as clues to sounds.
3. The child identifies these sounds in new words.
4. The child develops generalizations concerning the function of these sounds.
5. The commonest phonic elements are met in a variety of words until the child recognizes them whenever he finds them in regular words.

Heilman gives the following steps in teaching phonics.[1] This list is

---

[1] Arthur W. Heilman, *Phonics in Proper Perspective* (Columbus, Ohio: Charles E. Merrill Books, Inc., 1964).

not arranged entirely in the sequence in which phonic elements are introduced.

1. Various types of auditory discrimination with words.
2. The introduction and teaching of consonant sounds.
   a. The introduction of initial consonants.
   b. The use of letter substitution with initial consonant sounds.
   c. The introduction of consonant sounds at the ends of the words.
   d. The introduction of consonant digraphs.
   e. The introduction of consonant blends.
   f. The introduction of consonant digraphs found at the ends of words.
   g. The introduction of consonants that are irregular.
   h. The introduction of silent consonants.
   i. The introduction of contractions.
3. The introduction and teaching of vowel sounds.
   a. The introduction and teaching of short sounds.
   b. The introduction of long vowel sounds.
   c. Teaching words contrasting long and short sounds.
   d. Teaching exceptions to vowel rules.
   e. Introduction of diphthongs.
   f. Introduction of short and long sounds of *oo*.
4. The introduction and teaching of syllabification.
   a. Introduction of rules for syllabification.
   b. Introduction of prefixes and suffixes.
   c. Introduction of compound words.
   d. Introduction of rules for doubling final consonants.
   e. Introduction of accent marks.
5. Teaching the use of the dictionary.

Suggestions for Teaching Beginning Consonants

Selection of the First Consonant. Most authorities suggest that regular initial consonants be taught as the first step in phonics. As words beginning with these letter sounds are met in stories in the pre-primers and primer, the teacher makes a note of the words that begin with the same initial sound. In one series, the children meet the words *make, me,* and *may,* as one of the first consonants that have been repeated at least three times. When the teacher is planning her lesson, she will notice that the children already know three words beginning with the sound of *m* and will realize that the word *my* in the next lesson is the fourth word to appear beginning with *m*. The children will be introduced to the new word, *my*, on the first day of work on their new story and will have met it in their silent reading.

Teaching the First Consonant. When the teacher has given practice on the new words in sentence context and alone in a particular lesson, she will be ready to give some help on phonics. She will put the review words *make, me,* and *may* on the board in a vertical list, reminding the children that these are words they know. After they have taken turns in reading these words, the teacher will ask them to see if they can find any parts of these words that look exactly alike. The children will be able to point out the beginning letter, *m,* either by name or by referring to it as the first letter. The teacher praises their success and says, "Now I am going to put another word on the board. This is the one we had in today's lesson," as she adds the word *my* to the end of the list. After the children have read this word, she may then say, "Do you see anything about the last word that looks like the others?" The children will again mention the beginning letter. A child is then asked to reread the four words to see if all the beginning letters sound alike. When the children have decided that the words do begin with the same sound, the teacher may call on a child to circle the *m* in the first word and to read it. She will follow the same procedure with the other three words. She may also ask the children to think of other words that begin with *m.*

Adding Words Beginning with the First Consonant. When in a later lesson, the teacher encounters the next word beginning with the letter, *m,* she may follow the same procedure, adding the new word, *much,* to the first four words. This step helps the children review the words with the beginning *m* sound taught earlier and to add the new word to their list, thereby reinforcing their concept of the sound of this letter. Even though no new words beginning with *m* occur in the next several lessons, the teacher will review these old words in sentences and ask the children to point out the similarities again.

Review of the First Consonant. The teacher may also review these words in multiple-choice sentences. She may write on the board,

> my
> "I will bring may doll," said Mary.
> make

In this case the children underline or circle one of the words beginning with *m* that will complete the meaning of the sentence. She may put several other sentences on the board such as the following:

much.	much
Give the doll to make.	Mary can make cookies.
me.	me

Review Applied to a Story. When the children know enough words beginning with a particular initial consonant, the teacher may use the multiple-choice sentences to test comprehension of the story read by the children. In this case all of the multiple-choice words should complete the thought of the sentence, but only one should be correct according to the story. All of the words in this sentence should be known by the children. An example of such a sentence is given below:

me.
Mary will bring her doll to Mother.
my house.

Although all of the choices are correct according to sense, only one, *my house,* is correct according to the story. Again the children will underline or circle one of the several choices beginning with *m* in order to complete the meaning of the sentence, but they will also take the content of the story into consideration. In the same way the teacher provides experiences with other single consonants after each has occurred at least three times in the previous lessons.

Use of Word Cards. Some teachers print the words they are teaching for beginning consonants in good manuscript on cards made of tag large enough to fit into a shoe box. The teacher may make alphabetical dividers for each of the beginning consonant sounds. As she adds new words beginning with the same sounds, she finds it very easy to review other words already in the box under a particular consonant. The box contains all the words already developed under an initial consonant which can be used for review along with a new word. In this case the teacher may use the pocket chart for the cards and let the children frame the initial sounds with their fingers.

Initial Consonants Followed by Vowels. Beginning consonants followed by vowels of different sounds such as *make* and *much* are often rather difficult for children to identify. When the teacher can begin the list with at least two words beginning with the same initial consonant followed by the same vowel sound, the children have less difficulty with beginning consonants. An example of two such words are *made* and *may. Have, had,* and *happy* are another group of words with the same initial consonant followed by the same vowel sound.

Use of Key Words. Cordts suggests the use of key words to help children with the particular sounds they are learning.[2] These key words are easier for the children to use if they represent nouns that can be pictured. A good key word for the *m* sound might be *man.* When a child meets a new word beginning with the *m* sound, he may look at a card hung in a convenient place showing a picture of a man with the con-

[2] Anna D. Cordts, *Phonics for the Reading Teacher* (New York: Holt, Rinehart and Winston, Inc., 1965).

sonant, *m*, printed in one lower corner and the word *man* printed in the other. The child can then use the *m* sound and the context to help him figure out the unknown word. A list of consonants with one sound only is given in the Appendix.

Consonants with More Than One Sound

As children progress through the reading in their primers and pre-primers, they will begin to meet consonants that have more than one sound. In many cases the second sound is rather unusual and rarely met on the primer level. A list of these consonants with two or more sounds is given in the Appendix. Some of these initial sounds are discussed below.

Letters with Two Sounds. The letter *d* usually represents the sound of *d* as in *dog*, which is by far the most common sound. An occasional unusual word contains *d* sounded as *j* when followed by *u*, as in the word *verdure*. Since primary children will not meet any words with this unusual pronunciation of *d*, the common sound of *d* may be introduced with no problem along with those of the other consonants. This unusual sound of *d* may not be met before the sixth or seventh grade and may be discussed when this type of word is met. A mention of this sound of *d* in primary teaching would merely confuse the children.

Letters with Two or More Sounds. The letter *f* is another consonant that has two sounds, the common sound as in *fun* and the *v* sound as in *of*. The wise teacher will work on the common initial sound of *f* and will teach the word *of* and any other word containing the *v* sound as sight words without reference to the difference in pronunciation. Primary children rarely notice such an exception to the sound of a letter if it is introduced as a sight word. If a child should notice the difference in sounds, the teacher may explain that *f* has two sounds. The second sound of *f* need be introduced only when older children meet the *v* sound in their spelling.

Some other letters that have two or more sounds are *x*, *j*, *q*, *z*, and *s*. The common sounds of all these letters may be taught in the usual way. When the less usual sound of the letter is met in occasional words, these words may be taught as sight words in the primary grades. When the exceptions are encountered more commonly in the middle and upper grades and when the irregularities are important in the teaching of spelling, the second or third sounds of such letters may then be taught.

Silent Letters and Homonyms. Some letters with two sounds occur often enough in the primary grades to be given consideration. The letter *w* represents the usual sound in such words as *way* and *week*.

This letter is silent in some unaccented syllables as in the word *answer* and is also silent in the one-syllable word *two*. In the primary grades only the common sound of *w* will be met, and its use as a silent letter need not be discussed until a later time. One of the very few words containing a silent *w* met by primary children is the word *two*. This word is best introduced and taught as a sight word with emphasis on its meaning with very little discussion of its spelling until the children need to use it in their own writing.

In reading, the homonyms *to, too,* and *two* are best dealt with as sight words in context. Each of these words is introduced in the first grade at a different time. The form *to* is usually met first. The teacher is likely to have the greatest success by teaching each of these words one at a time as they are met in context.

Mastery of One Word Form at a Time. Experience has shown that children encounter little difficulty if they are taught one form of a word thoroughly and if no mention is made of the other forms until the first one is well mastered. In reading it is often unnecessary to call attention to the similarities of these words. Experience has shown that confusions usually result from introducing several forms of words with similar appearance or several homonyms at one time while trying to help the children understand when each is used. A first-grade teacher found that the words *doll* and *ball* had never caused confusion in the children's minds until a new reader that made use of these two words in the same lesson was adopted. Thereafter, the problem caused continuous trouble.

In another case teachers used a pre-primer in which *Jane* as a child's name and *Jump* used with a capital were introduced in adjacent stories. Although these words had never been confused in the children's minds before, they produced constant confusion when introduced almost simultaneously. The confusion resulted from the identical beginning consonant and the similarity of length of the words.

Hard and Soft Consonant Sounds. The consonant *g* has two sounds, the hard *g* as in *get,* and the soft sound of *j* as in *George, giant,* and *judge*. Most of the words beginning with *g* used in primary readers have the hard sound. For this reason, the soft sound should not be mentioned until the children meet several words involving this sound. They are very likely to meet the name *George* in their own experience stories if a child by this name is a member of their own class. In such a case nothing need be said about the sound in the name *George* and the word may be handled as a sight word without reference to the soft sound which should be taught when the children meet this sound.

The letter *c* as in *cake* when followed by the vowels *a, o,* and *u* takes the hard sound like *k*. Examples of such words are *cat, coat,* and *cut*. The letter *c* takes the soft sound when followed by the vowels *e, i,* or *u* as in *center, circus,* and *cyclone.* The letter *c* also has the sound of *sh,* as in *social.* The *sh* sound of *c* is rarely met in the primary grades and should be taught as a sight word. In the middle and upper grades, this sound should be taught as a third variation of the letter *c.*

Teaching the Hard and Soft Sounds. The soft sound of *c* as in *circus* may be met as early as the second grade. When several words with these sounds are met in reading lessons, the teacher may help the children discover a rule for their pronunciation. For example, she may write on the board in a vertical list three words beginning with *c* followed by the vowels *a, o,* and *u* respectively. These words should have been met in earlier reading lessons and should be well known at sight. The teacher may then make another list of known words beginning with *c* and followed by the vowels *i, e,* and *y* respectively. Such a list is given below:

cake	center
coat	circus
cut	cyclone

After the children have taken turns reading the words aloud, the teacher may ask them to look at all the words to discover in what way they are alike. The children will soon discover that they all begin with the letter *c.* After assuring the children that they are correct, she may ask them why they think she has written the words in two lists. This question involves a more difficult problem and may bring forth a number of wrong conclusions before some child notices that the pronunciation of the *c's* in one list is different from the pronunciation of the *c's* in the second list. The teacher will then ask the children to tell her the names of the vowels following each *c* in the first list. As they dictate them, she may write them on the board beside the list of words beginning with the hard *c.* She may then ask for the vowels following the *c's* in the second list and will probably write these vowels near the second list.

Making a Rule for Soft and Hard Sounds. The teacher is then ready to ask the children to make a rule to help them pronounce new words starting with the letter *c.* If the children are not used to drawing conclusions, they may have some difficulty but will eventually decide that *c* followed by the vowels *a, o,* and *u* has the sound of *k,* or hard *c.* They will also decide that the consonant *c* followed by the vowels *e, i,* and *y* usually has the soft sound like the letter, *s.*

The teacher may then write some unfamiliar but phonetically regular words on the board for the children to read, following the rule they have just developed. She will put these new words in sentences, if possible, in order to tie the rule into a situation demanding a practical application. If the children forget their generalization when they meet other words involving the same problem, the teacher may review the original experience to help them draw the conclusion again.

Need for Review.   In a lesson or two later, the teacher will follow the same steps with the letter *g*. A few children will be sure of the application of the rule the first time they work it out, but many children will find it necessary to go through the steps again and again before they develop real insight into the situation. The teacher will also review this experience when children encounter words beginning with *c* and *g* in their spelling. The teacher always concludes such an experience with a reminder that almost all phonic and spelling rules have exceptions and that the use of the word in context is always the final proof of its pronunciation.

Values of Discovery.   Some teachers may feel that the process of discovery just described requires considerable time. The teacher can give the rule to the children in a very short time. She may then ask the children to memorize this rule and feel that her lesson is completed except for occasional review. She is likely to find, however, that time has really not been saved. Without insight the children frequently have difficulty in recalling which vowels demand the hard *c* and which take the soft *c*. On the other hand, they may rediscover the generalization for themselves once they have followed this inductive procedure. They know the names of the vowels and can think of words beginning with *c* followed by each of the vowels. From there it is a simple matter to pronounce each word silently and to restate the rule for themselves. The process of discovery, then, provides a tool for the children to use in case of need.

The process of making a discovery gives children a feeling of power, and the development of insight in such a situation acts as a strong reinforcement of the learning process. Many children become challenged by the process of discovering such a generalization and will search avidly through their spellers and readers to see if they can discover any exceptions to the rule. If the teacher encourages this search for exceptions and is enthusiastic if one is found, such a learning experience can be very challenging. The process of discovery also adds zest to teaching as well as learning. If, on the other hand, the teacher gives a rule to the children and asks them to memorize it, the procedure is boring, and the children tend to forget the rule soon after they have learned it.

Teaching Words with Consonant Endings

Just as beginning consonants are more easily heard by children when they are combined with vowels, so ending consonants are easier for children to hear when they are combined with vowels. Although a list of phonograms (groups of letters containing at least one vowel and one consonant commonly found as parts of words, such as *an* in *man*) are no longer given as much emphasis as formerly, ending consonants are more easily taught with a preceding vowel than alone.

Value of Phonograms. Lists of phonograms were formerly taught to children to help them analyze words. Some authors state that the phonograms as they were previously taught are not found in words of two or more syllables met by children in the intermediate and upper grades. As a result, their value is distinctly limited. It is true that some of these phonograms are less useful than others. However, some of these letter combinations met at the ends of words are also commonly met at the beginnings of some upper-grade words as well as in a medial position. For example, the letter combination *an* in *angry, animal, ankle,* and *another* is met twenty-six times at the beginnings of different words in one reading series. This phonogram is also met as a medial sound in many other words, such as *candles, candy, cannon, ran, rang, sand,* and *sandwiches.* The combination *en,* such as the sound met in the words *end* and *enjoy,* is met nineteen times at the beginnings of words in this series. It is also found many times as a medial sound in such words as *bench, bend, cents, century, center,* and others. On the other hand, the combination of letters *on* is not met as frequently and is not as dependable at the beginnings and endings of words. It is found in such words as *one* and *only,* neither of which use the short vowel sound. However, it is found frequently in a medial position in many words used in middle and upper grades.

Letter Groups as Prefixes and Suffixes. The combination of the vowel *u* and the consonant *n* is met not only in primary words but in a reasonable number of words in the upper grades when it is used as a prefix. It is also found in the medial position in many words. The letter combination *ing* is another phonogram of value to primary children because of the number of one-syllable words containing this letter group and because it is used with verbs as an inflectional ending, both in the primary and intermediate grades. Sometimes vowel and consonant combinations are of considerable value merely because they help the child recognize many of the one-syllable words which are used commonly in the primary readers and which constitute common words met in all reading.

Teaching Consonant Blends and Digraphs

A cluster of two or more consonants that appear together in a word and that are blended without the loss of identity of each of these sounds is called a consonant blend. For example, the consonants *b* and *l* in *blue* and *c* and *r* in *cry* are consonant blends because each consonant can be heard as these words are pronounced.

A consonant digraph is usually made up of two consonants that represent a single sound or phoneme. This sound is usually different from the sound of each letter when used separately. The combination *s* and *h* in *she* is a consonant digraph. These two letters together have one sound that is different from the sound of either *s* or *h* when used alone. Other examples of digraphs are the letters *c* and *h* at the beginning and end of the word *church,* the letters *g* and *h* in the word *laugh,* and *t* and *h* in the word *them.* Sometimes a digraph is combined with a single consonant to blend with it. The word *shrimp* blends the digraph *sh* with the consonant *r.*

Consonant Blends. Even in the pre-primers children are likely to meet words beginning with two consonants which form blends. Some of the words for colors start with consonant blends such as the words *green, brown, blue,* and *black.* When words containing blends are first met, these are taught as sight words. For instance, in one set of pre-primers the only blend is one containing the consonants *gr* in the word *green.* The teacher will not become concerned with work on the *gr* blend until the children have met several words containing this letter combination. Even in the primer in this set of readers, no other words containing the *gr* blend are introduced. The sight word *green,* however, is used frequently enough through the primer for review to maintain it as a sight word.

Place of Blends in the Program. Several words beginning with the *gr* sound are found in the first reader. In this series those words include *grandfather, grass, ground,* and *grow.* After at least three of these words have been met, including two that use the short vowel *a* following the blend, the teacher may put these words on the board and teach them in the same way that she taught single initial consonants described earlier in this chapter. When the children meet the word *grow* later in the first reader, the teacher will review the other four words and add the word *grow* to the list, again stressing the common elements. She will review these words from time to time so that the children will not forget them.

In the same way, each of the consonant blends should be introduced after the children have met a number of sight words containing them and should be taught in connection with words that contain them. In the primary grades the consonant blends are usually found at the beginnings or at the endings of the words. Blends at the beginnings of words are usually introduced first because they are easier to hear. Because so few blends occur in the pre-primers and primer, most of the teaching of these letter sounds will take place in the first and higher readers. By this time the children will have mastered most of the initial consonants and will find little difficulty in gradually adding the consonant blends. A list of the most common two-letter consonant blends and blends including three or more letters, some of which include digraphs, are given in the Appendix.

Use of Phonics Terms. The terms "consonant," "consonant blend," and "consonant digraph" need not be used with young children. Digraphs in words such as *she, the, then, them, what, when,* and *children* will be met in sight words, just as single consonants and blends are first met in sight words. The terminology has very little relation to the ability to recognize the sounds when met in words. These terms represent concepts or generalizations. A concept begins with a wide variety of experiences for its understanding. The children will not meet enough of the digraphs before the late second or third grade for the teacher to develop an abstract concept of the term. The terms "consonant blend" and "consonant digraph" are valuable to the teacher primarily in helping her realize that the consonants in some words are pronounced as they are blended, and in other words the consonants are combined to result in an entirely new sound.

Teaching Blends. To analyze a beginning blend, the teacher may help the child build from a known word as in the known word *late* by writing the letter *p* in front of it to make the word *plate*. The process of helping with ending blends is similar. For example, if the child has met the new word *mend,* the teacher may print the known word *men* on the board. After the child pronounces it, she may add the letter *d* to the end of it, changing the consonant *n* to the *nd* blend. The child should then be able to recognize the word *mend.*

Often groups of letters rather than words are involved. In developing the word *cream* the teacher may start with the phonogram *eam.* She may then place *r* in front of the phonogram to make *ream,* and then precede it again with the letter *c* to make the word *cream.* On the other hand, she may start with a *cr* blend in the word *cry* and substitute the *eam* phonogram for the vowel *y.*

This process is actually a synthesis in some cases, but lacks the disadvantage of requiring the child to pronounce the letter *p* alone in the word *plate.* If the child tends to do so, the teacher should go back to the use of other familiar words beginning with blends of the letters, *pl,* such as *play, place,* and *plant.* She should then add the new word to this list. The child should be able to recognize the new word from this help.

Consonant Digraphs. Consonant digraphs have been defined as a combination of two consonants that represent a single sound or phoneme, usually different from the sound heard in either of the consonants heard singly. Although teachers, linguists, and phoneticians disagree on the classification of digraphs, the most commonly accepted digraphs are given in the Appendix.

The teacher introduces each digraph after the children have met three or four words beginning with this particular digraph. It is taught in the same way as were the single consonants. One of the most important principles to remember in teaching the letter sounds in whole words is that children need to review words starting with the same sounds learned previously.

Teaching Digraphs. Digraphs must be taught by substitution of these letters in whole words. The teacher never adds consonants to build a digraph since the sound is completely different from that of each consonant sounded separately. For example, the teacher would never try to help the child recognize *bath* by starting with *bat* and adding *h*. Instead, the teacher goes back to three known words beginning or ending with the digraph she wishes to teach. If *bath* were the new word and voiceless *th* the digraph to be taught, she would find three known words with this digraph such as *path*, *with*, and *both* and follow the usual procedure of guiding the children to find similar elements among the words.

Teachers of intermediate and upper grades also need to understand the terms, digraph and blend, since they are important in the syllabification of words. Although many words are divided between consonants, they are never divided between the two or three letters of a consonant blend or the letters of a digraph. Syllabification is discussed later.

Frequency of Digraphs and Blends. In analyzing the same set of readers mentioned previously, three digraphs were found in the primer, each of which was repeated a number of times. In addition, one initial blend was found in the second pre-primer, two in the third pre-primer, and four in the primer.

Although more of the digraphs were found on the ends of words, the child does not meet enough words containing a specific digraph for the teacher to teach the sounds of these combinations before the first or second readers. The review of words previously learned in connection with each new word with the same beginning or ending digraph or blend not only helps to reinforce the letter sounds for the child, but it also serves to review words in the child's sight vocabulary. Older children use the same techniques for analyzing sounds in syllables when needed as younger children use for words.

Voiced and Voiceless Consonants

Some consonants are classified as voiced consonants, and others are classified as voiceless. The voiced consonants are produced with the vocal folds open. As the sound is made, it vibrates in the vocal cords and is modified by the lips, tongue, or other parts of the mouth. For example, the consonant *m* is sounded by a tone from the vocal cords modified by the lips in an almost closed position. As a result, a voiced tone or vibration can be felt in the throat. On the other hand, the consonant *s* is made without vibration in the vocal cords. It is produced with the breath only, which is modified primarily by the tongue. The sound of *s* is actually a whispered sound.

Some consonants are identical in sound with the exception of vibrations of the vocal cords for the production of one, and lack of vibration for the second one. For example, the consonant *d* is voiced and *t* is voiceless, but both are duplicates of the same mouth and tongue position. To make the *d* sound when enunciating a word beginning with that letter, the tongue is placed against the roof of the mouth accompanied by the vibration of the vocal cords. To make the sound of *t*, the tongue and lips are in the same position as for the *d*, but the vocal cords do not vibrate. This sound is really whispered. These sounds are slightly difficult for the adult to differentiate, but they are quite hard for the child. Therefore, the teacher tries to avoid word lists including both of these consonants, especially early in the phonics program. *B* and *p* are another pair of such consonants, the *b* is voiced and the *p* is whispered; otherwise the speech position is the same. *G* and *c* involve the same problem. A list of the voiced and voiceless consonants are given in the Appendix.

Voiced and Voiceless Digraphs

Some of the digraphs fit into the voiced category, and some into the voiceless category. The beginning teacher often has the greatest difficulty with the voiced and voiceless sounds of the digraph *th*. For example, the words *this, the, then,* and *than* all contain voiced *th* digraphs. On the other hand, the words *thin, thick, with,* and *bath* all contain voiceless *th's*. The teacher can tell the difference most easily by putting her hand against her throat as she pronounces each of these words. When pronouncing voiceless *th* words, she will feel no vibrations in her larynx, except for the ending sounds. When pronouncing the voiced *th* words, she will feel a definite vibration in her throat as she pronounces the *th* part of these words. She should know the difference between the types of *th's* in order to be sure to compare voiceless *th* words with each

Eighth-grade students collect clippings for a current-interest bulletin board. (Courtesy California Department of Education.)

other, and voiced *th* words with words containing similar sounds. Otherwise, the child may become confused if he listens to voiced and voiceless digraphs at the same time. The child does not need to learn the differences between these sounds until he is in the intermediate grades.

Consonant Groups Containing Silent Letters

The matter of silent letters in consonant groups is another problem with which the teacher must be concerned. Most of these words are met in the second grade or above. In this way the child gradually learns which letters are silent and becomes able to apply this knowledge in his reading. One of the common silent consonants is *k* when combined with *n* in such words as *knight* and *know*. In one reading series ten of such words are the only ones used in the elementary series of readers. None is found in the primer, one is found in the first reader, two in the second reader, three in the third reader, one in the fourth reader, none in the fifth, and three in the sixth. Obviously, all of such words met before the third grade may be taught as sight words.

After meeting several such words, the children may then begin to learn that the *k* is silent when it appears before *n*, but they will have little need for the generalization until they meet it in their spelling words in the intermediate grades. A list of consonants preceded or followed by a silent consonant is given in the Appendix. Each combination should be discussed when it is met in a reading situation. As the children become familiar with more of these silent letters, they will begin to remember the groupings, such as *k* before *n* and *p* before *s*, to help with words they will meet later.

Long and Short Vowel Sounds

Most reading manuals introduce short vowels before long ones because the former are the most common. Less variety is also found in their use. Some new trends are found in modern dictionaries such as the use of the schwa to take the place of å as in the word *about*, the *e* with the tilde as in *maker*, the italic short *i* as in *charity*, the italic short *o* in *connect*, and the italic short *u* in *circus*. The long vowels present more problems than the short ones due to the large number of exceptions in their pronunciation. Diphthongs also have an important place among the vowels.

Short Vowels. Short vowels are usually found in the middle of one-syllable words or in unaccented syllables. As with the consonants, the teacher usually watches until she finds four one-syllable words containing the same short vowel and ending with the same consonant since children are able to hear the vowel with a consonant more easily than the vowel alone. If the children know the words *red, bed,* and *fed,* the teacher may use these words to help the child analyze the sound of the new word *led*. She puts the first three words on the board, telling the children that these are familiar to them. After the children read them and find the common element in them, the teacher adds the new word *led* and asks the children to tell how this word is like the others. When they have found the common element, *ed*, she asks them to read the new word. Again the teacher reviews this list and adds later words to it as the children meet them in their readers.

In another step, short vowels should be introduced in words in which the final consonant is substituted, such as *big*, *bill*, and *bit*. As an even later step, both the beginning and ending consonants should be changed for contrast and to help the child hear the sound of the short vowel. Examples of such words are *did*, *tip*, and *miss*. To help in hearing short vowels in another way, the word *did* may be contrasted with *dad*, *tip* may be compared with *top*, and *miss* may be compared with *moss*.

Exceptions to the Short Vowel Rule. When *o* is followed by the blend *ld* the *o* is usually long. The teacher may teach the first several words in this combination as sight words. She then looks for several sight words following this rule, such as *cold*, *sold*, and *told*. When the children meet a fourth word, such as *fold*, the teacher follows the same procedures she used in teaching the short vowel sounds. She can, however, help the children make a rule from the use of *o* followed by *ld*. She may put three words on the board, such as *pot*, *not*, and *lot*. She may then ask the children to compare the two lists to discover why the *o* sounds are different in the list headed by the word *cold*. When the children discover the letters *ld* in one list, they may conclude that *o* "says its name" or is long when followed by the letters *ld*.

The children may make similar rules for the vowel *a* when followed by *l* as in *talk*, *ll* as in *call*, *w* as in *raw*, and *u* as in *caught*. They will discover that *a* takes the sound of *aw* in such cases. They will also discover that *i* takes the long sound when followed by *nd* as in *rind*, *gh* in *tight*, and *ld* in *wild*. In addition, they will discover that the letter *r* changes the sound of vowels, such as the sound of *a* as in *arm*, *e* as in *her*, *i* as in *bird*, *o* as in *nor*, and *u* as in *fur*.

Long Vowels. A description of the development of the rule for silent *e* at the ends of words to make the preceding vowel long was given early in the chapter under the heading, "Development and Application of Rules." In connection with this rule, the teacher must remind the children that exceptions often occur. The teacher herself will find that the children have great difficulty with the words *here*, *there*, and *were*, because the first one is the only word that follows the rule in these three problem words.

A very controversial rule concerns the one about two vowels together. The rule states that when two vowels occur together in a one-syllable word, the first vowel is usually long and the second is usually silent as in *wait*. One faction argues that this rule applies to only about half the cases. The opposition faction maintains that the rule is helpful when it does apply. The rule seems to be most consistent with words containing the letters *ea* as in *meat*, *ee* as in *feet*, and *oa* as in *boat*. The rule does not apply in the case of diphthongs and many exceptions are found in combinations of such letters as *ou*, *ie* and *ei*.

The wise teacher uses the rule for two vowels with words to which it does apply and teaches other words as sight words. However, the vowels *ea* have three alternative pronunciations which may be of some value. Usually the *e* takes the long sound and the *a* is silent, as in *meat*. Sometimes the *e* is silent and the *a* is long, as in *great*. At other times the *e* is short and the *a* is silent, as in *head*. The children may gradually learn these alternatives and use them when they need this combination of letters.

A few other generalizations are helpful. When the only vowel of a word of one syllable comes at the end, it usually has the long sound as in *fly*, *no*, and *we*. The children should derive this rule themselves from examples placed on the board by the teacher after the children have had considerable experience with such words. The vowel *y* takes the short sound when it comes at the end of a word of two or more syllables such as *noisy*. Some authors maintain that *y* takes the sound of short *i* in this case, and others state that it takes the sound of long *e*. Children are not concerned with such problems as long as they recognize the sounds of words they meet in their reading. The rules for vowels are given in greater detail in the Appendix.

Vowel Diphthongs and Special Vowel Groups. Although authors disagree in their classification of vowel combinations, the common pronunciation of the following vowel combinations are helpful for children to learn over a period of time. These diphthongs include *ew* as in *few*, *oi* as in *oil*, *ou* as in *mouse*, *ow* as in *cow* and *show*, *oy* as in *boy*, and *ue* as in *blue*. The letter combination *ou* is very difficult for children because of its great variety of pronunciation. When words are found containing these great variations, they should be taught as sight words.

The sounds of *oo* do not seem to fit into any of the other groups. This combination of vowels has two pronunciations, one classified as the long sound of *oo* as in *cool* and *room*, and the other as the short sound of *oo* as in *look* and *good*. Children have difficulty in hearing the difference between these short and long sounds. However, the children in the primary grades do not need to be concerned with the difference between these sounds. The teacher, however, should compare only long sounds with each other and short sounds with themselves when teaching words containing these sounds.

Inflectional Endings

Inflectional endings are added to words to show their change of function in a sentence. They may show change in the tenses of the verb, change of words from singulars to plurals, change in the gender of the person speaking, change showing possessive form, and other similar changes. For this purpose, suffixes are usually added. Sometimes, however, the entire form of a word is changed, as in pronouns such as *him* and *her*, and in irregular verbs such as *go, went,* and *gone.* Regular verb forms are usually changed by adding the suffixes *s, es, ing, ed, t,* and *en.* Examples of these various types of changes are given in the Appendix. The irregular verb which takes the *d* or *t* sound for the past tense instead of the obvious *ed* sound is most difficult for the children to hear. Verbs ending in *t* and *d* have a distinct *ed* sound on the end, such as *want, wanted,* and *fit, fitted.* When teaching the verbs ending in the less obvious past form, such as *jumped,* the teacher's best procedure is to help with the thought of the sentence. The knowledge of and use of inflectional endings covers a long extent of time in reading and even a greater extent of time in spelling.

Compound Words, Contractions, and Derivatives

The first compound word the child usually meets is playhouse. If he knows both the words *play* and *house* at sight, he will have no difficulty with this compound word. The teacher asks him to find a word he knows within the larger one. After he has found one familiar word, it is easy for him to find the second and to put the two together to form the compound word. In the case of contractions, the process is reversed. The teacher may write two sight words such as *can* and *not* separately on the board. When the child recognizes these, she will write the words together and again ask him to read them. She may then cross out the superfluous *n* and *o,* substituting an apostrophe and ask the child to read the word as it has been changed. Usually some child in the reading group can do so, and the other children gradually gain insight in the process, especially as it is repeated in other words such as *isn't* and *haven't.*

The use of prefixes and suffixes, except for inflectional endings, usually begins gradually in the high first or low second, but the burden of the work takes place primarily in the middle and upper grades. Some children become very interested in root words and the meanings of various suffixes and prefixes. Some children may also develop an interest in looking up the derivations of root words and their derivatives. The child's vocabulary expands rapidly when he begins to learn the meaning of such a root as *aqua* and looks up some of the many derivations of this word. In so doing, he may come across other roots, such as *duct* in *aqueduct,* and find that the latter root, *duct,* has many derivatives of its own. The study of root words and derivations may also help the child in his spelling.

Syllabification

Some children have difficulty in recognizing syllables in words. By the time they are ready for syllabification, they will be quite familiar with vowels and can follow the rule that the number of vowel sounds heard in a word serves as an indication of the number of syllables. The discovery of two vowels together should not cause the child to have difficulty because these usually form digraphs or diphthongs and therefore have one sound each. Rules for syllabification are given in the Appendix.

As in other aspects of phonics, the child will remember these rules much better if he draws them as conclusions from a number of specific examples. He will, of course, need to go back to original examples to review the conclusions he has drawn when he needs to apply these conclusions or rules to new words. This skill, too, takes much time to develop. The habit of using the dictionary to check the application of the rules is important since many exceptions are found.

Application of Phonics in Reading

Word analysis is needed only when an unfamiliar word is met. Some elements of sounds in words are helpful, and some should be avoided. Rules, also, can be helpful if only a few of the most reliable ones are used. The manuals provided by publishers are helpful in giving suggestions for teaching phonics and in guiding the teacher in the sequence of introducing the sounds of letters.

Need for Analysis of Words. The teacher should realize that words originally recognized by phonics and other word analysis techniques become sight words after they have been analyzed. If the reader had to break down every word he met even though he had analyzed it originally by phonics techniques, he would find reading a very difficult process. The adult rarely uses phonics to analyze a word unless this word is new in his reading vocabulary. Even then, the adult usually must use the dictionary in addition to phonics to discover the meaning and pronunciation of the unknown word. The only time a child is likely to need to analyze a word already met is in case he has forgotten it and needs to analyze it again to help him recall it. Once he has mastered the word, it becomes a sight word and is recognized at a glance.

Important Phonic Elements. Little words in big words sometimes constitute a problem for teachers as well as chlidren. One parent stated that every child in the second grade should be able to recognize the words *we, at,* and *her* in the word, *weather.* This parent fell into the trap encountered by some children. The best way to avoid this problem for children is to suggest that they look at the largest part of the word they can recognize. If they do so, they will not try to pronounce the letters *at* in *plate,* but will go on to identify the sound of *ate,* which carries the correct sound for analysis in this case.

Need for Rules. The generalizations given in the appendix are there to help the student who has forgotten the phonics he learned in the elementary school. Only the most common and reliable rules should be taught to children. Too many rules become confusing and tend to take the pleasure out of reading. The use of too many rules also tends to make the child afraid of failure, and he may therefore tend to build a block against the entire reading process.

Use of Manuals. The manuals that are provided by publishers of reading textbooks give excellent suggestions for teaching phonics. They also provide the teacher with a guide to the sequence of letter sounds as they are introduced in the readers. Not all authors follow the same pattern of sequence, although they follow the guidelines for a natural progression of skills.

Vowels were introduced after all the consonant variations in this chapter and in the list of skills to be developed. In actual practice, the teacher may introduce rhyming words after the children have made a good start in the recognition of consonants. The sounds in the rhyming words are easy for the children to hear. Again, the sequence used in the manuals is the best one for the teacher to follow.

Practice on Phonic Elements. Practice on the various elements of phonics can be very boring when these elements are found in words that are unrelated in thought. Therefore, there is no meaning to hold the child's interest.

SUMMARY

Some changes have taken place in the methods of teaching phonics over the years, though some procedures are being revived by a number of publishers. A logical sequence has been found most successful in teaching phonics. Consonants are introduced first because of their regularity, but vowels are gradually introduced along with the later elements of the consonant program. Review is important in all phases of the program. Some generalizations are helpful. The child is encouraged to discover them through their application rather than to be given them by the teacher and required to memorize them. The entire program of word analysis is spread over all the elementary grades because the elements are introduced when the child has had an adequate background for their use. He also remembers and applies them better when he needs them and when they are introduced gradually.

16

Reading for Thought
in Primary Grades

Reading skills vary from the most simple to the most complex. These skills are roughly categorized in five levels as follows:

1. The ability to recognize words, both from sight and from the use of clues such as phonics and context, is the first and easiest step. Mastery of these skills is not achieved at any one grade level. It is rather a continuous process of adding sight vocabulary and becoming increasingly adept at using various clues.

2. On the next level the comprehension of exact meanings of simple facts and the securing of information from the printed page is emphasized.

3. On the third level the child learns to relate his past experiences to the material he reads.

4. On a still higher level, the child acquires ability to use facts and information for purposes that are important to him. In order to do this, he must learn simple ways of locating information and organizing it so that it is most useful to him in solving his problems.

5. On the most advanced level, the child acquires ability to interpret reading material. He learns to read beyond the material by making inferences and drawing conclusions. He may observe relationships among ideas and look for cause and effect in situations described in the reading material. All of these steps are aspects of comprehension. Procedures for developing the first two levels have been given in Chapters 7 through 10.

The activities suitable for developing these abilities in the primary grades are very simple and might even be thought of as procedures for building readiness for these steps in the intermediate grades. The habit of thinking about and analyzing reading material should be taught from the very beginning so that children acquire permanent habits of active and intelligent reading. Ability to think about, that is to understand, organize, evaluate, and apply, information from reading matter is increasingly important to people in today's age since they are faced with many new and crucial problems.

SKILLS IN RECALLING AND LOCATING INFORMATION

Children enjoy retelling stories the teacher has told or read to them. Some stories are favorites, which the children ask to hear repeatedly. These lend themselves best to retelling by the children. Experience in retelling stories after listening to them is an important way to provide readiness for later ability to recall stories that have been read silently.

On the primer and first reader levels primary children are able with practice to recall most of the ideas in a selection. As they advance through the primary grades, they are also able to learn to use the table of contents, some alphabetical arrangements, and picture dictionaries. If children are not put under pressure but are merely encouraged and given purposes that are important to them for using these aids, many will be able to achieve considerable skill by the end of the third grade.

Ability To Recall Information

When children learn to read silently a section of a story, that is, from three to five pages, and recall the facts of the story, they are learning the first important skill prerequisite to later organization of facts and ideas. The mere repetition of facts or events in a story or selection in answer to questions can be stimulating at times but very dull when repeated with each selection. The teacher, however, can help to arouse interest if she makes use of children's experiences that relate to the reading material.

Using Personal Experiences. An example of the use of children's experiences is shown in the following situation. The story in a reader may be about a dog that lost a ball. His master cannot play ball either with the dog or his own friends until it is found. The teacher may help the children discover the problem either through pictures or through reading the first paragraphs of the story. She may encourage them to recall similar situations in their own experiences and to tell where they found their lost balls. The children may then continue to read the story to discover where the hero found his ball. When they discover how the ball was found, they will also be likely to recall other events in the story.

Anticipating Endings.   The procedure just described is one way to help childen anticipate the ending of a story. In another method children may merely anticipate endings instead of telling of their own experiences. One reading group in a second grade tried to anticipate the ending of a story about a boy who liked to throw a stick for his dog to retrieve. One day the stick landed in the crotch of a tree. The children were able to think of eleven different methods the boy might have used to get the stick down from the tree. They read the story eagerly to discover how the hero got his stick down, and they also recalled details relating to the action of the story.

Choosing Parts.   Another way of helping children recall information while maintaining interest is to suggest that they choose to be characters in the story they are reading. In the story of the "Gingerbread Boy," each child may tell what he did in the story. One child may be the Gingerbread Boy, and others may be the Little Old Man, the Little Old Woman, the cow, the dog, the pig, and the fox. They may choose their characters before reading the story in order to help them remember their respective parts. If the children have acquired considerable ability in recalling information, the teacher may prefer that they read the story first and then choose parts. General discussion after the story has been read is another informal way to help children develop ability to recall events in a story or ideas in a selection.

Skills in Following Directions

The teacher uses all the natural and functional reasons for helping children follow directions, not only on the readiness level, but in later stages as well. Dramatizing the action of a story provides experience in following directions indirectly since the story itself provides the directions through its context. Children may also learn to follow directions printed on sentence strips as a way of giving practice on vocabulary, comprehension, and interpretation expressed through action or the discussion of ideas gained from reading material.

Dramatizing Action.   On the pre-primer level, children may dramatize the action of the characters either personally or with flannel board figures. In dramatizing such a sentence as, "Run, Tippy, Run," the teacher may let the children take turns being Tippy. One child may choose a reading strip with the sentence, "Run, Tippy, Run," printed on it. Without telling what it says, he may call on another child to show him what the sentence says by dramatizing the part of Tippy. If the latter child carries out the action and reads the strip correctly afterward, he may become the new leader to choose a strip for another child to dramatize. Such a procedure helps vitalize the rather repetitious sentences used in the pre-primer and serves as a good check on immediate recall in silent reading.

Finding Toys. Later on in the primer and more advanced books, the teacher may use review words in directions. The teacher may permit one child to hide some toys that represent nouns used in a story. Such toys may include an airplane, a man, a woman, a boy, a girl, a car, a stop sign, and so forth. If it is difficult for the teacher to secure such toys, the children may make them of papier mâché or mount magazine pictures on cards. For review on the word "bring," the teacher may print on a reading strip, "Bring the toy airplane to me," and so on for the other objects. Again, one child chooses a strip and calls on another child to follow the directions. After he has found the object and brought it to the first child, he may read the strip orally. If the second child followed the directions correctly, he may have a turn to become the new chooser. In this activity, too, the child's silent reading and immediate recall are checked.

Skills in Using the Table of Contents

Children who have sufficient background to read in a primer without frustration due to lack of vocabulary or other problems can usually learn to use the table of contents. The titles of the stories are written in words that have been or that will be introduced in connection with the lesson. In the beginning the teacher prints the name of the story on the board and helps the children find the page on which the table of contents is located. Then she gives the children clues about where the title is located on the page. After the children have read the name of the story from the board, the teacher may say, for example, "The name of our story is near the top of the page. Frame it with your fingers when you find it." Some of the slower children may need a few more clues, such as, "Look a little higher, Paul," and "You're very close to it, Jessie."

When all have found it, the teacher will ask a child to read the title and the number of the page opposite it. The children may then turn to the proper page for their story. Children soon become very proficient in locating the titles and pages of their stories, and fewer and fewer will need clues to position in the table of contents. Most second- and third-grade children are able to locate specific topics in science and other books by using the table of contents, although some may need the teacher's guidance for a longer period than others.

Ability To Use Alphabetical Arrangements

One of the effective ways to help first-grade children become familiar with the alphabet is to guide them to make picture dictionaries for themselves. When the children use dictionaries they have made, they can more clearly understand the use of the alphabet. The use of spelling word boxes also helps familiarize children with the alphabet.

Making Dictionaries. Each child may be provided with a booklet made of 12″ × 18″ drawing paper which has been folded to make 9″ × 12″ sheets stitched down the middle, usually with yarn because the paper is less likely to tear out than when fastened with thread or paper fasteners. The child will need seven sheets to make twenty-eight pages, as well as a piece of colored paper for the cover. Because first-grade children often become confused when given more than one direction at a time, they may work on one letter at a time. They may cut out the letter A which has been duplicated on a small square of paper. They may then paste the square with the letter A on the first page of their booklets along with a duplicated picture of some object beginning with A. On the next day the children may work on a page for B, and so on day by day until the dictionaries are completed. Some of the brighter children may work ahead if they are sure they know the letter sequence. Children may wish to cut out pictures from magazines to paste in their alphabet books or to draw pictures for illustrations. They should check with the teacher, however, to be sure that the names of their pictures start with the proper letter. At this time double and triple blends may be allowed with single letters.

Using Word Boxes. Another functional use of the alphabet is to make a spelling word box from a shoe or similar box, using cards and alphabetical dividers to fit. The words may be printed on 4″ × 6″ filing cards and placed behind the dividers according to the appropriate beginning letter. As the children use the word box, they gradually learn the place of various letters and become more skillful in using the alphabet. Alphabet cards for manuscript writing that teachers usually pin or staple around the room are more functional if they, too, are placed in a box so that children are able to refer to them when needed. Objects that are left too long on the wall usually fade from the consciousness of the observers. After a few weeks children cease to see them. If the cards are in a box, a child may get the one he needs and use it directly next to the work he is doing so that its use is more functional. Second- and third-grade children may use alphabet boxes or may keep booklets to which they add needed spelling words. In this way they gain greater power in using the alphabet.

Using Picture Dictionaries. Picture dictionaries are provided in the second and third grades of some schools. If children have had considerable experience with the word boxes and alphabet books, only a little help will be needed in showing them how to use their picture dictionaries. Some children like to browse through these books. In this activity they may gain greater understanding of the use of the alphabet, and they may also learn some reading vocabulary. In the third grade many children are ready to start alphabetizing by means of the second letter of words. Some children may need special help, which may be given in connection with the reorganization of their spelling booklets, rather than in artificial exercises. The words under each letter will be rearranged by second letters. For example "bear" will be placed before "bicycle." Children learn better in functional situations.

Ability To Scan

Ability to scan is a very easy skill to establish if the teacher uses parallel stories and reading strips described in Chapter 7 as a technique for introducing the pre-primer vocabulary. (A word card is described in Chapter 3, page 65, and a diagram of sentence strips placed in a pocket chart is shown on page 64.) In the identification step the child merely scans to find the sentence strip the teacher calls for, but the child may need to run his eyes down several strips before he comes to the right one. Later when he is ready to do actual reading, the teacher calls for the reading of the strips in mixed order in answer to a question such as, "Find and read the line that tells what Tippy did." In this way the child scans from the very beginning of his reading. Later in the primer and other books much of the oral reading is carried on by asking the child to find and read a part that tells about a certain person or situation.

Ability To Use Maps, Charts, and Graphs

In the first grade maps may be used to record as well as to locate information. A child may wish to go to the nurse's room. In order to expedite matters at the moment, the teacher may send the child with another who knows the location of the room.

Making Maps. At a later time that day or the next, the teacher may help the children learn an easy way to find their way around school. Several sheets of wrapping paper may be pasted together to make a map large enough for the children to walk on it. The children may decide to locate their own room in relation to the school, perhaps at the end of a corridor. The room may be drawn in black crayon, and the corridor may be extended to the center of the school where the principal's office may be located. If the children have had an orientation trip around the school, they will know what the principal's office is like. At the next recess, the children may count the number of rooms between their classroom and the principal's office, and these rooms may be drawn on the map. At the same time the nurse's office may be located and drawn on the map. Little by little the map may be expanded as the children take trips around the school until the entire map is finished. The next time a child is not sure of the location of a particular place, he may be guided to walk there on the map first so that he knows which way to turn when leaving the classroom and where to go from there. In this way, maps serve both to record information and to provide it, when needed. The second- and third-grade children may make similar maps of the parts of the community they are studying in social studies. They may locate their homes, the near-by shopping area, and buildings where public servants are housed, such as the postoffice, firehouse, and so on.

Using Charts. Charts may be used in functional reading. Even in the later months of the kindergarten, simple and brief charts may be used when the children dictate ideas to the teacher. Such a chart may be prepared before taking a trip. A few simple statements may be recorded, such as, "We stay together, We wait for the teacher," and "We listen when people talk." Although some children may not be able to read the chart, the teacher may help them recall the statements from memory just before taking a trip. Longer and more functional charts may be used with older children to record such matters as, "Materials we need," "Books that will help us," and "Things we need to do." Since the children can read these charts, they are used for frequent reference to help the work progress. Other charts include the weather chart, the helpers chart, the show and tell chart, and a chart for committees for social studies.

Using Graphs. Bar graphs may also be used in the primary grades. A type of graph may be used in the first grade to show the number of days children must wait from Thanksgiving until Christmas. Squares of colored paper may be fitted and pinned on a background of plain paper to represent days before Christmas. Sometimes children like to draw a sun on each square. As each day passes, the children may take the square representing a particular day off the chart. Since young children become very excited about the advent of Christmas, such a graph gives them a little help in understanding the passage of time. In the third grade a bar graph to represent numbers of hours may be made to compare the time necessary to travel to a specific destination by airplane in contrast to the use of a bus or train. A circle graph may be used to help children in the third grade understand the parts of a dollar. Various other uses may be found.

SKILLS IN ORGANIZING

Primary children may make simple beginnings in organizational skills. One of the easiest is the skill of following the sequence of the story, which can be begun in the kindergarten. Classification can also be used in connection with pictures. Simple steps in selecting main ideas and brief summaries are also within the ability level of some primary children.

Skills in Following Sequence

One of the most appropriate organizational skills for children in the primary grades is the ability to carry a sequence of events in mind. Even on the reading readiness level children are able to organize pictures in a logical sequence. In any story that carries a number of events, children may be helped to recall these events in order. The ability to tell a story in proper sequence is also a skill to be developed on the reading readiness level.

When children are able to follow the sequence of a story as they retell it orally, they are ready for help in following the sequence of simple stories they read in the pre-primers and primers. To help children who have just read a section of a story in the primer recall the events, the teacher may ask the children to tell what happened at first. She then follows the story through asking for the next event, and so on, until the children can tell her the last event.

The children need consistent help in following sequences of stories in their early readers whenever the story lends itself to this type of organization. Some teachers put sentences giving the main events of the story in mixed order on the chalkboard. The children discuss the story and number the sentences to show the correct sequence.

Skills in Classification

Ability to make selections according to a particular classification is an important skill throughout all levels of reading. After children have learned to organize pictures according to various classifications, they are ready to apply this skill to ideas gained from reading. Some of the pre-primer stories are too simple to be used for developing this skill on a reading level. Some workbooks, however, have pages of pictures of such articles as tools mother uses compared with tools father uses.

Children in this eighth grade made a large outline map for the location of pertinent geographic areas in their study of trade. (Courtesy of California State Department of Education.)

When the stories in the readers become longer and involve more ideas, children may learn to classify them from various standpoints.

In a story, Raymond may go to the store to choose a birthday present for his sister. The children may tell the various toys Raymond considered before he actually bought the present. In another story, Judy may have helped her mother by running several errands after school. The children may recall the errands Judy ran. In a science story, children may read about a number of small animals including birds. The children may classify those that lay eggs such as birds and reptiles in a separate list from those whose young are born alive such as most animals. (The term "mammals" can be used for very mature children.)

Early Steps in Outlining

Even immature children can begin a very simple and brief type of outlining. For example, as they dictate to the teacher several things they want to see when they go to Paul's home, they may list the radishes Paul planted, his Bantam hen and chickens, and his pet white rabbit. The teacher may jot down the names of these objects on a large piece of paper. She may also use this list, when the children return, to help them recall what they liked about each thing they saw. When first-grade children dictate a letter of invitation to their teacher, they may be helped to discuss what information their visitor will need. As they discuss these points, the teacher may print on the board "who, where, when, why, and what" as words to guide the dictation of the letter. In a later grade they may discuss the parts of a letter and may dictate the names of these parts, which the teacher puts on the board in a list.

In the second and third grades, opportunities may arise for making lists of topics found in reading selections. A story may tell about foods eaten by various animals. After reading the story, the children may dictate the names of the animals and their foods for a list as it is printed on the board. This list may be used at a later time to help the children review the ideas they acquired from their reading. Ways in which animals help people may serve as another topic for a similar listing. In later grades, the children will learn how to organize these topics and to put them in outline form.

Ability To Summarize

Children may be able to make simple summaries at about the level of their ability to outline. The kindergarten children who visited Paul may summarize what they saw in a simple way. For example, the radishes were big enough to eat. The chickens and the rabbit both ate lettuce and grass; however, the chickens had milk to drink but the rabbit didn't. In the first grade the children may summarize the events in a story, for example, by telling several things the hero did after school. As the children read on a more mature level, they may summarize various ways in which seeds are scattered after reading a selection in a science book. These summaries may be made into a list on the board or may merely be discussed.

SKILLS IN INTERPRETING

Some of the interpretive skills are simple enough to be taught to young children. Many children can become skillful in interpreting pictures and relating the events in stories to their own experiences. They may also make simple comparisons and observe relationships, especially among concrete objects. In addition, they may be able to make a few simple generalizations if these are closely related to their personal experiences. Primary children may be able to acquire considerable skill in making interpretations of various sorts from their reading material.

Interpretation of Pictures

Interpretation of pictures is an ability which can be fostered as long as the pictures are large, clear in color, and simple. This activity is useful on the reading readiness level and has values for older children as well. Some aspects of the child's maturity can be evaluated by his ability to interpret pictures (see Chapter 5). The skillful teacher makes use of ability to interpret pictures in many of her introductions to new stories in readers. From the pictures, the children may derive the problem to be met by the children in the story.

Ability To Relate Content to Experience

Most kindergarten teachers help relate the stories she tells to the children's experiences as a standard way of helping them identify themselves with the characters in the story. The teachers of older children also follow this same practice in their story telling period. Most teachers introduce stories in readers with the same type of activity in order to help children identify themselves with the characters. Teachers even help children relate their personal experiences to stories about children in other times and other places in order to bring the stories closer to the lives of the readers. This activity is very important in all reading and story-telling activities.

Ability To Make Comparisons

Even pre-school children are able to make comparisons about objects they see. For example, "Jimmy's apple is bigger than mine," or "I'm too small to reach the top shelf, but my brother, Ted, can. He is bigger than I am."

Comparing Ideas on a Readiness Level. On the reading readiness level, children may sort pictures of objects that vary in size. The big cake may be placed with a small cake, the big ball with a small one, and so on. Moving objects may be discussed by comparing those that go fast with those that go slowly. In science the children may compare objects that float with objects that sink and objects that can be picked up by a magnet with objects that cannot.

When listening to stories, the way children play with the dog may be compared with the way they play with the cat. The kinds of help mother gives them may be compared with the things father does with them. When the children read on a sufficiently advanced level, they may be able to compare plants that grow below the timber line with those that grow above it.

Comparing on a Reading Level. On an early reading level, the child is helped to use picture clues to identify unknown words. Older primary children may preview their story by means of picture clues. If the characters wear clothing of an earlier day, the children may compare the clothing with that worn today and may decide that they are Pilgrims. The children may have some idea of the historical setting of the story from the use of pictures. From another picture the children may decide upon the occupation of the hero. Work clothes with a miner's cap and reflector may be compared with the uniform of a fireman and may help the children set the story in a mining town. According to a study of students in high school by Robinson, a preview of the headings and the summary of a selection just before reading helped increase the reader's comprehension.[1] In the same way, the use of picture clues and comparisons of their settings may be used to help primary children plan what to look for in reading a story, thereby increasing their comprehension.

Ability To Make Inferences and Draw Conclusions

The interpretation of pictures provides excellent opportunities for children to learn to draw conclusions. A picture of a family packing a car with lunch, bathing suits, and fishing poles leads the children to conclude that the family is going to the seaside, a lake, or river for a picnic. On the other hand, a picture of a family that is packing ice skates, toboggans, skis, and ski poles in a car and wearing heavy clothes provides clues to lead the children to infer that they are going to a spot where they will find snow. When reading a story that tells that mother is in the kitchen and is assembling flour, eggs, sugar, milk, and chocolate chips, the children may conclude that mother is going to make either cake or cookies. If a rolling pin and cookie cutters are also mentioned, the children may be practically certain that she is going to make cookies. If father is in the yard sawing boards while the family dog stands by, the children may conclude that father might be making a house for the dog. Some kindergarten children are able to draw conclusions on this level.

In a story about a ship in a storm, for example, the children may read to discover what in addition to the storm caused the boat to sink and how the people were rescued. The captain and crew may be very concerned about the cause of the catastrophe. In such a selection the children may be led to anticipate a variety of possibilities concerning the cause of the sinking of the boat. They may then be encouraged to read to discover which was the actual cause in this story.

Ability To Observe Relationships

In the kindergarten, for example, children may be helped to see a relationship between an hour glass type of egg timer, which the teacher

[1] F. P. Robinson, "Study Skills for Superior Students in Secondary Schools," *The Reading Teacher,* XV (Sept. 1961), 29–33, 37.

may bring to class, and the clock in the room. In order to stimulate the children to see the relationship by themselves, the teacher may show the timer while the children discuss it. She may pass it to each child so that he may have a chance to manipulate it. She may then ask if anyone can tell what the timer is used for. If the children mention that it tells time or tells how long some activity takes, the teacher may ask them to name something else found in the room that can be used for the same purpose. The more mature children will be able to identify the clock, especially if the teacher has made them conscious of periods of time for the occurrence of particular events.

Certain types of classifications on the readiness level carry relationships. The child may sort cards on some of which are pictured objects that fly and on others objects that swim. As the child classifies, he is learning to see a relationship between an airplane and a bird in terms of flight.

Relationships in terms of size occur rather frequently in stories. For instance, a child's older brother may play baseball but refuse to let a little sister join because she is too small. On the other hand, an older brother may try to ride on a little sister's tricycle with obvious difficulties because he is too big. On a more mature reading level, children may be led to draw conclusions regarding the similarities between alligators and turtles. For example, if children know that both animals lay eggs, the relationship is easily drawn.

Skill in Making Generalizations

If kindergarten children have had an opportunity to have a variety of pets visit their classroom, they may notice that all these animals must have food and water, whether birds, rabbits, kittens, or puppies. If the teacher encourages them to think about what they had to do to care for each animal, they will be able to draw the generalization that all the animals they had in the room require food and water. First-grade children can draw generalizations about plants as well. They may carry on simple experiments to discover that plants need air, sunlight, and water. They may also discover that plants kept in the room for a period need fertilizer, a type of food. In addition, they may find that plants kept for any length of time need soil, although tubers can grow for a considerable time because of the nutrients they contain. From simple stories in primers, first-grade children can make generalizations about some differences between men's and women's work. These children can also draw generalizations in regard to safety and compose their own rules.

Second- and third-grade children have more opportunities than younger children to make generalizations from their readers. They may generalize concerning the fact that children are often able to help their parents by running errands and doing other small tasks. In the third grade they may read stories of older days when children were responsible for an important part of the work in the home. On another topic they may make generalizations about the fact that fruits usually grow on trees and berries grow on vines and bushes. They may also reach the generalization that farmers usually produce food, whereas people in the cities usually do other kinds of work.

Ability To Determine Cause and Effect

The ability to determine cause and effect is a very valuable skill needed to help children try to solve their problems of living as well as an important one in the organization of reading material. Young children make many mistakes primarily because they are unable to anticipate the results of their activities. As an example of cause and effect in children's work in the kindergarten, they need help in learning that too much food will kill the fish in the aquarium. Therefore the food must be measured, and a schedule must be followed. They must also learn that scissors should be carried with the points covered to avoid hurting others when they are moving around the room.

First-grade children can learn simple aspects of cause and effect in the stories they read. In a story children might analyze the cause of Jerry's loss of his top. Perhaps he left it in his pocket when doing stunts on the bars. From such a situation children may learn the concept of gravity. In reading in the social studies, they may learn the reason for crossing the street at the corner. From a story they will find that drivers of cars may not be able to stop in time to avoid hitting children if they cross the street at the wrong place. They may also read to find why the pilots of airplanes must wait for instructions from the conning tower before they land.

Skills in Appreciating Literature

Skill in learning to appreciate literature is another aspect of the interpretive program in the primary grades. Appreciation may be developed both through stories that are told or read to children and those they read by themselves.

Developing Appreciation Through Story Telling. Children have opportunities in a good classroom to listen to many stories. Teachers usually have a regular story-telling period when new stories are told or read and familiar stories are retold at the children's request. The teacher takes the responsibility for choosing good literature for this level.

When the teacher shows a picture to introduce a story, children usually ask questions. The teacher makes use of these to help arouse the children's interest in the story. The teacher makes use of children's experiences to help them relate themselves to the characters in the story. As the reading goes on, she may ask an occasional question concerning how a character feels or what the character may do next. Some teachers let the children make some anticipatory guesses at this point. Others prefer to build enough background for the story so that these questions arise before they begin to read, because they feel that the reading should be interrupted as little as possible.

If the children have made guesses concerning the action or feelings of the character, the teacher helps them discuss these after the story is finished. She may ask if they remember who guessed the right ending and how they thought the hero or one of the characters felt after certain events. Other clues may be discussed concerning the appearance of one or more of the characters and any changes that might have resulted from the events in the story. They may also discuss the setting of the story.

Developing Appreciation Through Reading in Pre-Primers. In the early levels of the first pre-primer, most of the work is done to help children interpret pictures. Informational questions may be discussed first, such as what the children in the pictures are doing and the children's own experiences with this type of activity. Even on this level some questions about the characters, their actions, and their feelings may be brought in, such as the following: "Do you think the children like baby to play with them? Does Don look happy? Do you think baby can do what the other children do? Does Karen mind helping baby?" and "Is baby having fun?" In an example of a longer story, the children may take their dog and cat for a ride in the wagon. Again, feelings can be discussed, such as the following: "Do cats and dogs like to ride in wagons? Do you have a cat or dog that likes to ride? Why do you think these animals jumped out of the wagon?" and "Do you think that the little boy was doing something they didn't like?"

By the time the children have progressed to a higher level, a story may tell that a little boy wants his father to help make a playhouse, a house for the dog, or some other type of construction. Questions to help children develop understanding may include the following: "Does your father like to build things? Did he ever build something for you? Do you think Don's father is too busy to help him? Does he look as though he likes to work like this? Do you think he likes to have baby and the dog so close to him? Can the boy or girl do anything to help father? What do you think Don and Karen can do to keep the dog from bothering father? How would you feel if your father made a playhouse for you?"

**Developing Appreciation Through Reading in the More Advanced
Books.** As the children read in more advanced primary books, the
teacher may help them observe clues regarding the hero's character, appearance, motives, actions, and feeling. Conversational clues may be
obvious, but children still need help in discussing their interpretation.
When a character in a story says his mother will be surprised about
something, the teacher may help the children analyze whether that surprise will be a happy one or a disappointment. Descriptions of action in
stories often carry clues to feelings and motives. Questions arise when
one child in a story suggests that another climb a ladder. The reader
needs to know why the children want to climb a ladder. The question
arises concerning why the first child suggested that the other climb the
ladder rather than that he, himself, do the climbing. If mother finds the
child on the ladder, might she be angry? Might the first child, therefore, prefer that the second child take the risk? Is the first child afraid
to climb the ladder or does he feel that the other child is older and
stronger? Might the second child, therefore, succeed better than the
first?

Children sometimes need help with suggestive details. Sometimes
motive is involved. For example, when Don climbed up in the tree to
try to catch a squirrel, mother asked him to come down. She suggested
that he come into the house to get some nuts and try to catch the
squirrel on the ground. She didn't say anything else until Don got down
from the tree. Children may be helped to analyze why mother didn't
say more while Don was in the tree. Was she afraid to scold him then
for fear he might fall? Did she think that Don would have a better
chance to catch the squirrel if he lured it with nuts from the ground?

Emotional words may sometimes give children the feeling of fear,
awe, excitement, or enthusiasm without stating this emotion directly.
In "Juan's New Boots" by Russell and Wulfing,[2] Juan went out in a row-
boat from a little village on the Mexican seacoast with his father, mother,
and sisters to a trading vessel anchored in the bay. He was permitted
to go into the hold of the ship to look around. The family members
chose things they needed, but Juan saw only a pair of boots that he
knew should belong to him. They were beautiful, soft, brown leather
and were trimmed in silver like his saddle. Before asking his father if
he might have them, he decided to try them on. He had two fears,
first that his father had not brought enough hides to trade for family
needs as well as the new boots, and second, that the boots might be too
small. His feelings are suggested in the statement, "Then he held his
breath while the man brought out a new pair and slipped them on his
feet." The second fear was resolved when Juan discovered that the

boots fitted him, and the first was taken care of when the father gave his permission for Juan to keep the boots. The teacher may ask, "How would you feel if your father had just given you a beautiful pair of new boots with silver trimming on them?"

Figures of speech are not usually found in primary books. When they are found, they are simple and obvious for children. For example in the story "Today We Fly" in *Friends Far and Near*[3] when the children were taking off in the airplane with the pilot, Uncle Joe was standing behind the plane. The effect of the take-off is reported in the words, "The wind from the propeller made a snowman of Uncle Joe." A little later in the story Peter was extremely anxious that his model airplane should win some sort of prize in the contest where hundreds of model airplanes were competing. When he saw the other models, "A lump came into Peter's throat when he thought of his little fighter." Later when Peter found that he had won a blue ribbon, his emotion is described in a sentence that states that, "Peter tried to swallow the lump in his throat." The allusion to Uncle Joe as a snowman is fairly obvious. Some discussion of the expression, "A lump in his throat" may be needed if children are not familiar with this rather common expression.

Children may also need some help with expressions descriptive of mood. When Jonathan in "Jonathan Goes Hunting" by Russell and Wulfing,[4] looked for a bee tree in order to help his family find honey, he succeeded only in arousing a nest of white wasps to stinging madness. When he returned home covered with wasp stings, his family said, "You're too little to hunt bee trees, . . . That's a man's job!" Many children have had a similar experience that resulted in the same feelings of belittlement. The teacher may ask, "How do you feel when someone tells you that you are too little to do something that you especially want to do?"

Appreciation of the literature and customs of children whose parents or grandparents came from other lands is an important phase of the literature program.

THINKING SKILLS IN THE PRIMARY PROGRAM

Since each of the study skills described in this chapter has been illustrated by fragments of stories, a need seems to exist for a picture of an integrated program in which these study skills are used. The second grade has been chosen for the first example because children's ability levels may range from kindergarten to above the third grade. A study of the airport was used to illustrate the use of study skills in the third

---

[3] *Ibid.*, "Today We Fly," pp. 6–16.
[4] *Ibid.*, "Jonathan Goes Hunting," pp. 293–304.

grade, and the study of the home and family was selected to illustrate work in the first grade. Examples of locating information are given in the second-grade study, skills in organizing are applied to the third grade, and skills in interpretation are illustrated in the first-grade study. No attempt has been made to illustrate the previously described skills in the order in which they were presented in the previous section of the chapter.

The Farm

Mrs. Jacks' second-grade children had been studying the grocery store in their social studies program. As time went on, they became increasingly interested in the source of the products. Since spring was about to arrive and the weather was becoming warmer, Mrs. Jacks decided that the time was ripe for a study of the farm. She brought to school some pictures, some books about the farm, a film strip and projector, and a bunch each of radishes and green onions that had just appeared in the markets. She placed the pictures on the bulletin board and put the books in a conspicuous place on the library table. The vegetables were left on a tray on her desk. The children noticed the new things at once and were eager to look at the books.

Planning Questions. Since the children had some idea of the vegetables and fruit raised on the farm from their study of the grocery store, Mrs. Jacks decided that they were ready to set up some questions. To secure some questions, she showed the film strip about truck gardening. Before she started to show the film strip, she told the children a little about its content and suggested that they watch it to see what else they would like to know about truck farming. She told them to raise their hands whenever they thought of questions, and she would jot them down on a piece of paper. On the following day the children organized these questions in logical order. The teacher printed them on a large chart at a later time. These questions served as a beginning to guide the study of truck farming and also provided experience in functional reading. Because the children had dictated the questions themselves, they were able to recall them from memory and very soon to read them with ease.

Locating Information in Supplementary Books. As time went on Mrs. Jacks secured more simply written books about farming from the school and public libraries. Most of the children had been able to use the table of contents in their books even in the first grade. When Mrs. Jacks found a selection in a book which directly answered one of the children's questions, she made a note of the book and pages in her lesson plans. On the following day she showed these books to the children and told them that the answers to some of their questions could be found in these books. She also mentioned that the titles of the selections would be very helpful in locating them, and that these could be found in the table of contents. She then asked for volunteers of children who would like to work in committees of two each to use these books. Volunteers came mostly from the top reading group.

Locating Information in the Library. Grace was a very rapid and efficient reader. She told Mrs. Jacks she would prefer to read by herself. Since she read on about sixth-grade level, Mrs. Jacks suggested that she choose a topic to look up in a *Childcraft* book in the library. Mrs. Jacks had previously asked the librarian if she might send one of the children to the library to look up references. The librarian had been happy to permit the child to come and said she would be able to give her a little help even though she was working with an upper grade class at that time. Grace was very happy to work in the library. While some of the children in the room went about looking up material in their reference books, Mrs. Jacks helped the rest of the class start work on scrapbooks. Some of the pictures she had brought to school had been torn out of magazines for the children to use in this way.

Following Directions in Science. Don and Richard were very much interested in science. They read on about fifth-grade level and had found a book by Leaming describing some science experiments.[5] They asked Mrs. Jacks for a glass jar, a drinking glass, and a piece of blotting paper. They showed her the place in the book where they had found the directions and told her that they had brought some bean seeds. They also showed her another picture of celery standing in a glass of colored water. They told her that they had brought food coloring and a piece of celery. Mrs. Jacks told them they would find jars and, she thought, a jelly glass in the cabinet beside the sink. She also told them to get a blotter from the supply cabinet in the back of the room. The boys left and went about busily setting up their experiments.

Reporting Information. At the end of the period Mrs. Jacks asked the children who had been reading to bring their books to their seats. She then gave them an opportunity, by committees, to tell one or two things they had learned from their reading. Grace gave a rather complete report on the growing of lettuce in the Salinas Valley in California. Kathy and Pauline each remembered two interesting points from a book they used. David and Gerald thought of three points between them and disagreed on the fourth. When they began to argue vigorously,

[5] Joseph Leaming, *The Real Book of Science Experiments* (Garden City, N. Y.: Garden City Bks., by arrangement with Franklin Watts, Inc., 1954), 178, 182–3.

Mrs. Jacks suggested that they find the place in their book and read it to the class. They sat down to locate the place while Karen and Debbie showed the pictures from their book and talked about them. It was fairly obvious that they had recalled very little from the rather difficult text, but Mrs. Jacks felt that they had made a good beginning in their ability to interpret pictures. When David and Gerald were called back, David said very smugly, "I was right," and then read the supporting paragraphs from his selection.

Evaluating the Reports. Mrs. Jacks complimented both boys on their ability to locate information and then asked the class for one or two comments on how to be a good sport when winning a point. Mrs. Jacks then asked Don and Richard to show their experiments and tell what they had done. Don showed the jar in which he had placed a blotter upright inside the glass. He told that he had placed the bean seeds between the glass and the blotter and had put a small amount of water in the bottom. When Kathy asked why he did not cover the beans with water, he explained that the beans would drown because they needed air. He stated that the blotter would suck up all the water the beans needed but still permit the beans to get air.

Richard then showed the celery in the glass of red colored water and was about to tell that the celery would pull up the red water in its veins when Mrs. Jacks stopped him. She said, "Richard, I think it will be more fun if you let the children find out what happens. Suppose you just tell the children how you colored the water and let them wait to see what the celery looks like tomorrow. We know, but let's keep it a secret." Richard was happy to keep the secret. When the boys finished, they put the experiments on the science table.

Mrs. Jacks continued the evaluation with a discussion of the positive features of the reports. She also asked the children working on scrapbooks to show one picture each, by rows. The children then brought out the positive aspects of the work on scrapbooks. At the end Mrs. Jacks asked for a general comment on anything that could be improved but suggested that the children did not mention names. A few suggestions were made regarding more careful cutting, neater pasting, and the need to put a picture in the center of a page rather than to one side.

Using Skills in These Experiences. The children who had used the reference books had demonstrated ability to recall information from the reading material. Grace had shown a high level of this ability and was also able to locate her topic through her skill in using alphabetical arrangements. Karen and Debbie had demonstrated that they had made a beginning through ability to acquire information from pictures. Mrs. Jacks would continue to work on this skill in her reading groups, giving especial help to those children who were weakest. All of these children had been able to use the table of contents successfully without help. Don and Richard had shown ability to follow printed directions on a fairly advanced level. The entire class was learning to use the chart of questions to guide their work. Mrs. Jacks felt that the children in her most advanced reading group were making good progress in ability to locate information with independence.

The Airport

Mrs. Peterson's third-grade children had made considerable progress in their study of the airport. One of the committees had used reading material to follow a family from the time they purchased their tickets at the airport until they arrived at their destination.

Using Lists as Work Guides. Before the children had begun work, they had dictated a list of the steps to take when going on a trip, and the members of a committee had each chosen to draw a picture of one step. Mrs. Peterson had printed this list of topics and the names of the children on cards and had given them to the children to place in a pocket chart. This chart was used to help the children follow the sequence as they worked and would later be used to help them put their pictures and story together to make a booklet.

Each child on the committee had worked on a step in the sequence, making an illustration and writing a brief story about his own step. Each child used a large piece of drawing paper for his illustrations and mounted his story below. These sheets were to be combined to make the story book about this family and their trip.

Using Classification. Another committee was working on a frieze, or a series of pictures, to show various types of passenger and cargo planes. The children drew and painted their own illustrations and printed their own captions below the pictures. These pictures were eventually mounted on a large bulletin board. Joe and Fred were interested in fighter planes. Although Mrs. Peterson realized that these did not belong in the airport, she felt that the interest was related closely enough to the study to let these boys pursue their own interests. They collected pictures from magazines and other sources and were working on a scrapbook to illustrate their topic. They, too, printed their own captions under the pictures. Mrs. Peterson suggested to these boys that they make a table of contents for the front of their book to show on which page each type of airplane might be found.

Culminating the Study as a Summary. As the unit came to a close, the children invited another class to see their model airport, booklets, and displays. They set up part of their room to look like the interior of an airplane. The pupils took the roles of the dispatcher in the control tower, the pilot, co-pilot, navigator, stewardess, and passengers. The visiting class took the part of new passengers boarding the plane at a stop. Mrs. Peterson's class dramatized the take-off, following the directions from the dispatcher. They flashed directions for the passengers to fasten their safety belts by holding up a printed card. When in flight, Mrs. Peterson's class entertained the new passengers with songs, stories, and poems about airplanes. They demonstrated some of their science experiments and told about the exhibits in their room. Several of the girls took the part of stewardesses and served fruit juice and cookies to all of the passengers and the airplane crew as well. They flashed signals for landing and bade their guests good-by as the visitors left the airplane.

Organizing Skills in the Study of the Airport.   The children who organized their reading around the trip taken by a family were gaining experience in following a sequence of events. The children who worked on the frieze and Joe and Fred, who made a booklet on fighter planes, were carrying on activities in classification. Each time lists were made, the children were gaining experience in outlining. The culmination of the unit provided an opportunity for the children to summarize many of their learnings in order to present them to the visiting class.

The Home and Family

The home and family are usually studied in the first grade. This topic in the social studies offers opportunity for children to learn and use skills in interpreting pictures and reading material.

Interpreting Pictures of the Home.   Since most first grade children are limited in their reading ability, they are guided to gain as much information as possible from pictures. Mrs. Baker had an excellent collection of mounted pictures showing types of homes, rooms, furniture, and various activities of people working and enjoying leisure in their homes. She had helped the children collect questions by making notes of those asked by the children when she read stories, showed pictures, and presented film strips and slides. These questions were later organized by the children under her guidance. Mrs. Baker printed them on large charts. Since many of the children could recall them from memory and some could read them, she helped the children use these questions to guide their search for information.

Answering Questions with Pictures.   Often these questions could be answered by interpreting pictures. Although some of Mrs. Baker's children were still in the stage at which they named objects in pictures, and some were in intermediate stages, others were able to interpret and secure considerable information from pictures.

A picture in one of the children's readers showed an elderly man and woman visiting a family of a mother and father and three children. The older man was offering a ball to the baby. When discussing other members of our families who do not live with the family Mrs. Baker showed this picture to the children. Some of them knew at once that the family had company because they were sitting in the living room. Sharon thought that the visitors were grandmother and grandfather because they looked like her grandparents. Joyce decided that the baby had a birthday. He looked just about like her baby brother who had a birthday last week. Besides, the grandfather in the picture had brought a ball for the baby. That must be his birthday present. Mrs. Baker felt that her more mature children were able to interpret this picture with considerable success.

At another time, Mrs. Baker showed the children a picture of a family in the kitchen, in connection with the study of work in the home. More children were able to offer interpretive suggestions at this time. Frances said that the children were helping with the dishes. She added that her older sister and she often wiped the dishes, too. Phillip laughed and said that father looked funny because he had on an apron and was washing the dishes. Ted explained that mother was busy with the baby so father was helping with the dishes. His father washed dishes sometimes when mother had to take care of the baby. Mrs. Baker felt that these children had analyzed this rather complex picture with good interpretive skills. Throughout the interpretive activities the children had related the content to their experience. They were also able to bring their experiences to bear on their other reading lessons.

Making Comparisons Concerning the Home. Many opportunities both in listening to stories and in reading simple material were provided in comparing mother's work with father's work. The children decided that father did some things because he was stronger than mother. He also earned the living while mother took care of the home. They compared rooms and furniture in relation to the activities carried on in each. In addition, they compared games and activities that older children carried on with things the baby liked to do. They also compared toys that were suitable for play indoors with those that were suitable for play outdoors, and talked about why mother usually objected to their playing with skates, tricycles, and balls indoors even when it was raining. These discussions usually took place in group reading of stories about the home. Sometimes comparisons were made by mounting pictures on large charts, such as by cutting out furniture belonging to different rooms and putting each type on its own chart.

Drawing Conclusions About the Home. As the children selected pictures for each chart, Mrs. Baker usually asked them why they put certain furniture in certain rooms. The children decided that cabinets were needed in the kitchen to hold the dishes and to store the food. The refrigerator was also needed to store food. The stove and sink were obviously important in the kitchen for preparing food and washing dishes. The baby's crib went in mother's and father's room so that mother could take care of the baby during the night. Father sometimes also gave the bottle to the baby during the night. The children were able to draw conclusions about the placement of all the furniture although an argument arose about television in the children's room.

When the problem arose concerning why some food was kept in the refrigerator and some in cupboards, Mrs. Baker guided the children to carry on an experiment. They placed some milk in one sauce dish and some corn flakes in another. They watched for several days, until the milk soured, but the corn flakes were unaffected. They then concluded that milk must be cold in order to keep. To test this conclusion, they put milk in two saucers and placed one in the school cafeteria refrigerator and left the other on the science table in their room. From the fact that the milk on the science table soured before the milk in the refrigerator, they decided that their conclusion had been correct.

Observing Relationships in the Home. People and objects have many kinds of relationships to each other, such as part to whole, position, condition, and shape. For example, the children in Mrs. Baker's class read a story about a little boy whose wagon was broken. One of the wheels had come off. When introducing the story, Mrs. Baker asked if the children could ride on anything with only three wheels. The children named a tricycle. Mrs. Baker then asked if they could ride on anything with only two wheels, and they named a bicycle and a scooter. She next asked why the wagon could not go with only three wheels. The children eventually arrived at the conclusion that the wagon had two axles and therefore needed two wheels on each axle. They also mentioned that some trailers have only one axle and can go as long as they have a tongue and two wheels. Although most of this thinking in regard to relationships was verbal, it was a way of laying the groundwork for later ability to see relationships when reading.

In another story a little girl received two new dolls on Christmas Eve. Although she was very happy about the dolls, she decided to take an old rag doll to bed with her as usual, because of familiarity and because she endowed it with feelings such as jealousy and loneliness. This situation called for a discussion of children's feelings about old and new toys.

Making Generalizations About the Home. As the children discussed various types of homes, including family residences, hotels, and apartment houses, they dealt with generalizations. They learned that the usual home with a yard around it is built for one family, that duplexes are built for two families, and that apartment buildings are built for a larger number of families. The children also learned that, regardless of size, each family unit contained a living area, kitchen, and bathroom. They also learned that the living area and sleeping quarters are sometimes combined and sometimes contained in several rooms. In most hotels, on the other hand, they found that living and sleeping quarters are usually combined, and bathrooms are provided, but eating facilities are usually omitted because people eat in public dining rooms.

Discovering Cause and Effect in the Home. Most health books include lessons in safety. Mrs. Baker's children read about the danger of overloading the electric circuits with too many plugs and the danger of playing with matches. They conducted a simple science experiment in connection with this problem by setting two candles in two saucers, respectively. Mrs. Baker lighted both candles and then placed a jar over one. The children watched to discover that the candle under the jar went out. When the children had difficulty in discovering the cause, Mrs. Baker removed the jar, relighted the first candle, and then placed the jar over the second one. When some of the children still had difficulty in discovering the cause, Mrs. Baker asked them what the word "smother" meant. Most of the children knew that the word meant that air was withheld. They were then able to apply the principle of the need of fire for air to the candle. In order to help the children apply the principle, Mrs. Baker followed the experiment with ways of putting out fires when clothing, curtains, and other materials are burning.

SUMMARY

The teaching of thinking in connection with reading and the use of study skills are classified into three types, skills in recalling and locating information, skills in organizing, and skills in interpreting and appreciating reading matter. Primary children are able to apply some of these skills to their reading and can work with others through discussion and the use of pictures. Readiness for the application of these skills can and should be built through most stories in readers and social studies books. Except for recreation, reading has little value if the reader does not use the information as a tool for thinking. Examples of locating information are given in connection with the second-grade study of the farm. Skills in organizing are applied to the third grade study of the airport, and skills in interpreting are applied to the first grade study of the home.

17

Reading for Thought in Intermediate and Upper Grades

By the time the children reach the intermediate grades, most of them will have acquired a rather large sight vocabulary and will have mastered the ability to use a variety of clues in word recognition. They will also be able to comprehend the exact meanings of simple facts and to secure information from the printed page. In addition, they will have had many opportunities to relate past experiences to their reading material and to organize and interpret material on a simple level.

The teacher in the middle and upper grades helps children learn a variety of more advanced techniques for organizing and interpreting reading material. If these skills are to be applied and mastered, children must have opportunities to use them in meaningful and purposeful situations. The teacher of these grades reviews past work and takes the children where they are in their reading levels. She fills in any lacks or gaps before she makes an attempt to add further skills. If the teacher fails to fill in the gaps, the children will have difficulty in making progress on higher levels. They will also tend to become frustrated and to give up any effort to make an improvement in their reading.

SKILLS IN LOCATING INFORMATION

In addition to the skills learned by primary children, older children add the use of the index and glossary in books and also extend their ability to the use of regular dictionaries, encyclopedias, and the card catalog. They increase in ability to use maps, charts, and graphs and also to read more extensively in newspapers and magazines.

Skills in Using Alphabetical Arrangements

Children use alphabetical arrangements primarily in their work with the index, the dictionary, encyclopedia, and card catalog. Upper-grade children may also use yearbooks, the *Readers' Guide to Periodical Literature*, biographical dictionaries, and the thesaurus. A number of other skills must be taught in connection with these guides, such as the use of diacritical markings, accent markings, and syllabification. Fourth-grade children may need review in the use of tables of content, especially when they use books with increasing independence to solve problems. Some of the previously mentioned skills will help in the use of the glossary.

Although these skills are only preliminary to the actual use of information in the solution of problems, nevertheless they involve a certain degree of thinking in order to apply them successfully. Slower children will need a repetition of introductory help. If the need for the use of alphabetical arrangements of various types arises in connection with the social studies or other content fields, children will have a strong purpose for using them.

Using the Glossary. Some reading texts have glossaries. The children should be taught how to use these glossaries and given considerable help in interpreting the diacritical markings and accents. In the primary grades most of the emphasis is placed on the diacritical markings for long and short vowels only. Few children are able to use the other marks and need help in using the key words to aid pronunciation. For example, when the child looks up the word *gargoyle* he finds it marked as gär′goil. When he looks for the symbol called *two-dot a* in some glossaries and dictionaries, he finds that it is pronounced like the *a* in *arm*. He also finds that the second syllable is pronounced as though it were spelled *goil*, and therefore it rhymes with *soil* and *boil*. He also finds that the accent is on the first syllable. The teacher helps the child use these aids in pronouncing the word. As the teacher helps the child learn how to use these aids, he becomes increasingly able to use them independently.

Since glossaries are like small, simple dictionaries made to help with the unfamiliar words of the particular book in which they are found, guidance in their use will also help children with the use of the full size dictionary. As with all aids of this type, the teacher should help children work with the glossaries until they feel completely secure in

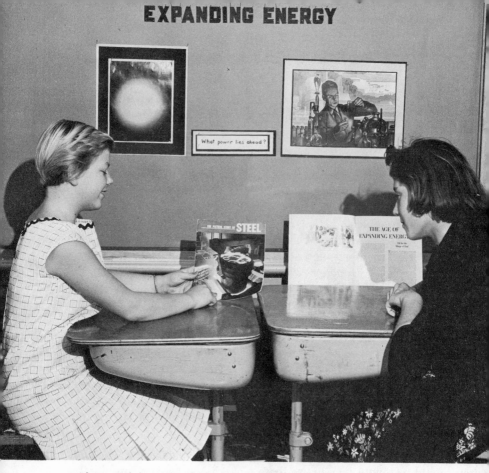

EXPANDING ENERGY

What power lies ahead?

STEEL

THE AGE OF EXPANDING ENERGY

These eighth-grade children are mature enough to study such abstract subjects as chemical and physical energy. (Courtesy California State Department of Education.)

using them independently. Some children will be able to work independently long before others. If they are required to use glossaries before they understand and feel secure with them, the children tend to become confused and frustrated. They also tend to develop a dislike of such aids instead of an appreciation of their value.

Using the Index and the Dictionary. Most intermediate-grade children are able to master independent use of the dictionary and indexes. Over the years modern school dictionaries have been greatly improved, especially from the standpoint of simplicity of definition. In order to help children locate topics in the index and words in the dictionary, they will need to review alphabetizing with the first and second letters of words and will also need to add alphabetizing with the third and fourth letters. For example, they will discover that "straight" comes before "street." By the time they are able to alphabetize with three and four letters, they can usually handle a fifth and sixth if necessary with a little help from the teacher.

In order to use the dictionary as a help in pronunciation, the child must become increasingly familiar with diacritical markings and should be helped to know where to look in the dictionary for the key to pronunciation. In most dictionaries the key is located in the front of the book. In some, added keys are also given at the bottoms of the pages. Children need help with primary and secondary accent marks such as those in sa'crile'gious. The light accent over the first syllable indicates a secondary or weak accent, and a dark one over *le* indicates a primary or strong accent. Another needed skill is the ability to use the dictionary in order to be able to divide words into syllables.

Some children are confused by the lack of separation marks between syllables when the accent mark is used. They must be helped to understand that either one or the other indicates a division between syllables. Use of the dictionary to divide words when writing stories or selections for the social studies and other content subjects gives children excellent functional practice in syllabification without extra drill. Durkin gives a few rules that may help older children with this skill, but they must realize that they will find some exceptions to the rules.[1]

Another dictionary help which children must learn in order to save time is the use of the guide words at the tops of the pages to indicate the first and last words on the pages. Ability to open the dictionary at a point near where a particular word is located also saves time. By asking children, for example, where they would look for such a word as *mileage* or any similar word to find how it is spelled and by encouraging them to try to see who comes nearest to the correct page at the first try, the children may enjoy the activity and gain ease in locating words.

Using the Encyclopedia. The use of the encyclopedia demands considerable skill in the ability to alphabetize. Teachers should help the children understand the fact that a single book may cover only one or two letters, even less in a large, complete set. The children must learn how to use the letter guides to help them locate topics. They also need help in knowing how to look up specific topics, since these topics may be listed under words that are different from those used by the child. In addition, some words have several meanings, such as worms in the garden (zoological); worm, a type of gear in an automobile; Ole Worm, a Danish author; worm, a type of grass; worm, a type of lizard; worms, the parasites; and Worms, the Edict of. Often a few individuals in the classroom will learn to use the encyclopedia sooner than others merely

[1] Dolores Durkin, *Phonics and the Teaching of Reading* (ed.: Alice Miel), Practical Suggestions for Teaching, No. 22 (New York: Bureau of Publications, Teachers College, Columbia University, 1962).

from looking for particular answers to problems. These children, then, may serve as helpers for other children. They must be coached, however, to learn to help another child rather than to do his work for him.

Using the Card Catalog. The card catalog is usually easier than the encyclopedia for children to use. The best method of helping children learn to use the card catalog is to take them either to the school library or to the local neighborhood library. School librarians understand children and can use language geared to their level. Children usually enjoy such a trip, and some will master the ability to handle a card catalog at one explanation. Others will need further help as time goes on. Children need to know that books are listed both under author and title. By the end of the upper grades, most children who are able to read on their own grade level should be able to use the dictionary, card catalog, and encyclopedia with reasonable ease. Upper-grade children should also be helped to use the atlas, the *Readers' Guide to Periodical Literature,* yearbooks, biographical dictionaries, and a thesaurus. Only the better readers, however, are likely to acquire skill in their use. Further help for some children will be needed in high school.

Ability To Scan

Scanning on the intermediate level is different, to a degree, from the scanning used on the primary level, which was limited to a short selection. The child on the intermediate grade level learns to scan through a larger section of material, such as a chapter. He may learn to jump from paragraph to paragraph, taking in a few words in each lead sentence. Sometimes the first sentence in the paragraph does not carry the main thought. He may then try scanning the last sentences in the paragraph, since the topic sentence is usually found at the beginning or at the end of each paragraph. If he fails to find the topic sentence at either of these places, he must scan over the most important words in each paragraph. It is usually not necessary, however, to carry the search this far.

As an example, a child on the eighth-grade level recalled a story about homing pigeons and had vague memories that they were used in Olympic Games at some time. He was not, however, able to give the exact information. He remembered the book in which he had found the story, so he turned to the index to find the topic of pigeons. He found a number of pages listed under the main topic and a page each for two subtopics, that is, "the breeding of" and "the training of." Since he was not interested at the moment in the breeding or training of pigeons, he turned to the first page listed under the main topic in the index. On turning to this page in the text, he found the story for which he was searching. He now scanned the first sentence in each paragraph until he came to the one that started with the words, "The first Olympic Games. . . ." He then read that paragraph carefully to find that pigeons were used to carry news during the original Olympic Games in Greece two thousand years ago because they were the fastest means of communication then known. Most scanning serves a purpose similar to the example just given.

Children may scan the newspaper, making use of the headlines to find an interesting article to share with the class concerning some topic they are studying or for a general news period. When the child locates a topic that interests him, he may scan through the article rapidly to decide whether or not his class might also be interested in this topic. If he decides that they would, he will then read the article carefully to decide whether or not he wishes to read it to the class or to summarize it for them. Many purposeful situations should be provided for scanning in the upper grades until the children are proficient in this ability.

Skills in Following Directions

Intermediate- and upper-grade children can learn to follow more complex and abstract directions than young children. One important use for the ability to follow printed directions is found in filling out forms. Some practical forms such as applications for positions, order blanks for merchandise, checks, and post-office orders should be used with upper-grade children to help them learn how to complete these forms properly. Printed traffic signs may be copied and discussed. Especial attention should be given to the colors used for no parking and loading zones.

Ability to follow directions may be used in connection with children's work in social studies and science when making authentic models of boats, railroad engines, airplanes of various types, electric motors, and so forth. Children may need some help from the teacher, but she should rarely read the directions to the children or explain them in her own words unless a particular child completely lacks the ability to interpret the directions for himself. She may help with unfamiliar terms or with the interpretation of the most difficult elements in the directions if help is requested by the children. Children achieve both a feeling of satisfaction in accomplishment and growth in ability to think when they do most of the work themselves, including the reading.

Ability To Select Suitable References

One of the techniques for helping children evaluate the suitability of the reference material they use is to guide them to check the date of publication. So many changes have taken place in the fields of science and industry that much information is out of date within a year or two.

Intermediate children are old enough to learn that the printing of an article or other written material in no way indicates that the statements included are factual. Even some adults tend to believe anything they read in print. If children are helped to check one biased newspaper article with another in which the opposite view is stated, they may develop a healthy scepticism. If biased newspaper articles are checked against articles in reputable magazines, the children will learn to use this technique for evaluating the material they read.

When using newspaper and magazine articles, upper-grade children can learn to check the bias of the author or publisher. Near election time, children should know whether a given newspaper is in favor of a particular party and what that party's platform may be. Some candidates write or speak in terms of broad generalizations such as belief in the family, the church, and the flag. Others are willing to make definite statements about specific issues.

The background of the author is another important aspect that needs evaluation. If an author is noted in one field but writes in another, the writing should then be checked with that of another author who is an authority in the latter field. Authors who are scholars in their fields refer to the writings of other authorities and to experimental work to support their statements. Some writers make statements based only on their personal opinions and emotional feelings. If no specific reference is made to other authorities in the field, the article or book may well be checked against that of other authors to decide if the original writer has made a statement of fact or opinion. Specific references should give the name of the author, the book, the publisher, the date, and the page.

The purpose of the author is helpful in evaluating reading material. An author who tries to convince the reader or uses high pressure arguments in support of a certain position usually does not mention any arguments in support of the other side. An author who tries to present a subject fairly will give arguments in support of both sides. He may also present criticisms of both positions. Another helpful criterion for evaluation may be applied to the types of proof the author uses. He may draw a doubtful conclusion from the evidence he has presented, or he may make a generalization based on one example that represents an exceptional situation rather than a normal or average situation. For example, an author may describe a two-year-old child who learned to read and therefore conclude that all children can learn to read at two.

Ability To Use Graphic Representations

Maps have little meaning for children until they have had some experience in travel. Some children will not have an opportunity for this type of experience so the teacher helps them by substituting films and other audio-visual aids.

Using Local Maps. An exception to this need for extensive travel is found on the primary level when children make their own maps to provide background for later map work. Children may first start with a map of their own city and will need to become oriented in regard to directions both in the classroom and on the map. They may then locate important places on the map, such as the main library, the main post office, the depot, the airport, the nearby fire station, and some of the municipal buildings. Since many children will have seen these places first hand, this map will have more meaning than many other kinds of maps.

Using Outline and Relief Maps. In the fourth grade children will probably study about their own state. The teacher may place a large piece of paper on the wall and project on it an outline map of the state, which a committee copies from the projected image. Some features, perhaps the major rivers, will also be indicated. From then on, the children may fill in their own and other important cities and other various features, such as mountains, lakes, deserts, and so forth as they study these particular areas. If pictures are pasted on the map to show forests and other features, the map will gradually come to life under the children's fingers. As children add main highways, they will find that they need to use a scale of miles. The teacher will need to help them compute their scale since the map has already been made. When the scale of miles has been computed, the children will use it to help them place their cities at the proper positions and in correct relationship to each other.

Using Symbols on Maps. A published map may be referred to for symbols for cities and to show different types of highways. The children may also refer to a published map to discover how various altitudes are shown and how the mountains are indicated. A topographical or relief map may be necessary for this type of help. The lakes, bays, and rivers should be made according to the scale of miles so that their sizes and locations will be accurate.

As the children carry on this type of work, they may notice that lines are drawn horizontally and vertically on the maps. When they ask their teacher about this, she may take them to the globe to introduce them to longitude and latitude. They may locate their own state in terms of longitude and latitude and may read stories about the use of these terms and their importance to navigators. Some children who are especially interested may wish to follow this topic to learn about the instruments used on shipboard and may be able to borrow a sextant, a barometer, and a few other of the instruments used by navigators. Stories of early navigators may be very challenging to children in the upper grades.

In the same way, all of the various symbols necessary for map reading are developed gradually with the children. If they have an opportunity to use them to meet their needs as they make their own maps, these symbols will have meaning, will be easy to remember, and will have importance in the children's minds. If children are merely given workbook exercises in tracing maps and in placing symbols on these, they will tend to become bored and to dislike map work. Workbooks, however, may be used with children who feel the need to clarify some of their concepts and to practice for greater experience in the use of the symbols. The pupils' feelings of need are of the utmost importance in teaching skills that may be thought of as either satisfying tools or boring details.

Using Charts. Children often make charts as a way of interpreting information they have gained from reading matter or as a way of presenting information to the class. When they do so, they will also tend to gain a far better understanding of the use of these aids than if they were merely taught to read them in a book.

One type of chart which children may enjoy making is used to show the products of a state or country. Fourth-grade children who are studying their state may wish to put samples of dry products in cellophane bags and to mount these bags on a chart with labels below each one. Strings or ribbons may be attached to the bags and may lead to the area on the map of the state where these products are found or grown. Some teachers help the children arrange the map on the chart between two rows of the samples of products. When no dry product is available, as in the case of tomatoes, a picture from a magazine or a child's own painted illustration may be substituted. After children have made a few charts to present information to the class, they will be interested to see how authors of books have used them.

Using Tables. Factual information concerning such matters as income from various resources or population figures are difficult to present interestingly to a class audience. The committee presenting the information may put it on a large graphic table printed on wrapping paper. They may then point out the interesting facts concerning the table and make comparisons without reading all the figures. After using tables themselves, the children will be more likely to be interested in those used in books and may enjoy finding different ways to present their figures to hold the interest of the class.

Using Graphs. Graphs have many applications. Upper-grade children may use pie graphs, for example, to show the proportion of various national and cultural groups in the population of a particular city, state, or county. These graphs may be used in the same manner to show the income received from various agricultural or industrial products. A pie graph may also be used to show the percentage of land in forests, under cultivation, in deserts, and in untillable areas such as mountains. Bar graphs may be used by children studying the pioneers to compare speed of travel of the wagon trains, pony express, stage coaches, steam boats, early steam trains, modern trains, and airplanes. A square of paper may be used to represent a day, and these squares may be repeated to show the number of days required to travel from one point to another by various types of transportation. In an active social studies program, many other needs will be found for various types of graphs. As with maps, charts, and tables, children will be much more able to read graphs in books and be more interested in them after they have made some of their own.

Ability To Read Newspapers and Magazines

A number of good newspapers and magazines are published especially for school children. The newspapers are often printed specifically for each grade level, and the magazines are written for a group of levels such as the intermediate grades. *My Weekly Reader* and *Junior Scholastics* are two of the most widely read newspapers. Some good children's magazines include *Children's Digest* and *Children's Play Mate Magazine,* which are used in both primary and intermediate levels. *Boy's Life, American Girl, Junior Natural History Magazine,* and *Model Airplane News* are written for use in the intermediate and upper grades.

Reading Newspapers. In most situations teachers order some newspapers for the grade level they teach and add a few for the grade below and the grade above to meet the needs of the slower and faster readers. When different news items appear in the newspapers on these various grade levels, the children may share information from their reading. If a child chooses to read an article aloud to his class, he should prepare it carefully, making sure of the meaning and the pronunciation of the words. Some teachers suggest that two children practice reading their individual articles aloud to each other in order to be sure that the articles are read with smoothness, accuracy, and expression.

When a child reads an article, he should be the only one who has a copy in his hands. The other children should be encouraged to listen, to add points they may have heard at home, and in other ways to discuss the article. They may also be encouraged to evaluate the reading briefly with emphasis on the successful aspects. Suggestions should always be given in terms of improvement rather than on what was wrong. Any newspaper clipping brought from home should be handled in a similar fashion. Standards for choosing worthwhile articles should be set up by the class in order to avoid sensational news. Some teachers have a news period once a week or schedule it in their program in some definite way.

Upper-grade children need help in learning how to use and apply many of the organizational skills when reading the newspaper. A class may be interested in following and keeping a day-to-day record of a specific trend in the news possibly in the form of a scrapbook or a series of charts. The remodeling of a civic center to provide more space for parks, to add buildings, and to widen streets may be a topic of interest over a period of time. Children may learn to scan the newspapers to find articles about this reconstruction and to report on the latest happenings as they occur. The teacher and children may bring in copies of a newspaper for a certain day so that she may help them learn how to scan the headlines. When they keep their continuous record, children may list in an abbreviated form the events as they occur in order to have a brief running account of the work. Some topics may fit under others as subtopics. In this way the children learn to use the beginning steps in outlining.

Analyzing News. Children in the upper grades are able to read more deeply than younger children. They can discover writers' points of view and can learn to analyze propaganda features of newspaper articles and advertisements. Propaganda techniques are described more fully in the next chapter. The writer's point of view is often apparent in newspaper articles during an election campaign. At that time children can be encouraged to bring papers that support opposite sides of issues and competing candidates. The children may carry on simple debates regarding their candidates and issues. As long as the teacher does not take sides, the practice should not be subject to criticism. The teacher should make very clear the fact that she is taking a neutral stand. She may admit that she has an opinion and a position, but that she feels she should not reveal her political beliefs at school. To evaluate advertisements in magazines, newspapers, and other media, another skill in analysis, children may use *Consumer's Reports*.

Reading Magazines. Some magazines provide excellent material for children to use in their social studies and science work. *Life Magazine* carries outstanding pictures of a variety of science interests, usually with captions that upper-grade children can read. Current affairs are also pictured graphically and, as such, are helpful even for the slower readers in these grades. *The National Geographic* is outstanding. It contains material primarily concerned with travel and is invaluable as a help in the geographical phases of the social studies. Some science articles with illustrations are also included.

Field and Stream, Look, Mechanix Illustrated, Popular Mechanics, Popular Science, and *Sports Illustrated* are also good magazines for older children. Some of these magazines may be very valuable for use with children who reject book reading but who may be deeply interested in sports or mechanical matters. Their interest may often be captured through the pictures. Sometimes slow readers are willing to put a great amount of energy into reading on an advanced level about a topic that is of intense interest to them. The stories in adult magazines are often inappropriate for use in school, but the articles may be of value. If children bring full length articles, they should learn to report on them briefly and to read only the most interesting paragraphs. The reading of a long article can be very tedious to listeners.

Ability to Follow Sequence

Many children learn to follow the sequence of a story and to retell the main events in proper order in the primary grades. If children have not mastered this simple skill by the fourth grade, the teacher should begin at this point.

Listening to Follow Sequence. An easy way to help children learn to follow a sequence of ideas or events is to start on a listening level. The teacher should select a short story with a clear, simple sequence of events. Although folk tales and fairy stories usually carry a good sequence, children may resent these because of their familiarity with them in the primary grades. When the teacher has found a story that is of interest to the children and that has a good sequence of events, she may determine the number of events in the sequence and let the children know this number when she introduces the story. She should be careful to introduce the story from the standpoint of the children's interest. She may suggest that the children jot down a word or two each time they hear a new step in sequence, or she may prefer to have them listen and recall the steps.

She will then read the story to the children and follow this reading with the children's recall of the steps in sequence. One child may record the suggestions made by members of the group. The children will discover that some have described the same steps in words that are different from others when referring to a given step. The superfluous topics will then be eliminated. Children may also find that some have listed events within a step instead of listing the main topic. Through discussion these, too, will be eliminated.

When the sequence has been decided upon, the teacher may guide some of the children to retell the story using the guide words or topics to help them. Although this latter activity is part of the language program, the reading and language programs frequently overlap when developing children's skills. The retelling of the story is also an application and use of the reading material.

Reading to Follow Sequence. After the children have had sufficient experience with following the sequence of events or ideas when listening to a story, the teacher may help them learn to take brief notes on the story while reading silently. If some children find this step difficult, the teacher may list the steps in mixed order on the board or reproduce them on paper. The children may then renumber the steps as they read the story silently. After working independently, they may discuss their choices to see if all agree on the same sequence of steps. If a disagreement arises, those who disagree may try to prove their choices by reading orally from the story to convince the other members of the group of their point. The copy on the board may be corrected when the children agree on the order of the steps. To give purpose to the activity, one of the children in the group may be chosen to tell the story to another group or to another class by using the steps in sequence as notes. As various stories are organized in this manner, other children should have turns to retell the stories in purposeful situations.

SKILLS IN ORGANIZING

The teaching of organizational skills to intermediate- and upper-grade children is greatly needed because children have uses for these skills in oral and written work. Some children have been known to reach junior and senior high school without these skills. When required to make reports from articles in encyclopedias, newspapers, and magazines, these children often resort to the extremely tedious task of copying and memorizing entire articles. Others, less willing to spend energy, copy articles and read them, regardless of inability to pronounce words and understand their meaning. This activity is not only a complete waste of the reporter's time, but it is also an utter waste of the listeners' time. Often the children develop negative attitudes toward the giving of reports because of acute boredom due to listening to such a process. Children do not necessarily resort to these techniques because of laziness. Usually they do not know how to take notes and report from them.

Skills in organizing include skills in classifying, outlining, and summarizing along with the minor skills involved in each. It is difficult to test for each of these skills separately because they overlap and reinforce each other. The child, however, needs help in all aspects of organizing so that he will be able to use each appropriate skill when he has a need for it in reading and reference work.

Skills in Classification

Skills in classification are basic to organizational skills since subtopics must be classified under main topics. Classifications may be made according to a wide variety of criteria such as size, physical position, shape, color, time, quality, quantity, mood, use, speed, direction, personal relationships, and many others. In the elementary school many opportunities for classification occur in science, the social studies, and arithmetic. The examples given here will be taken from science and the social studies.

Classifying in Science. At one time science, especially biological science, was taught almost entirely as a matter of learning various classifications and of classifying organisms into categories. Although one of the main objectives of scientists over the ages has been to organize and classify plants and animals, this activity can be very boring and has little value for children. Usually too many organisms are introduced so that children's memories are crowded with details, resulting in loss of recall and interest. In schools today, classifications are used only to help children understand the function of an organism such as that of animals that lay eggs and animals that bear their young alive. A few technical terms such as cold-blooded and warm-blooded or the thorax and the antenna of insects may be needed. Children in upper grades may add more technical terms than those in intermediate grades. Children remember more and are more deeply interested when they study one animal or insect at a time to learn about its characteristics. Whenever possible, the animal or insect should be kept in the room for a period of time so that children can observe it and discover its characteristics for themselves.

Classifying in Social Studies. Sometimes children may classify the resources of an area according to minerals, animal life, and farm crops. Again, the element of classification should not be overemphasized. If children make a large resource map, they may put samples of the products on a table below the map. The mineral, vegetable, and animal products may be grouped separately. One color of ribbon or cord may be strung from the map to the samples of minerals, another color to the samples of farm crops, and still another to the samples of animal life. When real samples cannot be secured, pictures are satisfactory substitutes.

Another type of classification may be made in connection with a study of the kinds of work carried on by pioneer men as compared to that carried on by pioneer women. The children may be classified as helpers to one or the other group. Such classification should never be given to children to memorize; rather, the children should discover and organize the classifications as a part of their reading experience.

Steps in Outlining

Many children find outlining to be a very difficult skill and one which demands a great deal of thinking. Even some college students are insecure in dealing with this procedure. If outlining is taught in a number of steps and if these steps are introduced gradually over a considerable period of time, the learning can be greatly simplified, and children will also become secure in its use. One of the first steps is to help children select the main idea in a paragraph. Another step closely related to this is to organize the main ideas to aid recall. The selection of subtopics under main ideas is added after children have considerable skill in the other steps. The actual construction of an outline is the last step and makes use of all the other previous abilities.

If teachers continue some of the very simple procedures suggested in the chapter on "Reading for Thought in the Primary Grades," the children will make the transition to more formal outlining without undue effort. The making of lists of materials needed for the social studies, objects to be made, new words acquired in the study of a unit, steps in planning and preparing for a trip, and so forth will give children experience in organizing related topics. The preparation of simple lists of topics read and discussed in connection with stories will also provide experience in selecting main ideas. Choosing titles for experience stories and children's individual stories helps provide readiness for selecting main ideas. The more formal process of selecting main ideas may be begun in the fifth or sixth grades. By the seventh and eighth grades, average and superior readers are likely to have mastered the preparation of an outline with independence if all teachers of these grades have consistently helped them master the skills, step by step.

Organizing for Main Ideas. When introducing formal outlining, the knowledge that the main thought is usually given in either the first or last sentence in the paragraph is helpful to children. They must also know, however, that the main idea is occasionally found in the body of the paragraph. As a first step the teacher may select several paragraphs with main ideas in the first sentences since these are the easiest to analyze. Without telling the children of the location of the main idea, the teacher may guide them to select the sentence in each paragraph which they feel is most important and which tells most about the rest of the paragraph. Children volunteering their choices must justify their reason for choosing a given sentence. If several choices are made, the children should evaluate each and eventually select the best sentence. A little practice of this sort each day is much better than a long period spent at one time.

Eventually the children will notice that the main thought in these paragraphs chosen by the teacher is always in the first sentences of the paragraph. When this occurs, the teacher may move to the second step without telling the children of her strategy. To do this she may select paragraphs containing the main ideas at the ends of the paragraphs. Some strong arguments may take place when some children expect to find the main idea at the beginning and others realize that the pattern has been changed in the new paragraphs. Children should always be permitted to make these selections and tell their reasons for so doing.

When the children begin to realize that the main ideas are now located either at the beginning or the end of the paragraphs, the teacher may follow the third step. She may now add some paragraphs that contain the main thought in sentences in the bodies of these paragraphs. More time may be required for children to master the ability to locate these sentences than was required for the other types. Eventually, children should be able to locate the main thought, regardless of position in the paragraph.

The last and most difficult step for children is to analyze paragraphs in which the main thought is not definitely stated and to put this main thought into their own words. If sufficient time has been taken to help children master the previous steps and if children's security has been built with care, this last step in the thinking process should be mastered without undue difficulty.

If the children have difficulty in selecting the sentence containing the main idea during any step, the teacher may select these sentences in advance and put them on the board in mixed order. In this way the children are not required to select the sentences containing the main idea but merely to identify them when they are listed out of proper sequence. When the children gain self-confidence in this skill, the teacher may go back to helping the children select the main idea without a crutch. After practice in identifying main ideas, they should have a clear idea of the procedure and should be able to select main ideas independently.

Some children progress much more rapidly than others. Progress through these steps must be paced to each child's level, or frustration and later difficulty will result. Whenever this process can be taught in connection with a real problem in the social studies, it will carry more interest, and children will later be able to apply it more successfully.

Organizing to Take Notes. When children are able to select key sentences, they are ready for help in reducing them to phrases or even words. Hovious [2] suggests that the children may be guided to word sentences as though they were telegrams. They must eliminate every nonessential word. The remaining words may then serve as notes to remind the children of the thought in each paragraph. If several ideas are included in a paragraph, the sentences containing these may also be restated to eliminate surplus words. For example, the key sentence, "The wagons were strong and well made," could be reduced to "Wagons" and "Strong." These words should then be inverted to read "Strong wagons." These two words should serve as the key to help children recall how they were made, the materials used, and the reinforcements added to give strength.

The wise teacher carries on this work with children as long as they seem to need help. The children who are able rapidly to master this ability to take notes may be released to work on problems of their own while the teacher continues to work with the slower readers until they have also mastered this ability. Teachers should provide help for children in their reading groups until they have real insight into and mastery of this process so that little reteaching will be required in later grades.

After the children have learned to select key words to represent the thought of a paragraph, they may take turns telling what they remember about the paragraph without their books. This technique is an important one in helping children use notes in making reports. An example of the use of key words to represent a thought may be illustrated by the use of the words "Making Camp." After the children have read the paragraph, these key words should help them think of various information which they found in the paragraph. They may recall what the men did to set up camp, how the women and children helped, what they did with the horses and oxen, how they cooked their food, where they slept at night, and the reasons for the things they did. As the children practice with key words, they will learn how to use notes in giving simple reports.

Upper-grade children will probably deal with more abstract material. They may read about such a topic as "The Invention of the Cotton Gin." A key word for one of the paragraphs may be stated as, "The Inventor" and another one may be stated as, "Need." The children will then use these words to guide them in recalling as much as they can

[2] Carol Hovious, *Flying the Print Ways* (Boston: D. C. Heath and Co., 1938), p. 163.

about each topic. If the children are studying in the social studies about how people in the south live and earn their livelihood, such topics will have more meaning than they would if concerned with mere isolated topics in a book.

Organizing to Aid Recall. When children are able to select the key sentence in each paragraph and to reduce it to a word or phrase, they will be able to apply these abilities to a plan of study that should be of considerable value to them. The SQ3R method described by Robinson has been found to be very helpful with older students and can very easily be adapted for the use of children in the intermediate and upper grades.[3] Suggested steps adapted for children of this age and suitable for application in the content fields, such as the social studies, are:

1. Guide children to read and discuss the introductory paragraphs of a selection to discover the particular aspect of the topic to be considered. Also survey the summary in the same way, if one is provided.
2. Guide children to read the first caption or key sentence and to change it into a question.
3. Guide the children to read silently to answer this question.
4. With the books closed, help pupils discuss the answer to the question. Also, guide pupils to review other ideas gained from the part of the selection they read. Jot down words or phrases on the board to help in recalling these points as pupils decide and dictate which are important and what words to use.
5. After the whole lesson has been studied in this manner, help children review all the notes. Then cover the notes on the board with wrapping paper or other material and help children recall the important ideas from memory.

In the beginning, selections may be limited to one paragraph. Paragraphs may be added gradually, but the selections should be kept short when working with younger intermediate children. Most upper-grade children should be able to cover a part or all of a chapter, depending upon the length and complexity of the material. A testing type of review immediately after the last step was found to reduce forgetting from 80 per cent to 20 per cent with high school students. Perhaps an informal review without notes on the second day might serve as well as a test for intermediate children. This technique could well be applied to preparation for making short reports in the intermediate grades.

Organizing to Make an Outline. When children are able to select the main idea or topic sentence in a paragraph, they should also have help in selecting subtopics as the next step in making an outline. The

[3] F. P. Robinson, "Study Skills for Superior Students in Secondary School," *The Reading Teacher*, XV (Sept. 1961), 29–33, 37.

teacher should select a paragraph that contains a clear-cut topic sentence and very definite subtopics. She should then explain that the subtopics must either add to or give more details concerning the topic sentence and must, therefore, relate to the latter. As the children make suggestions for subtopics, a child may write them on the board under the main topic. The teacher may take all the ideas suggested by the children and then help them evaluate these to make sure that they are true subtopics and do not overlap each other unduly.

To help the children, the teacher may sometimes select and put a list of several main topics on the board. Opposite these she may put in mixed order several subtopics for each paragraph. For example, the subtopics for the first item may be scattered so that one is opposite the second main topic, another is opposite the third main topic, and the third is opposite the first main topic. Other subtopics will be scattered in the same way. An example of a scrambled outline on a very simple topic is given in Figure 17-1.

SAN FRANCISCO HARBOR IN EARLY DAYS

Main Topics	Sub-topics
1. Use of ships	Mexico Tools River boats
2. Places from which ships came	City prison Hotels Whaling ships
3. Kinds of boats and ships	Food China Clothing
4. Goods needed by people	South America Stores Ferry boats Machinery Clipper ships

(The above outline concerns the San Francisco harbor in early days during the gold rush. Some of the smaller ships were used for buildings such as stores, hotels, and even the city prison because of a shortage of buildings. The other sections are self-explanatory.)

Fig. 17–1. A sample exercise to help children learn to use sub-headings.

The children may then discuss each topic to decide where it belongs. A child may serve as a recorder to list each main topic and the proper subtopics underneath it as the children make suggestions so that the final result is in the form of a simple outline. Whenever possible, topics should be taken from the social studies or some content material in order to serve some real purpose as part of the activities of the class. Outlines should be kept as simple as possible in the intermediate grades. Children in the upper grades may learn how to make more complex outlines, but unnecessary complexity should be avoided.

Steps in Summarizing

Ability to summarize involves some of the skills learned in outlining, particularly ability to select main ideas. In summarizing the material from a few pages, the child may depend heavily on the main ideas in each paragraph. Some may be eliminated because they are not sufficiently important for inclusion. If the summary includes the thought from longer material or an entire chapter, several main thoughts may be grouped under one topic, if possible.

A chapter in one of the sixth-grade readers by Yoakam and others tells the story of ships.[4] Very helpful captions are used to guide the reading. Some of these captions that may be grouped include "Ships of the Period of Discovery," "The Development of American Ships," "The First Great American Ship of War," and "American Packet and Clipper Ships." The information on these eight pages may be summarized in the following manner:

The ships used by Columbus and some of the other explorers were known as caravels. They were faster than the early cargo ships, but were rather heavy and sturdy with a square stern. The British built lower and still faster ships and were therefore able to defeat the Spanish Armada. Ship building became an important industry in America because of trade with distant places. The clipper ships were long, streamlined, and very fast. Because of their speed they helped make shipping an important occupation in the early days of America.

When captions are not included in the text or reference book, the children may be able to make their summaries from sentences containing the main ideas. Even some of these topic sentences which refer to details will be eliminated. When the number of sentences has been reduced as much as possible, the children may then restate the ideas in their own words, eliminating all the unimportant words and combining as many ideas as possible. Writing titles for stories and headlines for articles are activities that help children state important ideas briefly.

THINKING SKILLS IN THE CONTENT FIELDS

In order to choose a grade level that would apply most widely in helping teachers from the fourth to the eight grade, an example of a

[4] Gerald Yoakam, M. Madilene Veverka, and Louise Abney, *From Every Land* (River Forest, Ill.: Laidlaw Brothers, 1941), 209–32.

social studies unit in the sixth grade has been selected for description. Only those phases of the work that lead to or illustrate thinking needed in locating and in organizing information are discussed.

Initiating the Unit

The children in Mrs. Stone's sixth grade had just completed a unit on Mexico and were ready to study how people in Canada work, live, and enjoy leisure time as their next unit in social studies. In order to arouse interest in the new unit, Mrs. Stone had mounted a large, clear, colored map of Canada and had placed it in the center of the bulletin board. Above the map she had pinned the caption, "Who Are These Neighbors?" Around the sides of the map and across the bottom she had pinned bright, clear pictures of various places and people at work in different sections of Canada.

On her last trip to a large city, she had secured several Canadian newspapers and travel magazines showing and describing scenes in Canada. These she placed on a table under the bulletin board. She had located some interesting books about Canada geared to a variety of reading levels and had placed these on the library table. She had arranged several books on holders opened to attractive pictures and had placed book markers in other books at interesting places. She had secured a few samples of wood typical of the timber grown in Canada, a piece of beaver fur, and a pair of ski poles and had placed them on a display table. She had also secured a good general film for introducing the topic of Canada to the children.

When the children arrived the next day, Mrs. Stone encouraged them to browse among the books, newspapers, and magazines and to look at the bulletin board and display table. As they moved quietly around the room, they began to ask questions. When they returned to their seats, Mrs. Stone asked them to dictate these questions to be put on a chart. They dictated the questions while one of the children put them on a large, lined sheet of newsprint clipped over the chalk board. In this way they started their use of maps and charts even during the initiation of the unit. After some questions had been recorded, Mrs. Stone suggested that the children view the film to see if they might find some of their answers while watching it.

Using Reference Materials

When the children began work on their unit, they formed committees, about seven in all, and chose problems for their work. Some of them chose to work on the construction of models such as that of a fishing weir, fur-bearing animals of papier mâché, and boats used in carrying

These children have begun the writing of a play and will submit their work to their editor as they progress. (Courtesy California State Department of Education.)

freight on the Great Lakes. Other committees chose to work on the making of costumes worn by groups during celebrations, a diorama of Niagara Falls, a diorama of a northern hunter using dogs and sled in a snow scene, and a map of resources and products of Canada. As work went on, questions arose and were recorded on charts. The children used many references in order to make sure that their models and other articles were correctly made and authentic. Most of the reference techniques had been introduced at a previous time, but some children needed help in remembering how to use glossaries, encyclopedias, and the card catalog. The slowest readers gained a good deal of information by referring to some of the many excellent pictures Mrs. Stone had collected for her file.

Applying and Reviewing Reference Skills. When the children used magazines and newspapers for reference, they skimmed through headlines and captions in order to find material applicable to their problems. When they found sections that seemed applicable, they also skimmed these to make sure that the material was of value. As they read articles in newspapers, magazines, and books, the children applied their note-taking techniques.

When Mrs. Stone found a number of children who were insecure in ability to take notes and use outlines despite their earlier knowledge, she usually called them together in a group for special help. She selected a set of reading books that were easy enough for the slowest readers in this group. She located an explanatory selection with clear-cut topic sentences and subtopics. She then helped the children understand why they were having difficulty and used this selection to review techniques in the choice of sentences containing main ideas, in reducing these to words and phrases, and in selecting subtopics. Releasing the children who grasped the techniques easily, she sometimes spent several days working with those who had the most difficulty until these children felt that they were ready to go back to independent work.

Clarifying Concepts. Sometimes children needed help with vocabulary and the development of concepts. Mrs. Stone helped them use pictures whenever possible and encouraged a discussion of some of the new words by the class, as a whole, during the planning or evaluation period. Children who had more experience than others were often able to add interesting points in the clarification of some concepts. The children who had traveled in at least one or more parts of Canada made especially valuable contributions. When an average reader had difficulty with the terminology in an encyclopedia, Mrs. Stone usually encouraged him to choose another child to help him. Children became very adept in selecting helpers who had adequate background and skill. If a few children wanted to re-project a film or film strip, Mrs. Stone suggested that they secure the help of one of the children who had been trained to use the projector and to work in a corner of the room that could be most easily darkened.

Applying Map and Globe Skills. The children decided to make a relief map in addition to the products map on which they were already working. After the members of the committee projected the outline of the map and were ready to begin work on the terrain, they found that they had forgotten how to compute the scale of miles. Mrs. Stone encouraged the children to bring the problems before the entire class during the planning period so that other children might help them with suggestions and, at the same time, review this process. With the help of the entire class, the scale was computed and another scale was selected for use in making the elevations. If the scale of miles for the map as a whole had been applied to the elevations, the difference between the valleys and the mountain peaks would have been too small to observe. The children therefore used a half inch to represent a thousand feet in elevation, a figure they had used and found successful when making the mountains for their relief map of Mexico.

The children working on the products map decided to use lines to show longitude and latitude on their map and needed some help from the class and teacher in making these correctly. The members of both committees discussed the influence of latitude and altitude on the climate of various parts of Canada and its effect on the types of crops that can be raised in this country. The group working on distribution and cultural backgrounds of the population applied the knowledge gained from these committees to help them understand why most of the people lived along the southern borders of the country. At times, the members of these committees needed the help of the class members in using symbols for various types of highways, airports, railroads, the capitals of the provinces, national parks, and fish hatcheries. Some children also needed help in the use of the globe when estimating distances of air routes to other parts of the world.

Evaluating Progress.   Each day the work of one or two committees was evaluated in detail, and brief constructive comments were made regarding the work of the other committees. The evaluation was usually carried on with the entire class. If members of a committee had been using reference materials to discover needed information, for example, for their products map, they reported as much information as they had been able to secure when their turn came for evaluation, even though they had not finished their task. If they were looking for information regarding the types of grain produced in Canada and the areas where the grain was grown, for example, they would share with the class whatever information they had discovered. Since they knew in advance on what day they would be expected to make their detailed report, this committee usually spent their time before evaluation on that day summarizing what they had learned up to that point. Each child made notes to summarize his reading and to remind him of the part he would discuss during the evaluation. The committee chairman usually brought the model under construction to the front of the room to demonstrate progress, and each committee member tried to find a picture or some visual aid to illustrate his report. Mrs. Stone usually encouraged each member of the committee to share in the report so that he would have a need to use techniques of summarizing and reporting. By sharing in the report, each child's part was brief. It was also easier for the children to prepare brief summaries and to keep the class interested while they gave the reports.

When children brought in articles out of magazines or newspapers, Mrs. Stone encouraged the children to ask about the source of this material to be sure that it was authentic. If any differences were found between the information in articles and information found in textbooks and references, the children checked a third source such as an encyclopedia in order to discover which information was authentic.

SUMMARY

Teachers review alphabetizing and provide purposeful situations to help children learn techniques in locating needed information. They also guide children to develop the ability to use tables of content, indexes, and glossaries. Ability to use the dictionary, encyclopedia, the card catalog, maps, charts, and graphs are also taught in the intermediate grades. Children need help to improve their ability to use headings, captions, and skimming techniques in order to locate information in books, newspapers, and magazines and must learn how to use films to add to their information and understandings. As they organize information for use in making reports and in producing authentic models and other articles, they gain ability in using skills in classification, outlining, and summarizing.

18

Interpretive Reading

In the previous chapter, suggestions have been given for developing skills in locating and organizing information for purposes that are important to the child. In addition to skills in organizing, the child needs to develop skills in interpreting and appreciating reading material.

SKILLS IN INTERPRETIVE READING

Interpretive skills demand ability to read between the lines and beyond the material. The reader comprehends the information provided but goes beyond this step by making comparisons and inferences and drawing conclusions. He may also observe relationships among ideas and look for cause and effect in situations described in reading material. He tends to make greater use of his own background of experience in its relation to the content he is reading than when organizing information. Relationships are rather easy to observe when they apply to concrete objects, but more difficult when the child must see relationships among abstract ideas.

Interpretation of Pictures

Pictures may be interpreted on three levels: (1) the child may merely enumerate the objects in the pictures, (2) he may describe the objects, adding some detail, or (3) he may interpret the meaning of the pictures. Work with pictures in the intermediate and upper grades involves the third level, that of interpretation. Interpretation of pictures may seem to be a rather simple ability for children in the middle grades, but many new understandings may be added as the child acquires greater depth and ability to see more complex relationships.

Using Pictures to Relate Experience and Make Inferences. A newspaper picture, showing a political speaker in a South American city talking to a crowd of people behind whom are located several policemen, has little meaning to most primary children. To an advanced middle-grade child and most upper-grade children, however, this picture would suggest that the situation was probably political, and that the speaker might be trying to start a revolution against the government in power. Although these children would have no realization of the types of oppression and the poverty experienced by some groups of people, discussion should help deepen the implications and make the picture more meaningful. The teacher uses picture interpretation as a readiness step to more advanced interpretive skills through reading material. She also helps children extend their experiences vicariously through the interpretation of pictures.

Some of the ways the teacher helps children with pictures are very similar to those she will later use with reading material. The first step is to relate the content of the picture to the children's experiences in order to carry them as far as possible in their understandings. She may then help the children compare the economic situation in the United States, including labor strikes, with the political situation in the country pictured. She helps the children observe the clothing of the revolutionists, which may indicate their impoverishment. She may also help the children observe the drawn faces and undernourished bodies of the revolutionists. The buildings in the background may help the children understand more about the people if the scene is laid in a slum or factory area. The time of day may help the children draw conclusions regarding whether or not the people are employed. From all these aspects of the picture, the children are guided to make inferences and draw conclusions regarding not only the revolutionary characters of the scene, but also the apparent justification of the actions of people who are trying to better their lot.

Using Pictures to Discover Relationships in Size. As children extend their experiences vicariously through reading, they meet new concepts and add new vocabulary to their present stock. Children need help in understanding relationships in size of various objects to acquire accurate concepts. Although many children have seen jet airplanes in flight, some may not have seen them on the ground. The size of jet airplanes, especially those used for crossing the continent and flying to other countries, is impressive. Even the knowledge of the number of passengers carried by such a plane does not prepare the observer to expect their

tremendous size. When a child sees a picture of a jet on the ground beside a DC plane, a local transport plane, he can begin to gain an idea
of the size of the jet. If small private passenger planes such as the Piper
Cub are also shown in the picture, the child begins to realize how huge
the jet airplanes are and has a better concept of the relationship in size
of these various planes.

Children are fascinated by the new modes of space travel. When children had an opportunity to see on television the various space capsules,
they discussed them with great excitement. They were impressed by the
fact that they were smaller than they had expected. The opportunity
to see astronauts standing beside the capsules provided the children with
a very clear concept of the relationship of its size to the size of a man.

Using Pictures to Discover Relationships in Time. After children
have had an opportunity to study various eras in history, they are able
to use pictures to give them clues to the approximate era illustrated.
When they see men riding on horseback costumed in mail with spears
and shields, they are likely to decide from the picture that the scene is
located in the age of knighthood or in the Feudal Ages. A picture of
women costumed in hoop skirts and men in fitted velvet jackets and knee
trousers may help the child relate the picture to the colonial era in
America.

A picture of a biplane with one set of wings below the fuselage and
the other set above and with an open cockpit tells the child who knows
about airplanes that such a plane might have been used in World War I
or near that period. A picture of an early steam automobile on the street
near a horse drawn carriage would help the child relate the picture to
the early twentieth century.

Using Pictures to Discover Relationships in Position. A picture showing an automobile driver sitting on the right hand side of the front seat
and driving in the left lane would help a child who knew something
about customs in other countries realize that the picture was located in
a foreign country. Other details would be needed to decide upon the
specific country. If a picture shows a driver sitting on the right hand
side of the front seat but driving in the right hand lane, the child who
knows about foreign cars will notice the relationship of the position of
the driver to the position of the car. He will then be able to conclude
that the driver is probably driving a car which he purchased in a foreign
country but is now driving in this country. Some teachers begin a study
with a large wall map of the area of interest to help children understand
relationships of position.

When children study about the Feudal Ages they may learn about
the custom of seating serfs at the dining table below the salt, that is,

nearer the kitchen, and seating the nobility above the salt. When a child knows this custom and sees a picture of a table divided in this manner, he is able to interpret the relation in position of the people at the table to the era in which this custom was followed.

Ability To Relate Content to Experience

The teacher helps children interpret their reading by relating content to their experiences from the very beginning. The use of experience is of great value in helping children develop concepts. As children progress through the middle and upper grades, they increase their experiences gradually both through real and vicarious activities. As a result, the teacher has more and more background upon which to draw. Even fourth-grade children extend their experiences vicariously through the use of pictures, listening, reading, and viewing television. All these experiences provide more background. The teacher continues to help the children discuss their experiences in order to relate new vocabulary and ideas to their reading.

Using a Variety of Sources. Children in the fourth grade are beginning to expand their vocabularies by means of the dictionary. The teacher should continue to give guidance to some children in helping them relate the dictionary definitions to their experiences to help them build this habit. Children also need continuous help from the teacher as they meet new sources of ideas, such as the newspaper, magazines, and the encyclopedia. Pictures often accompany articles in these materials which the teacher can use to help the children clarify their understandings. It is very important to give the children help in the beginning in uses of the atlas, the globe, maps, tables, charts, and graphs so that they will have experience to draw upon when they begin to work independently.

Using Experiences to Generalize. As children acquire an increasing background of experiences, the teacher may begin to help them interpret these experiences by guiding them to draw the ideas together by means of generalizations. In the fourth grade, for example, the children find that the crops grown in their own state include apples, pears, and other fruits. Turnips, cabbage, some corn, carrots, potatoes, and other vegetables are also raised in the state, and beef and dairy cattle are commonly produced. The teacher may then guide the children to decide the general type of industry most common in the state. The children may conclude that farming is a good name. By asking for further synonyms, however, some child may be able to supply the word, agriculture. The children may also add the word, agrarian, as an adjective applied to an agriculture population. Although not all of the children may incorporate these words in their own vocabularies, they will have some ideas of their meanings.

Ability To Make Comparisons

Comparisons have been made in very simple terms in the primary grades. Young children have been able to compare objects for size, color, and location. In the intermediate and upper grades comparisons are also used as a means of helping children interpret reading material. The teacher's role is that of arousing and challenging interest in problems involving comparisons. She then makes sure that material is available in reference and supplementary books. She helps the children with skills in locating material and in taking notes so that they may be used in later comparisons. She may help the children with various types of presentations, such as general discussions, panels, and even an occasional debate. Whenever ideas may be compared successfully with pictures, graphs, tables, and other types of charts as well as pictures, she helps the children to decide on and plan the type of pictorial presentation they wish to use and makes material available to them. She carries on these activities with suggestions when needed and gives children freedom to make their own choices.

Comparing Partially Abstract Ideas. The younger intermediate children are able to compare abstract ideas if they can see or make use of objects along with these abstract ideas. They are beginning to have a little better concept of time and can make some comparisons in this area. They can compare ways people lived in early days with the way people live today, especially if they are able to see some of the artifacts, such as kerosene lamps, wood- and coal-burning stoves, and old firearms, probably in a museum.

Comparing Abstract Ideas. Older children may compare the use of apprenticeships in early days with the training provided by today's trade schools. They may compare ways of farming in underprivileged countries with agricultural methods used in the United States today. In making such comparisons, the children should realize how and why the underprivileged peoples are handicapped, both in terms of financial ability and overcrowded conditions which make the use of large farm equipment impossible. They may compare the factory of a few years ago with today's automation and may relate it to problems resulting from the displacement of labor. A comparison of the attitude of American statesmen toward international affairs from Colonial times to the present gives children an understanding based on a comparison of trends to move away from isolationism and toward responsibility for the people of other countries.

Ability To Analyze Propaganda

Another aspect of interpretive reading is the ability to analyze propaganda. Children need help in learning to detect propaganda clues since many people tend to believe everything they see in print, and others also believe all they hear on the radio and television.

Analyzing Name-Calling. One of the most common propaganda techniques in political life is that of name-calling. If one political group wishes to undermine the other, they use such words as "red," "communist," "socialistic," "radical," and "bureaucratic" among others.

Analyzing Glittering Generalities. Political parties also use glittering generalities, thereby avoiding a discussion of the real issues. Some generalities that have been mentioned in connection with the analysis of news include belief in the family, the church and the flag. Others include the country, democracy, and free enterprise, which is usually applied to competition among small business firms rather than among corporations.

Analyzing Identification with Prestige. Identification with prestige is very commonly used on television and in the newspapers. A moving picture star is shown smoking a cigarette. The public, of course, is supposed to believe that the film star is smoking the cigarette advertised below. In another type "young" folks choose a certain type of soft drink to be popular and have a good time socially. Society matrons are shown using various types of cosmetics in order to provide a touch of glamor to the product.

Analyzing Testimonials. Testimonials are often used in connection with a class of people, always mentioned vaguely. Four out of five physicians, dentists, or veterinarians sponsor a certain product. The number of professional people questioned is left to the imagination of the reader.

Analyzing the Bandwagon Effect. In the bandwagon effect a statement is made that everyone uses a certain product, votes a certain way, or goes to certain places. If the reader does not follow the crowd, he may seem queer to other people.

Analyzing Card Stacking. Card stacking refers to a variety of ways of misusing statistics or distorting facts. One of the most common is to make a vague statement that one product is twice as good as other leading brands, or three times as effective, or lasts four times longer. The term "twice as good" is left for the reader to fill in mentally. No actual statistics are ever given in connection with these claims. Another form of card stacking is the use of the expression "pennies a day" in reference to a variety of commodities. When the reader goes to the trouble of finding out the price, he may suffer a rude shock.

Ability To Discover Relationships

The ability to interpret reading by discovering relationships among various factors demands a high degree of comprehension and considerable thinking in the reading process. Simple relationships are found in terms of size, time, and position, among others. The sequence of ideas and the relationship of specific to general ideas are also an aspect of this problem. The same sort of relationship may be found in terms of subordinate ideas to main ideas, in cause and effect, and in other similar areas.

The most important point for the teacher to emphasize is the element of discovery. If the teacher points out relationships, they will have little meaning for the children and may soon be forgotten. If the child is guided to discover the relationships for himself, they will have much more meaning for him and will tend to be retained for a much longer time.

Discovering Relationships in Size. When children study about the pioneer movement they may compare the size of covered wagons with today's automobile and house trailer to discover the relationship in size of one to the other. When intermediate children study about their state, their country, and the world at large, the wise teacher helps them relate the size of each new country to be studied with their own state. If children have made an outline map of their own state on lightweight wrapping paper according to a specific scale of miles, they may make the same type of map according to the same scale for the new country to be studied. They may lay one paper directly over the other to compare the sizes of the two areas. If the outline has been made with a wide tip fountain brush, the heavy black lines on the lower map will show through on the upper map. In this way, the children may directly compare the size of this new country with that of their own state.

Discovering Relationships in Time. Relationships in time are more difficult for intermediate-grade children because they lack experience due to their own lifespans. Upper-grade children have a somewhat better understanding of time relationships. The use of symbols can be very helpful to children in seeing these relationships. Children may be interested in comparing Lindbergh's first flight time across the Atlantic with the time spent in traveling across the Atlantic by jet today. Time may be represented on a chart by squares or circles to stand for hours or days.

A time line is valuable in helping children discover relationships in time. A time line of inventions since revolutionary days in the United States would show a few scattered early inventions followed by pyramiding of inventions in modern times. Many would be omitted from the area representing modern times because of lack of adequate space and because of inadequate opportunities to know about all modern inventions. A time line is set up to scale using an inch or foot as a unit to record a specific amount of time. For example, a foot may represent twenty-five or fifty years. Children may draw pictures of the inventions, paint them so that they will stand out clearly across the room, and mount them on the time line at the proper date.

Discovering Relationships in Position. Children today are deeply interested in spatial relationships as they follow the work with space missiles, satellites, and rockets. They are much more able than adults to encompass the idea of men traveling in space, not only to the moon but to the planets and stars. Because of this interest, they are eager to read about the relationships of the position of the earth to the moon and planets and also to stars and constellations. They enjoy reading directions for making small-scale planetariums, which show the correct relationship of objects in the sky.

Discovering Relationships between Specific and General Ideas. Children as well as adults tend to generalize about the characteristics of other peoples. Oriental people may all seem to look alike and to possess certain characteristics in common to the child who does not know these people personally. If, however, an Oriental child enters the class, he becomes an example of the specific. The children become accustomed to his features and personality. When another Oriental child enrolls in the same class, he is found to be a distinct personality and is widely different in many ways from the first Oriental child. Gradually children learn through experience and reading that the general ideas they had about Oriental people were too limited, and they eventually expand their concepts to cover a wide variety of characteristics. Elizabeth Foreman Lewis and Pearl Buck have written stories to help acquaint children with the human qualities of the Chinese.

Children may discover relationships between general and specific ideas when they study about astral bodies. The child who is interested in space may think that stars and planets are the same. As he begins to read more about these heavenly bodies, he finds crucial differences between them. He later learns that even planets differ greatly among each other in size, position, surface temperatures, and other characteristics.

Discovering Relationships between Cause and Effect. Younger intermediate children are often interested in weather and can be helped to discover the cause of rain through a few simple science experiments. Children may discover the loss of water when two jars containing equal amounts of water are placed side by side. The water level should be marked on each glass. If one jar is covered and the other is left un-covered, the children will discover that the water level in the uncovered jar gradually lowers. They may make various guesses regarding the cause. These guesses, whether correct or not, are written on the board. The teacher then guides the children to read to discover if they were cor-rect in any of their hypotheses concerning the loss of water in one jar. They may also observe a terrarium and refer to books to find the causes of the evaporation and condensation in the water cycle.

Older children may observe soil erosion, usually in the gullies in their immediate areas. The teacher may help them with the meanings of the terms and guide them to hunt for causes in reference materials. Older children may also be interested in causes of such problems as unemploy-ment in the early days of inventions when hand labor was replaced by machinery. As the children discover the feelings and attitudes of people when machinery replaced hand work, they may be guided to look for the effects of automation on today's labor market. They may also read to discover the effect of automation in terms of a gradual shift in employ-ment from unskilled and skilled labor to increased employment in the service areas.

Ability To Make Inferences and Draw Conclusions

Although much literature provides opportunity for children to make inferences, some factual material also makes this provision. Inferences from factual reading material may be made in regard to climate, for ex-ample. If the coldness of the climate is emphasized in a story, the pupil may infer that the site of the story is the north or in a high altitude. The drawing of conclusions requires this ability to use clues.

Making Inferences Regarding Location. The teacher uses questions to help the children look for clues regarding the setting of a story. She may use the questions to guide the children before they begin to read, or, with a more advanced group, she may use the questions later to discover if the children are developing the habit of noticing such clues. For ex-ample, if children in a story are dressed in mukluks and fur coats with hoods, the readers will probably infer that the story is about Alaska or some other cold area. If the story includes a reference to a cyclone, children may infer that this story is set in the middle western states. If monsoons are mentioned, the children may decide that the story is prob-ably set in India, and the mention of earthquakes leads them to infer that the story is set in California, Japan, or South America. Other clues in the story, such as the type of clothing worn, some of the buildings, or some of the occupations of the people may help the child locate the setting of the story more definitely.

Making Inferences Regarding Status.   Although economic status is not of vital importance to most intermediate grade children, some of its implications or deprivations may affect them profoundly. A story of a little girl who is heartbroken because her rag doll has lost a leg may lead the children to infer that this doll may be her favorite toy. If the child writes a letter for a new doll to Santa Claus, the children may infer that the broken doll was not only deeply loved but also the only one she had. Privileged children may have difficulty understanding how such a child would feel, but their understanding may be increased if the teacher helps them apply the situation to the loss of a beloved pet. Another story may tell of a child who has many toys, but who lives in an apartment. He has no one with whom to play and spends much of his time looking out the window at children passing by. From such a situation, the children might infer that he is lonely and that his many toys do not take the place of a playmate.

Older children may make inferences from the story of a boy who enters junior high school from another area. From his actions (he walks through the hall alone, he seems afraid to speak to other children, and he eats his lunch alone) the children may infer that he is shy, has difficulty in making new friends, and needs the help of a sensitive peer who will make the first advance. Another type of inference may be made from the story of a wealthy boy who has only one close friend, another child of a wealthy family. These boys stay by themselves and refuse other children's invitations. If another child asks them to go to the movies with him, they reply that they have their own projector and movies. If they are invited to join a scout troop, they reply that they are not allowed to associate with most of the boys in the troop. The implications from such a story would be fairly clear to any upper-grade child. How these children feel and what could be done to improve their situations would serve as the focus for challenging and vital discussions.

Drawing Conclusions from Several Clues.   The ability to draw conclusions is closely related to the ability to make inferences but may be based on a wide variety of clues. For example, several clues in a story about a woodsman following a path through the forest may lead to a conclusion. The first clue may be a few small broken branches, suggesting that either a man or a tall animal has passed by. Later the woodsman may see a man's footprint in a bog in the forest. Still farther along he may notice a wisp of cotton print cloth caught on a thorny branch, and even later he may find the footprint of a woman in another marshy spot.

For evaluation and improvement of the dialogue and quality of action, children are reading the parts in a play they have written. (Courtesy of the California State Department of Education.)

By this time the children reading the story, as well as the woodsman, have concluded that at least two people have gone along the trail ahead of the woodsman. If a further clue of rain the previous night is added, the children will decide that the people have gone along the trail the same day as the woodsman. Again the teacher uses questions to help the children draw their conclusions. Without help, the children may merely read for the adventure but fail to take account of the more subtle and challenging elements of the story.

Ability To Solve Problems

Dewey, along with other educators, lists a number of steps in the solving of a problem including the feeling of need, the development of a purpose, the collection of data and its organization in relation to a problem, the establishment of an hypothesis, the testing of the hypothesis, and some conclusion concerning the problem. In children's thinking, most of the worthwhile problems of value to them will be likely to arise in the content fields.

Solving Problems in Play Writing.	An example of such a process may be found in the desire of a committee to write a play about village life in Mexico. The children have chosen the topic and will need to decide upon a way of presenting their information to the class, thus providing the feeling of need. After discussing a variety of ways to organize the information, the children may decide that they would like to write a play, thus developing a purpose. In order to be sure that the costumes, the market place, the home that will be included, and all other properties are authentic, the children must read from a variety of sources. After they have secured enough information to go to work, they must decide on the material to represent the home and the market place and also what part of each will be chosen.

Since children will take part in this play, they will want to make the properties full size. They may discuss the use of wrapping paper, cardboard, and wood as possible materials. Since they want the material to look like adobe bricks, they may set up the hypothesis that paper is most easily painted to look like the authentic materials and is most available. They will need tall slats or other wood for supports. They must then decide how large to make the room in the home they are planning, how large to make the market place, and where to put these features. They must consult the teacher and other members of the class regarding the space in the room which they wish to use in order to avoid interfering with other activities.

When they have concluded that the use of paper, supported by wood, is the best material for their undertaking, they may proceed with the writing of their play and the construction of their props. Changes in plans may be made from time to time if, for example, the play is found to lack plot or if heavier wood is required for supports for the properties. Many minor adjustments will be made as the children proceed in the solution of their problems. The teacher serves as a consultant and may occasionally prevent rather disastrous mistakes that would be too costly in time or materials and, thus, too discouraging to the children. Errors in minor ways are permitted by the wise teacher, since children learn greater foresight when they make some mistakes. The problem is solved when the children present the play to the class.

Solving Problems in Science.	Science procedures follow problem solving steps rather closely. For example, a small group of children in an upper-grade class were interested in the variation in the length of sound waves resulting from differences in pitch. By skimming through a variety of science books, they found an experiment that might help them discover the effect of pitch on the length of sound waves. After reading the directions, they put sand in a long, glass tube and closed the ends with corks. They then attached a tuning fork with a low pitch to the tube by means of a clamp. When they tapped the tuning fork, the sand in the tube formed mounds at specific intervals which showed, according to the text, the wave lengths for that particular sound. The children made another sound tube in the same way and attached to it a tuning fork with a much higher pitch. When they tapped the second tuning fork, the sand formed into mounds at closer intervals than those in the first tube.

The problem solving steps are clear in this situation. The need arose when the children became interested in finding the differences in the wave lengths of tones, and their purpose was to find an experiment that would help them see or measure the differences. They actually collected their data from one book, but they looked through others to find plans for carrying out their purpose. They accepted the hypothesis from the book that differences in wave lengths can be demonstrated by mounds of sand in a glass tube attached to a tuning fork. They found that the hypothesis was correct when tested and decided that each tone must have a different wave length as shown by the mounds of sand. Apparently the higher tones had shorter wave lengths than the lower tones. These children might wish to experiment with wave lengths of other tones if they were able to find other tuning forks to use in their work.

SKILLS IN APPRECIATIVE READING

Appreciative reading is very closely related to and depends upon interpretive reading. Interpretive skills may be called for in both informative and fictional material. Appreciation usually applies to literary material and depends on clues in relation to motives, emotions, character, mood, and similar aspects of style. The methods of literature are indirect, whereas the methods of informative writing are usually direct. In the latter, the reader is told almost all he needs to know. In literature, only enough is told to challenge the imagination, arouse vivid imagery, and stimulate thought and feeling that the reader himself contributes. If literature is read after the manner of content material or even after the manner of the pulp type of western stories, the child may lose all the values that he might have gained from a deeper type of reading.

Levels of Appreciation

Six levels of fiction are listed by Gainsburg.[1] 1. The first level refers to action alone and includes violence and suspense. 2. In the second level, an element of understanding, motive, or character may be implied

[1] Joseph C. Gainsburg, "Critical Reading is Creative Reading and Needs Creative Teaching," *The Reading Teacher*, XV (Dec. 1961), 185–92; from *The Reading Teacher*, VI (Mar. 1953).

in an action or suspense story. An adventure story, illustrative of courage or persistence in the face of difficulties, may fall in this category. 3. The character of the hero or heroine is less obvious, and the reader's personal reactions may shift as he learns more about the development of a character. The story may also be of the adventure or action type, but the plot is more plausible and the characters are genuine. 4. Although not necessarily of greater complexity, the fourth type of story may describe backgrounds and ways of life that are different from those of the reader. 5. These stories on this level too, are not necessarily more complex, but the emphasis is found in the mood of the story. On the adult level, some of Charlotte Brontë's stories fit into this category as does Lillian Smith's One Hour. 6. Stories of social, personal, and other problems are listed as the sixth level of fiction. The first, and probably the second, level may not be considered of literary quality; however, the other levels should be found in literature.

Use of Clues To Increase Appreciation

The use of clues to discover the character of the hero, his feelings, and his motives are rather difficult for children. If one type of clue is considered at a time, although minor references may be made to others, children may learn how to use these clues to help them in more deeply appreciating the stories they read.

Discovering Clues to Appearance. Many descriptions of fictional characters are found in literature, but sometimes the author gives hints or clues that may throw a spotlight on the most telling aspect of a character's appearance. The discovery of these clues is one of the easiest appreciational skills because the interpretation is made of an objective quality. The following selection beginning with a severe snow storm and taken from "The Fourth Day" in On the Banks of Plum Creek gives a clue to appearance.

Sideways from the peep-hole, Laura glimpsed something dark. A furry big animal was wading deep in the blowing snow. A bear, she thought. It shambled behind the corner of the house and darkened the front window.

"Ma!" she cried. The door opened, the snowy, furry animal came in. Pa's eyes looked out of its face. Pa's voice said, "Have you been good girls while I was gone?" [2]

In a book of myths for older children, the story of "Phaëthon" is taken from the book Gods and Heroes.[3] The meeting of Phaëthon with his

---

[2] Laura Ingalls Wilder, On the Banks of Plum Creek (New York: Harper & Row, 1937).

[3] Gustav Schwab (translated by Olge Marx and Ernst Morwitz), Gods and Heroes (New York: Pantheon Books, Inc., 1946).

father, Phoebus, the sun god, carries clues to the appearance of Phoebus, who sat in his palace, brilliant with gold and flame-red rubies. When Phaëthon came to the palace where he found his father, "He dared not approach too closely, but stopped at a little distance, because he could not endure the glittering, burning nearness."

Sometimes clues to the appearance of animals are found, especially when the animal may be the hero of a story as in the following selection, "The Pulling Bee," from *Justin Morgan Had a Horse.*[4] The "Pulling Bee" referred to a contest to see which horse or team of oxen could pull a large log from the place where it was felled to the saw mill in three attempts. Several dray horses had tried and failed when Evans rode up on his horse called Little Bub. The following is the statement made by a snickering member of the crowd when Evans boasted that his horse could pull the log: "*That* little flea? Why, he's just a sample of a horse. He ain't no bigger than a mouse's whisker! Besides, his tail is so long, he's liable to get all tangled up and break a leg."

Discovering Clues to Story Setting. Clues to settings of stories or situations within stories are rather easy to interpret, although direct descriptions are found more commonly. Sometimes the two are combined, but the following selection by Sperry from *Call it Courage*[5] gives clues only. In the story Mafatu had strong feelings about the sea by which he had been surrounded ever since he was born. The following quotation implies his fear and gives clues to the location of his home: "The thunder of it filled his ears; the crash of it upon the reef, the mutter of it at sunset, the threat and fury of its storms on every hand, where-ever he turned—the sea."

In a selection from "Hitty Goes to Sea," in *Hitty: Her First Hundred Years,*[6] a clue is given to the situation both from the standpoint of the setting and the reason why the old peddler, who carved Hitty, decided to stay and help Captain Preble. "Even when the weather cleared, the roads were impassable for many days and all vessels stormbound in Portland Harbor." In a later part of the story after the family had gone to sea, the following gives some clues to the violence of the storm: "The noise grew to be so great that even the men's shrillest shouts to one another could scarcely be heard above the sloshings and poundings, the thud and crash of waves breaking over and about us."

Discovering Clues to Character. In the case of character, too, inferences tell the reader a great deal. Children do not necessarily learn to

---

[4] Marguerite Henry, *Justin Morgan Had a Horse* (Chicago: Wilson and Follett Co., Follett Publishing Co., 1945).

[5] Armstrong Sperry, *Call it Courage* (New York: The Macmillan Co., 1940).

[6] Rachel Field, *Hitty: Her First Hundred Years* (New York: The Macmillan Co., 1929).

make this kind of inference by themselves. As the teacher guides the discussion of stories with questions, the children begin to become more observant and to learn more from the wording used in a selection in the same way that the woodsman reads stories about people and animals as he travels along the path of a forest. The city dweller, on the other hand, would probably fail to notice animal tracks, broken leaves and small branches, and occasional footprints made by animals or people.

In "The Snow Storm" from *Smoky Bay*,[7] one aspect of Helga's and Sigga's characters is contrasted. Helga had warned Eric to be careful when he went out into the snowstorm to help the farm hands take care of the sheep. Sigga, however, had been worried about the milk that had been spilled because it was a bad sign. The way in which the two waited for Eric to return as they sat in the light of the kerosene lamp is described as follows: ". . . she appeared peaceful in contrast with the nervous Sigga but Nonni saw the knotted frown between her eyes and noticed that her hands lay frequently idle on the embroidery frame." In the meantime Sigga paced the floor and shuddered every time a gust of wind shook the house.

In "Hitty Goes to Sea" by Rachel Field a strong clue to Bill Buckle's character is given in his relation to a little girl and her doll in the following: "Bill Buckle, a big sailor, was our constant companion and we were on such intimate terms with him that he even went as far as to loan Andy his jackknife and showed his tattoo marks."

Discovering Clues to Feelings. Opportunity is provided for children to infer feelings from such words as smiled, frowned, clenched his fists, stamped his foot, and yawned. Sometimes some feeling is reflected by words that tell how an individual enters the room, as "he crept into the room, he stormed into the room, he barged into the room, he entered with head high and back straight, he came in hesitatingly," and so forth.

Much of the discussion of words and expressions may center around the meanings derived from the inferences. The teacher may ask, "Why did John barge into the room? Was he supposed to be there? What did he interrupt? Why didn't he knock before he entered? Did he annoy the people who were already in the room?" Some of these questions may help children understand the situation and some may help them learn more about John. In the same way, the teacher may ask why another character crept stealthily into the room. She may also ask, "Did he belong there? What time of day or night was it? Why did he want to go into the room? Why didn't he want anyone to know that he was there?" Again, the inferences tell much about the feelings of the character.

[7] Steingrimur Arason, *Smoky Bay* (New York: The Macmillan Co., 1942).

Discovering Clues to Mood. In "Hitty Goes to Sea" from *Hitty: Her First Hundred Years* some good examples of foreboding are found. The first sign that trouble might be at hand is found in the expression of Captain Preble, "Everything was *drawing* 'most too well.'" A little later in the story Hitty tells us that, "No more sunny hours of leisure and yarn spinning on deck, but two days and nights of pounding, tossing, and buffeting such as no pen can describe." Later on in the story Hitty quotes Phoebe as follows: "'What's happened, Mother? Are we going to sink?' Phoebe cried seeing the fright in her face." Children's empathy may be developed or increased by discussing how they might have felt had they been in Phoebe's place on the ship. Interesting figures of speech are also found in the same story. Before the storm becomes unduly violent, Captain Preble reassures his wife and tells her that, "I mean to heave to and lay under bare poles till this is over with." Although Andy answers Phoebe's question regarding the meaning of "bare poles," children may need some help with Andy's reply when he said, "Means he don't dast have an inch of sail up." When the storm had subsided Hitty tells us that the boat headed east into the calm and placid South Seas, ". . . heading for what the men all agreed was the best whaling ground, though what ground there was about these miles of sea I could not make out." Since no explanation of whaling grounds is given, children as well as Hitty would need help with this expression. Another figure of speech is found in Andy's remark when he said the following: "'Now they're off for a Nantucket sleighride,' he told Phoebe. 'That's what they call it,' he explained, 'when the harpoon's in fast and they can just pay out the rope an' follow him round.'" Several expressions in this quotation may call for discussion with children who are not familiar with sea-going terms.

WAYS OF HELPING CHILDREN USE CLUES

Some teachers hesitate to bring up a discussion involving clues to interpretive and appreciative reading, because they feel it is necessary to interrupt the children in order to do so. There seems to be no justifiable reason for breaking the children's thought to discuss these clues when the children meet them. The entire selection may be read to the end without interruption. The discussion following the reading can very well center around the implications of the story after a few of the facts have been mentioned by the children. If children have failed to observe some of the important clues to character, feelings, setting, or other matters, an excellent opportunity would be provided for the children to turn back and skim to locate these words. As each child locates a clue, the reading group may turn to the proper place while the child reads the part that gives the clue and justifies his choice. In some cases the choices may be pure description rather than clues. If so, the other children in the group should help the reader analyze his selection to decide under which category it falls. As children take part in such discussions, they gradually learn to observe more carefully and to interpret clues more skillfully. The effect of one discussion will influence the reading of the next story. In this manner children are able to build up skills in interpretive and appreciative reading.

SUMMARY

Skills in interpretive and appreciative reading are needed by intermediate and upper-grade children. Even pictures may need interpretation because of children's lack of familiarity with the setting, the situation, or the people depicted. Children's own background of experience can be brought to bear on the pictures, but often more information and a greater understanding are demanded if children are to discover the full implications of the type of pictures used in the intermediate and upper grades. Pictures may be helpful to children in their discovery of relationships in size, in time, and in position. Children's own experiences are also brought to bear in helping them understand the content of the references they find in a variety of sources and in learning to generalize on the basis of experience and information. Children need help in comparing abstract ideas and in analyzing various types of propaganda. After children have learned to use pictures for discovering various relationships of objects to each other, they may learn to discover these relationships in content and may add skill in discovering inferences from abstract ideas. Inferences of various sorts are found in reading material. Some are adequate as a basis for drawing conclusions. Children may learn to solve problems in connection with their work in social studies, science, and other content fields. A variety of clues may serve to increase children's appreciation of literature. Teachers make use of discussions and guiding questions in helping children learn increasingly better skills in interpretive and appreciative reading.

V

IDEAS FOR
BETTER TEACHING

19

Individualized Reading

In order to avoid some of the weaknesses of reading organized in groups, some teachers prefer to work with children on an individual basis. The trend to teach children individually has been in existence for many years, but each plan offers some modification and some values not found in older plans. The first teaching of reading was carried on individually when the father or mother taught the child the alphabet and helped him spell and pronounce words at a time when many children had no access to schools.

A strong trend toward individualization of instruction in school took place early in the century under the direction of Frederick Burke, who was president of the San Francisco Normal School. Washburne worked with Burke in the early years and later established a plan of individualized instruction in the Winnetka Schools where he was an administrator. Individualization of instruction was also carried on in the Dalton Plan, a plan whereby children signed contracts for the completion of a given amount of work in a specified length of time.

In 1925 Zirbes, Keeler, and Miner compared two programs.[1] In one program individualized reading was practiced and in the other a program of developmental reading was followed. These authors found that the most able readers made the most progress in the individualized program, whereas the slower readers made the most progress in the developmental plan. No difference was found for the average reader. The individualized as well as the developmental programs were probably somewhat different from those practiced in recent times. Studies of the

[1] Laura Zirbes, Katherine Keeler, and Pauline Miner, *Practice Exercises and Silent Reading in the Primary Grades* (New York: Lincoln School of Teachers College, Columbia University, 1925), 4–5.

relative merits of both programs are being made today, and findings seem to vary, with advantages first to one plan and then the other.

PLANS FOR INITIATING AND TEACHING THE PROGRAM

Teachers have used the individualized plan of organizing the reading program on all grade levels beginning with the first grade. The program is more easily managed with older children but has been successfully used with primary children.

Individualized Reading in the First Grade

At least two ways of introducing individualized reading have been followed with success. Both the use of experience stories and group work with basic readers help children acquire a fundamental vocabulary so that they may read simple books with reasonable independence.

Initiation with Experience Stories. Some teachers guide the children to dictate experience stories along with the usual program of readiness activities. At first the teacher may work with the whole class. As soon as she knows the children's levels of reading, she usually finds it more convenient and easier for the children if she groups them. After this program gets under way, one of the children who is most ready will discover that he can read an easy book from the library table. He has acquired a sight vocabulary from dictating and reading experience stories, and he finds in his library book many of the same words he has read in the experience stories. He undoubtedly uses context clues to help him recognize other words in the text. When this first child is able to show that he can read easy books independently, the teacher may encourage him to read alone during the time when she is working on the readiness program and further experience stories with the fast group. This fast reader may join the group on occasion if he wishes. He should be encouraged to read parts of his books orally and to discuss them either individually with the teacher or with the members of his group as a part of his work with them. Other children will soon find that they, too, are able to read simple books from the library table.

Initiation of Reading with Groups. Some teachers help their children begin reading by using the usual groups for readiness and for later work in pre-primers. The customary developmental type of reading program is followed until a number of the best readers give evidence of sufficient sight vocabulary to read independently. Children are then released in the same way as in the other plan. Eventually the teacher may work with only a small group which is still in the readiness stage. The teachers using experience stories and those using group reading in books help their children in much the same way when the children are working individually. Some teachers, however, do not schedule the children for turns in reading. These teachers may observe the children and offer help if any child seems to have difficulty with a book, or they may make themselves available for children who wish to come to them for help.

Books for Independent Readers. Some of the books on the library table may be pre-primers from basic and supplementary reading series. Others may be "Easy-to-Read" and other trade books, including picture books with short captions under the pictures. A problem results due to the difficulty of retelling pre-primer stories because the plot is carried primarily by means of the pictures. Picture books with captions are also difficult. Some of the "Easy-to-Read" trade books have good plots written in very simple language, and these more easily lend themselves to retelling.

Work with Independent Reading. As more children begin to read, they may be freed from the group to read by themselves. The teacher may work with each child individually. She may listen to each child read orally from his book either on material covered recently, or she may make a spot check of earlier reading. She may discuss the story with the child in order to estimate his comprehension, or she may ask specific questions. On the other hand, she may form the independent readers into small groups to share their stories by reading short selections orally to the other children in their group and by discussing the content of their stories with others.

The teacher must make provision for help on difficult words. The abler children may take turns, each taking one period, to help the slower children with the words they need. This task should be passed to a different child each day in order to give every child an opportunity to achieve status and to avoid using too much of one child's time in a service to the class.

Use of Records. As the child reads orally, the teacher makes notes regarding difficulties such as the need for help on beginning consonants, consonant blends, digraphs, and other types of phonics. The teacher may also find needs for help with ability to recall the sequence of events in the child's story, ability to read for cause and effect, and similar problems. She may give a little help on a particular problem at a sitting and may record the problem in her notebook to be sure that she follows up with it at the child's next turn for help, which may be several days later.

Work with Slower Children. The teacher will continue working on readiness skills and experience stories with the rest of the class, releasing children to read individually as they demonstrate an adequate sight vocabulary and ability to work independently. Some of the slowest children may be unable to begin reading in books at any time during the first year and may not read until the middle or end of the second grade. Some children may begin to read even later, depending upon the mental maturity, emotional adjustment, and other factors. In many classes all but a few children will have made a beginning in reading by the end of the first year. A large proportion of these delayed readers may be found among children whose parents take no interest in reading. Although some handicapped children normally begin to read at a later time, the teacher would be wise to ask to have such children tested individually by a psychologist to discover if special kinds of help are needed.

Time for Each Individual. By the time most of the children are reading independently, the teacher may plan to work individually with a certain number each day, but time must also be provided for the readiness group. Some teachers try to work with each child twice a week. In such a case the time allotment for each child must be very short.

Supplementary Activities. The short attention span of many first graders constitutes one of the greatest problems in the use of the individualized plan of organization. Teachers need a fifty or sixty minute period for working with the reading program. Very few first graders, and not very many older primary children, can concentrate on reading for a period of this length, depending, of course, upon their experience and background. Other activities are needed if boredom and misbehavior are to be avoided.

When a child has finished reading as long as he wishes, depending upon his attention span and maturity, he should be able to go to other activities. Many activities of a creative nature, as well as work with puzzles and other manipulative materials, must be planned so that all children are challenged and provided with satisfying activities. Early in the first grade some children will drift from one activity to another with almost the same frequency as kindergarteners.

The wise teacher will use the first few weeks of the school year for helping children learn how to take part in activities without undue interference with others. She also helps them learn how to secure materials for themselves and to clean up and return materials to their proper places after work. Unless children are carefully taught to handle this procedure, the teacher will find great difficulty in concentrating on work with individualized reading.

The teacher must also spend time helping problem children learn how to achieve recognition and to satisfy their emotional needs in positive ways. Help on such problems will be needed during the entire year, but some of the rough edges may be smoothed down before children actually undertake reading. Parent conferences are necessary for work with children to alleviate problems concerning both the aggressive type of child and the one who withdraws into a dream world. The beginning teacher, especially, does not try to work with children individually from the very beginning. While upper-grade teachers may start the year with individualized reading by carefully explaining the program to the children and by helping them set up standards, most first-grade teachers would merely confuse the children by such a procedure.

Individualized Reading in the Second and Third Grades

The teachers of the second and third grades use many of the same procedures that are used in the first grade. Some modifications may be needed because the program may be new to the children.

Orienting the Older Primary Children. The teachers of the second and third grades may have to change children's habits, a problem not met by the first-grade teacher. The children who come to them may have been accustomed to reading in groups and may have carried on formal seat work during the previous year or two. For this reason these teachers would be wise to work with their children in a formal program for a few weeks while they help them learn how to work in a permissive situation using free activities. Many of these teachers will begin the individualized program with one group only, almost always the top group because these children can read more independently and because the plan will succeed better with children who have few reading problems. Again, a few children at a time may be released until the plan has been put into effect with all of the children.

Helping Children Use Time Wisely. The provision of a variety of genuinely worthwhile activities for children who tire of reading before the end of the period is the greatest demand in these grades. The teacher may have a problem with a child who would rather draw, paint, or work with puzzles than read. This child may leave his book at the earliest opportunity in order to carry on other work. The teacher must make sure that he has a book that is easy enough for him to read with satisfaction. She may help interest him in stories through her own story telling period and may try to read part of a story that appeals to him in the hope that he will volunteer to take it to his seat to finish it. Pressure to force him to read against his will tends only to make him dislike reading.

Keeping Records for Older Primary Children. Most teachers feel that it is important to keep records of each child's progress. The child's own notebook is an excellent place for him to keep his records. The child may record the name of the book, the author, and the number of pages he has read each day. He may add notes regarding special difficulties and suggestions made by the teacher in conference. An example of such a difficulty may be the need to find familiar roots in unfamiliar words such as "happy" in "unhappy" or to learn the meaning of a new suffix such as the "er" in "worker." The teacher also keeps a record of the difficulties and the suggestions she makes in her own notebook to help the child. When reading to the teacher, new sight words may be listed in the child's and teacher's notebooks, particularly those new sight words on which he needs help.

Some teachers use a system of filing cards in addition to the notebook for keeping a record of the books read by each child. The child writes the name of the author and the title on the top lines of the card. The child usually writes some comment, perhaps the reason he enjoyed the book or a comparison of this book with some others he has read. He then signs his name at the bottom of the card. These cards are kept in a filing box, sometimes made from a shoe box. When several children have prepared cards about the same book, they may enjoy comparing their reactions. One child may have enjoyed the book more than another or may have enjoyed it for different reasons. In this type of file no thought is given to the number of cards prepared by each child. The fact that the reader's name is at the bottom of the card and therefore not easily accessible tends to discourage other children from checking the length of their friends' reading list. The child's progress is a matter between him and the teacher, and both have notes in their own note books to help evaluate such progress.

Example of a Mature Primary Group

Mrs. Dexter taught a mixed second- and third-grade group. Because of the mixed grades, she had been given rather mature second-grade children and slower and average third-graders. She taught individualized reading in groups that were organized on the basis of children's choices. One day eight children had come to work as a group to share information and stories.

A Fast Reader. Melvin was in the second grade but read on an average fifth-grade level. When asked for volunteers to report on books, Melvin said that he had decided to look for a book about anemometers because he was working with a committee that planned to make one for the airport. He had found an excellent book that not only told the uses of the anemometer but also had pictures and drawings to illustrate how a simple one might be made. He read a selection from his book for the children and showed the picture to them. When asked what materials he planned to use, he told the children that paper cups were suggested to catch the wind, but he would talk with the other members of the committee before making a final decision. During evaluation, the children complimented Melvin for his success in finding so much information about anemometers.

An Average Reader. June was an average reader in the third grade. She had chosen Hansel and Gretel from one of the easy second readers and volunteered to give her report next. She said that she had enjoyed her story very much. She told the name of the author and the title of her story and showed the children the book in which she had found it. She then explained why she liked it. She thought the gingerbread house was beautiful, and she was very happy that Hansel's and Gretel's father had found the children and rescued them from the witch. When asked if she would like to read a selection, she decided to read the description of the gingerbread house. Some of the other children had also read the story and took pleasure in recalling it, a point they brought out in the evaluation.

A Slow Reader. Although Marilyn was in the third grade she read on a first-grade elvel. She had chosen a story from a second-grade book and had made a peep show in a shoe box. The peep show was well made because Marilyn had good muscular coordination and had learned to work neatly. She gave the name of the author and title of the story and showed the children her peep box, which she passed around the group so that the children could look inside it. Mrs. Dexter was somewhat skeptical of Marilyn's ability to read with comprehension in the second reader. She also noticed that the peep show had been copied from a large picture on one of the pages. After praising the peep show, she asked Marilyn one or two questions on the content of the story, but found that Marilyn was somewhat vague in her knowledge. Mrs. Dexter ignored the lack of reading and encouraged the children to evaluate the peep show from a constructive point of view.

Because she didn't wish to embarrass Marilyn before the group, Mrs. Dexter waited until later in the period after the other children had gone to their seats to work with Marilyn alone. She helped her read a paragraph orally but found that Marilyn was defeated by too many unfamiliar words. Again, Mrs. Dexter praised the good work Marilyn had done on the peep show and helped her find an easier book with a fairy story which she felt sure Marilyn could read. The child was happy to find another story and planned to read it on the next day.

A Mentally Retarded Reader. Sam was a slow learner and read on an easy primer level. He was working on the model firehouse which was located at the classroom airport. Mrs. Dexter had helped him find a picture book of fire equipment with captions under the pictures. She

Children in a sixth-grade class select a variety of fiction and non-fiction books. (Courtesy California State Department of Education.)

had suggested that he work with another child, who was a much more capable reader, to help him learn some of the captions under the pictures. Sam had been able to remember several of these captions because of the clues the pictures gave him. When his turn came to report, he showed the pictures, told about the equipment, and read the captions that he had learned. Because Mrs. Dexter helped her children develop a strong sense of understanding and a desire to evaluate the good points, the children were very complimentary about Sam's reading. One of his friends mentioned that Sam had remembered some hard words, and Sam was very pleased at the recognition.

Examples of Individualized Reading in the Intermediate Grades

As children become older, they are able to carry on more extended reading and to apply it more widely. These children still read widely

for recreation but tend to read more informational material and literature including poetry. They also extend their reading more deeply in
the content areas as in social studies and science. Written work in connection with purposeful reading may be used more frequently in the
middle grades. Reading will also be used in more functional ways to
help children understand and carry out directions for such activities as
making models, using chemistry and science sets, and following recipes
in cooking.

Some teachers make use of reading in the social studies and other
content areas in connection with the individualized reading program
but allow the children to read in these fields as a matter of choice. On
a certain day a child may wish to continue reading on a social studies
problem that he began in the social studies period. He may prefer to
read for recreation, or he may wish to work with a group that is planning
a play. Sometimes reading may be very closely related to writing. The
group planning a play may spend part of its time listing costumes and
properties it needs. The children will check frequently with books,
however, to make sure that their properties are authentic for the period.

Some children may spend a large part of their time on science reading and experimentation. Procuring the equipment necessary and setting
up a science experiment requires very careful reading for detail. If some
of the children spend a great deal of time on science, the teacher may
encourage them to read for recreation at other times and may help them
find science fiction stories which appeal to their interests.

Reading in the Social Studies. When, for example, Steven, a fifth-
grade pupil, chose to work on a social studies problem, he looked for
books on the library table that might contain some of the information
he needed. He was interested in the hardships of the pioneers crossing
the plains. He had had some help in using reference material so he
looked in the table of contents and also used the index to find references
concerning the pioneer's hardships. After skimming, he discarded an
occasional book about the pioneers because he could find very little concerning their hardships. He then found another book with several pages
listed under this topic.

When he turned to the first of these pages, he discovered that one of
the hardships was the loss of prized possessions that could not be brought
to the west in covered wagons. A little girl could choose only one doll
of her precious six, and an older boy could bring only one of his games.
The mother had to leave most of her beautiful furniture, and the father
sold all of his dairy cows. Steven had been taught to take notes, so he
had jotted down a word or two to represent each of these crucial
problems.

When he had finished the references to the hardships in St. Louis, he turned to the index to find another series of pages to read. There he found that these hardships concerned problems on the trail, such as lack of water between springs, sickness, and trouble with the wagons. When Steven had listed these hardships and made an outline of his topics, he joined another member of his committee, Robert, who was working on native foods used by the pioneers on their journey. The children compared progress and Steven, who had completed his outline, looked for some references for Robert, who had been progressing more slowly.

When the children had completed their reading, they talked about ways of presenting the information to the other members of the class. Steven decided to draw a series of pictures to represent the hardships experienced by a certain family in crossing the plains. Robert, who did not like to draw, decided to try to find pictures in magazines and to use samples of real three-dimensional materials to make a collage. When the children were given time to make their presentation during the social studies period, they followed their outlines in the discussion and showed their pictures and materials. The visual aids helped hold the attention of the other members of the class by reinforcing their interest in hearing about these topics.

Reading in Science. During the science period, Howard and Martin decided that they would like to build an electric motor. When questioned, their teacher assured them that this construction would not be too difficult if they used parts from their science kits. She suggested that the boys ask members of the class if any of them had a good book on electricity at home that he would be willing to lend. Before going home that afternoon she made a point of checking the library table to see if any of the books gave directions for making an electric motor. She did not find any so she stopped at the school library for one and went on to the public library to locate more books on this topic. In reading period the next day, these boys decided to read the book with directions for making the motor. Since directions are always somewhat difficult to read and since they must be followed very accurately, the boys asked the teacher for an explanation of some of the terms. She helped them and also checked their progress occasionally to make sure they were following the directions accurately.

Reading in Music. Esther, Mary, and Hazel decided to look for pioneer songs and went to the library to secure some music books they wanted. They read these songs together to decide which ones they wished to select. When they had chosen some appropriate songs, they asked the teacher for permission to use the melody bells to help them learn the songs. The teacher suggested that they work in a corner and try to be as quiet as possible. She also asked if these children could read the music. Hazel assured the teacher that she had taken piano lessons and was sure she could. After several days of practice, when the songs had been learned, the children decided to present their work by dramatizing a campfire scene. They consulted the teacher, who suggested they teach the songs to the other members of the class so that all could enjoy the singing.

Reading to Plan a Play. Phyllis, Helen, and Bessie who were interested in stories about pioneer life, decided to write a play. As they undertook their work, they first decided what type of costumes should be worn. Since they had not read specifically on this point when browsing in their books, they found it necessary to go back to the books to look at the pictures and to read to discover what materials were used, the colors and patterns of the cloth, and other such details. As they planned the play, other problems arose. The children wondered if the pioneers ever used stoves in the covered wagons or if they always stopped to build campfires. They also wondered if the pioneers slept on real beds in the wagons or if mattresses were spread on the wagon bed the way their fathers did when they allowed the children to sleep on the patio. As the children wrote, they returned again and again to books to help them with their problems. When they had difficulty in finding answers, their teacher wisely helped them locate books, articles, encyclopedias, and other materials rather than yielding to the temptation of giving them answers. The play was filled with romance as well as Indians, scalps, buffalo, and other lurid details. The children, nevertheless, had learned a great deal about the life of the pioneers in their undertaking, had excellent practice in using resource materials, and had a good experience in assembling their information in dramatic form. The other members of the class enjoyed the play, despite its amateurish character.

ADVANTAGES AND DISADVANTAGES OF THE PROGRAM

The plan of individualized reading has many valuable features and has contributed ideas to enrich the teaching of reading. Occasionally weaknesses may be found, but the strengths are important. Some of these advantages and disadvantages may be grouped in terms of the factors that facilitate the reading procedures. Others are related to the emotional and social factors in the reading situation.

Factors Relating to Reading Procedures

Some of the methods in the individualized program are of help both to the teacher and to the pupil in facilitating the pupil's progress. A few of these methods have weaknesses. Not all methods are peculiar to the individualized program but have been used also in the developmental program.

Adjusting to Reading Levels.   In any classroom a wide range of reading abilities will inevitably be found.   In the third grade, children may read on any level from first to fifth grade or even higher.   As children increase in age, their reading levels increase in spread and may cover an eight-grade span.   It is very difficult for teachers properly to place children in groups in order to achieve a reasonable homogeneity in their reading ability.   Children in any one group may differ from each other in reading by two or three grade levels.   Although the plan of using three groups is most common, some teachers divide the class into five or more groups in order to provide for the wide difference in the reading abilities of these children.

The individualized program makes its best contribution in providing opportunity for children to choose books on their own levels.   At first, the teacher must give children considerable help in selecting books, while they gradually learn to make choices for themselves on the basis of interest and reading level.   It has been found that children may choose and succeed in reading some books above this level if these books are closely related to their interests.   At other times children may choose books that are rather easy for them.

Pacing.   Pacing is another advantage of the individualized reading program.   Although pacing has been recognized as an important psychological principle of learning and has been applied to educational methods for some time, it has received special emphasis in the individualized reading program.   The child who is properly paced in his reading works with material which he can master without difficulty and yet which gradually increases in difficulty as he grows in ability. One skill depends upon another, and the child takes on each new skill as he achieves competency in the older ones.   Pacing at each new step depends on readiness for this step.   The child who is able to select a book that he can read successfully, but which demands the development of few new understandings and which gradually adds a limited number of new words to his vocabulary, is properly paced in his reading.

Pacing may be more precise when used in the individualized program than when used with an entire group, even though the teacher may make minor adjustments within the group.   Ideally in the individualized program, the reading material should be perfectly matched to each child's reading level.   Certain child needs, however, may interfere with, rather than facilitate, pacing.   If a child has a strong need for status, he may select books that are far beyond his reading level in order to keep face with the other children.   He may fear that he will be accused of reading "baby books" if he chooses books that are on his actual level of reading. An understanding and skillful teacher is needed to cope with this situation. On the other hand, some children may deliberately choose books that are too easy for them because of a strong need to feel secure. While both of these kinds of choices meet personality needs of the child, they may seriously interfere with his improvement in reading, if prolonged.

Some children come from homes in which reading is either considered "sissified" or in which it is merely ignored. James, a fifth-grade boy, had developed a tremendous resistance to both spelling and reading. The resistance was partly due to school frustrations resulting from a less-than-average intelligence and partly due to the fact that his father and all his male relatives were fishermen, who put their values on outdoor life and adventure. He lived for the day when he would be able to leave school and join this group. Despite the fact that some interest in reading might have been developed by a skillful teacher who would have found books on fishing for him, reading was not a part of this child's culture. In addition, poor pacing had been typical of all this child's reading experience. It is very difficult for one teacher to undo the damage of five or six years of frustration. Good pacing in the reading readiness level and continued pacing thereafter, might have helped teachers arouse and maintain an interest on the part of such a child whether or not individualized reading was used.

Making Choices. The opportunity for children to choose their own books, called self-selection, is another characteristic of this program. Children are encouraged to choose books that appeal to them. They usually find the reading material that they have been allowed to choose more enjoyable and satisfying than reading material chosen for them. Children who have been somewhat discouraged in the group organizational plan of reading may respond with enthusiasm to the opportunity of selecting their own books.

Providing a Variety of Reading Materials. In this program children may read a very wide variety of materials to meet their diverse interests. They may browse among many interests from fairy stories, boating, and biography to science and space ships. Teachers must help children learn how to locate information since so many interests are found among the members of one class. Storybooks, science books, basic reading texts, biographies, magazines, children's newspapers, reference books, and encyclopedias are all used to meet children's interests and needs. A child with a limited interest may not necessarily read a wide variety of material unless encouraged and stimulated by his teacher. In the older reading program, too, basic texts used in group reading are often augmented by supplementary reading materials and research reading in committee work in the social studies. Children who read in basic texts may also read at least as wide a variety of books and materials as those read by children in the individualized reading program.

Giving Help When Needed. Each child may receive help on a particular skill when he needs this assistance. He has an opportunity to ask for the teacher's help and may become more able to analyze his own needs through this procedure. This advantage would be greater for the teacher who reserves her help for those children who need it than for the teacher who schedules a different group of children each day. In the latter case, a child might need help on Monday, but might not be able to approach the teacher until Thursday, when he would have forgotten about the difficulty. This advantage is also greater for the child who is conscious of the need for help than for those who have merely a vague feeling of frustration. Only as the teacher helps each child to analyze his problems and to record his progress is he likely to develop a real understanding of his own needs.

Providing for Critical Thinking. Some teachers feel that the individualized reading program provides opportunity for critical thinking. Some opportunities for critical thinking during reading are natural to the reading material itself, but the teacher must help each child recognize these opportunities when he meets them. The fact that people do not critically evaluate newspaper articles, television speeches, or even political issues is evident daily in conversations with many people. These skills must be taught.

When children take turns discussing the books they have read in terms of what they enjoyed about the story or why they liked another story better, they are engaging in a limited type of critical thinking. A child in the middle grades, who looks for information about a given topic, such as the process of locating oil to find where to drill wells, evaluates each article or selection from a textbook or the encyclopedia in terms of whether or not it provides the information he wants. This phase of critical thinking has been developed extensively in social studies committees.

Any further critical thinking must be developed consciously by the teacher. The child must be helped to think critically in regard to whether an article he selects is factual or if it has been written to spread propaganda. Children are not able to make such evaluations without help. Since almost all children need such a skill, the teacher would be wise to help children in groups based on reading level. Obviously, a child cannot evaluate an article for propaganda unless he can read the article with ease. Such a skill might much more easily be developed in a group reading program.

The ability to select topic sentences, main ideas, subheadings, to interpret pictures, to apply information from reading to solve problems, to draw inferences and conclusions, and to make comparisons and judgments are skills that can most economically and effectively be taught in groups. Children help each other gain insights in such processes as well as receive crucial help from the teacher. After children have learned to use various techniques of critical thinking, individual reading provides excellent opportunities for them to apply and utilize these skills. This application may be carried out in the reading period, in work in social studies, science, or in any field in which it applies.

Flexibility of Grouping with Change of Interest. Once this individualized program of reading has been organized, pupils read individually during a specific time of the day, or they may work together in small groups when they are reading about some topic of mutual interest. Three sixth-grade boys may be interested in sailboats and may wish to read orally to each other parts of the books they have selected because of their mutual interest. Instead of reading orally to each other, they may prefer to discuss the information they have found in these books. When interests change, the group membership also tends to change.

Providing Uninterrupted Time. The individualized reading period may provide those children who are able to make use of it with uninterrupted time for reading without pressures or demands. Good readers lose themselves in the stories or material while they are reading and must have time to concentrate on this material if they are to maintain this ability. The ability to concentrate is extremely valuable in later school and adult life.

During the reading period no need occurs for the activities of the other children to be suppressed since mature readers usually can, and should be able to, concentrate regardless of the reasonable sounds of activity of those about them. The less able readers will need continuous help in developing the ability to concentrate for an increasing period, regardless of minor distractions. Young children, however, have a much shorter attention span than older children, and some of the younger ones cannot be expected to spend more than fifteen or twenty minutes in reading at one time. Others may be able to concentrate for a longer time, depending upon age and other factors, but no time standard should be set for the group as a whole.

Integrating with Other Subjects. Whenever other subjects are integrated with reading or whether individualized reading is used as a tool for work in the social studies and science, many opportunities occur for integration. The two procedures are closely related. In the social studies, choices of reading material are more often made to meet the child's needs for information and understanding. Sometimes information is used to provide help when children wish to make such objects as authentic doll costumes for a period in history or models of fishing weirs or oil wells. Sometimes information from reading is used to help the children carry on authentic dramatic play, dramatizations, or panel discussions. If the reading arises from the individualized program, some children may choose to read for enjoyment, whereas other children may wish to pursue a subject that arose in the social studies or other content field. If the reading originates during the social studies period, children do not usually choose to read for enjoyment at that time unless that reading relates in some way to the main interest.

Extending to Home Reading. Children often take home books they have started in school in order to read further or to finish them. The fact that children become deeply involved in a story and want to discover what happens next naturally leads them to want to take the book home. When children read supplementary books in the group plan, they also plead to take them home.

Any good teacher can stimulate most children's interest in books by reading stories to them. Occasionally, for example, she may read a short story as far as the climax and then allow children to finish it by themselves at the library table or at home. In such a case the demand usually exceeds the supply. Whenever a child is given an opportunity to tell what he likes about a book or to read a part of a book without revealing the climax, other children become very anxious to have an opportunity to read the same book. Children's interest in reading is also stimulated by television and library programs.

Individualized reading provides opportunity for purposeful reading on the part of the pupil. The child who is encouraged to choose a book in which he is interested has a built-in purpose. If a child has no immediate purpose, he may browse until a book strikes his fancy. He may develop an interest in a book and a purpose for reading as he looks at the pictures and browses in the text. As he reads, questions come to mind and a purpose is formulated. On the other hand, a child may read without a purpose despite the fact that he is allowed to select the book. If he does not have a genuine interest in reading, his teacher should help him develop purposes just as the teacher of group reading helps her group members select a common purpose in reading a story.

Factors Relating to Social and Emotional Adjustment

Some of the advantages of the individualized reading program relate to social and emotional adjustment. Children have an opportunity to develop a feeling of responsibility for their own reading progress and may share their interests with others when they find a book they enjoy. Competition and boredom resulting from poor methods should be eliminated, and the slow readers should feel that they have a position of greater status in this program.

Developing Responsibility. A characteristic of the individualized program is the development of responsibility on the part of the child for his own choices of books to read and for his ultimate progress. Some children who resent working for the teacher, as they feel it, will respond with enthusiasm when they accept the responsibility for their own advancement. A considerable time may be needed, however, for some children to develop a sense of responsibility if they have spent several years in classrooms in which they have always followed the teacher's directions. The goal of developing responsibility was one of the outstanding aims of the "Progressive Movement" in which much the same type of reading was encouraged by some of its followers. The pupil's use of some form of record, such as that described earlier in this chapter, is important in helping him learn to work toward his own improvement.

Sharing with Others. Some teachers give many opportunities for the child to take advantage of his natural desire to share stories he enjoys and the information he may have discovered that other children may need. In order to take part in this type of activity, the teacher must work with children to develop skills in telling stories and sharing information. Some children may be interested in telling the parts of their stories they liked best, in retelling or reading orally the most exciting parts, or in recommending books for other children. For example, one child may recommend a good book on boats with directions for making models to another who he knows has been looking for such a book. The inclusion of this sharing process in the individualized program is valuable because children develop new interests from each other and absorb each other's enthusiasms about reading. This phase of reading, too, was part of the supplementary program.

Eliminating Competition. In the individualized reading program competition and stigma for the slower children are eliminated if the program is properly managed. Since there are no groups, as such, parental pressure for membership in the highest group is automatically eliminated. On the other hand, some teachers have unconsciously set the stage for an even more vicious type of competition. The teacher who uses stars or other symbols to represent the number of books read is setting up a situation in which the slow child cannot possibly compete. Prestige for only those children with the most stars is just as bad, if not worse, than prestige for only those children in the fast group. All records should be kept where they are accessible to the teacher and the child concerned, unless the teacher and children record their reports briefly on cards in a file. These reports may be alphabetized by the title or author of the book, and no attention is given to the number of books read by each child.

Eliminating Boredom. In individualized reading the children who read to the teacher orally by turns in their own books are not delayed by waiting for other children to read orally as they might be in the group plan. It is obvious that the other children cannot be required to follow the sentence with their eyes since they do not have the same book. One of the greatest criticisms of group oral reading has been in regard to this problem. The accusation is justified. This type of oral reading should have been eliminated many years ago when it was first criticized.

The weakness does not lie in the plan of organization by groups, but in the method. In the group plan when reading orally in a basic text, the teacher who directs the children to skim to find certain information, to find the answer to a question on which the children disagree, or to find the next step in a sequence of events does not have this problem. These children are taught to skim rapidly until they have found the proper place. The teacher watches until all have located the place in the book and then calls on one child to read his selection. All others listen, rather than follow the text, to see if the reader agrees with their opinions in regard to the correct information. If a disagreement occurs, the child disagreeing with the first child reads his choice of the selection. Other children may also have different ideas regarding the choice of the selection. The group then decides upon the best choice. In this method too, boredom is eliminated and important reading skills are developed as children read rapidly to find specific material. In addition, social skills of lasting value are developed as the children learn to disagree politely and to listen courteously and open mindedly to other children's opinions.

Observing Interests and Feelings. Opportunity for children to choose books and materials to read provides the teacher with an excellent situation for observing children's personal feelings toward books, their interests, and sometimes their attitudes toward life. The mere list of books chosen by a given child is a helpful index to his interests if no pressures have been exerted to influence his choice. In many cases the child's reactions to books helps the teacher understand his personal feelings and sometimes his problems and anxieties.

For example, a child may like a book because the hero was a little boy without a father just as he lacks a father. In another story the child hero may be afraid of diving just as the reader fears diving from high places. He may like the book because the hero found a way to overcome his fears. In the same way the teacher of group reading, if she is sensitive to children and encourages the expression of feelings, may discover much about her children. This opportunity is especially great if she also carries on a supplementary reading program and encourages children to report on and discuss the books they read.

Avoiding Deception. The advocates of the individualized reading program state that the teacher in their program does not try to deceive the children in regard to their reading abilities by giving special names to the reading groups as is quite often done in the group program. Actually, few teachers who use the group plan of teaching reading attempt to deceive the children. The names of books read by the groups are often used as a way of designating different groups. The teacher may say, for example, "The children reading *Tiny and His Friends* please come to the reading circle." This is a polite way of asking the slow group to come to the reading circle. It is a mere courtesy, since teachers as well as children try to be courteous.

The question of deceiving children may also be applied to the individualized program. In this program too, slower readers are not deceived by thinking they are reading as well as the more able children when they are reading a second-grade book in an individualized program while in the fifth grade. Neither are they deceived by sitting in a group with better readers. The good teacher helps children improve on whatever level they may be able to work and emphasizes improvement rather than reading level. A slow reader may gain considerable prestige for making outstanding improvement, whereas an outstanding child may fail to make little, if any, progress and therefore receive no special recognition.

Giving Confidence to Slow Readers. The lack of a slow reading group is one of the most important characteristics of the individualized program. If teachers of the group plan have failed to give the children in the slow reading group material that they can read with ease and satisfaction, these children often develop pronounced feelings of inferiority and a dislike for reading. They may respond to the individualized program with enthusiasm because they are no longer stigmatized by membership in an inferior group.

In one class a slow reader, two average readers, and two advanced readers all needed practice in oral expression. Although the slow reader read his own material, he felt increased status through his opportunity to work with children who read on a higher level than he. In such a case it is very important that the teacher insists that the better readers listen with understanding and appreciation to the slow reader; otherwise, more harm than good may result.

The lack of definite slow, middle, and fast reading groups is a great help to the teacher. Many parents put pressure on both the teacher and on their own children to have them work with the fast group. Sometimes the placement of these children in the fast group may be very detrimental to them if they are not ready to read at this level. Much of this pressing problem is usually eliminated by individualized reading.

The teacher of both the group and the individualized plans can help the children in the slow reading group in several ways to give them feelings of personal adequacy. First, she must sincerely like these children and must respect them for their good qualities. A teacher who is truly fond of children will have no difficulty in finding fine qualities and abilities among these children. Second, this teacher must give these children material that they can read in the sense that the adult reads. For the first year or two this requirement may seem impossible to meet. The use of experience stories and various types of matching activities has been suggested for these children until they begin to acquire a sight vocabulary. Third, these children must be given status in every possible way without making them seem different. This status must be given for reading activities as well as for other kinds of contributions. Suggestions for helping the children in the slow reading groups in these ways are given in the following chapter.

SUMMARY

Individualized reading may be introduced in the first grade by means of experience stories or through regular developmental reading in groups. Second- and third-grade children will need an orientation to the program if they have not worked in an individualized program in the first grade. Record keeping is essential if each child's program is to be followed and each child's difficulties analyzed and corrected. In a good program children will learn to share information and stories with other members of a group. Even the most retarded child in a class can take part in the sharing. When used in the content areas, individualized reading is extended to the work of committees.

The individualized reading program is valuable in providing for choices in reading paced to each child's level of ability and for meeting each child's interests, which are often extended to reading at home. The teacher tries to give help when the child needs her assistance and makes available a wide variety of reading materials. She also tries to help children to develop good social attitudes. Each child takes the responsibility for his own progress and does not compete with other children in a good program.

20

Evaluation of
Organizational Plans

Some of the procedures followed in the individualized reading program and a number of its values were discussed in the previous chapter. Some problems arising from this plan, on the other hand, seem apparent if it is to be thought of as the total reading program. Other organizational plans offer advantages and have disadvantages that should be considered. A plan utilizing three reading groups has been described in a previous section of this book in connection with the methods suitable for use with this program.

Several ways of organizing the reading groups or the reading program itself have merit. One of the plans making use of groups is known as split session grouping. The ungraded plan is another way of meeting the needs of children. This plan has values for the reading program as well as for other areas of the curriculum.

PROBLEMS OF THE INDIVIDUALIZED PROGRAM

Some of the problems that arise in connection with the individualized reading program include the difficulties in providing help for children such as the limitations of time, the availability of the teacher when needed, the provision of other activities for the immature reader, the complexity of the many skills that should be taught, and the type of oral reading followed by the pupil when reading alone to the teacher.

Difficulties in Providing Help

The improbability of the same need arising for help at the same time by children in a reading group has been stressed by those who oppose the group program. In such a plan, all the children in the group must work on a particular skill needed perhaps by only one child. The point has merit, but such an interpretation is very misleading since children need review. On the other hand, it is suggested that children's needs are met at once when they arise in the individualized program. The limitation of time as well as the difficulty of providing for practice are involved in these implications.

Limitation of Time. Actually, the needs of each child are not always met immediately when they arise in the individualized program. Most teachers who follow the individualized program, even those who teach first grade, do not try to work with each child every day. Some teachers schedule each child for a specific day and plan to reach all the children once during the week. Some are able to schedule each child twice a week but must give each one a very brief period of time since the reading is rarely taught for longer than an hour a day in the primary grades. When following this type of schedule, it is very difficult to give help immediately when a child encounters a problem, and some children do not secure help when they need it.

Many teachers in graded schools have an average of thirty-five children in their classes, whereas some have larger classes, and some have smaller ones. If a teacher of thirty-five children devotes sixty minutes a day to reading, she will spend three hundred minutes a week on this subject. If each child is given an equal share of this time, he will receive eight and a half minutes of the teacher's time during the week. The teacher who has fewer children faces a less difficult problem. Eight and a half minutes per child per week is a very limited extent of time for all the direct teaching needed in the primary grades, especially for children in the first grade.

In the early primary grades sixty minutes a day is probably the maximum length for a reading period because of the limited attention span of the children and the long periods of time when the children at their seats are required to work independently, a matter of fifty-two minutes a day for each child to work alone. Most primary children must be provided with a number of different types of activities and adequate supervision if they must work alone over such a long period.

Children in the intermediate grades fare better in the individualized program. The teacher is usually able to allot ninety minutes to reading and probably has also an average of thirty-five children in her class.

This teacher, then, spends four hundred forty minutes a week with her children and is therefore able to give each child approximately thirteen minutes each week. Many of these children are able to read independently with at least satisfactory speed and comprehension and have acquired the ability to use phonic, context, and other clues with reasonable efficiency. Except for the introduction of and practice on new skills, such as those needed for organization, interpretation, and appreciation, these children can read widely without a great deal of help from the teacher. Thus, the teacher is able to give more time to the children who have problems in reading or to those on a lower reading level, but this time must be taken from the more capable pupils.

Availability of the Teacher.   When children are scheduled to work with the teacher only once or twice a week, they will inevitably have needs for help when the teacher is not available. Pupil helpers can assist the children with unknown words but cannot usually assist in other ways. Sometimes the child who is having difficulty will recognize his problem. If he is sufficiently mature, he may be able to make a memorandum in his notebook to help him remember to discuss the difficulty with his teacher and to show her the place where he met it. Other children, more predominantly slower learners and children in the primary grades, may not recognize their specific problems and are almost certain to be unable to tell the teacher about the problems because these difficulties are too vague in their minds. In the oral spot check the teacher may or may not discover the problem, depending upon what she asks the child to read.

If, on the other hand, the teacher gives help when needed, rather than on schedule with each child for one or two definite periods a week, she may spend a large part of her time with children who recognize their needs for help. She may therefore neglect some who may need help as much as the others but who may not recognize their problems or who may be too shy or diffident to ask for help.

Need for Activities for Immature Readers.   In the primary grades a wide variety of activities, primarily creative, must be provided for children who have not yet learned to read and for those with limited reading ability or with limited attention span. At least a little of the eight and a half minutes with each child will be lost in helping some of these young children change from one activity to another as they complete work or tire of one activity.

The problem of time spent independently must also be faced in the intermediate grades, although it is not as serious as in the primary grades. Not all members of every class are able to concentrate on reading with satisfaction for ninety minutes each day. Some variety of work must be provided for these children, and a little supervisory time must be given to enlist their interest and help them begin a new activity. The children who need this type of help are usually the slower learners and those with emotional problems.

Need for Review and Application of Skills. The method or way in which a need for a skill is met must be considered. Is it met once for all time when a child first asks for help? Possibly a few needs are met in this manner, but teaching would be a simple process if the teacher could discover a pupil's need for help with even one skill and eradicate that difficulty with one simple explanation during a period of eight to thirteen minutes. A skill needed by one child or a group of children may be complex such as the skill needed to select the main idea in a paragraph and to use it in the making of an outline. On the other hand, a skill may be rather simple, such as the skill required to recognize the triple blend *str* and to use it as a key to pronounce words beginning with these sounds.

In group teaching most needs even for such a simple skill as the recognition of the triple blend *str* and its application are met in somewhat the following manner. When a word beginning with this blend is met by the children in the group, the teacher usually puts a sentence on the board containing the word. Such a sentence might be about a kite and the sentence might be, "John needs a long piece of string." The children know that John has a kite, so the teacher may ask a child to read the sentence or as much of it as he can. When he hesitates on the word *string* she may ask what John needs. Some children will suggest that he needs a strong wind or an open place to run, but at least one child who uses phonic aids along with context clues will conclude that he needs a string. The teacher gives this child reassurance and then asks the first child to finish the sentence. The child who analyzed the word *string* will probably remember this blend and may be able to use this phonic clue when he meets the *str* blend again. One or two other children may also be able to do so. The teacher then reviews familiar words containing the *str* blend.

During this lesson some of the group members will be able to follow the original child's thinking but will be unable, without help, to make the application of this blend to a new word. Still other children in the group will fail to acquire adequate insight into the process of applying the *str* blend even though they participated in the procedure. The next time these children meet the *str* blend in a new word such as *straight*, the teacher will repeat the original process again. Each time the process is repeated with a new word, more children will gain insight and will be better able to apply the skill to new words. The process is gradual, and insight and understanding increase with each new experience with this blend.

Need for Procedures to Meet Individual Differences. In order to meet various differences in rates of learning and in levels of understanding due to experience, the process of teaching a skill, as illustrated above, may be analyzed and classified in the following steps: (1) the introduction of the skill, (2) guidance to help the child discover the principles involved in the process and to help him understand the use of the skill, (3) further clarification of the use of the skill and review of its application, (4) review and application until mastery is achieved by the child, and (5) new applications of the skill for review to increase power in its use and to prevent forgetting. Each child must progress through this procedure at his own rate if he is to achieve mastery and retain the skill. A very few children will reach mastery almost at once, whereas the slowest children in the group will need a number of repetitions and many applications before the skill is mastered.

When the teacher of the developmental group program is working on a skill that has been mastered by several children in the group, she may include these few only long enough to give them a brief review to prevent their forgetting the skill. She may then dismiss them to work at their seats on independent reading of their own selections while she continues to help the children who need further practice. Nothing inherent in the developmental group plan of teaching demands that the teacher keep all of the children in a reading group if some of them do not need the practice. If those who have mastered the skill are dismissed, the need for help with a skill in the developmental program may be met satisfactorily and to the point of mastery.

In the individualized program the need may be met satisfactorily for a few children the first time it is discovered by the teacher. If help is to be continued to the point of mastery for most children, the expenditure of a great deal of time and the control of meticulously kept records are essential. The teaching of the organizational and interpretive skills makes even greater demands upon the teacher.

Diagnosis and Help with Organizational Skills

The teacher, who carefully analyzes the chart of skills (see page 464) needed for organizing, interpreting, and appreciating reading material of an informational, recreational, and literary nature, as well as an organized plan for presenting word analysis skills, is usually impressed and even awed by the tremendous task and responsibility of the teacher of reading. On the other hand, some teachers feel that children will acquire these skills by themselves as they read broadly.

This second-grade chart helps children recall the various items of preparation for their work. (Courtesy N.D.E.A. 1967 Demonstration School and Sacramento City Unified School District.)

Needs for Organizational Skills. Anyone who observes children in upper-grade classes knows how many children are without the ability to take notes, to make outlines, or to organize material and give simple reports, despite their ability to pass standardized tests successfully. Numbers of high school students, including some of the most intelligent, are also without these skills. Many of the freshmen with college ability who fail during their first year in college do so because of inadequate reading skills, lack of ability to take notes from lectures and books, and lack of adequate vocabulary arising from failure to read widely. Even seniors in college sometimes express lack of security in working with outlines, and many seem to depend upon good memories rather than study techniques when preparing for tests. It is obvious on all levels that few children pick up these skills without help.

The teacher who tries to teach all these skills to one child at a time or even to children in temporary groups faces a tremendous problem. The effective teacher who uses the developmental group plan does not depend solely on the discovery of all the children's needs for help through their oral reading. Instead, she follows a carefully organized plan adapted to children's needs discovered through all their reading activities.

Many of these skills are more wisely taught in the developmental program with children in groups because of the need for review and practice as the children become more able to apply these skills. Suggestions are given in the best teachers' manuals for teaching and applying these skills in the stories and non-fiction provided in the developmental readers. Inexperienced teachers are especially in need of these suggestions for following a plan to provide a balance of skills through the year. In the individualized program, the teaching of skills in organization, interpretation, and appreciation are often overlooked because of the many demands and pressures for time in this program. In some cases the teachers are not conscious of the need for these skills and are not sufficiently experienced to plan and organize the reading of each child to introduce and provide adequate practice in such a series of skills.

Unless the individualized program is planned to include many types of reading activities with a variety of applications of organizational skills and unless careful plans are made to discover and analyze needs for a wide variety of skills, the needs for many of these skills will not be apparent to the average teacher. The teacher of the individualized reading program seems to meet children's needs for help in phonic analysis and in the use of context clues better than she meets the needs for the other types of skills.

Use of a Check List for Diagnosis. The teacher of individualized reading who maintains that she can tell whether or not children understand their reading material without a check of some sort is missing the point of the program in organizational, interpretive, and appreciational skills. It is true that children's absorption in their reading indicates a degree of comprehension of a recreational level, but the teacher cannot depend on the child's degree of concentration to tell her how well he is using his reading to develop or increase his abilities to organize ideas. The following list will help the reader appreciate the complexity of these needed skills.

Study Skills

1. Recall information.
2. Follow printed directions.
3. Locate information through use of the table of contents.
4. Locate information through the use of the index, glossary, and encyclopedia.
5. Select suitable references.
6. Skim for specific information.
7. Read maps, charts, graphs, and tables.
8. Classify information acquired through reading.
9. Make inferences and draw conclusions.
10. Observe relationships.
11. Make generalizations.
12. Determine cause and effect.
13. Read newspapers and analyze news.
14. Follow a sequence of events or ideas and recall these when needed.
15. Take notes.
16. Select main ideas.
17. Make an outline.
18. Make a summary.
19. Analyze propaganda.
20. Solve problems.
21. Appreciate reading material through use of clues to appearance and emotions of characters, story settings, story mood, and qualities of the characters.

Use of Subject Areas. Some teachers teach the skills in organization, interpretation, and appreciation of reading material and literature in connection with the social studies program. One of the greatest difficulties in such a procedure results from the fact that a third or more of the children in most classes usually cannot read the social studies text for the grade. The teacher, therefore, must resort to the use of many different books for children on various levels of reading. She must also spend much of her time in helping the poorer readers acquire at least some of the content of their grade. She may help the more advanced readers with organizational techniques, but this work should be in the nature of review and application. Otherwise, the teacher will spend her time teaching reading techniques instead of social studies.

It has been suggested that some of the work in appreciation and interpretation of reading material may be carried in the language program, but here, too, the time is limited and the requirements for developing and improving oral and written skills is great. Children can read some literary selections with limited individual help, but they will miss much of the beauty and depth of literature if not given more adequate help at times. A fair share of the teaching of the organizational and appreciative skills must take place in the reading program, whether with each individual at a time or with groups.

Some teachers find that they are most successful when teaching the group plan of reading, and some find their greatest success in teaching the individualized reading program. The teacher must follow the plan that gives her a feeling of security and success. One great danger inherent in the individualized program is that it may be foisted upon those who do not understand it or who have no real interest in it. Some teachers have accepted the plan as an opportunity merely to let the children read while they, themselves, catch up on other work. Such an attitude toward the program will result in disaster.

Some authorities have suggested that the individualized and the group program be carried on alternately, using part of a week for one program and the remainder of the week for the other. Other authorities have suggested alternating the program in the same way but over a period of two or three weeks for each type of plan. Not all groups of children would necessarily follow the individualized program at the same time.

OTHER ORGANIZATIONAL PLANS

The plan of dividing and teaching the class in three groups is the one most commonly followed and is usually referred to as the developmental program because most teachers use a developmental series of books with it. In still another plan teachers who have a longer school day carry on a developmental program of fifteen or twenty minutes for each group in the morning and provide an additional individualized program for half an hour in the afternoon. Any special problem discovered in the afternoon period may be taken up in the morning developmental group work with the basic texts. Self-selection or free choice in reading may also be substituted for some of the formal seat work that is used so constantly with many children.

Use of Three Groups

The use of three reading groups is likely to be the surest way for the beginning teacher to reach her objectives in the teaching of reading. As she gains self-confidence and skill, she may supplement this group work with other plans of organization and may vary her procedures to challenge the children and to find ways of teaching best suited to her own abilities and personality.

The division of the class into three groups seems the most practical for many teachers. One of the basic advantages in limiting the groups to three is the resultant limitation of the time to two periods that children must work independently. In this way each child spends one period reading with the teacher and two periods working alone or in small groups. Each of these periods varies from fifteen to twenty-five minutes in the third grade. Even in the intermediate and upper grades, the total reading period is seldom longer than ninety minutes.

Problems of Status

Many of the advantages and disadvantages in various plans of organization are the result of the methods used in each and the ways groups and individuals are managed. The stigma attached to children who read in the slow reading groups in the developmental program and to those reading easy books in the individualized program is one of the greatest problems with which the teacher must cope. To partially eliminate emphasis on the slow reader, children may be grouped in a variety of ways in other subjects. The use of classroom helpers and of a variety of activities for all children described by Morrison and Perry may help both good and poor readers forget differences in reading skill.[1] The teacher must have genuine respect for and must be willing to stress each child's strengths. The selection of reading material also has an influence on children's concerns regarding their ability to read.

Use of the Social Studies. Slow readers may work to advantage with capable readers on social studies committees. The good readers may help the slower readers with difficult words in their respective books, whereas the slow readers can often help the others with problems in art and construction. Although the slower readers do not always have

---

[1] Ida E. Morrison and Ida F. Perry, *Kindergarten-Primary Education—Teaching Procedures* (New York: The Ronald Press Co., 1961), Chap. 13.

good muscular co-ordination, they sometimes have more patience than the faster readers. Through this type of co-operation mutual respect is developed.

Use of the Class Newspaper. Slower readers in the intermediate and upper grades may work with the better readers in the language program. A weekly class newspaper in the intermediate and upper grades provides excellent motivation for writing. Slower readers may work with fast readers as reporters. When these pupils complete an article, they may take it to one of the class editors for help. Because of the joint authorship, the interest of the slower child may be enhanced both in reading and writing. The slower readers may bring in news, notices, and free advertisements from other classes for inclusion in the newspaper. In this way they have opportunities to work with children without regard for ability and to gain status for contributions to class activities.

Use of Classroom Helpers. The wise teacher provides many opportunities in the classroom for children to serve on committees to help with room chores. Even in the kindergarten and first grade, children can secure materials and put them away. They can clean their work areas, take care of the chalk and erasers, clean the chalk boards, feed the fish, and water the plants. Some mature primary as well as older children can keep the library table, the teacher's desk, and supply areas in order. They may also help with arranging flowers, changing the water, throwing out dead bouquets, counting the scissors to be sure that all have been returned, picking up scraps, cleaning the paint easel, cleaning the tables after nutrition or the use of paste, opening the windows and closing them as needed, sharpening pencils, filling paste jars, and mixing paints if the children are mature enough. Children of all ages can also serve as host or hostess to meet visitors at the door and seat them in a convenient place. They can also help by leading the flag salute and taking the balls or other play materials out to the playground and returning them after play. Older children can help in even more ways.

Many suggestions for ways of helping in the classroom have been suggested because of the status-giving value of this work. Dickinson studied the value of such activities in giving status. [2] She took sociometric tests of the children in the first five grades, beginning with the first, to discover the number of isolates to be found in each class. She asked for three choices of friends for three types of activities, a total of nine choices in all. When she totaled the number of times each child was chosen, she found approximately two isolates in each class.

---

[2] Anna Dickinson, "The Use of Guidance Techniques to Increase Sociometric Status." (Unpublished Master's Thesis, Sacramento State College, 1952).

For the next four months the teachers encouraged each of the children in their classes to volunteer for work on one of the room committees. These committee members continued their work for about three weeks before the committees were dissolved and re-formed for other duties. The teachers tried to make reassuring comments about the contributions of each committee member each day when possible, but they made sure that the isolates received recognition for their work every day. On retests at the end of the four-month period, only one isolate was found in the entire five grades. This child was new to the school, having entered two weeks previous to the tests. The use of slow readers along with others as helpers is an excellent procedure for giving them status.

Use of a Variety of Activities. The types of reading activities used with the children in the slow group can be valuable in giving status to these children. After preparing a dramatic reading or "play," the children in this group may present it to a lower grade whose teacher is understanding and sympathetic. The story should be practiced until the reading is fluent and the expression is good so that the younger children can really enjoy it. Individual children may take turns reading stories to the kindergarten children if their teacher appreciates this service. Again, the reading must be well prepared.

The children in the slow group may dramatize their stories with puppets, using a large carton with the front removed to serve as a stage. They may also use such a device for taking parts as actors in television plays, another way of motivating the reading through dramatization. A variety of games should be used to practice with the children in this group since they are likely to need more motivated practice than the other groups. If the other children observe the slower reader's enjoyment of the reading period, their status will be enhanced because these other children will not feel sorry for them.

The Attitude of the Teacher. Usually the attitude of the teacher is the most influential factor in the self-concepts of the slow readers and in the attitude of the other children toward them. If the teacher approaches the work with this group with a feeling of a chore to be endured, the children are certain to absorb this feeling, even though it is not expressed. They will also recognize the enthusiasm with which she turns to the children in the fast group who respond so easily. If the teacher dreads a visit from her principal or supervisor while teaching the slow group, this negative feeling will also be unconsciously felt by the children.

The teacher who has honest respect for the slow readers and who can teach them with enthusiasm usually does not need to be concerned about their feelings of inferiority because these feelings are minimized by her attitude. The attitudes of adults toward children's reading is often the cause of their unhappiness. Since concern over slow progress in reading and feelings of inferiority interfere with learning, whereas success stimulates effort, teachers should respect these children and give them books they can read as well as every encouragement possible to succeed, to enjoy reading, and to acquire a strong desire to read. The teacher must also help the better readers to respect the slower ones for other strengths these slower children often possess.

Selection of Reading Material

Another factor in children's feelings of inferiority in reading is often the result of the difficult level of the books selected by the teacher for the children in the slow reading group. Because of concern that the teacher in the grade above or the parents will expect the children to read in a book near their own grade level, teachers often select books that are too difficult for the members of this group. As a result the children are forced to struggle with too many unknown words and are unable to enjoy the stories because they cannot follow them when frustrated by the difficult vocabulary. If children in the slow reading group are given books on their levels of confidence, that is, books that they can actually read, they have a better opportunity to acquire skill in reading, to enjoy the work, and to find satisfaction in reading. A list of easy books with interest for retarded readers is given in the Appendix.

Split Session Reading

One of the most demanding tasks of the primary teacher is to provide adequate material for the children who must work independently while she works with one of the reading groups. This task also includes the need to supervise these children while they work and to keep the room quiet enough for the children who are reading with her to concentrate on their work.

Those schools that use the split reading program in the primary grades add an extra hour to the teaching day. Half of the children come for the first hour, usually from nine until ten in the morning. These children have their reading during this first hour when they are alone with the teacher. They also go home early in the afternoon, usually about two o'clock. The remaining half of the children join the others for the second hour of the morning, usually at ten o'clock. They then stay for an hour in the afternoon after the morning children have left for home, usually until three o'clock. All of the children work together from ten in the morning until two in the afternoon.

Advantages of the Split Reading Program

Smaller sized groups are possible in the split session reading program because the teacher has more time to teach reading. The children who are working independently may have more freedom because of the smallness of their number, and the teacher is able to give each child more time.

Size of Reading Groups. The reading groups can be smaller than in the usual grouping plan because the teacher may easily work with four groups, two during the morning period and two during the afternoon. In a class of thirty-six children each group may be made up of nine children, more or less. If an unselected group of eighteen children are taught in the morning, the teacher may work with eleven or twelve children in the fast group and six or seven in the slower group. The afternoon group may be divided in the same way. During this period of approximately fifty minutes the teacher will work with each group for about twenty minutes if they are sufficiently mature and will spend about five minutes, before or after each group reads, to assign independent work and check this work after the children have completed it.

Activity and Materials. During each hour the teacher has no more and usually less than twenty children in the room. The children may be more active in a room with twenty or fewer children than in a room of thirty-six children because fewer children will make far less noise and will distract the readers less. Even a few less metal tipped boots can be a relief. When the children working independently have finished their assigned work, such as a page in a workbook, they should know what creative or free activities they may choose and should be able to go to a work center without special direction from the teacher. Fewer puzzles, games, and other teacher-prepared reading materials are used at one time, so fewer need to be made.

Time for Each Child. The teacher who has fewer children in each reading group is able to meet each child's reading needs more easily and successfully. If children have questions, she has more time to answer them. She can give each child more opportunities to respond to her questions at the end of the silent reading or to find answers to the questions she uses to guide the oral reading. Each child will also have opportunities for more responses during the games and activities.

Disadvantages of the Split Reading Program

One of the disadvantages of the split reading program for the primary teachers is a longer teaching day. Integrated learnings may be more limited, and the sharing period must be delayed in this program. In addition, parents may object to the program if the school divides the children by ability grouping.

Teaching Day. The split reading program requires a longer teaching day than the usual program in which the children all stay together until the usual dismissal time. Most teachers feel that the expenditure of more time with the children is compensated for by the two periods when only half of the children are present. The demands for control are greatly decreased at this time, and the teacher can work in a much more relaxed atmosphere. In addition, the teacher needs to spend less time after school or in the evening preparing work for the use of the children who are working independently. This program is of particular help to the first-grade teacher since the demands for teacher-prepared material are particularly great in this grade. These children are far less able to work on their own initiative or to read directions for self-help than older children.

Limitation of Integrating Learnings. The split reading program may limit some opportunities for the integration of the reading program with the social studies, science, and other content fields. If the teacher plans carefully, however, some of the reading of the social studies or other material may be taught during the reading period. The primary teacher must usually use different social studies books with each group, and these may be used during the early hour when only part of the children who need this special help are present. These or other suitable books may be used with children for whom they are appropriate during the late hour. The two groups may bring together the ideas they have gained when they work together during the regular social studies period. In order to make the discussion brief and to the point, the teacher will help the children use key words printed on the chalk board. In this way the older primary children will learn the early steps of speaking from notes and will gain some ideas regarding the use of outlines.

Delay of the Sharing Time. In the split reading program the sharing period is usually delayed until all the children are present at ten o'clock. For this reason, treasures must be put away for a while. The young child is usually eager to show immediately the things he has brought for the teacher and his classmates to see. A compromise may be made by allowing the younger children to show their articles briefly to the teacher and children in the early group and to show them again while they discuss them in detail when all the children are present. Older children may be satisfied to show the things they have brought to the teacher and to withhold the display and the discussion until all members of the class are present.

Parent's Objections. If the children are divided according to slow and fast groups in the split reading program, the parents soon learn about it. If the slower children are taught in the morning period and the faster children are taught in the afternoon, most parents will demand that their children are placed in the afternoon group. They seem to assume that the label will influence the product rather than the reverse. Parents also fear that their neighbors will see their children going to school early and that they will lose status and prestige as a result of this situation. This fear is often justified because some parents are not above making unkind comparisons between their children and those of their neighbors' in the presence of their "less fortunate" neighbors. Such comparisons may cause the slower child's parents to push him, thus making his reading problems greater than they already are. For the sake of parent's feelings and the danger that these may rebound on the child, morning and afternoon groups should be heterogeneous. Other considerations may be taken into account such as arrangements for parents who leave for work early or who must make special provisions for baby sitters.

Reading in the Ungraded Program

The ungraded program has special value for readers who are slow to make a beginning. Because promotions are not made during the primary grades, frustration is eliminated due to failure while the child is quite young.

Example of Reading in an Ungraded Program. For example, a teacher carried an average group of six-year-old children through two years of an ungraded primary program. The highest intelligence quotient in the class was about 140, and the lowest was a little above 80. The upper third of the class ranged from 111 to 140, and the average group ranged from 81 to 102. Some children in this class were emotionally disturbed, but the parents co-operated to improve greatly the adjustment of these few children.

The teacher used experience stories completely unrestricted in vocabulary and a wide variety of other functional types of reading. Surprises were announced in simple sentences on the bulletin board. A class calendar, daily newspaper, labeled boxes holding supplies, social studies planning charts, charts of growing vocabulary lists, charts reporting science experiments, group dictated letters, individual and group booklets, and many other interesting and challenging uses of reading were carried on along with many firsthand experiences and an extensive use of oral language.

Achievement in an Ungraded Reading Program. The brightest and most mature child in this class was able to read preprimers at sight after six weeks of participation in this program. Within two or three more weeks a group was ready to take part in a regular developmental reading program. Enough children were ready to make up another reading group after about two months, and a third reading group was organized in January. By the end of the first year, on the other hand, five boys were unable to do more than memorize sentences as wholes in their own very short experience stories. These boys were able to recognize their own names, but could not recognize any other words when they met these words out of the context of a memorized sentence.

By the middle of the second year, the five boys made a sudden spurt. One by one they started voluntarily to read stories in a first reader that had special appeal to them. In the beginning the teacher thought that they had memorized these stories from hearing other children read them. When the boys brought her stories that had not been read by any of the children in the regular group reading, the teacher was forced to have faith in this unprecedented situation and tried working with them in a first reader of special interest that no one in the class had used before. These boys were able to read with success in this set of first readers and went into a developmental reading program at that level. They never were taught to read in pre-primers or primers. By the end of the second year, these five boys were able to read well enough to be promoted to the third grade with the rest of the class. There was no greater spread in their reading abilities than in any normal third grade. In fact, no child read below the first reader level.

The work with this class in an ungraded program over a period of two years showed that all of these children had learned to read by acquiring a beginning vocabulary from unrestricted experiences of a creative nature. The process required a long period of time for the most immature children.

Advantages of an Ungraded Reading Program. The success of this ungraded type of reading program, however, depended upon a number of factors, particularly in regard to the work with the most immature beginners. These factors are given as follows: (1) These children were not under pressure to achieve reading at any previously stated level at any time and therefore had no reason to develop a fear of reading. The teacher had excellent relations with the parents, who were willing to rely entirely on her judgment and had faith in her ability. Therefore the parents did not put pressure on the children. (2) The teacher expected performance from these children only in matters in which they were able to succeed. The slow beginners worked with their experience stories on charts by matching strips to the sentences on the charts, one of the few activities they could carry on successfully.

(3) As far as possible, these children carried on activities similar to those followed by the other children. They came to the circle for their readiness experiences just as the other children did. Thus, they did not feel that they were different from the others. The other children, too, were not conscious of differences. (4) No failing marks on report cards were sent home since conferences took the place of report cards. Because the children were to remain in one class for two years, the parents were not concerned about promotion or retention during most of the time the children were in this class. No bicycles or talking dolls were promised for which scoldings were substituted later. By the time the problem of promotion did arise toward the end of the second year, all the children were reading well enough to be assured of promotion.

(5) A very rich social studies program provided many opportunties for these less mature children to work with their hands. They helped other members of the class in a variety of ways and made articles for the use of the group. Everything was done to help these immature children feel that they were successful and valued members of the group and that they were completely accepted by their teacher and peers.

Lack of Pressures. The two-year program for these children was carried on informally. No grade level requirements were set up, and only the minimum standardized tests were given. Other teachers have used similar programs on an informal basis and have achieved similar results. All of these teachers, however, had good techniques and were skillful in working with children, along with the other factors involved in the success of these programs. These successes illustrate the fact that even immature children can learn to read in an ungraded program by beginning with creative experience stories, providing a considerable period of time, depending on ability, is allowed for their progress. Good teaching and a good general program are probably paramount in the success of such a procedure. Pressures and distrust from some of today's parents might result in criticism of the schools if teachers used similar procedures with immature children in school districts populated by Caucasian, competitive, climbing parents who measure social status by the grade of the book Junior is reading.

A Modern Ungraded Program. In recent ungraded programs, primary children are divided into as many classes as the numbers permit on the basis of tests of readiness or intelligence. Thirty or thirty-five children of homogeneous ability, as nearly as possible, are placed in one class. The children are then encouraged to progress in reading at their own rates. If a child becomes too advanced for the class group with whom he is working, he is moved into the next higher class. If he fails to keep up with the children in his own class group, he may be placed in the next group below his.

Children may move from teacher to teacher according to their progress, but no annual promotions are made until the children are ready for the fourth grade. All those who are able to work on the fourth-grade level are then promoted. Others who have progressed more slowly may continue to work in their own classes another year before being promoted to the fourth grade. The greatest advantage of this plan is the lack of failure, at least until the end of the third grade, which minimizes discouragement and frustration. As the plan was originally advocated by Goodlad and Anderson the levels were not meant to serve as arbitrary hurdles similar to grade hurdles used for promotions.[3]

Homogeneous Grouping

Homogeneous grouping has been tried many times in various ways as a plan for improving the teaching of reading. The procedures for dividing groups of children are usually similar to those followed in a study described by Balow.[4] The *Iowa Silent Reading Tests* were given to ninety-four fifth-grade children who were then divided into four groups on the basis of their total scores. These scores were given in terms of grade equivalents, that is, the grade level of the average pupil as standardized on tests. The analysis of the subtests for these fifth-grade children provides some insight regarding the meaning of such "homogeneous" grouping.

Division into Groups. The children were divided into four groups as follows: Those who had scores in the highest quarter with a median score equivalent to the sixth grade, seventh month were placed in Class A. Those who had scores in the second quarter with a median of fifth grade, seventh month were placed in Class B. Those with scores in the third quarter with a median score of fourth year and zero months were placed in Class C, and those with scores in the lowest quarter with a median of third year and third month were placed in Class D.

Each of the fifth-grade teachers taught one of these class groups for an hour a day. Each child left his own classroom and went to another room taught by a teacher who was responsible for his reading class. Some children who happened to belong to the particular classes taught by their regular teachers stayed in their own rooms. Each teacher ad-

3 John I. Goodlad and Robert H. Anderson, "Educational Practices in Nongraded Schools: A Survey of Perception," *The Elementary School Journal*, LXIII (Oct. 1962), 33–40.

4 Irving H. Balow, "Does Homogeneous Grouping Give Homogeneous Groups?" *Elementary School Journal*, LXIII (Oct. 1962), 28–32.

justed her teaching to the average of the group she taught. Many
teachers like this plan because they feel that it is easier and more efficient
to teach children that are similar in achievement. Some feel that groups
within the class are unnecessary because all the children in the class
have the same problems and read on about the same level. Since these
children's reading achievements are average for their class group, the
teachers feel that they may teach the entire class together using the
same book.

Analyzing for Homogeneity. Perhaps the word *average* is more confusing than helpful. The story of the man who drowned in the middle
of a river that averaged four feet in depth underlines this point. To discover what is really meant by teaching children who make an average
of a particular score and to find out if the children in each of these
groups had similar problems, Balow analyzed their tests. He was particularly interested to see what kind of scores these children made on the
seven parts or subtests that made up the total reading test given to them.
The charts in Figure 20-1 show the range of scores on each subtest for
each of the classes, A to D. Median scores are also shown on these
charts for each class. The median score indicates that one half of the
children had higher scores than the median and half had lower scores.
The median score, then, is the midpoint and is usually close to the
average.

The range gives the highest and lowest scores found on a particular
subtest in each class. The other scores are scattered between the highest
and lowest scores. No one particular pupil usually receives the high
scores on all the subtests nor does any one usually receive all the low
scores. The range helps the teacher know that some of her pupils have
low scores in some skills and therefore need help and that some of her
pupils have high scores. A particular pupil, however, may have a high
score in comprehension and a low score in alphabetizing, even in Class A
shown in Figure 20-2.

A glance at the range of the subtests for Class A shows at once that
this teacher cannot use one book for all the children in this class. It also
tells that none of these particular needs for help are the same for all the
children in this class. Although the smallest difference is found between
the lowest and highest scores on word meaning, a gap of four grades
is found in this one skill.

Even in Class D a gap of almost two grades exists between the lowest
and highest scores in word meaning, the subtest with the smallest range.
Apparently none of these teachers can use one textbook for her entire
class, nor can any of them help all of the children on the same problem
if they are to meet the needs of these children. Even in Class D one

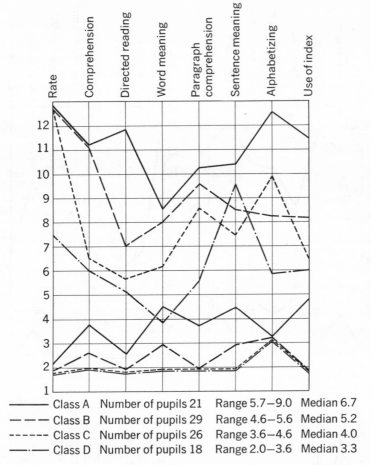

———— Class A Number of pupils 21 Range 5.7–9.0 Median 6.7
– – – Class B Number of pupils 29 Range 4.6–5.6 Median 5.2
------ Class C Number of pupils 26 Range 3.6–4.6 Median 4.0
—·— Class D Number of pupils 18 Range 2.0–3.6 Median 3.3

Fig. 20–1. Range in grade equivalent in reading for four fifth-grade classes after homogeneous grouping.

child reads as slowly as a first-grade child and another reads as rapidly as a seventh-grade child. It is obvious that each of these teachers will need to put some children in one group within his own class for one type of problem and some in another to help them on a different problem. They will also find that some of these children may need to take part in several groups. This study has been described because the data is typical of all so-called "homogeneous" grouping.

Achievement in Homogeneous Groups. Balow carried on another study to discover if children taught in homogeneous classes learn to read better than those in groups of mixed ability. In one school the children in the sixth grades worked with their regular teachers. In another sixth

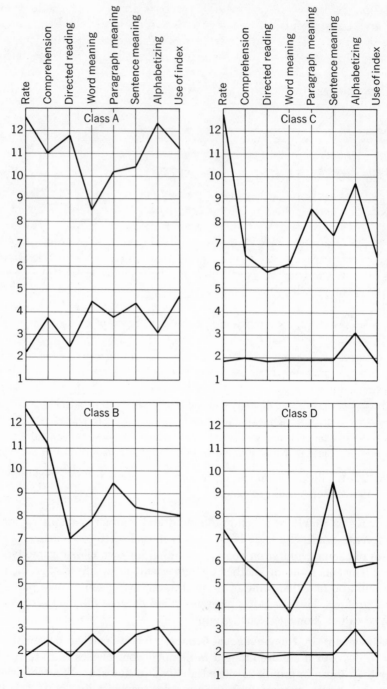

Fig. 20–2. Grade equivalents in reading.

grade the children were divided into groups of those above grade, average, and below grade. Three teachers divided these children among them by groups. The average intelligence levels of those in the homogeneous groups were three points higher measured by raw scores than those of the other children. The gain in reading ability for the children in the homogeneous groups was slightly less than the gain of the children in the mixed groups.

One school district, on the other hand, found excellent results for below-average groups after they had changed to homogeneous grouping. It was discovered, however, that they had placed their best teachers with the retarded readers.

Results of Teachers' Enthusiasm. Sometimes another factor influences the results when teachers request a change to homogeneous grouping or when they are asked to try to plan for their district or school administration. If the leaders are enthusiastic about the idea, they often inspire the teachers who unconsciously put enthusiasm and extra effort into the plan. If another group is used as a control to follow the old plan without the inspiration or enthusiasm of a leader, they may lack this same challenge.

Sometimes children, too, become enthusiastic about a new plan. The parents who are told that their children will read in an upper group often feel pleased and proud and sometimes even smug, and their attitudes may carry over to the children. Even the slower children may feel that the special help may solve their problem, and they, too, may work with greater enthusiasm and therefore achieve on a higher level. This feeling of increased hope is often called the *Hawthorne* or the *placebo* effect. This latter word is a medical term used to refer to a sugar pill given to patients who seem to have no physical cause for disorders. If the patients improve, the results may be due to faith in the doctor rather than to the actual treatment. If the plan of homogeneous grouping is continued for a number of years, the placebo effect is usually lost, and the difference between the achievement of the two plans usually disappears.

Preference by Children. Some parents who may have been enthusiastic about this type of grouping because their younger children were selected to read with the highest group may change their minds after the program has been under way for some time. Bright fourth-grade children who are grouped with sixth graders may find that some of the material is not very interesting to them or that some of it may be beyond their understanding. These children can read the words, but they may not understand the thought because it is appropriate for older children.

On the other hand, the sixth-grade child who is below average in reading may feel affronted by material that is of interest to children two years younger than he. He may also feel self-conscious about reading with younger children. If these slow readers remain in the lowest group over a period of years, they tend to lose enthusiasm and self-confidence and to become frustrated.

Reading in Other Subjects. A fifth-grade teacher was delighted when he was given the highest reading group in a school that grouped homogeneously for reading in the fourth, fifth, and sixth grades. Slow sixth-grade readers read with average fourth-grade children, whereas excellent fourth-grade readers read with average and advanced sixth-grade children. The fifth-grade children were scattered among the classes of various reading levels. As he began to teach his fast reading class, he was delighted with their ability and the challenge they gave him to provide them with books on a great variety of topics. He found little difficulty in helping them with their occasional problems in reading skills because they learned rapidly.

This teacher, however, began to become concerned with the children in his fifth-grade class, especially in social studies and science. He checked with the other reading teachers who worked with his children and found that some had been taught reference skills but needed review and others had not yet been taught these skills. He found that he needed to give much help of this kind as well as with the development of concepts during his social studies and science periods. He realized that he knew the skills and habits of his advanced fifth-grade readers, but he had to consult other teachers often and refer frequently to test records to learn more about his average and slow fifth-grade readers.

He wanted to learn more about the causes of these children's difficulties, but his time was limited because he had to learn about the problems, interests, and abilities of the children in his own special reading class. As the year progressed he realized that many of the subject-matter problems of the children in his regular class tied in with or arose from their reading problems, but he was unable to give them needed help except during out-of-school hours. He decided he could have worked more successfully with his fifth-grade class if he had taught their entire program in a self-contained class.

SUMMARY

Although the individualized reading program has some excellent values, described in the previous chapter, it also has some problems that should be considered. The teacher has a very limited time with each pupil alone, and she cannot always be available when individuals need her for help. She must also provide a variety of activities for the

EXTRA THINGS TO DO

MOTHS
by Dorothy Childs Hogner

1. Read a book.

2. Draw a picture.

3. Write something.

Do a puzzle
a game.

rk on a special
oject.

Two first-grade children are consulting a chart of activities to choose from when their work is finished. (Courtesy N.D.E.A. Demonstration School and Sacramento City Unified School District.)

children, especially on the primary level, who must spend a long time each day working by themselves. Time is needed for most children to provide review and application of study skills, a difficult matter if children are to be helped individually.

Other organizational plans have values and also present difficulties. The developmental program with three reading groups is the plan followed most widely. The tendency to acquire feelings of inferiority by the members of the third group is a serious problem, but many activities can be used to give these children self-respect and status. The teacher's attitude is particularly important in her effort to help the slower readers.

The split reading plan provides time for the teacher to work with half the class in the morning before the others arrive at school and to work with the other half after the other children have left in the afternoon. In this way the teacher can give the children more time in group and individual work, and she needs less prepared work for the independent work period.

The ungraded program permits all primary children to learn at their own rates of speed without concern about failure or promotion until the child is ready to enter the fourth grade. Flexibility in moving pupils from one group to another when needed is an important aspect of this plan.

Homogeneous grouping is a plan that has been used from time to time, especially in the intermediate grades. Teachers often feel that this plan is more efficient than most and makes it easier for them to teach more effectively. When the subtests of the *Iowa Silent Reading Tests* were given to a group of fiifth-grade children who had been divided into four class groups on the basis of ability, these subtests showed a great range of high and low scores typical of apparently homogeneous groups. These children would need help in various types of groups on a wide range of skills. Total average scores on tests tell very little about the individual pupil's problems and needs.

21

The Culturally-Deprived Child

Approximately one quarter of the population is culturally-deprived, some more severely than others. The teacher who works with these children must be conscious of some of their important characteristics and the circumstances under which they live to avoid frustration for herself and the children she teaches. She must have some idea, too, of teaching procedures that may be more suitable for these children than others.

CHARACTERISTICS OF THE CULTURALLY-DEPRIVED CHILD

Many of the characteristics of the culturally-deprived child tend to work against success in school. The teacher must realize that the culturally-deprived do not wish to live as they do and would try to make a better adjustment if that were possible. These people are, however, gripped in a vise of poverty and ignorance from which very few are able to escape. Some of these characteristics that act as obstacles to learning are discussed in this chapter.

The Self-Concept

The term, *self-concept*, refers to the kind of person each individual feels he is and includes the individual's attitudes toward himself. The attitudes of the culturally-disadvantaged are made up of feelings of inadequacy, lack of self-confidence, and lack of worth. They feel excluded from the culture. They also feel that they are, at the best, victims of circumstances and of the lack of concern of the middle and upper classes. In more extreme situations the deprived feel that they are the prey of the politicians, hoodlums, and criminal organizations. In many situations, this feeling is based on fact.

Self-Concept of the Children. The children acquire their feelings of inadequacy both directly and indirectly from their parents. The parents may talk about and react on the basis of their own feelings of inadequacy and failure, which leads the children to take the same attitude toward themselves. In addition, the parents often criticize the children harshly and also talk about them to others in terms of a disparagement while the children are present. These people have no understanding of the tremendous needs of their children for feelings of success, achievement, belonging, and love. Fundamentally, they love their children, but they do not know how to help their children and are usually too busy and harassed to express these feelings.

Low Self-Concept in School. Often the young children are responsive, warm, and appreciative when they enter pre-school or kindergarten. The tendency of teachers to look down upon them because they may be dirty and poorly clothed and use very poor English undermines their already limited feeling of adequacy. Their lack of experience also tends to limit their self-concepts. Other children who have a little more security and material advantage may also absorb the teacher's attitude and look down upon these children.

Influence of the Curriculum on the Self-Concept. The curriculum in most of the Headstart Programs and most of the kindergartens are well adapted to the needs of the culturally-deprived, although they may not provide enough experiences and enough opportunity for growth in language. If the predominant attitude toward these children is hostility and disapproval, they will reflect these feelings in their attitudes toward others. The child who hates himself also hates others, and these attitudes pervade the entire adult life. The school must begin early to help build self-respect.

On the other hand, the Headstart Programs taught by teachers of older children, who have no idea of the preschool program and who try to give these children a watered-down, academic curriculum, do untold damage. Only the very brightest and those who come from the best situations are able to cope with this type of curriculum. Their lack of language readiness tends to defeat them in every area of academic work. In their first experience, then, in school, their feelings of inadequacy and lack of belonging are sometimes greatly intensified. Children who learn fear and dislike school at this age have little hope of achieving success in academic work throughout their lives in school.

Kindergarten teachers who put the blocks and creative materials on the shelves and substitute outlines of pictures to be colored within lines and endless pictures to be matched fail to provide any of the real skills these children need. These teachers also convince the children that school is a boring, frustrating place, where they are required to sit still far beyond the limits of their physical maturity. This waste of human resources is vicious and criminal. If the teacher does not know better, someone in a responsible position should insist that teachers be trained for these positions. If these teachers refuse to carry out the proper type of curriculum, they should not be employed even though children will remain in their homes.

Methods of Improving the Self-Concept. A sensitive teacher who is deeply interested in the problems of these children should be selected to teach them. She should provide very simple experiences in which she feels sure the children can succeed and should gradually add activities that are slightly more difficult to challenge them but also to insure success. The teacher should consciously give recognition and praise for all efforts. This recognition must be sincere but should emphasize good effort rather than a finished product. She should also take a personal interest in each child, talk with him in a warm and friendly manner, and listen to him whenever possible.

Obstacles to Education for Culturally-Deprived Children. Fewer than one out of ten of these children read at or above grade level, and most read two to four years below grade level. Their reading disability increases with each year, and their measured I.Q. declines from grade to grade. If I.Q. serves to predict school achievement, then these I.Q. figures predict that children will do poorer and poorer work as they advance through the grades.

The language of these children is impoverished, and they speak a dialect that is different from that used by middle-class children. They may therefore have difficulty in understanding the teacher, shown by lack of attention. These children are also poor listeners because communication in the home is very brief and usually consists of a command for immediate action. These children's language is poor also because they lack a background of hearing stories in childhood and carrying on discussions with their parents. Questions directed to their parents are discouraged. Efforts to change these children's dialect too early may inhibit their speech. The dialect in the basic readers differs from children's own dialect and may be difficult for them to understand. The stories in these books have no interest for the children because they represent situations of which these children are completely ignorant.

The shortage of well-trained teachers who understand these children's problems is another obstacle to their advancement in school.

These children have little or no opportunity for contact with middle-class children because they live in congested islands in large cities. Any family that is able to rise in social class tends to move to the suburbs. In addition, the culturally-deprived in remote areas tend to move to urban centers for work and thereby become enmeshed in the slums.

The Family of the Culturally-Deprived Child

Many of the families are headed by a mother alone, although sometimes both parents are found in the culturally-deprived families. The father often deserts the family because the struggle for survival, food, clothing, and shelter is too great for him. Some of these fathers are victimized by criminal gangs who use them to act as "go-betweens" and "cats' paws." They are the ones who are most often caught and put in jail while the real criminals go unscathed.

When the mother is left alone, she must work as many hours as possible. Even so, she is still unable to provide satisfactorily for the children's needs on the inadequate wages she gets for the only kind of work she is capable of doing. She must be away from the children all day and cannot supervise their activities. Adolescent children are often drawn into gangs where they begin to carry on acts of rowdyism and vandalism.

The girl is often taken advantage of by these boys and by older men. She then starts life as an unwed mother and may continue to have one child after another, each by a different father. These children may never know their fathers, and the mother may not be sure of each child's last name.

Cleanliness. The home is often dirty and the children and their clothes remain long unwashed. Five or six families may live on one floor in a run-down building with cold water only. Other families may live in situations where only outdoor plumbing is available, and water must be carried a distance and possibly up several flights of stairs. The mother may never have learned that cleanliness of the children and the home is desirable. Even if she does know, she is too tired after her work away from home and her efforts to feed the children to do much about their cleanliness.

Health. Because of the lack of cleanliness, the over-crowding, the poor diet, and the lack of dental and medical care, these children are susceptible to many diseases and are usually poorly nourished. The doctors and dentists in the Headstart Program were shocked at the condition of the pre-school children they tried to help.

Condition of Employment. The culturally-deprived family is caught in an endless struggle for food, clothing, and shelter. Because of the lack of education of the parents, they must take the lowest paying jobs. This type of work has the least security because it often depends upon the harvesting of crops or construction work. The men are frequently laid off work and spend long periods of time unemployed. For this reason they have no way of getting ahead or of getting out of the slums. The situation is becoming worse as the demand of the economy for un-educated and unskilled workers decreases with automation.

Deficiencies in the Home. An attitude of discouragement and pessimism usually pervades the home, which is extremely drab. The parents are not interested in trying to make the home attractive and cannot afford to spend money on it if they wished. Flowers and other objects of beauty are rarely seen by the children. Almost no toys are found in the home, and the children have no books or even pencils and paper. The children escape from the over-crowded homes and spend most of their time playing in the streets unless they are old enough to work. Nothing in the environment directs their interests toward reading or school.

Effects of Frustration. These people do not get together for social activities and have almost no recreation. Their struggle for existence seems to submerge other interests, even their interest in their children. Due to discouragement and frustration, one or both parents may try to escape through alcohol and sometimes narcotics. Men also turn to gambling to try to make a little extra money or to try to forget their problems. If they become addicted to narcotics, they become even more severely trapped because they must have money to get their supply.

The families resent the services of the agencies they most need. They fear and hate policemen because they interfere with some of the things these people do. They resent the school because of its authority and because of what these people think of as interference. Other agencies, such as social service, fire protection, and public health are resented for the same reason.

Discipline. Discipline is authoritarian, because the parent does not have the time, energy, or possibly even the verbal skills to discuss why certain acts are wrong or dangerous. The parent uses physical punishment. Great variation is found from those who give the child a quick spat and then go on without grudge or resentment on either side to those who actually beat their children. Many of the children are sweet and co-operative at school although their frustrations may result in lack of interest, resistance to work, or even resentment of the school by the time they are in the upper grades. Those children who are beaten and commonly see violence in the home tend to take out their resentments and aggressiveness physically at school. These children are taught to stand up for their rights at home by fighting and are considered sissies if they do not. A great deal of time and energy is spent by the teacher in such situations to reduce this constant defensiveness at school.

Language Deprivation

The greatest weakness of culturally-deprived children is their lack of language, which is the result of their extremely limited experiences. For this reason, some authors use the term, language-deprived, in reference to these children. Most of the parents left school at the elementary level, even as early as the fourth grade. They therefore have a limited vocabulary. They usually have large families and must work so they have little time to spend on their children. As soon as the children are old enough, they too must work. The older ones must also take care of the younger ones.

Directions from parents are usually limited to gestures or two or three words at the most. These parents do not have time to reason with their children or to carry on discussions of any sort. Therefore, the children are exposed to a very small vocabulary. The children's play is primarily active and does not provide opportunity to make much use of even the language they know. These children may come to school with a vocabulary of only a few hundred words, many of which are learned on the street and are not suitable for use at school. These children use language primarily to tell others of their concrete needs, whereas the middle-class child uses language additionally for the relating of concepts. They also use their own idioms. For example, in some areas a teacher is a "mink job" or a "sad sack," ice cream is "snow," and skin is "velvet." The culturally-deprived cannot effectively operate in the same kind of school situation that is provided for children who may have up to an 8,000-word speaking vocabulary and a vastly greater understanding vocabulary with many well-established concepts. Young language-deprived children use single words and phrases in their speech and cannot work successfully in a situation which is adapted to children who in many cases are able to use simple, compound, and complex sentences.

Unless these children are helped to bridge the gap between their inadequate level of language development and that used by the middle-class child, they will not be able to cope with the curriculum planned for the latter. Such activities as coloring pictures already outlined will not in any sense of the word help them bridge this gap. Language maturity is basic for all success in academic work especially in the first grade of the elementary school. Children who are unable to use simple sentences are not ready to begin reading. These children need both a background of many experiences and a great many opportunities to express their ideas through language as they acquire this experience.

Intellectual Development

According to Kirk, children with the same native intellectual equipment may operate anywhere on the level of from 80 I.Q. to 120 I.Q., depending upon the environment in which they are brought up.[1] Most thinking seems to be carried on in terms of language. The language-deprived child is thus seriously limited in his ability to think.

Help of the School. The school must provide this child with many experiences not only to develop language but to provide language as a basis for thought. The greatest growth in mental ability, that is, the greatest growth toward achieving the child's maximum potential I.Q. comes between birth and three or four years of age. Some improvement can be made between the ages of four and six, and a little improvement can be made after six. Therefore, the education of children in pre-school kindergarten and first grade is extremely important in determining whether they will be able to operate at any level near their potential intelligence. The interpretation of I.Q.'s as a predictor of school success should be recalled. An I.Q. of 80 in terms of school achievement implies that the child is a slow learner and may be retarded one or two years in school. The child with 120 I.Q., on the other hand, will be very successful in elementary and high school and can succeed in college. This comparison emphasizes the tremendous importance of the educational program. Although the school alone is not entirely responsible for such a limitation of achievement, the school can make a tremendous contribution in helping the child attain his maximum potential achievement.

Children's Questions. Another factor that limits the child's intellectual growth is the unwillingness of parents to answer children's questions. Part of this unwillingness is due to fatigue, discouragement, and anxiety. The other part is due to the parent's fear that he does not know enough to give the child adequate answers and that he therefore will lose face with the child. In comparison, the life of the middle-class child in his early years is filled with one question after another. Most middle-class parents try to answer these children's questions to the best of their ability. The psychologists believe that the ability to formulate questions is one of the basic ways in which the child acquires information and forms concepts. Therefore the gap between the experiential background

[1] Samuel A. Kirk, "Language, Intelligence, and the Educability of the Disadvantaged," *Language Programs for the Disadvantaged* (Champaign, Ill.: National Council of Teachers of English, 1965).

of the culturally-disadvantaged child and the middle-class child is seen to be even greater than that which results from lack of language development. Questioning is not only desirable; it is essential to intellectual growth.

Slowness in Unfamiliar Tasks. The fact that the culturally-deprived child is relatively slow in performing intellectual tasks and that he is likely to have difficulty in forming generalizations may give his teacher the impression that he is a slow learner. However, he is fast when he is secure. He can verbalize in his own idiom, that is, use street language with considerable effectiveness. He can perform rapidly in athletic activities and games, and he may be very perceptive and quick in judging the expressions on people's faces. He is usually able to visualize well and may be creative. However, he is often a slow reader and a slow problem solver and may be slow at making a beginning in his work. He is particularly slow in taking tests which may seriously handicap him in school. If the teacher takes the results of intelligence tests at face value, this child will be considered a slow learner and may never be challenged to use his real intelligence.

Interests and Attention Span

This child's attention span may be very short when he is engaged in verbal activities. He may have trouble in listening to the teacher because he does not understand the meaning of some of the things she says and may only partially understand other things. He is interested in activities of various sorts rather than in discussions because he is used to playing on the street a great part of the time. His play primarily involves physical activities rather than language or dramatic activities. As he grows older, however, he may respond well to verbal activities if he becomes deeply involved in a problem that is important to him. He has difficulty adjusting to a school situation where he often must sit still for long periods at a time and take part in language activities and those that demand abstract thinking. He may understand meanings and concepts if he is able to make models or look at concrete examples of the things he is studying. He also needs more illustrations and more examples than other children when he tries to draw conclusions or form concepts. This child may also have considerable creative talent, but needs opportunities to express his creativity through the use of concrete materials.

Lack of Success in School

A high rate of school failure is found among the culturally-deprived because many of these children have disabilities in learning to read. As a result of discouragement and frustration in trying to meet the demands of the school, these children tend to drop out in large numbers in high school. They seem to change from the curious, affectionate, and likable children they are in kindergarten to children who are apathetic, who tend to withdraw, and who tend frequently to show anger and frustration by the time they reach the sixth grade, according to Riessman.[2]

Many factors besides those met in school affect the child as he is growing up to make this change. He absorbs much of the parent's feelings of discouragement, defeat, and resentment of society. The school, however, often reinforces these attitudes and builds new frustrations to add to those the child already meets in his environment.

Variety in Backgrounds

In almost all slums, the homes range from the most ravished to well-kept but cheap lodgings. Some families make a tremendous effort to keep the home and their children clean, to send them to school regularly, and to hold firmly to as many middle-class standards as possible. Some Negro families are much more religious and much more strict with their children than many white families. They know that very high standards are necessary to their eventual acceptance in the middle class.

Mexican parents are often very gentle but firm with their children, and the latter are usually sweet and co-operative in school. Japanese and Chinese people also handle their children with a firm hand, although they never cause them to lose face, and they insist that their school work be excellent. Some of the parents of Oriental and Negro children are professional people who are very intelligent and have very high standards. They may be required to remain in the slums, however, because other people refuse to let them live elsewhere.

The teacher is likely to find children in her classroom from the poorest homes to a few excellent homes and from slow learners to highly intelligent children. Most culturally-deprived parents want their children to learn in school but have no idea of how to help them. Attitudes also vary greatly. The parent's attitudes toward violence, school achievement, and honesty are widely divergent. Some children are taught to steal and are punished severely if they fail to bring any stolen goods home. Other parents are crushed if any of their children take things belonging to others even when they are too young to know better.

READINESS AND READING FOR CULTURALLY-DEPRIVED CHILDREN

Much can be done by the school to provide experiences in which the child can succeed and to give him continuous reassurance and recogni-

[2] Frank Riessman, *The Culturally Deprived Child* (New York: Harper & Row, 1962).

tion for his successes. The school should be able to give the child continuous success and encouragement to help him stay in school until he can acquire enough education to suceeed in a well-paying and reasonably secure occupation. The school can also help to improve the conditions in the home by providing parent-education programs starting at the time when the child first enters school.

Culturally-deprived individuals occasionally move to better occupations and are then able to move to better residential areas. The number of successes is pitifully small and should be greatly increased as the school is able to begin the education of the children at the pre-school level and provide a more appropriate curriculum on all levels.

Misinterpretation of Standards

Criticism of the school's promotional policies and so-called "lack of standards" has seriously handicapped the adjustment of the curriculum to the needs of culturally-deprived children. The effect on the schools of the second World War and the post-war period has been described in detail in an earlier chapter. Since many trained teachers left the schools and a large part of the teachers who replaced them were untrained, the education of the children was seriously handicapped. The fear aroused among the people of the nation by Sputnik, the first satellite placed in orbit by the Russians, caused many people to blame the schools for America's failure to compete and to feel that our educational program was not as effective as that in Russia.

The program that resulted from work by untrained teachers was considered to be education's best. College professors of academic subjects and army officers, neither of whom had any knowledge of the elementary school situation, filled the magazines with demands for a return to the three R's, which were presumed to have disappeared from schools due to so-called "progressive education."

As do all people who have no understanding of schools and the educational program, these people demanded that teachers go back to the academic requirements and "high standards" of the era when they were educated since this early era produced such paragons, that is, themselves. By "high standards" these self-appointed experts meant that the school should fail every child who did not attain a level of achievement decided presumably by the class average. If this so-called standard of success was based on the average, these people forgot that the *average* is made up of all those below as well as those above the standard.

The school had at one time failed many children, particularly on the basis of reading, because they did not meet certain artificial standards. Two thirds of these children who were failed did no better, and many did less well during the repeated year than they had during the initial year. Failure was shown to produce dropouts in high school, and the dropouts sometimes became delinquents. As long as the dropouts could get work in unskilled labor, they could manage to subsist. This group can no longer find steady employment.

The purpose of the schools in a democracy is to provide education for all children, to help them make the best of their intellectual potential, and to help them make a satisfactory adjustment in society. Only those schools that provide the best education for every child have truly high standards. Failure has been shown to do more harm than good in most cases. The basic purpose of the Headstart Program is to give these children a background so that they can take advantage of a good educational program and make better progress in school. It may not, however, serve to bring them up to first grade "standards." The school must still adjust to the needs of each child. In many cases, more experiences must be provided for the culturally-deprived child than for the middle-class child, and he must be provided with a curriculum that allows him to make use of his own talents and to learn in his own way. Failure in school is no answer to this problem.

Education for Pre-School and Kindergarten Children

The Headstart Program, planned and supported by the federal government, is one of the most forward-looking procedures that has been introduced in the school. The program is sponsored co-operatively by the schools, the social welfare department, and the public health department of local communities. All these people are co-operating to give young children the best beginning possible for their educational program. Children are provided with one meal and one snack during their attendance in order to provide physical stamina. They are examined by doctors and public health nurses, and the latter assist in the follow-up program to remedy defects.

Attention to the visual and hearing defects of children as well as to other physical defects is basic for school success. Nutritionists help in meal planning and also help with educational programs for parents. Social workers locate people needing help, serve as liaison between home and school, and make their records available so that the schools can reach most of the children whose needs are the greatest. Parents are required to register their children for these preschools. Since some parents are too indifferent to bring their children to the preschools, a few of the most needy children are not reached.

Most education directors of the Headstart Program have started with the usual nursery school program and have tried to expand it in every way. They have found nursery school experiences that are adequate for middle-class children to be far from adequate for culturally-deprived children. A great variety of first-hand experiences are needed to help these children develop readiness for school. A full-length mirror in the room may provide the child with his first opportunity to know what he looks like, a first step in self-identification.

The Pre-School Environment. Cooking facilities and cots for napping are provided to help meet the physical needs of culturally-deprived children. A sand box, centers for creative experiences, apparatus for physical activities, and a library of pictures and story books should be provided for these children.

Toys have even greater value for culturally-deprived children than they do for others since these toys represent objects they may have never seen. Toys designed particularly for young children should be selected. They are simply made and are sturdy so that children may play with them freely. Elaborate mechanical toys have no place in the preschool.

Informal discussions with teachers in play situations are needed to help the children expand their concepts regarding the actual size of the objects these toys represent and their purpose or use. The teacher should start with some type of object such as a toy truck to represent something that the children know at first hand. They may discuss the fact that these trucks look like real trucks, but they are small enough to use for play. The teacher can then encourage the children to lay out streets, bridges, and tunnels to represent these facilities in their own area.

If the children have not seen bridges or tunnels, however, play with these facilities will be delayed until the children can be given some experience with them. The teacher may talk with the children as they play, encouraging them to tell her what they are doing and helping them to use their gradually acquired vocabulary in their discussion. Although some children may not respond, the more verbal children will make a beginning, and the others will gradually imitate them. Other toys are introduced one at a time such as buses, trains, boats, dolls, and play dishes. The teacher always makes sure that the children understand what these objects are and what purpose or use they serve.

Water Play. Some teachers hesitate to provide young children with water because they may get their clothing and the floor wet. Solid tubs that will not tip over and a large mop to take care of any water that may be splashed on the floor simplify routines. Clothes dry quickly in warm weather. In winter they may be hung near a source of heat if any child gets wet enough to require this help. Most children can play with water without getting too wet and they should be taught to use water sensibly.

Water has a very soothing effect on children, and play in water is very calming to a disturbed child. One mother told a story of her emotionally-disturbed pre-school child. When he became very upset and acted aggressively toward other children, the teacher put a pan of water in front of him. The water always fascinated him, and he settled down to play happily as soon as it was placed before him. Soon the other nursery school children helped take water to him in emergencies. The teacher might not even know that the little boy was having a tantrum until she saw some children rushing toward him with a pan of water.

Water provides children with an opportunity to discover how toys and other objects react in a liquid medium. They discover that some things will float and others will sink. They also discover that certain materials will absorb water and that some of this water may be squeezed out of objects such as cloth and sponges after they have become wet. They may also discover that warm air helps to cause water or dampness to leave these objects.

Opportunities for Manipulation.   Children develop through a number of stages in their use of art materials such as crayons and paint. At first, they will manipulate each of these materials, partly to see what it can do for them and partly because they do not yet know what they can do with it. These stages include: (1) manipulation, (2) use of materials to symbolize objects although they may have no relation to the objects themselves, and (3) representation, a stage in which the child draws an object as it actually appears, although it may be very crude. The second stage is sometimes called the "naming" stage because children may apply the paint first and decide what the object means to them afterward. Some children also use design as another stage.

Children's ability to move from one of these stages to another is related to their mental growth and also depends upon the experiences they have had as well as their opportunties to use creative materials. Children go through stages in the use of materials whether it be applied to paper, or whether it be a material he uses for modeling. According to Lowenfeld, children are ready for reading when they draw on the representative stage and uses a baseline in their pictures.[3]

Art experiences, then, are one type of reading readiness experience. Pre-school children should have opportunities to use tempera paints, finger paints, crayons, clay, flour dough, or other modeling materials. As they progress through the kindergarten, they may make collages out of torn paper along with other materials pasted to paper background, and later they may cut paper with scissors for their collages.

Play in the Sandbox.   Such a simple activity as play in the sandbox has been questioned by some authors as a waste of time for children who must catch up to middle-class children in their language develop-

---

[3] Viktor Lowenfeld, *Creative and Mental Growth* (3rd ed.; New York: The Macmillan Co., 1957).

ment. Children, however, can acquire vocabulary or develop any learn-ing only at a limited rate and must have opportunities to use each new word frequently before this word is absorbed in their speaking vocabulary. New experiences may stimulate children and add more words and con-cepts to their vocabulary than they might acquire in a given time with-out such experience, but no child can learn under high pressure. In addition, each child learns at a rate that is different from others.

The best procedure for the teacher is to provide experiences in a normal situation in a relaxed atmosphere and to give opportunities for children to use their newly acquired vocabulary in natural play situa-tions. Play in the sandbox provides as many opportunities as any other type of play for children to dramatize with language or discuss any of the experiences to which they have been exposed. The child must have opportunities to assimilate his experiences, to reorganize his ideas around his experiences, and to make use of these ideas in his play. This pro-cedure cannot be accomplished by any short-cut or pressure technique. The children who grow at a more rapid rate than others will grow best in a rich environment from which they may select the experiences most meaningful to them and in which they express their own ideas in natural situations.

Story Telling and Activities with Books. One of the most obvious and greatest differences between the background of the culturally-deprived child and the middle-class child is the lack of opportunity for the former to hear stories, look at books, and observe adults who put importance on the value of books. Listening to stories is one of the most important activities that can be provided in the preschool and kindergarten. Many good stories for the child of this age are available, and a large selection of books should be provided for each room. At least one story-telling period a day should be provided for all young children.

The teacher of culturally-deprived children must try to start with books telling of activities that are within their background of experience. Little by little as the children are taken on trips to expand their experi-ences, stories about these new experiences may be added. Eventually, stories of situations beyond the child's environment may be read, but the teacher must make sure that the children understand the vocabulary.

Sturdy picture books should be available for children so that they may look at them in their free time, and teachers should encourage chil-dren to look at the books. When possible, the teacher or a teacher's aide may sit down with a few children to discuss the pictures as the children look at them. As soon as children give any evidence of retell-ing or dramatizing these stories, they should be encouraged to do so.

Care of Pets. The value of caring for pets was discussed in a previous chapter among other reading readiness activities. The care and study of pets, however, has even greater values for culturally-deprived children. Most of these children do not have pets because of the time that would be needed to care for them and because of the expense of feeding them. A kindergarten teacher in an underprivileged district asked her supervisor for suggestions to help two emotionally-disturbed children. The supervisor suggested either water play or care of pets. The teacher decided to get a guinea pig and kept it in the classroom. She was amazed at the gradual change that took place, particularly in one of the disturbed children. His greatest problem was lack of love and attention at home, and his constant disturbance of the other children in the class had been an effort to get attention. He became very fond of the guinea pig and gradually improved to a surprising degree because of his love for the animal and its love for him. The other disturbed child did not respond particularly well to the animal. The other children in the class, however, were very fond of it, and it had a beneficial effect on their attitudes and behavior.

The children learned about the kinds of food it needed and its other needs for water, cleanliness, and affection. They were all eager to take care of it and developed attitudes of responsibility in this work. They increased their vocabulary as they learned to talk in more detail about the kinds of food it ate and its other needs.

Other Science and Nature Activities. These children also increased their vocabulary and concepts by watching a bird build its nest outside the classroom window and discussing its behavior. They developed sufficient auditory acuity to recognize its song and were gradually able to recognize the songs of other birds around the school. In addition, the children planted seeds and learned to eat vegetables they had grown, although they had not known them before. They were acquainted only with potatoes, turnips, cabbage, and dry beans. They grew radishes, lettuce, carrots, and other vegetables in their garden and developed a taste for them as well as learned that these vegetables were good for them.

These children brought in bugs of various sorts and developed visual acuity and extended their vocabulary in learning the names of a number of them. At no time were they ever forced to learn the names of insects or birds, but their curiosity and constant discussion helped them gradually acquire these names. The children also developed general concepts as they learned that all birds lay eggs, make nests of one kind or another, and raise their young. They learned concepts when they discovered which bugs were helpful and which were harmful to their vegetables. They also developed concepts about weeds and learned which ones should be pulled out of their garden.

These experiences added a great deal to the learnings of these children because they lived in an industrial area. Although they saw many

A first-grade child has written a story in i.t.a. (see Chapter 23) and illustrated it, and is ready to read it to the other children in his class. (Courtesy Georgetown School, Placer County, California.)

things around them, they had little understanding of their meaning or use. Science activities of all kinds for children in the heart of an industrial area are valuable and serve to extend their concepts.

Music. Although these children had never heard any music other than the poorest of the contemporary noise that is considered music by adolescents, they learned to be very fond of Bach and could even identify one or two of his selections. They were also very fond of light classical music such as Brahms' Lullaby, the Strauss waltzes, Beethoven's Minuet in G, Schubert's Military March, and Tchaikovsky's Andante-Cantabile. They used music of this type for their rhythm band and for interpretive dancing in a very simple way. They became more and more creative as the year advanced.

Good taste in music and the ability to enjoy time-tested selections of real worth are easily acquired by young children. All people learn to like the things they know, and children can learn to appreciate and develop a taste for good music as early as they can develop a taste for meaningless noise.

Physical Activities. Pre-school and kindergarten children need opportunities to develop large muscle activity of all sorts. The culturally-deprived children have access to no equipment or play material at home and need experiences with them. They should take part in large muscle activities, which are needed before small muscle activities and eye-hand co-ordination can be developed. Play with large balls is a good activity. The jungle gym helps them learn balance and gives them feelings of self-confidence as they learn to climb. The bars help them build strength in their arms and help strengthen muscles in their hands. Walking boards are good for an increasing sense of balance.

As these children learn to play with each other under supervision, they develop a sense of responsibility for the safety of others and also learn to handle the equipment with safety for themselves. These children also learn new, wholesome play activities to add variety to the few that they learn when they play on their street. Ideas for wholesome recreational activities are important for these children.

Trips. The value of trips has been discussed in connection with reading readiness activities. Walks and trips of various sorts are even more valuable for culturally-deprived children than for middle-class children. Allison Davis emphasizes the need for children to learn the names of many objects and to develop concepts in connection with these objects.[4]

The need for the development of a thorough understanding of the immediate environment for pre-school and kindergarten children was emphasized in the chapter on reading readiness activities. The service station was given as an example of a place in the environment that children have seen frequently but about which they know very little. Children may know the local corner grocery store slightly because they spend occasional nickels for candy there. They do not know, however, many of the other types of foods carried by this store. They do not know such general ideas as the fact that vegetables and fruits may be purchased

---

[4] Allison Davis, "Teaching Language and Reading to Disadvantaged Negro Children," *Elementary English* (Nov. 1965), pp. 791–97.

in several forms such as fresh, canned, and frozen. These children rarely see frozen foods because their parents cannot afford to buy them. The members of one kindergarten class took turns buying lettuce and carrots for their pet rabbit. Eventually, they cooked carrots in the classroom and some of them ate this vegetable for the first time. Later they cooked frozen carrots to give them an experience with two forms of this vegetable. They may also learn about various types of bread, rolls, and pastries that are carried by such stores.

Excellent opportunities for discussing the values of foods are provided by an acquaintance with a store of this sort. Children may even have opportunities to learn about the type of goods carried in wholesale warehouses and industries near them if the owners permit visits by children. They may never have seen various types of furniture and certainly have no idea of the names of many of the pieces. Owners of various businesses are usually willing to allow children to visit their buildings and often go out of their way to help children to understand the things they see.

Formalized Experiences. A number of programs have been developed over the last few decades for children with extreme reading difficulties. One program provides for large muscle activities such as crawling, tumbling, and learning to change the dominant foot while walking in order to establish dominance of a particular foot, eye, and hand, as one remedial approach to these problems. In another program, an effort is made to improve perception by presenting the child with an extensive series of geometric drawings. These drawings are usually presented in pairs. The diagram in one drawing in the pair is always complete. One element or line is omitted in the drawing with which it is paired. The child is trained to find this omitted line and fill in the second diagram so that it is identical with the first.

Some educators are grasping at these more formal and sometimes mechanical procedures to use them as a way of providing readiness for culturally-deprived children. A procedure that might be useful for children with extreme perceptual handicaps such as the brain-injured might be completely without value for a normal child who has not had as many experiences as other normal children.

Middle-class children are successful in reading, on the whole, not because they have been trained in mechanical and formalized exercises but because they have been exposed to a rich program of living. The best pre-school and kindergarten program tries to provide the experiences that the deprived family cannot provide. Language and experiences that develop language make up the big gap that exists between the culturally-deprived child and the middle-class child. The directive is plain. The school should try to provide for these children those things which the family has been unable to provide. Until very sound proof is available to assure the teacher that other procedures are better for the child, she should not blindly follow programs that were meant for children who are brain-injured or neurologically handicapped.

Education of Primary Children

Children in the primary grades have a need for many of the experiences described above for the younger group. These activities, however, will be extended to include more complex experiences and concepts. Trips will include places farther afield and may even include those that necessitate bus trips for the children. These children may expand their concepts by a visit to a cannery, the neighborhood post office and later the main post office of the city, the neighborhood library and the main library, the bus station, the railway depot, the airport, and many other of the more complex centers of service in the community. They will also study community helpers and learn that the policeman is a friend who provides important services for people. They may also learn about health and acquire some ideas of how to control contagious diseases and why cleanliness is important in the homes and streets of the neighborhood. The entire social studies program of the primary grades has tremendous contributions to make for these culturally-deprived children as well as for middle-class children.

Reading. The balanced program for the preprimer, primer, and more advanced books has been described in detail in earlier chapters in this book. Many of the procedures described in this program were used experimentally with culturally-deprived children, sometimes in desperation, to find some approaches that would be more effective with these children than the more usual procedures. For any program to be successful, the reading material must be paced to the children's ability to progress in reading. The material must not contain more than a few new words and must otherwise be made up of words that are well-known by the children.

To aid the children to gain meaning from the story, an introduction must be presented to help them understand the pictures and the concepts utilized in the story. Children's discussion of their experiences that relate to the story is essential to help them identify themselves with the children in the story.

The Parallel Story for the Culturally-Deprived. The parallel story was used especially with these children because it provided large print. It was also valuable because the teacher could hold the pointer under a particular line, thereby helping all the children concentrate on the same line at the same time. Because these children had difficulty in holding their attention on anything for a long enough time for it to impress them, the use of the chart was particularly helpful. The games and activities that have been suggested for use with the charts fulfilled the need for these children to move physically, which also helped hold their attention. The game element had a strong appeal even for the more immature of these culturally-deprived children.

Silent Reading and Practice for the Culturally-Deprived. The silent reading step was not introduced as early with these children as with middle-class children because their ability to handle an abstract skill such as silent reading developed much more slowly than with children with more mature language. Silent reading was therefore introduced later, and great care was taken to see that the children had thoroughly mastered the sentences, words, and phonic elements needed for each story before a new story was introduced.

The practice period was sometimes placed before the silent reading to give these children thorough mastery of all the words they would need in their story. A variety of games and activities were provided for the practice period because the teacher found that she sometimes needed to continue this type of activity for more than one day. Practice might be given on the same sentences and the same words over a period of several days, as long as the activities engaged in were varied. The children enjoyed the games very much, and this enjoyment tended to result in interest in and enjoyment of the entire reading experience.

Oral Reading for the Culturally-Deprived. Oral reading by turns line by line down the page was very ineffective with these children as well as with most others. They had a greater tendency to read word by word than middle-class children and had difficulty in getting meaning from the sentences. Instead of meaningless oral reading, the teacher often used dramatic activities of all kinds. If a sentence read, "Come, Rover, come," one child took the part of Rover, and the child reading the sentence was challenged to make Rover really want to come. Although the reader usually struggled with the sentence several times, he finally called Rover with enough expression to make him want to come. The child taking the part of Rover enjoyed resisting the command as long as he could, and the audience was intrigued by the situation.

In another part of the story, the sentence to be read was, "Rover jumped over the fence." If it was read word by word, a new Rover volunteered to dramatize the action. The teacher asked him to jump over a large block to represent the fence in order to encourage the reader to read what Rover did with understanding and expression. Dramatic activities, pantomime, and pictures eventually helped these language-deprived children learn to read naturally and to understand what they were saying when they read orally. These oral reading activities also provided opportunities for the children to leave their seats and move around in order to break the tension and increase the interest.

Experience Stories. One of the difficulties in helping language-deprived children dictate experience stories is their lack of ability to use complete sentences. After many readiness experiences had been provided in one classroom, the teacher began her work in dictation with titles for the children's paintings. The children were able to dictate these titles because single words and phrases were sufficient. Many of the children's paintings were mounted with captions dictated by the children. A few were placed on display on the bulletin boards for a short time and were soon replaced with others. The dictation of these captions helped the children understand the use of printed titles, and they often brought their mothers to see their paintings and listen to them read the captions whenever their mothers came to school with forgotten lunches, rubbers, or other belongings.

Dictated letters saying such things as, "Dear Mother, Thank you, Love, Miss Jones' Kindergarten," also helped the children develop an understanding of written communication. These letters were printed by the teacher at dictation on large news sheets, folded and sent home just as they were for cookies contributed for a party or any help given by the mothers. Sometimes the teacher added a note at the bottom of the page to explain the message in greater detail.

Eventually, stories of one sentence were dictated although the teacher might need to ask several children for help before the sentence was complete. The words, *He came* might require some work before the children changed the words to *Harold came*. Further questions might be needed to add *to school today*. The sentence was finally pieced together to make a "story" to place under a child's painting. Harold might have been a younger brother, but the children might have been too immature to add this fact. After the dictation of many one-sentence stories, the children began to add more sentences with less difficulty, and the teacher was eventually able to secure stories of two or three sentences.

Silent Reading of Directions. The use of direction strips is a technique teachers of deprived children have used successfully. Some suggestions for helping the children get meaning as they read orally have been given, but they need special help with the meanings of sentences in silent reading. One of the best ways of helping children get meaning as they read silently is the use of direction strips. The teacher prints directions on sentence strips described in an earlier chapter. In order to work with these directions, she finds toys to represent nouns that are introduced in the pre-primer that she plans to use with her children. She then uses the nouns in her printed directions such as, "Find the ball, Find the boat," or "Find the airplane." Later she adds other directions such as, "Bring the boat to me, Bring the ball to me," and so forth, always using words the children will read in their pre-primers at a later time.

If the pre-primers are too inappropriate in content for these children, some teachers develop a beginning vocabulary entirely by means of experience stories and direction strips. This vocabulary is used to lead to reading in books of high interest and low vocabulary. This procedure can be used instead of using one of the basic reading series, if the teacher finds the latter are too remote from the children's experiences and interests.

Use of Toys for Directions. The teacher may begin by setting out four toys such as a car, an airplane, a boat, and a house because the stories in the pre-primer tell about these things. The teacher and the children discuss what the objects represent. Some of the culturally-deprived children may have never seen a detached house. This house must be compared to the tenements in which they live, and the differences must be discussed without disparaging the tenements. Boats must also be discussed, unless children live near a river or a harbor and see boats frequently. Even so, the children will need help in relating their ideas of full-sized boats of various types to the model represented by the toy. The car and the airplane must be discussed in the same manner.

Introduction of the Direction Strips. The teacher may then hold up a reading strip on which is printed such a direction as, "Give me the airplane." She may inform the children that this sentence tells them to give her one of the toys. She may repeat by saying, "This sentence says, 'Give me something.' I want you to guess what you should give me. Who would like to give me one of the toys? Then I will tell you whether you guessed right." The children may then volunteer to take turns trying to bring the teacher the correct toy.

When a child brings the correct toy by trial and error, the teacher responds enthusiastically, directs the child to replace the toy with the others, and to whisper to her which toy he wishes to choose for someone else to give to her. The teacher then holds up the appropriate strip, while the new leader chooses some child to select a toy to bring to the teacher. The leader tells the child whether or not he is right. When one of these children finds the appropriate toy, he is the new leader and the process is continued. This type of game should be stopped while the children are still enjoying it. It may be repeated on the following days for short periods.

The Addition of Directions. When the children have discovered which sentence demands each toy, that is, when they can read each strip silently and follow the directions, a new toy may be added, and a new strip may be made to correspond to it. In this activity no oral reading is permitted; the strip tells the secret. The only way for a child to know whether he has guessed the secret is by the teacher's acceptance of the toy he brings. The procedure provides no opportunity for children to move their lips while trying to guess what the strip tells them to do since they never read it aloud.

The teacher may add interest to the activity and develop new vocabulary by changing the action. She may add sentence strips saying, "Give the airplane to George." Since the children now know the direction says to give the ariplane to someone, they must guess to whom the toy should be given. This direction is followed easily if the teacher has helped children to identify each other by name. Many of these culturally-deprived children do not know their own names when they come to school. They have been called, *Junior* or *Hey, You* all their lives until they come to school.

The teacher may also add very slowly to the vocabulary by changing one part of the sentence at a time. The teacher may add one strip at a time to say, "Put the airplane on the table." She will tell the children that the new strip tells them to put one of the toys someplace. Since they now know the word *airplane* in the sentence, they must now guess where to put the toy. Again the children learn through discovery by trial and error. The teacher adds the new strips, but continues to review the old ones in order to make sure that every child has an opportunity for success. She is very careful always to give recognition for and praise every correct response. When a child guesses the wrong response, she always reassures him by saying, "That was a good guess. Next time, I'm sure you will find it."

Need for Success. Davis stresses the importance of success for culturally-deprived children.[5] The child must be able to look forward to rewards if he is to retain any interest or desire for accomplishment. Success and the resulting feelings of self-respect and personal worth are the greatest rewards these children can have. The child must have continuing opportunities for success, achievement, and recognition if he is to build an adequate self-concept to support him through all the demands the school makes upon him. Therefore, the teacher is careful that the child that guesses the wrong object is given a strip which he can read successfully the next time he has a turn.

[5] *Ibid.*

Need for Self-Identification. Lesnik, along with many other authors and teachers, stresses the difficulty in the use of readers from a basic series.[6] The stories in these books depict the lives of middle-class children with which the culturally-deprived cannot identify. These stories have no appeal or interest for these children, who live in a shabby, brutal, sordid, antisocial environment. Experience stories and direction strips have been used successfully to bridge the gap until these children are ready to read in some of the new series which are more appropriate for their backgrounds. As their experiences are increased, they will eventually be able to gain further experiences vicariously until they can work more comfortably in books in use in the general classroom.

Reading Programs for the Intermediate and Upper Grades

The greatest problem in teaching reading to older culturally-deprived children who have not had appropriate help is the tremendous defense they have built against academic work, particularly reading. The constant failure and the utter lack of ability to succeed in the type of reading to which they have been exposed results in feelings of frustration, inadequacy, and anger at themselves, which turns into hatred of the reading act and sometimes of the school.

Remedial Help. Jean Lesnik describes her effort to teach a group of boys, aged 9-12 years, some of whom had barely made a start in reading. Others were able to read in the pre-primers and primers, and a few were able to read in a book as high as a third reader. Regardless of the fact that some of these children had achieved a degree of success in reading, they all had acquired an extreme dislike of the subject. Their reactions varied from sullen withdrawal to temper tantrums, which seemed to begin from no particular situation. The children had read some of the same books as often as five times. They were not only bored, but also resented the necessity of reading stories that were suitable for young children. These children rightly felt that such stories were insulting to their self-respect. Mrs. Lesnik was able to begin to get some co-operation when she and the children worked on a plan for a morning snack because these children came to school without breakfast. A hungry child cannot put his energy into learning. Success in any activity can help establish confidence.

Because these children had almost no self-discipline, she decided to work with them on physical activities. She felt that this type of child is almost equal to the normal child in this type of work. The children improved to some extent. She tells, however, that two months were re-

[6] Jean N. Lesnik, "Problems in Developing a Reading Program for Retarded Educables," *Elementary English* (Mar. 1965), pp. 249–253.

quired to teach a simple game that could be played without an argument or display of temper. Mrs. Lesnik was able to help these children improve in reading and general school work, but she felt that even her best attempts were too little and too late.

Activities for Furthering Reading. Some activities are helpful in improving children's attitudes toward reading and developing interests, although some of them may not serve to teach actual reading. Time spent on breaking down resistance and developing interest is of utmost value before reading can be taught successfully. The teacher should provide a period for reading stories to the children daily. She should select stories of adventure, danger, fantasy, courage, and strong emotional appeal in the face of opposition, in order to meet the interests of these children. At first these stories should concern children who live in impoverished situations. Some of the stories about Mexican children depict situations of great deprival although the children are able to live normal and happy lives despite their environment. Stories of situations less familiar to the children can be selected as these children acquire more experiences and have more background for understanding them.

Use of Visual Aids. Films, filmstrips, slides, and pictures of all sorts are valuable in helping these children develop vocabulary and a background of understanding. Television programs are often useful in providing a subject on which these children have common experience. One teacher was successful in helping these children dictate and learn to read stories about the cartoon programs, such as the *Flintstones,* which they all followed. The children illustrated their own stories with their own cartoon-like drawings.

Use of Varied Activities. Some teachers have found success in using many dramatic activities in connection with the stories these children were told and also those they were able to read. The making of tape recordings by the children when retelling parts of stories they enjoyed hearing or reading also helps to arouse interest in their own accomplishments. These children should be encouraged to make models of the things which they have discussed or read in order to help them develop a thorough understanding of these terms. Directions are given in science books for the making of a realistic type of volcano that erupts when elements are ignited inside it.

Children who read the *Cowboy Sam Series* might enjoy carving and decorating leather belts and purses to give them identification with the cowboys in their stories. Children may work on dictating a set of rules for their own conduct in the classroom to help solve some of their own problems of lack of self-discipline. These children should be provided with many walks around their own neighborhood and with excursions beyond their own neighborhood when they overcome their fears of going that far afield. Plans may be made for parties, and lists of things needed may be dictated to the teacher and read later to serve as reminders of what each child may do in preparation for the party.

Opportunity to read stories, on which they have practiced, to younger children in the primary grades is helpful in building confidence and motivating reading. These children will usually respond to games. Much of the reading content may be presented and practice provided through games. These games should be first played with sentences, words, or phonically-related words with which the children are completely familiar so that they can play each game with strong feelings of success. New sentences and words may be added very gradually for growth.

Cultural Experiences. Various types of cultural experiences should be given to these children. They can understand and enjoy simple narrative poems. On the junior high school level, they can expand their interest in poetry primarily if the teacher reads much of it to the children and makes copies of it available so that the children can read the poems to themselves, partly from memory. One group attended an opera in New York City and were very much impressed by the beautiful costumes and the drama of this production. The technical aspects of such music should be avoided except for an occasional explanation by the teacher, who feels that such an explanation will add to the children's understanding and appreciation of the production. Replicas of great masters' paintings and sculptures may be brought to the classroom for the children to discuss. They should never be required to learn the names of the paintings or sculptures or the names of the artists who produced the works. The names may be brought up in the discussion, and children may remember them incidentally. Pressure to remember such facts and tests to be graded on them will inevitably result in the children's rejection of interest in art or music. The junior high school children, mentioned previously, were happy that they had been taken to see things that were new in their experience. Sometimes guests may be invited to talk to the children. Lists of plans of what to do to make these people feel welcome and to thank them for their help may be printed on a chart and reviewed to remind the children of the responsibilities they have accepted.

Bibliotherapy. The term "bibliotherapy" refers to the use of books to help children with emotional problems. Guidance through books can be used to help children discover that others have problems similar to those that are disturbing them. The teacher helps each child find books that contain stories about his problem. If a child wishes to discuss his opinion of a book or express any of his feelings about his problem this discussion usually helps him. Books serve the purpose of most approaches to emotional problems, that is, they help the child consciously face his problems and release tensions by discussing them. The child often improves considerably when he is able to bring his problems to the surface and recognize them.

Heaton and Lewis have written a book entitled *Reading Ladders for Human Relations*.[7] Various types of problems met by children are listed in this book, and suggestions are given for books that children may read about each problem. A shorter list is given by Bertram in a volume of *The English Journal*.[8] Further bibliographies for use in this problem are suggested in the bibliography given in the Appendix.

Sociodrama. Sociodrama is another technique that may be used by teachers to help children understand their problems and possibly find solutions for them. The teacher selects a problem that seems to be somewhat common among members of the class and presents it to them in an impersonal way. She then asks for volunteers orally to make up a play about the problem and to try to find a solution for it. She chooses children among the volunteers who are not personally affected by this problem so that they may deal with it in an objective way. In this way, those who are concerned can observe this problem handled in an objective manner. Several groups of children may take turns presenting plays about the problem. Any child who is concerned about the problem but who seems to see it in a more objective way may participate with one of these latter groups. The problem is open for discussion and any child may make suggestions for changes or improvements in the play or merely discuss the problem involved.

Discovery of Interests. The interests of Puerto Rican children living in New York City differ greatly from the interests of Mexican children in small rural communities in New Mexico, Arizona, or Southern California. The teacher's greatest need is to discover what these children's interests are so that she can follow them in providing experiences and reading material for the children. A picture file is valuable for discovering children's interests. A few pictures may be shown and discussed each day. Some of those about which the children have expressed enthusiasm can be mounted on bulletin boards. As time goes on, the teacher will make notes of the pictures that interest the children most and in this way gradually find their interests.

As she reads stories to the children, she may make notes about the ones they enjoy most. She may also put a variety of books on the

---

[7] Margaret M. Heaton and Helen B. Lewis, *Reading Ladders for Human Relations* (Washington, D. C.: American Council on Education, 1954).

[8] Jean DeSales Bertram, "Books to Promote Insights into Family and Life Problems," *English Journal*, L (Nov. 1956), pp. 477–82.

library table and shelves and observe which books the children take to their seats most often for the pictures or to read. If books are allowed to be taken home, the teacher may also note the ones that are most in demand in order to assess their interests.

Developing Interests.   A good social studies program on the level of the children's understanding provides opportunity for them to acquire interests as they use a variety of art materials in making models and displays on charts of various sorts. These activities are extremely important with these children to help them develop the necessary concepts and to stimulate their interests in subjects that are remote from their personal experiences. When studying Mexico and South America, children may make papier-mâché dolls to be dressed in authentic costumes. They may make rhythmic instruments to represent some of the instruments used by people in these countries. They may also learn native songs and accompany their singing with instruments they have made to increasingly expand their interests.

Need of Concepts for Reading in the Social Studies.   A sixth-grade colored child transferred from a school in a small town in one of the southern states to a school in a metropolitan area in California. When the teacher realized that the child was having a great deal of difficulty in the social studies, the teacher listened to her read several paragraphs in one of the social studies books. The topic concerned the conservation of water by means of dams and other facilities. The child was unable to read and completely unacquainted with the meanings of fifteen words in three paragraphs on a little more than one page. The teacher had a conference with her aunt and uncle with whom the child was staying. Since many facilities for conservation, including a dam with an electric generator, and various types of agriculture could be found within twenty or thirty miles of the child's home, the teacher suggested that the child be taken on as many trips as possible. She also asked the relatives to explain the things that she was shown and discuss them with her from time to time to help her remember them. Although the child's schoolwork is still somewhat below that of the other children, she has made enormous improvement as a result of her relative's systematic efforts to provide many experiences for her.

Teachers of culturally-deprived children must use many types of activities to help the particular children with whom they work. They should learn as much as they can about their children's home lives and the local environment and try to adapt the school activities to the needs of their particular children. Curriculum requirements and grade level standards cannot be depended upon nor can they be used to limit the type of learning that are of most benefit to culturally-deprived children.

Report Cards and Parent Conferences

More damage has probably been done to the culturally-deprived child by the use of report cards than by any other procedure used by the schools. Parent conferences have been attacked by the supporters of so-called "high standards in the schools." However, educators are working again with parent conferences throughout the elementary school and even on the junior high school level. They have been found to be helpful on all grade levels.

Report Cards. Middle-class parents of bright and gifted children often demand that the teachers send home report cards. These report cards serve the purpose of giving status to children and parents who do not need this type of status. These parents have strong competitive feelings and want some symbol to show that their child is one of the best in the class. They often display these report cards to relatives and friends as a form of status seeking. One parent wanted report cards to send to a grandmother who would tie them up in pink ribbons and keep them for display. The parent of a child who gets C grades or lower rarely demands report cards. The status seekers are not concerned about the effect of the report cards on the children who have less ability or a less adequate background of experience than their own. The school, however, was not established to provide status seekers with success symbols.

Need for Success. The child who succeeds in academic work does not need report cards to reassure him of his success. Unless the parents over-stress the importance of report cards, these children work for the daily satisfaction of achievement and to follow their interests. The child who really needs motivation is discouraged rather than motivated by report cards. He is not able to achieve the rewards for efforts which are even more necessary for the culturally-deprived child than for middle-class children. Much more harm has been done to this child by the use of report cards than by almost any other procedure used in school. Grades on report cards require this culturally-deprived child to compete with others of greater ability although he hasn't the slightest chance to achieve on his level. Competition of this sort is comparable to asking a child of four and a half feet in height to compete in hurdle jumping with boys of six and a half feet in height.

Adjustments to Failure. The culturally-deprived child of lower ability has two kinds of recourse. He may completely withdraw from the field, intellectually and emotionally, thereby refusing to attempt any work. This approach is followed by many children whose teachers label them as lazy and unco-operative and whose peers label them as stupid. This child usually withdraws because he has no opportunity to achieve or receive recognition, which is one of the basic needs of all children.

The more aggressive type of child withdraws from the competition in academic fields but seeks status in antisocial behavior. He misbehaves in many ways in order to get attention. When the teacher says, "Jim, you are the worst boy in this class," he has gained a certain level of recognition. When she says, however, "Jim, you are the worst boy in the school," he has achieved the maximum in recognition and status. This child also seeks to join gangs who do things in which he can succeed, such as taking part in minor thefts and acts of vandalism. Report cards more than anything else probably serve to put the stamp of rejection on a child.

Parent Conferences. School personnel have found that parent conferences are successful with culturally-deprived parents. The parent participation in the Headstart Program has been very effective. The teacher and parent sit down together to discuss what can be done to help his particular child. Most parents want to help their children and are willing to do so when given some idea of how to go about this task. Most parents usually try to do their best to work with the school. Teachers often visit homes of the parents who are unable to come to school or provide babysitters at the school if the parents are tied down at home by younger children. The schools often hold conferences in the evening for parents who work in the daytime.

Successful conferences with parents depend to a very great extent upon the teacher's attitude toward the parents. They should be welcomed at the door in a friendly manner to show respect and should be escorted to the door after the conference for the same reason. The teacher must meet the parents on an equal footing with respect and liking. Any understanding teacher must respect the parents who try to meet as many obstacles as are met by the culturally-deprived, and she must do her best to like them for whatever virtues they have. She should talk to the parents from some part of the room other than her desk in order to avoid emphasizing her position of authority.

The teacher should avoid giving parents advice which may be impractical in their situations. She should try instead to ask the parents to suggest various plans for things they can do to help the child after giving general ideas of types of needed help. Parents are much more likely to follow the plans they themselves have made. If their plans do not succeed, they realize that the teacher was not to blame for their failure because she did not make the suggestion. The teacher should seek other suggestions for holding good conferences with parents. Often the mere fact that the child knows that the parents and teacher are on friendly terms will serve to improve his co-operation.

SUMMARY

The culturally-deprived child is usually characterized by a low self-concept and extensive language deprivation. The child receives minimum care in the home and tends to be inadequately nourished. This child's lack of experience in language usually results in his entering school with a year's handicap which increases as the child grows older. The young child needs many opportunities for physical and mental growth including first-hand experiences and much use of audio-visual material. His reading program should be adapted to strengthen his weaknesses.

22

Activities for
Independent Work

Problems of materials and activities for the independent work period are the greatest in the primary grades, especially the first. Young children have a short attention span and are in the process of learning to become independent. Many of these children, however, come from homes where they have considerable help. Often the mother in the family would rather do things herself than take time to show small children how to do them. Sometimes a mother has only one child or is left with the youngest while the others have gone to school. She may spend time taking care of the child as one outlet for her energy.

On the other hand, parents of the culturally-deprived have too many children to give them much time or attention. The older children may learn to take responsibility, but the younger children are often sent out to play in order to get them out of the way. So little opportunity for any type of activity exists in these homes that these culturally-deprived children are, in many cases, also unable to work independently.

CLASSROOM ORGANIZATION

If children in the kindergarten have had a good experience, they may be able to take some responsibility for their own activities and may have some initiative. On the other hand, they must learn new routines in the first grade. They must also learn to work without help from the teacher for two periods of approximately twenty minutes each. In most kindergartens, the children were able to go to the teacher for help at any time.

This step toward greater independence demanded of a first-grade child requires one of his greatest adjustments.

Organizing Routines

One of the earliest steps taken by the first-grade teacher is to teach children how to bring up their chairs to the reading circle without disturbing others, how to return to their seats, what to do when they return to their seats, and where and how to secure materials for themselves. Time spent on these routines early in the year saves time throughout the rest of the year.

Preparing for a Reading Period. The teacher can save herself time and energy and wear and tear on the children by teaching them to walk into the room quietly and to go directly to their seats after they have entered the room. The teacher should supervise this process and insist on quiet voices and responsible behavior, until the children have established this habit. Even afterward, she supervises the children's entrance, but her vigilance is not as great. The teacher who lets the children enter while talking in loud voices, slide across the room to their chairs, and push other children around in friendly camaraderie may have to spend five or ten minutes getting them ready for work.

Locating Materials for Drawing. The easiest way for the teacher to help children learn the location of materials and routines for securing them is to plan periods in which one activity at a time is introduced to the entire group. The teacher's first lesson may be merely one of using drawing paper and colored crayons. The children may draw anything they wish. Some teachers, however, encourage the children to draw pictures of their families, including themselves. She is able to gain some insight from these pictures in regard to the members of the family living at home. Broken homes are obvious and the child's place in the family is usually revealed.

Although the teacher may usually pass paper when the entire class is engaging in one activity, she will probably prefer to have children secure the paper themselves in order to learn the procedure. She will have the paper available either on a shelf, or in a labeled box. Because of the number of children helping themselves to the paper, she may have the children go to the usual source but spread the paper out in several piles so that they can help themselves without crowding. She then supervises this activity to establish taking turns without pushing and habits of walking quietly to and from the children's seats. In a middle-class school such a routine is easily and quickly established. In a culturally-deprived school in which fighting is a common procedure, the teacher will need to give a great deal of help over a considerable period of time.

Intent first-grade children are enjoying listening to stories they and their classmates have written and recorded. (Courtesy Georgetown School, Placer County, California.)

Some culturally-deprived children, on the other hand, are very responsive.

Putting Away Finished Work. Some teachers provide each child with a box of large colored crayons. Others put crayons in several boxes to be used by children seated at grouped tables. In other situations, children provide their own crayons. The routine which provides for the most learning is that which demands the sharing of crayons. Discussions should precede the latter situation, and children should decide what to do if another child is using the crayon he wants. Again, supervision of the sharing is important to establish good habits.

Some routines should be established for putting the drawing papers away. Some teachers have a labeled box on an open shelf or on the top of the counter. When each child has finished his drawing, he may put it in the box. He may also return his crayons to a central box if this procedure is adopted. Again, the teacher supervises this procedure carefully in the beginning. The teacher may start to read a story while the last children finish their pictures, or she may suggest to these children that they put their unfinished pictures in their desks and finish them at a later time. The teacher will probably discuss the pictures with the children after she has had an opportunity to look at them.

Making Collages

The use of collages during the independent work period provides for much creativity. The time needed to teach children how to handle these materials is worthwhile. A collage is similar to a drawing, but is made by superimposing one material on the top of another. The possibilities for creativity are almost endless. This activity, therefore, is very challenging to children.

A Box for Materials. Some teachers keep a gadget box to which both she and the children contribute. Anything that can be pasted or glued on drawing paper may be included in the box. Some of these objects include cotton, string, cloth, colored rice, pipestem cleaners, tongue depressors or ice cream sticks, toothpicks, seeds, grasses of various sorts, pieces of sponge, buttons, scraps of fur, ribbons, and various types of paper such as cellophane, paper-backed tinfoil, designed wrapping paper, tissue paper, corrugated cardboard, newspaper, and others. Colored construction paper of various sizes serves to meet a great variety of needs. A separate box for left-over pieces of this paper makes it easier to find. The children are always encouraged to return any useful scraps of this paper, since the supply is usually limited. Library paste or rubber cement may be used for attaching the collage material to the paper.

The children may be taught to spread newspapers on their desks when they are working with collage materials. If they use a double sheet of newspaper, it will help protect the desk. It will also hold most of the scraps which can be gathered up inside it and all thrown away together.

Introduction of Collages. The teacher may introduce the use of collages to the entire class at one time, or she may select a quarter or a third of the group to work on them while the other children listen to her read or tell a story. The latter method is the simpler. The entire class takes part in planning what materials are needed and how they are to be shared so that the children who are not participating will be acquainted with the procedure. The children may decide that they will need scissors, paste or rubber cement, a piece of drawing paper, a piece of newspaper, and something from the gadget box for their work.

The teacher will help them discuss how to avoid crowding at one area. They may decide that each child should get the material that is most available first. For example, if he sees a number of children at the gadget box, he may secure his piece of newspaper first, get the other things next, and go to the gadget box last when it is less crowded. The other children will watch those in the small group secure their materials and begin to work.

The teacher will then ask for favorable comments about the procedure of securing the materials to help the children develop pride in following good routines. She may also ask for one or two suggestions for improvement but will insist that these be stated positively. For example, Warren may suggest that some of the children could have gone to get paste and scissors instead of so many children trying to get something from the gadget box at one time. In this way, standards of work procedures are gradually developed.

Putting Away the Collage Material. After the story is finished, the teacher may suggest that the children working on collages should put away their finished work and other material. They should also pick up any scraps or objects that have fallen to the floor. The remainder of the class watches the members of the small committee as they put away their things.

Again, the teacher is wise to provide a box for the finished collages. Children have difficulty putting such work in neat piles. If the box is a little larger than the finished work, they can put their papers in it so that the effect is neat and orderly. Scissors and paste may also be returned to boxes for the same reason. Some teachers permit their children to keep scissors, paste bottles, pencils, and other supplies in their desks. Such a procedure may result in this material falling out from time to time to the inevitable distraction of other children. Whether or not these materials may be distracting depends on the maturity of the children and the type of desks they have.

Evaluation of the Clean-Up Period. The teacher may check on the completion of this activity. If she spends her time pointing out scissors and scraps that have been overlooked, she is likely to have to continue this procedure all year. If, on the other hand, she suggests that one of the children from the class, for example Shirley, look around to evaluate the clean-up work, the procedure may be more effective, and the learning may be greater. When, for example, Shirley reminds George to put away his scissors and suggests that Marilyn pick up the rest of her scraps, she tends to be more conscientious when she cleans up her own materials. She remembers the suggestions better because she herself made them. She also prefers not to provide the opportunity for another child to remind her to put away her scissors. George and Marilyn will also take the suggestions from Shirley much more seriously than from the teacher.

The teacher chooses a different child each time to serve as the helper to remind others in order to avoid prudishness on the part of such a child. She also desires to provide opportunity for every child at one time or another to look at the clean-up procedures from an objective point of view. As the children become accustomed to supervising their own clean-up activities and as the teacher gives generous recognition for good effort, the members of the class develop a strong pride in the neatness of their room and will straighten it up willingly and efficiently.

The Contested Scrap. One problem remains. Marilyn, for example, may decide that the scraps she has been requested to pick up were dropped by Ronald, who sits in front of her. Ronald will obviously deny the accusation. Some teachers handle this situation by presenting the problem to the class. A teacher may say that Marilyn feels that the scraps belong to Ronald, and Ronald feels that they belong to Marilyn. The teacher may therefore ask if anyone in the room would like to pick up the scraps in order to have a clean room that all can enjoy. Many children will volunteer, and the teacher makes a point of choosing a child from another part of the room in order to make the assistance obviously unselfish. The teacher then enthusiastically praises the volunteer for his public spirit. If Marilyn or Ronald try to pick up the contested scrap in the meantime, the teacher will insist that they had their chance and must leave the paper for the child who has volunteered to do it. Children like Marilyn and Ronald usually try to avoid this kind of "help" in the future.

Considerable detail regarding the handling of the clean-up period has been given because this procedure can be difficult and frustrating for the teacher if she does not have some procedure for successfully dealing with it. On the other hand, she is able to use a wide variety of activities with the children when she knows how to organize this routine smoothly.

Procedures for Working with Art Materials

The use of art activities is valuable as part of the interests followed during the independent work period. To introduce one of these activities, such as painting at the easel, the teacher may bring the children up to a semicircle before her. If she has chairs for all the children, they may bring these up to form a double semicircle. If she has only enough chairs for the reading circle, she may use these for the smaller and less mature children and ask the other children to fill up the seats in the front of the classroom. Primary children are attentive in proportion to their nearness to the scene of action. They also like to see in detail everything that is going on.

Acquisition of Material. Before the children are seated, the teacher may have brought an easel to the front of the room, along with the paints and brushes that are needed. She may tell the children that she would like to help them make a co-operative picture. She then sends one child to get a smock or coverall and another to get a large piece of painting paper, probably newsprint, twenty-two inches by twenty-eight inches in size or larger. The children who were sent after the materials tell the others where they found them so that the other children will know how to get these things for themselves. Some child is asked to fasten the painting paper on the easel, and another child is chosen to paint some object on the paper. The teacher may tell the children that this picture may be made up of anything they like to add to it. The first child may put on his smock and paint a sun on the picture. The next child may then take the smock, put it on, and paint some grass at the bottom of the page. The children take turns adding to the picture as long as their interest and the piece of paper hold out.

Establishing Habits in Using Materials. As each child takes a turn to paint, various problems arise. One child may be unable to fasten the button of his smock at the back of his neck. The teacher then guides the children to discuss his problem and decide what to do when she is not available to help them. Some child always volunteers to help the other in this situation which the teacher encourages to develop co-operation. In another case, a blot of paint falls on the floor. This problem is discussed, and the children are guided to decide to wipe it up in case someone else steps in it or it becomes dry and hard to wipe up. The teacher always helps the children think of the reasons for each procedure because then they behave more intelligently and develop habits of assuming responsibility.

Some teachers keep a package of paper towels nearby for such an emergency. Others keep large sponges. At this time the children are also taught how to wash out the sponge and squeeze excess water from it to avoid dribbling water across the room. When the picture is finished, the children discuss the need to hang up the smock in the proper place, to put away the finished painting (probably in a large shallow box), and to wipe the paint smears off the easel. The teacher probably returns the easel to the proper place, since it is heavy and awkward for the children to carry.

Substitutes for an Easel. The teacher need not eliminate this activity for the lack of an easel. Some teachers and children's art specialists prefer to have the children spread out newspapers on the floor and paint there. The problem of dripping paint is less acute in such a situation. Others make an easel from a large sheet of double-faced, corrugated cardboard, which is folded in the middle and placed on a table in a tent position. The cardboard is covered with oilcloth or some nonpermeable material. Clothespins, clips, or some other means of attaching the paper is fastened to the top of the easel at each side. The back and front of the easel are fastened together about halfway from the top with string or some other material to prevent the back and front from sliding apart at the base to cause the easel to collapse.

Procedures for Use of Other Art Materials. The introduction of each type of art material is valuable despite the time it takes. If children have never had this type of work before, this introduction helps them know what is expected of them. If they have done this type of work before, they are given a chance to know what this particular teacher expects. As they develop habits of securing their own material and taking care of their own needs, they are developing important habits of independence. When one helps another, they are learning to co-operate, and the child who gives help is gaining status for his maturity. As they learn to return materials to their proper place and clean up the area where they have been working, they learn habits that are valuable for a lifetime and that are necessary in any type of adult work.

The wise teacher always reviews work habits even if very briefly before the children begin their work. She asks the children to state the standards rather than doing so herself. If the teacher reviews the habits, the children think about something else while she is talking. If they, themselves, review the habits, they will remember them better.

The wise teacher always evaluates the clean up. Children's memories are short, and they are eager to go on to the next activity. Unless the teacher makes sure that they clean up their work space well, some children will neglect this duty. As time goes on, they will become more indifferent toward their responsibilities and will learn poor habits instead of good ones.

Planned Activities Suitable for Independent Work

Teachers who use three groups in their primary reading program provide three types of activities for each of their reading groups. Each period consists of fifteen to twenty or more minutes, depending on the age of the children.

Group Reading and Follow-up Work. Reading with the teacher in a group is obviously one of these activities. A second type may consist of follow-up work to give practice on the reading material. Most teachers make use of workbooks during this time, or they may put work on the board for the children. If the teacher does not have workbooks for first-grade children and possibly for some immature second-grade children, she may prepare material to be duplicated rather than use the chalkboard. Immature readers find it difficult to work from the board but are able to succeed when the material is duplicated on paper.

Creative Work. Some teachers use the third period for creative work. Young children are able to work with reasonable success for fifteen to twenty-five minutes, depending upon their maturity. If they are given further abstract assignments of a workbook or of a paper and pencil type, they become tired, bored, and frustrated. Even though the teacher insists upon their finishing the work, they are unlikely to learn any more in forty minutes than they can in twenty, and they will tend to dislike this type of work more and more as time goes on.

Many primary children are under a strain when they must concentrate on work with their eyes and with their finger muscles. They therefore become fatigued from doing this work for too long at one time. For example, a first grader had written a letter to his aunt to thank her for a birthday gift. He asked his mother what he needed to add to the letter to complete it. When she told him to add the word *love* at the bottom and his name, he said, "But Mother, if I write *love*, I'll be too tired to write my name."

Values of Creative Work. The use of creative activities provides an excellent break in pace from the more formal work. The children are given a legitimate reason for moving around when they secure the materials and later when they put them away. Most creative activities provide use of the larger muscles, which children can control with less effort than the smaller ones. In addition, they may stand up for some of their creative activities which breaks the strain of sitting still too long.

The use of creative activities, however, has greater values than those just mentioned. The intellectual processes used for creating are to a large extent the same as those used in thinking. Often more thinking is demanded for creative activities than for use of workbook material. Since automation has practically eliminated unskilled work, more workers will need initiative and ability to think for the types of work they will do than was formerly true.

Creative work also provides opportunity for the young child to express himself. Some ideas which he may not be able to express verbally can be expressed with other materials. Creative activity provides another important service in giving an outlet for children's emotional tensions. The child who can paint when he is concerned about his problems has acquired an outlet to help him live with his problems more successfully.

Value as an Emotional Outlet. Sometimes the art produced is too crude for the teacher to understand. If encouraged when alone, a child will often tell the teacher about his picture. In this way, she gains insight into some of his problems. Whether or not she is able to secure help for the child, she is at least able to understand him better and to work more sympathetically with him.

Continuous repetitive drawings on one theme usually indicate that the child is unconsciously trying to find a way of expressing a problem that concerns him. Some teachers feel that the children are not working when they are expressing their ideas with creative materials. Actually, their creative work may be one of the most valuable experiences they have during the day. Sylvia Ashton-Warner was able to help the Maori children, who were lost between two cultures, adjust to the school situation with remarkable success and improve tremendously in their relationships with other children.

Modeling Materials. Some creative activities are particularly useful in the independent work period. Clay, flour dough, and asbestos flour are all good materials for modeling. Sawdust mixed with non-toxic wheat paste and water makes another good modeling material, although it tends to have a coarse texture. When they are mixed, they may be kept in plastic bags closed with a rubber band or clip to keep the air out when not in use. When the children finish with this material, they should return it to the bag. Objects made of the flour dough or asbestos flour are less likely to crumble when dry than the objects made of clay. Those made of clay, however, can be fired and kept permanently if desired.

Easel Painting. Painting at the easel with tempera paints is one of the most satisfying activities for the primary child. He should use large brushes and 22″ × 28″ or larger newsprint, because it is satisfactory and inexpensive. This activity has all the values of any good creative experience.

Finger Painting. The materials for use for finger painting are easy to handle if the teacher teaches the child to secure these materials for himself. A table large enough for two or four children may be covered with oilcloth. Such a protective covering is not needed if the tables are finished with some type of material such as formica which is easily cleaned. The children should learn to wet the surface of the table with a sponge dipped lightly in water. They should then spread their paper on the table. The film of water between the table and the paper will hold it still while the children work on it.

If fingerpaints are not mixed, the child may pour some liquid starch onto the paper from a plastic squeeze bottle. This type of bottle will not break if dropped, and only a little starch will come out of it at a time. The child may then use a plastic shaker such as a large, plastic salt shaker to add paint to the starch, which he mixes directly on the paper. Finger painting provides one of the best materials for helping children relax and lose their tensions.

Colored Chalk. Large sticks of chalk one inch thick should be used by primary children. The chalk may be applied to the paper dry or dipped in any of a number of liquids to provide a glaze so that it will not easily rub off onto other things. One of the most practical materials for wetting chalk is liquid starch. It does not sour easily or become mouldy as does milk or buttermilk. It is easy to keep available for the children to use. Some teachers like to provide a little water saturated with sugar for the children to use as a glaze for dipping their chalk. The sugar and water solution probably gives the most brilliant colors. It tends, however, to harden the ends of the chalk, but this crust may be rubbed off easily before the chalk is used again.

Spatter Printing. A child may cut out his own design and pin this over a piece of drawing paper. The object, such as a tree, is pinned on the paper. The color will then silhouette this object. If the paper from which the object is cut is pinned on the drawing paper, the space the shape of the tree will receive the color.

Some teachers use a toothbrush which is dipped in tempera paint to make the spray. The child then pulls a tongue depressor over the bristles to apply the drops to the paper. Some teachers prefer a screen and a toothbrush dipped in paint. Others use a fly spray gun instead. The latter must be cleaned after each use because the nozzle becomes clogged with paint unless cleaned at once.

Block Printing. Some teachers let children work with half a potato and a tin spoon for carving their designs. Older children may prefer tubing from an automobile tire. They cut the designs in the tubing and then glue them to blocks of wood. Even though the designs may be crude, the final result is usually interesting because of the repetition.

Weaving. Some second- and most third-grade children are able to weave successfully. This activity provides an excellent way of helping children understand how cloth is made. An apple box with nails fastened a quarter of an inch apart along the ends and strung with roving cotton provides a loom that even some first-grade children can use. Looms may also be made even of cardboard with pins fastened in the ends. Simple looms for the use of primary children are described by Morrison and Perry.[1] First-grade children with good co-ordination can make simple things such as a rug for the playhouse or a pot holder for mother.

[1] Ida E. Morrison and Ida F. Perry, *Kindergarten-Primary Education—Teaching Procedures* (New York: The Ronald Press Co., 1961).

They should use coarse roving cotton. Second- or third-grade children can use four-ply wool successfully.

Papier-Maché. Children can cover some fruits and vegetables with papier-mâché in connection with the study of foods or the grocery store. Vaseline or liquid soap should be used to coat the object before the papier-mâché is applied. If the object is covered with about ten coats of paper each of which have been dipped in wheat flour paste, a very solid object can be made that is suitable for children to use for a long time.

Each layer should be allowed to dry at least over night before another layer is applied. The fruit or vegetable inside the shell will tend to dry and draw away from the outer layers. When ten or more coats of papier-mâché have been applied, it may be cut in half by the teacher for safety, and the object removed. A mark across the cut will help the child match the pieces when he puts them together again. At least two or more additional coats should be applied after the object in the center has been removed. When it is dry, it may be painted and shellacked if desired. The objects may be then used for buying and selling in the store, involving the counting of a quarter dozen, a half dozen, a dozen and a half, and so on to help the children understand the value of these quantities.

Crayons. Crayons are often overused in the primary grades. Their great advantage is that they are clean, easily available, and quickly put away. They serve a good purpose when they are used to illustrate children's experience stories that have been pasted in booklets. They are also of value to illustrate duplicated copies of dictated reports of science experiments, dictated questions in the social studies, dictated lists of plans for the social studies, and dictated daily newspapers. They may be used occasionally for work during the independent work period, but they should be balanced with a variety of other materials. Their best purpose is as a quick activity for a child who has finished other work a short time before recess and needs to occupy himself for about five minutes. If he has not finished his picture, he may put it in his desk and finish it at a later time when he has another short period left.

ADDITIONAL ACTIVITIES FOR THE INDEPENDENT WORK PERIOD

In order to give the children a variety of experiences, the teacher occasionally changes the type of activities they engage in at their seats during the independent work period. She drops some from the list and adds new ones. Some activities have value for creative work. Others provide opportunity for developing eye-hand co-ordination and for learnings of various sorts. Some activities for enriching the independent work period are given below.

Work with a Variety of Materials

1. Make scrapbooks.
2. Make picture dictionaries or pictures for homemade "moving pictures" to be pasted on a long roll of paper.
3. Make booklets of duplicated experience stories or daily newspapers.
4. Illustrate experience stories or dictated news stories in the booklet.
5. Make pictures using various types of seeds. The seeds may be attached to the paper with glue.
6. Make paper bag masks to fit over the head for holidays like Halloween. Make paper fringe to attach to the top of the bag for hair. Cut two short pieces of fringe to paste over the eyes for eyebrows. Cut out ears to be pasted on the sides of the masks. Fold a triangle of paper on the face for a nose.
7. Make paper doll puppets, paper bag puppets, or puppets with faces of papier-mâché.
8. Make dolls and doll clothes.
9. Make silhouettes for shadow pictures.
10. Work on models such as cars, trucks, boats, and so on.
11. Make gifts for holidays.
12. Build with small blocks.
13. String colored beads on shoelaces in designs.

Puzzles and Games

1. Work with jigsaw puzzles.
2. Play phonic games.
3. Work with arithmetic puzzles or games.
4. Work with reading puzzles or games.
5. Work with clock faces with a partner.
6. Use number wheels for practice with a partner.

Literature and Reading Activities

1. Make a picture of one of the favorite characters in the reader which is used by the children. When in the reading circle, each child asks the other children to guess which character the picture represents.
2. Listen to stories at the listening center. Some teachers also record directions for various activities the children may follow. Such directions might be used to check the comprehension of a story in the reader. Four to six children sit around a table on which is a tape

recorder or record player. Each has a set of ear phones. Directions given by the teacher may say, for example, "Fold your paper into four rectangles. First fold it from the bottom to the top. Then fold one side over the other. Now you have four rectangles or spaces. In the upper left hand corner draw the number of apples that Peggy sold to Mrs. White. In the upper right hand corner draw the amount of money Mrs. White gave Peggy. In the lower left hand corner draw the number of cookies Bill sold to Mrs. White. In the lower right hand corner draw the amount of money Mrs. White gave him." These directions may be spaced widely apart to give the children time to follow each direction.

3. Look at library books, stereographs, or view masters.

4. Look up information in books. This information may be needed for some activity in the social studies.

Writing Activities

1. Write a story or a letter.

2. Write a story about one of the pictures in the picture file. The teacher may keep a file of pictures mounted on nine by twelve inch tag cardboard which show interesting situations. The child who wishes to write a story but cannot think of a theme selects one of these cards as a source of an idea for his story. He then returns the picture to the file so that it may be used by another child at a later time.

3. Write a brief book review (for older children). Such a review may give the name of the author, the title of the book, the child's name, and one reason why he liked the story.

4. Write price tags to be used on articles in the class grocery store.

5. Write signs for various departments to be used in the grocery store such as Meat Department, Bakery, and so on.

6. Write labels for exhibits on the bulletin board such as various kinds of seeds, various kinds of wild flowers, or other materials.

Dramatic Activities

1. Write and practice a play for puppets in a small group of two or three children.

2. Write and practice a play with paper dolls in a small group.

3. Practice taking parts in oral reading for a "reading" play.

4. Play in a small group in the play center.

Activities for Classroom Use

1. Classify or label materials for exhibits.

2. Arrange books on the library table and bookshelves.

3. Make scenery to use with reading lessons.

4. Make place cards, decorations, or other things needed for a party.

5. Make pictures for a homemade "moving picture machine."

6. Make pictures of homes, stores, gasoline stations, and other buildings to be placed on a large wall map of the community.

7. Make scenery and characters for dioramas (a scene made in a cardboard carton with the front and top of the box removed and arranged so that the carton serves as a frame for the scene).

8. Work on a mural that has been developed in connection with a social studies unit such as the farm, the community, the dairy, or a similar topic.

9. Serve as a librarian to check out books to other children. A child who can keep records and read and write to some degree may serve as librarian. He may have a series of envelopes or pockets open at the top. The name of each book in the classroom library is printed at the top. The pocket should be large enough to hold a three by five inch index card with ease. Keep each of the index cards in a box. The name of each member of the class is printed at the top of each of the cards. When a child in the class takes the book home for overnight use, the librarian inserts the card with the child's name in the envelope on which the name of the book has been printed. When the child returns the book, his name is removed from the pocket and is replaced in the box with the names of the children who are not reading books at that particular time. The librarian is helped to keep the children's names in alphabetical order using first names with last initials added when two children have the same first names. The child is also helped to keep the envelopes used as pockets in alphabetical order by the authors' last names.

10. Make a time line to help keep track of the days before Thanksgiving, Christmas, or other important holidays. Use a strip of wrapping paper twelve inches wide measured into twelve inch sections, each divided from the other by a heavy black line. The date of each day should be printed at the bottom of the square which it represents. Children draw and paste a large picture of a sun in each section to represent each day. The children may count the number of days left before such a holiday as Christmas. Christmas day may be represented by the last square on the paper on which a Christmas wreath or other symbol has been painted. As each day passes, a child may put a large "X" through the sun representing that day. In this way, children can answer their own constant questions concerning how many days they have to wait for Christmas or a similar holiday.

Activities in Science

1. Use the magnifying glass to look at insects, seeds, or other objects of interest.

2. Work on science experiments such as testing materials to see whether they float or sink.

3. Look at the insect collection with a magnifying glass.

4. Work with a box of materials that can be picked up with a magnet and those that cannot.

Puzzles Made by the Teacher

1. Make cards by pasting pictures of objects that belong together such as a pail and shovel or a knife and fork, each on separate cards. The pupils sort to put together the things that belong together.

2. Make sets of cards by classification. Collect sets of pictures on such things as vegetables that grow above the ground and those below, things that fly and things that walk, and things that can move and things that cannot move. Mount this series of pictures on cards. Put these related sets in an envelope. Copy one pair of pictures on the outside of the envelope. The pupils sort the pictures according to the proper classifications.

3. Paste a picture of a clock on plywood and cut up like a jigsaw puzzle. The child puts the pieces together.

4. Make a set of cards by printing a word on one card that can be combined with another to make a compound word. On another card, print the other half of the compound word. Make a series of these cards which children can sort and put together to make compound words. Put a sample on the outside of the envelope. The teacher listens to the child read the compound words after he has finished arranging them.

5. Print a series of questions on a cardboard folder using the vocabulary of the children's reader. Draw rectangles with paper clips on top of them opposite each question and make cards to fit the rectangles. On the folder, print such questions as, "Can a boy jump?" "Can a wagon eat?" "Can a girl fly?" and so on. Print a series of answer cards with *yes* on some of them and *no* on others. The child selects the proper answer and slips it under the clip after the appropriate question. The words used in this exercise should either be well-known, sight words or should be easily analyzed by known phonics procedures.

6. Make envelopes of two sheets of a heavy quality of transparent acetate bound together with tape. These envelopes may be made large enough to hold pages from workbooks on which the children need extra practice. The answers may be circled or underlined on the acetate with a china marking pencil. After the teacher has checked the work, the pencil marks can easily be rubbed off with a cloth or paper tissue so that another child can use the material. Some teachers use old X-ray films that have been washed in warm soapy water.

INITIATING GROUP READING

When the teacher has taught enough activities for the children to be able to work alone at their seats and has established habits of independence and good housekeeping routines, she may select the children who are ready for reading to work together in a fast group. Either at the end of the kindergarten or during the first few weeks of the first grade, reading readiness tests will have been given. These readiness tests have not been proven to be particularly good predictors of success in first-grade reading. The teacher, however, may use the results from these tests as one criterion of readiness.

Selection of Members of the First Group

During the first few weeks in the first grade, some teachers take very brief notes regarding children's reactions and behavior, especially in regard to the criterion listed in the checklist at the end of Chapter 3. The language factors merit special attention. Shortly after the children leave for the day, the teacher may jot down brief comments regarding any child who has shown some type of growth or who appears to have a particular problem. Such comments might include the following. "Marilyn recognized several words in the experience stories today." "Donald still has difficulty matching." "Ronald is beginning to hear beginning consonants in two or three words." If she saw no particular new reaction on the part of another child, she makes a note concerning some child about whom she has made few comments in the past. The third note might say, "Georgia's work is consistent. She seems about average for a potential middle group." These notes might be made on half sheets of paper or filing cards and dropped into each child's folder.

On the following day the teacher will make notations concerning the progress of another two or three children. This way she will have notes on the progress of about half the class at the end of each week or two. When she is ready to set up her first group, she may take out the folders of the children who received the highest marks on the readiness test and whom she recalls as having evidenced the most readiness traits. She may then look at her check list and annotations and compare them with the results of the readiness test. She may also take into consideration any other comments or data from the folder that might be pertinent.

She may feel, for example, that Mervin is ready as far as his test records and her comments indicate. She may also notice, however, that Mervin was very shy and tended to withdraw in the kindergarten. She may realzie that he is still quite insecure. She may therefore decide to keep Mervin in a readiness group until he seems more secure. Any difficulty in beginning to read he may have at this time might result in a fear of reading he might have difficulty in overcoming.

She may find that Debbie's case, on the other hand, is very clear. Debbie has a high mark on her readiness test, is able to recognize words in the experience stories, can retell a story in detail, and has plus marks after all the items on her checklist. The notes from the kindergarten teacher indicate that Debbie is mature, poised, and well-adjusted. The teacher will therefore decide to put Debbie directly into the first reading group. In this way, she will make up her list of members of the first reading group.

Beginning of Group Work

On the following day the teacher will help the children get started on their activities as usual, except for the children she plans to start in the reading group. She will then ask these children to bring their chairs to a circle in front of her. In the meantime, she will remind the children at their seats that she does not wish anyone to come to the circle to ask her for help. She will appoint a child to give the children help and will tell them to go to the helper rather than to her. She will also ask them to tell her what they think they may do if they finish their work before she is ready for them. Since this question has been brought up each day, the children will know that they may color a picture with crayons, work on a jigsaw puzzle, or look at books at the library table. The teacher is then ready to begin work with her first parallel story.

Work with the Second Group

The teacher may work with the remaining children on readiness activities in one large group, or she may divide them roughly into two groups if she feels that the children are ready to work on two different kinds of activities over a period of approximately forty minutes in length. Little by little she may shift these remaining children from one group to another on the basis of her check list, anecdotal records, and readiness test results. When she feels that the second group is ready to read after their readiness work, she may start her first parallel story with them. She continues to use readiness work with the third group until she is sure that they are ready to begin reading.

Need for Success

Young children have a great need for success. The work in reading in the first grade is their first real test in accomplishment. At this time they develop attitudes toward reading and toward school that are likely

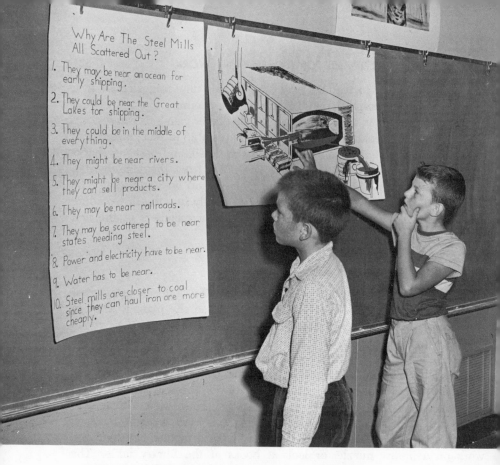

Children in this fifth-grade class thought of a variety of reasons for the existing distribution of steel mills in this country. Their next step was to check the validity of their guesses. (Courtesy of California State Department of Education.)

to become permanent. If every child were given activities in which he could be sure to succeed, his future in school would be a much happier and successful one than that of many children in school today. The time required for readiness for assured success in reading is a very small amount of time in the child's life. If he were allowed time to become secure in each of the readiness and early reading steps, this security would be one of his greatest assets throughout his school life.

If a variety of readiness activities are used with the children in the slow group including work with the matching of reading strips to the sentences in experience stories and also the matching of words to the words in the stories, the child on the readiness level is unlikely to be conscious of the difference between his work and that of the children who are getting ready to read in books. Even when the other children are able to read in books, the slow child tends to show little interest or concern because printed matter in books has as yet little interest for him. The development of security on the part of the culturally-deprived child is even more crucial than that for the middle-class child, if any one level could be said to be more important than another.

CLASS ORGANIZATION FOR READING AND WORK

Some suggestions for organizing the work carried on during the reading period are given in this section. If the teacher uses three groups, each child may take part in three types of activities, reading with the teacher, working in his workbook or on follow-up work, and taking part in a variety of creative and other planned activities. If the use of a workbook is not required, any of a variety of activities listed in the previous section of the chapter may be used for this independent work.

A Chart for Organizing Independent Work

A chart with movable pictures is useful for helping children remember the activity they will follow during the work period. A large sheet of cardboard is divided into six or seven columns, one for each type of activity the children may follow.

The Pictures. Space enough is allowed at the top of each column for a picture to illustrate each of the types of activities the children may engage in during their independent work. Six or seven activities provide an adequate variety. These pictures are mounted on tag cardboard and attached to the chart by means of paper clips put through the cardboard at the top of the space allowed for each picture. The rest of each column is divided into six rectangles for six children's names. A paper clip is also inserted through the cardboard at the top in the center of each rectangle.

The Name Cards. A name card for each child in the class is made to fit the rectangles under the pictures. The name cards of two children from each reading group may be printed on cards and fastened under the paper clips below each picture. In this way, six names will be found under each picture representing an activity. The first two may give the names of two children from the fast group. The second pair may give the names of two children from the middle group, and the last pair may give the names of two children from the slowest group.

The cards are kept in the same order across the chart, although no designation such as fast or slow is ever given to a group. If the cards are kept in the same order by groups across the chart, the teacher can review the names of the children working on activities at a glance. The children can also remember where their names are located on the chart in order to find the activity in which they are to engage. The limit of two children from each reading group for each activity prevents too many children from participating in any one activity for which adequate materials may not be available. This limit also makes sharing of materials easier. Figure 22-3 shows a slightly different type of planning chart.

Change of Activities. Each day, the pictures with the titles under them may be moved one column to the right, and the last picture may be brought back to the extreme left column. In this way, each child has an opportunity to participate in each activity before he begins to repeat. The teacher may remove certain pictures and titles on occasion and replace them with others in order to vary these activities. She may also move the children's names if a need occurs. The name of a child who has left the class may be removed and the name of a new child may be added.

Activities for Each Reading Period

The chart shown in Figure 22-1 will give the teacher an idea of how the activities for the three groups may be scheduled.

Group	First 20-minute period	Second 20-minute period	Third 20-minute period
Slow 3	Reading with teacher	Follow-up or workbook	Planned activities
Middle 2	Planned activities	Reading with teacher	Follow-up or workbook
Fast 1	Follow-up or workbook	Planned activities	Reading with teacher

Fig. 22–1. A plan for scheduling the reading periods.

Activities for the First Period. Most teachers work on reading with the third group during the first period. These children have a short attention span and tire easily. While the third group is reading with the teacher, the second group may participate in creative or planned activities. The term "planned activities" is used to include any of the activities described in the first part of the chapter. The first group will probably work on their workbooks or some type of follow-up work planned to give practice on problems they may have met in their reading.

Most of the children in the first group may not have met difficulties in their reading and may not need workbook or follow-up material. Individual reading at the library table is one of the best activities for such children. If books on a variety of levels from the ones easy enough for the slowest children to those difficult enough to meet the reading needs of the best readers are included on the library table, these children may gain a great deal from supplementary reading at this time.

The children who do have need for workbook activity may be given sheets torn out of workbooks to meet their specific needs. Follow-up work was suggested for the first period for the most advanced reading group, because they are able to remember directions for exercises they may be given from the previous day. The teacher may help the children plan this work on the previous day and review it very briefly before the children work on the following morning.

Transitions to the Second Period. Before the children in the slowest group who have been reading with the teacher go to their seats, the teacher will carefully explain their workbook or follow-up material. These children are then allowed to go directly to work before they forget what it is they are to do. These slowest children understand their directions best if the teacher supervises one step in the workbook to make sure the children know what they are to do and how to do it.

A five-minute period is valuable for supervising children as they put their work away and clean up before changing to another activity. At first, the children will need more than five minutes for the teacher to help them with the transition until their habits are established. The teacher should insist that the children working on planned activities put their things away and clean up properly. Otherwise, the last children to work on the planned activities will be burdened by cleaning up for all of the others. Usually the teacher checks the workbook or follow-up material of the group participating in that work before calling a new group to the circle. If only a few of the fast group are working on their workbooks, this correction will be simple.

Activities for the Second Period. Many teachers read with the middle group next because they are less flexible than the children in the fast group. While the second group is reading with the teacher, the children in the slow group work in their workbooks or on other follow-up work, and the children in the fast group take their turns at planned activities. Usually a glance at the chart is sufficient for them to know what they may do at this period. At first, the teacher may call their attention to their names on the activity chart and remind them of what they are to do. Later, she merely asks the children to raise their hands for each activity, and still later, she merely reminds them to look at the chart.

At the end of this period, the teacher plans the follow-up or workbook activities with the second group before they go to their seats from the reading circle. She then checks the work of the slow group and carefully plans their work from the chart with them. Although they may know their names and use the pictures to identify their work, they may forget to look at the chart and may not understand how to use it clearly. If the teacher plans carefully with them before they undertake this work, she tends to avoid later confusion.

Activities for the Third Period. A recess usually follows the second period. Some teachers continue with the reading immediately after the recess. Others break the schedule for another subject and return to the reading after the lunch hour. The latter plan provides greater variation in the program for the children and seems to be effective. If time has elapsed since the teacher discussed the planned activities with the third group, she must review them carefully. On the other hand, she may have delayed this planning until just before the children are ready to go to work. She will also review the directions for follow-up or work-book activities for the second group before she starts the reading period with her fast group. At the completion of the third reading period, the teacher checks the follow-up or workbook activities of the second group, who has just finished this activity and makes sure the slow group puts away the materials they were using during their planned activities.

Participation in Group Work

The sponsors of the individualized reading program are concerned because some children may take part in practice activities in the reading group for which they have no need. With rare exceptions, children need some teaching in all skills. For example, most children need some exposure to the sound of the digraph, *ch*, or on a more advanced level, to the activity of picking out main ideas and other steps in outlining. Some very intelligent students reach the college level without the ability to make an outline.

As the teacher reviews the teaching of a skill, she can soon discover the children who seem to have adequate mastery from those who need more practice. She can dismiss the children who have learned the skill to carry on reading individually while she works with the remainder of the group. Each time she reviews a skill, even the better readers should be exposed to this review before they are freed to go to other reading, or they will tend to forget the skill. If the teacher has the children practice in this manner, she can feel sure that every child has had some review of each skill, and those who need it have had the practice neces-sary for them.

Use of Workbooks

A basic principle in the use of the workbooks which bears repeating is that children should be given only the workbook activities they need. The teacher will usually discover the children who need less practice by the speed with which they usually finish their work. Individual reading would be much more valuable for these children than working on exercises that they do not need.

The teacher checks the seat work material as soon as the children have completed it before bringing up the next group. She also corrects the work with each individual child to make sure that he understands the corrections and so that he might avoid the same mistake later. Unless the teacher does correct the work of each primary child as soon as his group has finished this work, he tends to have lost his identity with the material. If in the afternoon a teacher tries to find the owner of a paper completed in the morning, she will have difficulty trying to find a child to claim it, especially in the first grade. He may not even recognize his own writing. In a similar situation, young primary children do not even recognize their paintings when asked to identify them on the following day. The younger and more immature child must have his corrections made at once. The more mature child and the faster readers in first grade and higher grades may be able to benefit by help later in the day. Most of the children learn almost nothing from the papers if the teacher takes them home and passes them back on the following day. The teacher's time could be much more advantageously used in planning new work.

Interruptions

Some teachers permit children who are engaged in working at their seats to come up to them to ask for help while they are teaching the reading group. Sometimes these children merely want the teacher to tell them a word, but others want help with more time-consuming things. These interruptions break the thought of the children who are working in the reading circle. In some cases, the work is so badly disrupted that the children in the reading circle gain nothing from the lesson.

Some teachers permit interruption only for emergencies; however, they appoint one of the better readers who is working at his seat to give this help for one period at a time. A different child serves as helper for another period and still a different one helps on the following day. These helpers are not required to do their regular work at this time, unless they wish to do so.

To help with work some teachers put a completed piece of work for each group on the bulletin board with the instruction that the children may look at it if they have difficulty. Most children will not copy it in its entirety, but will refer to it only if they need to do so. Other puzzles and game materials of various sorts may be made with self-checking devices on the backs.

SAMPLES OF PERMANENT MATERIALS FOR USE IN THE INDEPENDENT WORK PERIOD

Examples of puzzles and games are given for a series of grade levels in reading. This work is planned primarily for first- and immature second-grade children who are unable to read library books with satisfaction. Some teachers like to keep permanent material in a box so that children may work with this material in their free time. The material is made up to use the vocabulary of the current series of readers in use in the classroom.

Various plans are suggested for holding the cards in their proper places after the child has sorted them. Unless the cards are held in position, they may fall on the floor if the child moves the materials. Pockets and paper clips are two of the devices suggested for holding these materials in place until the teacher is able to check them. Self-checking devices have also been suggested when possible.

Puzzles for Practice on Sight Words

Permanent puzzles made of cardboard may be kept in a box for children to use when they have finished other work. They should not be used to replace creative work. They are valuable, however, for review of follow-up work, to give extra practice on recognition of sight words, or for supplementary work on comprehension. Each puzzle along with the matching cards should be given a number which is placed on the back of each piece and on the envelope. Then if a card belonging to one of the puzzles is dropped on the floor, a child can match its number to the number on the envelope and replace it where it belongs.

The puzzles suggested for use in this section are planned to give the children practice on sight words used alone. Because they are used with pictures, they are almost completely limited to practice on nouns. Some may be used for verbs such as the words *run* and *jump,* if the pictures are obvious and the teacher discusses them with the children.

Matching Word Cards to Pictures. A puzzle may be made to help children become familiar with printed words which they may not have yet mastered at sight. The puzzle provides opportunity for the children to match words on cards to words that have been printed under pictures pasted on a manila folder.

To make the puzzle, draw a row of three rectangles each two inches wide across the top of the inner left side of the folder and draw another row of the same number of rectangles across the inner right side of the folder. Make the rectangles each an inch and a half in depth. A picture may be drawn or pasted within each rectangle.

Draw lines between the pictures through to the bottom margin of each page. Draw horizontal lines across the vertical lines at intervals of one and a half inches. Thus, three columns of rectangles will be made below the set of three pictures on each page. The horizontal lines may be spaced wider apart if preferred. Print the words represented by each of the pictures in the first rectangle directly below each picture.

On a separate piece of tag or on index cards draw rectangles of the same size as those drawn on the pages of the folder. Print the words represented by the pictures on enough cards to fill the spaces below each picture. Put paper clips through the cardboard folder at the top center of each of the rectangles. Each card may then be matched to the proper picture at the top and slipped under a paper clip to hold it in place. The cards may be kept in an envelope made of tag. If the envelope is stapled to the folder along one edge but left loose along the other edge, the children will be able to remove the cards without tearing the envelope. Another folder may be attached as a cover to the original one to prevent the paper clips from scratching the desks. The folders should be bound together around the edges. A diagram of this matching puzzle is shown in Figure 22-2.

Sorting Words for Picture Titles. A puzzle may be made similar to the one just described without the words under the picture. The series of pictures similar to those used in the other puzzle are pasted across the top of the page. Lines are drawn in the same way to make a column of rectangles under each picture. Word cards are made to fit the rectangles under the pictures. Enough cards with the word printed on them are made to fill the spaces under each picture.

In this situation, no word is printed under each picture to help the child match the words. Therefore, duplicate pictures are pasted on the back of the puzzle with the name of each printed under its picture. If the child does not recognize a word on the card, he may turn over to the back of the folder and match the word to the correct word under its appropriate picture. He may then put the word card in its correct place. Paper clips are used at the top center of each rectangle so that the cards do not fall out of place when the child turns the puzzle over to check the words on the back. This puzzle constitutes a higher level

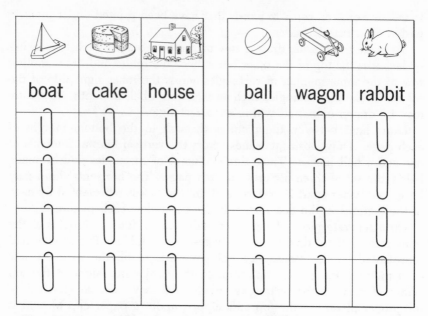

Fig. 22–2. A puzzle to help children review sight vocabulary. Cards one and a half inches wide by two inches long on which the words under the pictures have been printed should be prepared to be matched under the names of the pictures. For this puzzle, four cards are needed for each word.

than the one that allowed for matching on the face of the sheet. A diagram of this puzzle is shown in Figure 22-3.

Jigsaw Puzzles. The teacher may look through the word list in the backs of the pre-primers for nouns which can be illustrated by pictures. She will probably be able to find suitable pictures to go with these nouns in the workbooks. Two workbooks may be used to cut up for this purpose; one for the front of each page, and one for the back. If, for example, the teacher finds that *airplane* is one of the nouns in the stories the children are reading, she may cut out a picture of an airplane and mount it on the upper half of a 3″ × 5″ or 4″ × 6″ index card. She may then print the word, *airplane,* in manuscript on the lower half of the card. She will then draw several zigzag lines to divide the upper part of the card from the lower part and will cut the sections apart on these lines. Such a puzzle is shown in Figure 22-4. She will prepare nine or ten similar cards made with other nouns and place these in a durable envelope for the children to put together. The word printed on the back of the part of the card with the picture helps the children to check the words of which they are not sure.

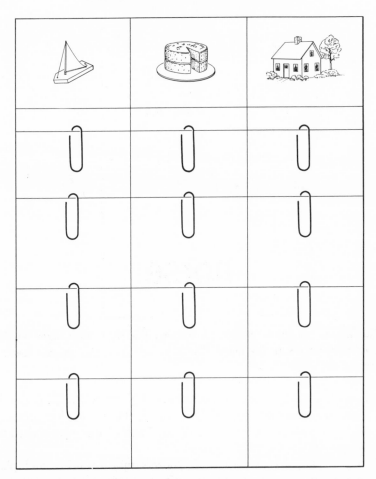

Fig. 22–3. This puzzle is similar to the one shown in Figure 22–2, but the words under the pictures have been omitted. Word cards are made to be placed in the rows under each picture.

The number of cards included in any one set of puzzles will depend upon the maturity of the children who work with them and on their mastery of sight words. The teacher is wise to start with six or seven pairs of cards to be sorted and to add to these as the children need practice on new words and are able to complete the work in a fifteen- or twenty-minute period.

Small Pockets and Cards. Two cards are needed for each part of this type of puzzle. To make the pocket use a 4″ × 6″ card and fold the bottom up one inch to make the flap of the pocket. Staple the sides

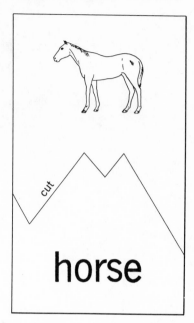

Fig. 22–4. A jigsaw puzzle for helping the child learn sight words. If the two parts of the puzzle match, the child will know that he has found the correct word.

of the pocket to the back. Print the word to be learned on the flap. Put a picture corresponding to the word on the flap on the upper half of a 3″ × 5″ card. Print the word on the back of the picture card as it was printed on the flap of the pocket.

Nine or ten pairs of cards and pockets may be made and placed in an envelope. The child sorts the picture cards and puts each in the pocket that has the appropriate word printed on the flap. If the child is not sure which picture should be placed in a particular pocket, he can turn over the picture card and match the word printed on it to the word on the flap of the pocket. He then turns the card with the picture side up when he puts it in the pocket. He may also check the accuracy of the other cards in the same way. In this way he learns what each word represents. A picture of this type of puzzle is shown in Figure 22-5. A similar type of pocket with cards for comprehension of a paragraph is shown in Figure 22-6.

Folders with Paper Fasteners and Yarn. A 9″ × 12″ manila folder used for filing provides two pages and enough space for an adequate number of pictures to challenge the child. To make this puzzle paste a row of pictures down the left side on the inside of the folder, and paste

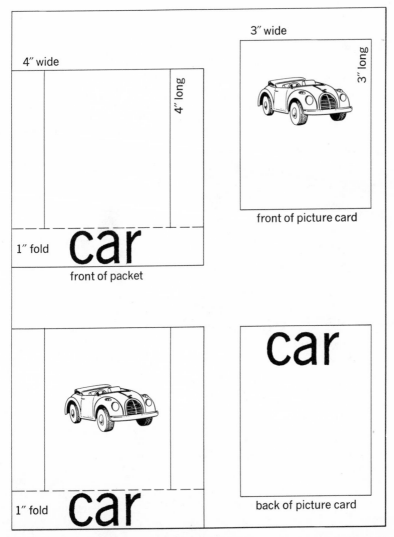

4" wide

4" long

1" fold **car**

front of packet

3" wide

3" long

front of picture card

1" fold **car**

car

back of picture card

Fig. 22–5. The child places in the pocket the card with the picture that has the appropriate word printed on it.

another row of pictures on the left side of the facing page. Opposite each picture on the right hand side of each page print the words that represent each picture. These words should be opposite pictures found on the same side of the folder, but opposite those that are different from the ones to which the words belong.

A piece of yarn is then knotted and threaded through a hole near the inside of the picture. Each piece of yarn should be long enough to reach

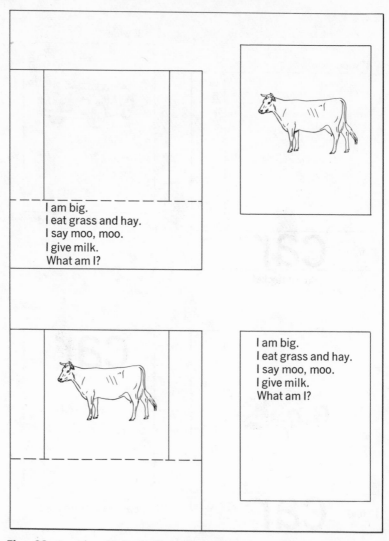

I am big.
I eat grass and hay.
I say moo, moo.
I give milk.
What am I?

I am big.
I eat grass and hay.
I say moo, moo.
I give milk.
What am I?

Fig. 22–6. The child places in the pocket a card with a picture and the appropriate word, sentence, or paragraph.

any of the words on the page with enough left over to wrap around the head of a paper fastener. Paper fasteners are inserted through the folder opposite each picture and beside each word. The head of the fastener is placed on the inside of the folder, and the prongs are on the outside. To prevent the prongs of the paper fasteners from scratching the children's desks, another folder is used as a cover for the first. The two may be bound together around the edges with colored plastic tape or similar material. The child draws the yarn from the picture to the corresponding word and wraps it around the head of the paper fastener beside this word.

To help the child who is not sure of recognizing the words, a second set of pictures may be put on the back of the cover with the words to which the pictures belong printed immediately below them. These pictures may be only outlines, since the children do not need detail for them. An upper-grade child who draws well is often willing to help the teacher with such work. Some room mothers are also happy to help. This type of puzzle is shown in Figure 22-7.

Puzzles for Work with Sentences

The words used in the sentences in this type of material should be primarily those that the child knows because self-checking devices are difficult to use with this material. Any unfamiliar sight word should be very easy to recognize by the types of phonics the child already knows. The purpose of this type of work is to give practice on comprehension of silent reading material. The pictures are used to test the child's understanding of the meaning of the sentences.

A Puzzle for Comprehension of Sentences. Each of the inner pages of a manila folder may be used for this work. Paste a series of pictures in a column down the left hand side of each page. The rest of the page should be divided into rectangles, each of which is opposite a picture. Cards are made to fit the rectangles so that they may be sorted and placed under paper clips opposite the appropriate picture. Examples of such pictures and sentences for first-grade children which may be placed opposite them include the following: a ball, opposite which the child places the sentence, "I can catch it"; a doll, opposite which the child places the sentence, "Girls like to play with it"; a doll buggy, opposite which the child places the sentence, "A doll can ride in it"; and a dog, opposite which the child places the sentence, "It likes to play with me."

A Puzzle for Comprehension of the Words "Big" and "Little." This puzzle is set up in the same form as the puzzle described above. However, pictures are pasted in pairs, one below the other, to show an object that is big and the same object in a smaller form. A picture of an airplane may be pasted at the top on the left hand side. Another picture of a smaller airplane but similar in shape should be pasted immediately below it. A picture of a wagon may be placed below the airplanes, the first one to be larger than the second, and so on down each side of the page. The names of these pictures should be known sight

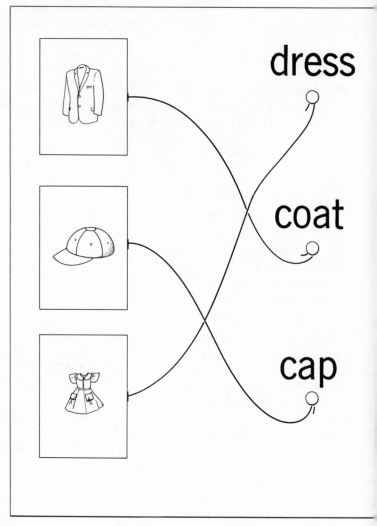

Fig. 22–7. A puzzle with paper fasteners and

words unless they are easily analyzed by phonics of a type the children know. In this puzzle, the practice is focused on the words, "big" and "little." As in the previous puzzle, cards are cut to fit the rectangles opposite the pictures. On each will be printed a sentence appropriate for the picture such as: "Here is a big airplane"; "Here is a little airplane"; "Here is a big wagon"; "Here is a little wagon"; and so on, for each of the pairs of pictures. Each sentence is printed on a separate card, so that the child must sort not only for the object but for its size as well.

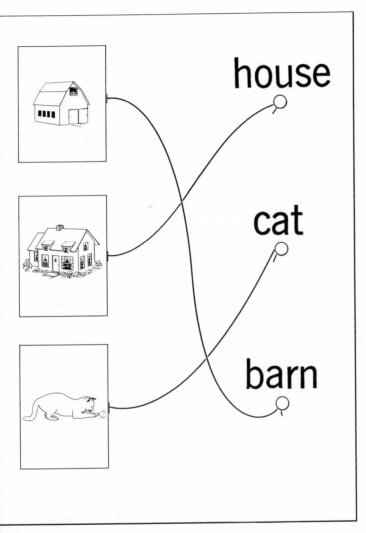

arn for helping the child learn sight words.

A Puzzle with Paper Fasteners for Sentences. The concept for practice may be things that go fast and things that cannot go fast. A series of pictures of vehicles or animals may be placed down the left hand side of each page. Print a sentence on a card to be placed opposite each picture. The objects may be some of the following: an airplane, a train, a boy walking, a sailboat, a car, a snail, a deer, a motorboat, a boy on a scooter, and a cow. These objects have been listed in mixed order so that the child is not able to pick alternate sentences for each picture.

The sentence opposite each picture should state either, "It can go fast," or "It cannot go fast." These sentences may be alternated as long as the pictures are in different order.

A knot is tied at the end of a piece of yarn and it is threaded through the folder immediately to the right of each picture. A paper fastener with the head up is put through the folder under each of the sentences. The child then draws the yarn from the appropriate picture to the appropriate sentence and wraps it around the head of the paper clip. The teacher should discuss the various objects pictured with the children to give them an idea of the comparative speeds represented by each picture so that their reading will be tested rather than their concept of speed. The folder should be backed in the way described for the other puzzles.

A Puzzle for Sequence. A very short story containing a number of definite steps in the sequence of the action is needed for this puzzle. If the teacher is not able to find one she can use, she may condense the steps in a story in one of the children's readers. Paste or print the story on the left hand page of the folder. On the opposite page, make a series of rectangles wide enough for sentences to be placed under a paper clip on each. The sentences should give the steps in the story, but these should be worded in a different way so that the child cannot match the sentences to the story without understanding their meaning. The children then read the story silently and put the sentence cards in correct sequence under the paper clips.

Puzzles for Work with Paragraphs

Any of the devices for holding cards in position may be used with paragraphs. Two samples of such puzzles are given in this section.

A Puzzle for Identifying Objects. Pockets and cards similar to those shown in Chapter 8 for use with sight words may be made. Place a picture on the folded section of the pocket which may be two inches in depth. On each card to be placed within a pocket, put several lines of description to be matched with a picture. The sentences may be similar to the following:

I am big.
I eat grass and hay.
I say moo, moo.
I give milk.
What am I?

The child will place the card with the paragraph above in the pocket on which a picture of a cow has been pasted. Eight to ten of these pockets with matching paragraphs may be placed in an envelope. A sample should be drawn or pasted on the outside of the envelope in which the pictures are placed.

A Puzzle for Rhyming Words. Pockets and cards similar to those described in the previous puzzle may be made for use with rhyming words. A paragraph such as the following may be printed on a card to be placed in a pocket:

> You can play with it.
> You run after it.
> It rhymes with fall.

An appropriate picture is then pasted on the flap of the pocket in which the card is to be inserted, in this case a picture of a ball. Eight to ten of these pockets with matching paragraphs on cards should be placed in an envelope. A sample should be drawn or pasted on the outside of the envelope in which the pictures are placed.

USE OF MATERIAL FOR INDEPENDENT WORK

Most of the puzzles or permanent seat work material has been described to meet the needs of the younger primary children. Older children can work from books and material on the chalkboard. The workbook supplied for these children is adequate for some. Others need more review or more emphasis on special aspects of the work. Permanent materials can be given to individuals to help them with particular skills on which they may need help. It also has an appeal for some children and provides worth-while work for children when they have finished a regular assignment.

Work in workbooks and with other materials does not take the place of the teacher's guidance. The teacher must give children help in the use of this material, make sure that they can read and understand it, and correct it with each child personally so that he can learn from his correct responses as well as his mistakes. Supplementary material of this type is not useful for the first teaching of a skill. It is valuable primarily for supplementary help with a skill that the child has at least partially learned. This material is then used for review and extra practice.

Practice materials should not be used with children who do not need them. If they are capable readers, these children should be encouraged to read widely both in books for recreation and in supplementary books and materials in other subjects in the curriculum. They are likely to gain much more skill in comprehension and improved rate in reading from this type of material. Capable readers should be guided to work on problems in the social studies, science, and other fields, even in the second and third grades. Many excellent books are written for children of this age, and they deal with problems on these children's levels of interest and understanding. These mature children can help find answers to some of the questions in social studies that demand reading material that is too difficult for the slower readers.

SUMMARY

First-grade teachers should teach their beginners to work independently and to be able to secure their materials and return them to the proper places before they begin to teach formal reading in groups. Care in such training saves time and smoothes the routines for the entire year. Children should be taught how to work with and care for creative materials as one aspect of their independent work. They should also learn to work in workbooks or on practice material for a period of fifteen or twenty minutes without disturbing the teacher.

Charts of activities help children remember what they may do while the teacher is busy with another reading group. A plan for a variety of types of activities breaks the pace for children and provides greater learnings than too much time spent on one type of activity. Children in each group spend some time with the teacher in the reading group, some time in reading or follow-up activities of various sorts, and some time in creative activities.

A variety of permanent material is provided by some teachers to give review and extra practice on skills needed by some children. This material is placed in a box for easy selection by the teacher or by the children who wish to work on these reading puzzles.

23

Trends in
Reading Instruction

Probably at no other time in this century has so much experimental work been carried on in the area of reading. One of the most spectacular trends is that of teaching children to read at an early age. Another strong trend is the teaching of beginning reading by means of the alphabet, phonics programs, and linguistic systems. In Great Britain an "Augmented Roman Alphabet" has been developed in an effort to reduce the great variety of letter sounds in the English language. An experiment in teaching beginners to read by means of writing has been carried on for some time. Other trends include team teaching, programmed learning, and machine teaching. On the other hand, courses have been rapidly increasing in speed reading for college students and adults who have failed to achieve effective speed and comprehension in childhood.

VALUES AND HAZARDS OF NEW TRENDS

Innovations must be included in the reading program if progress is to be made. There are hazards, however, in these innovations when they are introduced by people without adequate understanding of modern educational principles, present methods of teaching reading, or experience in teaching children.

Values of New Programs

An effort has been made to point out some of the advantages of these trends and to mention any problem that may arise if some of these plans were adopted generally in the public schools. Although reading teachers and specialists may not feel that some of these programs should be adopted in their entirety, some have aspects that may be of value if incorporated with or used to supplement a general developmental program. Experiments in teaching reading can bring important values, additions, or changes to the school program, but similarities and differences between the experimental and the public school situations should be examined carefully before the public schools adopt practices that may not apply to the circumstances under which they must operate.

Dangers Inherent in New Programs

Although some well-planned and thoroughly researched innovations in reading are introduced, some serious dangers exist in this variety of conflicting and competing programs. Sometimes the designers or supporters of new plans for teaching reading can see no values in any other approach but their own and may be very adamant and emotionally rigid in their rejection of other plans. Some of these people have no idea of acceptable reading programs nor the basic principles underlying them. In some cases, no research has been conducted to prove the values of the new program. On the other hand, the program may have been tested on unsuitable subjects such as adults, or it may have been compared with some "regular" undefined program or a program that makes use of practices that are no longer considered acceptable by reading teachers.

Interpretation of Research Findings

Other supporters of new programs may have some ideas of the principles underlying a good reading program but may have refused to give them credence because of the existence of exceptions to the research findings. An example of this latter viewpoint is held by those who have read that some readers who have slow eye movements and fixations are as accurate in their reading as those with faster movements and fixations. While this statement is true, it does not justify the refusal to accept any of the studies of eye movements or to support programs that violate the basic principles underlying such studies. The fact that the most efficient readers have rapid eye movements and short fixations is ignored by this critic of modern reading procedures.

Extreme Programs

The danger to the public schools of some instigators of limited programs is that they may sweep away satisfactory reading programs already established in school districts due to their enthusiasm and their pressures to adopt their particular plans, sincere as their arguments may be. During the last two decades two extreme and unbalanced plans of teaching reading have been adopted by numerous districts over the country. In each case fairly satisfactory developmental programs have been exchanged for these extreme and limited plans which were dropped later. Sometimes these innovators work with parents who have less understanding of basic principles underlying good programs than teachers and administrators and who are more easily persuaded to adopt an extreme and unbalanced practice. Some phonic programs are examples of pressured selling campaigns. Reading texts based on some of these new plans are in the process of being published and others are on the market, despite the fact that no careful and convincing research has been pursued to prove their value.

Need for Understanding of Principles

One of the most fundamental causes of failure on the part of people outside the field of teaching to understand the modern program is the lack of understanding of the change in educational viewpoints during the last four or five decades. The formal program of the schools during the earlier period was based on the idea of passing down to the child the facts and information that mankind had spent centuries in acquiring.

Organized Learning. Since man had spent so much time acquiring experiences and organizing them into neat bundles such as the addition, subtraction, multiplication, and division tables, the obvious way to teach was to pass these facts on to the child in their organized and condensed form without wasting his time with the experiences upon which these facts had been based. Man had also neatly organized information concerning the various sounds of the letters and had packaged these in a subject called phonics. The linguists have now organized the basic principles underlying the use of language and have packaged these in another plan of organization. Why, then, shouldn't the efficiently organized material be passed to children just as soldiers were given K rations to take the place of bulky, wasteful, unprocessed foods?

Interest. Perhaps the two situations depend upon the same factor, palatability. This factor is not the primary one, but it is very important in both situations. The soldier will eat K rations when away from camp because the desire to survive is a basic drive. The soldier also knows he will get something better when he gets back to camp or home. The primary child must accept these indigestible packages of facts as long as he attends school. In the days before compulsory attendance, he did the logical thing, that is, he dropped out of school.

The teachers in the days of compulsory attendance found that children might sit in their seats at school and still refuse to swallow these hard, lumpy subjects. When the teacher broke them up and provided the children with some of the experiences from which these organized packages had been made up in the first place, the children became very interested and even enthusiastic. The teacher also became enthusiastic, and discipline (actually, resistance) dropped to the minimum. Many teachers still present children with the tight packages, but those who know how to develop interest are vastly more successful because they have the horsepower of thirty-five children with them instead of against them. The bright child suffered the least in the formal program because he could better understand it than the slower child. Even he, however, enjoys a challenge.

Experience and Understanding. A primary factor more basic than interest or flavor is one of digestibility. Man's digestive system was not made for K rations nor was man's mind made for condensed systems of learning without at least some underlying experiences. The child tends to develop mental indigestion when he is handed solid packages of knowledge which he is supposed to swallow whole. He needs to get his teeth into the raw material of experiences and his inner mental organs need raw material to keep their digestion up to par. In educational terms the child needs to *discover* ideas and information for himself through experiences, reading, and discussion. He retains only a small part of the predigested, organized information handed to him.

To some people this matter of discovery seems to be too wasteful of time. The process including the idea of challenging children through interest has been called *pampering* and a program of *fads and frills*. Nevertheless the modern program is the challenging one and has been proven the more effective in an important series of studies carried on during the nineteen thirties. Time is not wasted because the child develops not only a better understanding of the subject, but he also remembers many of the facts he would otherwise have forgotten.

In regard to reading, the child can discover phonic principles for himself under the skillful guidance of a good teacher. He enjoys the challenge and understands and remembers the principles far better and for a much longer time. Other skills in reading also profit greatly from this type of stimulating teaching. Unfortunately, this thought-provoking program demands much more understanding, planning, and skill on the part of the teacher than the formal program. Such a teacher is the filet mignon of the teaching world and is not found in every snack bar.

PRESCHOOL READING

Two investigations of reading by preschool children have attracted general interest. In one situation children had learned to read at home before or during kindergarten. The other study involved children of two and three years who were taught to read by means of a special typewriter.

Readers in the Kindergarten

In a study by Durkin forty-nine children who had learned to read at home before attending school or during the kindergarten year were studied.[1] These children comprised almost one per cent of the kindergarten children in a particular school district.

These forty-nine children had learned to read either by the help of older brothers and sisters, an interested parent, or by incidental observation of signs, television commercials, labels on foods, and similar material. Most of these children had depended primarily on answers to their questions by other children or adults. In all cases, these children had a very strong interest in reading.

When the children in this study entered first grade, they were on the average a year ahead of the normal children of their own age in reading, although some read on a much more advanced level. At the beginning of the second grade they averaged six months above the normal reader of comparable mental ages. Another test was given at the beginning of the third grade to see if the experimental group had maintained their lead or if the gap had diminished still more.

On this second test only twenty-five children of the number tested originally were available. Due to failure to select tests that measured the achievement of the brightest children in either the control or the experimental group, Durkin used a statistical procedure for estimating the expected reading achievement from the intelligence test scores. At this time the reading achievement of the children whose IQ's ranged from 121 to 161 were about a third of a year above expectancy. The children of 91 to 120 IQ's were almost two thirds of a year above expectancy at the time, but they dropped to approximately average for their mental age by the time they were in the fifth grade.[2]

[1] Dolores Durkin, "An Earlier Start in Reading?" *Elementary School Journal,* LXIII (Dec. 1962), 146–61.

[2] Dolores Durkin, "Fifth Year Report on the Achievement of Early Readers," *Elementary School Journal,* LXV (Nov. 1964), 76–80.

An Experiment with Typing

Dr. Omar K. Moore, a sociologist at Yale University, has worked with a group of children between the ages of two and five years. According to a report by Maya Pines, Moore has taught them to read, write, type, take dictation, and compose their own stories.[3] Moore stated that only two of the children in his study ranked as gifted and that the intelligence of the others fell within the normal range. Moore used the term "normal" to refer to children under 140 IQ, a much broader interpretation of the term than that used by most educational psychologists.

Procedures. During this experiment each child worked alone in a soundproof booth. As he struck the keys of a typewriter in a haphazard way, an unseen adult outside the booth named each letter or symbol. After the child had passed the haphazard stage, the adult outside the soundproof booth projected a letter which was shown on an exhibitor, a frame on which printed matter could be displayed, and named this letter, which was heard through a small speaker. At this point all other keys except the one named were blocked so that they would not print when struck. Only the letter named was printed when the child happened to strike that key. In this way the child learned the names of the letters. Eventually words were printed, and a similar procedure was followed to guide the child to print the letters in the proper order. The teacher named each letter as it was printed and then named the word. The child gradually discovered that he was learning to type and spell words. More advanced procedures were followed after the child mastered the beginning steps.

Possibilities for Application. Because Moore realized that the use of one adult as teacher of one child was an expensive procedure, he invented a fully automated talking typewriter to replace the adult who guided the child's learning. The development of this machine cost an estimated $400,000. No mention was made of the probable selling price if this machine is put on the market.

The use of such a machine might be of considerable help to a teacher who might wish to use it with a child who has been absent for a time or with one who needs extra practice in order to keep up with his reading group. On the other hand, a particularly able child might work on advanced material as one way of enriching the program for him.

Some problems might be encountered in using this machine with very young children in the public schools. The children who partic-

[3] Maya Pines, "How Three-Year-Olds Teach Themselves to Read—And Love It," *Harper's Magazine*, CCXXVI, No. 1356 (May 1963), 58–64.

ipated in Moore's study were from a culturally advantaged population, the area around Yale University. Although Moore spoke of these children as normal, he used the term to refer to all children under 140 IQ, as stated above. Undoubtedly these children were highly intelligent. Few school districts are able to work with such a limited population level. In addition, Moore worked with only those children who were interested in co-operating in the program. Since the children were quite young, any child who wished might leave the program. Very few public schools could be operated on such a plan.

The program was very time consuming. Moore's three year old daughter had an IQ of over 140, yet Moore spent more than half an hour a day for a period of thirty-three weeks according to Barton in teaching the alphabet to her.[4] This period is the equivalent of two college semesters. Moore's daughter could undoubtedly have learned the alphabet in a week or two at six years of age.

Part-to-Whole Reading. These children were taught to read letters before words, and words before sentences. This method is typical of the part-to-whole approach. Pines reported that ". . . the first grade class is reading fourth grade geography books, . . ." She added that these children were "plodding" through school workbooks at third and fourth grade levels, but "without enthusiasm." Referring to a copy of the *Scientific American* opened at random, Pines states, "Although they stumbled over some words which they did not understand, they could clearly handle anything phonetically." Emphasis seems to have been placed on phonics and word pronunciation. The correspondence of the children's level of comprehension to their level of ability to pronounce words was apparently not considered. The use of the typewriter for learning to read, however, might have been programmed for a more effective and more modern type of reading program.

The ordinary typewriter has been successfully used in earlier investigations to help motivate first-grade children to read and write. It was found helpful in writing because the children were able to write without the strained muscular co-ordination resulting from efforts to use manuscript or cursive writing.

Reading by Mentally Retarded Children. In the same article Pines reported that five kindergarten children whose IQ's ranged from fifty-nine to seventy-two were taught to read simple material after a year of work in Moore's laboratory. Since these children seemed to have learned to read to some extent despite their mental retardation, Moore's study should be followed carefully for the values which it seems to provide.

[4] *Ibid.*

ACHIEVEMENTS OF EARLY AND LATE SCHOOL STARTERS

To discover the eventual achievement of children who began school early compared with children who began school at a later chronological age, Richard Hampleman studied fifty-eight sixth grade children who had attended the same school since they entered first grade.[5] He divided these children into two groups. Those who were six years and three months of age or younger at entrance to first grade constituted group one, and those who were six years and four months of age or over when they entered first grade constituted group two. The average IQ's for both groups were approximately 106.

Findings from Hampleman's Study

In the sixth grade the children in group two, the older group, were found to have an average reading achievement of slightly more than four months above the children in group one, the younger group. When the median score, that is, the middle score by rank, for the children in group one was compared with the median score for group two, the older group was found to achieve an average of seven months above the younger group. Similar findings were secured in a variety of studies that were followed to investigate this problem.

English and Scottish Children Compared

Ruth Strang, a well-known authority, discloses that Scottish children are taught to read at five years of age but that they read no better at eight than English children who begin reading at six.[6] She adds that word analysis may lead to confusion at five years of age. Strang's information tends to support the existence of a normal growth curve which results in a leveling off of the achievement of readers who were taught at an early age.

INTRODUCTION TO READING THROUGH WRITING

Some investigations have been carried on in a few of the California schools, originally in San Diego County. In this study beginners are taught to read by first teaching them to dictate and later write stories of their personal experiences.

[5] Richard S. Hampleman, "A Study of the Comparative Reading Achievements of Early and Late School Starters," *Elementary English*, XXXVI (May 1959), 331–34.

[6] Ruth Strang, "Should Parents Teach Reading?" *PTA Magazine*, LVII (Mar. 1963), 7–9.

The San Diego Study

The San Diego Study involved sixty-seven teachers from eleven school districts that volunteered to take part in the study. Two plans were followed, the development program using a basic developmental series with the teacher's manuals and the language experience approach.

Children's Creative Stories. In the language experience approach the skills including listening, speaking, writing, and reading were taught together. Teaching was based upon each child's own particular experiences or upon experiences shared by the group. The individual stories were initiated through drawings or paintings followed by the child's dictation of a sentence or story about each picture. As each child told the story of his picture, the teacher printed it for him. He copied the story later if he wished.

Phonics and Spelling. The use of the alphabet, phonic analysis, configuration, and spelling were all taught through this writing program. As the teacher wrote from the child's dictation, she would call the children's attention to beginning sounds of words, the shapes of the letters, the length of words, the use of capitals, and other technical aspects of writing.

Some teachers feel that this procedure interrupts the thought. They prefer to accept the story in rough draft first. They then enlist the children in the rewriting of the story when they work on the techniques. In this way the children can concentrate on the creative aspect of the writing without interruption.

Dictating and Writing Stories. Dictation can be carried on by an individual, children in a small group, or the members of the entire class. Some topics are of a personal nature and therefore lend themselves best to individual stories. Other experiences may be shared by a group or by an entire class and therefore lend themselves to group dictation. Sometimes the children prefer that the teacher write the story they dictate on the chalk board or on another paper. These children like to copy their own stories under their own drawings or paintings.

The children should never be required to copy either their individual or group stories. Writing demands intense concentration and a high degree of small muscle co-ordination for young children. Because of the strain involved, many young children are frustrated by copying two or three sentences. They may therefore grow to dislike the experience approach if copying is required.

The stories dictated by a group of children are bound into books and placed on the library table or reading center. Some teachers help the children read their own and others' stories in small groups. High interest is maintained because the stories belong to the children. Often individual children volunteer to read their own stories to others and sometimes enjoy reading other children's stories if they are sure of the words.

As time goes on children acquire the ability to write their own stories. Some teachers help the children by putting an open ended or unfinished sentence on the chalk board to help children begin writing stories of one sentence in length. If the child does not know how to spell the word he has chosen to complete his story sentence, the teacher may write the word on the board or on a paper. Some teachers encourage the child who wishes to write stories individually to tell a story to other children first. As the child does so, the teacher writes down words on which she expects him to need help. He is then able to write independently at his seat. Later the children may be able to look up needed words in their own spelling word books or in picture dictionaries. Some teachers encourage the children to look up needed words in other children's stories bound together on the library table.

Outcome of the San Diego Study.[7] The study that was reported by Kendrick and Bennett was carried on in San Diego County for a period of two years.[8] A variety of skills in reading, speaking, spelling, and attitudes toward the reading program were compared with the same skills achieved by the control group using basic developmental readers. The achievement of boys was also compared with that of girls.

At the end of the first grade study, test results of eleven of the skills showed better progress on the part of the children taught by the developmental reading program, whereas test results of twelve of the skills showed better progress on the part of the children taught by the language experience program. Ten of the skills achieved in the developmental reading program were significantly higher than those achieved in the language experience approach.

At the end of the second grade, test results of thirteen of the skills showed better progress when the children were taught through the basic developmental readers, whereas test results of ten of the skills showed better progress on the part of the language experience group. Only five of the comparisons, however, showed a significant difference.

In general, the writing skills were especially good in the language experience program. The results of the study indicate that both types of programs resulted in effective achievement in the language arts.

[7] Dorris M. Lee, and R. V. Allen, *Learning To Read Through Experience* (2d ed.; New York: Appleton-Century-Crofts, 1963.

[8] William M. Kendrick, and Clayton L. Bennett, "A Comparative Study of Two First Grade Language Arts Programs—Extended into Second Grade," *The Reading Teacher* (May 1967), 747–55.

Suggestions for the Language Experience Approach

A few suggestions for ideas for children's writing may help the teacher who is following this program. Charts needed to facilitate the routines of the day and the children's activities may also be dictated by the children and will serve as functional reading because they will be read or reviewed when they are needed. Suggestions are also given for some of these charts.

Topics for Children's Stories. If the child's painting is used as a basis for his writing, he usually has no problem with ideas for stories. Experience in dictating group stories from the children's own experiences also helps them realize that stories are to be found all about them. Some topics that provide opportunity for individual and group stories are listed below:

Animals	Mother's work
Pets	Father's work
Trips	Community helpers
Plants	Weather
Flowers	Dreams
Insects	Safety
Birds	Holidays
Fish	New clothes

Some teachers make a collection of pictures to show interesting child and family situations. They put these in a file which is available to the children. Any child who needs an idea for a story, may borrow a picture from this box to help him get started. An experience chart dictated by a small group of children is shown in Figure 23-1.

Charts of Various Types. Charts needed by the children for a variety of reasons may be dictated to the teacher, who prints them and hangs them in the room where they can be of use to the children. Examples of such charts are given below.

Words we know	Standards of behavior
Songs we know	Records of daily temperature
Duties of committee members	Guessed answers to social studies
Duties of committee leaders	problems for later evaluation

Figures 23-2 and 23-3 show two of these types of charts.

Use of ITA in Writing. One teacher taught her children to use the ITA alphabet, described below, for writing to help them become more independent in their spelling. As the year advanced the children's stories became longer and more involved. They were also able to use their own spelling work books and picture dictionaries. In this way they became increasingly independent. The children were provided with a wide variety of experiences to stimulate their writing, and an outstanding creative writing program was developed, especially with the more able children. Toward the end of the year the class and teacher invited the parents to come to school for an author's tea. Each child read one or more of his stories to the parents who were very pleased with their children's progress. Even the most immature child had written a few simple stories and was able to read them.

ADULT SPEED READING

Sometimes trends in the business and industrial world influence trends in education. It is possible that the increased demand for semi-professional and professional workers accompanied by the decreased demand for unskilled and skilled workers, especially those in the manufacturing trades, has had an effect on the need for more efficient reading by adults. The increase in the number of people working on the semi-professional and professional levels has resulted in an increase in the number of people who have needs for more effective reading procedures.

As a probable consequence of this increased demand, many courses in speed reading for adults have sprung up in the college as well as those given by trained and untrained lay teachers. Rather extreme claims have been made by some of these reading schools. In general, college students and adults have greatly improved their abilities in reading with speed and comprehension.

THE AUGMENTED ROMAN ALPHABET

The University of London Institute of Education has sponsored an investigation of the use of an Augmented Roman Alphabet with twelve hundred children in the British Infants Schools. The Augmented Roman Alphabet was planned to provide a very simplified and consistent form of spelling for use in beginning reading.

Downing'uses T. O. for traditional orthography or spelling, as opposed to A. R. (now ITA) for Augmented Roman Alphabet.[9] An illustration of the need for simplified spelling is given in the following: "For example, in T. O. that phoneme which makes up the whole of each of the words 'I,' 'eye,' 'aye,' and which occurs at the ends of the words 'die,' 'my,' 'high,' and 'buy' can be spelled in at least forty different ways." A phoneme is the smallest unit in the sound system of a language, such as the "t" in top, or the "n" in notice. About forty phonemes are found in English according to Downing. Only eighty or ninety dif-

[9] John A. Downing, "The Augmented Roman Alphabet for Learning to Read," *The Reading Teacher*, XVI (Mar. 1963), 325–36.

ferent ways of spelling these forty phonemes are used in ITA as contrasted to more than two thousand ways of spelling these same phonemes in traditional orthography. Children are obviously extremely confused by the many different spellings for the same sounds that they meet in traditional reading.

Procedures with Small Groups

At this point in the study, the results have been quite successful. This program was carried on with two small groups of children who had encountered difficulty with reading. The children in the experimental group succeeded in learning to recognize more than twice as many words at the end of sixteen hours of remedial teaching, than the children in the control group. The ITA children were found to be more independent in their reading, and definite improvement was found in their attitude toward school work. Later studies show approximately the same results as found for the developmental program by the end of the second grade.

The application of phonics was heavily emphasized in the methods used in the teaching in these schools, and word-by-word reading was quite evident in the films shown by Dr. Downing when he presented his report at the Sacramento State College in July, 1963. The word-by-word reading, however, although not mentioned by Dr. Downing, was apparently the result of the emphasis on phonics and single words rather than the result of the use of the ITA alphabet. As Dr. Downing stated, the alphabet should be of value regardless of the method used. If a method aimed toward more emphasis on comprehension and speed in reading were used with the ITA alphabet, abilities in speed and comprehension should be included in the tests to evaluate the plan.

Conversion to Traditional Spelling

According to Dr. Downing, the basic problem that concerned the experimenters in the use of the ITA alphabet was the need for later conversion to reading matter using traditional spelling. The English children made the conversion much more easily than the experimenters had expected. In fact, some of the brighter children made the change without help. The children, in general, were very successful in making this type of adjustment.

THE LINGUISTIC APPROACH TO READING

Several authors have discussed the application of linguistics principles to instruction in beginning reading. The student and teacher should have some understanding of this trend. At least two programs have been planned to teach reading, both of which introduce the child to reading by means of phonemes and morphemes.

Elements of the Linguistic Program

A knowledge of the meaning of some of the terms used frequently in linguistics is helpful in understanding the program. An effort has been made to select terms that seem to represent elements used in teaching procedures.

Consonant Phonemes. A phoneme is a single functioning or signaling unit of a word pattern. Alphabetic writing represents the phonemes of the language. Some examples of phonemes listed by Fries may clarify the definition.[10] Thirteen consonants each represent a single phoneme or sound. They are *b, d, f, j, k, l, m, n, p, q, r, t,* and *y.* The letter, *s,* represents three phonemes or sounds. The letters, *c, g,* and *z,* each represent two phonemes. Some authors disagree; for example, they list two sounds for *f,* as in *fun* and *of.*

Consonant Clusters. Four consonant clusters, according to Fries, each represent a phoneme. These consonant clusters are combinations of two consonants and include *ch* as in *chicken* or *chorus; sh* as in *sheep; th* voiced in *this* and unvoiced in *thin;* and *ng* usually found at the ends of words. Fries classifies *q* as a phoneme although most dictionaries interpret it as representative of two phonemes, *kw.* He classifies the consonant blends as consonant clusters representing two or more phonemes as *bl* and *ck* in *black* and *str* in *street.*

Vowel Phonemes. Fries finds eleven single vowels and three vowel clusters that he seems to feel represent all the vowel phonemes in English. They include long *a* as in *pale,* short *a* as in *hat,* long *e* as in *peal,* short *e* as in *get* (long *i* is listed in the vowel clusters), short *i* as in *pill,* long *o* as in *pole,* short *o* as in *hot,* long *u* written *oo* as in *pool,* short *u* as in *hut,* and *au* as in *Paul.* The vowel clusters are long *i* written *ai* as in *aisle, ow* as in *foul,* and *oi* as in *foil,* each representing two vowel phonemes. Fries mentions that other experts recognize more vowel sounds, but these are the only ones he recognizes. This list is very much more limited than the sound of vowels listed in most dictionaries.

Morphemes. According to Goodman "Morphemes are the minimum units of language that can carry meaning, but they have no existence outside of syntactical structures. Syntactical structures, such as sentences, have reality only in the stream of language." [11] Therefore, words

---

[10] Charles C. Fries, *Linguistics and Reading* (New York: Holt, Rinehart and Winston, Inc., 1962), 159–85.

[11] Kenneth S. Goodman, "The Linguistics of Reading," *The Elementary School Journal,* LXIV (Apr. 1964), 355–61.

are morphemes. Prefixes and suffixes are also morphemes because they are added to words to modify the meaning. Examples of prefixes are *trans* and *ex,* and examples of suffixes are *ing* and *ed.*

First Set of Spelling-Patterns. According to Fries, "The major spelling-patterns consist of consonant frames which contain one or more of the five vowel letters." Fries uses a variety of spelling-patterns programmed in a related sequence. A number of types are listed in the first set which is made up of one-syllable words and the pattern of consonant-vowel-consonant making use of different initial consonants with the same vowel and final consonants, as *bat, cat, fat, gat,* and *hat.* In a second type the contrast comes in the final consonant instead of in the initial consonant as in *cat, cad, cam, can,* and *cap.* A third set of patterns is made up of words that hold the consonants in fixed position but use contrasting vowels as *bag, big, beg, bog,* and *bug.* In other types of spelling-patterns the initial or final consonants are made up of consonant digraphs representing phonemes such as *ash, bash, dash, gash, lash, mash,* and *sash* or *chin, chip,* and *chit.* Other spelling patterns are illustrated by those beginning and ending with consonant blends representing two or three phonemes such as *pack, peck, pick, pock,* and *puck* or *ball, call, fall, gall, hall, mall, pall, tall,* and *wall.*

Second Set of Spelling-Patterns. The second set of spelling-patterns makes use of three-letter words followed by the same words ending in *e* for another type of contrast. Examples of these spelling-patterns are *bad, bade,* and *fad, fade.* Many variations of beginning and ending phonemes, digraphs, and blends are used to illustrate this set of patterns. Two vowels are used in the center of words or the silent *e* is added to the ends for other variations such as *bet* with *beat, back* with *bake, fed* with *feed,* and *rod* with *road.*

The schwa is apparently taught in connection with all five vowels to represent the sound of these in unaccented syllables of various words. Words making use of the schwa for each vowel are *a* in *about, e* in *silken, i* in *pencil, o* in *pistol,* and *u* in *circus.* All examples of spelling-patterns have been taken from Fries' lists. These words are in the dictionary.

Definitions of Programs

Condensed statements of three approaches to the analysis of language are given to clarify the differences among these programs. Confusion sometimes arises in discussions of the various aspects of these programs.

Fries' Plan for a Linguistics Program. Lefevre makes the following statement to summarize Fries' thesis or plan of teaching.

All the experience lying back of the conclusions presented in this book seems to justify the assertion that only a tremendous amount of practice on reading materials that have been adequately programmed and streamlined to lead the developing reader by small steps through all the important spelling-patterns will lead to the high-speed recognition responses of efficient reading.[12]

Phonics. Since the terms, phonics and phonetics, are often confused, the student or teacher should be clear concerning the meaning of these terms. The word *phonics,* in a teaching situation, is used to represent various methods or practices used by teachers to help children acquire the power to analyze and thereby recognize words by the sounds of the letters that make up these words. These letters may be recognized singly or in groups. In contrast to linguistics, phonics makes use of generalizations or rules. Although many exceptions to these rules occur, some of them are helpful to primary children, especially when they are used along with context clues. In another contrast to linguistics, phonic elements are taught in connection with new words when they are introduced in stories. In this way phonic elements are introduced and reviewed when the child needs the specific phonic elements and rules. In linguistics and some phonic plans, phonemes and letter patterns are introduced and taught with much practice before actual reading is taught. Phonics is taught in the elementary school.

Phonetics. Phonetics is the science of the speech sounds that serve as elements of language. This science includes the study of the formulation of speech sounds as they are registered by the ear and produced in the speech organs, including the anatomy and physiology of these organs. The attributes of each sound are analyzed and their relation to other aspects of language are studied. This science has its own alphabet, which is used in the application of this science to the understanding and speaking of all languages. Phonetics is taught in colleges.

Bloomfield's Method of Linguistics

Leonard Bloomfield and Clarence Barnhart have published a combined textbook and manual to guide teachers in the use of materials and methods in teaching reading by the linguistic approach.[13] Two hundred forty-five lessons in beginning reading are described in detail in this book called *Let's Read: A Linguistic Approach.* In this particular approach spelling-patterns stressing the short vowel sounds are given in monosyllables in the first thirty-six lessons. Consonant blends and words including plurals and possessives are presented in the next thirty-five lessons, whereas vowel combinations are stressed in the following thirty-

---

[12] Carl A. Lefevre, "Linguistics and Reading," *The Elementary School Journal,* LXIV (Apr. 1964), 400.

[13] Leonard Bloomfield and Clarence L. Barnhart, *Let's Read: A Linguiustic Approach* (Detroit: Wayne State University Press, 1961).

five lessons. In the remaining lessons irregular letter sounds of various types, polysyllables, and suffixes are presented. Much after the McGuffey method, a list of monosyllabic words and nonsense syllables representing particular vowel phonemes such as long *a* or short *a* are given at the top of the page. These monosyllabic words are then used in a series of unrelated, meaningless sentences. In contrast to some of the linguistic authorities, Bloomfield and Barnhart teach the names of the letters of the alphabet as an essential step in learning the sounds of these letters, although single letters are not sounded in isolation.

Fries' Method of Linguistics

Charles Fries has planned a program under three stages. In step one, the transfer stage, the children compare the letters of the alphabet, first one letter to another and later groups of two letters with two others. Groups of letters called spelling-patterns are then learned. Step two is the stage of "Productive" reading, and step three is called the stage of "Vivid Imaginative Realization" which involves the teaching of literature.

Learning in the Transfer Stage. According to Fries, the transfer stage includes two processes. The first is called learning the letters, and the second is called learning the spelling-patterns.

Learning the Letters. Capital letters, only, are used in a large part of Fries' program because he believes that they are easier for children to recognize. He has organized these letters into groups including (1) those using only straight lines or strokes, (2) those using parts of circles, and (3) those using circles. The letters of the first group selected for teaching, that is, those using strokes only, are taught first in pairs of single letters. The entire teaching at this stage consists of helping the child recognize letters that are alike from those that are unlike as *N N* compared to *N M*. The children are taught to recognize the likenesses or differences at a glance. They may learn the names of the letters, although Fries believes that letter names are not important at this stage. Later the child learns to recognize matching pairs of letters grouped in twos as *AM AM* compared to *AM EM*. When the child has learned to make comparisons between these two-letter groups, he proceeds in making comparisons between three-letter groups.

Providing Readiness. According to Fries, the ability to distinguish between like and different groups of letters comprises the readiness step which should be taught in kindergarten. He selects letters that are as similar as possible for teaching these distinctions, based on the idea that the greater the similarity, the easier the differences are to observe. All other phases of readiness are completely ignored with the following statement:

This ability to identify the difference between three-letter groups is so important a basic skill at this stage that the variety of practices necessary for its full development should become the chief activity of the pre-reading child.[14]

As far as this author is concerned, ability to speak is the only factor of importance in readiness to learn to read. This position is clarified in Fries' statement that, "From the evidence available, we believe that we can assume that *any* child *can* learn to read within a year after he has learned to 'talk' his native language satisfactorily." (The italics are part of the quotation.) No definition is given of talking at a "satisfactory" level and no research is quoted to support the statement. The volumes of research on readiness and reading disabilities are completely ignored.

Learning the Spelling-Patterns. The teaching of the recognition responses to the spelling-patterns is delayed until the habits of recognizing contrasting letter shapes are thoroughly established in order to avoid confusing and frustrating children. At this point the spelling by types and sets as described above are learned by intensive practice. The child does not learn the sounds of the vowels or consonants in isolation but learns them rather in spelling-patterns. This statement is greatly emphasized as a point of contrast between the phonics and linguistic approaches.

All of these spelling-patterns actually represent words rather than nonsense syllables. These words, according to the author, are within the average first grade child's understanding vocabulary even though such words as BAN, BANE, FATE, DEAN, and FEAT are included. Much emphasis is given to the automatic habits of response and high speed recognition of these spelling-patterns, but no techniques for developing speed are suggested. When the child arrives at the level of ability to recognize groups of words, he goes through a series of exercises such as the following: BAT–BATS, PAT–PATS, CAT–CATS, RAT–RATS, HAT–HATS, followed by A CAT BATS AT A RAT, and CATS BAT AT RATS.

Achieving at the Stage of "Productive" Reading. This second stage is taught after the child has systematically and thoroughly mastered all the major spelling-patterns and some of the minor patterns. This next step in the child's learning, according to Fries, consists of the following procedures:

He must develop recognition responses (high speed recognition responses to read efficiently) to the bundles of graphic shapes that now represent the

---

[14] Fries, *op. cit.*, p. 193.

language signals formerly represented for him only by bundles of vocal noises.[15]

The linguistic program is basically aimed at replacing auditory word signals with visual word signals through the procedures described above. Eventually these spelling-patterns are presumed to "sink below the threshold of attention" so that the child is conscious only of the meaning of the printed material. No research is quoted to support this statement.

Achieving at the Stage of "Vivid Imaginative Realization." This section concerns literature. Its purposes and the need to help the child achieve a complete vivid imaginative realization of the content of literature are stressed. Further discussion centers around the rhythm of poetic expression and the quality of rhyme.

Fries devotes a chapter in his book to research regarding methods of teaching reading before the end of the nineteenth century. This author has probed deeply into these early practices and quotes from and describes in detail the literature regarding the alphabet and phonics method, the word method, the methods used in the McGuffey readers, the sentence method, and some research regarding eye movements. Most of the methods are described fairly, and the arguments regarding the advantages of each method are often presented in quotations from authors supporting each type of procedure.

Implications of the Linguistic Method

Some questions arise concerning the effects on the learner of some of the linguistic procedures. One question concerns the effect of practice on letters and words isolated from thought over a prolonged period. Other questions pertain to the unit of learning and the use of capital letters.

Early Reading Habits in the Linguistic Program. The research regarding eye movements is criticized because effective comprehension has been found on the part of both slow and rapid readers. No recognition is given to the problem of word-by-word reading, previously discussed as the outstanding difficulty met by many college students and adult readers.

The child's first work in the readiness step consists of differentiation between very similar pairs of capital letters. In many cases the differences lies in only one extra stroke as in the difference between N and M. Time spent by the child focusing his eyes on such minute differences must inevitably result in habits of looking carefully at letters and parts of letters. When such habits have been established as the beginning step in reading by day after day practice, as Fries advocates, these habits tend to be firmly fixed in the child's mind and may have a lasting effect on later speed of reading.

When the child reaches the stage of recognition of spelling-patterns, he is presumed to learn to recognize these patterns with great rapidity. However, he will repeat these words or spelling-patterns in lists, whether vertical or horizontal, many times in order to know them well. When children learn words in lists rather than in sentences, many of them acquire the habit of reading word-by-word. Once this habit is thoroughly established, it is very difficult to break. Even today with our present confusion in the use of methods, many adults are word-by-word readers and may never learn to read more efficiently.

Use of Capital Letters. The assumption that children can read capital letters more easily than lower case letters and that the most similar elements are the most easily differentiated by children is not supported by research. The part played by the configuration of words in beginning reading is recognized by all reading authorities, and the help gained from the maximum differences in configuration is also known to teachers of beginning reading.

The Unit of Learning. Some of the linguists differ among themselves regarding the unit of learning for teaching reading. Bloomfield uses the letter and small groups of letters as the units for his program. Although Fries teaches the child to differentiate between similar capital letters and to learn the alphabet, he uses the word as his basic unit for teaching reading. Lefevre and Goodman both support the sentence as the unit of learning. Goodman is not a linguist but a professor of elementary education who feels that educators can make use of applications from linguistics to improve the reading program.

In the balanced reading program, as well as in the writing of Goodman and Lefevre, the sentence is considered the basic unit of learning because some words out of context have little, if any, meaning of their own. Some words, on the other hand, have so many meanings that they are not intelligible when presented alone. Even the frequently used word, *can*, has a variety of meanings. It may be used as an auxiliary verb followed by one form of the verb, *be*, as *can be*. It may also refer to physical or intellectual ability or the possession of necessary physical or mental courage. In other situations it may be an enabling verb supported by law, agreement, or circumstances. When used in regard to food or other products, it may refer to a vessel made of tinned iron for holding materials of various sorts or to the act of preserving food sealed in a container. It may even be used to refer to the discharge or dismissal of a person from his work. An unabridged dictionary would undoubtedly provide many more meanings for this word. An example of the ambiguity of this word is found in the sentence which states, "We eat what we can, and what we can't, we can." The definitions of this simple and frequently used word emphasize the ambiguity of many words read out of context.

All new programs and revivals of old ones must be evaluated at least through the intermediate grades before their value can be accepted. Only then can the program show whether the child has the comprehension and flexibility of rate necessary for effectively meeting the demands of his academic work.

Agreements Between Developmental Reading and Linguistics

Some of the agreements between principles underlying a balanced reading program and those accepted by the linguists concern the importance of speech. The fact that single letters or phonemes should not be pronounced or sounded alone is another point of agreement.

Language Patterns. The linguists state that children enter school with well-established language patterns, both from the standpoint of vocabulary and sentence structure. Teachers, however, find that some children have vastly more limited vocabularies than others as well as immature sentence patterns. Culturally-deprived children usually have very limited language patterns or patterns that differ greatly from those used in schools. Children's need to communicate with others provides the purpose and the desire to stimulate them to grow and improve in their ability to express their ideas in increasingly mature language. Reading is an important aspect of this communication process. Reading must always have meaning of importance for the child and must be learned in connection with concepts that are on his level of development. The agreement that words should be met in sentences from which they have meaning is repeated in Goodman's statement, "Morphemes are the minimum units of language that can carry meaning, but they have no existence outside syntactical structures." [16] He also adds, "Syntactical structures, such as sentences, have reality only in the stream of language."

Isolated Phonemes. Most reading specialists agree with the linguists that single letters or phonemes should not be pronounced or sounded alone. The effort to pronounce consonant phonemes alone usually results in the addition of a vowel before or after the consonant that warps the correct pronunciation. Phoneticians stress the fact that the letters

[16] Goodman, *op. cit.,* p. 360.

b and *d* are impossible to pronounce in isolation and also object to the habit of adding a vowel before or after any consonant in isolation. For example, when helping a child with a beginning *b* sound in *boy*, the teacher may say that it begins with *bu* or *ub*. Both are incorrect. *Bu* can not be correctly combined with most other sounds as *bu-at*, *bu-ed*, *bu-ird*, *bu-oy*, or even *bu-urn*. Some words beginning with *bu*, however, can be blended with this sound such as *bulb*, but the procedure of pronouncing *b* alone is poor.

Influences on Phonemes. The fact that some phonemes are influenced in their pronunciation by adjoining letters is another reason why they should not be pronounced in isolation. The sound of the letter *c* is one that illustrates this point. If the hard *c* is used at the beginning of the words, *celery*, *circus*, or *cyclone*, these words will be pronounced incorrectly and will therefore be unrecognized by a child trying to analyze them. On the other hand, if the soft *c* is used at the beginning of the words *carrot*, *crossing*, or *cushion*, the same problem will arise. These phonemes must be recognized in groups, especially word groups, if they are to be recognized correctly.

PROGRAMMED LEARNING AND TEACHING MACHINES

All teaching machines make use of programmed material. This material must be planned in carefully developed sequence. Several types of machines are on the market. Some expose one question after another on a tape. Others make use of multiple-choice materials using a push button type of response.

Programmed Material

The content of programmed material is carefully selected and planned. It is divided into small increments or steps to cover each detail of the reading material. The sequence of the lessons must be selected from the standpoint of the logical order of the material and the developmental growth of the pupil. Some machines are used to help the student increase his reading speed and comprehension. Other machines are used for programmed teaching.

Use of Machines

Machines to help the student read more rapidly have been on the market for several decades. The tachistoscope is one of the older machines. Other devices have also been used to help the reader move his eyes down the page more rapidly and thereby increase his rate of reading. Newer and more elaborate machines to be used with programmed learning have been introduced more recently.

Machines for Increasing Rate of Reading. The tachistoscope is a piece of equipment for exposing a very short piece of printed material for a limited period of time such as a second, a tenth of a second, and even shorter periods. Letters, numbers, or words are exposed for increasingly shorter periods to help the student take in the visual image more rapidly. Sometimes a series of sentences are exposed, a word or a short phrase at a time in sequence, to help the reader acquire greater speed in this type of reading.

These machines have been used with students all the way from the age of beginners to adults. Goins worked with beginners but found no advantage in the use of this tachistoscope with children of that age.[17] In some cases older children and college students have been able to increase their speed while reading from the tachistoscope. This increased rate, however, does not necessarily carry over to improve speed in other types of reading material. Additional help must be given in the reading of the printed page.

Some machines are designed to be used with books or printed material. The book is inserted into the machine which lies on the student's desk. An arm or an exposure device of some sort drives the eye of the reader down the page. The material read is usually covered as the exposure device moves down the page. The student may adjust his own rate of reading which is usually gradually increased as the reader acquires greater speed. These machines have been used with success, primarily with junior high school and older students.

Machines for Use in Programmed Learning. More recently, rather elaborate machines have been produced for use in programmed learning. The pupil, usually in the intermediate grades or in high school, may be provided with reading material designed for this type of instruction. After a specified amount of material has been read, a question may be exposed by the machine that uses a tape on which the pupil writes his answers. He next pushes a lever, which covers his answer with a sheet of glass and which then moves along to expose the correct answer. Although he can not change his answer, he knows at once whether or not he was correct, and he scores himself accordingly. He then moves the lever to expose another question. The teacher may examine his responses after he has finished working.

Another type of machine presents a multiple-choice item on a card. The pupil chooses the answer and presses a button to indicate his choice. If his answer is correct, a green light comes on. If no light is shown, he knows his answer is incorrect, and he pushes another button to indicate

---

[17] Jean Turner Goins, *Visual Perceptual Abilities and Early Reading Progress,* Supplementary Educational Monograph No. 87 (Chicago: University of Chicago Press, Feb. 1958).

his second choice. He continues to push buttons until the correct response is made. In this way, too, he knows when he has selected the correct answer or response. The machine may record the number of errors made. Other types of machines use variations in the way the questions are presented or in the way the responses are made.

Applications of Machine Learning. This type of learning has been suggested for various types of subject matter and for various types of reading activities. Some of these suggested uses are given below. Exercises in comprehension can be programmed on cards or work sheets and corrected automatically. It has been suggested that readiness pictures might be placed under transparent keys. The child might make the response by touching the picture or symbol that matches another. Vocabulary exercises might be used with these machines. A picture might be exposed, and the child would locate the word that names the object. Vocabulary help might be given to older children by listing words with multiple-choice responses containing synonyms for the original word. Ability to use context clues might be practiced through the use of sentences each containing a blank space. The child would then choose the appropriate word for the space. Practice in phonics might be given by means of clue words followed by multiple-choice words from which the child could select the words that began with the same letters as the matching word.

Evaluation of Machine Learning

Some of the advantages of machine learning include the fact that the child knows at once whether or not his response is correct. On some machines he can repeat the step until he gets the correct response. The pupil is active at all times. He can advance at his own rate of speed without waiting for slower children. The slower child does not become lost because the other members of the group are ahead of him.

Automatic Correction and Motivation. Since the material on the machine shows both the correct responses and the errors made by the child, the teacher is saved time correcting the papers. The use of the machine is highly motivating when the child first begins to use it because of the mechanical element. If a classroom were supplied with a few machines used for specific purposes, the machines would continue to be attractive since children would not use them often enough to become bored.

Lack of Challenge and Pacing. The use of machines for programmed learning presupposes that the child has a strong purpose for desiring this type of help. If used too frequently, the lack of discussion and exchange of ideas normally found among a group of children might fail to provide the challenge of a live situation and would eliminate the learnings children acquire from each other. Some practice material lends itself well to the development of items on a scale of incremental steps in programmed learning. Material requiring the use of organizational skills by the child might be less useful because the child should have opportunity to create his own organizational plans at times. Another factor involves pacing. Although the amount of material may be adapted to the speed of the learner, extra review for the slow child or the elimination of unnecessary steps for the fast child is not so easily controlled, although it is sometimes provided by this type of programmed learning.

Limitations of Stimulus-Response Material. As stated above, the use of machines for programmed learning presupposes that the material to be read has been carefully organized in small steps and planned in sequence to develop gradually increasing skills. This type of learning is almost always applied to factual material and is usually based on Skinner's theories of stimulus and response. In much of the work the mind responds somewhat in the manner of the older switchboard used by telephone operators. A specific stimulus, the telephone plug, is applied to a specific situation, the socket on the switchboard, to result in a specific response. The stimulus and the response are preplanned and are one to one in their relationship; that is, only one response is correct.

This type of learning is of a very rudimentary type. While this level of learning is needed in some situations, it is far from adequate to meet the needs of those who must adjust to new elements in the environment. Almost no individual can survive on the basis of stimulus-response learning. He must be able to adapt to new situations and creatively to solve problems, particularly in this modern age of tremendous and very rapid change. While the use of programmed learning of this type may be adequate to help the child develop simple skills with objective material, many other procedures must be used with reading to give the child experiences in adapting to new situations and solving problems.

Use as Supplementary Material. A good use of programmed material might be made in situations in which a child who has been absent for some time might use the machine to make up the learning he has missed. A bright child might turn to the machine for advanced work of a factual or objective type on material beyond the level of the class average if he needed this type of practice.

A NON-ORAL METHOD

An older approach to beginning reading was used with considerable success during the past several decades. This plan has some possible applications for supplementary work in today's program. McDade used a non-oral approach in the Chicago schools.[18] He planned a program of directions for action that utilized a basic reading vocabulary in order to eliminate oral reading for the first two years. By using silent reading, only, he hoped to eliminate vocalization or silent speech. This vocalization in silent reading varies all the way from actually pronouncing the words in a mumble to movement of the lips, only, to minor contractions of the vocal cords without any sound, described in Chapter 2. Too much vocalization tends to limit silent reading speed to the pace of oral reading. McDade hoped that comprehension, as well as speed, would be improved by eliminating the effects of the vocalization.

Direction Strips

McDade planned a series of carefully developed sentences giving directions for action in short but complete sentences. For example, the sentence, "Get the ball," would be printed in large manuscript on a strip of manila tag. When this card was held up, a child would go to a table, pick up the ball, and hand it to the teacher. At no time did the children read any of the directions aloud. The fact that the children were able to carry the directions into action served to prove their understanding, and also to prove that young children can comprehend reading material without reading it orally. They do, however, need immediate reassurance. After the children had acquired a rather extensive vocabulary through this technique over a two-year period, they were given a general developmental program in reading textbooks in the third grade and were on their way to becoming rapid and efficient readers.

Some later experiments in the field of psychology, also mentioned in Chapter 2, proved that some vocalization takes place even in the muscles of rapid readers. These movements are less pronounced, however, in cases of fast readers than in cases of slow readers. McDade's study did not prove that vocalization can be completely eliminated, but it did show that considerably better comprehension and speed resulted from his procedures than from other methods using much purposeless oral reading.

Success of the Non-Oral Program

Buswell worked on a ten-year study of seventy thousand children in the Chicago schools to measure the results of this non-oral program at the end of the eighth grade.[19] These children who were taught by the

[18] James E. McDade, "A Hypothesis for Non-Oral Reading: Argument, Experiment, and Results," *Journal of Educational Research*, XXX (Mar. 1937), 489–503.
[19] Guy T. Buswell, *Non-Oral Reading: A Study of Its Use in the Chicago Public Schools*, Supplementary Educational Monograph No. 60 (Chicago: University of Chicago Press, 1945).

non-oral methods were compared by matched pairs to children of the same age who were taught by procedures using some oral reading from the beginning. The children taught by the silent or non-oral reading procedures were superior to the other groups on all the criteria which were evaluated. Buswell concluded that silent reading should be stressed from the first in a beginning reading program. He also concluded that methods that establish oral reading habits before silent reading habits tend to result in silent reading which is only noiseless oral reading. The pupil and often the adult must think or say each word to himself as he reads, that is, he uses word-by-word reading. For this reason the values of teaching silent reading from the first were emphasized. Buswell found support for his conclusions in his work as director of the adult reading clinic at the University of Chicago. He was able to help adults make an average of fifty-four percent gain in rate of reading without loss in comprehension.

Adaptations of Non-Oral Methods

The non-oral method has not been widely adopted by teachers, possibly because they felt it must be used on an all-or-none basis. It has some elements, however, that can very well be incorporated in a more balanced program by the teacher of beginning readers. The emphasis on the early establishment of effective silent reading techniques is very important. The procedure involving physical participation for the young children is also very helpful since they have short attention spans and find it difficult to sit still. The overt responses made to direction strips by the children serve as proof that they are able to read with thought. Children enjoy activities of this sort and think of them as a type of game. They can call on each other to carry out the direction, which further intensifies the game spirit and adds social learnings to the process. Buswell's findings also support the use of procedures such as those suggested in Chapters 7 through 10 of this book.

USE OF FILM STRIPS

In the New Castle experiment McCracken reported success by introducing a reading vocabulary through the use of film strips.[20] These strips were prepared to accompany a basal reading series and provided at least one frame of material for use with every lesson in the basic books. The frames were used with the readiness book and with all the primary reading books from the primer through the third reader. A

[20] Glenn McCracken, "The New Castle Reading Experiment—A Terminal Report," *Elementary English*, XXX (Jan. 1953), 13–21.

picture in bright, clear colors accompanied the text on each frame. The picture and story were introduced through discussion, and the children participated actively by going to the screen to point to objects of interest in the pictures. Various games were played to give all children, including the shy ones, an opportunity to share in the reading experience.

Teaching from the Screen

The lessons were actually taught at the screen, and the book was merely used as "a testing instrument," according to the author. The lessons on the screen were similar to those in the book but shorter. After the introduction on the screen, the children found that they could read the story in the book without difficulty and therefore felt the power that comes from success.

Standards for Equipment

The author stressed the need for ventilation and good quality projectors and screens so that the images are large, clear, sharp, and have good color. The type of screen which can be used without darkening the room is preferable. Wall-type screens are more stable and convenient than those on stands for work with little children. A yardstick or pointer wrapped with adhesive tape saves the screen from scratches and wear.

McCracken found that the large colorful projections held the interest of the children very successfully. Since most young children are far-sighted, it was easier for them to concentrate on a large image at a distance than on small pictures and print in a book. In this experiment the same lessons were used with the entire class so that problems of grouping were eliminated.

Advantages and Problems

Dr. McCracken has had consistent success with this program. Apparently the motivation is excellent, the children have an opportunity for physical movement in going to the charts for learning activities, and large colored pictures not only hold the children's interest but seem to help them recall the text. These film strips were used with the entire class in the original situation.

Most teachers prefer to use groups in teaching reading. The problem of preventing the distraction of the children working independently when the film strips are used with groups is one of the difficulties involved in their use. If the screen is placed in such a way as to be useful with one group without disturbing or interfering with other groups, the technique may be successfully adjusted to group work.

The greatest value of the film strip technique seems to be its high motivating quality. Children are delighted with and look forward to their "moving pictures." This procedure would seem to be a good method to use occasionally for supplementary work even with a set of books that are not provided with accompanying film strips. Homemade slides can be adapted to children's needs. Materials for making slides of either glass or a type of cellophane material are usually available in schools along with other audio-visual supplies. Black and colored ink can be used on this material, and it can also be used in a typewriter. The teacher can make slides to supplement sections of any reader for further practice or duplicate exercises of various sorts to demonstrate how to work with them.

SUMMARY

Many investigations are being conducted to study new methods of teaching reading. Although new investigations are necessary for progress, new ways of teaching reading should be carefully practiced over a number of years and meticulously evaluated before their adoption. Some of the new programs offer excellent contributions. Certain phases of other studies offer help, although the entire programs may not always be practical for adoption in the public schools. Other investigations seem to tend toward a return to older practices and need even more careful scrutiny.

Children who have learned to read before they have entered first grade have been studied, particularly by one investigator. In other studies the sixth-grade achievement of children who were taught reading early was compared with the achievement of children who entered school and were taught reading at a later age.

Some schools have experimented with teaching children to write before they have learned to read in an effort to facilitate the reading process. The experience story has also been used to introduce beginners to reading. Others have been taught the Augmented Roman Alphabet in an effort to eliminate the difficulties of the non-phonetic aspects of English. Linguists have been developing programs for teaching beginners by means of phonemes, morphemes, and spelling-patterns, although other linguists prefer the sentence as the unit of learning.

Programmed patterns of learning and the use of machines have been studied as other forms of teaching reading. A non-oral method of teaching reading was studied in an attempt to eliminate vocalization with beginning readers. Film strips have also been used for the teaching process to accompany a selected set of readers.

Booklist for Slow Readers

Books for Easy Reading. University of Michigan, Library Extension Service. Titles chosen for junior and senior high school students who find reading difficult, selected for reading interest, clarity and directness of style, and for simplicity of language.

Carpenter, H. M. *The Gateways to American History: An annotated graded list of books for slow learners in junior high school.* New York: The H. W. Wilson Co., 1942.

Provides criteria for judging books for slow learners and recommends and analyzes more than 200 books for historical fiction, biography, and other informational literature.

Carr, C. "Substitutes for the Comic Books." Part I: *Elementary English,* **28**:194–200 (Apr. 1951). Part II: *Elementary English,* **28**:285–99 (May 1951).

Fifty-eight authors listed in Part I and their titles; seventy-seven authors listed in Part II and their titles, suitable for slow readers. Under groupings: Below 4th grade, 4th–6th grades, and above 6th grade. Annotated under many broad subjects. List of publishers and addresses given on page 285.

Children's Catalog, 8th ed. New York: The H. W. Wilson Co., 1951.

Arranged in alphabetical order by author and title in Part I and Dewey Classification in Part II. These books are selected and suitable for elementary and junior high schools. Full buying information given. Graded levels given.

Clark, Margaret M. *Adventuring with Books.* Elementary Reading List Committee of the National Council of Teachers of English, 1950.

Lists and annotates over 1,000 books for grades kindergarten through 6th. Indicated books useful in personal development, for understanding human relations, and for use by readers of limited ability. Indexed.

Dunn, Anita E., *et al. Fare for the Reluctant Reader.* Books, magazines, audio-visual materials for the slow learners in grades 7–10. Committee for the Capital Area School Development Association. New York State College for Teachers, Albany, 1952.

Brief annotations are given for the 800 titles grouped in three sections: grades 7–8, 9–10, 11–12. Within each group, titles have been grouped by categories such as Animal Tales, Popular with Boys, Favorites of Girls, Tall Tales, Choosing a Career, etc. Also includes lists of series, abridgements, and adaptations that are easy to read.

Durrell, Donald D., and Helen Blair Sullivan. *High Interest Low Vocabulary Booklist.* Educational Clinic, Boston University, School of Education, 1952.

List under grade vocabulary levels and interest levels starting from grades 1–7 and interests reaching grades 10–12. Author, title, publisher, and price given for each.

Heaton, Margaret, and Helen B. Lewis. *Reading Ladders for Human Relations.* Revised and enlarged edition. American Council on Education, Washington, D. C., 1954.

Interesting list of titles to increase understanding in the areas of human relations. Arranged by themes; many titles are annotated. Reading ladder bibliographies are given at the end of theme sections. Listing of books by author, title, publisher, price. In three parts, for young readers, intermediate readers, and mature readers.

Massingill, Alberta. "Remedial Reading and the Public Library," *Wilson Library Bulletin*, June, 1954.

Discussion of the remedial reading collection at the Grand Rapids Public Library. Bibliography of 700 titles graded as to difficulty and grouped according to subject or interest area.

Matthews, Pauline, and Helen Perdue. "Reading is Fun," *Library Journal*, December 15, 1953.

A graded reading list for the child whose interests have outdistanced his reading skills. Titles have been tested for difficulty and reader appeal.

Orr, Kenneth N. *Selected Materials for Remedial Reading.* Indiana State Teachers College, 1954.

In addition to the list of children's books, this also contains a bibliography of progressional books for teachers who are concerned with remedial reading.

Rue, Eloise. *Subject Index to Books for Intermediate Grades* (2nd ed.). Chicago: American Library Association, 1950.

1,800 titles in print listed, 75 titles out of print listed. By subject content in alphabetical order under subject. Full buying information given. Grade level given. Part I is the list of books indexed.

Sprague, Lois. "Non-Fiction Books for Retarded Readers in the Upper Grades," *Elementary English*, 28:28–34 (Jan. 1951).

Under broad subjects, such as Science, Social Science, Physical Science, and Personal Guidance. Author, title, publisher, annotation given. Also grade level. Illus. listed.

Strang, Ruth, Gilbert and Christine B. Strang, and Margaret Scoggin. *Gateways to Readable Books* (2nd ed.). New York: The H. W. Wilson Co., 1952.

An annotated graded list of books in many fields for adolescents who find reading difficult.

Teachers' Resources

BOOKS FOR RETARDED READERS

Reading at First, Second, and Low Third Grade Levels
Compiled on the Basis of Children's Responses and Objective Data

Title	Author	Spache Readability Score	Minimum Instr. Rdg. Level of Child for Reading Bk.
Beginner Books			
(Random)			
Big Ball of String, A	Holland	2.9	High 1
Big Jump & Other Stories	Elkin	1.9	High 1
Cat in the Hat, The	Seuss	2.1	High 1
Cat in the Hat Comes Back, The	Seuss	2.1	High 1
Fly Went By, A	McClintock	2.3	High 1
Sam and the Firefly	Eastman & Benchley	1.8	High 1
You Will Go to the Moon	Freeman	2.1	High 1
I Can Read Series			
(Harper)			
Danny and the Dinosaur	Hoff	2.5	High 1
Emmett's Pig	Williams	2.2	High 1
Little Bear	Minarik	2.3	High 1
No Fighting, No Biting	Minarik	2.2	High 1
Sammy the Seal	Hoff	2.1	High 1
Seeds and More Seeds	Selsam	2.5	High 1
Beginning-to-Read Series			
(Follett)			
Big New School	Hastings	2.2	High 1
Boy Who Would Not Say His Name, The	Vreeken	1.9	High 1
Four Friends, The	Hoff	2.4	High 1–Low 2
Gertie the Duck	Romano & Georgiady	2.1	Low 2
Hill that Grew, The	Meeks	1.9	High 1
In John's Back Yard	Meeks	2.0	High 1

BOOKS FOR RETARDED READERS—Continued

Title	Author	Spache Readability Score	Minimum Instr. Rdg. Level of Child for Reading Bk.
Mabel the Whale	King	2.4	Low 2
Miss Hattie and the Monkey	Olds	2.1	Low 2
My Own Little House	Kaune	2.6	High 1–Low 2
Nobody Listens to Andrew	Guilfoile	2.3	High 1–Low 2
Peter's Policeman	Lattin	2.6	Low 2
Something New at the Zoo	Meeks	2.3	High 1
Easy to Read Books (Benefic)			
Big Top	Derman	1.7	Primer
Monkey Island	Derman	1.9	High 1
Poker Dog	Derman	2.0	High 1–Low 2
Pony Ring	Derman	1.6	Primer
Pretty Bird	Derman	1.3	Primer
Surprise Egg	Derman	1.7	Primer
Photo Story Books (Reilly & Lee)			
Billy Buys a Dog	Steward	1.7	High 1
Come to the City	Tensen	1.8	High 1
Come to the Farm	Tensen	1.5	Primer
Come to the Pet Shop	Tensen	1.5	Primer
Come to the Zoo	Tensen	1.4	Pre-Primer
Frisky-Try Again	Fox	1.7	Primer–High 1
Funny Squirrel	Steward	1.9	High 1
Little Cowboy	Jones	1.7	Primer
Little Dog Tim	Steward	1.7	Primer
Patch . . . You Just Be You!	Steward	2.1	High 1
(Garrard)			
On the Farm	E. & M. Dolch	2.1	High 1–Low 2
Tommy's Pets	E. & M. Dolch	2.2	High 1–Low 2
Zoo Is Home	E. & M. Dolch	2.6	High 1–Low 2
I Want To Be Series (Childrens)			
I Want To Be a Baker	Greene	2.1	High 1
I Want To Be an Animal Doctor	Greene	2.2	High 1–Low 2
I Want To Be a Bus Driver	Greene	2.1	High 1
I Want To Be a Coal Miner	Greene	2.6	Low 2
I Want To Be a Dairy Farmer	Greene	2.2	High 1
I Want To Be a Doctor	Greene	2.8	High 1–Low 2
I Want To Be a Fisherman	Greene	2.6	Low 2
I Want To Be a News Reporter	Greene	2.4	High 1–Low 2
I Want To Be a Nurse	Greene	2.3	High 1
I Want To Be an Orange Grower	Greene	2.3	High 1–Low 2
I Want To Be a Pilot	Greene	2.2	High 1
I Want To Be a Policeman	Greene	2.6	High 1–Low 2
I Want To Be a Postman	Greene	2.3	High 1
I Want To Be a Road-builder	Greene	2.5	Low 2
I Want To Be a Storekeeper	Greene	2.6	High 1–Low 2
I Want To Be a Teacher	Greene	2.5	High 1–Low 2
I Want To Be a Telephone Operator	Greene	2.4	High 1–Low 2
I Want To Be a Train Engineer	Greene	2.1	High 1
I Want To Be a Truck Driver	Greene	2.6	High 1–Low 2
I Want To Be a Zoo Keeper	Greene	2.3	High 1

BOOKS FOR RETARDED READERS—Continued

Title	Author	Spache Readability Score	Minimum Instr. Rdg. Level of Child for Reading Bk.
The True Book Series *(Childrens)*			
True Book of Air Around Us	Friskey	2.5	High 2
True Book of Airports and Airplanes	Lewellen	2.5	High 2
True Book of Animal Babies	Podendorf	3.6	High 2
True Book of Animals of Sea and Shore	Podendorf	3.1	High 2
True Book of the Circus	Harmer	3.0	Low 2
True Book of Farm Animals	Lewellen	2.5	Low 2
True Book of Freedom and the U.S. Family	Witty	3.2	Low 2
True Book of Health	Haynes	3.0	High 2
True Book of Houses	Carter	2.8	Low 2
True Book of Indians	Martini	3.1	High 2
True Book of Insects	Podendorf	2.9	High 2
True Book of Moon, Sun, Stars	Lewellen	2.5	High 1
True Book of More Science Experiments	Podendorf	3.2	High 2
True Book of Our Post Office	Miner	3.1	Low 2
True Book of Pioneers	Harmer	3.7	High 2
True Book of Policemen and Firemen	Miner	2.9	Low 2
True Book of Reptiles	Ballard	2.9	High 2
True Book of Rocks and Minerals	Podendorf	3.0	High 2
True Book of Schools	Elkin	3.7	High 2
True Book of Science Experiments	Podendorf	2.7	Low 2
True Book of Time	Ziner	2.8	Low 2
True Book of Tools for Building	Leavitt	2.9	Low 3
True Book of Transportation	Posell	3.5	High 2
True Book of Trees	Podendorf	3.2	High 2
True Book of Weeds and Wildflowers	Podendorf	3.3	High 2
What Is It Series *(Benefic)*			
What Is a Chicken	Darby	2.2	Low 2
What Is a Fish	Darby	2.3	Low 2
What Is a Season	Darby	1.6	High 1
What Is a Turtle	Darby	1.7	High 1
Cowboy Sam Series *(Benefic)*			
Cowboy Sam	Chandler	2.1	High 1
Cowboy Sam and Dandy	Chandler	1.6	Primer
Cowboy Sam and Flop	Chandler	2.1	High 1
Cowboy Sam and Freddy	Chandler	2.2	High 1
Cowboy Sam and Miss Lily	Chandler	1.8	Primer
Cowboy Sam and Porky	Chandler	1.7	High 1
Cowboy Sam and the Fair	Chandler	2.3	Low 2
Cowboy Sam and the Rodeo	Chandler	2.4	Low 2
Cowboy Sam and Sally	Chandler	2.1	High 2
Cowboy Sam and Shorty	Chandler	1.9	High 1
Button Series *(Benefic)*			
Bucky Button	McCall	1.8	Pre-Primer
Buttons and Mr. Pete, The	McCall	1.9	High 1
Buttons and the Boy Scouts, The	McCall	2.6	Low 2–High 2
Buttons and the Pet Parade, The	McCall	1.8	Primer
Buttons and the Whirlybird, The	McCall	2.0	Primer

BOOKS FOR RETARDED READERS—Continued

Title	Author	Spache Readability Score	Minimum Instr. Rdg. Level of Child for Reading Bk.
Buttons at the Farm, The	McCall	1.7	High 1
Buttons at the Zoo, The	McCall	1.4	Primer
Buttons Go Camping, The	McCall	2.2	Low 2
Buttons See Things that Go, The	McCall	2.2	Low 2
Buttons See Things that Go, The	McCall	1.6	High 1
Buttons Take a Boat Ride, The	McCall	1.8	High 1
The Basic Vocabulary Series *(Garrard)*			
Animal Stories	E. & M. Dolch	2.6	Low 2
Bear Stories	E. & M. Dolch	3.1	Low 2
Circus Stories	E. & M. Dolch	2.7	Low 2
Dog Stories	E. & M. Dolch	2.3	Low 2
Elephant Stories	E. & M. Dolch	2.9	Low 2
Folk Stories	E. & M. Dolch	2.7	Low 2
Horse Stories	E. & M. Dolch	2.7	High 2
Irish Stories	E. & M. Dolch	2.6	High 2
Lion and Tiger Stories	E. & M. Dolch	2.9	Low 2
Lodge Stories	E. & M. Dolch	2.9	Low 2
Navaho Stories	E. & M. Dolch	2.7	Low 2
Pueblo Stories	E. & M. Dolch	2.4	Low 2
Tepee Stories	E. & M. Dolch	2.6	High 2
Wigwam Stories	E. & M. Dolch	2.7	Low 2
Why Stories	E. & M. Dolch	2.8	Low 2
Dan Frontier Series *(Benefic)*			
Dan Frontier	Hurley	1.5	Primer
Dan Frontier Goes Hunting	Hurley	1.8	Primer–High 1
Dan Frontier with the Indians	Hurley	2.3	High 1
Jerry Series *(Benefic)*			
Jerry	Battle	1.3	Pre-Primer
Jerry Goes Fishing	Battle	1.7	Primer–High 1
Jerry Goes on a Picnic	Battle	2.1	High 1–Low 2
Jerry Goes Riding	Battle	1.7	High 1
The Jim Forest Readers *(Harr Wagner)*			
Jim Forest and the Bandits	J. & N. Rambeau	2.2	High 1
Jim Forest and Dead Man's Peak	J. & N. Rambeau	2.6	Low 2
Jim Forest and the Flood	J. & N. Rambeau	2.6	Low 2
Jim Forest and the Mystery Hunter	J. & N. Rambeau	2.4	Low 2
Jim Forest and Ranger Don	J. & N. Rambeau	1.9	High 1
Walt Disney Story Books *(Heath)*			
Donald Duck and His Nephews	Brumbaugh	2.0	Low 2
Here They Are	Wayle	1.7	High 1

BOOKS FOR RETARDED READERS—Continued

Title	Author	Spache Readability Score	Minimum Instr. Rdg. Level of Child for Reading Bk.
Pinocchio	Baruch	2.1	High 2
Water Babies Circus and Other Stories	Browne	2.1	Low 2
The American Adventure Series (Wheeler)			
Friday, the Arapaho Indian	Anderson	2.5	High 2
Portugee Phillips and the Fighting Sioux	Anderson	2.8	High 2
Squanco and the Pilgrims	Anderson	2.7	High 2
The Deep-Sea Adventure Series (Harr Wagner)			
Pearl Divers, The	Coleman et al.	2.8	Low 2
Sea Hunt, The	Coleman et al.	2.5	Low 2
Submarine Rescue	Coleman et al.	3.0	Low 2
Treasure Under the Sea	Coleman et al.	2.6	Low 2

Title	Author	Publisher	Spache Readability Score	Minimum Instr. Rdg. Level of Child for Reading Bk.
Trade Books				
All Around You; A First Look at the World	Bendick	McGraw	3.2	High 2
And to Think I Saw It on Mulberry Street	Seuss	Vanguard	4.1	High 2–Low 3
Apron Strings and Rowdy	McKee & Aldredge	Benefic	2.9	Low 2
Boats on the River	Flack	Viking	3.6	High 2
Circus Baby, The	Petersham	Macmillan	3.1	Low 2
City Boy, Country Boy	Schlein	Childrens	3.8	Low 2
Cloud Hoppers	James	Childrens	3.0	Low 2
Cowboy Small	Lenski	Oxford	3.0	Low 2
Fireman Fred	Barr	Whitman	2.7	Low 2
Fluffy and Bluffy	Dalton	Childrens	2.8	High 2
Great Sweeping Day	Wood	Longmans	3.6	High 2
I Like Trains	Woolley	Harper	3.6	Low 2
I Live in So Many Places	Hengesbaugh	Childrens	2.3	Low 2
Little Airplane, The	Lenski	Oxford	3.6	High 2
Little Eagle	Deming	Laidlaw	2.1	Low 2
Little Stone House, The	Hader	Macmillan	3.2	Low 2
Little Train, The	Lenski	Oxford	2.7	High 2
Littlest Circus Seal, The	Gehr	Childrens	3.3	Low 2
Mike Mulligan and His Steam Shovel	Burton	Houghton	3.4	High 2
Mr. Plum and the Little Green Tree	Gilbert	Abingdon	4.8	High 2
Mrs. Mallard's Ducklings	Delafield	Lothrop	4.5	High 2–Low 3
Mystery of the Broken Bridge	Friskey	Childrens	1.7	High 1
Mystery of the Gate Sign	Friskey	Childrens	2.2	High 1
900 Buckets of Paint	Becker	Abingdon	3.0	Low 2
Papa Small	Lenski	Oxford	2.5	Low 2
Perky Little Engine	Friskey	Childrens	3.2	Low 2

BOOKS FOR RETARDED READERS—Continued

Title	Author	Publisher	Spache Readability Score	Minimum Instr. Rdg. Level of Child for Reading Bk.
Policeman Paul	Barr	Whitman	2.5	Low 2
Scatter the Chipmunk	Coblentz	Childrens	3.0	High 2
Schoolroom Zoo	Woolley	Morrow	3.8	High 2
Skiing with Per and Kari	Murstad	Childrens	3.2	Low 2
Sleepy Little Lion, The	Brown	Harper	2.3	Low 2
Trip for Tommy	Friskey	Childrens	3.5	High 1
Twelve O'clock Whistle	Beim & Crichlow	Morrow	3.3	High 2
While Susie Sleeps	Schneider	Scott	3.4	Low 2
Whopper Whale	Vaughn	Childrens	3.6	Low 2

This list is the result of a study made by Sister Mary Ruth, O.S.F., under the direction of Sister Mary Julitta, O.S.F., Graduate Division, Cardinal Stritch College, Milwaukee, Wisconsin.

Award Winning Books

The Caldecott Medal is awarded annually for the best picture book for children. Both the Newbery and the Caldecott awards have been established by Frederick C. Melcher. The selection is made by a committee of children's librarians of the American Library Association. The date given is the year in which the award was made.

The John Newbery Medal is awarded annually for the most distinguished book for children published in the United States.

THE CALDECOTT MEDAL BOOKS

Ness, *Sam, Bangs and Moonshine,* Holt, Rinehart and Winston, Inc., 1966.
Alger, *Always Room for One More,* Holt, Rinehart and Winston, Inc., 1965.
De Regniers, *May I Bring a Friend?,* Atheneum Press, 1964.
Sendak, *Where the Wild Things Are,* Harper and Row, 1963.
Keats, *The Snowy Day,* The Viking Press, Inc., 1962.
Brown, *Once a Mouse,* Charles Scribner's Sons, 1961.
Sidjakov, *Baboushka and the Three Kings,* Parnassus Press, 1960.
Ets, *Nine Days to Christmas,* The Viking Press, Inc., 1959.
Cooney, *Chanticleer and the Fox,* Crowell-Collier Pub. Co., 1958.
McCloskey, *Time of Wonder,* The Viking Press, Inc., 1957.
Simont, *A Tree Is Nice,* Harper and Row, 1956.
Rojankovsky, *Frog Went A-Courtin',* Harcourt, Brace & World, Inc., 1955.
Brown, *Cinderella,* Charles Scribner's Sons, 1954.
Bemelmans, *Madeline's Rescue,* The Viking Press, Inc., 1953.
Ward, *The Biggest Bear,* Houghton Mifflin Co., 1952.
Mordvinoff, *Finders Keepers,* Harcourt, Brace & World, Inc., 1951.
Milhous, *The Egg Tree,* Charles Scribner's Sons, 1950.
Politi, *Song of the Swallows,* Charles Scribner's Sons, 1949.
Hader, *The Big Snow,* The Macmillan Co., 1948.
Duvoisin, *White Snow, Bright Snow,* Lothrop, Lee & Shepard Co., Inc., 1947.
Weisgard, *The Little Island,* Doubleday and Co., Inc., 1946.

Petersham, *The Rooster Crows*, The Macmillan Co., 1945.
Jones, *Prayer for a Child*, The Macmillan Co., 1944.
Slobodkin, *Many Moons*, Harcourt, Brace & World, Inc., 1943.
Barton, *The Little House*, Houghton Mifflin Co., 1942.
McCloskey, *Make Way for Ducklings*, The Viking Press, Inc., 1941.
Lawson, *They Were Strong and Good*, The Viking Press, Inc., 1940.
D'Aulaire, *Abraham Lincoln*, Doubleday and Co., Inc., 1939.
Handforth, *Mei Li*, Doubleday and Co., Inc., 1938.
Lathrop, *Animals of the Bible*, J. B. Lippincott, Co., 1937.

THE NEWBERY MEDAL BOOKS

Hunt, *Up a Road Slowly*, Follett Publishing Co., 1966.
De Trevino, *I, Juan de Pareja*, Bell Books (a Division of Farrar, Straus & Giroux, Inc.), 1965.
Wojiechowska, *Shadow of a Bull*, Atheneum Pubs., 1964.
Neville, *It's Like This, Cat*, Harper and Row, 1963.
L'Engle, *A Wrinkle in Time*, Farrar, Straus and Cudahy, Inc., 1962.
Speare, *The Bronze Bow*, Houghton Mifflin Co., 1961.
O'Dell, *Island of the Blue Dolphins*, Houghton Mifflin Co., 1960.
Krumgold, *Onion John*, Crowell-Collier Pub. Co., 1959.
Speare, *The Witch of Blackbird Pond*, Houghton Mifflin Co., 1958.
Keith, *Rifles for Watie*, Crowell-Collier Pub. Co., 1957.
Sorensen, *Miracles of Maple Hill*, Harcourt, Brace & World, Inc., 1956.
Latham, *Carry On, Mr. Bowditch*, Houghton Mifflin Co., 1955.
De Jong, *The Wheel on the School*, Harper and Row, 1954.
Krumgold, *And Now Miguel*, Crowell-Collier Pub. Co., 1953.
Clark, *Secret of the Andes*, The Viking Press, Inc., 1952.
Estes, *Ginger Pye*, Harcourt, Brace & World, Inc., 1951.
Yates, *Amos Fortune, Free Man*, E. P. Dutton & Co., Inc., 1950.
De Angeli, *The Door in the Wall*, Doubleday and Co., Inc., 1949.
Henry, *King of the Wind*, Rand McNally & Co., 1948.
Du Bois, *The Twenty-One Balloons*, The Viking Press, Inc., 1947.
Bailey, *Miss Hickory*, The Viking Press, Inc., 1946.
Lenski, *Strawberry Girl*, J. B. Lippincott Co., 1945.
Lawson, *Rabbit Hill*, The Viking Press, Inc., 1944.
Forbes, *Johnny Tremain*, Houghton Mifflin Co., 1943.
Gray, *Adam of the Road*, The Viking Press, Inc., 1942.
Edmonds, *The Matchlock Gun*, Dodd, Mead & Co., 1941.
Sperry, *Call It Courage*, The Macmillan Co., 1940.
Daugherty, *Daniel Boone*, The Viking Press, Inc., 1939.
Enright, *Thimble Summer*, Holt, Rinehart and Winston, Inc., 1938.
Seredy, *The White Stag*, The Viking Press, Inc., 1937.
Sawyer, *Roller Skates*, The Viking Press, Inc., 1936.
Brink, *Caddie Woodlawn*, The Macmillan Co., 1935.
Shannon, *Dobry*, The Viking Press, Inc., 1934.
Meigs, *Invincible Louisa*, Little, Brown and Co., 1933.
Lewis, *Young Fu of the Upper Yangtze*, Holt, Rinehart and Winston, Inc., 1932.
Armer, *Waterless Mountain*, David McKay Co., Inc., 1931.
Coatsworth, *The Cat Who Went to Heaven*, The Macmillan Co., 1930.
Field, *Hitty, Her First Hundred Years*, The Macmillan Co., 1929.

Kelly, *Trumpeter of Krakow*, The Macmillan Co., 1928.
Mukerji, *Gay Neck*, E. P. Dutton & Co., Inc., 1927.
James, *Smoky, the Cowhorse*, Charles Scribner's Sons, 1926.
Chrisman, *Shen of the Sea*, E. P. Dutton & Co., Inc., 1925.
Finger, *Tales from Silver Lands*, Doubleday and Co., Inc., 1924.
Hawes, *The Dark Frigate*, Little, Brown and Co., 1923.
Lofting, *Voyages of Dr. Dolittle*, J. B. Lippincott Co., 1922.
Van Loon, *The Story of Mankind*, Liverwright Publishing Corp., 1921.

Phonic Generalizations

This brief summary of generalizations relating to phonics and structural analysis was prepared for the convenience of the student and teacher. It includes generalizations concerning single consonants, blends, consonant digraphs, voiced and voiceless consonants, consonant groups with silent letters, vowels, vowel digraphs, and spelling and syllabification rules. This summary is not meant as an outline of content to be taught. It is to be used only for reference.

The use of phonics and word-analysis skills must be taught with the following cautions in mind: (1) Although some letters in the English language each have one consistent sound, others have several sounds. For example, the letter *s* has four separate sounds. (2) Some sounds in English may be spelled in a variety of ways. Cordts [1] lists fifteen ways for the spelling of the sound of long *i*. (3) While some rules and generalizations are helpful in the teaching of reading, most of these rules have many exceptions that result in confusion for the reader. Because of these problems, the teacher should not depend unduly on the use of word analysis and should help children constantly use context clues to check the accuracy of their word-analysis procedures.

CONSONANT SOUNDS AND GENERALIZATIONS

Although authorities in both phonics and linguistics disagree on the number of sounds carried by some particular consonants, the following classifications are agreed upon by at least two authors. In cases of disagreement the classification of the phoneticians has been consulted.

---

[1] Anna D. Cordts, *Phonics for the Reading Teacher* (New York: Holt, Rinehart and Winston, Inc., 1965).

Single Consonants

Some consonants have only one sound each, whether used alone or in groups. These consonants are easy for the children to learn because of their consistency. Other consonants have two sounds, and still others have more than two sounds. The teacher should know what these sounds are and have some idea of how they should be taught.

Consonants representing one sound. The following consonants are considered to represent one sound or phoneme each: *b, h, j, k, l, m, n, p, r, t, v, w,* when used as a consonant, and initial *y.*

Consonants representing two sounds. The letter *d* represents two phonemes. The sound of *d* as in *dog* is the most common. On rare occasions *d* has the sound of *j* when followed by *u* as in *verdure.*

F represents two sounds: the common sound of *f* as in *fun,* and the sound of *v* as in *of.*

G represents two sounds: the hard sound as in *get,* and the sound of *j* as in *George, giant,* and *judge.*

J is classified as a consonant representing one phoneme by some of the linguists. On the other hand, phoneticians use two symbols for *j: d,* indicating that *j* has the normal sound of *d,* plus another sound similar to the sound of *zh;* and therefore *j* represents two phonemes. Although two sounds are represented by the sound of *j,* however, these sounds are always consistent.

Q followed by *u* normally takes the sound of *kw,* as in *quick.* In rare cases *q* followed by *u* may take the sound of *k,* as in *queue.*

W represents the usual sound heard in *way* and *we.* The sound of *w* is heard in a few words that omit the *w* in the spelling of a word, as in *one.* In addition, *w* is silent in unaccented syllables in some words, as in *answer. W* is also silent in some one-syllable words, as in *two.*

X represents the sound of *ks,* as in *expand.* It occasionally represents the sound of *gs* as in such words as *exact.*

Z represents two sounds. The common sound of *z* is that heard in the words, *zone* and *zoo.* On rare occasions *Z* takes the sound of *zh* as in *azure.*

Consonants representing more than two sounds. *C* represents three sounds, or phonemes. The letter *c* takes the hard sound when followed by *a, o,* and *u,* as in *cake, cost,* and *cut. C* takes the soft sound of *s* when followed by *e, i,* or *y* as in *center, circus,* and *cyclone.* Less commonly, *c* may take the sound of *sh* as in *social.*

S is another letter that represents several sounds. The common sound of *s* is heard in the word *sat. S* also takes the sound of *z* in such words as *cousin, his,* and the plural *suns.* Less commonly, *s* may take the sounds of *sh* and *zh,* as in the words *sure, sugar,* and *treasure.*

Consonant Blends

A cluster of two or more consonants that appear together in a word and are blended without the loss of identity of their separate sounds is called a consonant blend. Some consonant blends include the blending of a single consonant with a digraph. Here are the most common consonant blends; with examples.

bl, *bl*ack	*nk*, i*nk*
br, *br*ead	*nt*, we*nt*
cl, *cl*ean	*pl*, *pl*ay
cr, *cr*y	*pr*, *pr*etend
dl, can*dl*e	*rd*, ha*rd*
dr, *dr*op	*rk*, da*rk*
fl, *fl*y	
fr, *fr*ee	*sc*, *sc*arce
ft, le*ft*	*sk*, *sk*ip
gl, *gl*ad	*sl*, *sl*ow
gr, *gr*een	*sm*, *sm*all
kw [2]	*sn*, *sn*ow
lk, mi*lk*	*sp*, *sp*eak
lm, e*lm*	*sq*, *sq*uirrel
lp, he*lp*	*st*, *st*op
lt, me*lt*	*sw*, *sw*ay
mp, ca*mp*	*tl*, li*ttl*e
nd, ha*nd*	*tr*, *tr*ain
	tw, *tw*in

Following are some consonant blends of three or more letters.

sch, *sch*ool	*spr*, *spr*ing
scr, *scr*atch	*str*, *str*aw
spl, *spl*ash	

As discussed before, some blends combine a digraph with a consonant.

lfth, twe*lfth*	*sph*, *sph*inx
nch, ra*nch*	*thr*, *thr*ee
shr, *shr*imp	

Consonant Digraphs

Consonant digraphs are defined as a combination of two consonants that represent a single sound or phoneme, usually different from the sound of either of the consonants. Although language specialists, linguists, and phoneticians disagree on the classification of digraphs, the following letter combinations are fairly well accepted.

[2] According to Cordt the blend *kw* is represented by two different spellings, as *qu* in queen and *cho* in choir.

ch, church	*th* (voiced), *th*an
gh, laug*h*	*th* (voiceless), *th*in
ng, si*ng*	*wh* (sound of *hw*), *wh*at
*sh, sh*e	*wh* (sound of *h*), *wh*o

Voiced and Voiceless Consonants

Some consonants are produced with the vocal folds or cords open. In such a case, these consonants are formed with the breath, which is modified by other speech organs, such as the lips and tongue. In other words, these consonants are whispered and are classed as voiceless.

*c, c*ome	*p, p*ie
*f, f*un	*s, s*un
*h, h*ouse	*t, t*op
*k, k*ing	*x,* e*x*it

Other consonants are produced by the breath modified by the vocal folds or cords closed to the point of vibration and further modified by other speech organs, such as the lips and tongue. These sounds are called voiced consonants.

*b, b*all	*r, r*un
*d, d*oes	*s,* ro*s*e
*g, g*o	*v, v*ery
*j, j*ump	*w, w*alk
*l, l*ong	*x,* e*x*act
*m, m*e	*y, y*es
*n, n*o	*z, z*ero
*q, q*uick	

Silent Letters in Consonant Groups

When certain consonants appear in groups or clusters of two, one of these consonants is usually silent. Sometimes these groups occur at the beginning of syllables and sometimes at the end.

bt   The consonant *b* is sometimes silent when it precedes *t*, as in *doubt* or *debt.*

ck   The consonant *c* is silent when joined with *k*, as in *kick.*

gh   Both consonants, *g* and *h*, are silent when combined with *t* or when found near the end of a syllable or word, as in *thought, through,* and *night.*

gn   The consonant *g* is usually silent when it precedes *n*, as in *gnaw.*

kn   The consonant *k* is silent when it precedes *n*, as in *knight* and *know.*

lm   Sometimes the consonant *l* is silent when it precedes the letter *m*, as in *calm* and *salmon.*

mb   The consonant *b* is usually silent when it occurs after *m* at the end of syllables or words, as in *climb.*

pn   When the consonant *p* precedes *n*, the *p* is usually silent, as in *pneumonia*.

ps   When the consonant *p* precedes *s*, the *p* is usually silent, as in *psalm* and *psychic*.

rh   When the consonant *h* follows *r*, the *h* is usually silent, as in *rhubarb* and *rhyme*.

sl   The consonant *s* preceding *l* is usually silent when it occurs in the middle of a word, as in *aisle*.

t   The consonant *t* is sometimes silent when it occurs in the syllable *-ten* following another consonant, as in *often*.

tch   The consonant *t* is usually silent when followed by the digraph *ch*, as in *watch* and *pitcher*.

wh   The digraph *wh*, when it precedes any vowel except *o*, is pronounced *hw*, as in *what* and *where*. When *wh* precedes the vowel *o*, it is usually, though not always, silent; only the *h* is heard as in *who*.

wr   When the consonant *w* precedes the consonant *r*, the *w* is usually silent, as in *write* and *wrist*.

Double Consonants

In words containing double consonants, only one of the consonants is usually sounded, as in *rubber*. Two exceptions to this rule are:

1. When the consonant combination of *cc* is followed by *e* or *i*, the first *c* is usually hard, and the second *c* is pronounced *ks*, as in *eccentric* and *occidental*.

2. When the double consonant *ss* is followed by the letters *ion*, it takes the sound of *sh* as in *impression* and *omission*.

VOWEL SOUNDS AND GENERALIZATIONS

The vowels are usually listed as *a, e, i, o, u,* and sometimes *y*. The letter *w* sometimes combines with *o* to form a diphthong. The uses of *w* and *y* as vowels, as well as the most common generalizations concerning the pronunciation of the vowel sounds are given below. The newest dictionaries omit the diacritical mark for the short vowel, although they continue to use the other diacritical marks.

Vowel Sounds

Although a number of different diacritical markings are used to indicate a variety of sounds for each vowel, these sounds can be grouped under such headings as short vowels, exceptions to the short vowel rule, long vowels, sounds of *y*, sounds of *w*, and the schwa.

Short vowels. One vowel alone in the middle of a word or syllable is usually short, as in *cap, handle, met, ship, riddle, rod,* and *but*.

Exceptions to the short vowel rule. O is an exception to the short vowel rule when followed by the blend *ld;* this *o* is usually long, as in *sold.*

The vowel *a* is an exception to the short vowel rule when followed by the letters *l,* as in *talk; ll,* as in *call; w,* as in *raw;* and *u,* as in *caught;* where *a* takes the sound of *aw.*

The vowel *i* is also an exception to the short vowel rule when followed by such consonant blends and digraphs as *nd* in *rind, gh* in *tight,* and *ld* in *mild,* where the *i* has a long sound.

Vowels followed by the consonant *r* are also exceptions to the short vowel rule. Each vowel is modified by *r,* as *a* in *arm, e* in *her, i* in *bird, o* in *nor,* and *u* in *fur.*

Long vowels. When two vowels occur together in a one-syllable word, the first vowel is usually long and the second is usually silent, as in *wait, meat, feet,* and *boat.* This rule does not always apply to vowel digraphs. All vowel diphthongs are exceptions to this rule, and combinations of *i* and *e* are often irregular. In words of more than one syllable, this rule is more likely to hold true in accented than in unaccented syllables.

When a word of one syllable or an accented syllable ends in *e,* the preceding vowel is usually long, as in *gate, here, fire, rode, sure,* and *locate.* The sound of this vowel does not change when inflectional endings are added. For example, when the *e* is dropped at the end of the word *rate* for the addition of *-ing,* the *a* remains long.

When the only vowel in a word of one syllable comes at the end, it usually has the long sound as in *fly, no, gnu,* and *we.* This rule also tends to apply for root forms of words to which inflectional endings or suffixes have been added.

Sounds of y as a vowel. *Y* is a vowel and is usually long when it occurs at the end of a one-syllable word that contains no other vowel, as in *by.*

Y takes the part of a vowel and is usually short when it comes at the end of a word of two or more syllables as in *noisy.* The sound of *y* in this case is similar to that of long *e,* although it is sometimes described as similar to short *i.*

Y is a vowel when it follows another vowel, as in *stay,* and is classed as a digraph.

Y takes the part of a single vowel when it occurs in the middle of a syllable, as in *symbol* and *type.*

Sounds of w as a vowel. *W* usually takes the part of a vowel when it follows the vowels *a, e,* and *o,* as in *paw, few,* and *blow.* Sometimes the *w* is silent, and sometimes it combines with vowels to form diphthongs. In the word *snow,* the vowel *o* is long and the *w* is silent. As in the words *now* and *cow,* however, *ow* is listed among the diphthongs.

The schwa. Some vowel sounds are classified under the term *schwa.* The sounds of *a, e, i, o,* and *u* are almost identical in unstressed syllables.

Formerly each was listed separately in the dictionary with the use of a different diacritical mark. In some new dictionaries this sound, which is almost identical in each of the vowels, is listed under the symbol for schwa (ə).

The use of the schwa to take the place of the various diacritical marks placed over each vowel simplifies the problem of pronunciation for children when they use the dictionary. For example, the vowel sound in the unstressed syllables in each of the following words may be represented with the symbol for the schwa and are pronounced in almost the same way: *a* in *about, e* in *kitten, i* in *pencil, o* in *ribbon,* and *u* in *minute.*

Vowel Digraphs

When two vowels occur together to represent a single sound, they are called vowel digraphs as *ea* in *meat* and *oa* in *coat.* Authorities differ in their listings of digraphs, but most are included in the following vowel combinations.

ai	wait	*ei*	ceiling
ai	aisle	*ei*	neighbor
ai	said	*eu*	neutral
au	author	*ey*	valley
au	Paul	*ey*	they
ay	may	*ie*	pie
ea	meat	*ie*	histories
ea	feather	*oa*	boat
ea	break	*oe*	foe
ee	feet		

Vowel Diphthongs

A diphthong is defined as a combination of two vowels that occur together and are blended to form a continuous sound. Although authorities disagree in their classification of vowel combinations as diphthongs, the following vowel combinations are usually included.

ew	few	*ow*	cow
oi	boil	*oy*	boy
ou	bough	*ue*	blue

Special Vowel Groups

The sounds of *oo* do not seem to fit into any of the other groups. This combination of vowels has two pronunciations, one classified as the long sound of *oo* and the other as the short sound of *oo.* The long sound is found in such as *boot, cool, room, soon.* The short sound is found in such as *took, look, good,* and *stood.* Children have difficulty in hearing the difference between these short and long sounds; however, this difference is not usually confusing in the primary grades. The teacher would be wise to use a word containing the long sound of the *oo* as a key word when comparing it to the new words with the long sound. The same suggestion applies to the words containing the short sound of these vowels.

Other sounds are formed for the combination of *oo*, such as the long sound of *o* in *floor* and *brooch*, and the short sound of *u* in *flood*. These words are best taught as sight words.

STRUCTURAL ANALYSIS

The term structural analysis usually refers to the consideration of the inflectional endings, prefixes, and suffixes to root words. The use of each type of change is treated separately.

Inflectional Endings

Inflectional endings are added to words to show change of function in a sentence: They may show change in tense of the verb, change from singular to plural, change in gender of the person speaking, change to possessive, and similar changes. For this purpose, suffixes are usually added. Sometimes, however, the entire form of the word is changed, as in such pronouns as *him* and *her* and in such irregular verb forms as *go*, *went*, and *gone*. Verb forms are usually achieved by adding the suffixes *-s, -es, -ing, -ed, -t,* and *-en.*

VERB FORMS

run, run*s*
fix, fix*es*
fix, fix*ing*
want, want*ed*
send, sen*t*
forgot, forgott*en*

SINGULAR AND PLURALS

boy, boy*s*
box, box*es*
man, m*en*
penny, penni*es*

ADJECTIVE COMPARISONS

pretty, pretti*er*, pretti*est*

POSSESSIVES

girl,   girl'*s*,   girls'
boy,   boy'*s*,   boys'
people, people'*s*, peoples'
child,   child'*s*,   child*ren's*

PRONOUN FORMS

they, thei*r*, the*m*

Compound Words

The combination of two root words to make a compound word should be understood by children. Some of these compound words, such as *playhouse,* combine the meanings of the two parts. Some, such as *broadcast,* take on new meanings. Some are hyphenated, and others are written as total words.

*play, play*house
*fire, fire*men
*foot, foot*steps

*dog, dog*cart
*dress, dress*maker

Contractions

Some letters are omitted from particular compound words. In the contracted form, an apostrophe is used to show the position of the omitted letter or letters in words.

cannot, can't   have not, haven't
do not, don't   of the clock, o'clock
is not, isn't

Derivatives

A root word is an uncompounded word or element to which no suffix, prefix, or inflectional endings have been added. A derivative is a word which has been changed by the addition of a prefix or suffix. Children may be helped to find root words in their derivatives. They should also learn to analyze the root word for its meaning and to understand the new meaning resulting from the addition of a prefix or suffix.

Prefixes. Some common prefixes, along with their meaning and a root word for each, are as follows.

*ab-, ab*normal — The prefix *ab-* indicates the absence of the state indicated by the root word.

*ad-, ad*join — The prefix *ad-* means a change toward; here, to join an object or person to another.

*be-, be*witch — The prefix *be-* sometimes means to affect with; a person who is bewitched is affected with witchery.

*bi-, bi*monthly — Here the prefix *bi-* indicates two; an event occurring bimonthly occurs every two months. (Note that biannual, however, means twice a year.)

*com-, com*mensurable — The prefix *com-* often indicates the idea of with or together; an object that can be measured is measurable, and an effect that can be measured by the same number, quantity, or measure is commensurable.

*de-, de*part — The prefix *de-* means away; when people part from each other to go away, they *depart*.

*dis-, dis*connect — In *disconnect* the prefix *dis-* is used to mean to reverse or counter the meaning of the root word.

*en-, en*close — The prefix *en-* is often used to indicate an internal relationship; here, to close inside another object.

*ex-, ex*change — The prefix *ex-* implies from or away from. In *exchange;* goods may be changed from one owner to another (for some, hopefully, equivalent consideration).

*fore-, fore*see	The prefix *fore-* is used to denote the concept of before or in advance, either in time or position; to foresee is to see beforehand or to anticipate.
*il-, il*logical	The prefix *il-* in this usage means lack of or negative of; hence, not logical.
*im-, im*perfect	The prefix *im-* has the same meaning, as il- mentioned above; hence, not perfect.
*in-, in*active	The prefix *in-* here indicates absence of the quality of the root word; hence, not active.
*in-, in*land	The prefix *in-* here indicates the quality of being within, in the center of an area of land as opposed to a position near the water.
*mis-, mis*spell	The prefix *mis-* means wrong, ill, wrongly; hence, wrongly spelled.
*out-, out*grow *out*run	In addition to such more obvious usage as in *out*doors and *out*bound, the prefix is also used for leave behind, or more strongly, surpass, as in *out*grow and *out*run.
*over-, over*flow	The prefix *over-* means upper, superior, or excessive; an excessive quantity of water causes a river to *overflow*.
*pre-, pre*fix	The prefix *pre-* often indicates before, beforehand, at the beginning, or in front of; a *prefix* is something that is fixed or put before, as at the beginning of a word.
*pro-, pro*motion	The prefix *pro* implies an advance; one who is *promoted* is moved forward to an advanced position.
*re-, re*pay	The prefix *re-* refers to the concept of back, backwards, or again; to *repay* is to pay back.
*sub-, sub*marine	The prefix *sub-* means under; marine carries the meaning of water, and a *submarine* is that which stays or moves under water.
*un-, un*happy	The prefix *un-* usually indicates absence of or the negative of the root meaning.

Suffixes. Some common suffixes, along with their meaning and a root word for each, are as follows.

-er, work*er* *-or,* participat*or* *-ant,* occup*ant*	The suffixes *-er*, *-or* and *-ant* are added to a verb to indicate persons who perform the action of the verbs.
-ist, pian*ist* *-ian,* librar*ian*	The suffixes *-ist* and *-ian* indicate the person who works with or in connection with the object referred to by the noun.
-n, America*n* *-an,* Mexic*an* *-man,* police*man*	The suffixes *-n*, *-an*, and *-man* indicate the person who is a member of a group or works in connection with an occupation.

-able, manage*able*	The suffixes *-able, -al, -ary, -ive, -ness, -ous, -ic,* and
-al, logic*al*	*-ful* indicate the idea of like, pertaining to, full of,
-ary, station*ary*	or the possession of qualities described in the root
-ive, act*ive*	words.
-ness, complete*ness*	
-ous, courage*ous*	
-ic, electron*ic*	
-ful, resource*ful*	
-y, honest*y*	The suffixes *-y, -ty,* and *-ity* indicate the condition
-ty, identi*ty*	or quality of the adjective or the root word.
-ity, legal*ity*	
-ion, violat*ion*	The suffixes *-ion, -tion, -ation,* and *-sion* indicate
-tion, interven*tion*	the act of or the end product resulting from the
-ation, tempt*ation*	action of the verb.
-sion, deci*sion*	
-less, odor*less*	The suffix *-less* indicates the lack of possession of the quality of the root word.
-ence, correspond*ence*	The suffixes *-ance* and *-ence* indicate the object
-ance, convey*ance*	that is capable of carrying out the work of the verb or the process or result of the action of the verb.
-ment, improve*ment*	The suffix *-ment* refers to the result of the action of the root word; *improvement* is the result of an effort to improve something.
-ly, kind*ly*	The suffix *-ly* is added to an adjective to transform it to an adverb; a man is kind, but he acts kindly.
-er, whit*er*	The suffixes *-er* and *-est* are added to the adjective
-est, whit*est*	to change it to the comparative and superlative forms.
-ism, pacif*ism*	The suffix *-ism* pertains to a condition, practice of, or doctrine; here, the doctrine of a pacific attitude of mind.
-ure, legislat*ure*	The suffix *-ure* refers to an act, process, or an agent involved in an action; here the *legislature* is the agent that carries out the action of the verb *legislate.*

Syllabification

Words should be divided only between syllables. The number of vowel sounds heard in a word serve as an indication of the number of syllables. For example, *tomato* has three vowels, all of which can be heard when the word is pronounced. Therefore, *to-ma-to* has three syllables. On the other hand, *release* has four vowels, but only two of them, the first two *e's* are audible. The *a* and the final *e* are silent. Therefore, *re-lease* has only two syllables.

1. Monosyllables should not be divided. Examples of monosyllables are *hoarse, which, might, friend,* and *jumped.* The suffix *-ed* is sounded as a separate syllable only after verbs ending in *d* or *t.*

2. A single letter should not be divided from the rest of the word even

though this letter is an audible vowel. Examples of such words are *among, event, ideal, oblige,* and *unite.*

3. Diphthongs and digraphs cannot be divided. Examples of such words, with hyphens to show where they may be divided, are laugh-a-ble, might-i-ly, diph-thong, as-sign-a-ble, or-tho-dox, and so-phis-ti-cate.

4. When two consonants occur together, the word should be divided between the consonants unless these consonants are parts of diphthongs or digraphs. Examples of words that can be divided between the consonants, are *thank-ful, kit-ten, sand-wich,* and *plen-ty.*

5. When a single consonant occurs between two vowels, this consonant usually goes with the second vowel: *sto-ry, be-gin, pu-pil, to-day, ba-by,* and *pa-rade.*

6. Usually prefixes and suffixes form separate syllables: *un-true, dis-ease, pre-cede, happi-ness, ex-ceed.*

Rule for Spelling when Adding Prefixes

A prefix is added to a root word without a change in either part. For example, when the prefix *un-* is placed before the root word *happy,* no change is made in spelling. The rule holds true even when a prefix ending with a particular letter is placed before a word beginning with the same letter. For example, when the prefix *mis-* is placed before the root word *spell,* the new word becomes *misspell,* because no change is made in either part. The addition of prefixes to root words should therefore result in no spelling problem.

Rules for Spelling when Adding Suffixes

The addition of suffixes does involve changes under certain conditions. Some suffixes are added without changes.

quick, quick*ly*	mean, mean*est*
pure, pure*ly*	actual, actual*ly*
achieve, achieve*ment*	

When suffixes are added in certain situations, spelling changes are made. An effort has been made to analyze these situations and to generalize these changes in spelling as follows:

1. The suffix *-es* is added to form the plural in words that end in *s, ss, ch,* and *x.*

ax, ax*es*	Santa Claus, Santa Claus*es*
class, class*es*	watch, watch*es*
fish, fish*es*	

2. To form the plural of words ending in *y* preceded by a consonant, change the *y* to *i* and add *es.*

baby, bab*ies*	cannery, canner*ies*
berry, berr*ies*	lady, lad*ies*
candy, cand*ies*	

3. When adding a suffix beginning with *i* to a word that ends with *y*, the *y* is retained.

buy, buy*ing*	hurry, hurry*ing*
carry, carry*ing*	play, play*ing*
fry, fry*ing*	

4. When adding a suffix to words ending with silent *e*, drop the final *e* before adding the suffix. Words ending with *ce* and *ge* are exceptions to this rule.

agriculture, agricultur*al*	dilute, dilu*tion*
decorative, decorat*ive*	live, liv*able*
blue, blu*er*, blu*est*	docile, docil*ity*
desire, desir*ous*	pure, pur*er*, pur*est*
fine, fin*er*, fin*est*	tribe, trib*al*

but

change, chang*eable*	notice, notic*eable*
courage, courag*eous*	trace, trac*ery*
manage, manag*ement*	

5. When a suffix that begins with a vowel is added to a word that contains only one vowel and ends in a single consonant, the consonant is usually doubled before the suffix is added. This rule also applies to polysyllables having the accent on the last syllable.

admit, admitt*ance*	metal, metall*ic*
big, bigg*est*	sum, summ*ary*
drug, drugg*ist*	

6. When a suffix is added to a word ending in *f*, the *f* is usually changed to *v* before the suffix is added.

elf, elv*es*	loaf, loav*es*
half, halv*es*	wife, wiv*es*
hoof, hoov*es*	

7. The root word is not changed when adding suffixes to words ending in *y* preceded by a vowel.

buy, buy*er*	joy, joy*ous*
gay, gay*ly*	play, play*ing*
key, key*s*	

8. A final *e* is usually retained in a root when adding a suffix beginning with a consonant. Some words ending in silent *e* preceded by *u* are exceptions to this rule.

excite, excite*ment*	like, like*ly*
hate, hate*ful*	live, live*ly*

but

true, truly

Index